PROPERTY AND THE LAW IN ENERGY
AND NATURAL RESOURCES

Property and the Law in Energy and Natural Resources

Edited by
AILEEN McHARG
BARRY BARTON
ADRIAN BRADBROOK
and
LEE GODDEN

OXFORD
UNIVERSITY PRESS

OXFORD

UNIVERSITY PRESS

Great Clarendon Street, Oxford ox2 6DP

Oxford University Press is a department of the University of Oxford.
It furthers the University's objective of excellence in research, scholarship,
and education by publishing worldwide in

Oxford New York

Auckland Cape Town Dar es Salaam Hong Kong Karachi
Kuala Lumpur Madrid Melbourne Mexico City Nairobi
New Delhi Shanghai Taipei Toronto

With offices in

Argentina Austria Brazil Chile Czech Republic France Greece
Guatemala Hungary Italy Japan Poland Portugal Singapore
South Korea Switzerland Thailand Turkey Ukraine Vietnam

Oxford is a registered trade mark of Oxford University Press
in the UK and in certain other countries

Published in the United States
by Oxford University Press Inc., New York

British Library Cataloguing in Publication Data

Data available

Typeset by Newgen Imaging Systems (P) Ltd., Chennai, India
Printed in Great Britain
on acid-free paper by
CPI Antony Rowe,
Chippenham, Wiltshire

ISBN 978–0–19–957985–3

1 3 5 7 9 10 8 6 4 2

Preface

This book is the result of a collective research endeavour by the Academic Advisory Group (AAG) of the International Bar Association's (IBA) Section on Energy, Environment, Natural Resources and Infrastructure Law (SEERIL). The AAG has been in existence for twenty-five years, as a small group of academics from different parts of the world, specializing in energy and natural resources law. It operates as an international research network within the IBA, demonstrating the value of close liaison between legal academics and law practitioners. For some time it has worked in a two-year cycle of research and publication, bringing together contributions from AAG members and other participants who can bring knowledge and insight to the research. The four previous AAG studies have been published by Oxford University Press. They have spanned the subjects of human rights in natural resources development, energy security, changing methods of regulation in energy and resources, and the consequences for law as we are impelled beyond a carbon economy.

For some time it had been clear to us that we should turn our attention to concepts of property as they operate in energy and natural resources law. It seemed right to do so at a time when the headlines often brought news—and indeed still do—on the merits of emissions trading schemes, fisheries quota, the security of investment, and the property claims of regulated industries. In any such matter, property questions are often underlain by pressing general questions of principle, whether relating to functional efficiency or distributional equity.

We thank the IBA and SEERIL for long-standing institutional commitment to the work of academics engaged in energy and natural resources law. We give sincere personal thanks to Alan Dunlop and Hunt Talmage, successive Chairpersons of the Council of SEERIL during the time of this study, for their cordial support. For the mid-term meeting in May 2009, at which took place a lot of valuable discussion and debate about the research project, our colleague Yinka Omorogbe invited us to Abuja, Nigeria, where she is now Secretary and Legal Adviser to the Nigerian National Petroleum Corporation; and we thank her warmly for her hospitality. We express our gratitude to Mr Mutiu Sunmonu, Managing Director of Shell Petroleum Development Company of Nigeria Ltd, and to Mr Mohammed Sanusi Barkindo, Group Managing Director of the Nigerian National Petroleum Corporation, for their generosity in providing financial support for the Abuja meeting; their assistance made a significant contribution. We express our appreciation to the anonymous reviewers of our book proposal for their thoughtful comments, and we thank Merel Alstein and her colleagues at Oxford University Press for their expertise and understanding of the time pressures in bringing the project to completion.

The Editors

September 2009

Contents

Detailed Contents

PART II. NATURAL RESOURCE REGIMES

PART III. PROPERTY RIGHTS, MARKETS,
AND REGULATION

List of Contributors

Nigel Bankes is Professor and Chair of Natural Resources, Faculty of Law, University of Calgary, Canada; email: ndbankes@ucalgary.ca.

Lila K. Barrera-Hernández is Adjunct Assistant Professor, Faculty of Law, University of Calgary, Canada, and Abogada, Buenos Aires, Argentina; email: lila.kbh@gmail.com.

Barry Barton is Professor of Law, University of Waikato, New Zealand; email: barton@waikato.ac.nz.

Adrian J. Bradbrook is Bonython Professor of Law, Law School, University of Adelaide, Australia; email: adrian.bradbrook@adelaide.edu.au.

Simon Butt is Senior Lecturer, Sydney Law School and a member of the Centre for Asian and Pacific Law, University of Sydney, Australia; email: s.butt@usyd.edu.au.

Terence Daintith is Professor of Law, University of Western Australia, and Professorial Fellow, Institute of Advanced Legal Studies, University of London, United Kingdom; email: terence.daintith@dbmail.com.

Yanko Marcius de Alencar Xavier is Professor of Energy Law, Department of Public Law, Federal University Rio Grande do Norte, Natal, Brazil; email: ymxavier@ufrnet.br.

Iñigo del Guayo is Professor of Administrative Law, University of Almería, Spain; email: iguayo@ual.es.

Luis A. Erize is Managing Partner of Abeledo Gottheil Abogados, Buenos Aires, and former Adjunct Professor of Constitutional Law, National University of Buenos Aires, Argentina; e-mail: erize@abeledogottheil.com.ar.

Lee Godden is Professor of Law, Melbourne Law School, The University of Melbourne, Australia: email: l.godden@unimelb.edu.au.

José Juan González is Professor, Department of Law, Universidad Autónoma Metropolitana, Mexico, and Director of the Mexican Institute for Environmental Law Research; email: jjgonzalez@gonzalezasociados.com.

Ulf Hammer is Professor, Scandinavian Institute of Maritime Law, University of Oslo, Norway; email: ulf.hammer@jus.uio.no.

Sarah Hendry is Lecturer in Law, IHP-HELP Centre for Water Law, Policy and Science (under the auspices of UNESCO), Graduate School of Natural Resources Law, Policy and Management, University of Dundee, United Kingdom; email: s.m.hendry@dundee.ac.uk.

Gunther Kühne is Emeritus Professor of Mining and Energy Law, Technical University of Clausthal, and Honorary Professor of Law, University of Göttingen, Germany; email: gunther.kuehne@tu-clausthal.de.

Tim Lindsey is Professor of Asian Law, Director of the Asian Law Centre, Director of the Centre for Islamic Law and Society and ARC Federation Fellow in Melbourne Law School, University of Melbourne, Australia; email: t.lindsey@unimelb.edu.au.

Alastair R. Lucas is Dean and Professor, Faculty of Law, University of Calgary, Canada; email: alucas@ucalgary.ca.

Aileen McHarg is Senior Lecturer in Public Law, University of Glasgow, United Kingdom; email: a.mcharg@law.gla.ac.uk.

Kazuhiro Nakatani is Professor of International Law, University of Tokyo; email: nakatani@j.u-tokyo.ac.jp.

Yinka Omorogbe is Secretary and Legal Adviser to the Nigerian National Petroleum Corporation, and formerly Professor and Dean, Faculty of Law, University of Ibadan, Nigeria; email: yinka.omorogbe@gmail.com.

Peter K. Oniemola is John D and Catherine T MacArthur Foundation Graduate Intern, Faculty of Law, University of Ibadan, Nigeria; email: petermola@yahoo.com.

Lavanya Rajamani is Professor, Centre for Policy Research, New Delhi, India; email: lavanya.rajamani@cprindia.org.

Catherine Redgwell is Professor of International Law, University College London, United Kingdom; email: c.redgwell@ucl.ac.uk.

Martha M. Roggenkamp is Professor of Energy Law, Groningen Centre of Energy Law, University of Groningen, and Of Counsel, Brinkhof Advocaten, Amsterdam, The Netherlands; email: m.m.roggenkamp@rug.nl.

Anita Rønne is Associate Professor of Energy Law, Faculty of Law, University of Copenhagen, Denmark; email: anita.ronne@jur.ku.dk.

Wang Mingyuan is Associate Professor and Executive Director, Centre for Environmental, Natural Resources, and Energy Law, Tsinghua University Law School, Beijing, China; email: wangmy@tsinghua.edu.cn.

Jonnette Watson Hamilton is Associate Professor, Faculty of Law, University of Calgary, Canada; email: jwhamilt@ucalgary.ca.

1

Property and the Law in Energy and Natural Resources

Aileen McHarg, Barry Barton, Adrian Bradbrook, and Lee Godden*

I. Introduction: mapping the property terrain

The law of energy and natural resources has always had a strong focus on property as one of its components. Property law has had a strong influence on the development of core legal principles in the governance of energy and natural resources, from the definition of rights of control and access, to the institutional structures for resource exploitation and conservation. In western countries, the history of energy and resources law has often been one of strongly embedded individual rights to natural resources exercisable and defensible as proprietary rights. In other legal systems, property in resources is more flexible, and can accommodate a range of models of collective and individuated utilization of resources.

As time has gone on, the state has played a greater role in the management of natural resources in most legal systems, co-existing with, but generally not displacing, systems of private property rights. Even where the state pursues a national model of resource and energy ownership and the vesting of resources *in situ*, it commonly grants legal instruments and title as the means to develop such resources, which are often considered to have proprietary characteristics. Other groups within the nation state also may assert claims to resources and energy based on customary, long-standing patterns of utilization and cultural connection.

In the energy industries, the facilities and infrastructure that generate, transmit, and provide electricity, natural gas, petroleum, and other forms of energy to consumers, often shift between public and private ownership. Regulatory controls of different kinds are often said to cut into the prerogatives of the proprietors of the regulated energy and resources industries. Claims of investment

* Senior Lecturer in Public Law, School of Law, University of Glasgow; Professor, School of Law, University of Waikato; Bonython Professor of Law, School of Law, University of Adelaide; Professor, Melbourne Law School, University of Melbourne. The financial support of the Section on Energy, Environment, Resources and Infrastructure Law of the International Bar Association for the research that underpins this chapter is gratefully acknowledged.

certainty or security are often asserted in terms of the importance of protecting proprietary rights. Property concepts have a new reach and significance when utilities for services such as water supply are privatized; and again when new needs appear in relation to resources, energy, and sustainability.

Thus whilst property law may have ancient origins, it has proven to be highly resilient and capable of adaptation in varied energy and resource situations. Accordingly, the aim of this edited collection is to explore the multiple dimensions of the contemporary relationship between property and energy and natural resources law. The genesis for the collection was the growing resurgence of global interest in questions of property in energy and resources, and how such property interests manifest themselves across legal regimes around the world. These questions were seen as significant ones at a practical and theoretical level for the group of energy and natural resource lawyers that form the Academic Advisory Group to the Section on Energy, Environment, Resources and Infrastructure Law of the International Bar Association, which is charged with a brief to examine emerging trends in energy and natural resources law.

The individual contributions to the book explore questions of the relationship between property law and energy and natural resources in a wide range of national as well as supra-national and international legal settings. The collection captures different views about the role that property plays in diverse energy and resource contexts: in civil law and common law systems; in market rules, in the law of customary and indigenous communities; and in public law and private law. It includes discussion of private rights and common property situations; and of competition for land use and resources. Given this breadth of coverage, the collection has relevance for a wide readership interested in the legal dimensions of property as an increasingly important aspect of the law for energy and resources.

At the same time, the volume recognizes the relationship between law and property that has always existed when societies seek to give formal recognition to particular 'choices' through legal frameworks for energy and resources. In this regard, the book investigates many of the fundamental issues about how property law infuses our legal, economic and social relationships.[1] The analyses in the collection therefore provide a particular 'view of the cathedral'[2] that comprises general property law scholarship. In this respect, the book seeks to make a contribution to legal literature, both in the area of property law and in energy and natural resources law. Although there is much fine scholarship on each topic—and indeed both have seen a burgeoning of interest in recent years—there are relatively few comparative treatments combining both disciplines.[3] Accordingly,

---

[1] F. von Benda-Beckman, K. von Benda-Beckman, and M. G. Wiber (eds), *Changing Properties of Property* (2006).

[2] See J. Watson Hamilton and N. Bankes, 'Different Views of the Cathedral: The Literature on Property Law Theory', in this volume.

[3] Although recent scholarship includes A. Scott, *The Evolution of Resource Property Rights* (2008) and R. Barnes, *Property Rights and Natural Resources* (2009).

this collection places property law squarely in the energy and resources picture, and it builds upon previous collaborative work by the Academic Advisory Group, on a range of emerging issues in energy and resources law. In this light, the international and comparative legal perspective adopted across the collection examines many key 'choices' for societies that property comprehends, when questions of resources and energy are engaged. As Barnes comments in respect of natural resources, although equally applicable to energy:

The regulation of natural resources poses important questions about the allocation of wealth and power in society. To what ends and in whose interest do we regulate such resources? Who can own these resources and in what form? Can and should limits be placed on the use of resources to protect other social values? Such questions are rightly the domain of both international law and municipal law.[4]

II. Property in energy and natural resources: emerging issues

Key questions that arise for examination include: the control of, and access to fossil fuels, mineral reserves and water resources; the relative merits of public and private ownership of energy and water utilities; the role of constitutional and international law in asserting sovereignty over resources and energy; and conversely, the role of these institutions in protecting individual property rights; and the counterclaims of access for cultural and ethnic groups; all of which has been highly influential in shaping regulatory regimes and ownership choices surrounding energy and resources. Property questions also impinge on a consideration of the land-use, planning and the wider social implications that surround the exploitation of natural resources and supply of energy and water services, especially for urban populations. In tandem with such service provision, significant regulatory trends such as competition policies have forged new understandings of organizational and institutional structures to which property might pertain.

The resurgence of interest in the perennial questions of property and law in oil and gas and mineral resources that is currently being played out against the backdrop 'realpolitik' of national claims to such energy and resources is testimony to the renewed level of attention being given to these sectors by governments, international organizations, and business and community members. A confluence of trends from globalization to privatization, from climate change to energy security, and from economic liberalization to looming economic recession has served to raise awareness of the central importance of energy and resources to the future of humanity, its security and well-being. Moreover, as fossil fuel reserves become more valuable, and by contrast, natural resources, including water and unpolluted air, become increasingly scarce, control and access issues become ever more important. Such trends have prompted a number of countries

---

[4] Barnes, ibid at 10.

to reconsider their ownership regimes, and have raised issues about the ownership of newly 'discovered' forms of natural resource. Perennial issues about the most effective governance and utilization of petroleum and natural gas remain as vexed as ever. But in tandem, as climate change and energy security impacts bite, they prompt a re-evaluation of resource and energy demands and utilization. Many changing energy demands find a legal response in the emergence of new forms of property rights in resources and enabling technologies, such as carbon sequestration. Long-term sustainability of energy and resources and the role that property and law might play in achieving such goals become the most fraught questions of all.

Changing legal and policy environments thus create new dimensions to the interface between property and energy and natural resources law. They also create wholly new conceptual problems to grapple with. For instance, changing resource ownership regimes create new questions about the precise nature and limits of the rights which are involved. The liberalization of gas and electricity markets has created new interest in patterns of ownership, where the demands of effective competition for de-concentration of interests and disaggregation may come into conflict with the creation of optimal conditions for investment, the protection of national champions, or legal protection of property rights. Property rights themselves may become an instrument of legal regulation, as much as the 'object' of regulation. The increased recognition of indigenous land rights may not only complicate questions of access to natural resources, but also bring different cultural understandings of the meaning of property in resources. Similarly, there is renewed interest in the responsibilities that accompany property, whether they involve obligations to facilitate and/or mitigate the impact of competition, or responsibilities to assist the exploitation or conservation of energy and other natural resources.

III. Property in energy and natural resources: thematic approaches

Given the diverse ways in which one can approach property and law in energy and resources, this book does not seek to provide an exhaustive account. Instead, it has been divided into four sections which reflect the main issues addressed by the authors. The first section deals with theoretical and conceptual approaches and encompasses an overview of property law theory, an examination of public and private rights to resources, the creation of property rights under statute, and the treatment of property at international law. The second section showcases the various natural resource law regimes that exist in specific countries, which highlights the diversity of perspectives upon property in such regimes. The third focus is on property in energy and resources and the interface with markets and regulation, while the final section explores emerging property regimes and examines cutting-edge forms of property in natural resources, such as sequestered carbon.

Notwithstanding that the focus of each chapter and group of chapters differs, an interesting aspect of our collective work is that a number of themes have emerged as common elements of the analysis of various authors, cutting across the sectional divisions of the book. Taken together, these themes give an insight into the directions in which property law developments are heading, and show the likely areas of relevance for property law in the energy and resources field in the foreseeable future.

The key themes hinge on distinctions between conceptual and instrumental views of property.[5] Conceptual views seek to define an essence or fundamental set of characteristics to answer the question—what is property?[6] In western legal systems, such notions typically are derived from Roman law categories and emphasize the primacy of property law as embodying strong legal rights enforceable against the world at large, and which typically privilege rights, such as the right to exclude.[7] Instrumental (also termed functional or utilitarian) views are more interested in determining the role that property plays as a social institution and the political and economic goals it can promote.[8] These debates surrounding the fundamental characterizations of the nature of property: ie what is property and its distinguishing features, *vis-à-vis* the functional role of property law impinge upon the following themes. Each theme is expounded further in the remaining sections below, and developed in more detail in specific chapters.

A. The purposes of property

As Watson Hamilton and Bankes contend, '[i]nstrumentalists are not so concerned about what property is; they want to know what purposes the institution of property can be made to serve'. Whilst Watson Hamilton and Bankes focus on the general functions that property as an *institution* might be said to fulfil, other contributions in this volume focus on the functional character of particular property rules, and more specifically on the changing instrumental demands that are placed on property rules at different times and in different contexts. Thus, for example, Daintith's discussion of the rule of capture is explicitly functional. Despite extensive criticism of the rule, he argues that 'the rule of capture is the least worst property rule for fugacious substances like oil and gas, so long as it operates within a context where the stimulus it gives to development can be married to an effective control of its side-effects'.

A similar concern about balancing the utilitarian benefits of specific legal rules against their detrimental impacts is noted by Wang in respect of natural gas

---

[5] Watson Hamilton and Bankes (above n 2) at 22.
[6] For an early discussion see F. Cohen, 'Dialogue on Private Property' (1954) 9 Rutgers L R 357.
[7] A. Bell and G. Parchomovsky, 'A Theory of Property' (2004–2005) 90 Cornell L Rev 532 at 535.
[8] Watson Hamilton and Bankes (above n 2) at 28. This approach has historical origins in the utilitarian philosophy of Bentham where property was held to advance the greatest happiness of the greatest number.

utilization in China: 'At present, natural gas resources have both a strategic value and an ecological significance. It is an urgent problem to weigh the costs and benefits of development'. From a civil law perspective, González's chapter examines the evolution and function of national property concepts in Mexico and the specific role that such constructs play in mediating between private investment interests and public oil monopolies.

As a response to historical patterns of colonization, the influence of national political and cultural agendas upon the contemporary social function of property is demonstrated in several chapters. In the analysis of the Indonesian energy utilities by Butt and Lindsey, they suggest that the approach to property rights entailed by 'Indonesian Socialism' embraces the view that property and resources have a social function in alleviating poverty. By contrast, Barrera-Hernández discusses how the failure to recognize and to enforce customary indigenous property rights in South America has played a major role in perpetuating the poverty of these groups. The classic question about the relationship between property and poverty that has played out across the centuries can be contrasted with contemporary debates. Today, the instrumental character of property rules is most obvious in the context of environmental regulation. There has been a clear trend in environmental policy in recent years towards the use of market-based regulatory instruments in order to tackle environmental harms. Such instruments depend at their core on the creation of tradeable property rights. This might involve the 'propertization' of hitherto 'common pool' resources such as air, water, and forested areas. Alternatively, it might involve carving out new forms of ownership rights over newly-valuable resources, such as carbon sequestration capacity. In his analysis of carbon-offset trading schemes in Canada, Lucas argues for a functionalist approach to the creation of a suitable property rights regime. He contends that this will require legislative intervention, rather than simply relying on common law categorization of the rights in question.

However, whilst instrumentalist perspectives on property rights can be very illuminating, Barton's chapter counsels against seeing property in purely instrumental terms, infinitely malleable to the purposes of the policy-maker. At least in relation to common law systems, Barton argues that the pull of formalist ideas of private law as an autonomous body of law, with its own internal logic, can produce consequences other than those intended by the legislature. The courts may be more willing to resort to proprietary concepts to resolve disputes than the legislature intended. This point also seems likely to hold for civil law systems, where, as McHarg discusses, the distinction between public law and private law is even more strongly entrenched. Godden echoes this conclusion in relation to water and atmospheric emissions trading schemes. She points out that, although market environmentalism offers innovative approaches for common pool resource governance, introducing the notion of property brings with it a long and contested history, which might therefore produce as many conflicts as it resolves.

B. The adaptability of property

Perhaps, however, the most striking theme across the collection is the continued relevance and evident adaptability of property law principles to meet the needs of the energy and resources sector in the twenty-first century. This development will be welcomed with open arms by traditional property lawyers, given claims by their colleagues about the obsolescence of property and its irrelevance to modern social and economic problems. In the common law, critics point to the law of perpetuities as an example, with its absurdities such as the 'fertile octogenarian'.[9]

Even more disturbingly, there have been statements from legal dignitaries that have suggested that property law may be incapable of developing at common law. One of the best-known comes from no less a reformer than Lord Denning, who stated in *Phipps v Pears*[10] that there should be no new negative easements and that the class of easements is closed.[11] Yet, as Bradbrook argues, opening up the class of easements, for example, to facilitate new solar technologies could constitute a significant social benefit. While it is possible to identify anachronisms of this type in the existing law of property in many jurisdictions, even in the context of modern legislation,[12] there is no conceptual reason why property law cannot be as dynamic as other aspects of private law.

Many chapters in this book do indeed illustrate the actual and potential adaptability of property law principles in formulating a dynamic, modern legal regime for the energy and natural resources sector. Daintith examines how in many jurisdictions, the rule of capture is the basis of the prevailing law determining property rights in relation to underground petroleum resources. This is so despite the fact that the rule was designed to apply initially to wild animals without any consideration of its possible application in the resources field. Barton shows that licences and other rights created by statutes may sometimes need to be analysed in relation to traditional property law rights and principles, a point echoed by Lucas in relation to carbon sequestration rights. From the perspective of India, Rajamani discusses how very ancient customary forestry rights have relevance for one of the most pressing questions of today; the reduction of greenhouse gas emissions through bio-sequestration.

The conceptual bases underlying the adaptability of property are explored by McHarg, who shows that the majority of theorists accept the notion that property rights should not be seen as a limitation on regulation, but rather as a social institution, created in order to perform valuable communal functions.

---

[9] *Jee v Audley* (1787) 1 Cox Eq 324; 29 ER 1186; *Re Dawson* (1888) 9 Ch D 155.
[10] [1965] 1 QB 76.
[11] ibid at 82–3.
[12] eg, under current land titles legislation in South Australia and Queensland restrictive covenants cannot be directly registered on a land title: see A. Bradbrook, S. MacCallum and A. Moore, *Australian Real Property Law* (3rd edn, 2002) 758.

In respect of how property might shape the future development of energy and natural resources law, a linked and perhaps surprising theme is that property consequences can arise unintentionally, sometimes accidentally, on the part of the legislature or courts. Such situations may occur when legislatures seek to define new rights or when courts interpret a factual instance by applying an incremental adaptation of the law. The analysis by Bradbrook, for example, shows that property law is a useful mechanism for promoting sustainable energy solutions. These range from advancing the use of energy efficiency measures in the building sector through to increasing solar energy production by protecting solar access via restrictive covenants or the law of private nuisance. In the case of easements, the argument is that the easement of light can serve as an appropriate property right even though easements of light were developed in medieval times for the purposes of securing adequate illumination, way before any issue of solar access for energy purposes became relevant to society. A similar issue applies to an easement of wind access, which is based on the ancient easement of air, which was developed for ventilation purposes rather than for any consideration of energy production.

Despite the capacity for judicial extension of the law, however, several analyses indicate that traditional property concepts in themselves may not be sufficient. For example, in Denmark, Rønne discusses a new statutory mechanism for resolving conflicts between neighbouring landowners over the adverse impact of wind energy installations that replaces reliance upon the law of nuisance.

C. Markets, privatization and globalization

The growing reliance on market-based instruments in the international, utility and environmental fields illustrates another theme that emerges strongly from the contributions to this book. This is the ongoing global influence of neo-liberal economic theories, which stress the virtues of private ownership and competition as the solution to problems previously addressed through state ownership and hierarchical regulation. One example, discussed by Godden, is the shift from centralized, state-based regulation to devolved regulation focused upon private property in relation to water and atmospheric emissions trading schemes. Another is the widespread privatization and liberalization of energy and natural resource industries which were until relatively recently characterized by strong state control and monopolization. A number of chapters in this volume document the impact of privatization and liberalization policies: in the United Kingdom (Hendry, McHarg); the European Union (del Guayo, Roggenkamp and Kühne); Latin America (Barrera-Hernández; de Alencar; Erize; González); Indonesia (Butt and Lindsey); and Japan (Nakatani).

For instance, the three chapters by Erize, González, and de Alencar, discussing Argentina, Mexico and Brazil, respectively, paint a similar picture of increasing private sector involvement in the oil and gas sector, despite constitutional vesting of the ownership of subsoil resources in national or provincial governments. In Argentina, Erize describes: '[a] sweeping privatization trend in the 1990s to solve the 1980s energy crisis [which] led to the oil and gas industry, as well as the power industry as a whole being trusted to the private sector'. In Mexico, similarly, González notes that 'the last three Mexican presidents have tried to modify the Constitution in order to have a more flexible model of absolute public dominion in the field of petroleum and hydrocarbons …'. As for Brazil, de Alencar discusses the 1995 amendment to the Brazilian constitution, which allowed greater private participation in the country's oil industry, which he attributes to a combination of the need for increased investment and the influence of the global wave of market liberalization of the 1990s.

Even in a country such as Norway, where state ownership remains important, the influence of neo-liberal ideas is apparent. Thus, Hammer describes how ownership and regulatory functions have been split in the Norwegian oil sector, with the owner of the petroleum resource, Statoil, now effectively constrained to act in its own commercial interests like any other private company, leaving wider resource-management and socio-economic considerations to a separate organization, Petoro. The phenomenon echoes the observation by Rønne as to the reduced role of state companies elsewhere in Europe, including Denmark. She notes the influence of European Community law in this regard. As McHarg explains, this subjects both public and private undertakings to the same market-based rules, thus requiring non-market objectives to be pursued via explicit regulatory rules rather than through ownership controls.

A notable feature of the examples analysed in the book, however, is how much resistance the neo-liberal model faces from other conceptions of property rights. For example, in her discussion of Argentina and Chile, Barrera-Hernández shows how the model of exclusive and tradeable property rights assumed by neo-liberal theory comes into direct conflict with the communal and inalienable rights to land and natural resources asserted by indigenous communities. In Indonesia, Butt and Lindsey explain how the conception of property rights enshrined in the Indonesian Constitution has acted as a barrier to the implementation of the International Monetary Fund's drive to privatization and liberalization policies, particularly in the electricity sector, since it has been interpreted as requiring extensive state control over natural resources and essential industries in order to benefit the people as a whole. Similarly, despite the privatization trends in Latin America, discussed above, ideas about the importance of national control over natural resources continue to be both politically and legally influential. Thus, in both Brazil (de Alencar) and Mexico (González), there has recently been some degree of backlash against private involvement in the oil sector, prompting experiments with new ways of balancing the need for capital investment with ensuring that society in general benefits from natural resource exploitation. Thus, according to González, Mexican opposition to private involvement is not based on a dogmatic rejection of private property *per se*, but rather 'is due more to the idea that privatization principally benefits foreign companies'.

However, even in jurisdictions where the liberal model of property rights is more firmly entrenched, its application to the energy and resources sectors still encounters resistance. For example, in the United Kingdom, which pioneered privatization and liberalization policies, Hendry argues that water is still widely seen as a 'public' good which should not be run on purely commercial principles. McHarg similarly explores how notions of the social obligations of ownership— which can be found in both common law and civil law systems, in tension with the absolutist, liberal conception—influence the legal regulation of energy utilities in both UK and EU law.

In Japan too, Nakatani explains how the government has sought to balance market liberalization trends and the promotion of inward investment flows, with rules on restriction of foreign investment in the national interest. This led the Japanese government to issue an order preventing foreign investment in one of the country's leading energy utilities being increased to a level at which the foreign investor would have been able to exercise *de facto* control over the company. While Nakatani stresses that the order issued by the Japanese government in this instance was regarded as exceptional, it raised the thorny question of the impact of national energy security requirements upon private property interests; a tension that reverberates across many other contributions in the book.

D. Private rights and the public interest

The protection afforded to private property in energy and resources contexts varies considerably across jurisdictions but there is a long-standing body of law that deals with questions of expropriation and compensation where government regulation impinges upon private property interests. Indeed, once private property rights have been created, they may, as Barton puts it, 'have a dangerous strength in environmental and natural resources law'. In other words, property rights may give their holders a powerful argument against future regulatory change which reduces the value or scope of those rights, or even eliminates them altogether. As Watson Hamilton and Bankes discuss, there is an extensive body of theorizing about the circumstances in which, and conditions upon which, such 'taking', or expropriation, of property is legitimate. They argue that this issue is particularly relevant in the energy and natural resources field—a claim that is borne out by a number of contributions to this book. In some cases, the use of property rights as a shield against regulatory intervention operates merely at the level of political argument. However, private property rights do receive constitutional protection in many jurisdictions (as Rønne discusses). International law may also provide support for property rights-based claims, either via human rights law or through customary and treaty-based rules providing protection for foreign investment (discussed by Redgwell, Erize and Nakatani).

In the energy and natural resources sectors, such claims have typically arisen in circumstances where governments have sought to restrict private participation—as, for example, Erize discusses in relation to Argentina. He notes the tensions introduced by ever tighter government controls on the energy industry. 'Reluctantly, the industry goes to court or arbitration, while being subject to severe criticism by public powers and the further menace of retaliation. The compound effect of these measures amounts to creeping expropriation: the deprivation, at the end of the road, of property rights.' Clearly, the boundaries between legitimate government regulation of energy and resources and undue interference with private property remain as fraught as ever.

In an interesting twist to the arguments about state expropriation, however, the chapter by del Guayo, Roggenkamp and Kühne shows that alleged interferences may also arise in circumstances where governing authorities are actually attempting to extend market principles. As they observe, constitutionally protected property rights have been invoked in a number of European Union member states to resist attempts to break up vertically integrated energy companies. Such companies have been identified as a major barrier to the creation of an effective European energy market. del Guayo, Roggenkamp and Kühne conclude that protection for property rights in both European Community law and in the constitutional systems of member states is relatively weak in the face of overriding arguments of public interest, such as the need to promote effective competition. This is a finding echoed by Rønne in relation to both Danish constitutional law and the European Convention on Human Rights, although other systems, such as Japan (Nakatani) may provide stronger protection. This might suggest that constitutional guarantees against interference with property rights often have more symbolic than legal value. Nevertheless, as del Guayo, Roggenkamp and Kühne show, the invocation of property rights as an apparent trump card can still have a real impact on policy development. Thus, they argue that the European Commission weakened its plans for full 'ownership unbundling', allowing member states to opt for less extreme measures, in the face of arguments from some quarters based on the sanctity of property rights.

E. Internationalization of property and national regimes

The question of the role of the state with respect to property interests is raised also by the internationalization of property law principles. Redgwell notes the interface between property in domestic jurisdictions and sovereignty under public international law. The interface between the two concepts is already important in the energy and natural resources sector as a result of offshore oil and gas exploration and development, and is likely to become even more important in the years to come as a result of recent developments such as offshore carbon capture and storage, offshore wind energy development, and the exploitation of wave energy.

Another point of comparison is with the sovereign rights of the state. As Redgwell explains, at international law, the property and investments of a foreign national are protected, but it is for the individual state to determine what property rights can be enjoyed under its legal system. Omorogbe and Oniemola examine these tensions closely in the relationship between host countries and multinational oil and gas companies. This kind of tension or competition is one of the main themes of energy and natural resources law: the tension between investment certainty and the sovereign rights of a legislature; or between security of tenure and regulatory flexibility. Much effort goes into the creation of legal mechanisms with which to deal with this tension or competition. Indeed property rules play a significant conflict resolution role. Omorogbe and Oniemola also provide an account of the United Nations General Assembly Resolutions on Permanent Sovereignty over Natural Resources. They explain the trend away from the traditional concepts of investor property rights to resources, towards the sovereign interests of the host state in its ownership of natural resources.

F. Property as a mechanism to resolve conflicting claims

Much talk about property is framed around property rights, not obligations, so there can be no surprise when the analysis of property becomes an analysis of competing claims. One very common kind of competition in energy and natural resources law is that between natural resource users and other property rights holders. Wang enters into a close examination of one example: the relations between natural gas pipeline operators in China with persons or communities holding different kinds of rights to land. He concludes that ownership arrangements that separate land from mineral resources are good for state planning and administration, and good for reducing natural gas development costs; but that they lay the foundation for conflict between natural gas development and land rights. After considering American and French law, he concludes that a more systematic legal framework is needed in order to deal with this kind of competition. As already noted, Rønne discusses new ways of balancing conflicting interests in relation to wind power and the impacts on surrounding land owners in Denmark.

Rajamani offers another perspective on conflicting claims and sources of property:

Natural-resource dependent communities, by virtue of their dependence on resources to which the State or others may have legal title, are vulnerable to losing their lands, access to resources and means of subsistence. Community based property rights typically encompass several rights, including rights to ownership, use and transfer. And they derive their authority from the local community in which they originate and operate.

Competition also occurs between claimants to the same resource. The chapter by Omorogbe and Oniemola discusses various models for 'ownership' of oil and gas resources. Their central focus however, is upon the situation in those countries such as Nigeria where domanial regimes exist and the hydrocarbon resources are vested in the sovereign state. Yet even under this 'absolute' model of national ownership, the authors illuminate the respective positions of the federal, state and local governments under a federated governance structure and the mediation with private interests that must occur.

Another perspective on 'stakeholder' interests is revealed by the rule of capture which is a property rights principle on competition between companies extracting oil and gas from a common reservoir. Daintith documents the origins and current strength of the rule, which inevitably is entwined with government regulation of well spacing and unitization. He concludes that the rule has virtues that counterbalance its more commonly mentioned ill effects. Modern oil and gas regimes tend to incorporate a number of functional substitutes for capture.

A different form of competition is that between the individual and the collective. The emphasis on private property means a tendency to see property rights as individualistic and in competition with social goals. McHarg notes this point. But she also observes that private and public property can be regarded as necessarily carrying with them obligations of a social nature. Such obligations of ownership are clearly stated under German law. In French law, the equivalent concept is the public service doctrine, which has effect whether or not public ownership or monopoly are present. A different aspect of this competition is where, as Barton notes, the sharper definition of property rights for an individual is not cost-free, and is often at the expense of the public, collective, or communally-held rights or interests.

G. Property as a dynamic reflection of change in the value of things

As we have stressed above, the property situation in respect of energy and natural resources is a dynamic one. Despite property being repeatedly proclaimed as the rights not the thing itself, it is remarkable that what is recognized and valued as property relating to 'things' also changes under the impetus of technological, social and economic change. In turn this affects the intensity of the property claims to them. Traditional natural resources (petroleum, minerals, and forests) have not lost value, but greater value is now ascribed to other resources and other values. Bradbrook examines the new value that must be ascribed to sustainable energy development. He notes a question of institutional choice between the legislature and the courts in recognizing that value.

Resources that can be described as common property resources, common pool resources, or simply not subject to proprietary claims at all, are being made the subject of new forms of property right. The reasons are not difficult to find; increasing population and wealth create demand and cause scarcity where once there was none. Fisheries and water resources are leading cases in point. We are seeing a great commodification, or 'propertization,' of such resources such as market-based systems in the form of individual tradeable quota (ITQ) for fisheries and tradeable rights for water. Property ideas are the fundamental building blocks of such systems. The decision to submit some element of the environment to a regime of individualized property rights is a profound one in policy terms. The implications are profound for legal systems as well. Nonetheless old assumptions about property are firmly entrenched. The cases analysed by Barton demonstrate the more prominent place of disputes over resources in terms of property. Lawyers bring property ideas to bear even where there is no legislative decision to do so.

Emissions trading systems (ETS) have emerged as one of the primary means for countries and groups of countries to reduce the emission of greenhouse gases. In twelve years, since the signing of the Kyoto Protocol, carbon trading has gone from the future-gazing of a few specialists to being a major commercial force. The proprietary character of emissions units or carbon credits and their legal character is now an essential consideration in large commercial transactions. Lucas makes a close examination of the manner in which a new property right can be structured in functional terms, to serve as an instrument to support a marketable carbon offset right. The new value of carbon sequestration produces a new need for property rights.

Godden makes a vital point that property rights are not a panacea; property concepts on their own will not solve entrenched problems of common resource use management. Such economic ideas may be useful in examining the allocation of property rights but are less effective at exploring the distributive consequences of property in energy and resources law.

H. Distribution: fairness and justice

Any system of individual property rights poses the question of equity in their distribution. Watson Hamilton and Bankes observe that a property regime almost guarantees that the distribution of wealth will not be equal, and that some will get richer than others. They consider the extensive literature on distributive justice. Much of the theoretical justification of the institution of property is concerned with equity. Both natural law and positivist justifications of property have to grapple with the matter.

Fairness and justice are natural preoccupations of legal thinking, but it is surprising how often the discussion of policy is couched entirely in instrumental terms of efficiency—in energy and natural resources policy as much as anywhere else. There is uneasiness about the messiness of fairness.[13] Thus in the introduction of a new system of property rights in natural resources, a great deal of attention will go into the efficiency of the trading system and very little into the initial allocation. While some strands of economics say that the initial allocation does not matter, everyone else seems to think that it does. Barton argues that the courts are more likely than the legislature to take a purely instrumental approach,

---

[13] L. Raymond, *Property Rights in Public Resources* (2003).

and more willing to consider fairness in determining liability between parties in dispute over natural resources.

The chapter studies in this book demonstrate different distributional issues implicit in different legal regimes. Barrera-Hernández and Rajamani write on relations between indigenous peoples and resource development. With respect to Argentina and Chile, Barrera-Hernández identifies property rights and individualization as a key element in distributional failure:

> The hand of the market is blind to issues of distributional justice. Welfare, which property is so uniquely designed to protect … becomes an abstraction shielding blatant inequalities. A system combining property and governance may be better able to bridge the gap between Western-style development and respect for indigenous culture and lifestyles.

With respect to India, Rajamani identifies precisely the same issue; community-based property rights are at the heart of the new legislation for traditional forest dwellers. She observes that the fundamental ideological shift that this represents raises questions about its implementation in practice.

Distributional concerns lie close to the centre of the policy debate about public and private ownership of key natural resources and energy industries. As noted above, Butt and Lindsey show how Article 33 of the Indonesian Constitution, which grants the state control over natural resources and important industries, was intended to benefit the people and poor people in particular. In Brazil, de Alencar discusses recent proposals for the reform of the oil sector which will, *inter alia*, involve the creation of a Social Fund on the widely-admired Norwegian model. The Fund will receive part of the proceeds of exploitation of new oil and gas reserves, and it will include amongst its goals poverty reduction and environmental sustainability. Hendry also notes, in relation to ownership of water utilities, that whilst ownership is less significant than is often thought for the economic efficiency of water undertakings, it can be a significant variable for social regulation, for both consumers and the environment, and when trying to manage socio-political agendas and improve governance. Public ownership may make it easier to resolve conflicting interests. For example, Hendry argues that where the service remains in the public sector, there may be less resistance to price increases necessitated by environmental improvements, as long as they can be justified by improvements in the service, and as long as there are adequate mechanisms for transparency in providing information and public participation in the decision-making process.

Nevertheless, Hendry's chapter, along with many others, calls into question the perceived dichotomy between the legal regimes of state regulation of energy and natural resources, and the private law constructs of property rights. The old divisions and firmaments of legal structures and social goals for property have shifted; and the public law/private law division is not the key (or at least not the sole) determinative of the outcomes for the community. Other factors, such as the influence of marketization and corporatization on the institutions of both public and private law contribute to a more nuanced understanding of the operation of property law in this sector.

IV. Conclusion

While this chapter has identified several themes, clearly, there are many points of intersection and overlap between them. For example, instrumental uses of property relate also to concepts of adaptation and the changing social and community values of resources and energy. More widely, as this book indicates, property takes on myriad definitions, institutional expressions and legal forms in its complex interactions with the law of energy and resources. Thus any understanding of exactly how property and law operate in respect of energy and resources will require a fine grained analysis, where long-standing assumptions of the role of property may need to be questioned. If property provides legal expression to the various choices that are made, even at times 'accidentally', about the manner in which energy and resources are managed, then this book will contribute to building an understanding of the perennial importance of property and the dynamics of its evolution, given the increased attention to energy and resources on the global scale.

PART I

THEORETICAL AND CONCEPTUAL PERSPECTIVES

2

Different Views of the Cathedral: The Literature on Property Law Theory

Jonnette Watson Hamilton and Nigel Bankes*

The literature on property law theory has burgeoned over the past twenty-five years. This may be because the concept of property was pronounced dead, or at least disintegrated, in 1980,[1] reinvigorating scholarly debate.[2] The recent proliferation of new forms of property rights in information and the emergence of ideas such as virtual property—notions that strain the boundaries of the concept—appear to have encouraged rethinking. It has also been suggested that the collapse of socialist regimes around the world played a role in reviving interest in private property's foundations.[3]

Recent writings have dealt with most of the important issues in property law theory, including the two most basic of all: 'what is property?' and 'what is the justification for (private) property?'. Issues related to the commons, a topic on which the writing was prolific before the 1990s, albeit not by legal scholars, is another area of legal theory that is now flourishing. The *numerus clausus* principle has also attracted a great deal of recent attention. There are, however, gaps in the literature. There is little written about public property, for example, except

* Associate Professor, Faculty of Law, University of Calgary, Canada; email: jwhamilt@ucalgary.ca; Professor and Chair of Natural Resources, Faculty of Law, University of Calgary, Canada; email: ndbankes@ucalgary.ca.

[1] T. C. Grey, 'The Disintegration of Property' in *Property: Nomos XII* (J.R. Pennock and J.W. Chapman, eds, 1980) 69 at 74.

[2] R. A. Epstein, 'Property as a Fundamental Civil Right' (1992) 29 California Western L Rev 187 at 187 (asserting that '[p]roperty rights are clearly back on the public agenda as a subject for discussion and debate'); L. C. Becker, 'Too Much Property' (1992) 21 Philosophy & Public Affairs 196 at 197 (noting that '[i]n the past fifteen years the usual steady trickle of philosophical work on property has grown to a steady stream'). cf T. W. Merrill and H. E. Smith, 'What Happened to Property in Law and Economics?' (2001) 111 Yale LJ 357 (beginning with the idea that '[p]roperty has fallen out of fashion. ...in the academic world there is little interest in understanding property').

[3] C. M. Rose, 'Property as a Keystone Right?' (1996) 71 Notre Dame L Rev 329 at 329. Heller's first article on the anticommons was stimulated in part at least by these events: see M. A. Heller, 'The Tragedy of the Anticommons: Property in Transition from Marx to Markets' (1998) 111 Harv L Rev 621.

in contradistinction to private property.[4] There is less recent work on justifications for private property than on the question of 'what is property'. This is perhaps because most recent work on justifications focuses on limitations on private property and is concerned with distributive justice and environmental issues. Furthermore, while the economists are interested in the emergence and bundling of rights to natural resources,[5] there is little theoretical work by legal academics in this area[6] beyond the considerable literature on open access resources and research that is more doctrinal in nature on the legal characterization of state-granted rights to public resources. We can speculate about the reasons for this. Historically, natural resources law was clearly a subset of property law for Blackstone and others and that tradition continued for many centuries. But the current dominant role of public ownership of natural resources in many jurisdictions leads to the characterization of issues relating to the use and control of such resources as administrative law problems, rather than as property law problems.[7]

This chapter provides a review of property law theory and its literature that aims to show how developments in general property theory may be relevant for energy and natural resources law. Given the purpose and length of this chapter, we do not purport to be comprehensive. For example, there is little coverage here of the extensive literature on intellectual property theories. Neither do we deal with the distributive justice literature, except in passing. That literature is certainly relevant to justifications for and limitations on private property, and even appears in a number of well-known treatments of property theory.[8] However, it is not usually thought of as being part of property law theory and it would be impossible to go into it in depth in this already lengthy chapter. The same could be said for the vast body of literature that focuses on environmental ethics and theory.

Our focus is on liberal Western understandings of property, and primarily those within the common law tradition, for a number of reasons. First, the vast majority of theoretical writing in English falls within these perspectives, or at least takes them as its starting point. Secondly, these perspectives are especially influential around the world, and increasingly so, due to global capitalism.[9] One

---

[4] L. Raymond, 'Sovereignty without Property: Recent Books in Public Lands Scholarship' (2003) 43 Natural Resources J 313 at 315 (noting that only one of the five books on public lands policy that she reviewed discussed property rights).

[5] See, in particular, A. Scott, *The Evolution of Resources Property Rights* (2008). See also the body of work by Liebcap on the evolution of mining rights on the 'frontier': G. Liebcap, *The Evolution of Private Mineral Rights: Nevada's Comstock Lode* (1978).

[6] A recent exception is R. Barnes, *Property Rights and Natural Resources* (2009) (focusing on international law, although early chapters deal more generally with property theory).

[7] R. L. Fischman, 'What Is Natural Resources Law?' (2007) 78 U Colorado L Rev 717 at 718.

[8] eg, F. I. Michelman, 'Property, Utility, and Fairness: Comments on the Ethical Foundations of "Just Compensation" Law' (1967) 80 Harv L Rev 1165; S. R. Munzer, *A Theory of Property* (1990); J. Waldron, 'Property, Honesty, and Normative Resilience', in *New Essays in the Legal and Political Theory of Property* (S. Munzer, ed, 2001) 10.

[9] A. Lehavi, 'The Universal Law of the Land' available at <http://ssrn.com/abstract=1260366>; E. Meidinger, 'Property Law for Development Policy and Institutional Theory: Problems of

of the most interesting current developments in property law theory is that defin-itions of property rights in national legal systems are increasingly subject to transnational influences. The growth of 'regulatory expropriations' law through multilateral and bilateral investment and treaties (eg the Energy Charter Treaty and the North American Free Trade Agreement) and the definition and enforce-ment of standards for property and resource management by non-governmental organizations both illustrate this influence.

This chapter divides the issues that the property theory literature addresses into the two basic types already mentioned. One is the question of subject matter: what is, and what is not, property? The other is the issue of justifi-cations for, and limits on, property. These broad categories are, of course, artificial distinctions. Indeed, our review of the literature suggests that C. B. Macpherson was right when, thirty years ago, he charged that justifications or criticisms go hand in hand with definitions: 'To formulate, or merely to accept, a particular concept of property is to justify or criticize a given insti-tution of property'.[10]

Section I of this chapter takes a broad look at the literature addressing the question of 'what is property?' and the issues raised by that question. We dis-cuss a number of conceptualist and instrumentalist approaches to the matter of definition, look briefly at the issue of commodification, examine the literature on the categories of property, and conclude with a consideration of the *numerus clausus* principle. Section II addresses the problem of justifying property, or at least private property. We outline the various explanations, dividing them into four types: the labour, desert, first possession (or occupation) and economic theories; personhood theories; liberty-based theories, and pluralist theories. We then look at explanations for the movement of property from one category to another, explanations that include the 'tragedy of the commons', the usual economic justification for converting an open access commons to either private property or state (or public) property. Section II concludes with a study of the justifications for (private) property as applied to the issue of expropriation.

I. What is property?

Some very fundamental questions about the nature of property are still controver-sial. Theorists writing in this area do not all mean the same thing when they use the term 'property'. Does property exist as a distinct legal category? Is it merely a

---

Structure, Choice, and Change' in *The Mystery of Capital and the Construction of Social Reality* (B. Smith, D. M. Mark, and I. Ehrlich, eds, 2008), available at <http://ssrn.com/abstract=876467>.

[10] C. B. Macpherson, *Property: Mainstream and Critical Positions* (1978) at 12. See also A. Clarke and P. Kohler, *Property Law: Commentary and Materials* (2005) at 372 (asserting that '[t]hose who seek to offer a definition that goes beyond this are simply attempting to make property support a philosophical, moral or political burden that it cannot bear').

concentration or aggregation of the law's usual entitlements, a bundle of rights, one or more of which must be present in order to earn the label 'property'? Does it have any value of its own or is it merely of instrumental use to an economic system?[11]

The literature answers the question of 'what is property?' in a number of different ways. We begin this part of the chapter by looking at two different methods for understanding property: conceptualism and instrumentalism. For some, property is a category worth analysing and understanding for its own sake (conceptualism); for others, it is merely a means to another end, such as economic efficiency (instrumentalism). We then turn briefly to the literature on commodification, a different type of answer to the question of 'what is property?'. Commodification looks at what can and cannot be the object of property. Next we discuss the literature on the various categories of property: open access commons, community commons, private property and state property. The forms of property are particularly important, if only because so much of the literature ostensibly addressing issues of 'property' is actually making arguments directed only towards private property. In the final section of this part, we review the literature on the *numerus clausus* principle—the idea that there are only a finite number of property interests that will be, or should be, recognized in law.

A. Conceptualist and instrumentalist approaches

Conceptualists tend to rely on notions derived from Roman law, insisting on the primacy of *in rem* rights—rights good against the world—and often privileging certain rights, such as the right to exclude.[12] Instrumentalists are not so concerned about what property is; they want to know what purposes the institution of property can be made to serve. In this section of the chapter, we first examine a number of conceptualist approaches to property. These approaches include property as 'thing' versus property as a bundle of rights, and property as the right to exclude versus property as the right to access and use. This discussion of conceptualist approaches ends, however, with the idea that attempts to give meaning to the concept of property are ill-conceived. This leads to a review of some of the alternative instrumentalist approaches to the issue, beginning with the notion that property is that which the law protects, a notion that focuses on enforcement. Also included are ideas of property as communication, as power, as sovereignty and as economic expectations.

1. *Conceptualism*

The simplest and easiest conception of property to grasp is the idea of property as 'things'.

---

[11] C. B. Macpherson, 'Property as Means or End?' in *Theories of Property Aristotle to the Present* (A. Parel and T. Flanagan, eds, 1979) 3.

[12] A. Bell and G. Parchomovsky, 'A Theory of Property' (2004–2005) 90 Cornell L Rev 532 at 535.

For example, one of the most famous descriptions of property—that of William Blackstone—focuses on the 'thing-ness of property', as well as the right to exclude: 'There is nothing which so generally strikes the imagination, and engages the affections of mankind, as the right of property; or that sole and despotic dominion which one man claims and exercises over the external things of the world, in total exclusion of the right of any other individual in the universe.'[13] While libertarian scholars such as Richard Epstein[14] may still celebrate this view of property, most writers think a focus on this paragraph is a distortion of the common law. David Schorr[15] and Carol Rose[16] insist that Blackstone himself did not have this view of property if one looks at the *Commentaries* in their entirety. Much of Blackstone's discussion of property is devoted to a consideration of concurrent and competing interests in land, including various gathering and harvesting rights, which suggests that the image of property as sole and despotic dominion was not true in Blackstone's time and is similarly inaccurate and unhelpful today.

The idea that property is only tangible things is a view held by few, although everyone credits laypeople with this (mis)conception.[17] In our so-called information age, the most valuable property rights are often in intangible goods. Almost all theoretical work on property is now disembodied. Few mainstream theorists pay attention to the time and physical space dimensions of property.[18] Even the vocabulary of 'things' has been replaced with the vocabulary of 'resources', with its connotation of instrumental value.

Nevertheless, there has been a fair amount of recent discussion of the idea of property as 'things', in part because of the challenges of virtual property, the information commons, and the like. Material conditions figure prominently in writing by many feminist,[19] environmentalist,[20] and indigenous scholars.[21] Some feminist engagements with property insist on a strategy of embodiment

---

[13] W. Blackstone, *Blackstone's Commentaries on the Laws of England* (1765–69), Book II, c. I, available at <http://www.yale.edu/lawweb/avalon/blackstone/blacksto.htm>.

[14] eg, R. Epstein's *Takings: Private Property and the Power of Eminent Domain* (1985) at 66 (asserting that 'private property gives the right to exclude *without* the need for any justification', with emphasis in the original).

[15] D. Schorr, 'How Blackstone became a Blackstonian' (2008) 10 Theoretical Inquiries in Law 103.

[16] C. M. Rose, 'Canons of Property Talk, or, Blackstone's Anxiety' (1998) 108 Yale LJ 601.

[17] eg, B. Ackerman, *Private Property and the Constitution* (1977) at 26–31, 97–103 (contrasting the 'scientific' perspective on the meaning of property with the 'layman's' perspective).

[18] But see the writings of Bell and Parchomovsky, above n 12, who write about the three dimensions of property (number of owners, scope of dominion and asset design (size)).

[19] eg, H. Lim and A. Bottomley, *Feminist Perspectives on Land Law* (2007) (insisting on a material grounding for critiques of the ownership model of private property).

[20] eg, A. Leopold, *A Sand County Almanac and Sketches from Here and There* (1949); E. T. Freyfogle, *The Land We Share: Private Property and the Common Good* (2003); and E. Freyfogle, 'Ownership and Ecology' (1993) 43 Case Western Reserve L Rev 1269 (emphasizing that a reconceptualization of property with an ecological understanding would need to recognize the importance of place, and of place embedded with a local and interlinked ecosystem).

[21] eg, F. Rose, *The Traditional Mode of Production of the Australian Aborigines* (1987); J. Y. Henderson, M. L. Benson, and I. M. Findlay, *Aboriginal Tenure in the Constitution of Canada* (2000); K. A. Carpenter, 'Real Property and Peoplehood' (2008) 27 Stanford Environmental L J 313.

and embedding.[22] These feminist legal scholars want to shift law's focus to tangible experiences with the corporeal and, specifically, the materiality of women's condition in relation to land. Similarly, personhood theories of property, whether within a feminist tradition,[23] or within a tradition of indigenous legal systems,[24] or other communitarian traditions,[25] tend to emphasize the relationship between people and particular property and resist the commodification and homogenization of property. The same is true of those who write about property law from an ecological perspective.[26] To take another example from the 'thing' side of the *summa divisio* in civil law between 'persons' and 'things', recent thinking has included work by scholars who limit the category to what the Romans called *res corporales*, that is, the natural and man-made objects that exist in time and space and that can be sensed, with everything else belonging to the category of rights and obligations.[27] How one views the re-materialization of the category of 'things' affects how one characterizes animals and new reproductive technologies such as cloning.

While the notion of property as a thing may dominate outside academic and professional circles and may play a role in critical perspectives, the 'bundle of rights' view of property is the prevalent conceptualist view in law. For example, Robert Coase's understanding of property, in his famous 1960 article, 'The Problem of Social Cost' (the starting point of most modern discussions of the economics of property rights), appears to be derived from a bundle of rights conception.[28] It is commonplace in the common law to think of property as a disaggregated set of interpersonal relations, based on Wesley Hohfeld's fundamental legal conceptions.[29] Hohfeld provided an account of legal relations that has been very influential in transforming understandings of property rights in Anglo-American scholarship. He is known today primarily for his theory of jural opposites and correlatives in which rights, privileges, powers, and immunities are paired with no-rights, duties, disabilities, and liabilities. Hohfeld did not use the metaphor 'bundle of rights' to describe property, but his theory of jural relations and his

[22] eg, H. Lim and A. Bottomley, 'Feminist Perambulations: Taking the Law for a Walk in Land' in *Feminist Perspectives on Land Law*, above n 19 at 9.

[23] M.J. Radin, 'The Liberal Conception of Property: Crosscurrents in the Jurisprudence of Takings' in *Reinterpreting Property* (M. J. Radin, ed, 1993) 120.

[24] Carpenter, above n 21 (applying and extending Radin's idea of personhood to the concept of peoplehood in the context of the property claims of indigenous people).

[25] N. Blomley, 'Landscapes of Property' in *The Legal Geographies Reader* (N. Blomley, D. Delaney, and R. Ford, eds, 2001) 118 (discussing the idea of community property by contrast with formal property and suggesting that residents of an area build community which becomes 'theirs').

[26] Freyfogle, 'Ownership and Ecology,' above n 20.

[27] J.-R. Trahan, 'The Distinction between Persons and Things: An Historical Perspective' (2008) 1 J Civil Law Studies 9 at 17.

[28] R. H. Coase, 'The Problem of Social Cost' (1960) 3 JL & Econ 1 at 44 ('We may speak of a person owning land and using it as a factor of production but what the land-owner in fact possesses is the right to carry out a circumscribed list of actions').

[29] W. N. Hohfeld, 'Some Fundamental Legal Conceptions as Applied in Judicial Reasoning' (1913) 23 Yale LJ 16.

efforts to reduce *in rem* rights to clusters of *in personam* rights provided the impetus for the metaphor.[30]

In the bundle of rights metaphor, each right, power, privilege, immunity or duty is one stick in the aggregate bundle that constitutes a property relationship. Whether the removal of one or more sticks from the bundle means that the remainder of the sticks can no longer be categorized as 'property' is not determined in advance. A. M. Honoré helped to popularize the bundle of rights metaphor with his list of the 'incidents' of property ownership:

Ownership comprises the right to possess, the right to use, the right to manage, the right to the income of the thing, the right to the capital, the right to security, the rights or incidents of transmissibility and absence of term, the prohibition of harmful use, liability to execution, and the incident of residuarity: this makes eleven leading incidents.[31]

This list of incidents proved to be very influential although different authors provide different lists of incidents and there is disagreement over the relative importance of the various sticks.[32] However, in the absence of agreement as to which sticks are required in order to label any particular bundle as 'property,' the conception is extremely malleable.[33] According to its critics, this view can succumb to nominalism,[34] even incoherence.[35]

Interestingly, the right to exclude is not one of the incidents of property on Honoré's list, although many consider it to be the *sine qua non* of property. Exclusion is considered essential, particularly to an *in rem* understanding of property rights, because it protects stable possession by prohibiting non-consensual takers and users. For example, Felix Cohen argued that private property describes a relationship among people that allows an owner to exclude or include others

[30] Hohfeld suggested that *in personam* and *in rem* rights were composed of exactly the same types of entitlements and differed only in the indefiniteness and number of persons bound by the relations. See Merrill and Smith, above n 2 at 364–5.

[31] A. M. Honoré, 'Ownership' in *Oxford Essays in Jurisprudence* (A. G. Guest, ed,1961) 107 at 113.

[32] eg, H. Dagan, 'The Craft of Property' (2003) 91 Cal L Rev 1517 at 1532 (asserting there is no *a priori* list of entitlements that the owner of a given resource inevitably enjoys); C. A. Arnold, 'The Reconstitution of Property: Property as a Web of Interests' (2002) 26 Harv Envtl L Rev 281 at 285 n 20 (describing different scholarly lists of the incidents of property); L. A. Fennell, 'Adjusting Alienability' (2008–2009) 122 Harv L Rev 1403 (arguing that limits on alienability could sidestep resource holdout problems and lessen resort to liability rules). See also Scott, above n 5, referring to three *powers* typically associated with property rights (the power to use and manage, the power to transfer and the power to take income) and six *characteristics* of rights to resources (exclusivity, duration, flexibility, quality of title, transferability and divisibility).

[33] The problems of conceptualization are particularly acute in the context of comparative work in property theory. 'Property' must be a meaningful term to evaluate similarities and differences in regimes. See O. L. Reed and F. A. Stamm, 'The Connection between a Property-Based Legal System and National Prosperity: Example from a Divided Germany Reunified' (2004–2005) 33 Ga J Int'l & Comp L 573 at 575.

[34] A. Mossoff, 'What is Property? Putting the Pieces Back Together' (2003) 45 Ariz L Rev 371 at 372.

[35] K. Gray, 'Property in Thin Air' (1991) 50 Cambridge L J 252.

from certain activities in connection with the owner's property, with the state backing either decision.[36] Thomas Merrill and Henry E. Smith distinguish contract and property rights by the fact that contract rights refer to very specific arrangements between particular people whereas property rights refer to very general rights relative to the world as a whole.[37] More recently, Thomas Merrill has also made the conceptual claim that property consists primarily of a 'right to exclude'.[38] The well-known work of Peruvian economist Hernando DeSoto gives primacy to the right to exclude, arguing that state-based legal systems should recognize and incorporate the informal property rights of urban squatters and rural villagers and 'listen to the barking dogs'. [39] Barking dogs guard boundary incursions. The property rights envisioned are those in which an owner has the right to exclude or permit entry by others.[40]

Generally speaking, property characterized by rights of exclusion is often called private property, while that which is characterized by rights of inclusion are termed public or common property. Some property law theorists push the contingent nature of property claims to the extreme. Thus, C. B. Macpherson, for example, has suggested that there would be nothing to prevent us from reconceptualizing property as the right to be included.[41] Still, many of the more moderate claims for distributive justice rest on the idea of individual and group rights to be included. The idea is not new. Some traditional property laws are framed in this way, including riparian law which affords rights of access and use for certain uses to a defined group of land owners based on their proximity to the water or, more specifically, ownership of the bank.

[36] F. Cohen, 'Dialogue on Private Property' (1954) 9 Rutgers L Rev 357 at 373 (arguing 'that is property to which the following label can be attached: To the World: Keep off X unless you have my permission, which I may grant or withhold. Signed, Private Citizen. Endorsed: The State').
[37] T. W. Merrill and H. E. Smith, 'The Property/Contract Interface' (2001) 101 Columbia L Rev 773.
[38] T. W. Merrill, 'Property and the Right to Exclude' (1998) 77 Nebraska LJ 730 at 748; T. W. Merrill and H. E. Smith, *Property: Principles and Policies* (2007) at v. See also T. W. Merrill and H. E. Smith, 'The Morality of Property' (2007) 48 William & Mary L Rev 1849 at 1850 (claiming that 'the differentiating feature of a system of property [is] the right of the owner to act as the exclusive gatekeeper of the owned thing'); S. Balganesh, 'Demystifying the Right to Exclude: Of Property, Inviolability, and Automatic Injunctions' (2008) 31 Harvard J L & Public Policy 593 (focusing on the duty of exclusion imposed on non-owners, rather than a mere entitlement to injunctive relief).
[39] H. DeSoto, *The Mystery of Capital: Why Capitalism Triumphs in the West and Fails Everywhere Else* (2000) at 163, 179.
[40] C. M. Rose, 'Invasions, Innovation, Environment' Arizona Legal Studies Discussion Paper No 09–14, available at <http://ssrn.com/abstract=1371256>. Interestingly, Scott, above n 5, writing in the context of the evolution of resource rights, uses the term 'exclusivity' rather than exclusion. What Scott has in mind is the extent to which the holder of a resource right is free to exercise that right without let or hindrance from others, including neighbours (spillover problems) or the state (through regulation).
[41] C. B. Macpherson, 'Liberal Democracy and Property' in *Property: Mainstream and Critical Positions*, above n 10, 199. See also H. Dagan, 'Exclusion and Inclusion in Property', available at <http://ssrn.com/abstract=1416580> (criticizing exclusion-centrism in property theory and arguing that inclusion is also a key component of property).

A variation on the 'right to exclude' conception—or perhaps a clarification—is the idea of an exclusive right to use. Some argue that exclusion excludes non-owners not from the *res* or thing, but rather from the 'dominion or indefinite right of user or disposition' associated with the thing.[42] Others, however, emphasize the importance of the free use of whatever one owns separate and distinct from a right to exclude. Those theorists who focus on use or access to resources tend to be those who adopt a more critical stance toward the traditional understandings of property.[43] For example, the literature critiquing the formalization of customary entitlements to land by the creation of market-oriented policies gives primacy to access rights.[44]

While some theorists emphasize the right to exclude and others the right to use, many environmentalists emphasize the opposite of rights, that is, the duties in the bundle of entitlements that make up the notion of property.[45] Even Honoré recognized 'the prohibition of harmful use' in his list of property's incidents.[46] The argument is that an owner's right to the use and enjoyment of the object of property is limited by inherent social and environmental obligations.[47]

This brief review illustrates that attempts to conceptualize property run into several problems. The different concepts enshrine different, incommensurable values.[48] It does not seem possible to reach agreement on what property is. Definitional attempts can also seem circular. It is often difficult to say whether the law protects property, or whether 'property' is the name given to that which the law protects.[49] Some scholars argue that 'property' does not hold together as a legal construct and so the conceptualist's project is ill-founded. One of the best known versions of this argument is that of Kevin Gray, who wrote that property

[42] E. Claeys, 'Property 101: Is Property a Thing or a Bundle?' (2009) Seattle Univ L Rev 1 at 14 (forthcoming), at: <http://ssrn.com/abstract=1338372>.

[43] eg, J. Waldron, 'Homelessness and the Issue of Freedom' (1991) 39 UCLA L Rev 295 at 296–9; M. Demian, ' "Land doesn't come from your mother, she didn't make it with her hands": challenging matriliny in Papua New Guinea' in *Feminist Perspectives on Land Law*, above n 19, 155; G. Cederlöf, *Landscapes and the Law: Environmental Politics, Regional Histories and Contests over Nature* (2008) (examining the role of law in consolidating early colonial rule from the perspective of people's access to nature in forests and hill tracts). But see J. C. Ribot and N. L. Peluso, 'A Theory of Access' (2003) 68(2) Rural Sociology 153 (developing a concept of access to differentiate it from property in order to enable a wider range of actors to benefit from natural resources).

[44] eg, J.-P. Chauveau et al, *Changes in Land Access, Institutions and Markets in West Africa* (2006); T. Sikora and T. Q. Nguyen, 'Why May Forest Devolution Not Benefit the Rural Poor? Forest Entitlements in Vietnam's Central Highlands' (2007) 35 World Development 2010; J. C. Franco, 'Making Land Rights Accessible: Social Movements and Political-Legal Innovation in the Rural Philippines' (2008) 44(7) J. Development Studies 991.

[45] eg, J. W. Singer, *Entitlement: The Paradoxes of Property* (2000); L. S. Underkuffler, ed, *The Idea of Property: Its Meaning and Power* (2003).

[46] Honoré, above n 31 at 113.

[47] M. Raff, 'Environmental Obligations and the Western Liberal Property Concept' (1998) 22 Melb U L Rev 657; C. Circo, 'Does Sustainability Require a New Theory of Property Rights?', available at <http://papers.ssrn.com/sol3/papers.cfm?abstract_id=1343228>.

[48] G. S. Alexander et al, 'A Statement of Progressive Property' (2009) 94 Cornell L Rev 743.

[49] S. Waddams, *Dimensions of Private Law: Categories and Concepts in Anglo-American Legal Reasoning* (2003) at 173.

is 'a vacant concept...oddly enough rather like thin air.'[50] Gray's point is that property is an illusion, an object of desire through which we are 'seduced into believing that we have found an objective reality which embodies our intuitions and needs'.[51] But, saying it is an illusion does not mean that it does not exist. It does mean, as Margaret Davies argues in her assessment of the ontology of property, that it is a construction with significant social and legal effects.[52] Instrumentalists focus on these social and legal effects and it is to that work that we now turn. The following section examines some of the main ideas here, including property as an enforcement institution, as communication, as power, as sovereignty and as economic expectation.

2. *Instrumentalism*

Property is often seen by economists as merely the institution or system of rules that protects people's entitlements with respect to the control of resources. Any discussion of the enforcement of property rights must begin with the oft-cited article by Guido Calabresi and A. Douglas Melamed, 'Property Rules, Liability Rules, and Inalienability: One View of the Cathedral,' published in 1972.[53] The authors set out a framework of entitlements and examined how the legal system protects these entitlements by different types of rules: property rules, liability rules and entitlements protected by inalienability rules. Entitlements protected by an inalienability rule may not to be transferred. Those protected by a property rule may be transferred only with the owner's consent and for a price set by or agreed to by the owner and the holder of the entitlement is generally entitled to injunctive relief. Entitlements protected by a liability rule may be taken by another in exchange for the payment of a price to be determined by a third party (for example, a damages award for a polluting smoke stack).

Most property rights are enforced through consent-based entitlements.[54] Trespassers to real property face injunctions, theft is a criminal offence, and so on. In some cases, however, property rights are enforced more weakly through liability rules. Expropriation is the most obvious example, but liability rules are also found at work in land title registration systems where an error by the registrar may work a dispossession, and in nuisance cases when the outcome is a damages award, not an injunction. There is no one-to-one correspondence between property and property rules, although the similarity is close enough to cause some analytical confusion.[55]

---

[50] Gray, above n 35 at 252. See also A. Pottage's 'Instituting Property' (1998) 18 Oxford J Legal Stud 331.

[51] ibid.

[52] M. Davies, *Property: Meanings, Histories, Theories* (2007) at 18.

[53] (1972) 85 Harv L Rev 1089.

[54] R. A. Epstein, 'A Clear View of the Cathedral: The Dominance of Property Rules' (1997) 106 Yale LJ 2091; H. E. Smith, 'Property and Property Rules' (2004) 79 New York University L Rev 1719.

[55] Indeed, it might be less confusing to refer to this form of entitlement as a consent entitlement; this has the advantage of allowing us to ask when property is protected by a consent entitlement

Since the original article, the literature has expanded the scope and applicability of the Calabresi and Melamed framework. Explications of the 'Cathedral' article have created one of the largest bodies of literature in law and economics.[56] There are also a number of extensive reviews of the legal literature influenced by the original 'Cathedral' article.[57]

If property is contingent and socially constructed, as it surely must be, then text, symbols, stories, and pictures are critical to the understanding of property. Much of property can be understood as the signalling of claims and the responses to those signals.[58] Seeing property as communication focuses on the effects of labelling something 'property'. Carol Rose is one theorist who has thoroughly explored property as an expressive endeavour.[59] For example, she has developed a narrative theory to explain the centrality of possession to property law.[60] Rose explained that property law, to function effectively, must take account of the intended audience and the symbolic context. In a similar vein, Henry E. Smith has argued that property law prefers possessors because possession conveys information efficiently to third parties. This is important not only in reducing the costs of discovering ownership prior to transfer of property, but also in reducing evidentiary costs should disputes arise about ownership.[61] The communicative value of property also underlies the approach of Merrill and Smith to the *numerus clausus* view of property,[62] discussed later in this Part.

Sometimes the message that property conveys is one of power. Some theorists see property as 'an abbreviated reference to a quantum of socially permissible

and when by a liability entitlement thereby avoiding the more tautological formulation, 'when is property protected by a property entitlement?'.

[56] A symposium was held to celebrate the article's 25th anniversary and the proceedings were published in 'Property Rules, Liability Rules, and Inalienability: A Twenty-Five Year Retrospective' (1997) 106 Yale LJ.

[57] eg, L. Kaplow and S. Shavell, 'Property Rules Versus Liability Rules' (1996) 109 Harv L Rev 713; J. L. Schroeder, 'Three's a Crowd: A Feminist Critique of Calabresi and Melamed's: One View of the Cathedral' (1999) 84 Cornell L Rev 394; I. Ayres, *Optional Law: The Structure of Legal Entitlements* (2005).

[58] C. M. Rose, 'Introduction: Property and Language, or, the Ghost of the Fifth Panel' (2006) 18 Yale J L & Humanities 1, available at <http://ssrn.com/abstract=934655>. Nestor Davidson has recently argued that the most important and ubiquitous messages that property communicates are messages about relative status: 'Property and Relative Status' (2009) 109 Mich L Rev (forthcoming), available at <http://ssrn/com/abstract/=1338917>. Davidson's analysis is similar to other work that has analysed property as a metaphor for 'the proper', that is, the idea that property reflects and cements propriety or the proper hierarchical order of the social and political spheres: M. Davies, 'The Proper: Discourses of Purity' (1998) 9 Law & Critique 147 (building on Jacques Derrida's identification of 'the proper' as embedded in language and knowledge); S. H. Razack, ed, *Race, Space and the Law: Unmapping a White Settler Society* (2002) (exploring the relationship between property, proper place and propriety).

[59] eg, *Property and Persuasion: Essays on the History, Theory and Rhetoric of Ownership* (1994).

[60] C. M. Rose, 'Possession as the Origin of Property' (1985) 52 U Chi L Rev 73 at 85.

[61] H. E. Smith, 'The Language of Property: Form, Context, and Audience' (2003) 55 Stan L Rev 1105 at 1115–25.

[62] T. W. Merrill and H. E. Smith, 'Optimal Standardization in the Law of Property: The *Numerus Clausus* Principle' (2000–2001) 110 Yale LJ 1.

power exercised in respect of socially valued resources'.[63] Among the most recent and influential accounts of property as social relations of power are those of Joseph William Singer.[64] The label 'property' conveys certain forms of power on owners, depending upon who can own, what they can own, and how they can own it. The ability to own, for example, is an incident of legal personhood, and the class of persons able to own property has expanded over the centuries, most notably to include women.[65] The liability to be owned, to be an object of property, was correlated to race prior to the abolition of slavery and, although outlawed in international law, today is correlated to gender, age and poverty.[66]

One of the themes that recurs through almost all discussions of property, building upon the understanding of property as power, is the idea that the concept of property delineates the private sphere from the public and, in doing so, privatizes and thereby hides the political power of property.[67] The western liberal conception of property insists, as did Roman law, on a distinction between *imperium*, or political power, and *dominium*, or private power. The distinction has, however, long been questioned. Morris Cohen stated long ago that 'we must not overlook the actual fact that *dominion* over things is also *imperium* over our fellow human beings'.[68]

The idea of property as power is closely related to the idea of property as sovereignty. Hugo Grotius treated sovereignty as property: 'Where the sovereignty is a full property right, it includes ownership of the land and people, and the right to dispose of all at pleasure'.[69] The emphasis here is on the power of the sovereign to change property relations. It does not follow from this that a change in sovereignty automatically effects a change in property relationships, a point of crucial importance in the context of Indigenous Peoples and their traditional territories.[70]

---

[63] K. Gray and S. F. Gray, 'Private Property and Public Propriety,' in *Property and the Constitution* (J. McLean, ed, 1999) 11 at 12. See also K. R. Minogue, 'The Concept of Property and its Contemporary Significance', in *Property: Nomos XXII* (J. R. Pennock and J. W. Chapman, eds, 1980) 3 at 5.

[64] eg, J. W. Singer, 'The Reliance Interest in Property' (1988) 40 Stan L Rev 611; J. W. Singer and J. M. Beerman, 'The Social Origins of Property' (1993) 6 Can J L & Juris 217. For a review of the social relations approach to property, see S. Munzer, 'Property as Social Relations' in *New Essays in the Legal and Political Theory of Property*, above n 8, 36. Among political theorists adopting similar views, see C. B. Macpherson, 'The Meaning of Property' in *Property: Mainstream and Critical Positions*, above n 10, 1; J. Nedelsky, 'Law, Boundaries, and the Bounded Self' (1990) 30 Representations 162; J. Nedelsky, 'Property in Potential Life? A Relational Approach to Choosing Legal Categories' (1993) 6 Can. J L & Jurisprudence 343.

[65] eg, the Married Women's Property Rights Act 1882, c 75, significantly altered English law regarding the property rights of married women, allowing them to own and control their own property. See A. L. Erickson, *Women and Property in Early Modern England* (1993).

[66] Davies, above n 52 at 77–80.

[67] ibid at 10–12.

[68] M. R. Cohen, 'Property and Sovereignty' (1927) 13 Cornell L Rev 8 at 13.

[69] Quoted in C. E. Merriam Jr., *History of the Theory of Sovereignty Since Rousseau* (2001) at 12. See also H. Grotius, *De Jure Belli Ac Pacis Libri Tres*, bk 2, c 8, para 1, at 295 (F. W. Kelsey trans, 1925); S. Pufendorf, *De Jure Naturae et Gentium Libri Octo*, bk 4, c 4, para 14 (Oldfather trans, 1934).

[70] For different perspectives on the relationship between property rights and territory rights, see C. Nine, 'A Lockean Theory of Territory' (2008) 56 Political Studies 148; A. Buchanan, *Justice,*

The relationship between property and sovereignty is reversed, however, by those who see property as a creation of the state.[71] Property is regarded as a kind of grant or delegation of personal sovereignty, with 'property becoming a microcosm of law and the proprietor a mini-legislature'.[72] Morris Cohen noted that property could represent a form of private sovereignty by the wealthy over the poor, a degree of personal control that rivalled the most coercive authority of any government.[73] In an innovative extension of this idea, Karen Merrill has applied Cohen's argument to the issue of sovereignty on public lands.[74] The relationship between property rights and claims to sovereignty could be seen as a key relationship in any shift of authority over public lands.[75] Nevertheless, the connection between the two concepts appears to be under-theorized in property.

More fundamental to natural resources and energy law are the economic ideas of property. The predominant instrumentalist view, developed over the past century by economists, is the idea that property is a legal right to draw a benefit from a valuable resource. This is an instrumentalist approach built on the idea that property is an institution uniquely qualified to protect utility or welfare. The function of property institutions, from this perspective, includes the establishment of rules about what owners, users, and others can expect to receive in the way of benefits flowing from a particular resource. The idea underlying this understanding of property is expectation. Armen Alchian and William Allen, for example, define property in terms of 'the expectations a person has that his decisions about uses of certain resources will be effective'.[76] The idea is not new. Jeremy Bentham began his chapter 'Of Property', in his *Theory of Legislation*, with the idea that '[p]roperty is nothing more than the basis of a certain expectation; namely, the expectation of deriving hereafter certain advantages from a thing (which we are already said to possess) by reason of the relation in which we stand towards it'.[77]

Legitimacy, and Self-Determination: Moral Foundations for International Law (2004); L. Brilmayer, 'Consent, Contract and Territory' (1989) 74 Minnesota L Rev 1. And on the continuity of indigenous property systems see L. B. Ederington, 'Property as a Natural Institution: The Separation of Property from Sovereignty in International Law' (1997–1998) 13 Am U Int'l L Rev 263 (examining the recognition of private property in *terra nullius*, the preservation of property rights after changes in sovereignty, and the protection of property rights during military occupation as embodying the notion that property rights precede government).

[71] N. Blomley, 'Remember Property' (2005) 29 Progress in Human Geography 125.
[72] Davies, above n 52 at 33, 109. See also K. Vandevelde, 'The New Property of the Nineteenth Century: The Development of the Modern Concept of Property' (1980) 29 Buffalo L Rev 325 at 328; K. Aoki, '(Intellectual) Property and Sovereignty: Notes Towards a Cultural Geography of Authorship' (1996) 48 Stanford L Rev 1293 at 1311–15.
[73] Cohen, above n 68.
[74] K. R. Merrill, *Public Lands and Political Meaning: Ranchers, the Government, and the Property Between Them* (2002).
[75] Raymond, above n 4 at 315.
[76] A. A. Alchian and W. R. Allen, *Exchange and Production: Theory in Use* (1969) at 158.
[77] J. Bentham, *Theory of Legislation*, vol 1 (1914) at 145. Bentham wrote mainly to quash the idea that property was pre-political. He famously said: 'Property and law were born together, and

In this section we have touched on a number of different approaches to property. Dominant ideas in the literature include property as a bundle of rights (especially the right to exclude) and property as the private equivalent of sovereignty protected and enforced by consent entitlements rather than a liability entitlement. These themes resonate within the energy and natural resources sector.[78] For this sector, the separation of the sticks in the bundle is crucial for both the state and the operator. While the operator will insist on exclusive rights to the resource in question within a particular geographical location, the state will typically confine the right to a particular resource or category of resources (eg oil and gas resources or hard rock minerals or coal) and rights will typically be framed in incorporeal terms as a right to extract or a right to harvest and reduce to possession, rather than ownership in place. Another stick in the bundle that is crucial for the operator is the transferability of the interest and in particular the question of whether or not the interest is transferable with or without government approval. Crucial too in many cases will be the proprietary status of non-working (and non-possessory) interests in the resource rights such as royalty interests and analogous interests such as net profits interests. The holder of such an interest will clearly prefer to be able to make an *in rem* claim that binds the world.

B. Commodification

In this section we leave the question of the subject matter of property and look at the object of property. What can be property? What type of thing or non-thing? This is an area of theorizing that has received some recent attention, particularly in the case of government benefits, bodies and body parts, sacred sites, certain natural resources and intellectual property. The issue is to what extent can and should these be commodified?

Nearly all valuable goods and services have become alienable commodities in our world. Richard Posner, an advocate of universal commodification, summarized his reasons for adopting that position in his book, *The Economic Analysis of Law*:

If every valuable (meaning scarce as well as desired) resource were owned by someone (universality), if ownership connoted the unqualified power to exclude everybody else from using the resource (exclusivity) as well as to use it oneself, and if ownership rights were freely transferable, or as lawyers say alienable (transferability), value would be maximized.[79]

Capitalism needs commodities and globalization is premised on increased commodification. If all goods can be priced, all prices can be compared, and all value is commensurable. Labelling goods with exchange values produces the fungibility

would die together. Before the laws property did not exist; take away the laws, and property will be no more': ibid at 146–7.

[78] See generally Scott, above n 5.
[79] R. Posner, *The Economic Analysis of Law* (5th edn, 1998) at 34.

necessary to engage in a cost-benefit analysis. Commodification focuses us on the instrumental value of the good for sale, leading us to undervalue or disregard its inherent worth. In the case of human beings and natural resources, this disregard is of moral concern.[80]

Carol Rose has emphasized that the objection to commodification is largely an objection to a particular feature of property rights, namely alienability, and especially alienability through sale.[81] This appears to be true for the bulk of the literature on the topic. However, one of the best known pieces of scholarship on the topic of what can be the object of property is not concerned with alienability. In an influential article published forty-five years ago, Charles Reich discussed the property-like characteristics of welfare payments and other government-created benefits.[82] He argued that claims to participate in state wealth—the 'new property'—served the same purpose as that traditionally served by property ownership, namely to secure individual autonomy against state interference. His article spawned a literature on the 'new property'[83] but, as the past forty-five years have shown, the general trend is that formal claims to government benefits have become less property-like rather than more.

Margaret Radin's *Contested Commodities* is another well-known look at how far society should go in permitting people to buy and sell goods and services.[84] Should it be possible to treat such things as babies, body parts, sex, and companionship as commodities that can be traded in a free market? Radin argues for a conception of incomplete commodification, in which some contested things can be bought and sold, but only under carefully regulated circumstances.

The issue of commodification is also a major one in scholarship concerning intellectual property. Most legal systems proceed from the basic premise that no one generally can 'own' knowledge. Instead, the default rule is that knowledge remains free for all to use. Of course, as with all default rules, there are exceptions. Intellectual property, such as patents and copyrights, is one of these exceptions justified by policy considerations, including the 'reward for creativity' version of the desert theory justifying property.[85] Most authors, working

---

[80] N. Smith., 'Commodification in Law: Ideologies, Intractabilities, and Hyperboles' (2009) 42 Continental Philosophy Review 1 at 4, available at <http://ssrn.com/abstract=1350369>.

[81] C. M. Rose, 'The Moral Subject of Property' (2007) 48 William & Mary Law Review 1897, available at <http://ssrn.com/abstract=926082>.

[82] C. A. Reich, 'The New Property' (1964) 73 Yale LJ 733.

[83] eg, M. A. Glendon, 'The New Family and the New Property' (1978) 53 Tul L Rev 697; K.J. Vandervelde, 'The New Property of the Nineteenth Century: The Development of the Modern Concept of Property' (1980) 29 Buffalo L Rev 325; R. H. Nelson, 'Private Rights to Government Actions: How Modern Property Rights Evolve' [1986] U Ill L Rev 361.

[84] M. J. Radin, *Contested Commodities* (1996). See also M. Ertman and J. Williams, eds, *Rethinking Commodification: Cases and Readings in Law and Culture* (2005); S. Wilkinson, *Bodies for Sale: Ethics and Exploitation in the Human Body Trade* (2003).

[85] J. T. Cross, 'Justifying Property Rights in Native American Traditional Knowledge', available at: <http://ssrn.com/abstract=1328473> (examining why legal systems choose to grant property rights in the products of the mind). See Part II.A.1. below.

within a variety of conceptual or instrumental frameworks, have concluded that statutorily-created intellectual property does indeed qualify as 'property'[86] but property sometimes protected by a liability rule rather than a property rule. Commodification of knowledge is, of course, highly controversial. Some authors draw an analogy between the privatization of intellectual production and the enclosure movement, the process of fencing off common land and turning it into private property. James Boyle, for example, argues that '[w]e are in the middle of a second enclosure movement... "the enclosure of the intangible commons of the mind"... [O]nce again things that were formerly thought of as either common property or uncommodifiable are being covered with new, or newly extended, property rights'.[87]

Although intellectual property readily raises the issue of commodification we can see a similar debate in an extensive body of scholarship on water.[88] According to Joseph Sax, the uniqueness of water is well recognized:

The roots of private property have never been deep enough to vest in water users a compensable right to diminish lakes and rivers or to destroy the marine life within them. Water is not like a pocket watch or a piece of furniture, which an owner may destroy with impunity. The rights of use in water, however long standing, should never be confused with more personal, more fully owned, property.[89]

The growth of emissions trading and carbon credit schemes raises new questions about the nature and extent of the rights involved.[90] For example, a carbon right may be a new form of property interest that confers upon the holder a right to the incorporeal benefit of carbon sequestration on a piece of forested land. Innovative legislation has been introduced in some jurisdictions that seeks to separate the incorporeal benefit of carbon sequestration from the traditional rights flowing from land ownership.[91] Indigenous land and resource claims based on different understandings of property and ownership

---

[86] M. Carrier, 'Cabining Intellectual Property through a Property Paradigm' (2004–2005) 54 Duke LJ 1 at 12; B. M. Hoffstadt, 'Dispossession, Intellectual Property, and the Sin of Theoretical Homogeneity' (2006–2007) 80 S Cal L Rev 909 at 917.

[87] J. Boyle, 'Second Enclosure Movement and the Construction of the Public Domain' (2003) 66 Law & Contemporary Problems 33 at 37.

[88] eg, C. M. Rose, 'The Comedy of the Commons: Custom, Commerce, and Inherently Public Property' in *Property and Persuasion*, above n 59, 105; E. T. Freyfogle, 'Water Rights and the Common Wealth' (1996) 26 Envtl L 27.

[89] J. L. Sax, 'The Limits of Private Rights in Public Waters' (1989) 19 Envtl L 473 at 482.

[90] eg, E. Meidinger, 'On Explaining the Development of "Emissions Trading" in U.S. Air Pollution Regulation' (1985) 7 Law and Policy 447; G. Sergienko, 'Property Law and Climate Change' (2007–2008) 22 Natural Resources & Env't 25 (arguing that, because of its traditional focus on tangible things, property law has been slow to recognize rights in the movement of air, water and photons, which has hindered the development of power sources such as in-stream hydropower).

[91] See, eg, the legislation reviewed in S. Kennett, A. Kwasniak, and A. R. Lucas, 'Property Rights and the Legal Framework for Carbon Sequestration on Agricultural Land' (2006) 37 Ottawa L Rev 171.

may pose more fundamental challenges which question mainstream understandings of property as a commodity within both international and domestic legal regimes.[92]

C. Categories of property

One of the foundational issues for the literature on property law theory is the classification of broad categories of property and the movement between these categories. While the categories or forms of property address the issue of 'what is property?', the literature on movement between these forms is usually literature justifying private property. The latter is therefore discussed in Part B of this chapter.

The broad categories are typically stated as open access commons, community commons, private property and state property.[93] Some would add additional categories, including anticommons,[94] semicommons,[95] and liberal commons.[96]

How does the literature use these terms?[97] An open access commons is a resource to which all have a liberty of access and use. Such a commons is a fundamentally anarchic and Hobbesian world.[98] Examples include the atmosphere and high seas fisheries beyond the limits of national jurisdiction. Since there is, by definition, no right to exclude others from using an open access commons and appropriating its fruits, it is best to think of an open access commons as

---

[92] eg, B. Bryan, 'Property as Ontology: On Aboriginal and English Understandings of Ownership' (2000) 13 Can J L & Jur 3 (arguing that a comparison of English and Aboriginal property yields insights into the ontologically specific grounds that inform institutionalized sociocultural practices like property); J. E. Anderson, *Law, Knowledge, Culture: The Production of Indigenous Knowledge in Intellectual Property Law* (2009) (looking at how indigenous knowledge has emerged as a discrete category within intellectual property law); L. Brunner, 'The Rise of Peoples' Rights in the Americas: The Saramaka People Decision of the Inter-American Court of Human Rights' (2008) 7 Chinese J Int'l L 699 (discussing a series of decisions applying the property rights protection clause of the Inter-American Convention to indigenous and tribal peoples).

[93] Socialist constitutions typically recognize three categories of property in addition to open access commons: state property, cooperative property, and personal property. Personal property is consumer, not productive, property. See K. Malfliet, 'The Hungarian Quest for a Valid Theory of "Socialist" Property: Still a Long Way to Go' (1987) 13 Rev Socialist Law 241 at 241, 256.

[94] Heller, above n 3.

[95] H. E Smith, 'Semicommon property rights and scattering in the open fields' (2000) 29 J Legal Studies 131.

[96] H. Dagan and M. A. Heller, 'The Liberal Commons' (2000–2001) 110 Yale LJ 549.

[97] For useful discussions, see S. Munzer, 'The Commons and the Anticommons in the Law and Theory of Property' in *The Blackwell Guide to the Philosophy of Law and Legal Theory* (M. P. Golding and W. A. Edmundson, eds, 2008) 148, and O. R. Young, 'Rights, Rules and Common Pools: Solving Problems Arising in Human/Environment Relations' (2007) 47 Natural Resources J 1.

[98] C. M. Rose, 'Property as Storytelling: Perspectives from Game Theory, Narrative Theory, Feminist Theory' (1990) 2 Yale J Law & Humanities 37 at 38 ('if there were no property rights in the berry patch, all of us would just have to fight all of the time for the berries'); F. I. Michelman, 'Ethics, Economics, and the Law of Property' in *NOMOS XXIV: Ethics, Economics, and the Lawn* (J. R. Pennock & J. W. Chapman, eds, 1982) 1 at 5 ('... in a state-of-nature regime there are never any exclusionary rights. All is privilege').

non-property.[99] An open access commons such as the high seas fishery is vulnerable to Garrett Hardin's tragedy[100] since each user enjoys the full marginal benefit of capturing additional fish but only a small fraction of the marginal cost which is spread among all fishers and others who depend on the resource. Each user therefore has an incentive to appropriate as much of the resource as possible in the absence of the mutual restraint of others. Game theory, and, in particular, the prisoners' dilemma, suggests similarly tragic outcomes, since, absent a means for coordination and enforcing commitments, each player is likely to engage in self-seeking behaviour.[101] Lee Anne Fennell has pointed out that commons problems arise not simply from the existence of open access but from the mix of open access commons with privately owned appropriations (ie the individual appropriator does end up owning the fruits of the chase).[102] This suggests that in developing solutions to commons problems we need to consider changes to either or both variables. Oil and gas unitization, for example, focuses on allocating ownership of the product without changing the ownership structure of the underlying assets: each working interest owner continues to own its own lease or share in a lease but has a percentage interest—a tract participation factor—in any production from the unitized zone wherever the producing well is located.

A second form of commons is the community commons. A community commons is a resource that is common to members of a particular group or community. It is indivisible; members are not joint owners and typically do not have even an abstract share in the commons.[103] Members have a liberty as between each other to use the resource and have the right to exclude non-members from using or accessing the commons. Non-members have neither a right nor a liberty to use the resource. From the perspective of an outsider, a community commons will look much like private property. A community may be formally and elaborately structured such as a Hutterite colony or other religious community,[104]

---

[99] Or perhaps, better still as 'anti-property', but Abraham Bell and Gideon Parchomovsky have already appropriated this term to describe a public space burdened by anti-development easements: A. Bell and G. Parchomovsky, 'Of Property and Antiproperty' (2003–2004) 102 Mich L Rev 1. James Boyle uses the terminology of the 'outside of property' or the 'opposite of property': J. Boyle, 'Foreword: The Opposite of Property' (2003) 66 Law and Contemporary Problems 1.

[100] G. Hardin, 'The Tragedy of the Commons' (1968) 162 Science 1243.

[101] Rose, above n 98.

[102] L. A. Fennell, 'Commons, Anticommons Semicommons' in *Research Handbook on the Economics of Property Law* (K. Ayotte and H. Smith, eds, forthcoming 2009), available at <http://ssrn.com/abstract=1348267> at 5. Fennell is actually discussing a true or community commons, but the point applies and perhaps with even more force in the context of open access resources. However, it might also be noted that in many societies the successful hunter will have obligations to share the harvest with family and kinship group.

[103] This is also true of the category of cooperative property in a socialist regime. Cooperative property is group property that combines appropriation with self-management, the collective organization of production, distribution or the satisfaction of needs. See Malfliet, above n 93.

[104] eg, A. Lehavi, 'How Property Can Create, Maintain, or Destroy Community' (2008) 10 Theoretical Inquiries in Law 43 (distinguishing between different types of communities: intentional communities (for example, religious communities, kibbutz), planned communities (for example, housing communities), and spontaneous communities (for example, friends of the park).

or a customary commons such as the type of manorial common that Hardin actually discusses in the 'Tragedy of the Commons'. Other communities may be more informal. Since resource use is limited to members, those members will likely be able to develop management, monitoring and use rules (either formally or informally) that prevent the resource from descending to the tragedy of the (open-access) commons described by Hardin. Such rules might include stinting rules that limit the number of animals that a member may be able to graze on the common lands or limits on the amount of the resource that can be appropriated or the equipment that can be used. Ostrom provides important empirical evidence to support the sustainability of these forms of commons, thereby emphasizing that there is nothing inevitable about tragedy.[105]

Traditional communal commons are closed to outsiders and marked by community involvement and few transfers and trades.[106] There is a body of scholarship suggesting that there are fundamental incompatibilities between traditional and modern legal systems, and that translating traditional relationships into a modern system will alter both of them.[107] There is a similar body of critical literature dealing with the problem of translation in the context of the recognition of indigenous ownership within the rules of a settler society.[108]

Both forms of commons—open access and community commons—are distinguishable from public goods, with which they share the quality of non-excludability, either generally in the case of open access commons or within the community in the case of community commons, because they are 'subtractable', that is, the use of the resource by one person lessens the amount or quality of the

[105] E. Ostrom, *Governing the Commons: The Evolution of Institutions for Collective Action* (1990).

[106] Rose, above n 40.

[107] eg, T. Kelley, 'Unintended Consequences of Legal Westernization in Niger: Harming Contemporary Slaves by Reconceptualizing Property' (2008) 56 Am J Comp L 999 (describing the adverse effects of titling on lower-status groups in rural Niger); B. Maragia, 'The Indigenous Sustainability Paradox and the Quest for Sustainability in Post-Colonial Societies: Is Indigenous Knowledge All That Is Needed?' (2006) 18 Geo Int'l Envtl L Rev 197 (describing disruptive effects of colonial titling project in traditional communities); C. Zerner, ed, *Culture and the Question of Rights: Forests, Coasts, and Seas in Southeast Asia* (2003).

[108] On the challenges associated with recognizing indigenous property interests within that of a settler society see, eg, S. Hepburn, 'Feudal Tenure and Native Title: Revising an Enduring Fiction' (2005) 27 Sydney Law Review 49 (arguing that the High Court of Australia did not go far enough in *Mabo* and should have embraced allodial tenure rather than radical tenure to allow a 'pluralist property culture' to develop). Other articles that grapple with this challenge include J. Webber, 'The Jurisprudence of Regret: The Search for Standards of Justice in Mabo' (1995) 17 Sydney L Rev 5 (although less focused on property issues), S. Motha 'Encountering the Epistemic Limit of the Recognition of "Difference"' (1998) 7 Griffith L Rev 79 (questioning whether it is possible for common law judges to capture (without destroying) the different ways in which indigenous people relate to land) and, more doctrinally, B. Slattery, 'The Metamorphosis of Aboriginal Title' (2006) 85 Canadian Bar Rev 255 (identifying three different ways of thinking about the recognition of indigenous title systems in settler law: (1) aboriginal title as a customary right rooted in the law and practice of particular indigenous groups, (2) aboriginal title as a translated rights expressed in the categories of the common law, and (3) aboriginal title as a *sui generis* right grounded in the ancient relations between the Crown and indigenous peoples).

resource available to others.[109] Public goods on the other hand, such as defence and weather forecasts, are non-rivalrous.[110] The characterization of resources as open access commons or as public goods may depend upon our understanding of the resource. Thus, historically, we might have thought of the atmosphere as a public good, but the science of climate change suggests that we need to revise our thinking to (re)conceptualize the atmosphere—or at least the ability of the atmosphere to absorb carbon dioxide—as an open access commons that is subject to degradation through overuse.

Henry E. Smith has sought to further clarify the nature of some community commons by coining the phrase 'semicommons'.[111] This phrase invokes the complexity of the norms and rules that may develop within a commons. Smith recalls that it was a feature of the English open field system that commoners/peasants had exclusive rights to certain strips for the purposes of growing things such as vegetables, grain, or even hay, but were required to open these lands up to collective grazing at certain times of the year. The semicommons form was thought to be reasonably efficient on the assumption of mixed farming practices because it allowed land to be used intensively as private land but also allowed the efficiencies of scale associated with livestock grazing. Several mechanisms were built into the rule structure to remove incentives for self-seeking behaviour. One such mechanism was a procedure for 'scattering' the strips to which parties might have exclusive rights. This removed an incentive that a party might have to cause the collective herd to spend more time in one area.

State or public property refers to property, the title to which is vested in the state or some other institution of the state such as a municipal government. State property is a large and diverse category.[112] State property differs from an open access commons insofar as citizens may have no general liberty or right to use the property or access the resource. For example, there is no general right or liberty on the part of the public generally, or citizens specifically, to use state-owned buildings or facilities. Similarly, in many jurisdictions, various resource interests (minerals, water, petroleum and natural gas, geothermal resources) may be owned by the state and, with some

---

[109] Another way to put this is that all public goods will be open access commons; but not all open access commons are public goods (because of the subtractable feature of open access commons).

[110] For discussions of the distinction between commons and public goods and concepts such as rival and excludable see Bell and Parchomovsky, above n 99 at 9–11, and Young, above n 97. Intellectual property is also non-rivalrous, making comparisons between the public domain and open access commons problematic. Such comparisons are made nevertheless because the two categories share the feature of non-excludability. See Boyle, above n 99 at 8.

[111] Smith, above n 95.

[112] The various types of public or state property found in Roman law are explored by Carol M. Rose in 'Romans, Roads, and Romantic Creators: Traditions of Public Property in the Information Age' (2003) 66 Law & Contemp Problems 89. For example, Roman law distinguished between *res nullius, res communes, res publicae, res universatitis,* and *res divini juris*; respectively, things that are unowned and open to all by their nature, things that are publicly owned and made open to the public by law, things owned by a public group in its corporate capacity, and things 'unownable' because of their divine or sacred status.

notable exceptions such as the public right or liberty to fish that exists in many jurisdictions, there is no general liberty of the public or citizens to harvest those resources.
Such property is therefore analytically very similar to private property. However, in
many cases, owners will be subject to additional statutory and administrative rules
and responsibilities with respect to the management of such public property that
would not apply to owners of private property. Futhermore, the state as owner will
be subject to political influence and lobbying in the manner (eg, the bundle of rights
and duration, etc) in which it elects to dispose of rights to those resources to others
(for eg, free entry systems, bidding systems, etc).[113]

As discussed in Part I.A.1, private property is typically characterized as a bundle of rights that an owner has as against strangers, or the rest of the world.[114]
Private property may of course be shared and held in some form of co-ownership;
co-ownership is particularly common in the natural resources sector where oil
and gas leases and the like will be held in some form of undivided co-ownership
(ie working interest) such as the tenancy in common of the common law tradition. Typically, theorists do not draw a sharp distinction between land that is
owned by a single owner and land that is held in some form of co-ownership.
The literature does, however, offer some discussion of the potential fragmentation
risks associated with co-ownership,[115] as well as doctrinal techniques that may be
used to reduce the risk of fragmentation or to reverse it. Examples include primo-
geniture rules of inheritance, the concept of survivorship in the law of joint tenancy, and the right of partition. Another theme in the literature is the 'thickness'
of the default rules in a particular jurisdiction to govern relations between co-
owners, or in other words the extent to which such relationships are governed by
contract (very few default rules) or property (more prescriptive as to the substantive content of the co-ownership relationship).[116]

Mention of the problem of fragmentation in private ownership serves as a useful introduction to the concept of the anticommons. This term, coined by Heller,
but apparently drawing inspiration from an earlier paper by Michelman,[117]
refers to a situation in which 'multiple owners are each endowed with the right
to exclude others from a scarce resource, and no one has an effective privilege of
use'.[118] In such a situation, where each owner has a veto over efforts to put the
property to an alternative and perhaps more efficient use, 'the resource is prone to
underuse—*a tragedy of the anticommons*'.[119]

---

[113] See generally Scott, above n 5.

[114] B. Rudden, 'Economic Theory v. Property Law: The Numerus Clausus Problem' in *Oxford
Essays in Jurisprudence*, Third Series (J. Eekelaar and J. Bell, eds, 1987) 239.

[115] eg, Heller, above n 3 at 685–7.

[116] H. Hansmann and R. Kraakman, 'The Essential Role of Organizational Law' (2000–2001)
110 Yale LJ 387.

[117] Heller, above n 3 at 624, n 9, referring to Michelman, above n 98 at 9.

[118] Heller, ibid at 624.

[119] ibid (emphasis in original). An anticommons is not its own category of property of the same
order as, say, community common property and private property. The traditional categories turn

Anticommons arise where there are disaggregated or fragmented rights rather than 'coherent' bundles with a single owner. Heller's article is principally concerned with societies in transition between Marxist economies and market-based economies and Heller suggests that, in that process, governments can create 'too many property rights and too many decisionmakers who can block use'.[120] But Heller also provided other examples including cases of individual allotments of land in Indian reservations in the United States. These allotments became further sub-divided over time as a result of intestate succession and it became practically impossible to make decisions in relation to these lands.[121]

Heller and others have argued that once an anticommons has been created it may be very difficult to find a way out to re-aggregate property. Fragmentation, as Heller puts it, is 'a one way ratchet'[122] and Fennell notes that, at bottom, all anticommons problems are problems of assembly.[123] One solution, purchase by a single owner, may be difficult to achieve because of holdouts, etc, and where an anticommons aggregation of property is created by the state—as in Heller's primary example where state assets were privatized—it may be difficult for the parties to develop the customary norms that allow them, as in the commons studied by Ostrom,[124] to avoid the tragedy of under or inefficient use and create a sustainable anticommons.[125]

In the natural resources field, it may be possible to see anticommons problems emerging in some societal responses to climate change. For example, in those jurisdictions where there are private fragmented titles it may be very difficult to aggregate large enough areas of subsurface pore space to accommodate saline aquifer carbon capture and storage projects.[126] And there may be similar problems in offering credible commitments to maintain biological sequestration, although here the problem may not be the existence of multiple vetoes, but rather, the existence of multiple use rights that make it difficult to deliver on promises to maintain a particular form of land use or vegetation cover.[127] But it may be possible to develop institutional responses to anticommons problems to allow vetoes to be

---

on the question of who has the right or liberty to make use of the resource while the antiproperty category is constituted by the size of the group that is able to veto the use or change in use of a property. In sum, an anticommons is perhaps better regarded as a characteristic of one or other of the forms of property, rather than as a distinct form of property.

[120] ibid at 625.
[121] ibid at 684–7 (providing a further example of property laws in Kobe, Japan).
[122] M. A. Heller, 'The Boundaries of Private Property' (1999) 108 Yale LJ 1163 at 1165.
[123] Fennell, above n 102 at 10.
[124] Ostrom, above n 105.
[125] Heller, above n 3 at 674.
[126] eg, A. B. Klass and E. J. Wilson, 'Climate Change, Carbon Sequestration and Property Rights' (2010) U Ill L Rev (forthcoming) (dealing with the situation in the United States where typically pore space ownership is vested in the surface owner; the same problems may arise where pore space is vested in the mineral owner and minerals may be privately owned).
[127] S. Kennett, 'Carbon Sinks and the Kyoto Protocol: Legal and Policy Mechanisms for Domestic Implementation' (2003) 21 J Energy & Natural Resources Law 252; Kennett, Kwasniak and Lucas, above n 91.

overcome. An example in the oil and gas sector is the idea of compulsory pooling, which serves as a means of overcoming the veto rights created by a combination of geographical fragmentation and oil and gas conservation spacing rules.[128]

If fragmentation is problematic and difficult to reverse then it is hardly surprising that writers list many examples of doctrinal measures designed to prevent or minimize fragmentation or what Heller refers to as 'extreme decomposition'. Heller's examples include:[129] no new forms of interest in land (also known as the *numerus clausus* rule and discussed further below); rules abolishing forms of estate (eg the fee tail) that are only inheritable by a specific class of heirs; rules dealing with conditions that are too restrictive; rules on escheat, or similar rules providing for reversion to government for non-payment of property taxes; and the rule against perpetuities. Parisi suggests that other techniques or rules that are designed to reduce fragmentation and facilitate reunification include rules dealing with the discharge of restrictive covenants and perhaps contracting rules relating to undisclosed principals which, by permitting non-disclosure of the agency, may make it easier to (re-)assemble the requisite geographical and other bundles of entitlements without encountering holdout problems.[130]

While Heller views the existence of multiple vetoes as problematic, Bell and Parchomovsky[131] have pointed out that it may be possible to use the antiproperty concept—and specifically the concept of an anti-development property easement—to correct for market imperfections in the manner in which we provide and, in particular, maintain green spaces such as parks. These authors argue that the market will tend to under-provide green spaces since such spaces serve as public goods or open access commons. Furthermore, once created it will be difficult for town managers and elected officials to resist the economic and political pressure to reclassify the land for development purposes. Bell and Parchamovsky explain that a developer will have a significant advantage in pushing the development agenda over those who would seek to maintain the green space. These advantages include the organizational and free rider challenges that will be faced by all those who benefit from the park, and who seek to organize to maintain

---

[128] N. D. Bankes, 'Compulsory Pooling under the Oil and Gas Conservation Act of Alberta' (1997) 35 Alta L Rev 945. There is a distinction here between pooling and unitization which operates at several levels. The concept of pooling is generally reserved for the geographical area of a drilling spacing unit while unitization generally refers to an entire oil or gas reservoir. While voluntary or compulsory unitization may best be seen as a response to a commons problem (too many straws in the pool), pooling and compulsory pooling truly is a response to a mutual veto. No party who owns part of a drilling spacing unit may drill a well except on behalf of all. But the distinction between too many liberties—a commons problem—and too many vetoes—an anticommons problem—will, in some cases, turn on the way in which the question is framed. For example, in a unitization setting, is the problem that each owner can continue to put its straw into the pool or is the problem that each has the right to veto the distributional arrangements that would allocate production to each tract as a part of a unitization arrangement? See the discussion below to the effect that every movement from commons to private property involves distributional issues.

[129] Heller, above n 3 at 664–5.

[130] F. Parisi, 'Entropy in Property' (2002) 50 Am J Comp Law 595 at 617–18.

[131] Bell and Parchomovsky, above n 99.

that park status, against the centrally organized and rent-seeking behaviour of the developer.[132] One possible solution that Bell and Parchomovsky suggest is to harness the self-interest of adjacent property owners, who benefit, but not in an exclusive way, from their proximity to a park and afford each of them an entitlement—a veto in the form of an anti-development property easement— to prevent development of the park. Now the developer faces significant transaction costs and hold-out problems to complete the property interests required to allow the development to proceed.[133] Parisi makes a similar point when he notes that environmental NGOs may deliberately use fragmentation as a strategy to oppose development.[134]

The veto idea that underlies the anticommons seems closely associated in the literature with concerns as to the undue fragmentation of property and the *numerus clausus* literature—to which we now turn.

D. *Numerus clausus*

Many writers now emphasize the reluctance of legal systems generally—and the claim is typically made very broadly and certainly in terms of both common law and civilian systems[135]—to recognize new property interests. Most, if not all, legal systems jealously guard the number and form of property interests that the legal system will recognize. This characteristic feature of property systems is generally referred to as the *numerus clausus* doctrine. What explains this practice? In his classic article on the subject, Bernard Rudden[136] canvassed three main categories of reasons: legal reasons, philosophical reasons and economic reasons.

Under the heading of legal reasons, Rudden includes the following: the argument that 'the present list of permitted property interests/real rights covers all that one could conceivably want …';[137] the problem of notice and the claim that purchasers of land should not be burdened or surprised by property interests that

---

[132] ibid at 11–18 and 20–31.

[133] ibid at 31–42.

[134] Parisi, above n 130 at 612. Parisi uses as his example wilderness protection in the United States. Another example in the news at the time of writing is the effort of NGOs to acquire land required for Heathrow's proposed third runway and to encourage literally thousands of people to acquire a beneficial interest in the land. See the website of the NGO 'Airplot' at <http://www.airplot.org.uk/>. When visited on 26 April 2009, some 43,044 people had accepted this invitation. Heller noted a rather bizarre example, albeit designed to facilitate marketing rather than a conservation agenda, when Quaker Oats provided square inch 'titles' to a block of land it had purchased in Yukon: M. A. Heller, 'The Tragedy of the Anticommons: Property in Transition from Marx to Markets' (1998) 111 Harv L Rev 621 at 682–4. cf E. Meidinger, 'Property Law for Development Policy and Institutional Theory: Problems of Structure, Choice, and Change' in *The Mystery of Capital and the Construction of Social Reality* (B. Smith, D. M. Mark, and I. Ehrlich, eds, 2008), available at <http://ssrn.com/abstract=876467> at 25 (noting that there is a relatively undeveloped functionalist-oriented argument against fragmentation from an environmental perspective).

[135] Rudden, above n 114 at 239.

[136] ibid at 239–63.

[137] ibid at 245.

others may claim; the importance of consent and the idea that a person should not be subject to positive obligations; and the problem of pyramiding or the building up of competing interests in the same property over time. We can expect this to be a particular concern where such interests are perpetual and there is no easy method for discharging that interest.

Under the heading of philosophical reasons, Rudden relies on Kant and Austin for the idea that, since property claims bind the world, individuals should not be able to create a property interest but this should instead be a legislative act, and on Hegel for the argument that, given the associations between feudalism and property, we must guard against clogs on property for 'we are fully free only when our property is (relatively) free'.[138] Here Rudden also refers to Hohfeld,[139] whom he credits with the insight that the creation of new property rights limits the freedoms of strangers, and not just the parties to the transaction.

Finally, under the heading of economic reasons Rudden notes the following arguments: new 'fancies'[140] may reduce the marketability of the property; standardization of property interests reduces transaction costs and particularly the information costs that buyers will face in terms of both screening ('can I buy that entitlement?') and suitability ('is this particular entitlement suitable for my needs?'); land utilization or sterilization; durability (while contracts are born to die, property is born to endure); and the expense, in terms of transaction cost, to terminate fancies.

Since Rudden's contribution in 1987 there has been an explosion of literature on the *numerus clausus* issue and related issues of fragmentation and the anticommons.[141] Much of the literature examines the issue from an economic perspective and seeks to explain the preference for a limited number of property rights and the aversion to fancies in terms of information costs. This strand of thinking is closely associated with the many contributions of Thomas Merrill and Henry E. Smith, alone[142] and together. In their classic article on the subject,[143] Merrill and Smith argue that property rights create information costs, not only for the parties to the transaction and their immediate successors in title, but also for others. This is because of the *in rem* nature of property rights—or, in more self-explanatory terms, the capacity of property rights to bind the whole world, or

---

[138] ibid at 250.

[139] Hohfeld, above n 29.

[140] 'Fancies' is the word coined for idiosyncratic property rights in *Keppel v Bailey* (1834) 2 My & K 517, 39 ER 1042

[141] Scholars have begun to explore the application of the *numerus clausus* to 'virtual' property, such as e-mail accounts and domain names and also entitlements that arise in increasingly popular online environments such as Second Life: J. A. T. Fairfield, 'Virtual Property' (2005) 85 BUL Rev 1047.

[142] Smith's contributions include H. E. Smith, 'Community and Custom in Property' (2008) 10 Theoretical Inquiries in Law 5 (distinguishing between the communicative aspects of well known customs and localized customs which may impose significant informational costs on outsider) and Smith, above n 95.

[143] Merrill and Smith, above n 62. See also Merrill and Smith, above n 2 and Merrill and Smith, above n 37.

at least some larger and more indefinite category of persons than those who are party to the original transaction (a category for whom Hohfeld coined the term multital rights).[144]

Merrill and Smith make the point that a bilateral transaction that creates a property interest cannot and does not internalize all the information costs. Other persons will still need to make inquiries to avoid transgressing the presumptively exclusive rights of the owner. This is unlikely to be problematic so long as the parties use a small number of well understood forms of property interests with known characteristics (and if they make full use of recording systems and the like), but the information costs imposed on others will rise if individuals are entitled to create 'idiosyncratic property rights' (ie fancies).[145] On the other hand, standardization lowers information costs and performs a communicative function. Thus, Merrill and Smith frame the *numerus clausus* issue as one of optimal standardization. How do we find the right balance between standardization and flexibility; when should we defer to the intentions of the parties and when should we insist on mandatory rules?[146] The answer to this question, however it is answered, draws the fault line between property and contract law.

For some, the *numerus clausus* issue also raises the question of institutional choice. Should decisions about the recognition of new property interests be made by the courts or the legislatures? Merrill and Smith suggest that economists prefer courts to legislatures because of the concerns of public choice theorists to the effect that legislatures will inevitably respond to interests with narrow distributional objectives. But other factors suggest that legislatures offer advantages over court adjudications. Thus, legislative decisions on property may be clear, universal, comprehensive, stable, prospective,[147] and may offer greater democratic accountability. But it can hardly be a question of 'either/or' since many such questions arise before the courts as questions of interpretation of statutory arrangements[148] and these interpretive responses will inevitably 'create' or refuse to recognize new property interests whether they reason by analogy—it walks and talks like property, therefore it must be property—or in a more functional or instrumental manner—we

---

[144]   See in particular P. Eleftheriadis, 'The Analysis of Property Rights' (1996) 16 Oxford J Legal Stud 31 at 42–3 (arguing that Hohfeld's terminology of paucital and multital is superior to the language of *in rem* and *in personam*). There is, Eleftheriadis notes, nothing particularly distinctive about rights *in rem*; they are not rights in relation to a thing; rather, they are claims, etc that may be maintained against all of the subjects of the legal order (perhaps subject to exceptions); whereas *in personam* or paucital rights can be maintained against specified individuals (determinate persons).

[145]   Merrill and Smith, above n 62 at 32 (noting that 'idiosyncratic property rights create a common pool problem').

[146]   ibid at 38. Hernando DeSoto opts for mandatory rules when he advocates a form of property rights that he calls formal property, which consists of relatively simple, standardized property rights that make property legible to anyone in the world and, more importantly, allows property to be divided into smaller standard pieces that can be mixed and matched, contracted and recorded: DeSoto, above n 39.

[147]   Merrill and Smith, above n 62.

[148]   For example, is a commercial fishing licence property for the purposes of bankruptcy or security legislation? See *Saulnier v Royal Bank of Canada* 2008 SCC 58.

should treat this interest as property because it will serve one or more of the justifications for property advanced in Section II of this chapter.[149]

Merrill and Smith acknowledge that there are some philosophical objections to the *numerus clausus* approach. For example, libertarians may prefer to respect the intentions of the parties at least unless they cause harm to others, but part of what Merrill and Smith claim to have shown is that idiosyncratic property rights do indeed cause harm to others insofar as such fancies impose information costs on third parties.[150]

There are traces of the *numerus clausus* debate in many different areas of natural resources law. The resources industry is characterized by large capital investments for which the investor seeks as much security as possible. But it is also an industry in which resource rights are frequently acquired from the state and may take quite novel forms of statutory rights. It is, in addition, an industry which tends to create fragmented interests (eg royalty interests, interests in particular substances such as natural gas but not petroleum, severed estates, and interests in particular formations). There is a significant body of case law and doctrine dealing with the legal characterization of these interests as property or as some other *sui generis* form of interest.[151]

Two lessons perhaps emerge from this. The first is that the *numerus clausus* doctrine still asserts tremendous hold notwithstanding these innovations. This is reflected in the sometimes tortuous efforts to shoe-horn innovative interests into an existing category of property (eg arguments to the effect that a royalty interest is, or is sufficiently like, a rent)[152] or that a state-granted resource right looks like a common law *profit à prendre*.[153] The second is that state-created resource rights may represent an exception to the general reluctance to create innovative interests. While this may run counter to the lessons offered by the information cost literature, information costs may be of limited importance in this context. For example, in many cases the state may be a monopoly supplier of the resource and there will be a direct contractual relationship between the

[149] The choice as to the 'supplier' of new forms of property is a key theme in Scott, above n 5. In his book Scott also emphasizes the role (both historical and contemporary) of custom in supplying new forms of property or modifying existing property bundles.

[150] cf M. W. Carroll, 'One for All: The Problem of Uniformity Cost in Intellectual Property Law' (2006) 55 Am U L Rev 845 (reviewing the literature arguing that, in the context of patents, economic inefficiency is caused by applying uniform rules rather than context-specific rules).

[151] eg, *Guaranty Trust v Hetherington* (1987) 50 Alta LR (2d) 193, varied (1989) 67 Alta LR (2d) 290; but see A. Quesnel, 'Modernizing the Property Laws That Bind Us: Challenging Traditional Property Law Concepts Unsuited to the Realities of the Oil and Gas Industry' (2003–2004) 41 Alberta L Rev 159 (discussing in particular the more robust approach adopted by the Supreme Court of Canada in *Bank of Montreal v Dynex Petroleum Ltd.* [2002] 1 SCR 146 where the Court ruled that a gross overriding royalty interest could qualify as an interest in land so long as that was clear from the intentions of the parties as demonstrated by the language used in the relevant document).

[152] *Guaranty Trust*, ibid. See also G. Davies, 'The Legal Characterization of Overiding Royalty Interests in Oil and Gas' (1972) 10 Alberta L Rev 232.

[153] *Saulnier v Royal Bank of Canada*, above n 148.

state and the interest holder. The statutory framework that allows the executive to create the interest also serves to communicate the boundaries of innovation and it is not uncommon to see government owners adopt standard form tenure documents. These measures all serve to minimize the information costs that would otherwise be associated with the creation of new statutory forms of interest. Furthermore, the interested community (the particular industry) may be quite confined. Finally, the international competition for capital will act as a general constraint on innovation and push aberrant regimes to standardize their terms.[154]

II. Justifications of (private) property

The lack of any agreed-upon core to the concept of property frequently leads theorists to a discussion of politico-philosophical justifications for property as an alternative. But, even for a conceptualist, property—or at least private property—has always required justification. A property regime almost guarantees that the distribution of wealth will not be equal; some will get richer than others. Property accumulation poses problems for distributive justice and democratic political processes.[155] In addition, the inequality associated with property is not distributed randomly. Rather, it is distributed systematically along dimensions of identity such as gender and race. A recent United Nations report reveals that the top one percent of the world's adult population owned about forty percent of the world's total net worth and the bottom half of the world's population owned only just over one per cent.[156] The question of whether it is morally right for wealth to be distributed unequally is usually seen as being of concern for theories of distributive justice, but not for theories of property law.[157] Still, the literature justifying property—which tends to be literature concerned only with justifying the one category of property, namely, private property—inevitably addresses this issue if only because of the right to exclude others, a right of central importance to the ownership of resources.

---

[154] See the discussion of the evolution of mining regimes and land settlement regimes in Scott, above n 5.

[155] J. Riedinger, 'Property Rights and Democracy: Philosophical and Economic Considerations' (1993) 22 Cap U L Rev 893.

[156] J. B. Davies, S. Sandström, A. Shorrocks, and E. N. Wolff, *The World Distribution of Household Wealth* (2008).

[157] But see Munzer, above n 8 (attempting to develop a grand but pluralistic theory of property based on three principles: (1) a principle of utility and efficiency, (2) a principle of justice and equality, and (3) a principle of desert based upon labour). See also R. Nozick, *Anarchy, State, and Utopia* (1974) (putting forward the libertarian claim that things that are justly acquired and justly transferred belong to the owner as a matter of right). Distributional concerns clearly underlay Locke's famous proviso to his theory of property, as discussed below.

This part of the chapter proceeds by first very briefly addressing the standard justifications for (private) property. These justifications are of three general types. One group is economic, another personhood-oriented, and a third political. Almost all economic justifications of private property view property as essentially an allocation of use rights. Property rights have a foundational role in incentivizing investment and allocating scarce resources and are therefore central to commerce and the private ordering that flows from transactions that yield the highest and best use of a given resource. Property rights serve this role primarily by granting exclusive rights that serve as the basis for free exchange (ie contract).[158] Personhood theories see property rights as important to individual identity. One important strand of property theory highlights the intersection between, in Hegelian terms, 'freedom of person and of things'.[159] Some theories relying upon political ordering are associated with certain strains of individual freedom.[160] Others focused on political ordering, however, see property as the site of mutual obligations, recognizing the expectations that arise from property's inextricable linkage to social relations.[161] The main varieties of each of these three groups is briefly canvassed below. In addition, an example of a pluralistic theory is briefly described.

After looking at the justifications for (private) property, we focus on the movement of property between categories. Here we revisit the parable of the tragedy of the commons, which is the main economic justification for the 'progress' from open access commons to either private or state property. The tragedy thus serves to justify the latter two categories of property. We then briefly look at other literature on the movement of property between categories, which tends to be overwhelmingly from some category other than private property to the category of private property. Finally, we conclude this part by looking at takings law in order to show how and why the various theories justifying private property matter.

A. The standard repertoire[162]

1. Labour, desert, first possession and economic theories

John Locke's well-known labour theory of property is a theory of natural rights. For Locke, property rights predate the creation of government, making them, in theory, much less vulnerable to government authority. The state does not create

---

[158] H. Demsetz, 'Toward a Theory of Property Rights' (1967) 57 Am Econ Rev 347.

[159] M. J. Radin, 'Property and Personhood' (1982) 34 Stan L Rev 957.

[160] J. Locke, *Second Treatise of Government*, c 5, Project Gutenberg eBook, available at <http://www.gutenberg.org/dirs/etext05/trgov10h.htm>; R. Pipes, *Property and Freedom* (1999) (advancing the traditional argument that support for private property was essential for the enjoyment of political freedom).

[161] Singer, above n 45.

[162] The phrase, 'the standard repertoire', as a reference to typologies of justificatory arguments, is that of Becker, above n 2 at 198.

property rights, but instead the state was created in order to protect individuals' property rights. His theory is concerned with how property is created and to whom it belonged and begins with the idea that '[w]hether we consider natural reason ... or Revelation ... 'tis very clear that God ... has given the Earth to the Children of Men, given it to Mankind in common.'[163] Therefore, everyone has 'an equal right to the earth and its natural produce'.[164] How does this commons become private property? Locke famously answers as follows:

Though the earth and all inferior creatures be common to all men, yet every man has a property in his own person; this, nobody has any right to but himself. The labour of his body and the work of his hands we may say are properly his. Whatsoever, then, he removes out of the state that nature hath provided and left it in, he hath mixed his labour with, and joined to it something that is his own, and thereby makes it his property. It being by him removed from the common state nature placed it in, it hath by this labour something annexed to it that excludes the common right of other men. For this labour being the unquestionable property of the labourer, no man but he can have a right to what that is once joined to, at least where there is enough, and as good left in common for others.[165]

The conclusion of the last sentence—the so-called 'Lockean proviso'—is essential to Locke's theory and he referred to it often. It is meant to ensure that appropriation of an unowned object does not worsen the situation of others. Locke also regarded property rights as carrying with them a duty of charity to help the needy.

For Locke, the value added by labour is so great and so inseparable from its object that property rights to both the value added *and* the object itself vests in the person supplying the labour. While this explanation may have intuitive appeal when applied to the products of a person's labour, its explanatory power in connection with land and other natural resources is contested.[166] Robert Nozick expressed some well-known doubts:

Why does mixing one's labour with something make one the owner of it? Perhaps because one owns one's labour, and so one comes to own a previously unowned thing that becomes permeated with what one owns. Ownership seeps over into the rest. But why isn't mixing what I own with what I don't own a way of losing what I own rather than a way of gaining what I don't? ... Why should one's entitlement extend to the whole object rather than just to the added value one's labour has produced?[167]

---

163 Locke, above n 160 at s 25.
164 ibid at s 26.
165 ibid at s 27.
166 A selection of recent expert commentaries on Locke's arguments include: J. Dunn, *The Political Thought of John Locke: An Historical Account of the Argument of the 'Two Treatises of Government'* (1969), R. Tuck, *Natural Rights Theories: Their Origin and Development* (1979), J. Tully, *A Discourse on Property: John Locke and his Adversaries* (1980), J. Waldron, *The Right to Private Property* (1988), J. Waldron, *God, Locke and Equality: Christian Foundations in Locke's Political Thought* (2001), G. Sreenivsan, *The Limits of Lockean Rights in Property* (1995), M. H. Kramer, *John Locke and the Origins of Private Property: Philosophical Explorations in Individualism, Community, and Equality* (1997).
167 Nozick, above n 157 at 174.

That labour should give rights to the product, the value added, seems fair and reasonable. That it should give rights to the land itself, which is Locke's central thesis, is for some an extravagant claim.[168] Jean-Jacques Rousseau, for example, acknowledged that occupants were likely to claim rights to land they had appropriated on the basis of labour, first to the produce and then to the land itself. But, for Rousseau, although '... it is not clear what, more than his labour, man can put into things he has not made, in order to appropriate them,' ... 'regardless of how they painted their usurpations, they remained just that, usurpations'.[169]

Desert theories are variants of labour-derived property rights and also related to economic justifications. As Lawrence Becker notes in developing his version of a desert theory, inherent to judgements that people are morally blameworthy or praiseworthy for their actions is the notion that such people 'deserve' reward or punishment for their actions.[170] Becker sets out three conditions that must hold for desert to justify property rights: the action must be morally permissible, it must be beyond what is morally required, and it must add value to the lives of others. The reward should be proportional to the value added and the type of benefit must fit the type of labour. Becker's theory is therefore more restrictive than Locke's, but both can be criticized on the grounds that each fails to establish a basis for property rights in land since land is not the product of labour.

Other theorists use first occupation (in the case of land), and first possession (in the case of chattels) as a justification of property.[171] Both claims are related to the labour and desert theories. The labour is the capture and reduction to possession. The role of first possession is illustrated by finder's rules, the rule of capture in oil and gas and groundwater law,[172] and the rule of free entry in mining law.[173]

As was the case with the labour and desert theories, the first possession justification for property also, and perhaps even more convincingly, allocates property to particular people.[174] The rule states why A should get to keep the fox or oil he captured and reduced to his possession but also allocates that fox or oil to A. It has

---

[168] P. Garnsey, *Thinking About Property: From Antiquity to the Age of Revolution* (2007) at 145–6.

[169] *Discourse on the Origin of Inequality*, Part II, 24, 30

[170] L. C. Becker, *Property Rights: Philosophical Foundations* (1981).

[171] For an extended inquiry into the role of possession in justifying property rights, see Rose, above n 60. See also J. G. Sprankling, 'Owning the Centre of the Earth' (2008) 55 UCLA L Rev 979 (using the inability to possess to support an argument that we should truncate the surface owners' claim to own lands to the centre of the earth, an extravagant claim that we should limit in the same manner in which courts have limited the owners' claim to the heavens or to airspace).

[172] For a collection of articles addressing the rule of capture, see the Symposium on 'The Rule of Capture and Its Consequences' in (2005) 35 Environmental Law.

[173] See generally Scott, above n 5.

[174] Becker, above n 170 at 23, distinguishes between general, specific, and particular justifications for property. A general justification explains why property rights of any kind at all should be recognized. A specific justification explains the existence of a certain kind of property. A particular justification is about priorities, as the basis of a decision as to which person or entity owns a particular

been argued that first occupancy, on its own, cannot justify private property.[175] For example, first occupancy is said to be only meaningful as a justification for the existence of property rights in something that 'is owned by no one, but is equally available to all'.[176] There are also other arguments based on distributive justice concerns. How can a principle that gives everything to the first occupier be just if everyone else is left destitute? Most famously, for Pierre Joseph Proudhon, a printer and one of the first to call himself an anarchist, writing in the early 1800s, it followed that property is theft.[177]

Labour, desert, and first occupation/possession theories can all be seen as subsets of economic justifications. The promotion of efficiency is the goal of economics and writers frequently put forward economic efficiency as a justification for private property. There are obvious affinities with the expectation and value conceptions of property. The economic justification for private property is most commonly made by telling the story of the 'tragedy of the commons', a story we discuss in Part B of this section of the chapter.

2. Personhood theories

In Locke's theory, people make property their own by extending themselves out into the world; property comes *after* the person has been defined. For Hegel, the usual starting point of personhood theories, property comes *before* persons are defined. Hegel's person appropriates or constitutes him- or herself in the process of appropriating external things; property helps make them who they are.

Hegelian theories justifying ownership have been developed by a number of contemporary scholars. The best known proponent of an Hegelian view of the person–property relationship is feminist legal theorist, Margaret Radin.[178] Radin introduced an important distinction between personal and fungible property.[179] Property belongs in the 'personal' category if its loss causes pain that cannot be relieved by its replacement. Personal property constitutes the self. It is within the fungible property category if it is replaceable with other property of equal market value.

Jeremy Waldron is another who has developed Hegel's basic idea of a right to property growing out of personality.[180] Waldron summarizes the conclusions of the Hegelian argument:

---

something. First occupancy or possession is generally seen as a better particular justification than general justification.

[175] J. Wolff, *An Introduction to Political Philosophy* (1996) at 158; Garnsey, above n 168 at 175.

[176] Pufendorf, above n 69.

[177] *What is Property?: An Inquiry into the Principle of Right and of Government*, B. Tucker, trans., available at <http://www.mondopolitico.com/library/pjproudhon/whatisproperty/toc.htm>.

[178] Radin, *Reinterpreting Property*, above n 23. The work of Jeanne Schroeder offers a challenging feminist Hegelian–Lacanian reading of property theory and the psychic dimensions of property as constitutive of the self. See J. L. Schroeder, 'Chix Nix Bundle-O-Stix: A Feminist Critique of the Disaggregation of Property' (1994) 93 Mich L Rev 239; J. L. Schroeder, 'Unnatural Rights: Hegel and Intellectual Property' (2005–06) 60 U Miami L Rev 453.

[179] Radin, above n 159 at 959–60.

[180] Waldron, *The Right to Private* Property, above n 166.

Property-owning is said to be important to the human individual since it is only through owning and controlling property that he can embody his will in external objects and begin to transcend the subjectivity of his immediate existence. In working on an object, using it, and having control over it, an individual confers on his will a stability and a maturity that would not otherwise be possible, and enables himself to establish his place as one in a community of such wills. Of course, he must not remain forever preoccupied with his status as proprietor; there are other tasks to be undertaken before ethical development is complete. But Hegel is adamant that property is necessary; unless he can establish himself as an owner, an individual's development in other areas of ethical life will be seriously at risk.[181]

If the Hegel-inspired lines of argument provide a convincing account of the importance of private property as a human good, then the development of personality would be relevant to egalitarian accounts of distributive justice. At the very least, no one could be excluded from the opportunity to acquire private property, or at least some types of private property. The consequences of accepting this view of property would be sweeping.[182] Attaching special significance to property rights in those parts of the physical world that people have invested with their inspiration and energy in ways that make that property partially constitutive of people's self-recognition or identity could affect, for example, the state's ability to take property, a point explored in the concluding example in this chapter.

3. Liberty theories

There are a variety of perspectives that justify property as freedom-enhancing. If the goal is to enhance negative liberty—the right to be left alone—recognition of private property would be a way to do so.[183] Charles Reich maintains that one of the functions of property 'is to draw a boundary around public and private power'.[184] Within the boundary, the owner enjoys greater freedom than outside it. Similarly, for Epstein, 'a system of private property which ... emphasises individual autonomy' allows individuals to develop their full potential.[185]

A very different type of freedom-based private property justification is that put forward by economist Amartya Sen. He has argued that the true measure of the market's success is the extent to which freedom is enhanced: '[t]he usefulness of wealth lies in the things that it allows us to do—the substantive freedom it helps us to

---

[181] ibid at 377–8.

[182] For a brief explanation of Waldron's project and its implications, see Becker, above n 2 at 201–6. See also Carpenter, above n 21 (applying and extending Radin's idea of personhood to the concept of peoplehood, especially in the context of the property claims of indigenous people, not just in relation to land, but also in relation to the remains of indigenous peoples).

[183] eg, Pipes, above n 160 (advancing the traditional argument that support for private property was essential for the enjoyment of political freedom).

[184] Reich, above n 82 at 771.

[185] Epstein, above n 14 at 138.

achieve.'[186] Charles Reich also wrote about the freedom to control one's own destiny that private property may afford. The extent to which private property enhances freedom depends a great deal on how widely ownership rights are dispersed.

4. *Pluralist theories*

Some of the more recent accounts of justifications for property are pluralistic. Stephen Munzer, for example, argues for a justification of private property on three different grounds: utility and efficiency; justice and equality; and labour and desert.[187] He refuses to put forward any one overarching justification for property. Likewise, although he explores various lines of argument and the tensions among those arguments, he does not put forward any one principle that could unify or solve priority problems.

The usual problems of pluralistic accounts have been briefly and well summarized by Lawrence Becker.[188] Pluralistic property theorists need to show that there are multiple independent justifications for private property. Pluralists must be able to show that the lines of argument they discuss cannot be adequately defined in terms of, or derived from, another. The second problem pluralists face is that of coherence. Does one principle lead to one conclusion when applied, and another principle to a different conclusion?

B. Movement between categories of property

One of the dominant justifications for private property, as opposed to property in general, is a theory about why property should move from another category to the category of private property. Hardin's tragedy of the commons[189] provides one explanation of why we might move from one category of property to another form of property. Hardin argued that we might avoid the conclusion that 'freedom in the commons brings ruin to all'[190] if the commons could be privatized or rights of entry and use could be regulated. He is widely cited as having said that resource degradation was inevitable unless common property was converted to private property, or government regulation of uses and users was instituted.

But the tragedy of the commons is not the only story about the movement to private property. Harold Demsetz offers a different analysis,[191] building on Ronald Coase's foundation[192] to advance an evolutionary theory of private property. Demsetz's point of departure is the Lockean hypothetical state of nature in which property was held in common. Demsetz argued that private

---

[186] A. Sen, *Development as Freedom* (1999) at 14.
[187] Munzer, above n 8.
[188] Becker, above n 2.
[189] D. Feeny, F. Berkes, B. J. McCay, and J. M. Acheson, 'The Tragedy of the Commons: Twenty-Two Years Later' (1990) 18 Human Ecology 1 at 2.
[190] Hardin, above n 100 at 1244.
[191] Demsetz, above n 158 at 350.
[192] Coase, above n 28.

property should arise wherever the gains produced by internalization exceeded the transaction costs involved in establishing the property right and the legal system to protect that right.[193] This evolutionary feature of Demsetz's work is, as Carol Rose points out, a recurring theme in property law theory: 'property rights evolve to meet changing needs for resource management'.[194]

Demsetz offers an account of 'the emergence of property rights' amongst the Montagnes of the Ungava peninsula in Labrador/Quebec.[195] He argued that private property emerged as a response to the fur trade. Prior to the fur trade, the hunting grounds were held in common. This resulted in certain externalities as the costs of a successful hunting expedition by one hunter imposed costs on subsequent hunters 'but these external effects were of such small significance that it did not pay for anyone to take them into account'.[196] The advent of the fur trade had at least two effects. It increased the value of furs to the Indians and it increased hunting activity. Both effects 'increased considerably the importance of externalities associated with free hunting'. This resulted in the development of rights to particular hunting territories[197] and led Demsetz to the general proposition that '[private] property rights arise when it becomes economic for those affected by externalities to internalize benefits and costs'.[198] In this formulation, the choice of property regimes is driven by efficiency concerns. The benefits of the new private property regime will include the exclusive right to harvest now (or to defer harvest into the future), while the costs will include such things as monitoring, enforcement, boundary delimitations and measures taken to improve the harvest. Others have emphasized that the transformation is a transformation from functional rights over a larger territory (overlapping and non-exclusive, such as the right to hunt) to a spatial organization of entitlements (exclusive and the entire bundle).[199]

While accepted as an important explanation, there are criticisms. One general line of criticism is that Demsetz's account is incomplete insofar as he never tells us how all of this happens. How did the Montagnes engineer this transformation? Was it a collective eureka moment or was it fraught and bloody? Who invested the time and effort to bring about this change? In either case, and whether brought about by a government (eg enclosure legislation), or by more informal and cooperative means, 'the production of a property right is necessarily a collective

---

[193] Demsetz, above n 158.

[194] C. M. Rose, 'Servitudes', Arizona Legal Studies Discussion Paper No. 09–13, available at <http://ssrn.com/abstract=1371251>.

[195] Demsetz, above n 158. Demsetz's use of the term 'emergence' of property rights suggests that for him open access and community commons do not really 'count' as property.

[196] ibid at 351–2.

[197] Demsetz is surprisingly vague as to the persons in whom these territorial rights vest. Both he and the sources he quotes refer variously to bands, groups, and families and whether the latter is nuclear or extended is never specified.

[198] Demsetz, above n 158 at 354.

[199] S. Banner, 'Transitions between Property Regimes' (2002) 31 J Legal Stud 359.

endeavour'[200]— an individual cannot create a new property regime. This serves to emphasize that the transformation of property regimes is an important collective action problem.[201]

Stuart Banner has discussed this collective action problem in the context of the colonial encounter—of which Demsetz's Montagnes example is but one— and the enclosure movement. Banner emphasizes that in both cases the trans- formation had significant distributional consequences and occurred within hierarchical political (and power) structures that benefited, respectively, settlers at the expense of indigenous peoples, and wealthy landowners at the expense of the rest.[202] The distributional issues will be particularly difficult to resolve where the relevant rule of decision that moves us from a commons to private property is unanimity or consent rather than majority or fiat. Wyman, for example, has offered an analysis of the transformation of open access fisheries regimes in the United States towards individual transferable quota (ITQ) fisheries seeking to understand why such regimes have been slow to evolve.[203] Wyman suggests that the delays are attributable to the fact that interest groups have many veto points that they can use to delay the rate of change—the anticommons problem—and because of conflicts in the allocation of the increased rents that tradeable rights are expected to generate.[204]

Carol Rose questions the consistency of the assumptions underlying Demsetz's account.[205] She points out that there is a problem if the move from a commons regime to a private property regime is premised on efficiency grounds and the idea that we are all rational utility maximizers. This problem arises because 'a property *regime* generally, taken as an entire system, has the same structure as a common property'.[206] If that is the case, then we must find individuals who are prepared to act in a disinterested way and to put the time and effort into setting up the new system rather than investing all of their efforts in their own harvesting activities. Or alternatively (and in more modern terms) somebody must be prepared to invest the time and effort to

---

[200] ibid at 358. See also Michelman, above n 98 at 31 ('... private property emerges as a possible device or instrumentality for social cooperation—available as such, only to agents *who have in first place, a capacity for cooperative action*' (emphasis in original)).

[201] See the discussion in Part I.D. as to who 'supplies' the property institutions and Scott, above n 5.

[202] Banner, above n 199.

[203] K. Wyman, 'From Fur to Fish: Reconsidering the Evolution of Private Property' (2005) 80 New York University Law Review 117.

[204] See also L. A. Fennell, 'Slices and Lumps' University of Chicago Law & Economics, Olin Working Paper No. 395 (March 1, 2008), available at <http://papers.ssrn.com/sol3/papers. cfm?abstract_id=1106421> (arguing that there are two fundamental challenges in reconfiguring property rights: (1) consent, and (2) dividing the surplus). Scott, above n 5 at 164, 171, 176, 181 also notes the distributional issues associated with moving from open access to licensed access.

[205] Rose, above n 98. Rose suggests that the similar accounts of others, including Hobbes and Locke, are also open to question at this critical point. See also Rose, above n 16.

[206] Rose, above n 98 at 37. Elsewhere Rose refers to this conceptualization of property regimes as a 'meta property': Rose, above n 59 at 5.

lobby the legislature or to bring the court cases to transform the nature of the property entitlements.[207]

Finally, if, as Demsetz argues, technological change may push us from a commons regime to private property, the reverse may also be true if the costs of monitoring and enforcing private property rights exceed the gains that flow from internalizing other costs. Bell and Parchomovsky have suggested that we may also be able to respond to technological changes by adjusting other dimensions of property rather than the basic regime characteristics.[208] These authors encourage us to think of property in terms of three dimensions: the number of owners, the scope of the dominion, and asset design. For example, one possible response to the challenge posed to the copyright owners of musical works by the development of file sharing technology is to reconfigure the asset from the bundled good of a CD or a long playing vinyl record to the individual selection of individual tunes through a vehicle such as iTunes.[209] Possible analogies in the natural resources sector include rules about the minimum and maximum size of mineral claims[210] and, in the oil and gas sector, pooling and unitization arrangements. Pooling, for example, may be effected either by cross conveyance (which changes both the size of the asset and the number of owners as the owner of each tract becomes a tenant in common of the entire pooled unit) or by a more limited administrative arrangement in which tract owners agree to collaborate for certain purposes (such as an application for a well licence and sharing costs and production).[211]

C. Justifications for private property and 'takings' law

The aim of this sub-section of the chapter is to offer an example of how theorizing about the different justifications for private property may be brought to bear on the practical reasoning[212] engaged in by lawyers in advising private clients or governments in the development of public policy. We have chosen the example of takings law (also known as expropriation or eminent domain law) because it has

---

[207] See Scott, above n 5. Scott's analysis deals with this type of problem across a range of resources (water, fisheries, mining, forestry). Furthermore he is interested in not just the big move from open access to private, but also the evolution of the different incidents or characteristics of resource rights. For example, he explores the evolution in the judicial understanding of the relationship between severed estates (eg mineral and surface estates) and between mineral owners and mineral lessees.

[208] A Bell and G. Parchomovsky, 'Reconfiguring Property in Three Dimensions' (2008) 75 U Chi L Rev 1015.

[209] ibid at 1029–30.

[210] See Scott, above n 5 at 264–70 (discussing both the apex rule in mining—the idea that the discoverer gains the extra-lateral right to follow its discovery—and variations in claim size as an alternative response but also as a response to changing exploration techniques).

[211] eg, Bankes, above n 128.

[212] C. R. Sunstein, 'Practical Reason and Incompletely Theorized Agreements' in *Current Legal Problems 1998* (M. D. A. Freeman, ed, 1999) 267.

attracted a particularly rich body of literature. Much of this literature is associated with the constitutional protection of property rights in the United States, but in recent years the advent of investor-state arbitrations in the context of bilateral investment treaties and their multilateral companions (for example, the North American Free Trade Agreement and the Energy Charter Treaty) has served to internationalize this debate.[213] We have also chosen this example because the issue of indirect expropriation is often of concern to those working in the natural resources and energy fields.[214]

A good starting point for this discussion is Frank Michelman's classic 1967 article entitled 'Property, Utility and Fairness: Comments on the Ethical Foundations of "Just Compensation" Law'.[215] In that article Michelman deals with two big questions. First, when is it legitimate for society to take the property of an individual? And secondly, when, if ever, is it legitimate to 'take' such property without paying compensation to those who suffer harm?

For Michelman the first question is largely, but not completely, a collective action challenge that arises because of market failure. Thus a taking, as opposed to a consensual acquisition, will be permissible where there is a market failure or holdout problem, and where the net benefits to society will exceed the private losses, ie, the taking is efficient. The issue is not always a market failure problem because there may be other legitimate reasons for a taking, most notably a redistributive taking, such as a progressive income tax, in the interests of securing a goal of substantive equality. But if the taking can be justified because it is efficient—and society cannot afford inefficient takings—we still need to deal with the question of whether society should compensate. In part the question arises because of two different ways in which we use the concept of efficiency, Pareto efficiency and Kaldor-Hicks efficiency. The concept of Pareto efficiency is associated with consent, property entitlements and contract, and necessarily entails the idea that a reallocation of resources will not occur unless all benefit from the reallocation. In a consensual arrangement, this will mean that the person who gives up their interest in the property will be actually and fully compensated for their loss.[216] By contrast, the Kaldor-Hicks idea of efficiency

---

[213] eg, C. McLachlan, L. Shore, and M. Weiniger, *International Investment Arbitration: Substantive Principles* (2007) esp. c. 8; C. Ribeiro, ed, *Investment Arbitration and the Energy Charter Treaty* (2006), c. 3 'The Concept of Expropriation under the ECT and other Investment Protection Treaties'; B. H. Weston, ' "Constructive Takings" under International Law: A Modest Foray into the Problem of "Creeping Expropriation" ' (1975) 16 Virginia J Int'l L 103.

[214] eg, J. M. Wagner, 'International Investment, Expropriation and Environmental Protection' (1999) 29 Golden Gate Univ L Rev 465; K. Tienhaara, 'Mineral Investment and the Regulation of the Environment in Developing Countries: Lessons from Ghana' (2006) 6 International Environmental Agreements: Politics, Law and Economics 371.

[215] Michelman, above n 8.

[216] There is a body of literature that suggests that expropriation statutes that use a market value basis for compensating tend to under compensate owners who in many cases will have a higher subjective valuation of the property. J. L. Knetsch and T. E. Borcherding, 'Expropriation of Private Property and the Basis for Compensation' (1979) 29 U Toronto LJ 237.

entails only the idea that the benefits of the taking exceed the costs incurred by those who suffer losses, so that those who gain can, in principle, compensate the losers. But the point is that Kaldor-Hicks efficiency does not require payment of actual compensation to all of those who suffer losses before a taking is deemed to be efficient.

Now one might say that society should always compensate for a collective action taking since it is unjust to require an individual to pay for a benefit that accrues to society at large, whether in the form of a bridge, a new highway, or even a park. But property rights holders suffer a variety of harms from a taking, from the direct physical acquisition of owned property to the more indirect losses suffered by those who now live adjacent to a new highway or airport runway. Must they all be compensated? If so, the transaction costs associated with tracking down and compensating such individuals might well eat up the efficiency gains of the project, and thus, a worthwhile project with welfare gains and net societal benefits may not proceed. So when should society compensate and what does property theory have to do with this question?

Michelman's response was that the existing American 'takings' jurisprudence did not provide an adequate answer and that it was necessary to inquire into the theoretical justifications for property on the basis that ideas of property somehow must justify or dictate 'some degree of permanence of distribution'.[217] His inquiry ranged broadly before settling on Rawlsian ideas of justice[218] and utilitarian ideals. Michelman drew on utilitarian ideas to suggest that the state only needs to compensate when demoralization costs exceed settlement costs (assuming of course that those costs do not exceed efficiency gains).[219] And he drew on Rawlsian ideas to argue that compensation would generally be due where 'settlements costs are low' (eg, where those affected are readily identifiable such as in the case of a physical taking), 'when efficiency gains are dubious' (the discipline of having to pay compensation serves to protect the liberty interests of the individual) and 'when the harm concentrated on one individual is unusually great'.[220] Rawlsian ideas, however, also suggest that we should not be concerned to track down every last individual who might have suffered harm as a result of public project because if we do so the transaction costs may defeat a public project which, all other things being equal, might make more of a contribution to those least well off in society.

---

[217] Michelman, above n 8 at 1203.

[218] J. Rawls, *A Theory of Justice* (1971). Michelman (note the timing) actually draws on Rawls's earlier writings that formed the basis for his famous *Theory of Justice*. See, for example, J. Rawls, 'Justice as Fairness' (1958) 67 Philosophical Review 164; J. Rawls, 'Justice as Fairness' in *Philosophy, Politics and Society, 2d Series* (P. Laslett and W. G. Runciman, eds, 1962) 132.

[219] Michelman, above n 8 at 1215 (and if settlement costs exceed efficiency gains, then Michelman would of course say that there should be no taking).

[220] ibid at 1223. See also H. Dagan, 'Takings and Distributive Justice' (1999) 85 Virginia L Rev 741 (discussing how American takings law could accommodate social responsibility and equality values).

Others have also used property theory to unpack takings doctrine. For example, Margaret Jane Radin uses the idea of personhood and human flourishing to argue that some (but not all) forms of property are deserving of special protection.[221] Thus for Radin, the use of property as a residence 'is much more closely protected to personhood', and therefore protection by at least some form of entitlement, 'than use of property as a garbage dump for one's factory'.[222] By contrast, Richard Epstein draws on liberty-based justifications of property both to limit the power of the state to take[223] and also to create and advocate for a robust and broad entitlement to compensation. Thus, for Epstein, the 'conception of property includes the exclusive rights of possession, use and disposition'[224] and for him government actions that limit any of these rights, including progressive taxes and welfare transfer payments, are prima facie compensable takings.[225]

III. Conclusion

This chapter has provided an account of some of the main strands in the literature on property law theory under two main headings, namely, what is property and justifications for private property. We have also tried to reflect on the implications of this literature for energy and natural resources law.

For the most part, the debates that have been occurring in general property law theory also resonate within the more specific fields of energy and resources law. For example, writers on energy and resources law and practitioners are comfortable with the concept of property as a highly functional bundle of sticks. They develop innovative ways both to fragment property and resources interests but also to re-combine them. By contrast, those who, like Freyfogle, write about property from an environmental perspective, are much more leery about disintegrated approaches to property, preferring to capture both the rootedness and place-based connections of particular land, but also the interconnectedness between particular property and ecosystems and landscape values.

While natural resources and energy law are a comfortable fit with the dominant (economic) ideas in property theory, it is more difficult to accommodate environmental values and ideas of distributive justice. Indeed, while some property theorists (for example, Waldron and Munzer) explicitly deal with the distributive justice issue most (given their economic focus) take the existing distribution as a given. Similarly, while some property theorists (notably Rose) engage with environmental values, and while some environmental lawyers (notably Freyfogle)

---

[221] Radin, above n 23.
[222] ibid at 139–40.
[223] Epstein, above n 14, ch12.
[224] ibid at 304.
[225] ibid, especially chs 18 and 19.

engage with property institutions, for the most part these are separate worlds. Property law theory therefore has tended to be isolated, traditional, and economic in its orientation. Pressure for change does, however, appear to be mounting on the institution of property law and, as a result, on property law theory.

We began this chapter with the observation that property law literature had flourished over the last quarter of a century. It seems safe to predict that this trend will continue, driven by a number of economic factors including globalization, commodification, the protection of international investments and the increased reliance on market-based measures (such as cap and trade schemes), rather than command and control measures, to achieve particular environmental goals (for such schemes inevitably exchange open access commons for property-like entitlements)[226] and, of course, the stark reality of the increasing demand for and the increasing scarcity of many resources. But we think that other factors will also ensure a continuing interest in property law theory, including the increased international recognition of the land and resource rights of indigenous peoples. This type of development, combined with both the increased interconnectedness and inter-dependence that is a necessary result of globalization and increased scarcity, will likely stimulate renewed interest in distributive justice and environmental ideas as a part of property theory. Increased interconnectedness and inter-dependence between resource rights is also observable at the local level in the form of multiple use rights (eg, forestry, oil and gas, carbon sequestration, and recreational activities) all within the same geographical area[227] and we anticipate that the conflict between these resource rights and their resolution and accommodation will continue to challenge theorists and practitioners alike.

[226] C. Rose, 'Expanding the Choices for the Global Commons: Comparing Newfangled Tradable Allowance Schemes to Old-Fashioned Common-Property Regimes' (1999) 10 Duke Envtl L & Policy Forum 45.
[227] Scott, above n 5.

3

Public and Private Rights to Natural Resources and Differences in their Protection?

*Anita Rønne**

I. Introduction

This chapter will analyse different entitlements to natural resources and the extent to which state ownership implies a different or less intensive regulation than where such ownership is not the case. It will focus on the prime regulatory instruments used to transfer rights of utilization, and will seek to identify the differences as to the protection of those rights—if any. The topic will be illustrated by different civil law examples. The analysis will be limited to three groups of natural resources (i) oil and gas, (ii) sand, stone and gravel, and (iii) wind and waves. This implies that metals, fish, forests and water resources are excluded from the coverage.

My approach to the work on property rights over natural resources started with a question relating to the creation of, and the background for, the different entitlements to natural resources. Why are some resources 'owned' by the state, and some by the landowner, whereas 'access rights' but not ownership to exploit others are vested exclusively with the state, and in other cases the right of access is common and free to anybody?

By way of illustration, the Danish Subsoil Act vests ownership rights to natural resources that have not been exploited prior to the adoption of the first Subsoil Act in 1936 with the state. The natural resources covered are oil, gas, salt, and geothermal energy; originally located only on land, but the area was expanded to include the continental shelf area in 1963. It includes a right for the state to issue licences to other parties to explore and produce the resources. As from 1981, the licensing regime was changed to introduce a right of state participation in the licences. Other natural resources like sand, stones, gravel, and chalk that were already (before 1936) subject to private exploitation continued to be either owned by the landowner or freely accessible depending on location. In 1972, however, this group of natural resources became subject to general regulation upon the

* Associate Professor of Energy Law, Faculty of Law, University of Copenhagen, Denmark; email: anita.ronne@jur.ku.dk.

adoption of the first Act on Raw Materials. Subsequently, this Act has been gradually tightened based on the introduction of a licensing regime. The most recent natural resources to become regulated are wind and wave resources offshore for use for energy purposes. In 1998, an amendment to the Electricity Act implied that the right to utilize wind or waves in the exclusive economic zone lies solely in the state. These exclusive rights are also combined with the introduction of a licensing system and since 2008 include requirements for the ownership of the production facilities and a compensation scheme for the landowners affected. I will return to these developments.

The gradual tightening of the natural resource regimes by general legislation, or by the imposition by the state of tighter licence conditions for exploitation, have given cause to many conflicts between the landowner or licensee and the state. Many governments have therefore also experienced legal claims that expropriation has occurred, rather than mere regulation that requires no compensation to be paid. Some illustrative cases will be included in the analysis.

II. The concept of property, its protection, and regulation

A. Historical background

To understand the concept of the relevant areas—property law, constitutional law and administrative law—it is useful very briefly to sketch out their roots and development. It is beyond doubt that Roman law has had an impact on the legal systems of all European states. The degree, however, varies considerably from north to south. The influence of Roman law in the Nordic countries and the common law countries is thus limited, compared to the rest of Europe.[1] Moreover, the Nordic legal systems are usually recognized as a separate legal family, distinct from both civil law and common law, although it must be admitted that there has been a considerable influence from continental legal thinking, especially from France and Germany and hence indirectly from Roman Law.[2] That being said, it is particularly within the areas of property law and tort law that the influence of Roman law is felt as those areas of law have not been subject to detailed regulation until recent times.[3]

In Roman law the term for the right of ownership is dominium. Different types of ownership exist and not everybody was entitled to be an owner.[4] It is

---

[1] See D. Tamm, 'The Danes and Their Legal Heritage' in *Danish Law in a European Perspective* (B. Dahl, T. Melchior and D. Tamm, eds, 2002) 43 ff.

[2] See K. Zweigert and H. Kötz, *An Introduction to Comparative Law* (3rd rev edn, 1998) 277 and J. Juergensmeyer and E. M. Basse, 'Civil Law and Common Law Systems' and E. M. Basse and J. Dalberg-Larsen, 'National Legal Systems' in *Legal Systems and Wind Energy—A Comparative Perspective* (H. T. Anker, B. E. Olsen, and A. Rønne, eds, 2008) 25 and 61.

[3] O. Due, 'Danish Law in a European Context' in *Danish Law in a European Perspective* (above n 1) 17.

[4] D. Tamm, *Roman Law* (1997) 70.

interesting to take note of the fact that the Justinian law already operated with *res communes omnium*—things that were in common to all such as air, water or the sea, along with *res publicae*, things that were public property such as harbours, theatres and marketplaces. Such things could not be objects of the law of private property.[5] Another area where restrictions in property rights were recognized was in the relationship between neighbours. Thus Roman law sets certain limits to an owner's exploitation of his property if it could annoy others.[6]

In most continental countries the nineteenth century was a period of major codification. Very few of the codifications are still applicable. Nordic legal co-operation implied the development of rather uniform legislation in certain areas such as contract law. Today, the influence of European Community Law is major in several areas of law that fall under the scope of Community treaties such as those relating to the internal market and environmental law.[7] Case law has never achieved the same authority in Continental Europe as precedents in the common law countries.[8]

B. The nature of property law

The law of property deals with rights to dispose of real or movable property. Ownership is normally defined negatively as a right to dispose of property factually and legally in all respects insofar as limitations do not apply by way of agreement, legislation or general legal principles.[9] Limited proprietary rights such as the right of use include only a right of disposal in certain respects. General limitations on the right to dispose of property are developed by court practice in the legal principles on nuisance which imply the limits that a neighbour must tolerate from the use of the adjoining property. Environmental protection legislation is mentioned below.

C. The protection of property rights: constitutional law

The protection of property rights against interference from others has three dimensions: the relation to third parties in connection with the transfer of the right; constitutional protection and the calculation of damages (constitutional law); and liability for damage to property (tort law). In our present context, it is only the second dimension that is relevant for the analysis.

---

[5] ibid at 71.
[6] ibid at 74.
[7] See Due (above n 3) 20.
[8] ibid at 18 and D. Tamm, 'The Danes and Their Legal Heritage' in *Danish Law in a European Perspective* (above n 1) 57.
[9] B. von Eyben, 'Danish Property Law', in *Danish Law in a European Perspective* (above n 1) 211. See also A. Scott, *The Evolution of Resource Property Rights* (2008) 6 ff, and A. Clarke and P. Kohler, *Property Law, Commentary and Materials* (2005) 17 ff and 153 ff.

The nineteenth century saw a return to the ideas of natural law and natural justice that were inaugurated in constitutions adopted by the majority of European states.[10] The constitutions include the protection of property as a fundamental human right[11] mirroring the wording of the 1789 French Declaration on the Rights of Man and Citizens that says: 'Since the right to Property is inviolable and sacred, no one may be deprived thereof, unless public necessity, legally ascertained, obviously requires it, and just and prior indemnity has been paid.'[12] The human right is thus based on three criteria: (i) no one can be deprived of his possessions unless in accordance with the law, (ii) full compensation must be paid, and (iii) the interference with the property rights is found to be necessary in the public interest.[13]

In Denmark, the courts have interpreted the concept of deprivation narrowly implying that many general regulatory measures affecting even only a small number of individuals will not necessarily be covered by the provision, and thus left without compensation, and without the measure being considered to be expropriation. Likewise the courts have been rather hesitant to review in more depth the grounds given for the steps taken by the executive or Parliament as to whether 'public interests' in real terms required the adoption of the restrictive measure; see further below.

The European Convention on Human Rights and its Protocols together with the European Court of Human Rights has increasingly become influential on national law. The Convention did not originally (in 1950) include an article on the protection of property rights, but such an article was adopted in the First Protocol to the Convention in 1952. It says:

Every natural or legal person is entitled to the peaceful enjoyment of his possessions. No one shall be deprived of his possessions except in the public interest and subject to the conditions provided for by law and by the general principles of international law. The preceding provisions shall not, however, in any way impair the right of a State to enforce such laws as it deems necessary to control the use of property in accordance with the general interest or to secure the payment of taxes or other contributions or penalties.[14]

Under international law the right to expropriate is recognized as being customary international law and is closely related to the development of the permanent

---

[10] See Due (above n 3) at 18.
[11] 'Property rights are one of the fundamental principles of the European legal order, with most national constitutions according property rights protection.' See *Energy Law in Europe* (M. M. Roggenkamp, C. Redgwell, I. del Guayo, and A. Rønne, eds, 2nd edn, 2005) 1272. See also E. E. Smith, J. S. Dzienkowski, O. L. Anderson, G. B. Conine, J. S. Lowe, and B. M. Kramer, *International Petroleum Transactions* (2nd edn, 2000) 203, 338, and D. N. Zillman in *Energy Law and Policy for the 21st Century* (The Energy Law Group, 2000) 3–40.
[12] See Art 17, available at <www.elysee.fr>.
[13] eg the Danish Constitution Art 73 and the Spanish Constitution Art 33. See also H. C. Bugge, 'Legal Issues in Land Use and Nature Protection—an Introduction' in *Land Use and Nature Protection* (H. T. Anker and E. M. Basse, eds, 2000) 28.
[14] See Art 1, available at <www.coe.int>.

sovereignty principle.[15] Likewise, several United Nations Resolutions and a number of arbitral awards have accepted the taking of foreign property. What is more doubtful are the criteria for the expropriation. Should it be according to national or international legal principles and how should full compensation be determined?

D. The development of administrative law

Modern administrative law in Europe outside the common law countries has to a large extent been based on the case law of the French Conseil d'Etat. The development has to some extent been supported by decisions by the German administrative courts.[16] This implies that within continental Europe administrative law is quite homogeneous. The principles of administrative law are founded on the balancing of public interests with those of the individual citizen and his or her legal rights. In the common law countries, administrative law has only more recently developed into a separate discipline of law.

Since the beginning of the 1970s, regulation of property rights has exploded concurrently with the development of environmental and planning law. The protection of the rights of neighbours based on case law—the law on nuisance—is much older as indicated above. When physical planning legislation was adopted in Denmark it followed a long debate concerning its consistency with the Constitution, because through planning property rights can be overridden without compensation. And this is indeed what the property owner has experienced during the last three decades. This should be seen in contrast to individual conservation orders including restrictions on the usage of land, where compensation has been paid if the limitation exceeded certain limits.[17]

III. Property rights to natural resources

The ownership of energy resources varies according to where such resources are located, onshore or offshore. Under general international law states have permanent sovereignty over natural onshore resources.[18] Hence, states are free to determine whether subsoil energy resources are owned by the state or by the individual landowners. As pointed out by Roggenkamp, Redgwell, del Guayo, and Rønne,

---

[15] C. Redgwell, 'International Regulation of Energy Activities' in *Energy Law in Europe* (above n 11) 142, R. Higgins, *Problems & Progress—International Law and How We Use It* (1994) 142 ff, and B. Taverne, *Petroleum, Industry and Governments* (1999) 84. See in general N. Schrijver, *Sovereignty Over Natural Resources* (1997).

[16] K. Revsbech, 'The Growth in Danish Administrative Law' in Dahl et al (above n 1) 149.

[17] E. M. Basse, 'Environmental Protection in Denmark' in Dahl et al (above n 1) 380.

[18] See eg UN Resolution 1803 (XVII) of 14 December 1962: Permanent Sovereignty over Natural Resources, Resolution No 2158 (XXI) and Resolution No 3281 (XXIX) of 12 December 1974: Charter of Economic Rights and Duties of States. See also R. Barnes, *Property Rights and Natural Resources* (2009) and references in n 15 above.

most civil law countries vest the ownership of the subsoil in the surface landowner, an exception is usually made for energy resources such as oil, gas, and coal. Hence, most countries reviewed claim State ownership of oil, gas, and coal resources onshore (Denmark, Norway, Poland, the UK, Spain, and recently also the Netherlands). Some other countries leave the issue of ownership to energy resources unresolved (Italy and previously also the Netherlands). It should be noted that the applicable energy legislation in these countries was usually drafted in the early 20th century; elsewhere, when replaced by modern legislation, all countries appear to opt for State ownership. Practical difficulties may, however, arise when determining how far the landowner's surface rights extend.[19]

As for offshore energy resources, international law recognizes the sovereign rights of the state over the resources of the continental shelf and functional jurisdiction for the purposes of exploring and exploiting these resources. Even in countries accepting private ownership of everything down to the centre of the earth these rights have been reserved to the state.[20] Under international law, states do not 'own' the resources but enjoy sovereign rights to explore and exploit them. Nonetheless, several states (eg Denmark, Norway, Spain, and the Netherlands) claim not only a right to regulate but also ownership of offshore oil and gas resources.[21]

In France, the Civil Code provides that 'ownership of the ground involves ownership of what is above and below the ground'.[22] However, mineral and oil deposits are distinct from ownership of the ground and vested with the state that may grant authorization and mining titles for exploitation pursuant to the Mining Code. This may happen without the land owner's agreement but is subject to consultation. The granting of the concession creates a special right of ownership distinct from the ownership of the land and the subsoil. The Mining Code covers oil, gas, coal, uranium, metals, salt, and geothermal deposits on land as well as on the continental shelf. The materials 'eligible for concession' include mineral substances, which were considered in 1810 as strategic and of prime importance for national sovereignty. The Mining Code has been regularly amended and reformed. The exploitation of materials defined as 'non-eligible for concession' is ruled by the regulations on quarries and covers mainly natural resources used for building materials; limestone, chalk, gypsum, slate, etc.

The German Federal Mining Act defines mineral resources as all mineral substances, solid, liquid, or gaseous (except for water) occurring in natural sediments or accumulations (deposits) onshore as well as offshore. Mineral resources are further classified into 'bergfrei' and 'grundeigen'.[23] Only mineral resources

---

[19] *Energy Law in Europe* (above n 11) 1273. See also B. Taverne, *Petroleum, Industry and Governments* (1999) 139, and Scott (above n 9) 187 ff.

[20] See Zillman (above n 11) at 3–4 and 7–8 and Scott (above n 9) 197 ff and 289 ff.

[21] *Energy Law in Europe* (above n 11) 1273.

[22] T. Lauriol, 'Energy Law in France' in *Energy Law in Europe* (above n 11) 554 ff, and C. Didier, *The French Experience of Post Mining Management* (2008) 6, available at <www.gisos.ensg.inpl-nancy.fr>.

[23] J. C. Pielow, H. M. Koopmann and E. Ehlers, 'Energy Law in Germany' in *Energy Law in Europe* (above n 11) 646 ff and 701.

classified as 'grundeigen' or land-owned run with the land and are protected as private property. This does not include the other mineral resources classified as 'bergfrei' (free from land-property) that includes, for example, metals like iron, gold, copper, coal, geothermal energy, and salt. The mineral resources of the continental shelf also belong to this category. Natural resources vested in the land owner comprise the rest and include, for example, basalt lava, quartz, and clay. The Federal Mining Law in this way suspended the land owner's access to the so-called 'bergfreie' resources which are regarded as goods that are not owned by anybody. They may, however, be exploited subject to the grant of an administrative permission. Utilization of offshore wind resources is subject to the Renewable Energies Act and relies on the initiative of private enterprises for the application of a building licence. Legislation is primarily concerned with planning issues and a minimum rate of return for the investor.

The Dutch Mining Act of 2002 replaced a Mining Act of 1810.[24] The new Mining Act applies to the exploration and production of minerals and geothermal energy—'minerals or substances of organic origin, present in the subsoil, in a concentration or deposit which is there by natural origin, in solid, liquid or gaseous form, with the exception of marsh gas, limestone, gravel, sand, clay, shells and mixtures thereof'. In contrast to the previous Act, it covers the Dutch territory, territorial sea, and the continental shelf area, whereas oil and gas were previously not included in the definition of onshore mining. The new Act makes use of a depth criterion and limits the scope of minerals to those located on land at a depth of more than 100 metres beneath the surface and determines that those natural resources are owned by the state. Before the adoption of the 2002 Act, the legal status of the minerals *in situ* was not settled. Minerals in the continental shelf are likewise owned by the state. Any exploration or production of minerals in the upper layers of the land is owned by the land owner and is governed by the Land Clearing Act. The Mining Act introduces one licensing regime for onshore and offshore exploration and production of minerals as well as geothermal heat. To some extent it codifies existing practice.

In many other countries as well, the general rule is that the rights of ownership of certain categories of natural resources are vested in the state. Thus in Spain all mines and other geological resources located in the Spanish national territory, in the territorial waters, or on the continental shelf, are declared by the Mining Act 1973 to be vested in the state, giving private individuals or companies the right to apply for an authorization to search for minerals or for a concession to work a mine, save in those areas where the state has reserved this right for itself.[25]

In Denmark, the general starting point is that the ownership to land includes 'items' that in a natural way are connected to or a part of the land. Beyond

---

[24] M. M. Roggenkamp, 'Energy Law in the Netherlands' in *Energy Law in Europe* (above n 11) 793 ff.
[25] I. del Guayo, 'Energy Law in Spain' in *Energy Law in Europe* (above n 11) 1099.

doubt this includes soil, stones, sand, and gravel.[26] However, this free access has gradually been limited through law, not least because of scarcity of the natural resources and the need for a rational utilization of them. Ownership to land has thus been constrained.

As early as 1932 it was established in Denmark's first Subsoil Act that natural resources such as oil and natural gas in the Danish subsoil belong to the state of Denmark.[27] The initiative came from the Danish Geological Survey and also had a background in the fact that private companies were planning to start exploration.[28] At this time, the Act only included the land and territorial sea. Following the Danish ratification of the 1958 Geneva Convention on the Continental Shelf on 31 May 1963, sovereignty was claimed over the Danish continental shelf area.[29] It was considered that Danish legislation, which was not expressly limited to the land and territorial sea, hereinafter also applied to activities on the continental shelf, but in order to eliminate any doubt the Act on the Continental Shelf was adopted in 1971.[30] The Continental Shelf Act states that 'the natural resources of the Danish Continental Shelf are the property of the State of Denmark and may only be explored or exploited by others under a concession or a permit' (s 1). Likewise, the Subsoil Act determines that 'this Act shall also apply to the Danish Continental Shelf Area' (s 1) and further that the 'raw materials ... belong to the Danish State' (s 2). It has thus exceeded its rights in international law, which only grants a state functional jurisdiction over the continental shelf ('sovereign rights' but not sovereignty).

The Subsoil Act of 1932 did not include all the natural resources of the subsoil, but limited its scope to the resources that had not been produced commercially

---

[26] B. von Eyben, P. Mortensen and P. Pagh, *Fast Ejendom* (Real Estate) (2nd edn, 1999) 14.

[27] In terms of territory, the Danish Constitution states in Art 1 that it applies to all parts of the Realm. This includes continental Denmark, the Faroe Islands, and Greenland. Both the Faroe Islands and Greenland, however, have their own home rule arrangements, established by a special statute adopted by the Danish Parliament. The legal regimes, though not quite identical, are based on the same model of local autonomy and have established a framework for extensive self-government, where legislative and administrative powers on specific matters are transferred to the Home Rule Authorities: the Home Rule Act of the Faroe Islands of 23 March 1948, and the Home Rule Act of Greenland of 29 November 1978. For more details see A. Rønne, 'Energy Law in Denmark' in *Energy Law in Europe* (above n 11) 446; A. Rønne, 'The Emerging Oil and Gas Law in the Faroe Islands' (2002) 8 International Energy Law and Taxation Review, 184; A Rønne, 'The Emphasis on Public Participation in Energy Resource Development in Denmark and the Rights of Greenland and the Faroe Islands' in *Human Rights in Natural Resource Development* (D. Zillman, A. Lucas, and G. Pring, eds, 2002) 355.

[28] See M. Hahn-Pedersen, *A.P. Møller and the Danish Oil* (1999) 20, and the explanatory notes to the Subsoil Act No 27 of 19 February 1932.

[29] Royal Order No 259 of 7 June 1963. Pursuant to s 3, a licence is required to explore and exploit the natural resources in the shelf, pursuant to the Subsoil Act.

[30] Act No 259 of 9 June 1971 as amended; cf Consolidated Act No 1101 of 18 November 2005. It is stated that 'Danish law shall apply to installations ... and in safety zones around'. Because of the adoption of special legislation, such as the Subsoil Act, and the Act on Offshore Safety which apply also to the continental shelf, the Act on the Continental Shelf has lost a lot of its initial importance.

before 23 February 1932 (the date the law came into force) in order to avoid claims of expropriation. The excluded resources included stone, gravel, sand, lime, chalk, peat, clay, and lignite, to which the rights of the land owner thus continued until regulation was introduced by the Act on Raw Materials in 1972, which also includes a licence system.[31] The Subsoil Act was amended in 1950, in 1971 and totally revised by the adoption of a new Subsoil Act in 1981. The latter was important as part of a strategy for reaching Denmark's energy goals, expediting self-sufficiency in energy by increasing the exploration for and production of oil and natural gas from the Danish subsoil.[32] In order to implement the EC Licensing Directive (94/22), it was necessary in 1995 to amend the Subsoil Act substantially. Criteria which gave preferential status to the Danish state and to national companies had to be abandoned together with special purchase rights of the state of oil and natural gas. Such developments can be observed in many other European countries as well.

IV. The licence system

Despite the different origins of the different national regimes in Europe, natural resources exploration and production is based on a system of licences, issued at the discretion of the responsible authority and including provisions aimed at continuing public control. As highlighted by Roggenkamp, Redgwell, del Guayo and Rønne,

> The rights typically allow the licensee to perform certain actions, and give some security for the investments of the licensee in the sense that the licence cannot be changed or withdrawn arbitrarily. The duties often reflect the social importance of the activity and require the licensee to perform, tolerate, or omit to do certain things.[33]

The central element of subsoil and mining legislation is the establishment of a licensing system permitting private and state-owned companies to explore for and produce hydrocarbons under the control of the authority for energy. The basic concept is that each licensee will enjoy, for a period, usually a long one of say, 20 to 50 years, within a delimited area, an exclusive right to explore for and produce, and an ownership interest in the natural resources won and saved. In return, the licensees must pay duties and commit themselves to certain obligations in carrying out their activities. The licence is strictly personal and cannot be transferred without the approval of the public administrative body. The state will in addition have a supervisory role and will require information from the licensee as activities develop and during the whole licence period.

---

[31] Act No 285 of 7 June 1972, now Consolidated Act No 1025 of 20 October 2008.
[32] Act No 293 of 10 June 1981 on the Use of the Danish Subsoil, with later amendments, cf Consolidated Act No 889 of 4 July 2007.
[33] *Energy Law in Europe* (above n 11) 1281.

Today the discretionary powers of the public authorities have become much more restricted and hardly any negotiations take place. For obvious reasons the area, the work programme, and to some extent the composition of the licensee are still subject to negotiations.

V. State participation

Direct state involvement in the energy sector through a wholly or partially state-owned company has been a feature of many European countries as an important element in securing society a share of the financial revenues from subsoil resources. Participation may also be seen as a way of providing the state with more insight into the oil and gas activities and making coordination and economic optimization possible. However, state participation has been subject to radical changes over the years—ranging from guaranteed participation and preferential status over private parties to abolition of the same, re-organization, and privatization. Generally speaking, the role of state companies has been reduced, partly because of general changes on the political agenda, and partly because of the requirements of the EC Licensing Directive.[34] Today a state participant must have the same rights and obligations as the other holders of licences.

State participation in hydrocarbon licences has been an inherent part of the Danish licensing system since the start of the 1980s. State-owned entities do not have control of production, as they hold only 20 per cent participation rights. If exploitable discoveries are made, the entity has in some licences an option to increase its share up to a maximum of 50 per cent, according to a negotiated sliding scale based on the magnitude of production. In the first and second rounds, however (1984 and 1986 respectively), and partly in the third round, this applied only in principle, as there was the crucial exception that the company was supported through the exploration phase on the basis of the 'carried interest' principle, that is, the other participants were required to pay the state participant's share of the exploration costs. As stated above, state participation now in principle takes place under the same conditions which apply to a private licensee.[35]

As a consequence of a political agreement on partial privatization of the state-owned company (DONG Energy), this company has not been able to manage the state's participation in new licences granted since 2005. As state participation in hydrocarbon licences was to remain an important element in securing for Danish society a share of the financial proceeds from subsoil resources, it was proposed to

[34] Directive 94/22/EC of the European Parliament and of the Council of 30 May 1994, OJ 1994 L 164/3.
[35] A. Rønne, 'A New Role For The State—Energy Regulatory Reform' in *Regulating Energy and Natural Resources* (B. Barton, L. K. Barrera-Hernández, A. Lucas, and A. Rønne, eds, 2006) 185.

set up a new state-owned entity tasked with managing the state participation in future licences. In 2005, the Danish North Sea Fund was formed by a special Act[36] to have responsibility for the state's participation in new hydrocarbon licences. Simultaneously, a state-owned entity, the Danish North Sea Partner, was established for the purpose of administering the Fund under the Ministry of Climate and Energy.[37] Placing the licence shares in a public Fund means that the state can transfer a possible profit to the Treasury. The Fund is not required to apply for its participation interest, rather, its interest is inserted automatically in all licences. In contrast to DONG Energy, the Fund cannot be awarded operatorships or act on its own initiative to acquire additional shares in excess of 20 per cent. Thus, the entity cannot act as a competitor to the oil companies. The Danish North Sea Fund has a pre-emptive right to buy shares in licences but has not made use of this option.[38] The 2003 Agreement on the specific terms of extending the A.P. Møller Sole Concession includes state participation. With effect from 9 July 2012, the state will participate as partner in the Consortium and will receive 20 per cent of the oil and gas produced. The state will also assume a 20 per cent share of the installations (platforms, processing facilities, pipelines, etc) without having to pay for the assets. In the Netherlands and Norway, state participation has experienced a similar total re-organization, as is described in other chapters in this book.

VI. New types of instruments in the balancing of interests

A. Legal rights to utilize the wind

Whereas utilization of wind on land is subject primarily to general planning requirements on the location of facilities in the landscape, several countries have introduced a special licence system for the utilization of wind offshore.[39] The Danish state has, however, taken some further steps which, to the author's knowledge, have not been adopted anywhere else. First, it has based the licence system on the concept of exclusive rights of the state to the utilization of wind offshore.[40] The purpose of the Act on the Promotion of Renewable Energy is indicated in its title. It provides that the use of renewable energy sources should be in accordance with climate, environment and macroeconomic considerations in order to reduce

---

[36] Act No 587 of 24 June 2005 s 1 and Order No 710 of 21 June 2007 include the regulations of the Fund. See also <www.nordsoeen.dk>.

[37] The Act s 4, see Explanatory Notes on the Bill No L 151 of 27 April 2005, 3. Annual reports for 2007 and 2008 may be found at <www.nordsoeen.dk>.

[38] Annual Report 2008, 7.

[39] See A. McHarg and A. Rønne, 'Reducing Carbon-Based Electricity Generation: Is the Answer Blowing in the Wind?' in *Beyond the Carbon Economy* (D. Zillman, C. Redgwell, Y. Omorogke, and L. K. Barrera-Hernández, eds, 2008) 287, and Danish Energy Authority, *Offshore Wind Power, Danish Experiences and Solutions* (October 2005).

[40] Originally set forth in the Electricity Supply Act but since the end of 2008 in a new Act on Promotion of Renewable Energy No 1392 of 27 December 2008.

dependence on fossil fuels, to ensure security of supply, and to reduce emissions of carbon dioxide and other greenhouse gases. The Act contributes in particular to ensuring fulfilment of national and international objectives on increasing the proportion of energy produced from renewable energy sources. Secondly, completely new instruments have been adopted to ensure public support for further development of renewables. These include a special compensation regime, purchase requirements, a Guarantee Fund, and a Green scheme.

B. The licence system

The Act merely lays down the framework for the licence system, and the more specific terms are included in the issued licence.[41] First and foremost there are limitations with respect to area and time, but if the activity may be assumed to have a significant impact on the environment, the permission may only be granted on the basis of an environmental impact assesment. When an installation is ready to produce electricity for the grid, a licence to exploit the wind energy is needed. The production period is fixed, in practice, at 25 years. A more detailed description of the area, including any special conditions applying to it, appears in the tender material and the Model Licence that is included as an attachment.

C. Compensation system

As a new principle, the Act determines that the loss of value to real property due to the erection of wind turbines shall be borne by the developer. Thus, any person who, upon erecting one or more wind turbines of more than 25 metres in height, causes a loss of value to real property, shall bear the costs (s 6).[42] Claims for payment pursuant to subsection 3 shall lapse if the loss of value constitutes one per cent or less of the total value of the property.

A valuation authority shall decide on the quantum of the loss of value on the basis of an individual assessment. The erector of the wind turbine and the owner of the real property may, however, choose to enter into an agreement about the amount to be paid. The valuation authority shall consist of a chairperson who satisfies the conditions for making a judgement and an expert in assessing the value of real property. In cases of disagreement, the chairperson's vote shall be decisive.

D. Purchase requirement

Another initiative concerns special purchase rights for local citizens to wind turbine shares. Any person who erects one or more wind turbines of at least 25 metres in height onshore, or offshore wind turbines established without a tendering

---

[41] See Conditions for Negotiated Tender on Offshore Wind Turbine Concession at Rødsand, 13 October 2005, available at <http://www.ens.dk>.
[42] Except for offshore wind turbines established following a tendering procedure.

procedure, prior to commencement of the installation shall offer for sale at least 20 per cent of the ownership shares to local citizens (s 3).

The proceeds of the sale shall cover a proportional share of the developer's project costs, so that the developer and the buyers inject the same amount per share. The sales material shall be accompanied by a report by a state-authorized public accountant declaring that the project fulfils the conditions and that the extent of the liability per share has been specified. The person must be over 18 years old and must at the time of the offer for sale, according to the National Register of Persons, have his or her permanent residence at a distance of no more than 4.5 km from the site of the development. Other incentives include a Guarantee Fund to support financing of preliminary investigations by local wind turbine owners' associations, and a Green scheme to enhance local scenic and recreational values.

As one might expect, the dependence on the law of nuisance is no longer considered an appropriate means of accommodating the concerns of neighbours about wind turbines. To ensure the further expansion of wind power, local support must be encouraged; and that provides the background for the new initiatives. The new compensation scheme has, however, been subject to considerable criticism. The influence of wind turbines is thus treated differently to the construction of other installations that have consequences on nature, landscape and neighbours—be it roads or solar panels. The issue is therefore whether the new compensation scheme may in fact have consequences for environmental regulation in more general terms and be in opposition to the principle that real estate owners must accept the influence of new installations resulting from general developments in society.

VII. The protection of development rights

The right to private property has for centuries been recognized as a fundamental human right that implies a right to fair compensation when property is taken for the sake of the public interest. There exists a difficult distinction between the land owners' right, regulation requiring compensation (expropriation or taking), and so-called compensation-free regulation—restrictions on the use and exploitation of land that must be accepted without compensation. It cannot be established by one single criterion, but rather on a combined evaluation of several different criteria, including generality, intensity, and purpose. However, these criteria are not very precise and often based on the facts of individual cases.[43] It is less likely to be expropriation if the restriction affects all or certain categories

---

[43] See O. Friis Jensen, 'The Role of Property Rights—Danish Perspectives' in *Land Use and Nature Protection* (H. T. Anker and E. M. Basse, eds, 2000) 48, and P. Pagh, *Miljørettens Almindelige Del* (Environmental Law—General Part) (2006) 67 ff. See also T. Allen, 'The Human Rights Act (UK) and Property Law' in *Property and the Constitution* (J. McLean, ed, 1999) 147, A. R. Coban, *Protection of Property Rights within the European Convention on Human Rights* (2004) 93 ff, and R. Higgins, *Problems & Progress—International Law and How We Use It* (1994) 142 ff.

of property, rather than specific property owners. Another issue of importance is how heavy the suffered loss is, whether the restriction applies to existing use or only future use, and the justification and purpose of the regulation. As has been noted, these criteria are not very precise, and they are difficult to interpret.

In all states there have been occasions where new and more restrictive legislation has been applied to a natural resource development. There have been many discussions of the legal characterization of natural resource licences, but in general terms it can be said that the freedom of the state to adjust the licence terms unilaterally is restricted. As pointed out by Roggenkamp, Redgwell, del Guayo, and Rønne,

> First, general principles of public law require that administrative authorities take all decisions on the basis of objective, non-discriminatory, and non-arbitrary considerations. The licensee is thus entitled to fairness, taking into consideration the negotiations conducted with the State, the pre-conditions on which the licence is based, and the risks and investments undertaken by the licensee. Even if the rights of the licensee are protected, changes can sometimes be justified by the strength of the public interests involved.[44]

If we use Denmark as an example, it is interesting to see that such general statutory amendments have indeed been adopted, and that licence terms have been revised quite substantially. It should be emphasized that under Danish law there is considered to be no legal difference between a concession, a licence, a permission, and a permit. All of them are regarded as public administrative decisions (as opposed to contracts) and the exact term is often chosen at random. The translation of the basis for the activities of Mærsk Oil and Gas is 'concession', whereas the Subsoil Act uses 'permission' and the Model developed by the Ministry is called a 'licence'. Consequently, the title on its own provides no basis on which to classify the arrangement, to determine the legal consequences, nor to determine the rights of the licensee. It is always necessary to analyse the regulatory framework, the negotiations conducted, the appropriate expectations derived from this process, the assumptions on which the licence is based, and the strength of the public interests involved.[45]

Interesting revisions of the existing Mærsk Oil and Gas licence have been the result of negotiations and subsequently agreements. The first licence was issued in 1935 and, following various licensee changes, was replaced by a 50-year Sole Concession on the exploration and production of hydrocarbons, granted to the Danish shipowner A. P. Møller (now Mærsk Oil and Gas AS) in 1962.[46] The licence was expanded to include the continental shelf area in 1963. Thus control

---

[44] *Energy Law in Europe* (above n 11) 1280.

[45] See further T. Daintith (ed), *The Legal Character of Petroleum Licences: A Comparative Study* (1981), A. Rønne and M. Budtz, 'The Legal Framework for Exploration for and Production of Oil and Natural Gas in Denmark' (1985) 3 JERL 168, and E. E. Smith et al, *International Petroleum Transactions* (2nd edn, 2000) ch 6(B).

[46] Over the years, A. P. Møller has involved different multinational oil companies in the activities under the licence, today operated by the Danish Underground Consortium (DUC), a joint venture by A. P. Møller, Shell, and ChevronTexaco, structured as A. P. Møller 39%, Shell 46%, and ChevronTexaco 15%.

of Danish territory onshore and offshore to explore and produce hydrocarbons was, until January 1982, in the hands of only one licensee. When activities to find oil and gas were started in the 1960s, knowledge of the actual probability of finding oil and gas in Denmark was scarce. Oil was first discovered in 1966, and oil production commenced in 1972 in the Danish part of the North Sea.[47] As a result of the oil crisis in 1973 and 1979, a debate started over whether the conditions in the Sole Concession were too light with regard to the size of the area, work obligations, and tax regime. A desire for change was specified in a mandate from the Parliament. The mandate contained several objectives. Arguments were put forward for some form of state participation. Against this background, the conditions in the Sole Concession were renegotiated several times and resulted in two agreements, in 1976 and 1981. The 1981 Agreement radically changed the original terms of the licence, one of the major changes being that over a few years Mærsk Oil and Gas relinquished nearly all of the Danish territory: 50 per cent in 1982, 25 per cent in 1984, and the remaining area in 1986, retaining only areas in the North Sea, where exploration and production activities were in progress, and a 'contiguous area' of about 1 per cent of the original licence area in the southwestern sector of the North Sea. No state participation was, however, introduced in the revised concession.

A. P. Møller's licence was to expire in 2012. In a protocol that was attached to the licence in 1962, the licensee was promised negotiations on the question of activities after the expiry of the licence, so that negotiations on possible continuation of the activities, and on what terms, should be opened well in advance. In September 2003, A. P. Møller/Mærsk reached an agreement with the Danish government.[48] It implied stricter taxation of income for the rest of the original licence period—that is, to 2012—and a state ownership share of 20 per cent from 2012. At the same time, however, the licence was extended by a further 30 years till 2042, that is, for a total of 80 years. The royalty was repealed as of 2004, and the pipeline tax terminated as from 2012. The agreement included a controversial clause on guaranteed compensation for consequences of any future changes in legislation to ensure that the economic balance between the state and the licensee is maintained—a so-called stabilization clause. Although heavily criticized by experts and some political parties, the majority in Parliament approved the terms for the extension, as did the EU Commission subsequently.

The result is that the changes to oil and gas licences have not been challenged in court. A few cases of the Danish Supreme Court on the revision of rights to exploit sand and gravel in more recent years can illustrate how the distinction

---

[47] For more information and statistics see also <www.ens.dk>.

[48] Agreement between the Minister for Economic and Business Affairs and the Concessionaires in accordance with Sole Concession of 8 July 1962 to explore for and recover hydrocarbons from the Danish subsoil of 29 September 2003, and implemented by amendments to the Subsoil Act, cf Act No 1230 of 27 December 2003. See also Minister of Economic and Business Affairs, *Report to the Danish Parliament on the North Sea*, October 2003.

is drawn in Danish law between compensation-free regulation and regulation against compensation within the area of natural resources rights.

A case from 1972 demonstrates that even in a situation where the regulation is general in its scope it may have very harsh effects on a limited number of land owners and still not be considered as expropriation.[49] A company was digging moler (clay) on its own property. The activity had started in the area before the new Nature Protection Act came into force that adopted a protection line system of 100 metres along the coast for first building activities, but was strengthened subsequently to include all activities altering the beach areas within the zone. It was emphasized that the prohibition applied to all coast owners, and that it applied to a fairly narrow strip of land. Moreover, the majority of judges added that the Act through its exemption clause opens up the possibility of mitigation in a situation where the effects were harsh on only a few land owners. This would usually imply relatively limited interference with the property rights. A modification had been used in the present case by reducing the restriction to 50 metres instead of the 100 metres and allowing digging in the area until 50 metres from the beach. In other words, in this case the general/specific criterion was combined with the question of intensity.

In another case from 1997, the rejection of an application for continued excavation was considered by the Supreme Court to constitute an expropriation, contrary to the decision of the High Court.[50] A company had been digging sand and gravel for several decades in an area called Robbedale on the island of Bornholm. In connection with the passing of the Raw Materials Act in 1972, these rights were notified as existing rights for which a licence was not required. By an amendment of 1977, the Act was restricted so that all old notified gravel digging rights were to cease on 1 July 1988. In the preliminary works to the Bill it was, however, implied that a licence to continued digging would usually be given. It was also stated that if such permission was not granted, the holder of the rights could be entitled to compensation pursuant to the Constitution (Art 73). In October 1988 the application of the company to be allowed to continue the activity was refused as it would adversely affect water resources. The Court did not find that the gravel digging had contributed to pollution of the ground water, but stated that the rejection could be considered an individual prohibition against further activity and should be compensated according to Art 73 of the Constitution. In other words, the Court did not consider the total prohibition of ongoing activities as general, but as a specific regulation, even though the company had received 10 years' warning about the prohibition. The rejection constituted a kind of exception applicable to very few, as it had been expressed that permission would usually be given.

[49] 'The Moler case', U.1972.603H (Danish Weekly Law Report).
[50] 'The Robbedale case', U.1997.157H (Danish Weekly Law Report).

As can be seen, there are no clear answers to how the line should be drawn between takings and compensation-free regulation. No single criterion determines the result but various considerations must be included in the evaluation and the balancing of rights. On one hand the essential concept of property rights is to protect the holders against inequity. Thus the general interests of society should not be promoted at the costs of a few randomly chosen property owners.

The requirement to balance the conflicting interests of environmental protection against economic development and natural resources development has also been addressed in human rights cases before the European Court of Human Rights. With reference to the first Protocol to the European Convention on Human Rights that includes the right to peaceful enjoyment of one's possessions, the Court has allowed states a wide margin to pursue environmental objectives, provided they maintain a fair balance between the general interests of the community and the protection of the individual's fundamental rights.

A Swedish national sought unsuccessfully to rely on the human right to property against the state revocation of a mineral exploitation permission.[51] In 1963, the applicants' parents had been granted, subject to certain conditions, a permit to exploit a gravel pit on a parcel of land. Over the years, the exploitation of gravel had become more and more regulated and, in fact, restricted. Thus, the amendment introduced on 1 July 1973 to the 1964 Act empowered the authorities to revoke, without compensation, old permits, such as the applicants', after 10 years had passed, that is, after 1 July 1983. The applicants became the sole owners of the land in 1977 and started to exploit the gravel in 1980. The permit was transferred to them in 1983. Acting under the Nature Conservation Act 1964, as amended in 1973, the County Administrative Board, which had previously given the applicants certain warnings on the subject, ordered in 1984 that the exploitation should cease as soon as possible. The Board decided, *inter alia*, that the permit should be valid until the end of 1987, by which time all work on the gravel pit was to be terminated and the area in question was to be restored, and that the security deposited by the applicants to cover restoration costs be increased. In 1985 the government extended the validity of the permit to 1 June 1988 and subsequently to 1 December 1988, on which date the extraction of gravel ceased. The applicants claimed that the withdrawal of the permit constituted a *de facto* deprivation of property and thus a violation of Art 1 of Protocol No 1 (right to peaceful enjoyment of one's possessions), whereas the government considered the revocation of the permit to be a measure for the control of use of property.

The Court noted that the revocation of the applicants' permit to exploit gravel cannot be regarded as amounting to a deprivation of possessions within the meaning of the first paragraph of Art 1 of Protocol No 1. It must be considered as a control of use of property, falling within the scope of the second paragraph

---

[51] See ECHR, *Fredin v Sweden (No 1)* – 192 (18.2.91) available at <www.manskligarattigheter. gov.se> and <www.echr.coe.int>.

of the Article (para 47). The Court also recognized that in today's society the protection of the environment is an increasingly important consideration. It held that it is well-established in case law that an interference must achieve a 'fair balance' between the demands of the general interest of the community and the requirements of the protection of the individual's fundamental rights (para 51). In determining whether this requirement was met, the Court recognized that the state enjoys a wide margin of appreciation with regard both to choosing the means of enforcement and to ascertaining whether the consequences of enforcement are justified in the general interest for the purpose of achieving the object of the law in question. Consequently, the Court concluded that it could not be said that the revocation decision was inappropriate or disproportionate (para 55), and no violation of Art 1 of Protocol No 1 was established.

The matter of conflicting interests has also been addressed by the International Court of Justice. As Rosalyn Higgins emphasizes, the earlier focus on the legal nature of concessions has been diminishing,

Since the evolution of the concept of the permanent sovereignty over natural resources, there has been a growing tendency to regard natural resources contracts as a temporary alienation of inherent rights, which may be 'called in' at any time, provided that proper compensation always is paid.[52]

In my opinion it is also correctly stated that the answer to classical issues as to what extent unilateral allocation or termination of concessions is permissible is not the same in 1990 compared to 1950: 'changing economic contexts and changing political perceptions condition legal answers'.[53]

The well-known Gabcikovo-Nagymaros case related to a joint project between Hungary and what became Slovakia for the construction and operation of a system of locks on the Danube. Hungary abandoned the work, justifying its action on environmental necessity. The claims were perceived as a clash between the classical law of treaties and the developing norms of international environmental law and of the law of state responsibility.[54] The Court affirmed that 'a state of necessity' is recognized by customary international law as a ground that precludes a determination of wrongfulness. It confirmed that 'ecological balance has come to be considered an essential interest of all States'. Importantly, the Court declared that 'environmental risks have to be assessed on a continuous basis' and require reference to current standards rather than the standards at the time of the relevant agreement. Most remarkable is the Court's reliance on the concept of sustainable development; 'new norms have to be taken into consideration' and moreover the 'need to reconcile economic development with

[52] R. Higgins 'Natural Resources in the Case Law of the International Court' in *International Law and Sustainable Development* (A. Boyle and D. Freestone, eds, 1999) 92.

[53] ibid at 95: 'These awards also illustrate the reality that was a legal truth in 1950 is not necessarily a legal truth in 1990.'

[54] ibid at 105 and Gabcikovo-Nagymaros Project (*Hungary v Slovakia*) (Judgment) (25 September 1997) ICJ Report, available at <www.icj-cij.org>.

protection of the environment is aptly expressed in the concept of sustainable development'.[55] As Higgins concludes, what is apparent 'is the change in focus from disputes about concessions and control of natural resources to disputes about sustainability and the limits of resource use'.[56] I would add that this is also why natural resources law is so interesting. We are not dealing with a static field of law, but on the contrary, a very dynamic one due to its outstanding importance to society.

VIII. Conclusions

The legal distinction between state-owned resources, land-owners' rights, regulation requiring compensation (expropriation/taking) and so-called compensation-free regulation (restrictions on the use and exploitation of land that must be accepted without compensation) touches upon crucial issues; issues that are indeed at the very core of the relationship between private rights and common rights. Today there may, however, be fewer differences between public and private ownership to natural resources than when the original legislation was adopted, due to the rapidly growing body of public administrative law and regulation. In other words, the traditional role of private property rights becomes less important.

The concurrent entitlement to compensation for restrictions on the individual use of land or rights to exploit natural resources may no longer have a higher value than the value of society in the protection of the environment. Society now seeks a sustainable development that includes a long-term perspective, including the interests of the next generations. Financial resources are limited, and to the extent that land owners are entitled to compensation, the environment will be protected to a lesser degree.

Conflicting interests in terms of the utilization of scarce natural resources on which the whole of society depends have provided comprehensive challenges to traditional law thinking, and present a need to redefine the traditional role of private property rights in order to ensure fair and equitable sharing of benefits. There are many ethical aspects and social justice issues to be considered as regards the distribution of ownership to land; the tragedy of the commons, differences in living conditions, and property rights to land. In his very interesting article from 1998, 'Where Would Mankind Stand Without Land', S. Westerlund raises the question, what would it take to make property rights to land compatible with the recognition of land as the basis for mankind? To answer this fundamental question the author emphasizes that it is 'an existential question how to regard land and rights to land'. He suggests 'that if property rights to land include an inherent

---

[55] ibid, para 140.
[56] Higgins (above n 52) at 111.

right also to degrade land, property rights are incompatible with sustainability' and implements a stewardship philosophy that 'implies an obligation to take care of the property so that it is not degraded, and so that it is not used in a way that degrades the biosphere anywhere'.[57]

It may be argued that along with the more widely-recognized concept of sustainable development, the precautionary principle, and the principle of intergenerational equity,[58] the balance point is moving away from the traditional strong legal protection of private property interests in favour of common environmental interests.[59] In other words, what we can see is a paradigm shift with implications for fundamental legal values and a new balance between economic growth and protection of individual property rights.

[57] Available at <www.imir.com>, see 31, 18 and 24.
[58] As for example adopted in the UN Framework Convention on Climate Change Art 3.
[59] See also H. C. Bugge, 'Legal Issues in Land Use and Nature Protection—an Introduction' in *Land Use and Nature Protection* (H. T. Anker and E. M. Basse, eds, 2000) 21 ff, and *Sustainable Development in International and National Law* (H. C. Bugge and C. Voigt, eds, 2008).

4

Property Rights Created under Statute in Common Law Legal Systems

*Barry Barton**

The granting of rights to resources is at the core of energy and natural resources law, whether the resources are minerals, water, or grazing land. The resources themselves are publicly-owned, and rights to them (whether called licences, permits, or something similar) are granted by a minister or a departmental official, under the procedures and on the terms set forth in a governing statute. More recently there have emerged laws that manage energy, resources, and environmental problems with cap-and-trade systems and other market-based systems. In fisheries, we have fish quota, and in air pollution and greenhouse gas emissions we have emission allowances of different kinds. In addition, we encounter authorizations under environmental or economic legislation that regulate company activity in different ways.

From time to time the courts must determine a claim that a statutory permit of this kind has the character of property. There are many reasons why such a claim may be made.[1] It may be to show that the permit comes within the statutory definition of property in another statute; or it may be to claim the benefits of a system of registration of instruments or of title to property. In common law systems, claims may arise out of common law and equity rather than statute. For example, when one of two holders of a statutory permit dies, does the general law of property distinguishing joint tenants with a *jus accrescendi* from tenants in common apply? If the holder of a permit grants an interest in the permit to one person, such as a lease or an overriding royalty, and then conveys the permit to a second person, is the permit in the hands of that second person bound by the lease or royalty? Commercial questions of this kind have always been a part of natural resources law. The legal status of overriding royalties has become a greater concern in the mining industry as they are used in new ways to finance mineral exploration and development.[2]

* Professor of Law, University of Waikato, Hamilton, New Zealand.
[1] Anita Rønne in this volume reflects similarly on the different circumstances in which a proprietary claim may be made.
[2] The classic Canadian case on overriding royalties in statutory mineral rights is *Saskatchewan Minerals Ltd v Keyes* [1972] SCR 703, where the Court of Appeal held that a Crown mineral lease, and

A second kind of claim is that the statutory permit is entitled to the special protection that property generally enjoys in law. Does the permit have the benefit of expropriation legislation if it is taken? Many constitutions protect private property from being taken without the payment of just compensation. International law has classically protected the private property of a foreign national from unlawful interference, although what property rights the foreign investor enjoys in the host state is purely a matter for the domestic law concerned.[3] Most bilateral investment treaties protect 'investments' which are defined in a broad way to include property but also every kind of asset.[4] Claims about the special place of property are common in political discourse as well as in legal analysis; it is often asserted that the government should not alter 'vested rights' of one kind or another without harm to the reputation of the jurisdiction as an investment destination.

Twenty or thirty years ago, the character of natural resource dispositions was particularly in issue in respect of the ability of sovereign governments to change the terms of resource dispositions, especially in consequence of the oil shocks of the 1970s. Terence Daintith observed that the central question was how a legal system could relate and balance the individual commitments of the state towards its licensees and the exercise of its general regulatory or legislative powers.[5] Petroleum licences could be statutory or contractual in form, but that did not necessarily express the extent to which the relationship is consensual or imposed. Nor does it determine whether a vested right exists for the purposes of international legal protection or whether property exists for the purposes of constitutional protections.[6] Andrew Thompson showed that a mechanism such as a 'compliance with laws' clause in a licence that has the form of a contract or property disposition can make its substance entirely dependent upon a changing regulatory regime.[7] Thompson also demonstrated that a natural resource tenure could operate as a conveyance of real property, as a contract, and by force of statute, and that these characteristics overlap in complex ways.[8]

It seems that in common law jurisdictions there is no generally accepted body of law for ascertaining whether the attributes of property ownership attach to permits granted under statutes. This chapter inquires into the way that different courts, mainly those of Australia, Canada, England, and New Zealand, have

a royalty granted out of it, were interests in land and was binding upon a subsequent assignee of the lease—it ran with the land. The majority of the Supreme Court of Canada decided the case on other grounds, but Laskin J agreed with the Court below.

[3] See Catherine Redgwell's analysis in this volume.

[4] L. Reed, J. Paulsson, N. Blackaby, *Guide to ICSID Arbitration* (2004) 44. Administrative rights are now usually included: M. Sornarajah, *The International Law on Foreign Investment* (2nd edn, 2004) 14.

[5] T. Daintith, 'Petroleum Licences: A Comparative Introduction' in *The Legal Character of Petroleum Licences: A Comparative Study* (T. Daintith, ed, 1981) 1 at 25.

[6] Daintith, ibid at 10–11.

[7] A. R. Thompson, 'Legal Characteristics of Disposition Systems: An Overview' in *Public Disposition of Natural Resources* (N. D. Bankes and J. O. Saunders, eds, 1983) 1.

[8] Thompson, ibid at 7–11.

approached the matter, and into the way that we may expect the interaction between legislatures and courts in common law jurisdictions, to proceed in the future.[9] There has been little systematic study of the law on the matter. Raymond has inquired into the allocation of resource rights under statute, calling them 'licensed property', and focusing particularly on the place of equity in the initial allocation of rights, but his investigation is in political studies, not law.[10] Like Raymond, we need to look from the allocation of traditional resources such as minerals or grazing rights ahead to market-based systems such as individual transferable quota for fisheries and greenhouse gas emissions rights. As we see an increasing individualization of rights in resources that were previously common property or public property, it is desirable to consider carefully the nature of what is being granted and put into trade, not only as a matter of public policy but also as a matter of commercial law.

I. What does the statute say?

The starting point must be the legislation that grants the rights under scrutiny. That is self evident. But we find a wide range of answers to our questions. Sometimes the legislature is clear; for example, the Mining Act of Ontario, Canada, declares that a patent is 'a grant from the Crown in fee simple or for a less estate made under the Great Seal, and includes leasehold patents and freehold patents'.[11] But the Mineral Tenure Act of British Columbia, Canada, says that: 'The interest of a recorded holder of a claim is a chattel interest'[12] which certainly intends property of some sort, but what kind is not so clear; the law recognizes chattels real (leases) and chattels personal. The courts of British Columbia determined that the section means personal chattels, so that a mineral claim is not 'land'.[13] On very similar provisions, the Australian courts agreed,[14] but the New Zealand courts disagreed.[15] Either interpretation is credible; the legislative

---

[9] The matter does not seem to come up in the same manner in civil law jurisdictions. Rønne, in this volume, says that under Danish law there is considered to be no legal difference between a concession, licence, permission or permit. All of them are looked upon as public administrative decisions as opposed to contract, and one analyses the regulatory framework to understand the rights granted.

[10] L. Raymond, *Private Rights in Public Resources: Equity and Property Allocation in Market-Based Environmental Policy* (2003). At p 14 he describes licensed property (for mining, grazing, SO_2, or greenhouse gases) as 'a private right that provides a significant degree of security and exclusivity to resource users but remains unprotected from future government adjustment or cancellation without compensation'.

[11] Mining Act, RSO 1990 c M.14 s 1.

[12] Mineral Tenure Act, RSBC 1996 c 292 s 24(2).

[13] *Cream Silver Mines Ltd (NPL) v British Columbia* (1986) 2 BCLR (2d) 392 (BC SC); further proceedings (1993) 75 BCLR (2d) 324 (BC CA).

[14] *Adamson v Hayes* (1973) 130 CLR 276 (HCA) on the Western Australia Mining Act 1904.

[15] *Tainui Maori Trust Board v Attorney General* [1989] 2 NZLR 513 (CA).

statement is deficient. In Queensland, Australia, for mineral resources the rule is that: 'The grant of a mining tenement under this Act does not create an estate or interest in land'.[16] But for carbon dioxide sequestration in forests, the rule is that: 'The benefited person's rights to the natural resource product under the agreement are a profit a prendre for the Land Act 1994 or the Land Title Act 1994'.[17]

At times the legislature seeks to eliminate all property law complications. New Zealand's Resource Management Act 1991 is a good example. It is the primary statute for environmental management and land use regulation, but it also allows rights—resource consents—to be obtained to divert and use water, to extract geothermal fluid for power generation, or to occupy coastal waters for aquaculture installations. Section 122(1) declares in crisp tones that 'A resource consent is neither real nor personal property'. However the next five subsections belie its simplicity, bringing property law to bear 'as if' the consent were personal property, to deal with death, bankruptcy, personal infirmity, charges, registration of interests under the Personal Property Securities Act 1999, and (for coastal permits) restrictions on exclusivity of occupation and rights to take sand and gravel and the like. The same words (in subs 1 and in relation to death, bankruptcy, infirmity, charges, and the PPSA) are found in s 92 of the Crown Minerals Act 1991 of New Zealand, governing rights to petroleum and hardrock minerals.

Even where the establishment of tradeable property rights is plainly an important element of the policy design, we may see little real legislative effort going into the definition of licence rights. The New Zealand Fisheries Act 1996 does not state the character of quota, but the Court of Appeal has referred to it as 'a statutory chose in action'.[18] Equally, the Climate Change Response Act 2002 identifies the New Zealand unit as 'a unit issued by the Registrar and designated as a New Zealand unit' without more.[19]

One finds therefore a wide range of legislative responses. In some cases the legislature states whether the permit is proprietary in character. Sometimes it does so well, but in other cases its work is general or ambiguous. In other cases it makes no effort to deal with the matter at all. It may be that policymakers who are concerned with environmental and natural resources matters are little engaged with such questions, dismissing them as 'lawyers' law' and of no real interest to their ministry. We can turn to consider how resource permits have been characterized

---

[16] Mineral Resources Act 1989 (Qld) s 10.

[17] Forestry Act 1959 (Qld) s 61J(5).

[18] *Antons Trawling Co v Smith* [2003] 2 NZLR 23 para 5. Generally on this subject, see C. Stewart, *Legislating for Property Rights in Fisheries* (2004).

[19] Climate Change Response Act 2002, as amended by the Climate Change Response Emissions Trading Amendment Act 2008, ss 4, 18–30A. Generally see D. Vogler, 'Linking the New Zealand Emissions Trading Scheme to Other Emissions Trading Schemes' unpublished LLM dissertation, University of Waikato, 2009. Also note amendments made by the 2008 Act to the Personal Property and Securities Act 1999, which defines units as investment securities so as to bring them under that Act.

in the cases, or at least a small selection of them, sometimes in reliance on such statutory provisions.

II. Australian cases

There are two main kinds of case in the Australian law on the characterization of resource tenures. The first is on the Commonwealth of Australia Constitution Act, s 51(xxxi), empowering the Commonwealth Parliament to enact laws for the acquisition of property on just terms, which operates to provide protection to property rights. One of the key cases is *Newcrest Mining (WA) Ltd v Commonwealth*[20] which concerned 25 mineral leases under the Mining Act 1980 (NT). In 1989 and 1991, the Commonwealth government extended the boundaries of Kakadu National Park to include the leased areas. In the Park, the National Parks and Wildlife Conservation Act 1975 (Cth) applied, prohibiting operations for the recovery of minerals. Newcrest sued for compensation on the ground that there had been an acquisition of property from it without just terms. By a majority, the High Court of Australia agreed. The main analysis of the character of the resource right was by Gummow J. Australian courts have considered mining leases in different ways over the years. They have taken note of the observation of Lord Cairns in *Gowan v Christie*[21] that a mining lease is really, when properly considered, a sale out and out of a portion of the land, but that it gives a liberty or licence to an individual for a time to go into the land and get minerals if they can be found, and to take them away, just as if he had bought so much of the soil. Windeyer J had made the link between these observations on the general law and mining leases granted under statute.[22] Gummow J endorsed this link. Newcrest's leases could not therefore be dismissed as no more than statutory privileges under a licensing system, as was the fate of some such claims.[23] Nor was there mere impairment; Newcrest's rights were effectively sterilized. Toohey and Gaudron JJ agreed with Gummow J, while others either noted that the leases under the Mining Act were property, or did not dwell on the matter.

The High Court of Australia reached a different result the next year in *Commonwealth v WMC Resources Ltd*[24] in respect of petroleum permits under the Petroleum (Submerged Lands) Act 1967, partly because the permits were on the continental shelf and therefore not carved out of the Crown's radial title, and

---

[20] (1997) 190 CLR 513. See M. Crommelin, 'The Legal Character of Resource Titles' (1998) 17 Australian Mining and Petroleum Law Journal 57.

[21] (1873) LR 2 Sc & Div 273. In fact a mining lease can be a conventional lease with additional rights to mine and remove minerals.

[22] In *Wade v NSW Rutile Mining Co Pty Ltd* (1969) 121 CLR 177.

[23] *Newcrest* (above n 20) at 130.

[24] (1998) 194 CLR 1.

partly because the statutory regime was more flexible and exposed the holder to a greater range of administrative actions; they were 'inherently unstable'.[25]

The other main reason to inquire into the character of resource dispositions in Australia has been to determine whether the issue of a disposition has had the effect of extinguishing aboriginal title. *Wik Peoples v State of Queensland*,[26] a year or two before *Newcrest Mining (WA) Ltd*, decided by a majority that pastoral leases did not confer exclusive possession on the leaseholder in a way that would exclude the interests of the indigenous inhabitants. The effect of a pastoral lease under the Land Act had to be ascertained by reference to the language used in the Act and reflected in the instrument of lease. It was not a necessary consequence of the description of the instruments as leases that they conferred a right of exclusive possession on the lessee. Whether a lease has been granted is determined by reference to the substance of the rights conferred. Gummow J is particularly useful.[27]

To reason that the use of terms such as 'demise' and 'lease' in legislative provisions with respect to pastoral leases indicates (i) the statutory creation of rights of exclusive possession and that, consequently, (ii) it follows clearly and plainly that subsisting native title is inconsistent with the enjoyment of those rights, is not to answer the question but to restate it.

Gummow J went on to refer to numbers of Australian cases that have emphasized that the rights under statutory dispositions under Land Acts and the like must be ascertained by reference to the statute, without attaching too much significance to similarities to interests under the general law. He quoted from Mason J in *R v Toohey ex p Meneling Station Pty Ltd*:[28] '[L]and law is but one area in which, while statute may appear to have adopted general law principles and institutions as elements in a new regime, in truth the legislature has done so only on particular terms'.

Wik Peoples was followed by *Ward v Western Australia*; notwithstanding 'its common law connotations, the nomenclature of a "lease" (when used as a descriptor for pastoral leases) does not of itself grant exclusive possession'.[29]

Matthew Storey has tackled the question of the characterization of resource titles in these Australian cases.[30] He contends that the characterization of a resource title should stem from an assessment of the attributes of the interest in question, and not from a comparison of these attributes to an interest 'known'

---

[25] ibid, Gummow J at para 194.

[26] (1996) 141 ALR 129 (HCA).

[27] *Wik Peoples*, ibid at 241.

[28] (1982) 158 CLR 327 at 344, quoted at p 242 of *Wik Peoples*.

[29] (2002) 213 CLR 1, para 180. The New Zealand High Court has held that a Crown pastoral lease grants a right to exclusive possession, diverging from the main Australian cases: *NZ Fish & Game Council v Attorney General* (unreported, High Court Wellington CIV 2008–485–2020, 12 May 2009, Simon France J).

[30] M. Storey, 'Not of this Earth: The Extraterrestrial Nature of Statutory Property' (2006) 25 Australian Resources and Energy Law Journal 51.

to the general law. He proposes five classes of statutory property as a means of analysis:

1) Statutory replication of a common law title.
2) Defeasible statutory replication of a common law title.
3) Statutory property bearing no common law parallel.
4) Statutory licence which only makes an act lawful which without it would be unlawful.[31]
5) Public right created by statute, without any permanence or transferability, conferred on all members of a class, and without any proprietary element.

Storey's classification is a useful attempt to impose order on the cases, but it is difficult to extract any consistent thread of principle from them.

III. *Saulnier v Royal Bank of Canada*

More useful, in my view, are two cases where judges sought to identify the characteristics of statutory licences that would require them to be treated as property.

Saulnier v Royal Bank of Canada[32] decided whether a commercial fishing licence under the Fisheries Act of Canada constituted 'property' available to a trustee in bankruptcy under the Bankruptcy and Insolvency Act (BIA), or to a creditor who had registered a general security agreement under the Personal Property Security Act (PPSA) of Nova Scotia. The bankrupt fisher argued that the licence was merely a privilege to that which would otherwise be illegal, and therefore did not pass to either such person. For the Supreme Court of Canada, Binnie J began his analysis with a useful reminder that the question was one of statutory interpretation, not one of the concept of property in the abstract. The Court's task was to interpret the definitions of property in the legislation in a purposeful way. It also cautioned that a fishing licence could be within the reach of the statutory definitions in the BIA and PPSA even if it did not qualify as 'property' for the general purposes of the common law. 'For particular purposes Parliament can and does create its own lexicon.'[33] The Court then outlined the three different approaches that could be seen in the case law.

1) *The Traditional 'Property' Approach.* Earlier cases concerning fishing licences and quotas to grow tobacco, such as *National Trust Co v Bouckhuyt*,[34] had referred to traditional indicia of property such as permanence or a significant term. The Court accepted that the PPSA required a broader concept of property. In any

---

[31] This phrase is used by Gummow J in *WMC Resources Ltd* (above n 24) at 71, acknowledging its origins in *Thomas v Sorrell* (1673) Vaugh 330, 124 ER 1098.
[32] (2008) 298 DLR (4th) 193 (SCC).
[33] ibid at para 16.
[34] (1987) 61 OR (2d) 640 (Ont CA).

event there was some analogy to a profit à prendre, which the Australian High Court in *Harper v Minister for Sea Fisheries*[35] had noted as well.

2) *The Regulatory Approach. National Trust Co v Bouckhuyt* resulted in a line of cases in which licences were held to be property if the regulatory authority was obliged, or almost obliged, to grant a renewal, showing that the licence is more than transitory and ephemeral. But the Supreme Court decided that this approach was of limited value; a lease of land is a property right even if only for one day or one hour, and there were no criteria to determine how much of a 'fetter' on the discretion is enough to transform a mere licence into a property right.

3) *The Commercial Realities Approach.* This view found favour at trial, where the evidence was that fishing licences, particularly for lobster, are commonly exchanged between fishermen for a great deal of money; fishing vessels of questionable value are traded for small fortunes because of the licences that are anticipated to come with them. 'To ignore commercial reality would be to deny creditors access to something of significant value in the hands of the bankrupt. That would be both artificial and potentially inequitable.'[36] Other decisions from Canada and England have followed this approach. But the Court held that many things that have commercial value do not constitute property, while the value of some property may be minimal. There is no necessary connection between proprietary status and commercial value. Binnie J said:[37]

I agree with the Court of Appeal that 'commercial realities' cannot legitimate wishful thinking about the notion of 'property' in the *BIA* and *PPSA*, although commercial realities provide an appropriate context in which to interpret the statutory provisions.

Binnie J's preferred approach was that the holder of a licence acquired more than merely permission to do that which would otherwise be unlawful. 'The holder acquires the right to engage in an exclusive fishery under the conditions imposed by the licence, and, what is of prime importance, a proprietary right in the wild fish harvested thereunder, and the earnings from their sale.'[38] One must look at the substance of what was conferred; a licence to participate in the fishery coupled with a proprietary interest in the fish caught, which bore a reasonable analogy to rights traditionally considered at common law to be property, so, reasonably, within the statutory definition of property in the BIA and PPSA. Essentially it is the first approach, the Traditional Property approach.

In this analysis, old common law terminology won an unusual significance. A 'licence' is defined in classical terms of private law as the right to do that which

---

[35] (1989) 168 CLR 314, [1989] HCA 47.

[36] *Saulnier* (above n 32) at para 41, quoting Kennedy CJSC at trial.

[37] ibid at para 42. On no necessary connection, he cited T. G. W. Telfer, 'Statutory Licences and the Search for Property: the End of the Imbroglio?' (2007) 45 Canadian Business Law Journal 224. On the earlier law on this matter, see R. C. C. Cuming, C. Walsh and R. J. Wood, *Personal Property Security Law* (2005) 109.

[38] *Saulnier* (above n 32) at para 43; also see para 34.

would otherwise be trespass, or illegal. The Court also relied on the old term for a profit à prendre, 'licence coupled with a grant' to shape the two factors that apparently made it possible to declare the Fisheries Act licence to be property.[39]

IV. *Re Celtic Extraction Ltd*

In 1999 the English Court of Appeal had to determine whether a waste management licence granted under the Environmental Protection Act 1990 might be property for the purpose of an insolvency. Two waste disposal licences were in issue. In each case the company became insolvent, and the official receiver applied to the court for directions whether he could and should disclaim the licence. (While the trustee in bankruptcy in *Saulnier* wanted to get in the licence, the receiver here wanted to get rid of it.) In the Insolvency Act 1986, s 178 allowed a liquidator to disclaim any 'onerous property'. Property was defined in the Act in very general terms, and many decisions had emphasized the importance of ensuring that a liquidator had access to the full range of the bankrupt's assets. The word 'property' is not a term of art but takes its meaning from its context. The key passage of Morritt LJ, speaking for the Court of Appeal, is as follows.[40]

[33] It appears to me that these cases indicate the salient features which are likely to be found if there is to be conferred on an exemption from some wider statutory prohibition the status of property.

First, there must be a statutory framework conferring an entitlement on one who satisfies certain conditions even though there is some element of discretion exercisable within that framework...

Second, the exemption must be transferable...

Third, the exemption or licence will have value...

The judge found that each criterion had been met in terms of the provisions of the 1990 Act. As for value, the trial judge had observed that there was a market in these licences, and it was common ground that money changed hands between transferor and transferee. The very substantial fees that the Environment Agency charged licensees was a good indication of the substantial value that a waste management licence possesses for the owners or occupants of the land to which it relates. (But it seems that there was little actual evidence on the matter.) The licences were therefore property. The effect was that the official receiver could disclaim the licences, without the costs of remedial works being a charge on the creditors' assets.

The Court of Appeal's list of three features has a precise look about it, but in truth it is rather loose. Are the features of general application? The Court relied on

[39] On this *Saulnier* (above n 32) at para 30 quoted Megarry and Wade, *The Law of Real Property* (4th edn, 1975) 779.

[40] *Re Celtic Extraction Ltd (in liq)* [2001] 1 Ch 475. The passage is repunctuated, and references to cases and the relevant sections of the legislation have been omitted.

cases from a general range, not confined to environmental regulation. Are the criteria both necessary and sufficient; if one establishes all three criteria, is the licence property? Property for all purposes, or only insolvency? Is it the test for disclaimer only? The question of the value of the licence seems little explored. Taken together, the criteria are easy to meet. The first is so wide as to encompass much of the work of the modern regulatory state. The second criterion, transferability, is present in much economic and resources regulation. The third, value, is often easy to establish, and in any event is more a matter of remedies and relief than of substance.

The waste management licence in *Re Celtic Extraction Ltd* did not allow any publicly-owned natural resource to be taken, and is therefore quite different from *Saulnier v Royal Bank of Canada*, where the Court set much store by the coupling of the regulatory licence with the obtaining of a proprietary right in the fish caught. There is no equivalent of the analogy with property interests known to general law, such as profits à prendre, mining leases or grazing leases, that was important in some of the Australian cases. Nor is there any equivalent of the grant of rights out of the Crown's radical title that was important in others. The requirement to obtain a waste management licence was a restriction on the use of all land that had no private law equivalent, however regular and ordinary as a matter of public law.

V. *Armstrong v Public Trust*

Armstrong v Public Trust[41] concerned two coastal permits in the name of a father and son to authorize whitebait stands for small-scale net fishing on the Moeraki River in Westland in New Zealand. Coastal permits are a form of resource consent. The official record of the holders of the permits was simply 'J & A Armstrong'. On the father's death, the son contended that he was entitled to be recognized as the sole holder of the permits by reason of the common law right of survivorship of a joint tenant. The Public Trust, as executor of the father, argued that there was no joint tenancy, and that the permit vested, presumably as to a one-half share, in the Public Trust, for transmission to his daughter under his will. The Trust relied on the absolute character of s 122(1), that a resource consent is neither real nor personal property, and on s 122(2)(a) as a specific and comprehensive provision, so that an interest capable of being held by the personal representative arose only on the consent holder's death.

However, Fogarty J did not agree. He held that the purpose of s 122(1) is to prevent the unfettered transfer of resource consents except where specifically provided. But whether the consent was held by one or more persons raised no readily ascertainable generic resource management issue. Such a matter is normally a result of private arrangements. Section 122(2)(a) implicitly recognizes the private ordering of affairs, including arrangements such as joint ownership, and there was no reason

---

[41] [2007] 2 NZLR 859, [2007] NZRMA 573 (HC).

that the common law on joint tenancies should not apply, including the right of survivorship. That meant that on his father's death the son became the sole owner.

The decision is a good simple illustration of how a court must decide a dispute between parties not related by contract even though the legislation provides no direct guidance. It also illustrates something to which we will return; the reluctance in legal thinking to oust property law as a means of dealing with such disputes. It shows a willingness to draw a line between the public aspects of a statutory scheme for the allocation of rights, where significant questions of policy are at stake, for which the legislature receives all due deference, and the private questions, where policy issues are less at stake, for which rather less deference is given.

VI. Criteria for deciding whether a permit is proprietary

In the cases from different countries, there are five possible candidates for a rule or principle for deciding whether a statutory licence is property of some kind. It is not easy to pronounce that one or the other is the best criterion, but they help us understand the issues in play.

1) *Assimilation*. If the statutory right can be assimilated to a property right known to the general law, then it is not *like* a lease or a profit à prendre, it *is* one. This is only sometimes seen. A striking difference of opinion on assimilation occurred in *Wik Peoples v State of Queensland*.[42] Brennan CJ maintained that where the Crown lands legislation used the term 'lease', then that is exactly what was meant, and the disposition could not be dismissed as a mere bundle of statutory rights. The majority replied that they were not turning their backs on centuries of history, nor impugning basic principles of property law; rather, they were recognizing historical development, the changes in law over centuries, and the need for property law to accommodate the very different situation in the particular country.[43] A variation of assimilation is *Telecom Auckland Ltd v Auckland City Council*[44] where the Telecommunications Act provided for ownership of lines by the network operator when they were in the soil, which was held to be an exclusive right of occupation, beyond an easement, and fell within the statutory meaning of 'land'.

2) *Analogy*. Analogy has always been an important method of legal analysis on a point not covered by existing rules or principles. Is the statutory right like a proprietary right known to the general law; as Jonette Watson Hamilton and Nigel Bankes say in this volume, does it walk and talk like property? *Harper v Minister*

---

[42]   (1996) 141 ALR 129, 155 (HCA).
[43]   ibid per Toohey J at 174.
[44]   [1999] 1 NZLR 426 (CA).

for Sea Fisheries[45] and *Saulnier v Royal Bank of Canada*[46] are good examples of reasoning by analogy. Analogy is less easy where a mineral exploration licence does not grant any right to extract the minerals, or for a water right, because the common law did not know rights to take natural water other than under riparian rights. It is less easy again for new rights like emission units.

3) *One Incident or Another of Property.* Another way to pose the question is whether the statutory licence displays the key one or more characteristics of property rights as known to the general law. Just what those key characteristics may be, of course, is eminently open to debate. Reference is often made to the set of standard incidents (or characteristics) identified by A M Honoré in his essay 'Ownership';[47] the rights to possess, to use, to manage, etc. However, exactly how such enunciations can be used to solve problems about the nature of statutory intention is by no means clear. (In fact, observations by Honoré, rather later in his essay, about rights in variable collections of things, and of funds, seem to be more useful.) *National Provincial Bank Ltd v Ainsworth* is another classical source, where, in considering whether personal rights could produce a new equitable interest in a property that would be binding on third parties, Lord Wilberforce said:[48]

Before a right or an interest can be admitted into the category of property, or of a right affecting property, it must be definable, identifiable by third parties, capable in its nature of assumption by third parties, and have some degree of permanence and stability.

Exclusivity has its advocates as a criterion.[49] But natural resources dispositions often only show exclusive rights in relation to the particular activity prescribed, and for fisheries quota or emissions units, it is even less useful. Term or duration is another such incident of property that is often looked for. However, a common law leasehold has the same legal status as a form of property whether it is for one hour or for one thousand years. *Saulnier v Royal Bank of Canada* discusses duration, under the possibly confusing heading of a 'regulatory' approach. Transferability is often referred to. Many statutory resources rights are transferable but subject to restrictions of one kind or another. Again, the common law justification of the criterion is not straightforward. The law has long known restraints upon alienation. Strict settlements restricted the alienation of much of the land of England in the eighteenth and nineteenth centuries.[50] Leases are very commonly subject to

---

[45] (1989) 168 CLR 314, quoted in *Aoraki Water Trust v Meridian Energy Ltd* [2005] NZRMA 251 (HC).

[46] (2008) 298 DLR (4th) 193 (SCC).

[47] A. M. Honoré, 'Ownership' in *Oxford Essays in Jurisprudence* (First Series, A. G. Guest, ed, 1961) 107.

[48] [1965] AC 1175, 1247–8.

[49] L. Fraser, 'Property Rights in Environmental Management: The Nature of Resource Consents in the Resource Management Act 1991' (2008) 12 New Zealand Journal of Environmental Law 145, discusses exclusivity thoroughly.

[50] E. Spring, 'Landowners, Lawyers, and Land Law Reform in Nineteenth-Century England' (1977) 12 American Journal of Legal History 40, 50. In 1872, 80 per cent of the land in Britain

a covenant not to assign without the consent of the lessor first had and obtained, and indeed the common law accepts a covenant that simply declares that the lease-hold shall not be assigned.[51] It seems to be more useful to refrain from elevating any one incident of property to the status of a deciding criterion, and instead to take a full view of all the incidents conferred by the statute. Effectively this is to argue by analogy, without seeking a close analogy with any particular existing estate or interest in property.

4) *Administrative or Statutory Aspects.* In *Re Celtic Extraction Ltd*, one of the three criteria offered was that there must be a statutory framework conferring an entitlement on one who satisfies certain conditions, as an exemption from a statutory prohibition. *Saulnier v Royal Bank of Canada* found value in the same criterion; the licence to participate in the fishery was coupled with a proprietary interest in the fish caught. However, it does not seem to be a very helpful way of distinguishing some kinds of statutory rights from others, because it simply describes one of the elementary characteristics of any system of statutory regula-tion. Any system of regulation invariably identifies a particular kind of conduct or activity—fishing, exploring for or extracting minerals, emitting pollution—and then prohibiting persons from engaging in it except on terms that the designated regulatory agency allows, whether by a general rule or by a particular permit. It is much the same for a system of disposition of public resources.

5) *Commercial Reality and Commercial Expectations.* Wishful thinking, said the Supreme Court of Canada in *Saulnier v Royal Bank of Canada*, will not jus-tify a 'commercial realities' approach to bringing a property right into existence. There is obvious truth in that; it takes more than commercial convenience to make something good law. And it must be agreed that the mere intention of the parties is insufficient to turn an arrangement into a proprietary one.[52] But the matter does not end there. Commercial reality takes us into commercial expect-ations, custom and practice. The thwarting of expectations may lead to unjust results. On another occasion, *Bank of Montreal v Dynex Petroleum Ltd*,[53] the Supreme Court of Canada took into account the context and customs of the oil and gas industry in recognizing a royalty interest as a new form of property right that could bind third parties. That case was not one of an interest carved out of a statutory permit, but it helps pose a relevant question for the characterization of statutory interests. If the parties have expressed their intention that a royalty based on a statutory permit runs with the land, if the purchaser of the permit property has notice of the royalty, if there is evidence of commercial expectations

was in the hands of 7,000 persons; and most of that would have been held under strict settlements which limited transferability and user.

[51] *Bocardo SA v S&M Hotels Ltd* [1979] 3 All ER 737 (CA).

[52] On the irrelevance of intention to distinguish leases from licences, leading cases are *Radaich v Smith* (1959) 101 CLR 209 (HCA) and *Street v Mountford* [1985] AC 809 (HL).

[53] [2002] 1 SCR 146.

within the industry that such royalties are intended to bind successors in title, and if the particular purchaser knew of this expectation, at what point should the purchaser be excused on the mere ground that the law does not recognize that the statutory mining lease, or the royalty carved out of it, is property? The same can happen in relation to dealings in water permits: 'they knew when they bought the farm that it was burdened with a water share agreement where I get one-third of the water, and everyone knows that you have to honour these agreements'.[54] To refer again to the analysis by Watson Hamilton and Bankes in this volume, this is functional or instrumental reasoning about the existence of property rights, drawing on justifications of property in desert and economic theory.

Argument by analogy or by assimilation causes one to ask whether statutory rights and common law rights are entirely separate. It quickly becomes apparent that they are not. At the very heart of the English common law of real property, for example, the estate in fee simple is actually a creature of the statute of *Quia Emptores* of 1290. The legislature has been active ever since, and it would take a great deal of courage to say of measures such as the Statute of Frauds or the English Law of Property Act 1925 that 'this is common law, but that is statute'. Registration statutes completely dominate the law of title to land and goods. Equally, much of administrative law is devoted to protecting entitlements of different kinds, including privileges and expectations. It has been argued that entitlements for social security benefits and the like must be regarded as property.[55] The law of substantive legitimate expectation has a potential to merge into property law, a potential that would be desirable to explore in detail.[56] If, then, property and statute are not entirely different realms, it becomes easier to envisage statutory rights that include property characteristics.

VII. The interplay between the legislature and the courts

We have noted that resources legislation often does a poor job of saying whether a permit granted under it carries a proprietary element. If the legislature's role is often one of inadvertence, then that played by the courts is a more active one. It is possible that lawyers and judges, even in non-constitutional cases, see questions about property rights and consequences in private law as being more properly in their sphere of expertise and constitutional responsibility, rather than in that of the legislature.

---

[54] In New Zealand *The Favourite Ltd v Vavasour* [2005] NZRMA 461 (HC) and *Hampton v Hampton*, High Court Christchurch CIV-2008-409-2394, Chisholm J, 9 March 2009, show that such claims are foreseeable.

[55] C. Reich, 'The New Property' (1964) 73 Yale Law Journal 733.

[56] *Aoraki Water Trust v Meridian Energy Ltd* [2005] 2 NZLR 268 relied *inter alia* on substantive legitimate expectation to buttress the rights held under a statutory water permit; an expectation that a council was committed to its grant in the sense that it could not deliberately erode the grant unless acting pursuant to specific statutory powers.

They distinguish the public law and the private law aspects of environmental and natural resources legislation. In the public law aspects, they are content to defer entirely to the direction of the legislature. They do not intrude on matters such as a discretionary decision to make a disposition of publicly owned resources. They do not substitute their views for that of the legislature or an agency about the proper level at which to set the total allowable catch of a species of fish, or the proper cap to impose on the emissions of greenhouse gases from different sectors. However, they are less deferential about the implications of legislation in private law. They appear to make a greater claim for the autonomy of the law in this respect.

Armstrong v Public Trust[57] discloses this claim to autonomy in respect of private ordering:

> This Court will not find that the legislature has so intervened to displace the common law position as to joint tenancy, by a side-wind, when pursuing control over the allocation of scarce resources, as it is doing in the RMA. To the extent that it does in fact allow property rights under the RMA, the common law as to real and personal property will apply, subject to constraints in the specific provisions of the statute.

These words show resistance to any general claim that the legislature has entirely occupied the field.

A similar claim to autonomy, in giving a narrow reading to a statutory declaration of the nature of a licence, is *Clarkson v Wishart*.[58] It held that a mining claim was 'lands' exigible under the Execution Act even though a section of the Ontario Mining Act stated that the holder was only a tenant at will of the Crown. The Privy Council held that the section did not constitute an exhaustive enumeration of the rights of the holder of an unpatented mining claim. The reference to tenancy at will dealt solely with the claimholder's relationship with the Crown. 'But such denomination, in [their Lordship's] view, cannot be allowed to destroy the substance and reality of the rights in the claimant as against other subjects of the Crown if such rights be in truth conferred by the Act.'[59] The Act gave the claimholder a right to work the claim and to transfer it; a certificate of record that gave protection against forfeiture; recording of instruments. It provided for recording to be deemed to be actual notice (provisions 'radically inconsistent with a mere tenancy at will'); and protected a claim of a deceased miner. One looks at what the legislature does, not what it says.

VIII. Formalism

An unexpressed rationale for this distinctive claim for judicial autonomy may lie in formalism; the perspective, as expressed by Ernest Weinrib, that private law must be treated as an internally intelligible phenomenon by drawing on what is

---

[57] [2007] NZRMA 573 (HC) para 23.
[58] [1913] AC 828 (PC Ont).
[59] ibid at 836.

salient in juristic experience and by trying to make sense of legal thinking and legal discourse in their own terms.[60] Formalism seems to provide a framework that explains or justifies four aspects of what we see. First, formalism emphasizes the role of the internal coherence of the law. Legal thinking seeks to develop the law in ways that increase, not decrease, its intellectual coherence. Different rules and principles, and different bodies of doctrine, are to be reconciled and made to work together in a rational manner. It is arguable that judges see themselves as having a greater role in that effort than does the legislature. The legislature can impose its will on the law, but it does not always do so intelligently. Weinrib argues that the law, especially private law, is an engagement of thought, of intelligence, not power.[61] In relation to our present question, this serves as a reminder that we seek a coherent evolution of the law, with rules that will make sense at a general level, in a variety of contexts, reconciling the intention of the statute with the dictates of particular problems. We can do without decisions that give us irrational distinctions and unnecessary exceptions such as 'it's property for the purposes of bankruptcy but not land taxes, except that if it's a coastal licence it's the other way round'. The ideal, perhaps, would be that if a statutory licence is determined to be property or statutory property, then a certain accepted set of consequences should follow, unless the legislation or the dictates of fairness require another result.

Secondly, because this coherence of law is an internal feature, with no external referent, law is argued to have an autonomous character. The standard view is that law is not an autonomous body of learning; that law cannot be separated from politics; and that legal concepts need not be taken seriously in their own right, but can only be properly understood in terms of external disciplines such as political or legal analysis. Weinrib argues that this view must be reconsidered. It is not necessary for us to decide how completely we agree on the question of the autonomy of the law. What we can perhaps agree on is that in making decisions about the legal character of statutory licences, especially their incidents in private law, the courts are more than usually willing to protect the autonomy of the law than in making decisions about the instrumental or policy-laden aspects of legislation.

This takes us to a third point, that it is desirable to distinguish the treatment of private law from public law. Again, the formalist view seems to have some explanatory power. The courts in cases like *Armstrong v Public Trust* and *Clarkson v Wishart* seem to be ready to make this distinction. There is room to reconcile a claim for autonomy in the private law aspects of natural resource disposition with proper judicial deference to the democratic character of legislation. While we can encourage the development of the law in directions that allow a wide range of principles of private law to apply to transactional disputes *inter partes*, we should refrain from

---

[60] E. J. Weinrib, *The Idea of Private Law* (1995). Also valuable is P. S. Atiyah and R. S. Summers, *Form and Substance in Anglo-American Law* (1987).

[61] Weinrib, above n 60 at 14.

using property ideas to decide matters which are substantially policy-oriented.[62] On such matters, we should avoid the importation of property ideas and stick to the statute. In particular, we should refrain from using property law ideas to expand the rights that have been granted under statute, and refrain from using them to extend their duration. *Saulnier v Royal Bank of Canada* warns against this.[63]

The fourth insight from formalism is its emphasis on the connection that private law makes between two particular parties through the phenomenon of liability. It reminds us that in the final analysis the question of property rights is not a discussion of a statutory framework, or a policy debate about natural resource management. If property rights are rights between persons in relation to things, then the ultimate question is which of two persons with competing claims to the thing will prevail. Liability or rights between parties is an aspect of property rights that must not be allowed to fall out of sight. The fundamental matter of justice between claimants must stay in sight as a criterion by which to judge the development of the law.

At this point the matter of commercial expectations or commercial realities seems to reappear. Expectations do not come out of nowhere. Nor can they be dismissed as wishful thinking, especially if they are shown to be spread right through an industry, and not merely the product of a plaintiff's hopefulness. Expectations that are based on a general perception of what are fair outcomes need more consideration than they have received thus far.

Formalism has been the subject of fashionable abuse for decades, but in the shape delineated by Weinrib it appears to have a good deal of explanatory and normative power in respect of claims of proprietary incidents for statutory licences.

IX. Restrictions on the creation of new kinds of property rights

Also relevant, in my view, is the idea that there is something natural and inevitable in the number of interests that legal systems recognize as proprietary. Bernard Rudden observes that all non-feudal legal systems lay down a restricted list of about a dozen 'real rights'.[64] He detects a pervasive general rule that we are not free contractually to create more than a handful of entitlements against

---

[62] I address this matter in more detail in relation to New Zealand's Resource Management Act 1991 in 'The Nature of Resource Consents: Statutory Permits or Property Rights' in *Environmental Law: National Issues* (2009), concluding that *Aoraki Water Trust v Meridian Energy Ltd* [2005] 2 NZLR 268, [2005] NZRMA 251 was wrong to use property ideas such as non-derogation from a grant in a way that strengthened the rights of the holder of a water permit.

[63] (2008) 298 DLR (4th) 193 (SCC). Also see A. Gardner, 'The Legal Basis for the Emerging Value of Water Licences—Property Rights or Tenuous Permissions' (2003) 10 Australian Property Law Journal 1, citing *National Audubon Society v Superior Court* (1983) 33 Cal 3d 419 on the power of an agency to vary licences without compensation.

[64] B. Rudden, 'Economic Theory v Property Law: The *Numerus Clausus* Problem' in *Oxford Essays in Jurisprudence* (Third Series, J. Eekelaar and J. Bell, eds, 1987) 239. By 'non-feudal' he includes Roman law, modern codified systems and modern non-codified systems. Watson Hamilton and Bankes, in this volume, also recognize the relevance of this characteristic of legal systems.

strangers, and everywhere the content is much the same. Generally, there are three possessory interests (in the common law, fee, life and leasehold estates); there are non-possessory non-security interests which may be described as servitudes; and there are security interests such as mortgages. All such rights can be held in co-ownership with others. Generally, legal systems prevent the imposition of affirmative burdens on a person merely because he or she has acquired a property interest.[65] All systems limit, or at least greatly restrict, the creation of other real rights: ' "fancies" are for contract, not property'.[66] This characteristic of legal systems is referred to as the *numerus clausus*, the closed number of property rights that are recognized. It is a characteristic that has received only incidental attention in the doctrine of most legal systems. (Some civil law systems say expressly that no real rights can be recognized other than those provided for in the Civil Code.) Similarly it has received little attention in the literature, although that is changing; an economic rationale for *numerus clausus* has been a particular focus.[67] Rudden's own preference is for a philosophical explanation in a combination of Kantian, Hegelian, and Hohfeldian terms.[68]

A duty-not-to may be imposed, but a no-duty-to cannot be removed. White's and Black's will alone can add another claimant (Black) to everyone's duty-not; it cannot do so in respect of a duty-to. ... Duties-not are frequently imposed on us without our consent, ... or by the law of tort. Duties-to are not.

Rudden usefully emphasizes that property rights are entitlements good against people with whom we have no contract, in short, strangers. A contractual right can be enforced only against a party who is privy to the contract; in contrast, a proprietary right can be enforced against anyone who interferes with it, even though they had not previously been in a relationship with the plaintiff, such as under a contract or trust.

The *numerus clausus* characteristic of legal systems provides us with further useful ideas about finding property rights in statutory licences. It explains why property rights should be restricted and why the courts should not expand the range of property rights carelessly. There is a philosophical rationale for caution in changing the law so as to impose new positive duties on strangers. Indeed, it is a rationale based on our notion of justice. There are economic rationales as well, such as information costs. In addition (as Watson Hamilton and Bankes in this volume put it) the *numerus clausus* characteristic asserts a hold on our thinking that explains our need to shoe-horn innovative interests into an existing category of property.

---

[65] Rudden, ibid at 242, 252.
[66] Rudden, ibid at 243, 260. By 'fancy' he adopts the word used by Lord Brougham LC in *Keppell v Bailey* (1834) 2 My & K 517, 535, 39 ER 1043, 1049.
[67] Rudden ibid took the view that none of the economic reasons for the characteristic seemed particularly convincing. T. W. Merrill and H. E. Smith, 'Optimal Standardization in the Law of Property: The *Numerus Clausus* Principle' (2000) 110 Yale Law Journal 1 find an economic rationale, primarily in the information costs of persons proposing to deal with property interests.
[68] Rudden, above n 64 at 252.

On the other hand, Brendan Edgeworth argues that one of the main rationales for the *numerus clausus* principle disappears where an effective title registration system is in place, protecting third parties who may be bound by interests that run with the land.[69] While he refers to the Torrens registration system, the same must apply to registration and recording systems for natural resource permits, along with tight statutory controls on duration and transferability. One might say that under such a system the real question is whether an interest is registered rather than whether it is one known to the law. Edgeworth also observes that the rationale of protection of the integrity of the science of the law is no longer a strong one; in recent decades we have seen highly intricate, multi-layered and novel regimes of rights created but without making property law chaotic or incapable of scientific classification.[70] Regimes for Crown lands, that is, public resources, are an example; novel rights can be specified and publicly registered, so there is no need for *numerus clausus* to protect third party purchasers from undue transaction costs.

There is certainly a need for new rights in natural resources and in environmental goods; the heritage that comes down to us from the Middle Ages is hardly adequate. There are new problems needing to be solved, both in public policy and in commercial activity. Anthony Scott has developed a substantial body of thinking about supply and demand for standardized property rights of different kinds in natural resources.[71] The supplier may be a legislature, a court, an administrative agency, or custom in the community or an industry. Innovations are often incremental. There is an interplay, and the question of institutional choice, whether the recognition of a new property interest should be made by the courts or by the legislature, really involves both.[72]

X. Conclusion

Even in this brief overview, we can see that the case law is not producing any consistent body of doctrine by which to determine whether a statutory resource permit has a proprietary character to it, or whether property law ideas can properly be

---

[69] B. Edgeworth, 'The *Numerus Clausus* Principle in Contemporary Australian Property Law' (2006) 32 Monash University Law Review 387. In this volume, Watson Hamilton and Bankes similarly note that state-created resource rights may be an exception to the general reluctance to create novel property rights, and that there may be sound reasons for the exception where information costs are controlled by a statutory framework, a state monopoly, a particular industry, and international competition.

[70] Edgeworth, ibid at 407. The language of 'the science of the law' is from the rationale for *numerus clausus* given by Lord Brougham in *Keppell v Bailey* (1834) 2 My & K 517 at 535, 39 ER 1042.

[71] A. Scott, *The Evolution of Resource Property Rights* (2008), especially p 48. In his earlier work, see 'Property Rights and Property Wrongs' (1983) 16 Canadian Journal of Economics 555 on the supply of new interpretations and new bundlings of rights.

[72] Watson Hamilton and Bankes in this volume make this point; Merrill and Smith (above n 67) consider it as well.

used to construe it. The legislature often pays little attention to such matters; often its general pronouncements fail to deal with the diversity of disputes that parties bring to the courts. It is unlikely that we can wait for legislators to provide comprehensively for all situations.[73] Given this legislative track record, it is interesting to discover that the courts are often reluctant to be entirely bound by the legislature's expressions of intention. We find that ideas about formalism and *numerus clausus* to some degree explain this behaviour. They also give us useful ideas about what we seek in the development of the law. One can identify the characteristics of coherence, justice between parties, and care in overextending the concept of property. We can see a need to inject a focus on relationships *inter partes* into a discussion that is sometimes excessively dominated by policy matters. That leads us to the possibility that commercial expectations or commercial realities require more care in judicial decisionmaking than they have done thus far.

It is arguable that we should encourage development of the law in directions that allow a wide range of principles of private law to apply to disputes *inter partes* where there is no significant policy point in issue, and where a just outcome should be the primary consideration. At the same time, we must be careful to ward off the misuse of property rights. Property rights claims are potent politically. Where natural resources or emissions rights are allocated to individual persons or companies, a commodification of the commons occurs. This is a well-understood phenomenon, even if its pace has accelerated extraordinarily in recent years. The particular risk is that property rights arguments can deter an agency regulator from reducing entitlements. At first sight, that may seem to be self evident; but there is much rhetorical strength in the argument 'I paid for these allowances, I was a purchaser in good faith, it is an invasion of my property rights in them to cut them back'. It is necessary to protect the regulators of the future against such claims. Property rights concepts have a dangerous strength in environmental and natural resources law. It is essential that we distinguish their legitimate uses from their illegitimate ones.

---

[73] cf L. Foster, 'Property Rights in Environmental Management: The Nature of Resource Consents in the Resource Management Act 1991' (2008) 12 New Zealand Journal of Environmental Law 145.

5

Property Law Sources and Analogies in International Law

*Catherine Redgwell**

I. Introduction

International law does not generally stipulate the ownership or property rights regime which states must apply to energy resources under their national law. It is thus open to a state to determine as a matter of its domestic law whether energy resources and facilities are publicly or privately owned, and whether the conditions under which, for example, petroleum exploration takes place, are pursuant to private contractual arrangements or by publicly regulated licence or other arrangements. Of course, it may not always be clear whether energy resources are public or private property, a position which may be clarified by domestic legislation. A case in point is the United Kingdom's 1934 Petroleum Act which vested all petroleum resources in the Crown—either an act of uncompensated expropriation if such resources flowed with private land tenure,[1] or recognition of the pre-existing public nature of such resources.

While international law is agnostic as to whether energy resources are subject to a regime of public or private property rights, it does, however, require certain international minimum standards of treatment with respect to foreign nationals'

* Professor of International Law, University College London, United Kingdom; email: c.redgwell@ucl.ac.uk.

[1] The first petroleum legislation in the UK dates back to emergency regulations made during World War I to ensure security of supply for the oil-burning navy. But during World War I the government also sought to encourage exploration for possible petroleum in Great Britain, and in 1917 a bill was introduced for this purpose. It failed because of controversy over compensation to land owners under whose land exploitable deposits lay. Instead the government used regulations under the Defence of the Realm Act 1914 empowering it to enter land for the purpose of searching for and getting petroleum, and to prevent others from doing so. In 1918 the Petroleum (Production) Act was passed which did not address property rights to the petroleum *in situ* but did establish the first licensing regime. This prevented competitive drilling by prohibiting the search for or boring for oil without a licence. In 1934 the property rights issue was finally resolved, establishing that all petroleum in the United Kingdom existing in natural condition in strata in the UK or beneath the territorial waters of the UK is vested in the Crown, by virtue of the Petroleum (Production) Act 1934 s 1. There is no compensation for a land owner who discovers he or she is sitting on top of a major petroleum deposit.

enjoyment of such rights, often now enshrined in bilateral investment treaties and in certain international instruments such as the Energy Charter Treaty and the North American Free Trade Agreement (NAFTA). There is now a significant body of case law expounding on the nature of property rights to be protected, and determining the permissible scope of state infringement. The purpose of this chapter is to explore property rights protection at international law, while also considering the relationship of 'ownership', sovereignty, and sovereign rights of states over their energy and natural resources at international law both within and beyond national jurisdiction, where international regimes of ownership and property rights may be applicable.

II. Property in international law

'Property' is used in a variety of international instruments and for a variety of purposes. One purpose is to establish 'ownership' of key chattels under international law.[2] Some international treaties address the relationship between domestic property regimes and recognition of international concern in its treatment and disposition. Relatively uncommon is the recognition of an obligation of international protection without prejudice to (national) property rights found in Art 6 of the 1972 World Heritage Convention,[3] which provides:

Whilst fully respecting the sovereignty of the States on whose territory the cultural and natural heritage ... is situated, and without prejudice to the property rights provided by national legislation, the State Parties to this Convention recognize that such heritage constitutes a world heritage for whose protection it is the duty of the international community as a whole to co-operate.[4]

More common is the need to define property in the context of liability and compensation regimes which define property damage for the purpose of harmonizing, and potentially limiting, compensation. Thus, for example, the 1993 Council of Europe Convention on Civil Liability for Damage Resulting from Activities Dangerous to the Environment[5] defines 'damage' to include 'loss of or damage to property other than to the installation itself or property held under the control

---

[2] See also brief discussion in I. Brownlie, 'Property in General' in *Principles of Public International Law* (6th edn, 2003) 432. In addition to some of the examples cited in the text, he adds that the rules of attribution at international law function as the counterpart of domestic concepts of ownership on the international plane for ships, aircraft, space objects, and national treasures.

[3] 11 ILM (1972) 1358. For general discussion of the impact of the Convention on energy activities, see the chapters by C. Redgwell and by G. Triggs in *Human Rights in Natural Resources Development* (D. Zillman, A. Lucas, G. Pring, eds, 2002).

[4] For commentary see G. Carducci, 'Arts 4–7 National and International Protection of the Cultural and Natural Heritage' in *The 1972 World Heritage Convention: A Commentary* (F. Francioni, ed, 2008) 119.

[5] Available at <www.coe.int> (not yet in force).

of the operator, at the site of the dangerous activity'. Similar language, which has been judicially considered, is found in the 1963 Vienna Convention on Civil Liability for Nuclear Damage[6] arising from a nuclear occurrence. Designed to establish international minimum standards in respect of compensation, it defines nuclear damage in Art 1(k)(i) as:

> loss of life, any personal injury or loss of, or damage to, property which arises out of or results from the radioactive properties or a combination of radioactive properties with toxic, explosive or other hazardous properties of nuclear fuel or radioactive products or waste in, or of nuclear material coming from, originating in, or sent to, a nuclear installation.

This definition of damage to property was judicially considered in *Merlin v British Nuclear Fuels Ltd*[7] in interpreting s 12 of the United Kingdom's Nuclear Installations Act 1965 (right to compensation). There the Merlins sought damages for the economic loss they suffered in consequence of their house reducing in price owing, the Merlins argued, to radiological contamination. Gatehouse J relied on this paragraph from the Convention which the Act was designed, *inter alia*, to implement to flesh out the definition of 'damage' in s 7 of the Act and held that:

A. property refers to tangible property not incorporeal property nor property rights;
B. damage is actual physical damage to tangible property and does not include pure economic loss.[8]

Perhaps one of the most fertile areas for development of concepts of property and property rights at international law is in the investment context. The classic example is the deprivation of a foreign investor's property by the host state in violation of international law.[9] Under traditional rules of state responsibility, the host state is responsible for the violation, and the home state may proceed with a claim against it for the wrong done to its national in the exercise of diplomatic protection. However, what property rights the foreign investor enjoys in the host state is purely a matter for the domestic law concerned; general international law does no more than impose standards of conduct with respect to the treatment of that property and the rights arising from it. Customary international law

---

[6] 1063 UNTS 265, in force 12 November 1977.
[7] [1990] 3 WLR 383; [1990] 3 All ER 711.
[8] ibid at 394 para G.
[9] Of course, it may be questioned whether rules on the protection of foreign investment are really property rules at all. Barnes observes that, '[s]trictly speaking the rules are part of the broader category of rules on State responsibility and are more akin to delictual rules'. But he goes on to observe that 'such rules are still concerned with the protection of proprietary interests' which is the justification for their inclusion here. See further R. Barnes, *Property Rights and Natural Resources* (2009) 230 n 54.

recognizes a broad measure of discretion of states in relation to the treatment of foreign nationals on its territory, subject to important limitations:[10]

- The host state must not, through its officials or courts, injure a foreign national through injury to his or her property.
- Foreign nationals must be allowed access to the courts in order to protect their property[11] and must have equality before the law in so doing.
- The host state has a duty to protect foreign nationals, a duty which applies to their property as well as to their persons;[12] and
- It has an obligation to observe certain minimum international standards in its treatment of the property of foreign nationals, and their persons.

There has been extensive analysis of the content of these international minimum standards in the case law and literature, with broad consensus on the following:[13]

(1) Expropriation must not be arbitrary.
(2) It must be based on the application of duly adopted laws.
(3) It should be in the public interest.
(4) It should be non-discriminatory as between nationals and aliens.
(5) Compensation should be paid for the expropriated property (though there is continuing disagreement as to the standard of compensation payable).

Property interests are also protected by treaty, the classical form being the treaty of friendship, commerce and navigation (FCN) prevalent in the nineteenth and early twentieth centuries, with its broad formula of 'property, rights and interest'.[14] This wording was also incorporated in the 1967 OECD Draft Convention on the Protection of Foreign Property deliberately to embrace a wider concept than investment alone.[15] More modern instruments focus more narrowly on investment, with over 2,000 bilateral investment treaties (BITs)

---

[10] See R. Jennings and A. Watts, *Oppenheim's International Law* (9th edn, 1996, vol 1) 916.

[11] At international law there is of course the requirement to exhaust local remedies before diplomatic espousal of claims by the home state, so long as such remedies are available and effective. The customary law position is codified in Art 44 of the non-binding but authoritative ILC Articles on State Responsibility 2001.

[12] *AAPL v Sri Lanka* 4 ICSID Awards 250; 30 ILM (1991) 577.

[13] See for example Jennings and Watts (above n 10); R. Dolzer and C. Schreuer, *Principles of International Investment Law* (2008); and N. Schrijver, *Sovereignty over Natural Resources: Balancing Rights and Duties* (1997).

[14] For interpretation of FCN treaties see for example *Electronica Sicula S.p.A. (ELSI) (United States v Italy)* ICJ Reports (1989) 15; *Oil Platforms (Islamic Republic of Iran v United States of America)* ICJ Reports (2006) 10.

[15] Art 9(c) and explanatory note 3(a), text available at <www.oecd.org> and 7 ILM (1968) 117. Though drafted by the OECD it was intended to have global effect, but failed to attract sufficient support for adoption. It was recommended as a model for investment protection treaties: Resolution of the Council of the OECD on the Draft Convention [C(67)102]. Dolzer and Stevens attribute the relative similarity of early BITs concluded by OECD members to the influence of this Draft Convention: R. Dolzer and M. Stevens, *Bilateral Investment Treaties* (1995).

concluded since 1959 for the protection of foreign investment. Amongst other things, these define 'investment' to include the property rights to be protected. Typically such definitions include: tangible or intangible, movable and immovable property; property rights such as mortgages, liens or pledges; and intellectual property.[16] A further feature of BITs is that, unlike the customary law position which amounted to an inter-state claim with the protection of foreign nationals' property dependent on the home state exercising diplomatic protection, modern BITs contain a dispute settlement clause permitting recourse by the investor directly against the host state through arbitration under the International Centre for Settlement of Investment Disputes (ICSID) or otherwise.

However, before enjoying the protection afforded to 'property rights and interest' or 'investment' under general customary law or treaty instruments, it is first necessary to consider whether international law *requires* the state to permit the acquisition of such property/investment. It is a natural concomitant to state sovereignty that, absent express obligations assumed to the contrary, states are not compelled to admit foreign investment. It remains open to the state in the exercise of its economic sovereignty to determine whether, and to what extent, it will open up its national economy to foreign investors. And this may fluctuate over time, as the recent experience of the oil industry in Ecuador reveals.[17] Once it does so, of course, then the customary obligations (and any treaty obligations) with respect to the treatment of that foreign investor and its investments are triggered. This balance is reflected in the 1967 Draft Convention, which recognizes the sovereign right of each state to regulate admission, and then elaborates upon the protection foreign investment must be afforded if and when admitted.[18] Today some, but not all, BITs contain reference both to entry requirements (admission) and to establishment (conditions under which the investor carries out its operations for the duration of the investment).[19] European practice has followed the 1967 evolutionary path in focusing on the standards and guarantees (protection) to be afforded investment once made, but does not tend to grant a right

---

[16] See, for example, the US Model BIT (2004); UK Model BIT (2005); see also the ECT Art 1(6) and the extensive definition of investment in Art 1139 NAFTA. For further discussion see Dolzer and Schreuer (above n 13) at 60–5.

[17] eg, a number of international arbitration claims by US oil companies were submitted for ICSID arbitration alleging, *inter alia*, breach of the US-Ecuador BIT. Changes in the regulatory environment, including a 2006 tax on petroleum company profits, led to claims amounting to over US$10 billion being made through the World Bank's ICSID arbitration facility. On 23 December 2007 Ecuador withdrew its consent to ICSID jurisdiction over matters 'relative to the extraction of natural resources such as oil, gas, or other minerals' and, in 2009, announced its withdrawal from the Convention with effect from 7 January 2010: see <icsid.worldbank.org>

[18] See Art 1(b) (above n 5) and T. Pollan, *Legal Framework for the Admission of FDI* (2006).

[19] See generally Dolzer and Schreuer (above n 13) ch V. The right of admission is not, however, unlimited, and is most commonly conditioned by requirements of national and most favoured nation treatment, or by enumerating lists of open (positive) or closed (negative) sectors.

of admission as such, which remains the unilateral decision of the host state.[20] North American practice grants a limited right of admission.[21]

Beyond the foreign investment context, international law may impinge upon the operation of private property rights through recognition of the right to property as a human right, the enjoyment of which is not dependent on the owner or rights holder being a foreign national. The right to property is recognized in a number of human rights instruments,[22] including the 1969 American Convention on Human Rights,[23] the non-binding European Union (EU) Charter of Fundamental Rights and Freedoms (2000),[24] and the African Charter of Rights.[25] Indeed, the first recognition of a right to property is found in the 1948 Universal Declaration of Human Rights adopted by the United Nations General Assembly, Art 17 of which recognizes the right to property and the right not arbitrarily to be deprived thereof.

There has been extensive consideration of the scope of the right to property under Art 1 of the First Protocol (1952) to the 1950 European Convention on Human Rights in particular.[26] It provides that:

Every natural or legal person is entitled to the peaceful enjoyment of his possessions. No one shall be deprived of his possessions except in the public interest and subject to the conditions provided for by law and by the general principles of international law.

The preceding paragraph shall not, however, in any way impair the right of a State to enforce such laws as it deems necessary to control the use of property in accordance with the general interest or to secure the payment of taxes or other contributions or penalties.

---

[20] ibid at 81. See also Art 10 of the Energy Charter Treaty which focuses on the promotion, protection and treatment of investments but does not accord a right of admission.

[21] See eg Art 3(1) of the US Model BIT (2004), which is couched in terms of market access.

[22] Notable exceptions are the 1966 UN Covenants on Civil and Political Rights and Economic, Social and Cultural Rights.

[23] Art 21 of the American Convention on Human Rights 1969 provides:

1 Everyone has the right to the use and enjoyment of his property. The law may subordinate such use and enjoyment to the interest of society.

2 No one shall be deprived of his property except upon payment of just compensation, for reasons of public utility or social interest, and in the cases and according to the forms established by law.

3 Usury and any other form of exploitation of man by man shall be prohibited by law.

[24] Art 17 of the Charter of Fundamental Rights and Freedoms provides:

1 Everyone has the right to own, use, dispose of and bequeath his or her lawful acquired possessions. No one may be deprived of his or her possessions, except in the public interest and in the cases and under the conditions provided for by law, subject to fair compensation being paid in good time for their loss. The use of property may be regulated by law in so far as is necessary for the general interest.

2 Intellectual property shall be protected.

[25] Article 14 of the African Charter on Human and Peoples' Rights provides:

The right to property shall be guaranteed. It may only be encroached upon in the interest of public need or in the general interest of the community and in accordance with the provisions of appropriate laws.

[26] See generally A. Riza Coban, *The Protection of Property Rights with the European Convention on Human Rights* (2004); see also the discussion in R. Desgagne, 'Integrating Environmental Values into the European Convention on Human Rights' (1995) 89 AJIL 263 at 277–82.

In *Marckx v Belgium* the Court observed that '[b]y recognising that everyone has the right to the peaceful enjoyment of his possessions, Article 1 is in substance guaranteeing the right to property'.[27] In *Sporrong and Lonnroth v Sweden* the Court identified three rules contained in the Article:

The first rule, which is of a general nature, enounces the principle of peaceful enjoyment of property... The second rule covers deprivation of possessions and subjects it to certain conditions... The third rule recognises that States are entitled, amongst other things, to control the use of property in accordance with the general interest, by enforcing such laws as they deem necessary for the purpose...[28]

The Commission has interpreted 'possessions' in Art 1 to include both tangible and intangible property, ie 'rights *in rem*, intangible rights, corporation shares, commercial good will, etc'.[29] The scope of peaceful enjoyment has been considered in the past by the Commission, which considered that environmental and other nuisances could indirectly amount to interference with the rights guaranteed by Art 1, and even to constitute *de facto* confiscation of property.[30] This economic thrust to the 'protection of the enjoyment of one's possessions'[31] was reinforced by the Commission in *Rayner*, where it observed that Art 1 is 'mainly concerned with the arbitrary confiscation of property and does not, in principle, guarantee a right to a peaceful enjoyment of possessions in a pleasant environment'.[32] Nor will there be a breach of Art 1 of Protocol 1 where impairment of the enjoyment of the property occurs without a substantial fall in the value of the property uncompensated by the state. Thus, in *S v France*[33] the applicant claimed breach, *inter alia*, of Art 1 of Protocol 1 owing to the construction of a nuclear power plant 300 metres from her house. The Commission took the same approach to the scope of the provision as in *Rayner* and found no breach since compensation had already been paid which was not disproportionate to the loss suffered. That the right is not an absolute one is clear from the second limb of Art 1 ('the third rule'), a fact underscored by the Court in *Fredin* when it held the Swedish authorities justified in revoking a minerals licence for reasons of nature conservation.[34] Further

[27] 31 Eur Ct H R (ser A) para 63 (1979).

[28] 52 Eur Ct H R (ser A) para 61 (1982).

[29] Desgagne (above n 26) at 277 n 104, who observes that 'ownership is defined in the extensive sense of general international law, that is, as "an acquired right/vested right"'. See also W. Peukert, 'Protection of Ownership under Article 1 of the First Protocol to the European Convention on Human Rights' (1991) 3 Human Rights Law Journal 37.

[30] Above n 28 at paras 60–3. In *S v France*, the Commission observed that noise nuisance, if very considerable, could significantly affect property value and even make sale impossible, thus amounting to a partial expropriation: Application 13728/88, 65 D & R (1990) 250.

[31] See S. Weber, 'Environmental Information and the European Convention on Human Rights' (1991) 12 Human Rights Law Journal 177 at 181.

[32] Application 9310/81, *Rayner v United Kingdom* 47 D & R (1986), 5.

[33] (1990) 65 DR 250.

[34] Ser A No 192 (1991). There are numerous other examples, in the environmental and other context, of the Court finding the impairment of property for a broader public purpose to be justified: see further discussion in Coban and in Desgagne (above n 26).

evidence of balancing of individual property rights against wider community interests is found in *Fagerskiold v Sweden*[35] where challenge by a holiday home-owner to the approval for the operation of wind turbines on adjacent property as nuisance impairing, *inter alia*, peaceful enjoyment of their property protected under Art 1 was held inadmissible on the basis that the interference with their rights was not sufficient to trigger Convention protection. Nonetheless, in rejecting the Art 1 claim as inadmissible, the Court observed, *inter alia*, that:

to the Court, there is no doubt that the operating of the wind turbine is in the general interest as it is an environmentally friendly source of energy which contributes to the sustainable development of natural resources. It observes that the wind turbine at issue in the present case is capable of producing enough energy to heat between 40 and 50 private households over a one-year period, which is beneficial both for the environment and for society.[36]

In balancing the interests of the community as a whole and the negative impact, especially of noise, on local inhabitants, the Court also noted that the local authorities had imposed limitations on the operation of the turbines to lessen their impact.

III. The parameter-setting role of international law for domestic property law

It is therefore clear that, while international law is agnostic as to whether energy resources within the state are subject to a regime of public or private property rights, it nonetheless imposes certain constraints on how such property may be regulated. One such constraint is grounded in domestic law concepts of property as private rights to be protected from unlawful interference through the exercise of diplomatic protection by the home state against the host state responsible for the interference. This customary law position has been enhanced by the conclusion of bilateral and multilateral investment treaties which provide a treaty foundation for standards of treatment and a dispute settlement mechanism permitting recourse directly by the foreign investor against the host state. A second constraint on state action with respect to private property rights may arise through the recognition of the right to property as a human right, the enjoyment of which is not dependent on the owner or rights holder being a foreign national.[37] Enforcement

---

[35] Application No 37664/04, decision of 26 February 2008, available at <cmiskp.echr.coe.int>.

[36] ibid at 18–19. Complaints about the negative impact of the turbines on property values were also dismissed, on the basis of the failure to exhaust local remedies.

[37] Although it is beyond the scope of the present chapter, it should also be noted that there has been extensive international harmonization of the protection of intangible property rights dating back to the nineteenth century with the conclusion of the Berne Convention for the protection of copyright, now under the auspices of the World Intellectual Property Organisation, and more recently with the TRIPs agreement under the World Trade Organisation. UNESCO

of such rights is dependent on incorporation of treaty rights in domestic law to enable recourse to national courts, or, once domestic remedies are exhausted and if established, through an international mechanism such as the European Court of Human Rights.

There are other, indirect, constraints on how states may treat property within their territory. For example, it was already noted above that the World Heritage Convention operates to impose standards of conduct with respect to designated heritage sites within the state.[38] It is not necessary for Convention protection that the site be publicly owned or even publicly designated as a park or reserve, though management obligations do arise with nomination and inscription. However, (i) it is up to the state to nominate the site which the World Heritage Committee then considers for inscription on the World Heritage List; and (ii) the Convention does not provide for an enforcement mechanism as such, beyond listing the property on the 'World Heritage in Danger List' and, ultimately, removing the property from the World Heritage List in the event that state (in)action has extinguished the outstanding universal value of the property. Thus, for example, a natural heritage site in Oman, established for the protection of the endangered Arabian oryx, was the first site to be removed from the World Heritage List in 2007. One reason for doing so was a diminution in area of protection below that needed for sustainability of the herd in consequence of petroleum licensing activities.[39]

In addition, states are not permitted to conduct or permit activities within their territory, or in areas beyond national jurisdiction, without regard for the interests of other states or for the protection of the global environment.[40] This has the twin prongs of imposing on states the duty to prevent, reduce and control transboundary pollution and environmental harm resulting from activities within their jurisdiction and control, and the duty to cooperate in mitigating transboundary environmental risks and emergencies, through notification, consultation, negotiation and, in appropriate cases, environmental impact

---

has also recently addressed intangible property in terms of protection for indigenous knowledge. Because such intangible property/resources cannot be physically limited, the chief legal tool here is excludability.

[38] Other international treaties relying on a site designation approach may impose similar constraints, such as the 1971 Ramsar Convention on Wetlands of International Importance Especially as Wildfowl Habitat, 11 ILM (1972) 969, which like the World Heritage Convention relies on a listing of sites approach, and the 1992 Convention on Biological Diversity, 32 ILM (1992) 818, which encourages the use of protected areas for *in situ* biodiversity conservation. The impact of these treaties on energy and resource activities is addressed in Redgwell (above n 3).

[39] See further the World Heritage in Danger List available at <www.unesco.org>.

[40] The best known soft law articulations are Principle 21 of the non-binding 1972 Stockholm Declaration on the Human Environment and Principle 2 of the non-binding 1992 Rio Declaration on Environment and Development. The 'no harm' principle was clearly recognized as a general principle of customary international law in the 1997 *Case concerning the Gabcikovo/Nagymaros Project (Hungary/Slovakia)* ICJ Rep 7.

assessment.[41] It is important to emphasize that this principle does not amount to a prohibition on activities which create a risk of transboundary harm, provided the two-pronged obligation above is observed. Rather, in the absence of express prohibition, states are required to exercise due diligence in regulating activities under their jurisdiction and control. 'Due diligence' embraces both the introduction of policies and legal and administrative controls to ensure the prevention, reduction and control of environmental harm, and adherence to best available (environmental) techniques or practices. Inevitably the exercise of such diligence will impact on the enjoyment of property rights under domestic law; such interference may even be challenged as a direct or indirect taking of property. But the obligation of the state to exercise due diligence is not contingent on ownership or the exercise of property rights directly by the state as the seminal *Trail Smelter* arbitration amply attests.[42]

IV. Property in internationalized domains

How does international law address property rights beyond the territory of the state? First, it should be recalled that while the coastal state enjoys sovereignty over its territorial waters and the resources of the seabed and subsoil below, on the continental shelf and in the exclusive economic zone (EEZ) the coastal state enjoys more limited sovereignty—sovereign rights—over the living and non-living resources located therein. Nonetheless such rights are exclusive and the coastal states still exercise exclusive domestic jurisdiction over the activities relating to the exploitation of the resources of these zones. But, as Higgins points out, the state itself does not own the resources: 'the State has no rights of ownership in the resources *in situ* the continental shelf—it has only sovereignty for the purposes of exploring and exploiting'.[43] Nonetheless state practice on this point appears to be inconsistent, with some states regulating offshore natural resources on the basis of ownership while others simply refer to the sovereign rights which international law recognizes without stipulating as to ownership of the resources *in situ*.[44] In practice, since it is the coastal state which has exclusive sovereign rights over the resources and exclusive jurisdiction to regulate access to them, no other states may claim title/ownership/property to the resources *in situ*. Unlike the traditional position with respect to unclaimed land territory which as *terra nullius* was susceptible to acquisition ('ownership') through occupation and other such means, developments offshore followed a different path, from the Truman Proclamation of 1946 onwards, of the recognition of sovereign rights over the

---

[41] P. Birnie, A. Boyle and C. Redgwell, *International Law and the Environment* (3rd edn, 2009) 56.

[42] (1941) 35 AJIL 684.

[43] R. Higgins, *Problems & Process: International Law and How We Use It* (1994) 138.

[44] Contrast for example the positions of Denmark and the UK, discussed in *Energy Law in Europe* (M. M. Roggenkamp, C. Redgwell, I. del Guayo and A. Rønne, eds, 2nd edn, 2006).

continental shelf as inherent, exclusive, and not dependent on express proclamation or use. In contrast, the EEZ concept which emerged through the United Nations Convention on the Law of the Sea (UNCLOS) negotiations also recognizes the exclusivity of coastal state sovereign rights. Those rights do not depend on being exercised for such exclusive enjoyment, but they must be expressly proclaimed.[45] However these provisions do not address ownership of the resources once extracted, nor the installations and devices associated with their exploitation; that is a matter for domestic law, although for transboundary installations and large transboundary resource projects it may need to be regulated additionally by treaty.[46] Thus installations and pipelines may be owned by the state or states, or by individual consortiums.[47]

How may domestic law address these issues of ownership of installations and of resources beyond state territory? With respect to regulation of property rights, it is clear that the sovereignty which the coastal state enjoys in the territorial sea includes the authority to extend its property regime(s) to this zone, and to do so exclusively—but not absolutely, given the obligations under the 1982 Law of the Sea Convention and at customary law to permit innocent passage and the duty not to hamper it unduly. However, it is unlikely that the extension of even an extensive system of property rights to the territorial sea would have this hampering effect, and would allow the regulation of natural resources through licensing and permitting systems for oil and gas exploration and production (including the construction of installations and pipelines) to proceed unimpaired.[48] The same general considerations apply for the regulation of energy activities on the continental shelf and in the EEZ for these resources purposes.

Beyond national jurisdiction, where domestic property rules do not apply as an extension of coastal state jurisdiction over territory and/or activities, the resources of the deep seabed are based on the notion of *res communis*, reflected in the status of its resources as the common heritage of mankind. The 1982 Law of the Sea Convention declares the Area and its resources the common heritage

[45] See Art 56 of the United Nations Convention on the Law of the Sea 1982, 21 ILM (1994) 1261 (LOSC).

[46] In areas of disputed jurisdiction, joint development of the resources of disputed zones may nonetheless proceed on the basis of mutual consent to pool exclusive rights, even if the exact territorial delimitation between the extent of the rights of coastal state A and coastal state B has not been determined. See, generally, D. Ong, 'Joint Development of Common Offshore Oil and Gas Deposits: "Mere" State Practice or Customary International Law?' (1999) 93 AJIL 771 and P. D. Cameron, 'The Rules of Engagement: Developing Cross-Border Petroleum Deposits in the North Sea and Caribbean' (2006) 55 ICLQ 559.

[47] An example is the Nord Stream pipeline, which when built will deliver gas from Russia to the European Union through the Baltic Sea, transiting the maritime zones of seven states. The NordStream pipeline is owned by Nord Stream AG, a joint venture of four companies, Gazprom (51%), BASF/Wintershall (20%), E.ON Ruhrgas (20%) and Gasunie (9%).

[48] Indeed, the *failure* to regulate such activities through the domestic law—whether by property or other legal mechanisms—may attract the responsibility of the state, a point considered in section III above, 'The parameter-setting role of international law for domestic property'.

of mankind and not subject to national sovereignty[49] or appropriation.[50] This is a rare acknowledgement at international law of the status of resources as common property resources to be enjoyed for the benefit of all humankind.[51] It is one illustration of the normative limits of the application of national (territorial) sovereignty and private property concepts; others are prohibitions on the possession and/or use of certain chemical and biological weapons, and of human beings as slaves. This reflects the moral limits of property, in that certain things should not be 'propertized' although this view will shift over time since it is culturally, socially, politically and temporally relative.[52]

What are the legal implications of common heritage status? The most commonly identified elements[53] include:

(1) the area in question cannot be subject to national appropriation;
(2) all states should share in the management of the resources of the area;
(3) actual sharing of the benefits derived from resource exploitation;
(4) dedication to peaceful purposes; and
(5) preservation of the area for future generations.

The distinguishing features of the common heritage principle are thus the emphasis upon international management and control and the sharing of resources. Common heritage status will usually entail some form of international institution or authority representative of the international community and for that community to share in the benefit of exploitation of the resources. The regime established by Part XI of the 1982 Law of the Sea Convention is one such example. For this reason, the concept is not 'self-executing' but requires institutional mechanisms for its implementation.[54]

---

[49] That said, this does not prevent property rights arising as a matter of domestic law. As Barnes (above n 9) at 13 rightly observes with respect to the deep seabed mining provisions of the LOSC, 'international law establishes a form of exclusive right for the benefit of private persons over the seabed of a kind more readily found in domestic property institutions'.

[50] United Nations Convention on the Law of the Sea 1982, 21 ILM (1994) 1261. See, in particular, Art 136 (declared the common heritage of mankind) and Art 137 (legal status of the Area and its resources).

[51] See also the Outer Space Treaty which explicitly acknowledges that outer space is the province of all mankind and not subject to national appropriation: Treaty on Principles Governing the Activities of States in the Exploration and Use of Outer Space, Including the Moon and other Celestial Bodies 1967, 6 ILM (1968) 386. See, in particular, Art 1 (province of all mankind) and Art 2 (no national appropriation). See also the Agreement Governing the Activities of States on the Moon and other Celestial Bodies 1979, 18 ILM (1979) 1434, Art 11(1) of which declares the moon and its natural resources to be the common heritage of mankind; however, unlike the deep seabed, no provision is made for institutionalization of the administration of these resources. Under Art 11 (5) and (7) this is postponed until exploitation is about to become feasible.

[52] See, generally, J. Penner, *The Moral Limits of Property* (2006) and Barnes (above n 9) at 16.

[53] See, generally, C. Joyner, 'The Common Heritage of Mankind' (1988) 32 ICLQ 443 and K. Hossain, *The Common Heritage of Mankind* (1998).

[54] This leads Boyle to conclude that '[c]ommon heritage is thus a concept of potential rather than actual legal significance'. A. Boyle, 'International Law and the Protection of the Global

V. Conclusion

With respect to the impact of international law on domestic property concepts, we have seen that international law is largely agnostic as to whether energy resources within the state are subject to a regime of public or private property rights. It does, however, require certain international minimum standards of treatment with respect to foreign nationals' enjoyment of such rights; additionally, some human rights instruments accord protection for the enjoyment of property rights regardless of the nationality of the rights holder. Constraints on state regulation of property rights may also arise through other explicitly assumed treaty obligations (such as the World Heritage Convention) or indirectly through obligations the state must fulfil in regulating persons and activities under its jurisdiction and control so as to prevent, *inter alia*, transboundary harm. In international-ized domains, we have seen that the state does not 'own' the resources of the continental shelf. Certain resources in areas beyond national jurisdiction, such as the resources of deep seabed, acknowledged as the common heritage of man-kind, are not susceptible to unilateral national appropriation or ownership. Property rights in such resources arise in the case of the continental shelf at the point the resources are reduced to possession (eg oil at the wellhead) and for the deep seabed, when permitted in accordance with the international framework for deep seabed mining established pursuant to Part XI of the 1982 Law of the Sea Convention. Sovereignty over natural resources,[55] whether viewed as 'absolute', 'full' or 'inalienable' or qualified as 'restricted', 'relative' or 'functional',[56] does not necessarily connote ownership of those resources at international law. Rather, as Schrijver observes, sovereignty is equated with non-interference, the exercise of domestic jurisdiction and 'discretion in the legal sphere'.[57] At international law it is not property but sovereignty which is 'the basic constitutional doctrine of the law of nations'.[58] Thus, while it is one of the fundamental ordering concepts of domestic jurisdictions, 'property' does not have a fixed meaning, nor does it per-form a dominant role, in international law.

Atmosphere: Concepts, Categories and Principles' in *International Law and Global Climate Change* (R. Churchill and D. Freestone, eds, 1991) 1 at 10.

[55] See, generally, N. Schrijver, *Sovereignty over Natural Resources: Balancing Rights and Duties* (1997).
[56] ibid at 2. See also D. French, *Sustainable Development and International Law* (2006).
[57] ibid.
[58] Brownlie (above n 2) at 297.

PART II
NATURAL RESOURCE REGIMES

6

Property Rights in Oil and Gas under Domanial Regimes

Yinka Omorogbe* and Peter Oniemola**

I. Introduction

This chapter is concerned with the various property rights that may arise in jurisdictions where the state owns all natural resources. Invariably, in these regimes, whilst absolute ownership rights remain vested in the state as the sovereign, there are various property rights which may be held by stakeholders such as:

- State/provincial or local governments;
- Holders of leases or other statutory rights that may be granted by the state;
- Contractors working on a licence or lease held by the National Oil Company or another entity on behalf of the state; and
- Communities within which the natural resources are located.

Ownership rights over oil and gas take various forms and vary from one country to another, depending on the country's socio-political and historical background, legal system, and in particular, the country's laws, which directly impact on the oil and gas industry and the various contracts between the government and the companies, or between companies. The enduring legal or regulatory regime provides the rules and procedures governing the allocation, maintenance, transfer and cancellation of oil and gas rights and the rights and obligations of the title-holders for the varieties of oil and gas rights available.

When ownership of a particular resource is vested in the state, as happens in domanial regimes, the rights of other entities are usually limited to the rights to use, management, control, or enjoy benefits as derived from the resources.[1] Put

* Secretary and Legal Adviser to the Nigerian National Petroleum Corporation, and formerly Professor and Dean, Faculty of Law, University of Ibadan, Nigeria; email: yinka.omorogbe@gmail.com. The views expressed within are my views and cannot in any way be interpreted to be the views of the NNPC.

** John D and Catherine T MacArthur Foundation Graduate Intern, Faculty of Law, University of Ibadan, Nigeria; email: petermola@yahoo.com.

[1] A. Clerk and P. Kohler, *Property Law: Commentary and Materials* (2005) 40.

differently, companies or individuals in countries where ownership is vested in the government cannot legally extract and sell any mineral commodity without first obtaining an authorization from the government, unlike in the United States and a few other countries, where ownership of mineral resources was originally granted to the individuals or organizations that owned the land surface.[2]

This chapter will examine the property rights over petroleum *in situ* between the federal, state and local governments in a federation. The chapter will also discuss the legal character of the various property rights given to companies for exploration and development under the various petroleum licences and leases, production sharing contracts, pure service contracts, joint ventures and other petroleum arrangements, as well as the rights of communities where petroleum exploration and production activities are carried out. The chapter focuses particularly on developing countries, although, where necessary and relevant, comparisons are made with more developed economies.

II. The concept of ownership

Ownership has been viewed and defined from various angles. The concept of ownership is amorphous as it cannot yield itself easily to a general definition. The concept is amenable to the different contexts in which it is used. To Blackstone, ownership is 'that sole and despotic dominium which one claims and exercises over the external things of the world, in total exclusion of any other individual in the universe'.[3] Waldron is of the view that 'ownership expresses the abstract of an object of being correlated with the name of an individual'.[4]

Honoré conceived ownership in terms of a bundle of separate, but related rights, which includes the following:[5]

(1) The right of possession (having exclusive control over a thing or to have such control as the nature of the thing admits).
(2) The right to use the thing at one's discretion.
(3) The right to manage the thing (the right of being capable of deciding how and by whom the thing shall be used).
(4) The right to the income and the capital (an owner has an unrestricted power to alienate and liberty to consume, waste or destroy the whole or part of it).
(5) The right to security (the ability to remain indefinitely as the owner, if he chooses and if he remains solvent).
(6) The incidence of transmissibility (the interest can be transferred to another).
(7) Absence of a fixed term (the interest is for an indeterminable term).

---

[2] 'Mineral Rights', available at <http://geology.com/articles/mineral-rights.shtml>.
[3] W. Blackstone, *Commentaries on the Law of England* (1979) 2.
[4] J. Waldron, *The Right to Private Property* (1988) 47.
[5] Clerk and Kohler (above n 1) at 194–205.

(8)   The duty to prevent harm (the owner of a thing has the liberty to use the thing subject to the condition that he must not harm others and prevent others from using the thing to harm others).

(9)   Liability to execution (the owner's interest can be taken away from him for debt either by execution for judgment debt or insolvency).

(10)   Residuary character (the interest of the owner is higher than any other interest as distinguished from the interest of the lessees, licensees, etc).

Ownership therefore connotes the totality of, or the bundle of the rights of the owner over and above every other person in relation to a thing. It is the ultimate property interest and the means by which we signify the person or persons with primary control of the thing.[6] It connotes a complete and total right over a property. An owner is one who has dominion over property, the right of possession and control of property, including the right to protect and defend such possession against the intrusion or trespass of others, the right to dispose of a thing as one pleases, provided that the rights of others are not thereby infringed or some laws violated.[7] Therefore, ownership should entail the power of enjoyment; the power to determine the use to which the thing is to be put; the right to deal with, produce or to destroy the thing, as the owner pleases; possession, which includes the right to exclude others; the right of alienation *inter vivos*; and the power to charge the thing as security.[8]

The vestee of ownership of oil and gas *in situ* may be a public entity or a private person depending on what is obtainable in the jurisdiction.[9] The ownership of petroleum may be determined by many factors. It may be determined by the political history of the people. It can also be determined by the provision of the laws of the state. Individual or state ownership varies depending on the circumstances.

Under the domanial regimes, determining what constitutes ownership of petroleum *in situ* may not raise the debate as to who owns the petroleum since the law specifically vests ownership of petroleum *in situ* in the state. Owing to the principle of sovereignty, states have right to determine what constitutes ownership. Put differently, the state has right to determine and organize its property rights. The conclusion can therefore be drawn that a sovereign state can accord itself certain rights, which include the right of ownership and the control of petroleum. However, the incidence of ownership or what constitutes ownership becomes necessary in determining the point at which the sovereign or the state may be divested of ownership of petroleum, or create an interest in the petroleum property (ie when petroleum has been discovered and evacuated from the land or

---

⁶ Clerk and Kohler (above n 1) at 194.
⁷ See *Higgins Oil & Fuel Co v Guaranty Oil Co* (1919) 145 La 233.
⁸ G. W. Paton, *A Textbook of Jurisprudence* (1936) 517.
⁹ See P. N. Oche, *Petroleum Law in Nigeria—Arrangement for Upstream Operations* (2d Impression, 2004) 24–5.

has been produced, the title may shift, depending on the provision of the law or arrangement reached by the state and oil producing companies). Also, the owner of a property can transfer certain property interests in the thing in his possession, and in this case the state which owns petroleum may transfer its interest in the resources or create a lower interest out of this interest.

III. Ownership theories relating to oil and gas

There are two possible ways of resolving the issue of ownership of natural resources, such as petroleum, which are located under land:

(1) they can be said to belong to the land owner; or
(2) they can belong to the state or either the federating part or part of the state where the resources are located, such as the province, state or local government.

A. Petroleum belongs to the land owner

From the inception of the oil industry in the United States of America, there has been private ownership of mineral resources, including oil and gas, unlike in the vast majority of other jurisdictions. In the United States, ownership of petroleum is vested in the public or private owner of the land surface, or of the subsoil where the petroleum is located.[10] In certain jurisdictions, ownership of oil *in situ* is not recognized, and ownership is said to occur only when the oil has been produced and reduced into possession. This position arose in the early days of the oil industry when there was little knowledge about the movement of petroleum in the ground. What was clearly evident was that it was capable of moving from under one piece of land to the other. In *Bernard's Case*, in 1906, the court refused to prohibit drilling by the adjacent land owner alleged to be draining oil from a reservoir under the plaintiff's land, holding that the remedy was 'self-help in drilling his own well'. In 1915, Texan courts adopted another ownership concept, reasoning that oil and gas beneath the earth belonged to the person who owned the land. This regime is supported by the maxim, *cuius est solum eius usque ad coelum et ad inferos*.[11]

There are two main theories of ownership in the United States. Under the absolute ownership theory, the land owner is regarded as having title in severalty to the oil and gas in place beneath his land.[12] A land owner who extracts oil or gas from a well within the subsurface of his land acquires absolute ownership of the

---

[10] B. Taverne, *Petroleum, Industry and Governments: A Study of the Involvement of Industry and Governments in the Production and Use of Petroleum* (2nd edn, 2008) 120.

[11] Whomsoever owns the soil, owns up to the sky and down to the depths.

[12] Y. Omorogbe, *Oil and Gas Law in Nigeria* (2003) 33.

substance, even if it is drained from the subsurface of another person's land.[13] He is not a co-owner even when the reservoir straddles two or more lands, each owned by a different person. However, he loses his title to an adjacent operator if the oil from his land migrates to the adjacent land and is produced from his neighbour's well as there is no cause of action for his divestiture of title by drainage.

The state of Texas in the United States has adopted the 'ownership in place' theory for oil and gas, holding that a land owner owns a corporeal possessory interest in the substances beneath his land, but his ownership is a determinable fee subject to the rule of capture.[14] In *Kelly v Ohio Oil Co*[15] the plaintiff was a lessee of the defendant company. He brought a claim that the defendant, which operated under an adjoining lease, had in the process of drilling drained the oil, to which the plaintiff maintained that he was entitled. The court, however, maintained that petroleum is a mineral, and while in the earth is part of the realty. When it moves from one place to another by percolation or otherwise, it forms part of that tract of land in which it lies for the time being. If it moves to the next adjoining block of land it becomes part and parcel of that block and the subject of a distinct ownership and the property of the person into whose well it came. In other words, the ownership of oil and gas can be likened to ownership of wild animals (animals *ferae naturae*), and the purchaser of oil and gas assumes the hazard of their absence through the possibility of their escape from beneath that particular tract of land.[16] It follows therefore that oil and gas can travel from one spot to another until they are captured by a person. This is known as the rule of capture. As explicitly put in the case of *Ellif v Texon Drilling* Co:[17] 'the owner of a tract of land acquires title to the oil or gas which he produces from wells on his own, though the part of the oil may have migrated from adjoining lands'. The first person to capture the oil or gas owns that resource and acquires absolute ownership rights over it even if it is drained from the subsurface of another person's land.

There also exists the qualified theory of ownership, which prevails in states such as California and Indiana. Under this theory, the land owner is said not to have title to the oil and gas *in situ* because of the fact that he can be divested by drainage without consent and without any liability on the part of the person causing the drainage.[18] The basic assumption is that minerals are an integral part of the soil, whether they are located on the surface or the subsurface. Thus, exploration and exploitation rights are granted through mining leases, which are an agreement between the land owner and miner.[19] All the owners of a common reservoir are designated as collective owners, with equal rights to take oil from the reservoir.

[13] *Ohio Oil Co v Indiana* (1900) 177 US 190, 203.

[14] *Michel T Halbouty and Ors v Railroad Commission of Texas and Ors* (1962) 357 SW2d 364.

[15] (1897) 57 Ohio St 317, 49 N E 399.

[16] *Texas Company v Doherty* (1915) 176 SW 717.

[17] (1948) 146 Tex 575, 210 SW 2d 558.

[18] Omorogbe (above n 12) at 32.

[19] 'Basic Instruments and Concepts of Mineral Law', available at <http://www.natural-resources.org/minerals/education/docs/Mineral%20Law%20&%20Policy-Unit2.pdf.>.

The respective owners do not have a title to the specific oil and gas underneath their respective lands. They also do not have title as tenants in common to an undivided share of the oil and gas in the common reservoir that is the equivalent to the amount of oil under their respective lands. What each land owner has is an equal right with his co-land owner to secure his proportionate part of the oil and gas in the common reservoir through wells drilled upon his land. Thus, he has a qualified interest in the oil and gas as one of the collective owners.[20]

B. Petroleum belongs to the state or is controlled by the state

The system under which petroleum belongs to, or is controlled by the state was first known as the regalian system and originated under Roman law.[21] After the Second Punic War the Roman Empire became the owner of all the conquered lands. Mineral resources came under the ownership of the sovereign, represented by the relevant political authority, which granted permits, licences and leases for the exploration and exploitation of mineral resources.[22] According to this system, the *dominium directum* (the dominion of the soil) was vested immediately either in the Crown, or in the feudal landlords, and was separated from the *dominium utile* (the possessory title), the right to the use and profits from the soil.[23] The regalian system has been applied with different modalities ever since and later integrated, according to various theories and approaches, into the modern concept of the mining domain of the state epitomized by the domanial system.

The domanial law system provides for the vesting of ownership rights of natural resources in the sovereign. In other words, the state vests in itself mineral resources, while the land owners only have a right of compensation for the loss of surface rights.[24] The sovereignty and the control of domanial states over oil and gas and other natural resources have been explicitly spelt out in their respective constitutions as well as in petroleum and mining legislation. Some examples are given below:

The Basic Law of Governance 1992 of Saudi Arabia:[25]

All God's bestowed wealth, be it underground, on the surface, or in national territorial waters, on the land or maritime domains under the State's control, all such resources shall be the property of the State as defined by the Law. The Law shall set forth the means for exploiting, protecting, and developing such resources for the benefit, security, and economy of the State.[26]

---

[20] Omorobe (above n 12) at 33.
[21] *Basic Instruments and Concepts of Mineral Law*, available at <http://www.natural-resources. org/minerals/education/docs/Mineral%20Law%20&%20Policy-Unit2.pdf.>.
[22] ibid.
[23] ibid.
[24] I. Sagay, 'Ownership and Control of Nigerian Petroleum Resources: A Legal Angle' in *Nigerian Petroleum Business: A Handbook* (V. Eromosole, ed, 1997) 177.
[25] Royal Order No A/91.
[26] Art 14.

The Petroleum Act of Iran:[27]

The petroleum resources of the country are part of the public domain (properties and assets) and wealth and according to Article 45 of the Constitution (of the Islamic Republic of Iran) are at the disposal and control of the Government of the Islamic Republic of Iran... The authority for exercising sovereignty and ownership right over the petroleum resources and installations is vested in the Government of the Islamic Republic of Iran ...[28]

The Constitution of Kuwait 1962:

Natural resources and all revenues therefrom are the property of the State. It shall ensure their preservation and proper exploitation, due regard being given to the requirements of State security and the national economy.[29]

The Oil and Gas Act 1998 of Papua New Guinea:

Subject to this Act, but notwithstanding anything contained in any other law or in any grant, instrument of title or other document, all petroleum and helium at or below the surface of any land is, and shall be deemed at all times to have been, the property of the State.[30]

The Petroleum Law 2001 of Mozambique:[31]

All petroleum resources in situ as natural resources in the soil and the subsoil, in interior waters and in the territorial sea, on the continental shelf, and in the exclusive economic zone are the property of the State.[32]

The Constitution of the Federal Republic of Nigeria 1999 clearly states that the entire property in the control of all mineral, mineral oils and natural gas in or upon the territorial waters and the Exclusive Economic Zone of Nigeria shall vest in the Government of the Federation.[33] In the same vein, legislative powers over mines and minerals including oil fields, oil mining, geological surveys and natural gas are exclusively vested in the Nigerian National Assembly.[34] The Petroleum Act 1969 of Nigeria also stipulates that the entire ownership and control of all petroleum in, under, or upon any land is vested in the State.[35] The domanial regime has been adopted by many countries.[36]

---

[27] Available at <http://www.alaviandassociates.com/documents/petroleum.pdf>.
[28] Art 2.   [29] Art 21.   [30] S 6(1).   [31] No. 3 /2001.   [32] Art 6.
[33] S 44(3).
[34] Constitution of the Federal Republic of Nigeria, Sch 2, para 39.
[35] S 1. The Exclusive Economic Zone Act of Nigeria, s 2(1) also provides: 'Without prejudice to the Territorial Waters Act, the Petroleum Act or the Sea Fisheries Act, sovereign and exclusive rights with respect to the exploration and exploitation of the natural resources of the sea bed, sub-soil and super adjacent waters of the Exclusive Zone rest in the Federal Republic of Nigeria and such rights shall be exercisable by the Federal Government or by such minister or agency as the government may from time to time designate in that behalf either generally or in any special case.'
[36] Constitution of the Republic of Bulgaria 1991 (as amended), Art 18; Constitution of Syria 1973, Art 4.1; Constitution of Ukraine 1996, Art 13; Petroleum Act of Bangladesh 1974, s 3(1); Constitution of Iran, Art 45; Constitution of the Republic of the Sudan 1998, s 9; Petroleum (Exploration and Production) Act 1991 of Namibia, s 2; Basic Statute of the Sultanate of Oman (Royal Decree No 101/96), Art 11; Constitution of Ghana, Art 257.6; Constitution of the Republic of Yemen 1994, Art 8.

The Nigerian Supreme Court has made a judicial pronouncement on ownership of oil and gas in the country, including the extent and size of the ownership, in the case of *Attorney General of the Federation v Attorney General of Abia State (No 2)*.[37] The case, *inter alia*, held that ownership of petroleum is vested in the federal government and that state and local governments are not vested with ownership rights over oil and gas, even where such resources are located in the land occupied by these states and local governments. According to the court, the only right which the states have is an entitlement to a certain percentage of the revenue accruing from the resources derived from the oil and gas within their boundaries.[38]

The rationale behind resource-rich states maintaining control over oil and gas in their domain has a direct link to the importance of oil and gas to the economy of the producing state, to its critical importance as the world's foremost source of conventional energy, and to the sizeable revenues that accrue from the petroleum industry activities.

As petroleum is an internationally traded commodity, the evolution of property rights and regulatory arrangements in the extraction of petroleum and natural gas has also been influenced internationally. The question of ownership there has received a lot of attention in the various host countries' international fora.[39] An historical look at trends and patterns reveals a shift away from investor ownership and control towards state control and permanent sovereignty over natural resources. In the nineteenth century and the early part of the twentieth century, the tendency was for the companies charged with exploration and production of natural resources to exercise rights that amounted to sovereignty over the resources and area in question. As the host countries became more aware of the need to exercise sovereignty over natural resources, they came to resent this state of affairs. In some instances there were nationalizations, as a result of which the nationalizing state found that the investor company and its home state were insistent on international rules of compensation, which required countries to pay amounts in excess of what they could afford, and which were often far more than they felt that the companies in question merited. Thus, the developing and socialist states attempted to redress what to them was an inequitable state of affairs, and expressed their sentiments through resolutions of the United Nations General Assembly.[40]

On 21 December 1952, the General Assembly Resolution No 626 (VII) provided that:

[37] (2006) 6 NWLR Part 764, 542–905.
[38] G. Etikerentse, *Nigerian Petroleum Law* (2nd edn, 2004) 52–3.
[39] See the United Nations General Assembly Resolution Nos 626 of 1952, 1803 (XVII) of 1962, 2158 (XXI) of 1966; Chapter II of the United Nations Charter of Economic Rights and Duties of States 1974, c II, Art 2. See also Taverne (above n 10) at 120–1.
[40] Attempts had previously been made to address this problem by Latin American countries, through for example, the Calvo Clause, which incorporates the standard of national treatment for the resolution of investment disputes, as opposed to the international classical standard of prompt, adequate and effective compensation.

The right of peoples freely to use and exploit their natural wealth and resources is inherent in their sovereignty.

On 14 December 1962, the General Assembly adopted Resolution 1803 XVII on Permanent Sovereignty over Natural Resources, which provided, *inter alia*, that:

The right of peoples and nations to permanent sovereignty over their natural wealth and resources must be exercised in the interest of their national development and of the well-being of the people of the state concerned.

The resolution also declared that:

Nationalism, expropriation or requisitioning shall be based on grounds or reasons of public utility, security or the national interest. In such cases the owner shall be paid appropriate compensation, in accordance with the rules in the state taking such measures and in accordance with international law.

The above statements were reinforced in 1966 by Resolution No 2158 (XXI), which provided as follows:

Taking into account the fact that foreign capital, whether public or private, forthcoming at the request of the developing countries can play an important role inasmuch as it supplements the efforts undertaken by them in exploitation and development of natural resources, provided that there is government supervision over the activity of foreign capital to ensure that it is used in the interest of national development:

—Recognizes the right of all countries, and in particular the developing countries, to secure and increase their share in the administration of enterprises which are fully or partly operated by foreign capital and have a greater share in the advantages and profits derived therefrom on an equitable basis, with due regard to the development needs and objective of the peoples concerned...

—Considers that, when natural resources of the developing countries are exploited in particular the developing countries are exploited by foreign investors, the latter should undertake proper and accelerated training of national personnel at all levels and in all fields connected with such exploitation.

On 12 December 1974, the General Assembly adopted Resolution No 3281 (XXIX), entitled 'Charter of Economic Rights and Duties of States', which *inter alia* stated:

Every state has and shall freely exercise full permanent sovereignty, including possession, use and disposal over all of its wealth, natural resources and economic activities...

Each State has the right....

(c) to nationalize, expropriate or transfer ownership of foreign property in which case appropriate compensation shall be paid by the state adopting such measures taking into account any relevant laws and regulations and all circumstances that the state considers pertinent. In any case where the question of compensation gives rise to a controversy, it shall be settled under the domestic law of the nationalizing State and by its Tribunals, unless it is freely mutually agreed by all States concerned that other peaceful means be sought on the basis of the sovereign equality of States and in accordance with the principles of free choice of means.

The Organization of Petroleum Exporting Countries (OPEC) has also through its policies emphasized control over oil resources. The policies and actions of OPEC have since its inception been geared towards member states having control of petroleum resources in their jurisdictions. At its Sixteenth Conference held in 1968, OPEC issued Resolution XVI.90, entitled 'Declaratory Statement of Petroleum Policy in Member Countries'.[41] This resolution enjoined member states to be involved in direct development of their resources or take measures for participation in and control over all aspects of resource operations where they cannot be directly involved in such direct development.[42] Other steps to be taken include the review of existing concession contracts, the relinquishment of existing concession contracts and the determination of oil pricing by member states.[43]

These resolutions significantly contributed to the emergence of new international legal standards for the legal taking of foreign property and what those in the developing world now regard as the principle of permanent sovereignty over natural resources. They reveal a definite trend away from the traditional concepts of investor ownership, which emphasized the protection of individual rights, towards host state ownership of natural resources.[44] The effect of the resolution is to stimulate the creation of alternative legal arrangements for petroleum development, which were structured not only to enable host states to retain ownership of the resources *in situ* in their national boundaries, but at the same time to allow oil companies to conduct petroleum operations in the country.[45]

IV. Allocation of rights

A. Contractual rights for exploration, production and development

Under domanial regimes, the state exercises exclusive legal dominion over its land area, including all natural resources, such as petroleum. The sovereign may grant rights to private or public entities for the exploration and production of the state-owned oil and gas. Thus, where the state is the owner of oil and gas, the rights can be granted to companies under licences or leases. These sovereign rights are usually exercised by the head of state or minister of the government according to the terms of the law in force.[46] For instance, in Nigeria[47] and Angola,[48] the minister has the

---

[41] L. E. Cuervo, 'OPEC from Myth to Reality', available at <http://www.entrepreneur.com/tradejournals/article/180517178_5.html>.
[42] ibid.
[43] ibid.
[44] Omorogbe (above n 12) at 37.
[45] M. Yalapan, 'Legal Nature of the Papua New Guinea Petroleum Arrangement', available at <http://www.paclii.org/journals/MLJ/2003/6.html>.
[46] *Basic Instruments on Concepts of Mineral Law* (above n 21).
[47] Petroleum Act 1969 s 2.
[48] Petroleum Activities Act (Angola) Arts 8 and 37.

responsibility for granting licences on behalf of the state. Where the licensed entity operates the licensed area directly what has been granted is in fact a concession.

The earliest type of petroleum arrangement between governments and companies was the traditional concession under which oil companies received the exclusive right to explore for petroleum, and if petroleum was discovered, to produce, market and transport it.[49] The concession is the earliest type of petroleum arrangement, the original ones being granted by various sovereigns in the Middle East towards the end of the nineteenth century. The earliest concession granted to oil companies in Nigeria was under the Mineral Oil Ordinances 1914, called Exploration Rights. Such rights were obtained from the British colonial government before Nigeria became an independent nation.[50] The traditional concession was inequitable by its nature and lopsided in favour of the companies and could not survive decolonization and the new international economic order.[51]

However, there exists the modern concession under which oil companies receive exclusive rights, in exchange for the payment of all cost and specified taxes, to explore for petroleum, and if petroleum is found, to produce, market and transport it. The oil company has rights over the produced petroleum and 'owns' it at the point of extraction. Today the modern concession is called by various names such as licence, lease, etc.

The Production Sharing Contract (PSC) is a method under which an oil company can acquire oil rights for the exploration and production through agreement with the state. The PSC originated from Indonesia and the Indonesian PSCs take the following forms: ownership of mineral resources are retained by the state and concessions are not granted to the IOCs, the IOCs are not liable for any related compensation, such as surface and/or proportional royalties, and have no ownership of petroleum production, but are only allocated cost oil and profit oil at an agreed location point, usually the connection point between storage and loading facilities. The PSCs are tax free as all operations are carried out in the name of the state.[52]

In a PSC, the oil company bears the risk of exploration, and is often in charge of the operations and management of the contract area. Where oil is discovered in commercial quantities, the company is entitled to recoup its investment from the crude oil produced from the contract area. A PSC allows the contractor a quantity of oil to ensure adequate return on investment, and the contractor can dispose of oil to meet its tax and royalty obligation.[53] The portion of oil meant for recouping is referred to as cost recovery, which is normally about 20 to 50 per cent,[54] while the remainder is shared between the National Oil Company

---

[49] Y. Omorogbe, *The Oil & Gas Industry: Exploration and Production Contracts* (1997) 58.
[50] M. M. Gidado, *Petroleum Development Contracts with the Multinationals in Nigeria* (1999) 119.
[51] Omorogbe (above n 49) at 59.
[52] N. Bonnefoy and G. L. Nouel, 'Petroleum Legal Regimes in the Gulf of Guinea', available at <http://www.gide.com/front/files/EuromoneyYearbook_GLN_PetroleumLegalRegimesinGuinea_oct2005.pdf>.
[53] A. Oshineye, 'Petroleum Industry in Nigeria: An Overview' (2000) 4 MPJFIL 325 at 338–44.
[54] But could normally even go as high as 100% as in the case of PSCs signed in Nigeria in 1993.

and the company in predetermined proportions.[55] The contractor is allowed to freely export its cost recovery oil and its share of profit oil but there may be certain restrictions, which include the right of the state party to purchase at market price.[56] However, ownership of petroleum under this arrangement is vested in the state and the oil company contractor can only lay claim to the proportion of petroleum it is entitled to after extraction. The legal rationale behind the use of the PSC is that from the host government's standpoint, it does not involve the surrender of the host country's sovereignty in the title to the resource; rather, by entering into such a contract, the company receives an interest in the oil, which is less than ownership.[57]

Within the Gulf of Guinea, with the exception of Congo-Kinshasa and Chad (which use only concessions), Nigeria, Sao Tome and Principe, Angola, Gabon, Congo-Brazzaville, Cameroon, and Equatorial Guinea have implemented the PSC regime.[58]

A variant of the PSC is the risk service contract, which has been extensively used in countries like Brazil, Argentina and Colombia.[59] Under the risk service contract, the contractor provides the entire risk capital for exploration and production, and where there is no discovery the contract ceases to exist with no obligation on either party.[60] Where there is a commercial discovery and subsequently development leading to the production of petroleum, the contractor is entitled to recover (with interest) its funding and to recover additional compensation in cash (not in production).[61]

The pure service contract is a simple contract of service. Under this arrangement, risks and costs are borne by the state. The contractor is in turn paid a flat fee for its services, as stipulated in the contract between the state and the oil company. This type of arrangement is common in Saudi Arabia, Kuwait, Qatar, Bahrain and Abu Dhabi.[62] The contractor is under the obligation to carry out the exploration, development and production operations, and the host government may take control of productions from the date of commencement of production.[63] One legal consequence flowing from this arrangement is that the oil company or contractor has no right or any claim to the petroleum discovered as it is paid for the services rendered.

---

[55] Omorogbe (above n 49) at 60.

[56] Taverne (above n 10) at 148.

[57] M. Yalapan, 'Legal Nature of the Papua New Guinea Petroleum Arrangement' (2003), available at <http://www.paclii.org/journals/MLJ/2003/6.html>.

[58] N. Bonnefoy and G.L. Nouel, 'Petroleum Legal Regimes in the Gulf of Guinea', available at <http://www.gide.com/front/files/EuromoneyYearbook_GLN_PetroleumLegalRegimesinGuinea_oct2005.pdf.>.

[59] The risk service contract originated from Iran under the Petroleum Act of 1974. See also Taverne (above n 10) at 157.

[60] Omorogbe (above n 12) at 42.

[61] Taverne (above n 10) at 156–7.

[62] ibid at 43.

[63] Gidado (above n 50) at 174.

Under the joint venture agreement, the state acquires participatory interests in exploration and production taking place within its territories. Most states under the domanial regime have in their legislative provisions the right to participate in oil and gas exploration, development, marketing and export. Often, the law in force will give the government the right to participate.[64] Usually the participation and the extent of the rights are negotiated between the state and the oil companies. Each partner in the joint venture contributes to the cost and shares the benefit or losses in accordance with its proportionate equity interest in the partnership.[65] Since the 1970s, participation by host countries in their mineral and oil rights has become increasingly common.[66] Participation can be exercised in respect of an area being produced under a concession, PSC or service contract, as the case may be.

The percentage of state participation may be fixed by legislation.[67] Under the Oil and Gas Act 1998 of Papua New Guinea, for instance, the State of Papua New Guinea has enshrined the state's right to a 22.5 per cent stake in any project.[68] Under the Petroleum Activities Law of Angola, Sonangol holds a participating interest, which shall exceed 50 per cent.[69] However, the government may authorize the National Concessionaire, in duly grounded cases, to hold a lesser participating interest.[70]

The participation relationship is governed by other agreements, which coexist with the fundamental contract. These agreements define the relationships of the respective parties. Invariably, there will be a participation agreement, which sets out the interest of the parties in the concession, and an operating agreement, which spells out the legal relationship between the owners of the leases and lays down the rules and procedures for joint development of the area and joint property.

Contracts for exploration and production are constantly evolving as the international investment climate changes, and in line with the need for host countries and international oil companies. However, all these arrangements are essentially concerned with the allocation of rights between the parties.

B. Rights of a licensee or lessee

The allocation of rights to oil and gas is also regulated through legislative processes, which in some instances are indistinguishable from the contractual process. The terms 'licence' and 'lease' are often used interchangeably. Thus, a licence in one jurisdiction can confer the same rights as a lease in another jurisdiction. In some jurisdictions a lease gives more power to a lessee than does a licence.

Licence and lease holders are regulated by the terms of the instrument creating them usually contained within laws or regulations, and have obligations to carry out petroleum operations within a defined time frame.

---

[64] Taverne (above n 10) at 131.   [65] Oshineye (above n 53) at 325–44.
[66] Omorogbe (above n 12) at 64.   [67] Taverne (above n 10) at 132.
[68] S 165.   [69] Art 15.1.   [70] Art 15.2.

There are different types of licences for different phases of activity, and these may be exclusive or non-exclusive. The rights granted under the licence therefore may be exclusive or non-exclusive. The initial licence is often an exploration licence.

In Nigeria, the law provides for an Exploration Licence (OEL),[71] which expires on 31 December of the year when the grant was made and may not be longer in duration than one calendar year. The right granted is non-exclusive and several persons may be issued with licences in respect of the same area.[72] The activities which the licensee has the right to conduct consist of 'preliminary searches by surface, geological and geophysical methods, including aerial surveys but excluding drilling below 91.44 metres'.[73] In practice, Exploration Licences are rarely given in Nigeria today. Instead, an exploration phase is included as part of the Production Sharing Contract and is therefore, in practice, exclusive to the Production Sharing Contract. It should be noted that under such contracts, the licences or leases are held by the national oil company.

In Nigeria, the Oil Prospecting Licence (OPL)[74] confers exclusive rights of surface and subsurface exploration for the production of petroleum in an area not more than 2,590 square kilometres. (1,000 square miles) in size. The OPL is granted in inland basins for an initial period of three years with the option of renewal for a maximum period of two years. For the deep water frontier blocks and basins the exploration period is ten years, broken into two five-year periods which automatically roll over unless otherwise withdrawn due to non-performance.

Nigeria also recognizes the Oil Mining Lease (OML),[75] which grants exclusive rights to explore, win, produce and carry away petroleum from the relevant area. The regulation size is 1,295 square kilometres (500 square miles) and the specified duration is 20 years. A licensee who has fulfilled the work commitment according to paras 30(b) and 31 of the Petroleum (Drilling and Production) Regulations 1969 and the conditions otherwise applicable to the individual licence may demand that the licence be converted to an OML. An OML is granted upon confirmation of the potential for economic production of petroleum from the licence. Only the holder of an OPL is entitled to apply for the conversion of an Oil Prospecting Licence to an Oil Mining Lease. The production of 25,000 barrels per day will be required as the minimum production level (commercial quantity) for the conversion of a deep offshore OPL to an OML. However, for other areas a production level of 10,000 barrels per day is required, as specified in the Petroleum Act 1969 (as amended).[76]

---

[71] Petroleum Act 1969 (Nigeria) s 2(1)(a).
[72] Etikerentse (above n 38) at 63.
[73] ibid.
[74] Petroleum Act 1969 (Nigeria) s 2(1)(b).
[75] Petroleum Act 1969 (Nigeria) s 2(1)(c).
[76] Sch I, s 2(8) and (9).

In Papua New Guinea, there are three types of upstream petroleum licences issued and administered by the government through the Department of Petroleum and Energy. These are: the Petroleum Prospecting Licence (PPL),[77] the Petroleum Retention Licence (PRL)[78] and the Petroleum Development Licence (PDL).[79] They can be granted to applicants by the state through the Minister for Petroleum and Energy. [80] The first three licences are granted during the exploration, production and development phases. As in the case of Nigeria, the Petroleum Prospecting Licence in Papua New Guinea is issued to a company for the purpose of embarking on petroleum exploration.[81] The Petroleum Development Licence, on the other hand, is issued to a holder of a Petroleum Prospecting Licence upon commercial discovery of petroleum, to produce and deal with the petroleum produced within the acreage.[82] Section 25 of the Oil and Gas Act 1998 states that:

A petroleum prospecting licence, while it remains in force, confers on the licensee, subject to this Act, and to the conditions specified in the licence, the exclusive right to explore for petroleum, and to carry out appraisal of a petroleum discovery, and to carry on such operations and execute such works as are necessary for those purposes, in the licence area, including the construction and operations of water lines, tests for appraisal of a petroleum pool (including the construction in accordance with the authorization and disposal), and the recovery and sale or other disposal of all petroleum so produced.

For the purpose of granting an exploration or a production licence, the earth's surface is divided up into gratucular sections (called 'blocks'), comprising five minutes longitude and five minutes latitude (the equivalent of 9 kilometres x 9 kilometres, ie 81 square kilometres).[83] An application for a Petroleum Prospecting Licence may be made in respect of not more than 60 blocks[84] and in special circumstances the minimum acreage may be increased to 200 blocks. A Petroleum Prospecting Licence is granted for a term not exceeding six years[85] and is renewable for a further term of five years but for a reduced area,[86] and is also subject to work and expenditure requirements.[87]

An exploration licensee may also exclusively apply for a Petroleum Retention Licence in respect of blocks within the exploration acreage in which petroleum is located.[88] The purpose is to allow holders of an exploration licence to retain and hold natural gas discoveries within the acreage pending the commercial

---

[77] Oil and Gas Act 1998 (Papua New Guinea) s 23.
[78] S 40.   [79] S 57.
[80] 'Papua New Guinea', available at <http://www.ccop.or.th/epf/png/png_terms.html>.
[81] Oil and Gas Act 1998 (Papua New Guinea) s 23.
[82] ibid s 57.
[83] M. Yalapan, 'Legal Nature of the Papua New Guinea Petroleum Arrangement' (2003), available at <http://www.paclii.org/journals/MLJ/2003/6.html>.
[84] Oil and Gas Act 1998 (Papua New Guinea) s 22(1)(c).
[85] S 26(a).   [86] S 26(b).   [87] S 22.
[88] ibid s 37.

extraction of the gas.[89] In Papua New Guinea, therefore, the treatment of title to petroleum *in situ* is consistent with the new concession arrangement, where title to petroleum is owned by the state, but upon production, the title in the petroleum produced shifts from the state to production licensees.

Where the licence issued to the licensee is a production licence, it confers ownership of the petroleum, if and when produced, on the holder of the licence.[90] A holder of the production licence can assert ownership of the petroleum once it has been extracted from the land or at the point the petroleum enters its well. However, before production the petroleum *in situ* remains the property of the state as a licensee cannot make a legal claim to it. As stated above, the same rule is applicable to the holder of a lease. It must be noted that though the licensee or lessor has a right over the petroleum produced, they are still subject to the payment of a petroleum tax or royalty, as the case may be.

A petroleum lease gives the lessee a property interest in the petroleum. In order to secure the lease, annual rental payments or a royalty on production is usually paid to the lessor by the lessee. The oil and gas lease has the legal nature of creating a right to take something from the soil owned by another person or entity.[91] It is an interest that authorizes the removal of a substance contained in the land. The lessee does not acquire an absolute ownership interest in the land but does acquire a proprietary interest in the substances removed when the petroleum has been brought to the surface.[92] Drilling companies do not always own the land they seek to drill on. Rather, the companies own the mineral rights, mineral estate, on a property owned by another party. Lessees of oil and gas rights have a right of reasonable access to the leased land to explore, develop and transport minerals.

C. Rights of contractors

Contractual arrangements within the petroleum industry have arisen from the desire of states to exercise both ownership and control over natural resources. The first change was to assert ownership through the various avenues described above, and then to enter into new legal arrangements that emphasized this fact. Under the various contracts, the oil company is the contractor to the licence holder, usually the national oil company, with the distribution of rights and duties depending on the type of contract.

In Angola, the ownership of the state is emphasized. Article 12.1 of the Angolan Constitution 1992, which upholds the domanial ownership principles, states that:

---

[89] M. Yalapan, 'Legal Nature of the Papua New Guinea Petroleum Arrangement' (2003), available at <http://www.paclii.org/journals/MLJ/2003/6.html>.

[90] Taverne (above n 10) at 177.

[91] L. Lytwyn, 'Oil and Gas Law', available at <http://www.articlearchives.com/law-legal-system/trial-procedure-jurisdiction/1519099-1.html>.

[92] Etikerentse (above n 38) at 66.

All natural resources existing in the soil and subsoil, in internal and territorial waters, on the continental shelf and in the exclusive economic area, shall be the property of the State, which shall determine under what terms they are used, developed and exploited.

Article 3 of the Angolan Petroleum Activities Law 2004[93] further maintains the fundamental principle of state ownership of petroleum resources, and states that:

petroleum deposits existing in the areas mentioned in Article 1 are an integral part of the public property of the State.

The areas mentioned in Article 1 are '... the surface and subsurface areas of the Angolan national territory, inland waters, territorial waters, exclusive economic zone and the continental shelf'.

Mining rights are granted by the government to the national oil company, Sociedade Nacional de Combustível de Angola, Empresa Pública, popularly known as Sonangol.[94] Sonangol cannot transfer its mining rights, whether in all or in part, and any actions to that effect are deemed null and void.[95]

Any company that wishes to carry out petroleum operations in the territory of Angola outside the scope of a prospecting licence may only do so together or in association with Sonangol.[96] The associates of Sonangol may only assign part or all of their contractual rights and duties to third parties of recognized capacity, technical knowledge and financial capability, after obtaining the prior consent of the supervising minister by means of an Executive Decree.[97] Also, the transfer to third parties of shares representing more than 50 per cent of the share capital of the assignor is deemed to be the equivalent to the assignment of contractual rights and duties.[98] Sonangol is also permitted to carry out petroleum operations by means of risk services agreements.[99]

The rights of the contractor are usually spelt out in the agreement of the parties. The contractor carries out its obligation with the understanding that it has no ownership of the oil and gas beneath the land and cannot exercise any right incidental to the ownership of the oil and gas *in situ* except as provided in the arrangement. The state is in all respects the owner of the oil and gas *in situ* and exercises sovereignty over them. The state therefore participates out of the desire to acquire a greater share of profit from oil and gas exploration and production within their domain, and at the same time exercises control over exploration and production.

D. Rights of communities

Under the domanial regime, the oil communities where the oil and gas are discovered cannot lay claim to ownership rights over the oil and gas *in situ*. However, they are entitled to certain rights. They may be entitled to compensation for

---

[93] Law No 10/04. [94] Art 4.1. [95] Art 5. [96] Art 13. [97] Art 16.1.
[98] Art 16.2. [99] Art 14.3.

environmental damage. People should have the right to participate in decision making and the rule of law is extended to their communities. With the damaging effect of oil exploration, the communities have the right to compensation and they should also be entitled to the right of development in their area. In Nigeria, oil production has had damaging effects on the environment of the oil producing communities. The extent of the damage is subject to dispute leading to civil litigation with the oil companies in Nigeria, which insists that their activities are conducted according to the highest environmental standards.[100]

Most communities would hold the view that oil wealth derived from their land should be theirs and the communities ought to be concerned with and involved in the management and distribution of the proceeds of petroleum production. Communities view their rights beyond a mere share in the proceeds, and want control and management of the petroleum located under their land. The rights of communities in the control and management of petroleum resources are inextricably linked with the desire to play a direct role in petroleum exploration and production. Thus, embedded in the community interest in the petroleum, is the right to participate in the development of petroleum and allocation of proceeds accruing from the resources in the development of their areas.

It is therefore normal that the state should return part of the proceeds to the communities where such resources are derived. The understanding that the communities are entitled to benefit from the petroleum exploration and production in their areas gives a clear indication that there exist in these communities certain levels of interest which they are to be ordinarily entitled to, since petroleum is derived from their land. Therefore, although the laws under the domanial systems vest ownership in the state, one cannot dismiss the fact that certain groups of persons reside in the area where the petroleum is located. Such communities may further rationalize that they should control the mode and management of commercial production of oil and gas discovered in their communities. In other words, since the land on which the oil and gas discovered are located lies within such oil communities, the communities should have far-reaching decision-making powers as to the organization and entitlement rights in relation to oil and gas exploration and production in their communities. Consequently, an oil company has the social responsibility of contributing to the development of the area of its operation through the provision of social amenities and ensuring that it takes all necessary steps to check against environmental degradation. It is immaterial whether the oil companies have paid their taxes, rents and royalties. Oil producing communities should have the right benefit from the revenue accruing from oil and gas exploration and production in their areas.

---

[100] Human Rights Watch, 'The Price of Oil: Corporate Responsibility and Human Rights Violations in Nigeria's Oil Producing Communities' (1999), available at <http://www.hrw.org/legacy/reports/1999/nigeria/>.

E. Rights of state/provincial and local governments where ownership is not vested in them

The domanial system, *stricto sensu*, vests ownership rights to oil and gas in the central government. This raises the issue as to the nature of the rights that can accrue to the state/provincial and local governments in states where the domanial regime operates. Such an issue may arise in countries where state/ provincial or local government ownership of petroleum exists. For instance, the Canadian Constitution explicitly grants ownership of all lands, mines, minerals and royalties to the original provinces of Ontario, Québec, Nova Scotia and New Brunswick.[101] Also, on the entry of the provinces of British Columbia, Prince Edward Island and Newfoundland into Canada, they were granted ownership of the mineral resources from the federal government. Only the prairie provinces of Alberta, Saskatchewan and Manitoba were not initially granted ownership of the mines and minerals upon entry into Canada as these interests remained vested in the federal government. In 1930, subject to certain exceptions such as land located in national parks and on Indian Reserves, the federal government transferred these interests to the prairie Provinces.[102] Section 92A of the Constitution Act 1867, added in 1982, now confers on the provinces exclusive jurisdiction to make laws in relation to the exploration, development, conservation and management of oil and gas and other non-renewable resources. With the exception of freehold estates, the federal government still owns and administers the mines and minerals located outside of the provincial boundaries in the three Territories.[103] The federal government has also retained mineral ownership in Canadian offshore areas,[104] but federal–provincial agreements implemented by legislation are in force for Newfoundland and Nova Scotia.

Unlike in some Canadian provinces, where oil and gas *in situ* may be owned by the provincial government, under the domanial regime oil and gas may be located in areas not under the control of the central government but in the control of the state/provinces. In this case, the oil and gas in such land is still the property of the central government. In such a situation, the rights that can accrue to the state or provinces may be in the form of compensation for the use of their surface rights, a share in the revenue accruing from production and exploration of oil and gas, and the acquisition of a participatory interest in an oil company through shares, etc.

Interestingly, the Oil and Gas Act 1998 of Papua New Guinea contains provisions for the grant of benefits arising from projects for the production of

---

[101] Constitution Act 1867 s 109.
[102] Blake, Cassels & Graydon LLP, *Oil & Gas Law in Canada,* available at <http://www.blakes.com/english/legal_updates/reference_guides/Overview%20of%20O&G%20Law%20In%20Canada.pdf>.
[103] ibid.   [104] ibid.

petroleum, the processing and transportation to land owners, provincial governments and local governments. Some of these provisions will now be examined.

These benefits include equity and royalty benefits. A part of the equity benefits accruing to the state for participation in petroleum projects must be granted to land owners and the local government where the petroleum production is situated.[105] Such equity benefits granted must be shared between the project area land owners and the affected local governments in proportions agreed by them in a development agreement, but in default of such agreement in the proportions determined by the minister, by instrument.[106]

Royalty benefits are granted by the state to the project area land owners, the affected local governments and the affected provincial governments of the land where the petroleum project is located.[107] Such royalty benefit granted is shared between the project area land owners and the affected local and provincial governments in proportions agreed by them in a development agreement, but in default of such agreement in the proportions determined by the minister, by instrument.[108]

If, in respect of a petroleum project, there is more than one affected local government, the equity benefit and royalty benefit granted to the affected local governments shall, unless otherwise agreed in writing by the affected local governments and the state, be shared between those affected local governments in proportion to the number of project area land owners who receive those benefits in respect of that project who reside within the jurisdiction of each affected local government.[109] If there is more than one affected provincial government, the royalty benefit granted to the affected local governments shall, unless otherwise agreed in writing by the affected local governments and the state, be shared between those affected provincial governments in proportion to the number of project area landowners who receive a royalty benefit in respect of that project who reside within the jurisdiction of each affected provincial government.[110]

In addition to equity and royalty benefits, the state must in a development agreement, and may in any other agreement, agree with the affected local and provincial governments of a petroleum project upon the amount, nature and timing of grants to be made by the state to those affected governments in relation to the petroleum project.[111]

On the extent of the benefit to be granted, s 174(1) provides that:

The total benefits granted in accordance with this Act to project area landowners and affected Local-level Governments and affected Provincial Governments and any other persons or organizations shall not, when added to other costs incurred by the State in the course of the development or operation of a petroleum project, exceed 20 per cent of the total net benefit to the State from that petroleum project as determined in a cost-benefit

---

[105] S 167(3).   [106] S 167(4).   [107] S 168(1).   [108] S 168(2).
[109] S 172(1).   [110] S 172(2).   [111] S 173(1) and (2).

analysis under Section 116 of the Organic Law on Provincial Governments and Local-level Governments.

Affected provincial governments, local governments and project area land owners of a petroleum project are at liberty to negotiate with a licensee to acquire from the licensee, on freely negotiated commercial terms, a participating interest in a petroleum project.[112]

V. Critical issues for states such as Nigeria

The nature of property rights in the Nigerian oil and gas sector raises critical issues: the issue of resource control and the emergence of militancy in the Niger Delta region, the environmental degradation of oil producing communities, the adequacy of compensation due to damage to subsurface and environmental pollution, and the extent of the corporate social responsibility of the oil companies carrying out petroleum exploration and production activities within the oil producing communities.

The issue of the allocation of rights is of great significance in Nigeria, and has been raging for decades. In fact, most of the festering conflicts in the Niger Delta area are rooted in the allocation of rights and benefits derived from natural resources, and the term 'resource control' within the country refers to any issue that is concerned with this matter.

The agitation for resource control raises three issues:[113]

- the power and the right of a community to raise funds by way of a tax on persons, matters, services and materials within its territory;
- the executive right to the ownership and control of resources, both natural and created within its territory; and
- the right to customs duties on goods destined for its territory and excise duties on goods manufactured in its territories.

For the communities of the Niger Delta, resource control signifies a change in the demands the communities from 'fairer sharing to total control of the natural resources found in a state by the state for use in its development at its own pace'.[114]

The fighting and agitation by various groups, ethnic militias, communities and political associations, and even the state government, have raise arguments as to the justification of the domanial regime in the country. Good examples of

---

[112] S 175(1).
[113] E. Osaghae, A. Ikelegbe, O. Olarinmoye, and S. Okhonmina, 'Youth Militias, Self Determination and Resource Control Struggles in the Niger-Delta Region of Nigeria', available at <http://www.ascleiden.nl/Pdf/cdpnigeriaRevisedOsaghae%5B1%5D2.pdf>.
[114] ibid.

the agitation are the Calabar-Ogoja-Rivers movement of 1953, the creation of the Midwest Region in 1963 and other Niger Delta states, the Isaac Adaka Boro-led Ijaw revolt of 1966, the Ogoni crisis and other resistance struggles, the increasing protests directed at oil companies' activities and the lack of development in the delta region, incidents of hostage taking, closures of flow stations, sabotage, and intimidation of staff. All of these activities are rooted in the agitation for resource control or sovereignty over natural resources.[115]

From a legal perspective, the case of *Attorney General of the Federation v Attorney General of Abia State*[116] typifies the struggle for resource control in Nigeria. Section 162(2) of the Constitution of the Federal Republic of Nigeria 1999, provides:

[T]he President, upon the receipt of advice from the Revenue Mobilization allocation and Fiscal Commission, shall table before the National Assembly proposals for revenue allocation from the Federation Account, and in determining the formula, the National Assembly shall take into account, the allocation principles especially those of population, equality of States, internal revenue generation, land mass, terrain as well as population density:

Provided that the principle of derivation shall be constantly reflected in any approved formula as being not less than 13 per cent of the revenue accruing to the Federation Account directly from any natural resources.

The proviso to the subsection, with respect to natural resources, entrenches the principle of derivation in any formula the National Assembly may come up with. By this principle 'not less than 13 per cent' of the revenue accruing to the Federation Account directly from any natural resources shall be payable to a state of the Federation from which such natural resources are derived. For a state to qualify for this allocation of funds from the Federation Account, the natural resources must have come from within the boundaries of the state, that is, the resources must be located within that state.

In February 2001 the federal government of Nigeria filed a suit at the Supreme Court of Nigeria in respect of a dispute between the federal government, on the one hand, and the eight littoral states of Akwa Ibom, Bayelsa, Cross-River, Delta, Lagos, Ogun, Ondo and Rivers States, on the other hand, as to the southern (or seaward) boundary of each of these states. The federal government contended that the southern (or seaward) boundary of each of these states is the low-water mark of the land surface of such state or the seaward limit of inland waters within the state, as the case so requires. The federal government, therefore, maintained that natural resources located within the Continental Shelf of Nigeria are not

---

[115] For instance, the Kaiama Declaration of 11 December 1999 states: 'All land and natural resources (including mineral resources) within the Ijaw territory belong to the Ijaw communities and are the basis of our survival.' See 'The Kaiama Declaration', *The Vanguard*, 25 January 1999, 7, cited in Oche (above n 9) at 36.
[116] (2006) 6 NWLR Part 764, 542–905.

derivable from any state of the Federation. The eight littoral states did not agree with the federal government contentions. Each claimed that its territory extended beyond the low-water mark to the territorial water and even to the continental shelf and the exclusive economic zone. The states maintained that natural resources derived from both onshore and offshore areas are derivable from their respective territory and in respect thereof each is entitled to the 'not less than 13 per cent' allocation as provided in the proviso to s 162(2) of the Constitution.

All the states in the Federation were joined as defendants in the action. The issues raised *inter alia* in the matter included:

- What is the southern or seaward boundary of each of the eight littoral states for the purpose of calculating the amount of revenue accruing to the Federation Account directly from the natural resources derived from the state, or what is the procedure for making provision for the formula for distributing the amount standing to the credit of the Federation Account pursuant to s 162 of the Constitution?
- As from what moment in time do the state governments become entitled to receive their share of the amount standing to the credit of the Federation Account?

The Supreme Court held that the seaward boundary of a littoral state within the Federal Republic of Nigeria for the purpose of calculating the amount of revenue accruing to the Federation Account directly from natural resources derived from that state pursuant to s 162(2) of the Constitution is the low-water mark of the surface or the inland waterways. Thus, the Supreme Court affirmed the federal government's ownership and control of natural resources within its territory and also affirmed that the states have no title to off-shore natural resources.[117] The consequences of this judgment include the fact that in Nigeria, states where natural resources have been derived are entitled to a certain percentage of the revenue accruing to the nation from such states. States/provinces and local governments cannot on any account exercise sovereignty over natural resources in their domain.

However, in spite of the settled position as to the ownership of natural resources, the issue of resource control still rages on as the people in the Niger Delta region still advocate that they should have the access to and control of the resources derived from their area. Central to the Niger Delta issue is the yearning to have a greater participation in petroleum resources in the region. It has been expressed as the need for freedom to dispose of petroleum resources and negotiate their alienation without the federal government's intervention. The majority of the Niger Delta people hold the view that oil-rich communities or states should be able to embark independently on the exploration and production of resources

---

[117] L. Atsegua, *Oil and Gas Law in Nigeria: Theory and Practice* (2004) 9–31.

and determine how the resources are to be utilized. Most oil communities wish to have ownership and control of the resources in their area.

Oil companies are expected to pay compensation for surface rights for trees, crops and properties on land acquired to be cleared for operations, damage caused to properties, including aquatic resources if impacted by spill or harmful chemicals, and inconveniences such as noise, etc.[118] Compensation has frequently been the subject of litigation between the communities and the oil producing companies. Communities have expressed concern as to environmental degradation caused by exploration and production. It must be noted that oil companies, whether enshrined in any legislation or arrangement or not, must ensure that they carry out their corporate social responsibility to ensure that there are development dividends in the communities where activities are conducted and that compensation is adequate and timely.

VI. Conclusion

The development of property rights in the developing countries that have adopted the domanial regime is largely shaped by the level of technology and the strategic importance of oil and natural gas to the economic development of the state. In other words, the nature of property rights in most oil producing countries has been largely influenced by the need for the state to exert control over petroleum and other natural resources. The level of technological development of the country goes a long way in determining the extent of the right granted to international oil companies. Thus, where the state lacks the technological know-how to explore and produce the oil and gas *in situ*, the proper step taken by it is to enter into negotiation or other forms of arrangement with international oil companies under statutory provisions or separate agreement, the incidence of which flows with the bundle of rights. Also connected with these rights are duties.

Under the domanial regime, the state exercises sovereign ownership over the oil and gas within its jurisdiction as well as legislative competence in the regulation of the oil industry. Most states have legislation governing the exploration, production and transfer of oil and gas rights. However, while there are variations among states as to the nature and extent of property rights granted, the area of convergence is that the state legally maintains the principle of sovereignty over the natural resources within its domain.

As examined in this chapter, it can be rightly concluded that there are various types of petroleum arrangements with varied rights and obligations arising from them. Many oil producing states that operate the domanial regime of ownership have opened their oil and gas sectors to investment by international

---

[118] C. Agim, 'Understanding Community Relations in Nigeria's Oil Industry' in *Nigerian Petroleum Business: A Handbook* (V. E. Eromosole, ed, 1997) 135–6.

oil companies through contractual arrangements such as concessions, royalty/ tax systems, production-sharing agreements and/or risk service agreements, joint venture and other hybrid arrangement, which have evolved to suit the needs of respective countries. In exercising its sovereignty over natural resources, the government must ensure that the rights of investors and other stakeholders are well defined without compromising the economic development of the state. In this context, suitable arrangements should be made to ensure a favourable investment climate.

In exercising its oil and gas rights, the state may often be faced by pressure in exercising control over the disposition of these resources in pursuit of economic development objectives by oil companies, the communities, states/provinces and the local government. In so doing the state must take into account the rights of the land owners and the communities. The resources, being the common heritage of the state, should be harnessed for the benefit of all.

7

The Rule of Capture: The Least Worst Property Rule for Oil and Gas

*Terence Daintith**

I. The capture rule

A. The American story

There can be few legal rules that have survived for so long in the face of constant criticism, indeed vilification, as has the rule of capture as applied to oil and gas. The rule states that oil and gas become the property of the owner of the land on which they are recovered by lawful drilling or other operations, regardless of whether they might have migrated from their original position under the land of another.[1] In the United States, where commercial oil production began in 1859, it has been judicially recognized since 1886[2] and is still in force there today, despite attracting such epithets as 'theft',[3] 'law of the jungle',[4] and 'absurd, almost idiotic'[5] during its long and unloved life. Its critics have had no difficulty in demonstrating that the rule has induced behaviour which has led to an extraordinary waste of oil and gas resources in the United States, notably—though not exclusively—in the period from the first beginnings of the industry in the 1860s through to the widespread

* Professor of Law, University of Western Australia, and Professorial Fellow, Institute of Advanced Legal Studies, University of London, United Kingdom; email: terence.daintith@dbmail.com. This chapter is based on research for the author's forthcoming book, *Finders Keepers? How the Law of Capture Has Shaped the World Oil Industry* (2010). Research support from the Australian Resources and Energy Law Association (AMPLA) is gratefully acknowledged.
  [1] R. Hardwicke, 'The Rule of Capture and its Implications as Applied to Oil and Gas' (1935) 13 Texas Law Review 391 at 393.
  [2] *Wood County Petroleum Co v West Virginia Transportation Co* (1886) 28 W Va 10 (W Va). This case preceded the more commonly cited *Westmoreland & Cambria Natural Gas Co v De Witt* (1889) 130 Pa 235; 18 Atl 724 (Pa).
  [3] Conclusions of Advocate-General Spier, para 8.02, in *Unocal v Conoco* Case (2005) C04/127 (Netherlands Hoge Raad).
  [4] J. Keen, 'Commonwealth Draft Guidelines for Trans-boundary Unitisations and the Rule of Capture' [1998] AMPLA Yearbook 433 at 438.
  [5] J. Ise, *The United States Oil Policy* (1926) 217.

application of limits on oil and gas production from the late 1920s onwards.[6] Where, as has been the norm in the United States, the land surface above an oil reservoir was divided into a number of separate holdings, and where the oil rights on each might be leased to a different operator, there inevitably followed a race among lessees, egged on by land owners anxious for their royalty cheques, to be the first to drill, and thus to exploit the high natural reservoir pressures that would drive the oil to the surface. Those pressures, however, would quickly be exhausted by the very fact of the drilling of large numbers of wells—numbers far greater than the efficient exploitation of the reservoir demanded or permitted. The waste of capital on unnecessary wells was enormous; so too were the waste of gas, flared or blown off as or before oil was produced in quantities large enough to meet the energy needs of several large American cities every year, and the waste of oil left in the ground as a result of loss of reservoir pressure through indiscriminate drilling. In addition, the sudden massive increases in production caused by the frenetic exploitation of major new fields resulted in vertiginous falls in prices, major storage losses, and the premature shutting in of higher-cost but still productive wells.

The nature and extent of these problems began to be appreciated in the early years of the twentieth century and by 1930 was acknowledged by almost all sectors of the industry: yet the campaign that had then begun to eliminate the effects of the rule—if not the rule itself—by requiring that each oil reservoir be developed as a unit, without regard for the man-made divisions of the land lying above it and hence without any need for competitive drilling,[7] enjoyed, and continues to enjoy, only modest success.[8] Achieving voluntary agreement to unitize a field, especially at an early stage of development when there is much uncertainty about reservoir characteristics, has always been difficult.[9] While most States (except Texas) now have some form of compulsory unitization legislation, its scope is limited and its operation burdensome. Most State oil industry regulators do not even know how much oil and gas in the State is produced from unitized fields and how much is not. Yet it is only under a unitization regime that the problems of capture can be fully addressed. Rather than address the problem of waste at its source, the governments of the oil-producing States, at the urging of the industry itself, set off down a regulatory path that led not to the irrelevance of the rule of capture but to its survival within a network of regulatory restrictions whose main aim was to restrain oil production to levels that would ensure an acceptable minimum price for crude oil. This form of control, known as prorationing, under which each well or lease was restricted to a fraction—sometimes

---

[6] For one among many sources see H. Williams, 'Conservation of Oil and Gas' (1951) 65 Harvard Law Review 1155.

[7] See generally R. Hardwicke, *Antitrust Laws, et al v Unit Operation of Oil and Gas Pools* (1961).

[8] The amount of production from unitized fields in 1975 varied between 82% (Wyoming) and 20% (Texas): G. Libecap and S. Wiggins, 'The Influence of Private Contractual Failure on Regulation: The Case of Oil Field Unitization' (1985) 93 Journal of Political Economy 690 at 701–3.

[9] See further below, text above n 45.

very small—of its potential output, originally promoted rather than restrained unnecessary drilling. This is because a producer's permitted output, or 'allowable', was commonly calculated by reference to the potential output of each of its wells. More wells therefore meant a higher total allowable. The alternative was to calculate allowables wholly or partly by reference to the acreage held by a producer. This latter approach, linked to rules setting minimum spacing between wells, with small tract owners being given the right to 'pool' their acreage with that of others so as to establish drilling units of the minimum size permitted by the spacing rules, could produce results approximating, albeit imperfectly, to those that might have been obtained by unitization, developing the field as a single unit.[10]

For most of its oil industry's history, the United States was the world's principal exporter. However as it became a net importer of oil and gas in the late 1960s, restriction of production through prorationing ceased to make sense, and the prorationing rules fell away. In 1971 the Texas Railroad Commission allowed wells in the State to run full open for the first time since 1930.[11] This left production from privately-owned land regulated—unless a field was fully unitized—essentially by spacing and pooling rules, coupled with measures to prevent the wastage of gas and to enforce a variety of other elements of good oilfield practice. And though most States had at some time included in their oil and gas legislation a so-called 'correlative rights' clause, providing that controls on exploration and production should be operated so as to ensure for each owner or lessee in an oil field a fair opportunity to recover the oil and gas under the land in which he or she had an interest, none of them had modified the rule of capture as the basic principle that determined the property rights of owners, or lessees, as between themselves. Even today, therefore, where regulations determining how many wells may be drilled and where, do not apply—for example where the State regulatory authority has not established a spacing plan for the field, or enabled the pooling of acreage into drilling units—the rule of capture will still operate. Consequently one lessee may quite lawfully draw oil from under the territory of its neighbour.[12] Advice to private lessors continues to be predicated upon the presumption that the rule of capture may apply, and that the lessee must protect against it by the use of appropriate provisions in the lease.[13]

While we can identify Texas as the State where suspicion of regulation is most firmly rooted and attachment to the rule of capture is strongest, doubtless because the rule has historically worked to the great advantage of the small independent producers that Texas counts in such large numbers[14]—this situation is common

---

[10] See generally R. Bradley, *Oil, Gas and Government: The US Experience* (1996) vol 1, ch 3, and for a more positive view, E. W. Zimmerman, *Conservation in the Production of Petroleum, A Study in Industrial Control* (1957).

[11] D. Yergin, *The Prize* (1991) 567.

[12] For an example see *Cowling v Board of Oil, Gas and Mining* (1991) 830 P 2d 220 (Utah).

[13] O. Anderson, 'David v Goliath: Negotiating the "Lessor's 88" and Representing Lessors and Surface Owners in Oil and Gas Lease Plays' (1982) 27B Rocky Mountain Mineral Law Institute 1029.

[14] See generally D. Prindle, *Petroleum Politics and the Texas Railroad Commission* (1981); D. Olien and R. Olien, *Oil in Texas: The Gusher Age 1895–1945* (2002).

to all oil-producing States. Indeed the rule also operates even in relation to areas in which the division of surface land ownership does not affect property rights in oil and gas, that is, in land in which the federal government has retained mineral rights. Because each lease granted under the federal Mineral Leasing Act covers a relatively small area, and areas of federal land are often held in chequerboard patterns with private land, a single oil and gas reservoir may be divided among a number of lessees. Here it has been easier to secure unitization, by making willingness to unitize a condition of obtaining a federal lease, but in its absence drainage legitimated by the rule of capture may still occur, notably to adjoining private lands. Even offshore, where there is of course no surface ownership, the rule of capture is assumed to apply, and drainage between the small blocks (nine square miles) into which the offshore is divided for leasing purposes needs to be controlled by effective compulsory unitization provisions.[15]

Capture thus remains today the property right principle on which the structure of United States oil and gas law and regulation has been erected. Indeed, the rule continues to conquer new territory. In Texas the rule has recently been deployed in order to deflect attack on the common practice of 'fracing' deep tight gas reservoirs by injecting fluids and particles that open up fractures in the reservoir rock that may extend well beyond the limits of the lease or drilling unit where the fractures originate. 'Fracing' may be a necessary procedure if such reservoirs are to be economically exploited, but is obviously open to the objection that it represents a sub-surface trespass of essentially the same nature as slant-hole drilling into one's neighbour's subsoil, opening an artificial path for the flow of hydrocarbons from his or her land to one's own well. For the Texas Supreme Court, however, if this is a trespass it is a non-actionable one, since the neighbour's loss of hydrocarbons is somehow excused by the law of capture.[16]

B. Capture in other countries

It is frequently assumed that the rule of capture is a peculiarly American phenomenon.[17] This is not the case. The rule has been of considerable importance in the development of oil and gas regimes elsewhere, exercising its influence both directly and indirectly. As for direct influence, capture was the general legal principle that applied in several countries where oil development was contemporaneous with that in the United States: Romania, Austrian Galicia, Russia. Indeed, the principle of capture was written into the influential French Civil Code,

---

[15] See eg *Clark Oil Producing Co v Hodel* (1987) 667 F Supp 281 (US Dist Ct La).
[16] *Coastal Oil and Gas Corpn v Garza Energy Trust* (2008) 261 SW 3d 1 (Tex). See also P. Burney and N. Hine, 'Hydraulic Fracturing: Stimulating Your Well or Trespassing?' (1998) 44 Rocky Mountain Mineral Law Institute 19–1; R. Thibault et al, 'A Modern Look at the Law of Subsurface Trespass: Does it Need Review, Refinement or Restatement?' (2008) 54 Rocky Mountain Mineral Law Institute 24–1.
[17] See eg M. Adelman, *The World Petroleum Market* (1972) 43.

promulgated in 1804, in the shape of the provision appearing in Art 552 that the owner of land was free to undertake whatever constructions and excavations he wished, and to take from them whatever products they furnished, subject to laws and regulations relating to mines and to public control ('police').[18] When the Code was used as the model for the Romanian Civil Code in 1865, no such specialized rules were adopted for petroleum, and the rule of capture accordingly applied.[19] Again, the history and problems of the Galician oil industry, in what is now southern Poland and western Ukraine, almost exactly reproduce, in miniature, those of the United States over the same period, with Galicia in fact conducting some of the first experiments in the use of anti-capture regulations like well-spacing rules.[20] Capture was likewise the working principle on which the prolific oil wells of Baku, in the Russian Caucasus, were exploited in the late nineteenth century.[21] In other countries, notably common law countries like England and her colonies and Dominions, it was assumed that the rule of capture would be the property law principle applied by the courts if called to rule on oil and gas property disputes. This belief, coupled with the fear that the industry might in consequence develop along the lines of waste and disorder visible in the United States, led to preventive regulation, or to the unification of petroleum property rights on the hands of the state, or both.[22]

There were of course other areas where the beginnings of the industry looked very different, notably in Latin America and the Middle East. The retention of mineral rights in state hands according to the principles of the Spanish Mineral Ordinance of 1783[23] or of Islamic mineral law[24] made it possible for concessions governing enormous areas—in some cases coterminous with the boundaries of the state itself—to be granted. Much of the demand for such concessions came from large American companies seeking opportunities for substantial oil production operations that would not be bedevilled by the problems encountered in domestic operations: the struggle to assemble adequate acreage via numerous leases, the obstacles to rational operation erected by those leases, the difficulties of reaching agreement on the cooperative development of fields, and the risks of losing production to small neighbours diligently exercising their rights to drain as much of the reservoir as they could. The history of the production side of the industry

[18] Art 552, third sentence. On the development of specialized rules for petroleum production in France, see J. Devaux-Charbonnel, *Droit Minier des Hydrocarbures. Principes et Applications* (2nd edn, 1987) 47–9.

[19] J. Cohen, *Le Régime des mines et du pétrole en Roumanie* (1926) 3–13; G. Buzatu, *O istorie a petrolului românesc* (1998) ch 4.

[20] See generally A. Frank, *Oil Empire: Visions of Prosperity in Austrian Galicia* (2005) chs 1–3.

[21] See generally C. Marvin, *The Region of the Eternal Fire* (1891).

[22] For the United Kingdom development see B. S. McBeth, *British Oil Policy 1919–1939* (1985) at ch 2.

[23] Reproduced with commentary in J. Rockwell, *A Compilation of Spanish and Mexican Law, in relation to Mines, and Titles to Real Estate, in force in California, Texas and New Mexico* (1851) 4–111.

[24] W. El-Malik, *Minerals Investment under the Shari'a Law* (1993) 44–70.

outside the United States, over most of the twentieth century, can be viewed as a struggle between companies and governments. Large American producing companies were convinced by their experience at home that they must enjoy a large measure of control over the pace and location of drilling, and the management of production over wide areas, in order to operate effectively. Governments for their part either resisted these demands out of fear of creating production monopolies or, having accommodated them, struggled in later years to recover some of the control over their country's natural resources that they had thereby granted away. While no two national paths of development have been exactly the same, most have converged upon a compromise position, in which oil and gas in the ground are state-owned, with the state seeking to grant exploration and production rights competitively and over limited areas, while retaining considerable powers of supervisory control over, or even managerial participation in, the activities of the successful companies. The size of areas offered continues to reflect the contest between the companies' desire for the maximum of operational discretion and the states' aim to engender, through competition, the maximum effort of comprehensive exploration of its territory and early production of its hydrocarbons. It is the relative prospectivity of the territory on offer that will determine the minimum size of the contract areas that a state can hope to offer successfully.[25] Effective unitization provisions are crucial to the successful management of territory attractive enough to be offered in small blocks, so that cross-block reservoirs may frequently occur. Where unitization powers are not exercised in such a case, competing operations on a common reservoir may still raise the issue of whether or not the state's control regime incorporates the principle of capture.

Obviously it is possible to imagine the current balance between state and oil company interests in this area being reached by different routes in a world which had never known the rule of capture. In reality capture was present at the very beginning of the chains of events which have led us to where we are today and has prompted, directly or indirectly, the behaviours typical of oil companies large and small, which in turn have shaped the corrective responses offered by governments. Like it or not, the rule stands at the starting point of the path of development that the industry has in fact followed.

II. Two puzzles

Two major puzzles emerge from this summary history. Why was such an inefficient rule adopted in the first place? Was it perhaps, despite its defects, the best rule available? Secondly, why, once adopted, did it remain in place in the United States, despite the major difficulties it was perceived to create, and when other countries were succeeding in creating more rational and efficient systems?

[25] M. Bunter, *The Promotion and Licensing of Petroleum Prospective Acreage* (2002).

A. Why was the rule adopted?

The standard economic explanation for the rule of capture is to see it as a response to the 'common pool' problem. Oil and gas, like fish and the water they swim in, are fluid resources, capable of moving from place to place without regard for property boundaries, so that ordinary property rules cannot work and a right to the ownership of what one can capture is the simplest rule that can be offered. A recent and sophisticated version of this theory has been offered by Dean Lueck, who seeks to provide a comprehensive economic analysis and explanation of the legal rules granting ownership not just of oil and gas but of land, personal property, intellectual property, water and other goods. Lueck posits a basic distinction between ownership of the *flow* of output from a given *stock*, such as the contents of an oil reservoir, or the whole of a herd of bison, and ownership of the stock itself.[26] Where it is possible to secure ownership of a stock, he argues that the tendency of the law will be to grant this by way of 'first possession' when this is the most efficient means of disposal, and to do so at a time which limits the possibility of wasteful races between claimants. Oil and gas, however, are identified by Lueck as presenting a likeness to a type of stock—the herd of bison is the common example—whose mobile nature means that the costs of enforcing possession of the whole stock would be prohibitive. In such cases, he argues, the law falls back on the rule of capture, allowing people to capture, and thereby obtain ownership of, some part of the flow of output: the individual animal.

In the case of oil and gas, Lueck's proposition is that '[t]he fluidity of oil and gas … can make it prohibitively costly for surface owners to establish rights to "their" stocks as against those of neighbouring drillers'.[27] Hence the rule of capture is the most practicable rule. There is a nice irony here. Academic lawyers, followed by engineers, have spent decades lambasting the judges who first recognized the capture principle for the ignorance they betrayed in relating the behaviour of oil and gas with that of wild animals. It was, they said, the judges' failure to understand that oil and gas did not roam free beneath the ground, but were confined in reservoir rocks, that set the industry on its path of wasteful competition.[28] Now we have an economist telling us that the judges were right all along. In fact both accounts tend to over-simplify by neglecting changes in industry understanding of the underground behaviour of oil and gas and its economic implications, and ignoring a crucial fact: that the first judicial reference to the rule of capture did not occur until the industry had been operating for twenty-seven years. At that time total annual United States crude oil production was

---

[26] D. Lueck, 'The Rule of First Possession and the Design of the Law' (1995) 38 Journal of Law and Economics 393.

[27] ibid at 425.

[28] See for early examples J. Veasey, 'The Law of Oil and Gas: I' (1920) 18 Michigan Law Review 445 at 453–5; E. Oliver, in *Federal Oil Conservation Board, Complete Record of Hearings*, 10 and 11 February 1926 at 93–5.

approaching 30 million barrels.[29] It is clear that capture was the general working principle of the industry from the very beginning, a reasonable position in that oil was at first thought to be tapped from crevices in the rock through which oil might run long distances from whatever accumulations existed.[30] In the absence of any notion that oil might have a stable existence in a stratum of reservoir rock covering a certain area, contesting a neighbour's actions in drilling a well nearby one's own made no sense. Nor did the idea of protecting one's own 'stock' of oil. Only when the understanding of reservoir geology developed in the 1880s did any basis for a possible legal attack on drainage appear. It was at this time that lessors began to attack their lessees in court for permitting such drainage to occur by reason of inadequate development of the lease: in particular, by failing to drill 'offset' wells, that is wells opposite those on the other side the property line that might be draining oil. In such cases courts showed themselves able to identify an appropriate measure of damages for loss of oil by drainage. Lueck's assumption that defending rights to one's 'own' oil would be prohibitively costly thus no longer obtained. Yet no one challenged the *legality* of drainage until the 1890s, and of the cases decided then, only *Kelley v Ohio Oil Co* in 1897 was an attack on capture as such.[31] Why was there not more litigation?

A general answer to this question is suggested by the economic analysis offered by Anthony Scott in his major study of how resource property rights have evolved over time.[32] Scott argues that resource property rights develop only when there is a clear demand for modifications and refinements that might be supplied by courts, legislatures, or perhaps by the development of custom, and suggests in very general terms that 'more demanders typically opposed than favoured individual rights to common-access resources'.[33] In the case of oil and gas, individual rights—in land owners and their lessees—certainly existed, but they were imperfect by reason of capture. To have tried to improve them, however, must have appeared to most participants in the industry in the 1880s as a negative-sum game. Success by a lessee in challenging drainage by a neighbour would immediately affect the drainage opportunities it might itself possess under this or other leases. Leases smaller than the area thought to be capable of drainage from a single well would immediately

---

[29] H. Williamson and A. Daum, *The American Petroleum Industry. 1859–1899: The Age of Illumination* (1959) 594.

[30] T. Daintith, 'A Pre-History of the Rule of Capture' (2008) 9 Oil-Industry History 143.

[31] *Acheson v Stevenson* (1892) 145 Pa 228 (Pa); *Hague v Wheeler* (1893) 157 Pa 324, 27 Atl 714 (Pa); and *Kelley v Ohio Oil Co* (1897) 57 Ohio St 317, 49 NE 399 (Ohio). Both of the other cases involved aggravating circumstances: in *Acheson v Stevenson* the drainage was arguably unlawful on other grounds, and in *Hague v Wheeler* it was accompanied by deliberate waste of the gas obtained.

[32] A. Scott, *The Evolution of Resource Property Rights* (2008). Scott offers a penetrating analysis despite being far from reliable on matters of history and law (eg, he offers two different dates for the US Oil Placer Act 1897, both wrong—1887, at 346, 1870–72, at 384; he also suggests at 359–60 that the United Kingdom and Australia negotiated individualized concession contracts for offshore oil and gas operations, when in fact financial and other terms were firmly fixed by regulation (UK) or even legislation (Australia)).

[33] ibid at 59.

become unworkable without the consent of neighbours. In general the value and attractiveness of the entire portfolio of leases would be restricted by the need to drill at a significant distance from border lines, even though the most promising locations for wells might be found there. Production could be expected to shrink significantly, and the consequent loss of profit might have greatly exceeded the costs of drilling unnecessary offset wells. When these consequences are taken into account, the odds against any lessee's embarking on the task of persuading a court to adopt a strict property rule for oil and gas seem long indeed. The few people we do find attempting litigation on this subject are those who have a limited range of operations and a heavy stake in a specific field: the larger producers are conspicuously absent from the lists. Lessors of course were far less concerned with such general production and leasing strategies. They would certainly have wished to sue to restrain drainage, but having assigned their oil and gas rights to their lessees, could not proceed directly against their neighbours. Accordingly they sought the aid of the courts to force their lessees to protect the lease against drainage by rapid development and the drilling of offset wells. The success they achieved in this by the first years of the twentieth century exacerbated the effects of capture by making competitive drilling a common law obligation.[34]

If we switch to the perspective of the judiciary as suppliers of property right development, the picture does not change much. Alternative property right rules for oil and gas were certainly available late in the nineteenth century; indeed one was offered for judicial consideration in the only direct challenge to the capture principle at that time, the case of *Kelley v Ohio Oil Co*[35] in 1897. Kelley was a lessee who claimed that the defendant company, operating under an adjoining lease, had systematically drilled wells along its side of the property line and thereby drained substantial quantities of oil to which he, Kelley, was lawfully entitled. This process, he argued, necessarily involved the withdrawal of the lateral support afforded to his oil, within a closed reservoir, by the oil of the defendants. Once the defendants drilled near the property line the plaintiff's oil, which had as it were been 'leaning' on theirs, was free to flow under a few yards of the defendants' lease and into their wells. Now the obligation to afford lateral support to one's neighbour's land has perhaps the longest recorded history of any principle of Western law: it is reflected in the laws of Solon, in sixth-century BC Athens.[36] Only two years after the *Kelley* case it was applied by the Judicial Committee of the Privy Council so as to prevent the common practice of digging pitch, which lay on or just below the land surface in part of Trinidad, in such a way as to allow pitch from one's neighbour's land to flow into one's own. There are legal grounds on which one can distinguish the two cases: in the Privy Council case, *Trinidad Asphalt Co v Ambard*,[37] the digging had the effect of letting down the surface of

[34] M. Merrill, *Covenants Implied in Oil and Gas Leases* (2nd edn, 1940) ch 5.
[35] (1897) 57 Ohio St 317, 49 NE 399 (Ohio).
[36] Plutarch, *Lives* (transl. J. and W. Langhorne 1845) 105.
[37] [1899] AC 594 (PC).

the neighbour's land, whereas the deep drilling in *Kelley* affected nothing but the valuable minerals themselves. Nonetheless, it is striking that the Ohio court dismissed Kelley's claim without even deigning to mention this at least plausible argument. The reason, one suspects, is that the Ohio court glimpsed in its mind's eye the chaos that might ensue if it turned oil property rights upside down in this way, and resolved to say absolutely nothing that could give the faintest encouragement to such an outcome.[38]

A question that needs a little more consideration is why arguments against capture like that based on lateral support were never raised in other States, where Ohio or Pennsylvania precedents were not binding and where significant oil developments came much later.[39] When *Kelley's* case was decided in 1897, the United States' very substantial production came almost entirely from those two States: the first significant production in Texas dates only from 1899, that from California from 1892. Courts in these and other southern and western States thus had a relatively clean slate to work on; but whatever the state of their slate, courts can only work if there are litigants to ask them to do so, and we have seen that oil men in this phase of the industry's development apparently had little interest in litigating against one another. As and when litigation did occur, normally between land owners rather than rival operators and usually years after oil development began in a State, courts of these newer oil lands, without exception, embraced the rule of capture as part of the legal environment for oil exploration and production. Walter Summers, one of the earliest legal critics of the rule, pictured such courts as justifying their decisions with the argument that oil development would otherwise be made impossible, by reason of the ability of land owners to stop their neighbours from drilling.[40] In fact we do not find courts explicitly relying on this rationale, but it is impossible to believe that it exercised no influence on their decisions.

While it might have been constitutionally feasible, in a case of first impression before a court of a 'new' oil State, to reject the law of capture and adopt a different rule, it is hardly surprising that this never happened. Such a ruling would have meant that a land owner could prevent or at least legally obstruct her neighbour's drilling for oil until she was ready to do so herself. As a consequence, the State's property laws would risk appearing unfriendly to oil development, with the tax revenues and economic prosperity that it would bring. Not a politically attractive position: and we should keep in mind that American judges, by reason of their background, of their pathways to the bench (often by popular election or politically influenced appointment), and sometimes also of their ambitions, were likely to be

[38] Its prudence was perhaps justified by what happened in Trinidad. Though the industry was minuscule compared with the United States oil industry at this time, though the Privy Council decision affected only a part of its operations, and though the legal relations involved were considerably simpler, the effects of the decision were serious enough to provoke the appointment of a Royal Commission and the construction of an entirely new legal regime.

[39] The argument was however later tried (unsuccessfully) in a Canadian oil and gas case that also ended up before the Privy Council: *Borys v Canadian Pacific Ry* [1953] 2 AC 317 (PC).

[40] W. Summers, 'Property in Oil and Gas' (1919) 29 Yale Law Journal 174.

closely integrated into their State's political life. A further point is that throwing the problem back to the legislature to fix, as the Privy Council did in effectively rendering Trindad asphalt mining practices illegal, might not have worked at all. To make oil and gas operations practicable, in the face of a 'no capture' finding, would have involved forcing land owners into a scheme whereby oil and gas could be drawn by drainage from under their land even though they were unwilling to consent to such production. Even if such schemes were required to make provision for full compensation, they would constitute a deprivation of property in the sense of the Fifth and Fourteenth Amendments by the very fact of their taking away the land owner's right to decide whether or not to develop the land, and if so, when. As late as 1929, the country's most experienced oil and gas lawyers felt that compulsory pooling and unitization schemes, imposing similar constraints in the interests of eliminating competitive over-drilling, could not be constitutional.[41] A judge ruling against the application of the law of capture in his State might thus have condemned it to decades of exclusion from the benefits of oil and gas production.

What the early American legal development evidences is a strong form of path dependence:[42] where decisions taken in ignorance at an early stage of industrial development produce a situation in which correcting the resulting, belatedly comprehended inefficiencies would be so costly, and would produce such massive and hard-to-foresee redistributive effects, as to be beyond reasonable contemplation. Indeed, there is plenty of evidence to suggest that by the time reservoir geology, and areal drainage, were well enough understood to make it theoretically plausible to litigate to prevent drainage from under one's lease, the idea that there could be any property right principle for oil other than capture was literally unthinkable.[43]

B. Why was the rule maintained?

Even if we accept that the United States industry was led by technological misunderstandings on to an inefficient path from which it could not escape by a radical change in property rights, it remains necessary to explain why management of the side-effects of capture proved so hard to achieve. Lueck's analysis really offers no answer to this question. American oil and gas law does not match his prediction that the law will mitigate the risks of waste occasioned by a rule of capture—in the shape of competitive over-investment in getting hold of the resource, and premature exhaustion resulting from such competition—by limiting access to the stock and restricting the transfer of rights in it.[44] For wild animals these protections were (tardily) afforded by close seasons for hunting and restrictions and prohibitions

---

[41] Report of Committee on Conservation of Mineral Resources, in *Annual Report of the American Bar Association* (1929) 741 at 751.
[42] See generally S. Margolis and S. Liebowitz, 'Path dependence' in *The Palgrave Dictionary of Economics and the Law* (P. Newman, ed, 1998, vol 3) at 17–22.
[43] Above n 30.
[44] Above n 26 at 410–11.

on wildlife product markets. While access is naturally limited in the case of oil and gas by the rights of exclusion possessed by surface owners, any restrictive effect was destroyed from the very first days of the industry onward by the frenetic subdivision of land for oil leasing. Quarter-acre leases were already common in the 1860s; at Spindletop, Texas in 1901 some shrank to less than 100 square yards, at Signal Hill in California in 1921 to 16 by 12 yards. Lessors and lessees alike went further by dividing and trading their respective royalty and working interests in individual leases: a single field might have thousands of royalty holders and hundreds of working interest holders. Subdivision of land enormously exacerbated the negative effects of the rule of capture; subdivision of interests has made any sort of contractual correction, such as voluntary unitization of a field, extremely difficult by reason of the number and variety of interests involved.[45] Lueck acknowledges that the cost of contracting is often prohibitive, but suggests that statutory rules like well-spacing and compulsory unitization have 'emerged' so as effectively to limit access.[46] These corrections, however, were introduced only in the 1930s and their coverage is still far from complete; in fact, no state legislature understood the need for restrictions on access and rights transfers until it was far too late.

There was, however, a potential line of common law development towards the kind of 'second-best' solution represented by well-spacing and similar regulations. Within three years of the *Kelley* case the United States Supreme Court demonstrated how, even if the rule of capture had to be retained, its worst side-effects might be controlled. This was made possible by a rare legislative intervention: an Indiana law seeking to conserve that State's vast gas deposits, on which the State already relied heavily for lighting, heating, and industrial fuel, against companies seeking to produce oil from the same formations and flaring or blowing vast quantities of gas in the process. One of these—as it happened, Mr Kelley's old opponent, the Ohio Oil Company—challenged the law as an unconstitutional taking of property. In its decision[47] the Supreme Court found a way of transforming the dysfunctionalities of the rule of capture into a basis for its control and even neutralization. On the basis that an unrestrained law of capture meant that there could be no secure property rights in a common oil and gas reservoir, the Court held that it was constitutionally legitimate for States to legislate to control the practice of those exploring for and exploiting oil and gas, for the protection of the correlative rights of the owners of interests in the reservoir, and perhaps for the prevention of waste in the interests of the general public also. The decision was thus of considerable importance in comforting the hitherto limited attempts of the oil- and gas-producing States of the north-east to enforce some basic conservation rules, and providing a platform for the more general prohibitions of waste that began to appear in legislation from 1915 onwards.

[45] J. Weaver, *Unitization in Texas: A Study of Legislative, Administrative and Judicial Politics* (1986) 29–33; G. Libecap, *Contracting for Property Rights* (1993) chs 1 and 6.
[46] Above n 26 at 426.
[47] *Ohio Oil Co v Indiana* (1900) 177 US 190.

The concept of correlative rights also had the potential to provide a basis for a modified *common law* of capture, the exercise of which would be subject to a number of constraints. Such constraints included restricting the ways in which a reservoir could be exploited[48] and possibly even requiring that production methods should not, as the Supreme Court put it in its *Ohio Oil* opinion 'result in an *undue proportion* being attributed to one of the possessors of the right, to the detriment of the others'.[49] This development never happened. Few cases came before the courts: no plaintiff ever tried to resist capture on the basis of a 'just distribution' argument, and courts were generally reluctant to impose or outlaw any particular production, methods as a matter of common law obligation.[50] This throttling of the potential for common law management of production through correlative rights may have owed something to judicial deference to a continuing industry commitment to the capture principle, but it was also linked to a change of judicial mood. The decades around the turn of the century were the time when, thanks largely though not exclusively to the power of the Standard Oil trust, popular suspicion of large resource corporations developed apace. Courts followed the trend: it is precisely in this period, from around 1895 onwards, that we start to find them vigorously reconstructing lease agreements so as to protect lessors from oil companies that tried to assemble blocks of leases and to drill within the block only where it seemed efficient to do so. They read delay rental clauses, designed to permit postponement of development, out of leases; they read prompt development and offset drilling obligations into them.[51] In these circumstances it is not hard to see why even the larger companies, with systematic policies of acreage acquisition and development aimed at low-cost production, would resign themselves to drilling unnecessary offset wells rather than seek to resist capture by judicial means. The platform for litigation offered by the *Ohio Oil* decision was a fragile and uncertain one. The penalties for failure might not only be loss of the oil to one's neighbour, but loss of the lease as well: better just to drill.

III. Nationalization of oil property rights

Oil became a matter of strategic concern in the first years of the twentieth century, when Britain and the United States realized the major advantages of substituting it for coal as the fuel for their navies. Those who advised the British government, most notably Lord Cowdray, who had extensive experience of oil operations in the

---

[48] *Manufacturers' Gas and Oil Co v Indiana Natural Gas and Oil Co.* (1900) 155 Ind 461, 57 NE 912.

[49] *Ohio Oil Co v Indiana* (1900) 177 US 190 at 210.

[50] See *Jones v Forest Oil* (1900) 194 Pa 379, 44 Atl 1074 (Pa); *United Carbon Co v Campbellsville Gas Co* (1929) 18 SW 2d 1110 (Ky); *Higgins Oil and Fuel Co v Guaranty Oil Co* (1919) 145 La 233, 82 So 206 (La).

[51] For details see Merrill (above n 34).

United States and Mexico, counselled strongly against allowing the development of American-style competitive drilling, with the waste and instability it brought in its wake. From the beginning of the century, therefore, Imperial policy was to keep tight control of oil development in territories, including the mother country, that were being opened up for oil exploration.[52] It soon appeared that the most effective way of doing this was to hold the totality of property rights in oil and gas in the ground. This enabled the state to control the rate and location of exploration, to promote competition between companies for acreage, and to eliminate the wasteful side-effects of the rule of capture through unitization where necessary. In contrast to the United States, where the grants of enormous areas of public land made as settlement moved westward had incorporated no reservation of mineral rights (though a largely unsuccessful effort was made to identify 'mineral lands' in advance and reserve them from grant),[53] nineteenth-century land policy in places like Canada and Australia had involved substantial reservations of minerals. These reservations were set out in terms broad enough to include petroleum, and were largely completed by what were in effect nationalizations of any petroleum rights that remained in public hands.[54] Queensland was the first State to legislate in this sense in 1915;[55] the United Kingdom followed in 1934.[56] Analogous moves were made in countries like the Netherlands[57] and France,[58] where rights to exploit minerals, including petroleum, had long been separated from surface ownership and held at the disposition of the state, but where exploration, anomalously, remained under the control of the surface owner.

These initiatives caused little disturbance because there was virtually no existing exploration or production activity in the countries concerned, and no inconvenient constitutional protection of property rights either. Nationalizations that took place against the background of an established oil and gas industry naturally provoked a good deal more controversy, even if their effect, as in Romania, was simply to substitute a publicly granted concession for a private lease.[59] These moves seldom involved expropriating one's own people, as opposed to foreign investors: unsurprisingly, unifying property rights in oil and gas by transferring

---

[52] See generally G. Jones, *The State and the Emergence of the British Oil Industry* (1981); McBeth, (above n 22).

[53] R. W. Swenson, 'Legal Aspects of Mineral Resources Exploitation' in *History of Public Land Law Development* (P. Gates, 1968) ch XXIII.

[54] See for Canada, above n 32 at 353–4; for Australia, J. Forbes and A. Lang, *Australian Mining and Petroleum Laws* (2nd edn, 1987) 17–26.

[55] Petroleum Act 1915 (Qld).

[56] Petroleum (Production) Act 1934 (UK).

[57] See generally M. Roggenkamp, *Netherlands Oil and Gas Law* (1991) ch 1; M. Roggenkamp, 'Energy Law in the Netherlands' in *Energy Law in Europe: National, EU and International Law Institutions* (M. Roggenkamp et al, eds, 2001) 629 at 637–44.

[58] R. Fehr, *Le régime juridique des recherches et de l'exploitation des gisements de pétrole en droit comparé: France, Angleterre, Allemagne* (1939) 50–1; J. Devaux-Charbonnel, *Droit minier des hydrocarbures: principes et applications* (1987) 47–9.

[59] On the Romanian nationalization of 1924 see M. Pearton, *Oil and the Romanian State* (1971) 112–25.

them from private American hands to public ownership was not seen, in the United States, as a first-line solution to the problems of waste and price instability, even amid the strategic concerns provoked by the experience of the First World War. Only President Wilson's Secretary of the Navy, Josephus Daniels, a Progressive Democrat who was already on record as favouring public ownership of armaments and munitions factories, dared to propose nationalization,[60] but achieved no more than the setting aside of some oil-bearing federal lands as a 'national petroleum reserve'. This half-loaf was possibly worse than no bread: much of this federal land was chequerboarded with private holdings, whose lessees, benefiting from the rule of capture, gratefully set out to drain the reserves the navy was trying to hold.[61]

In fact, the whole trend of American natural resources history pointed away from any movement of rights from private to public hands. For the government even to retain and then lease the mineral interest, rather than dispose of it outright, was, right up to the enactment of the Mineral Leasing Act in 1920, resisted as 'profoundly un-American'.[62] Texas, which inherited the Spanish system of reserved mineral rights through its former Mexican masters, gave most of them away to its land grantees in the second half of the nineteenth century, and in 1919 even relinquished the management of, and most of the revenue from, remaining oil rights held on behalf of its public school system to the overlying surface owners or lessees. Even had there been any public demand or political will to embark on the expropriation of private oil interests, the constitution and its legal consequences would surely have provided an insurmountable obstacle. The programme would have involved massive takings of property, requiring full compensation under the Fifth Amendment. The division of the property among (probably) hundreds of thousands of royalty and working interest owners, and the difficulty of placing values on partially developed or as yet undeveloped land, could have tied the industry up in a turmoil of regulation and litigation for decades to come.

IV. Time for a change?

I have written here about capture as a problem, one which bedevilled the industry in its early years not just in the United States, but in the European and Russian oilfields as well: a problem which countries outside the United States have largely

---

[60] McBeth (above n 22 at 57). R. Olien and D. Olien, *Oil and Ideology: The Cultural Creation of the American Petroleum Industry* (2000) 131 say that the legislature of Minnesota (not an oil State) had the same idea.

[61] J. L. Bates, *The Origins of Teapot Dome: Progressives, Parties and Petroleum 1909–1921* (1963) 24–32; G. Libecap, 'The Political Allocation of Mineral Rights: A Re-evaluation of Teapot Dome' (1984) 44 Journal of Economic History 381.

[62] Per Counsel in *Moore v Smaw* (1861) 17 Cal 199 (Cal), and see J. E. Wright, *The Galena Lead District: Federal Policy and Practice 1824–1847* (1966) 80, citing an 1841 newspaper description of leasing as a practice of 'our Spanish neighbors, a nation that broiled Montezuma for his gold'.

solved by taking oil rights into their own hands and managing them in such a way as to keep rivalrous behaviour among oil companies within strict limits. The United States has been able to reach this position only on land where the mineral rights are still in federal or State hands, notably on its continental shelf, which despite long-standing embargoes on drilling off most of the United States coastline, in 2007 accounted for 26.8 per cent of its crude oil production and 14.2 per cent of natural gas production.[63] On private lands, the rule of capture continues to function as the default rule in any case of where conservation regulations are not applicable. Indeed, it has been argued that the regulatory structure could not operate in the absence of a rule of capture, since the very approximate relationship of drilling units with the natural flows within any given reservoir means that in almost all cases, one operator will be taking oil or gas, at least at the margins, from under the lease of another.[64]

I have already shown some of the difficulties that would flow from adopting a property rule different from that of capture, and it would be well to recognize at this point that the rule has virtues to counterbalance its ill effects. It may be argued that the rapid development of the American oil industry owes much to the competitive pressures engendered by the rule, and that the very low prices for oil that followed major finds in the first decades of the twentieth century were largely responsible for the explosive growth of automobile use and the way that use, in turn, shaped the American way of life. The economist Joseph Pogue told an international energy conference in 1938 that—at least up to about 1920—the rule's effects were on balance positive, in that it drove the industry to achieve the rate of expansion that the market demanded.[65] A similar assessment was made by Paul Frankel, one of the leading authorities on petroleum economics, in 1946. '[T]hese somewhat primitive methods', he wrote, 'were exactly what was needed to make the young industry, in the first instance, aggressive and, in due course, great'.[66] Recently it has even been argued that spacing, prorationing and other regulations designed to control the effects of capture have produced more waste and less efficiency than would have followed from the unfettered operation of the rule.[67]

It is important not to neglect other factors contributing to the headlong pace of United States development, notably a very high capacity for capital formation, a large domestic market, a stable legal system, and low level of general regulatory

---

[63] Mineral Management Service, US Department of Interior, Federal OCS Oil Gas Production as a Percentage of Total US Production 2006 available at <http://www.mms.gov/stats/PDFs/June2008/AnnualProductionAsPercentage1954–2006AsOf6–2008.pdf>.

[64] E. Kuntz, 'The Law of Capture' (1957) 10 Oklahoma Law Review 406; B. Kramer and O. Anderson, 'The Rule of Capture: An Oil and Gas Perspective' (2005) 35 Environmental Law 899 at 951–4.

[65] J. Pogue, 'The Economic Structure of the American Oil Industry' in *Transactions, Third World Power Conference* vol 3 (1938) 221 at 236.

[66] P. Frankel, *Essentials of Petroleum, A Key to Oil Economics* (1969) 19.

[67] Bradley (above n 10, vol 1, chs 3 and 4).

restraint. America's nineteenth-century oil rivals in Romania, Galicia and Russia also operated the rule of capture, but were each handicapped in their development by the lack of one or other of these advantages.

We may nonetheless readily concede that capture provides a natural engine to drive early and thorough exploration, and that where it cannot operate—for example by reason of the sheer size of a concession or lease area enjoyed by a company—there will be a serious risk of under-exploration, postponed development, and 'warehousing' of acreage for future (possible) use. Such policies may make excellent sense in terms of the global or regional strategy of a substantial oil company, but are unlikely to respond to the economic, fiscal and energy security priorities of the granting state. Modern regimes for the exploitation of state-owned oil and gas resources, to the extent that they allow for private company activity at all, thus tend to incorporate a number of functional substitutes for capture: binding work or work expenditure programmes at the exploration stage (and indeed award of acreage on the basis of competitive programme bidding), obligations to relinquish substantial amounts of acreage at fixed intervals and on entering the production phase, continuing exploration obligations even on production acreage, and so on.[68] A residual role for capture may also be retained in such systems by offering blocks of acreage small enough to make cross-block reservoirs a likely occurrence, granting leases and concessions in terms that do not exclude capture, and making the exercise of compulsory unitization powers dependent on a showing that ultimate recovery will be impaired by competitive development. Such a regime can provide significant positional advantages for the first company to reach development stage on a shared cross-block reservoir.

A few years ago it would have been natural to hold that capture, in this interstitial or residual role to which, outside the United States, it is effectively reduced, was a benign influence in favour of development. Today, in the face of global warming, with the corresponding cooling of our enthusiasm for fossil fuels, we might not feel so sure. Should we not respond to our new situation by trying to leave the oil in the ground, reserved for the uses in which it may prove to be indispensable even as new fuel technologies take over and the slope down from peak oil production steepens? And if we readjust our goals in this way, should we not reflect this shift in the adoption of a property right principle for oil which, even if it does not explicitly block development, is at least, unlike the capture principle, neutral in this respect?

'Leaving the oil in the ground' was a proposition vigorously debated within the American conservation movement in the early years of last century, at the time when fears that the oil would soon run out were at their highest.[69] So far as

---

[68] For an analysis of four such systems (the federal offshore regimes of Australia, Canada and the United States, and the United Kingdom regime) see T. Daintith, *Discretion in the Administration of Offshore Oil and Gas: a Comparative Study* (2006).

[69] Olien and Olien (above n 60, ch 5).

mineral resources were concerned, the idea that conservation meant 'that they [natural resources] should remain as nearly undiminished as possible in order that this heritage of natural wealth may pass in full measure to succeeding generations'[70] was understood by most, even within the conservation camp, to be unrealistic; instead they sought to focus attention on efficient production and a sensible prioritization of use. In fact United States policy in relation to its own lands has since that period had the effect, at least from time to time, of leaving large quantities of oil in the ground, though with the exception of the naval petroleum reserves, of which the largest is on the Alaska North Slope, the reasons have been more environmental than strategic or economic. Most of the United States Continental Shelf remains unexploited for this reason. Elsewhere national leasing policies have to some extent provided *de facto* for reservation of areas from leasing, simply by opening up only limited amounts of acreage at regular intervals. Clearly, governments of small states with potentially large resources (like Norway, a particularly strong case because of its abundant alternative resource of hydropower) will find it easier to do this than states with large and energy-hungry populations, like India or China. Only Ecuador has so far attempted to link a specific proposed reservation of oil-bearing territory (in its Yasuní forest area) with an internationally-provided payment for the benefits—of maintenance of bio-diversity and reduction of carbon emissions—to be obtained from non-exploitation.[71]

However, unless a state is going to take the extraordinary step of forswearing development of all and any of its potential oil and gas resources, any policy of restraint is going to be exercised within the framework of a legally structured system of exploration for and exploitation of those resources. The right of capture can certainly be eliminated from such a system. The Dutch Supreme Court held in 2005 that general principles of Dutch law, coupled with the wording of the licensing provisions of the offshore petroleum legislation and regulations, allowed no room for the operation of the law of capture.[72] Different results would follow from the current wording of the production licences granted offshore the United Kingdom and Australia, but that wording could easily be changed, if desired, so as to eliminate capture.[73] The only result, however, would be to make offshore exploitation harder to manage, as a company holding a licence or lease giving impregnable rights to the petroleum in place under its block would be able to prevent drilling by its neighbours until it was ready to develop itself. The weapon of unitization might then have to be employed to force, rather than to control, development, a much more awkward option. This

---

[70] C. Van Hise, *The Conservation of Natural Resources in the United States* (1910) 1–2.

[71] T. Davis, 'Breaking Ground without Lifting a Shovel: Ecuador's Plan to leave its Oil in the Ground' (2007) 30 Houston International Law Journal 243.

[72] *Unocal v Conoco* (above n 3).

[73] See above n 4; T. Daintith, 'A Critical Evaluation of the Petroleum (Submerged Lands) Act as a Regulatory Regime' [2000] AMPLA Yearbook 91 at 103–7.

seems to subject the state to a quite unnecessary handicap in a situation where, having already opened acreage and granted licences, it must be presumed to desire prompt and efficient production. Capture has a useful marginal role even under current conditions.

In the United States, however, there is little ground for optimism about legal change. Path-dependency still reigns. Texas, still the largest producing State, has consistently refused even to enact a compulsory unitization statute: politically dominant small producers could not hope to enjoy thereunder the rewards they obtain from a capture-based system of production regulation.[74] Only if hitherto unexploited publicly-owned oil and gas resources, notably offshore, start replacing privately-owned reserves as the latter run down are we likely to see a significant reduction in the inefficiencies resulting from production under the rule of capture. Properly analysed, indeed, it is not so much the rule of capture that is at the root of American difficulties, as the American reverence for private property. European and Commonwealth experience suggests that the rule of capture is the least worst property rule for fugacious substances like oil and gas, so long as it operates within a context where the stimulus it gives to development can be married to an effective control of its side-effects. It was the refusal in the United States to contemplate the reservation of mineral rights in public hands, coupled with a constitutional frame-work and a political outlook that made the exercise of those rights, once granted to private persons, extremely difficult to control, that turned the capture principle from a spur to development into a monstrous engine of waste.

[74] J. Weaver, 'The Tragedy of the Commons from Spindletop to Enron' (2004) 24 Journal of Land, Resources and Environmental Law 187.

8

Models for State Ownership on the Norwegian Continental Shelf

*Ulf Hammer**

I. Introduction

Since the early 1970s, state ownership has been an important element in the management of petroleum resources on the Norwegian Continental Shelf (NCS). In recent years, however, important developments have taken place, both as regards the organization and the management of state ownership. The main purpose of this chapter is to analyse these developments.

In the following chapter, I make a basic distinction between state ownership of subsea petroleum deposits and state ownership of licence interests. In Part II, I will discuss state ownership of the subsea petroleum deposits. Then in Part III, I will discuss on how the state manages its ownership in the petroleum activities, ie exploration, production, transport, and eventually, abandonment. These activities are organized and executed through a licence system. But *within* this licence system, state ownership of licence interests—directly and indirectly—is an important element. In Part IV, I will further analyse how the state manages its licence interests through the state company Petoro. In Part V, I will sum up and make my concluding remarks.

In this chapter, I will focus on the management of petroleum resources. An important recent development concerns the management of capital accrued from state ownership. This capital is managed by the State Pension Fund and raises several issues, but capital management falls outside the scope of this chapter.

II. State ownership of subsea petroleum deposits

According to the Law of the Sea Convention (LOSC) Art 77(1), the coastal state exercises sovereign rights over the continental shelf for the purpose of exploring and exploiting its natural resources. This provision does not directly address the

* Professor, Scandinavian Institute of Maritime Law, University of Oslo, Norway; email: ulf. hammer@jus.uio.no.

ownership of natural resources; it is neutral in that respect. It is up to the coastal state to exercise its sovereign rights with regard to ownership of the natural resources on its continental shelf. In the Petroleum Act No 72 of 29 November 1996 (PA) s 1–1 the Norwegian state has claimed the proprietary right to subsea petroleum deposits.[1] This principle was first stated in Act No 12 of 21 June 1963 relating to exploration for and exploitation of subsea natural resources. This Act is still in force, but it now regulates subsea natural resources *other* than petroleum resources.

In this context, it can be discussed whether deep formations on the continental shelf can be regarded as a natural resource pursuant to the 1963 Act, when such formations are used as reservoirs for the storage of CO_2. In fact, the same issue arises with regard to the LOSC Art 77. The Norwegian government seems to be of the opinion that such formations constitute a natural resource. In the preparatory documents to a recent amendment to the PA, the government has signalled future regulation regarding carbon capture and storage (CCS). But this future regulation is not signalled within the scope of the PA, unless CCS is part of the petroleum activities or petroleum installations are used for the transport of CO_2. Otherwise, future regulation is signalled within the scope of the 1963 Act and the Pollution Act.[2] The international (jurisdictional) context is not discussed at all.

III. State participation within a licence system

A. Starting points

As a starting point, the state as a resource owner could have conducted all petroleum activities itself, or through a state-owned company. This is the situation in many petroleum provinces around the world. Instead, the Norwegian state has established a licence system where private companies participate as licensees together with the state. The reason for this was to attract technologically competent and financially strong companies to perform activities on the NCS, an area characterized by large water depths and harsh weather conditions. The licence system was introduced prior to the first licence round in 1965. The main structure of this licence system still exists. It consists of the exploration licence: PA s 2–1, the production licence: PA s 3–3, and the specific licence to install and operate installations: PA s 4–3. In addition, the development plan and the decommissioning plan belong to the licence system.[3]

---

[1] The same procedure has been adopted in many other jurisdictions. See N. Bankes and M. Roggenkamp, 'Legal Aspects of Carbon Capture' in *Beyond the Carbon Economy* (D. Zillman, C. Redgwell, Y. Omorogbe, L. Barrera-Hernandez, eds, 2008) 354.

[2] Ot prp No 48 (2008–2009) 11.

[3] For an overview, see F. Arnesen, U. Hammer, P.H. Høisveen, K. Kaasen and D. Nygaard, 'Energy Law in Norway' in *Energy Law in Europe* (M. Roggenkamp, C. Redgwell, I. del Guayo, eds, 2008, vol 2) 889–91.

The state does not need a licence to perform activities under the Petroleum Act: PA s 1–3. In practice, the state performs exploration activities without a licence. We are talking here mainly about seismic surveys.[4] These activities are performed by the Norwegian Petroleum Directorate (NPD). The purpose of these activities is to explore the resource potential in new areas on the NCS; ie areas which have not previously been opened pursuant to PA s 3–1. This has been firm practice for several years.[5] However, companies can acquire a separate exploration licence to conduct these activities.

A characteristic feature of the Norwegian licence system is the strong state participation within this system. The term state participation is wide and encompasses both state ownership of shares in companies holding a licence interest, ie indirect ownership of licence interests, and direct ownership of licence interests. Both pillars still exist, but over time the main emphasis of the state participation has changed from indirect ownership to direct ownership, as shown in this chapter. But first, it is necessary to present the purpose of the licence system: resource management.

B. Resource management

The PA s 1–2, para 1 introduces the resource manager: the King, who is the highest executive body of the Norwegian state hierarchy. In practice, the King only has a formal role. The real executive powers rest with the Cabinet, which has delegated its powers to the Ministries to a large extent. And the Ministries have further delegated some authorities to the Directorates.[6] This delegation of powers is reflected in the PA and in the regulations adopted pursuant to the PA.

According to the PA s 1–2 para 2, petroleum resources shall be managed in a long term perspective for the benefit of Norwegian society as a whole. The provision lists several broad concerns, which the resource manager, ie the licence authority and regulator, has to take into account. These include the generation of income, welfare and employment. Furthermore, the resource manager shall take into account a variety of interests affected by the petroleum activities, including the environment, Norwegian industry, and regional and local policy considerations. The scope of the resource management is—as a general rule—considerably wider than the scope of the management of state licence interests performed by Petoro. I will come back to that in Part IV.

C. The Statoil model

As a starting point, state participation in the licence system was carried out through Statoil, initially a 100 per cent state-owned limited company which was

---

[4] The term exploration is defined in the PA s 1–6(e).

[5] Ot prp No 48 (2008–2009) 1.

[6] F. Arnesen et al, 'Energy Law in Norway' in *Energy Law in Europe, vol 2* (M. Roggenkamp et al, eds, 2008) 884.

formed in 1972. The purposes were: (1) to increase state revenues, (2) to increase state influence in the sector, and (3) to increase Norwegian know-how compared to what could have been achieved through the normal licence system. In short, Statoil was meant to be a vehicle of the Norwegian state.

This had several consequences. As to the licence system, Statoil was granted a 50 per cent participating interest in all licence groups from the third licence round. The joint operating agreements (JOAs) contained several privileges for Statoil, including a carried interest in the exploration phase and an option to increase its participating interest if a petroleum deposit was found.[7] In addition, the JOAs contained voting rules which gave Statoil a dominant position in the decision-making process.

More generally, the Act on Limited Companies (ALC) of 13 June 1997 has separate rules for companies wholly owned by the state. According to these rules, the state can direct activities more directly as an owner. For example, the General Assembly elects the Board of Directors: the ALC s 20–4. The ownership function is exercised through the General Assembly (of the company). As to Statoil, these rules were supplemented by the company's rules of association section 10, according to which the Board of Directors should submit general activity plans to the General Assembly. The state could then—through the General Assembly—direct Statoil's activities as an owner, and promote general resource management objectives. In addition, the state could promote general resource management objectives as a licence authority and regulator.

D. The SDFI model managed by Statoil

With effect from 1 January 1985, the state's ownership was reorganized.[8] An arrangement was established between Statoil and the state whereby Statoil's licence interests were split into a Statoil economic share and a state economic share, called the State Direct Financial interest (SDFI).[9] But this was an internal arrangement between Statoil and the state. According to this arrangement a share of the costs accrued and a corresponding share of the revenues generated by Statoil in the licence groups were directly channelled to the state. Externally, towards the other members of the licence groups, contract parties and third parties, Statoil was still the formal licensee—with its previous licence interests. However, Statoil's dominant position in the licence groups was considerably reduced through changes of the voting rules in the JOAs. The latter changes were given retroactive effect for all licensees (including Statoil).[10]

---

[7] The JOA is entered into between the companies holding a production licence. The JOA is made by the Ministry of Petroleum and Energy (MPE), and entering into such an agreement is a licence term: PA s 3–3 para 4.

[8] Based on St meld No 73 (1983–84) and Innst S No 321 (1983–84).

[9] SDFI is a term covering the state economic share of all licences.

[10] This created no formal problems since these changes were beneficial to the other licensees. Statoil had to accept its owner's arrangement.

The privileges of Statoil were gradually reduced. From the fifteenth licence round Statoil was not granted an interest in all licences. This was a result of Norway's implementation of the Licensing Directive.[11] According to the Directive, Statoil must be treated as a normal commercial entity, which excludes any form of privilege in its favour. On the other hand, the Directive does not exclude or limit participation by the state. This principle has been implemented in PA s 3–6: 'The King may decide that the Norwegian State shall participate in petroleum activities according to this Act.'

According to Art 6 of the Directive, such participation can be managed by the state itself or through a legal person. In practice, Statoil managed the SDFI through its ordinary organization in licences where both Statoil and the SDFI had an economic interest. However, in some licences only the SDFI had an economic interest. In those cases a separate entity in Statoil managed the SDFI.[12] Externally, Statoil always was the licence holder.

E. The 2001 reform

In 2001, a major new reorganization took place. A basic distinction was made between the role as owner and the role as resource manager. The latter role was best executed by the licence authority and regulator.[13] Consequently, Statoil was no longer regarded as a vehicle of the Norwegian state. In addition, there was an international privatization trend regarding national oil companies.[14] Accordingly, Statoil was partly privatized and floated on the stock exchange. The state is still a majority owner.[15]

However, the special rules in the ALC regarding companies owned 100 per cent by the state do not apply to a partly privatized Statoil. Therefore, the state does not have full control as an owner (of the company). And the Norwegian Constitution does not allow a partly privatized Statoil to manage the SDFI.[16] Against this background the management of the SDFI has been transferred to a new company, 100 per cent owned by the state, called Petoro.

Statoil now functions as a normal oil company and no further mention of Statoil is required in this chapter.

F. The Danish model

In Denmark a model regarding direct state participation in the licence system has evolved that resembles the Norwegian model. State participation in the licences is

---

[11] Directive 94/22/EC of the European Parliament and of the Council of 30 May 1994 on the conditions for granting and using authorizations for the prospection, exploration and production of hydrocarbons. The implementation in Norwegian legislation entered into force on 1 September 1995.
[12] St prp No 36 (2000–2001) 38–9.
[13] See above Section III B.
[14] St prp No 36 (2000–2001) 28–30.
[15] The State (as of 15 March 2009) owns 67% of the shares.
[16] The Constitution s 19.

vested in the Danish North Sea Fund, a public foundation which is managed by the Danish North Sea Partner. The latter is a state-owned administrative entity.[17]

IV. The SDFI model managed by Petoro

A. Relationship to the state

The management of the SDFI is the main purpose of Petoro. Petoro's management of the SDFI is regulated in the PA ch 11.[18]

The relationship between Petoro and the state represents a prolongation of the previous relationship between Statoil and the state. Since Petoro is organized as a limited company 100 per cent owned by the state, the latter can direct Petoro's activities as an owner through the General Assembly pursuant to the special rules (pertaining to 100 per cent state-owned companies) of the ALC. But contrary to Statoil, Petoro's activities as a main rule are limited to activities under the PA: PA s 11–1 para 1. This means that Petoro's activities must be within the functional scope of the Act: PA s 1–4. According to this provision, the scope of the Act is petroleum activities in connection with subsea petroleum deposits on the NCS.

Petoro must manage the SDFI according to commercial principles. This represents a prolongation of the practice under the previous model, but is now directly stated in the PA s 11–2 para 1. Wider resource management objectives are pursued by the licence authority and regulator pursuant to the PA.[19] It is also specified that the state owns the licence interests, which it reserves for itself: PA s 11–1 para 1.[20] Petoro is only the manager of these licence interests.

The SDFI revenues generated and SDFI expenditures accrued from petroleum activities are directly channelled over the state budget. In addition, Petoro must render annual reports and annual accounts concerning the SDFI: PA s 11–8. Petoro's own activities are subject to separate accounts and reports pursuant to the ALC. As to taxes, both the SDFI and Petoro are exempted from these. In fact, the SDFI revenues is a part of Total Government Take, together with taxes, fees and share revenues from Statoil. And Petoro itself does not generate any revenues to a practical extent.

B. Relationship to the other licensees

In this regard, the 2001 reform implied important developments in a formal sense.[21] As a starting point, the state can take part in activities pursuant to the

---

[17] For more information on the Danish model, see A. Rønne, 'State Participation in Danish Oil and Gas Licences' in *European Energy Law Report VI* (M. Roggenkamp and U. Hammer, eds) 277–86.

[18] PA ch 11 is based on Ot prp No 48 (2000–2001).

[19] Ot prp No 48 (2000–2001) 8–9.

[20] This can also be derived from the PA s 3–6. See above Section III D.

[21] See above Section III E.

Act: PA s 3–6. This is further specified in PA s 11–1 para 1: the state participates in the licences and joint ventures established pursuant to the Act. Petoro—as manager of the SDFI—represents the state in the licences and joint ventures: PA s 11–2 para 1. Formally, Petoro then is a licensee and a party to the JOA which regulates the relationship to the other licensees in the joint venture: PA s 11–2 para 2.[22] As a party to the JOA, Petoro takes part in the decision-making of the joint venture. This implies that Petoro is a participant in all the committees of the Joint Venture, including the Management Committee (ManCom) which is the supreme organ (of the joint venture). But Petoro is never operator of the joint venture, the most attractive position for oil companies. The reason is that Petoro is not an ordinary oil company, but a manager of the SDFI. Therefore, Petoro is a relatively small company with approximately 60 employees.

The voting rules of the joint ventures had to be amended due to Petoro's entry into the joint venture as a new participant, but we are here talking about minor adaptations, affecting the voting rights of the other companies as little as possible.[23] Voting rights involving the General Assembly of Petoro, and Petoro's veto right in the ManCom, originated from the previous model for state participation (Statoil as manager of the SDFI). It should be mentioned here that Petoro's Board of Directors has a duty to submit major issues of a political and socio-economic interest to the General Assembly: PA s 11–7. Also, the duty to submit major issues to the General Assembly is expected to be executed according to commercial principles.[24]

As to the veto right, Petoro can oppose decisions by the ManCom that would not respect the conditions and requirements specified in the production licence regarding depletion policies and the state's financial interests: Petroleum Regulations s 12 para 3 and the JOA Art 2.3. These provisions reflect Art 6(3) sub-para 3 of the Licensing Directive. By exercising its veto right, Petoro functions as an instrument for state control.[25] In practice, the veto right has not been used. Today, it merely functions as a safety valve for state control.[26]

C. Relationship to Statoil

Under the previous model for state participation, ie the SDFI managed by Statoil, the latter was responsible for the sale of the petroleum owned by the state. Statoil managed this sale together with the sale of its own petroleum. This strengthened

---

[22] Note that in Denmark, the situation is the opposite. The licence interests are vested in the Danish North Sea Fund. The manager, the Danish North Sea Partner, has no formal role in the licence groups: see above section III F.

[23] Ot prp No 48 (2000–2001) 6.

[24] Ot prp No 48 (2000–2001) 14.

[25] See U. Hammer, 'Norway: Security of Supply in Liberalized Energy Sectors: A new role for Regulation' in *Energy Security: Managing Risk in a Dynamic Legal and Regulatory Environment* (B. Barton, C. Redgwell, A. Rønne and D. Zillman, eds, 2004) 331.

[26] The voting rules, including the veto right, are presented in F. Arnesen et al, 'Energy Law in Norway' in *Energy Law in Europe, Vol 2* (M. Roggenkamp et al, eds) 906–8.

Statoil's competitive position in the gas and oil markets, but was not regarded as a competition law problem.

Under the new model, ie the SDFI managed by Petoro, Statoil has continued to sell the State's petroleum, but now under the supervision of Petoro.[27] Supervision of this kind entails an administrative challenge for Petoro, but does not require the organization of an oil company.

D. Contractual obligations and third party liabilities

Externally, licensees will incur contractual obligations and liabilities towards third parties, for example liability for pollution damage pursuant to the PA ch 7. This is also the case as regards Petoro, but the state is directly liable for any obligations incurred by Petoro by contract or otherwise. Petoro will only receive the claims from contract parties and third parties, and forward the claims to the state. And bankruptcy proceedings cannot be instituted against Petoro: PA s 11–3.

Furthermore, Petoro cannot raise loans without the consent of Parliament: PA s 11–4. This is not a very practical provision, because operating costs and capital costs incurred by Petoro as a result of the management of the SDFI (in the joint ventures) are covered by the state budget. And funds for the operation of Petoro itself are also provided by the state: PA s 11–2 paras 3 and 4, respectively.

V. Conclusion

State ownership has always been an important part of petroleum activities in Norway. Since 1963 the ownership of the petroleum resources in the underground has been vested in the state. In addition, the state takes part in the petroleum activities together with the oil companies. But this state participation has been subject to substantial developments in the last 25 years. We have experienced a development from indirect ownership to petroleum resources through ownership of Statoil to direct ownership of petroleum resources through the SDFI, first managed by Statoil and later by Petoro. At the same time, the state perspective as to ownership has developed from a wide resource management and socio-economic perspective to a purely commercial perspective. Resource management objectives are today the responsibility of the state as a licence authority and regulator. In other words, the state manages separate roles as an owner and as a licence authority/regulator. This clear distinction is the basis for the 2001 reform.

---

[27] St prp No 36 (2000–2001) 67.

9

Natural Gas Development and Land Use: Conflict between Legal Rights and its Resolution

*Wang Mingyuan**

I. Introduction

Land is an important natural resource on which human beings depend for existence and development. Rights to land and rights to other natural resources such as mineral resources, water, forest, grassland, wild animals, and renewable resources make up a related and complicated system of rights. This chapter is based on the existing legislation of China on natural resources, taking the exploration, exploitation, and transportation of natural gas as example. It analyses the conflicts between rights of land use and rights of natural resource development, and puts forward suggestions for improvement.

II. An overview of related provisions in current laws

The development of natural gas not only concerns legislation on petroleum and natural gas, but also closely concerns related provisions of the Constitution, and provisions of the Real Right Law, the Mineral Resources Law, and the Land Administration Law.

The Constitution in Art 9 states that all mineral resources, waters, forests, mountains, grassland, unreclaimed land, beaches and other natural resources are owned by the state, with the exception of those owned by the collectives (rural and suburban communities); urban lands are owned by the state; land in rural areas and suburbs is owned by the collectives, except as otherwise provided to be owned by the state.[1]

* Associate Professor and Executive Director, Centre for Environmental, Natural Resources, and Energy Law, Tsinghua University Law School, Beijing, China; email: wangmy@tsinghua.edu.cn.
[1] Art 9 of the Constitution of the People's Republic of China (1982).

The Real Right Law, the Mineral Resources Law, and the Land Administration Law restate and implement the above-mentioned provisions on the ownership of the natural resources from their respective angles.[2] Article 52 of the Real Right Law enacts specific provisions on the ownership of infrastructures such as oil and gas pipelines, emphasizing that the infrastructure is owned by the state. Article 3 of the Mineral Resources Law declares that mineral resources should be owned by the state, and that state ownership of mineral resources is unaffected by any change of the ownership or rights to the use of the surface of the land. The ownership arrangements that separate land from mineral resources are good for the planning and administration by the state of natural resources, and good for saving costs in developing natural gas; but they also lay the foundation for conflict between natural gas development and land rights.

The Real Right Law fixes the nature and type of related rights in developing natural gas. With respect to the right of mineral exploration and the right of mineral exploitation, Art 123 of the Real Right Law gives them the nature of usufructuary rights, and makes them subject to that Law; meanwhile, in Part III of that Law, on Usufructuary Rights, the Law establishes the usufructuary rights such as the right to the contracted management of land, the right to use construction land, the right to use house sites, and easements.[3] These usufructuary rights exist affiliated to land, and may be important to support the development of natural gas, but also cause conflicts with the exploration, exploitation and transportation processes. For instance, Art 136 of the Real Right Law provides that:

> The right to use construction land may be created separately on the surface of or above or under the land. The newly-established right to use construction land may not injure the usufructuary right that has already been established.

Hence, pipelines for natural gas laid underground and above ground can establish rights to use construction land underground and above ground respectively, which can easily lead to conflicts with existing rights to the contracted management of land, rights to use house sites, rights to use construction land, and other usufructuary rights. A conflict resolution mechanism is necessary.

The Mineral Resources Law establishes the right of mineral exploration and the right of mineral exploitation in the development of natural gas. Article 3 of this Law requires that applications for exploration and exploitation of mineral

---

[2] Art 46 of the Real Right Law: 'Mineral deposits, waters and sea areas shall be in the ownership of the state'; Art 47: 'Urban lands shall be in the ownership of the state. As regards lands in the rural areas and suburban areas that shall be owned by the state as prescribed by law, they shall be in the ownership of the state'. Art 3 of the Mineral Resources Law: 'Mineral resources shall be owned by the state. The State Council represents the state to exercise the state ownership of mineral resources.' Art 8 of the Land Administration Law: 'Land in urban districts shall be owned by the State. Land in the rural areas and suburban areas, except otherwise provided for by the State, shall be collectively owned by farmers including land for building houses, land and hills allowed to be retained by farmers.'

[3] The Real Right Law, Arts 124–169.

resources shall be made in accordance with law. The right of mineral exploration and the right of mineral exploitation are granted after approval, and shall be registered. At the same time, Art 20 of this Law lists the areas in which mining is prohibited, and restricts the lands available for developing resources such as natural gas.

The Land Administration Law lays down rules for conflicts between the rights of land use and the rights of natural gas development. On one hand, Art 13 of this Law emphasizes that the ownership and right to use land registered according to law shall be protected by law, and that no unit or individual may infringe upon it. This requires the existing rights over land to be respected in the development of natural gas. On the other hand, this Law also provides for methods such as allotment, transfer, taking, and confiscation to resolve conflicts. For instance, in accordance with Art 54, state-owned land used for developing natural gas may be used by the method of transfer or allotment; according to Arts 44 and 45, if the land is owned by the collectives, it can be used for developing natural gas only after approval and taking so as to change it to state-owned land.

Besides, the Land Administration Law also sets rules for the temporary use of land in constructing natural gas pipelines. Article 57 provides that:

In the case of temporary using State-owned land or land owned by farmer collectives by construction projects or geological survey teams, approval should be obtained from the land administrative departments of local people's governments at and above the county level. Whereas the land to be temporarily used is within the urban planned areas, the consent of the urban planning departments should be obtained before being submitted for approval. Land users shall sign contracts for temporary use of land with relevant land administrative departments or rural collective organizations or villagers committees depending on the ownership of the land and pay land compensation fees for the temporary use of the land according to the standard specified in the contracts.

Users who use the land temporarily should use the land according to the purposes agreed upon in the contract for the temporary use of land and should not build permanent structures. The term for the temporary use of land shall not usually exceed two years.

What should be noted is that this section is interpreted to be that approval, once obtained, means that the owner of land has agreed.[4] This right of land use is, to some extent, similar in character to the public easement in foreign countries, ie establishing the priority of the right of land use.

The Regulation for the Protection of Petroleum and Natural Gas Pipelines covers the land use of related stakeholders with a view to maintaining security and protection of pipelines. Article 15 of this Regulation sets limits on third-party use of the land over or surrounding pipelines; Art 16 restricts the use of land for agricultural activities, in particular the use of explosives within 500 metres of a pipeline; and Art 19 provides that when a pipeline enterprise is maintaining a

---

[4] See 'The Interpretation on the Land Administration Law of PRC' available at <www.34law.com>.

pipeline or constructing protective works, units and individuals in the area that the pipeline goes through should provide for necessary assistance, and are entitled to compensation in accordance with law.

In addition, this Regulation sets rules for the confiscation of land-use rights, and compensation for the one experiencing this loss.[5] While there are no rules for the confiscation procedure and compensation standard, implementation shall consider together the Real Right Law and the Land Administration Law.

III. Conflicts between land use and the exploration, exploitation, and transportation of natural gas

A. Analysis of root causes

From the many laws concerned with the development of natural gas, we can see that there are unavoidable contradictions and conflicts between land use and natural gas development. A sound grasp of the root causes of these contradictions and conflicts is helpful in order to understand and to improve the legislation for natural gas development. The following discussion of the root causes of the conflicts between the development of natural gas and land use will be made from the natural level, the system level, and the practical level.

On the natural level, natural gas is inevitably associated with the land from which it comes; the two are naturally coexistent. In fact, ecologically, the concept of land is a natural synthesis which includes the mutual effects of natural resources and characteristics such as climate, physiognomy, rock, soil, vegetation, and hydrology.[6]

On the system level, on the one hand, China adopts a principle that the ownership of land is separate from the ownership of other natural resources. This can easily cause conflicts between land rights and rights in other natural resources. Considering many natural resources, especially those like natural gas, are not renewable while always connected with public interest and national strategy, many civil law countries claim that important natural resources belong to the state.[7] China is no exception. In this way, the owner of natural gas may not be the same as the owner of the land, and both the owner of land and the owner of natural gas have rights to develop their rights freely; so conflicts occur easily. On the other hand, generally speaking, China distinguishes civil legislation from natural

[5] Art 13, Regulation for the Protection of Petroleum and Natural Gas Pipelines: 'the pipelines enterprise is entitled to the right of land-use for the land it uses by confiscation in accordance with law, any unit and individual shall not violate the law to occupy it. Local peasants, after the approval of the pipelines enterprise, may plant crops with short root in the confiscated land. The pipelines unit will not compensate for the loss to the crops caused by petrol, maintenance or emergency repair.'

[6] See Sun Hongjie et al, *The Series of Natural Resources in China: Comprehensive Volume* (1995) 175.

[7] See Cui Jianyuan, Xiao Kun: 'The Discussion on Basic Problems of Mineral Rights' (1998) CASS Journal of Law, issue 4, 86.

resources legislation to land and other resources. A customized law is promulgated for each important natural resource, ie the Land Administration Law, the Mineral Resources Law, the Law of Water, the Law of Forest, the Law of Grassland. Current laws and regulations such as the Real Right Law, the Land Administration Law, the Mineral Resources Law and the Regulation for the Protection of Petroleum and Natural Gas Pipelines are concerned with the development of natural gas. A proposed special Law of Petroleum and Natural Gas is under research and draft. The multi-level and complicated system of legislation easily leads to repetition and conflict over rights to land and natural gas development.

In practice, the differences of people exercising their rights can easily lead to conflicts between land rights and the development of natural gas. In recent times, people have focused more and more on the use value of articles; attitudes towards articles have changed from static to dynamic. The focus on the realization of the value of an article is transferred from 'holding' it to 'using' it. In this light, the holders of rights will always find different ways to utilize the object in order to maximize profit. In this way, various real rights may be established on an object. The extension of the means of utilization of articles leads directly to overlaps of rights. As regards land use, the right holder of the land tends to set many rights other than ownership in the lands—*jus in re aliena*. The right holder also makes a selection of the methods of using land after weighing the alternatives in order to maximize profit. Then the choice is made whether to use the natural and ecological values of a parcel of land, or whether to use its economic and social values, and whether to use it for planting or construction. So it is not hard to understand the conflicts of rights between the development of natural gas and the use of land by the holders of rights in it.

At present, natural gas resources have both a strategic value and an ecological significance. It is an urgent problem to weigh the costs and benefits of development, and it is becoming more and more important to evaluate different methods of resolving conflict between development of natural gas and land rights.

B. Types of conflicts

In general terms, conflicts between development of natural gas and land rights may, from the perspective of land rights, be classified based on the rights system established in the Real Right Law. The development of natural gas may conflict with the ownership of land, or with the right of contracted management of land, the right to use a house site, and the right to use construction land; and it may be constrained by neighbouring relationships and easements. A detailed examination follows.

1. Conflicts between development of natural gas and ownership of land

In some countries which follow the accession theory of mineral ownership, the owner of land is entitled to the ownership of the natural gas in it, and that natural gas may belong to a private individual. However, in most countries, because mineral resources such as natural gas are not renewable, and have a public interest and strategic character, all minerals are the subject of state ownership and state control. China follows this pattern. In China, in accordance with the provisions of current legislation, rights to mineral resources are separated from the ownership of land. The acquisition of the rights of mineral exploration and exploitation do not depend on ownership of land. The sole requirement is the approval by the competent authority, subject to the procedures for application, approval and issuance of a certificate as prescribed in the Mineral Resources Law.[8] But the exercise of the right of mineral exploration and the right of mineral exploitation often brings about problems of conflict with land-use rights.

On occasions that the development of natural gas uses state-owned land, the natural gas and the land share the same owner, ie the state. The holder of the right of the natural gas (the developer) needs only to go through the allotment and registration of the right to use state-owned land and to pay related taxes and fees in accordance with Arts 54 and 55 of the Land Administration Law. In respect of land owned by the collectives, the natural gas right holder must obtain the right to use the collective land. So, in practice, the following two methods are adopted. The first is that the natural gas right holder negotiates with the collective economic organization that owns the collective land, to rent the land by contract. The second is that the state takes the collective land concerned in accordance with Arts 44, 45, 46 and 47 of the Land Administration Law, converting the collective land into state-owned land, and then the land administrative authority transfers the land-use right of this state-owned land to the natural gas right holder.

2. Neighbour relations in the development of natural gas

The development of natural gas always involves neighbouring lands in one way or the other. Natural gas development may affect the real right of neighbouring lands, such as with rights of way and construction activity, and the laying of pipelines. The development of natural gas is subject to the requirement of the neighbouring relationship as long as a neighbouring relationship exists. The Real Right Law has rules for these circumstances. For example, Art 88 of this Law requires that in case the right holder of land needs to use neighbouring land or buildings for the construction or repair of a building, or for the laying of wires, cables, water pipelines, heating pipelines, or fuel gas pipelines, etc, then the right holder of such land or building shall provide necessary convenience. Article 92 provides that where the right holder of land must use neighbouring land by virtue of using water, drainage, passage or laying pipelines, etc, he or she shall make efforts to avoid causing any damage to the right holder of the neighbouring land, and shall make suitable compensation in case any damage is caused.

---

[8] See Cui Jianyuan, Xiao Kun, ibid, 88.

3. Conflicts between the development of natural gas and rights to contracted management of land, to use house sites, and to use construction land

Natural gas development, especially natural gas pipelines, can occupy huge amounts of land, and restricts the cultivation of land and its use for construction. This will cause conflicts between the natural gas development and the right to the contracted management of land, the right to use house sites, and the right to use construction land.

First, the objects of the rights of natural gas exploration and exploitation and the objects of the rights to the contracted management of land can exist in different parts of the same land, which leads to the possibility of co-existence. Under general circumstances, there is no priority between the right of mineral resources and the right to contracted management of land; but natural gas is important to the national economy, because it is a mineral serving state strategic interests. So the exploration and exploitation of natural gas may apply 'the mineral land priority theory'. Article 16 of the Mineral Resources Law prescribes that the exploitation of specified mines such as petroleum, natural gas, and radioactive minerals shall be approved by competent authority of the State Council and that a mineral permit shall be obtained.

Secondly, the conflicts between natural gas development and the right to construction land are mainly those with the existing use right above and under ground over construction land. Article 136 of the Real Right Law provides that the right to use construction land may be created separately on the surface of, above, or under the land. The newly-established right to use construction land may not injure the usufructuary right that has already been established. The 'Reply Letter on Relevant Issues of Land Use in the Project of Transmitting Natural Gas from Western to Eastern Areas of 2001' (the 'Reply')[9] clearly prescribes the land right for underground land concerned in the long-term operation of natural gas pipelines after the completion of construction. The West-East Gas Transmission Project is an important infrastructure construction project of the state, approved by the State Council, subject to the Regulation for the Protection of Petroleum and Natural Gas Pipelines. After the completion of the Project, the construction unit is entitled to an underground passage right. The conflicts between this underground passage right and existing underground land right over construction land are to be resolved by contract between the right holder of the passage right and the land administrative authority of related county or city.

Lastly, the conflicts between natural gas development and the right to use a house site shall be resolved by negotiations between the right holder of natural gas and the owner of the house site. The key reason is that house sites are used mainly

---

[9] Reply Letter on Relevant Issues of Land Use in the Project of Transmitting Natural Gas from Western to Eastern Areas, issued by the Ministry of Land & Resources, No 327 of State Land & Resources Letter, 2001.

for the construction of residences for villagers, and the law sets strict limits on the transfer of the use right of house sites. Article 63 of the Land Administration Law states that the land use right of farmer collectives, including house sites, shall not be leased, transferred or rented for non-agricultural construction. So, in natural gas development, the taking of house sites is adopted, in order to carry out development in accordance with the provisions of the Land Administration Law. Subsection 4 of Art 2 of the Land Administration Law provides that the state may take or expropriate land according to law for public interests, but shall give compensation accordingly. Article 42 of the Real Right Law has related provisions.

4. *Easements in natural gas development*

Article 156 of the Real Right Law prescribes that 'an easement holder shall, according to the contract, be entitled to utilize the realty of someone else so as to enhance the efficiency of his own realty'.

Where natural gas development requires to use land that is not neighbouring to it, the construction, passage or laying of pipelines shall take place only after an easement is obtained over the servient tenement. If the natural gas developer fails to exploit, construct and lay in a way that minimizes the losses to the right holder to the land neighbouring the mineral area or working area, and also fails to sign an easement contract with the related right holder of the land, an infringement occurs and damages shall be paid. So, if the natural gas right holder needs to work beyond the allowance of neighbouring rules or to use land that is not neighbouring, it must sign an easement contract.[10]

IV. Resolution of conflicts between land use and the exploration, exploitation, and transportation of natural gas

A. Mechanism and principles for conflict resolution

Natural resources are always important commodities and are, to some extent, of the nature of public goods, which makes unavoidable occurrences of externality and market failure in the development of natural resources. So it is necessary to introduce some government intervention, based on market mechanisms, in order to reduce or avoid the side effect of externality and market failure. Based on this, it is common in all countries to combine the autonomy of private law with government intervention in order to allocate rights and obligations of related subjects, for the purpose of resolving conflicts of rights in the development of natural gas.

The administrative permit is a general method of governmental intervention. The legal theoretical meaning of such a permit is to adjust and regulate the

---

[10] See Cui Jianyuan, *The Research of Group Rights on Land* (2004) 348.

involvement of public power in private relationships over rights, in order to carry out public intervention and to protect the legal rights of the relative stakeholders and the social public interest. The exploration, exploitation, and transportation of natural gas involve various types of administrative permits, for example, mineral exploration permits, mineral exploitation permits, safe production permits in the exploration and exploitation period, project permits, land use permits (including transfer and allotment), planning permits, construction permits, rural area construction and planning permits in the construction period of the transportation pipelines. The common procedure is to acquire the permit for the project itself, then permits for land-use and land planning, then construction permits. Because in laying natural gas pipelines the area used for construction is, for a period, larger than the extent of the right of land obtained, a permit for temporary use of land must be obtained.

To sum up, the right holder for natural gas may, based on real needs and in accordance with the provisions of related laws, and subject to the principle of combining autonomy of private law with government intervention, resolve the conflicts between natural gas development and land right by way of methods in private law such as a leasing contract, or by an administrative permit, taking, and allotment.

B. Methods of conflict resolution

1. Taking and expropriation

As an instrument coordinating public interest and private interests, the taking and expropriation of land rights is widely used. The taking only applies to collective-owned land. In accordance with the current Real Right Law, the taking of land is limited to the whole ownership of collective-owned land.

The limited scope of land taking limits the coordination function of it, which is specially outstanding in the use of land for natural gas pipelines. The land occupied directly and affected by pipelines has a different value of use, based on the physical nature of pipelines and the distance from the pipelines. A complete taking of land will not only be costly, it will also do no good to maintain the original use of the land, as it is not helpful to minimize the loss of stakeholders and to make full use of the land. So it is rare to obtain the right to use construction land for natural gas pipelines by taking land. In practice, it is used only for temporary use of land, establishing right of temporary use of land by expropriation.

2. Allotment and transfer

Article 137 of the Real Right Law states:

The right to use construction land may be created through transfer or allotment, etc. As regards the land used for purposes of industry, business, entertainment or commercial dwelling houses, etc. as well as the land with two or more intended users, the alienation thereof shall adopt means such as auction, bid invitation or any other public bidding method. It is severely restrained to create the right to use construction land through allotment. For adopting such means, the provisions on land uses in the laws and administrative regulations shall be observed.

Among the two methods mentioned in this chapter for the right to use construction land, allotment is very controversial, because it is a method to obtain the land-use right for free and with no time limit. Along with the deepening reform of the land management system in China, the scope and procedure for land allotment are tending to be progressively more strict and standardized. Land transfer fees must be paid based on market value if the allotted land is used for commercial development and construction after having been approved in accordance with law. With respect to the transfer of the right to use the allotted land after approval by competent authorities in accordance with law, the transaction must be carried out publicly in the land market, and a land transfer fee shall be paid based on the market value; if it is lower than the market value, the government shall exercise a preference in purchasing the land.

Article 54 of the Land Administration Law lists the circumstances in which one may obtain state-owned land by allotment. Among them are 'energy, communications and water conservancy and other infrastructure projects supported by the State'. This means that once the land for developing natural gas (including pipeline construction and operation) satisfies the conditions for land used for energy infrastructure supported by the state, the right to use construction land may be obtained for free. Other natural gas development may obtain the right to use construction land by means of land transfer, including bidding, auction, and negotiation.

On the basis of the Law on Administration of the Urban Real Estate, the Real Right Law extends the scope of the construction land subject to public price competition, from 'luxury house' to 'commercial residence', and includes 'industrial land' in the scope of public price competition, and clearly states that once there are two persons intending to use a parcel of land, the transfer shall be made only after public price competition.[11]

But the Real Right Law does not exclude the former method of negotiation, where the transferor and the holder of the right to use construction land negotiate to transfer the land-use right. Although there have been suggestions to remove negotiation as a method, due to its lack of transparency, it is proper to transfer by negotiation for some industrial and large-scale facilities that need support in using land.[12]

---

[11] Art 137 of the Real Right Law: 'The right to use construction land may be created through transfer or allotment, etc. As regards the land used for purposes of industry, business, entertainment or commercial dwelling houses, etc. as well as the land with two or more intended users, the alienation thereof shall adopt means such as auction, bid invitation or any other public bidding method. It is severely restrained to create the right to use construction land through allotment. For adopting such means, the provisions on land uses in the laws and administrative regulations shall be observed.'

[12] See Liu Zhifei, Qin Fenghua, 'Further Standardization of Ways of Agreed Transfer Land: Reading the Provisions on Agreed Transfer State-owned Land Use Right' (2003) *China Investment*, issue 8, 24–6.

In order to avoid possible fraud or malversation, the Land Administration Law and related documents issued by the State Council and the Ministry of Land and Resources all strengthen the constraints on transfers of rights to use state-owned land by negotiation. The applicable scope of transfer by negotiation has become more and more narrow, and the procedure tends to be stricter. The Rules on Transfer of the Right to use State-owned Land by Negotiation promulgated in 2003 prescribe the scope of transferring the right to use state-owned land by negotiation, and the standard in deciding the lowest price of the transfer by negotiation. It establishes a new type of model for transfer by negotiation, and it regulates all procedures of the transfer, the time to publish the result of the transference, and the legal liability for all kinds of violations.[13] The Standard in Regulating Transfer of the Right to Use State-owned Land by Negotiation (trial) in 2006 tries to improve further the transfer by negotiation.

3. Leasing

Article 29 of the Implementation Regulation of the Land Administration Law points out that: 'The methods of compensated use of state-owned land include: transfer of the right to use state-owned land, leasing of state-owned land, and conversion of the value of the right to use state-owned land into investment and shares.' This legally defines the methods of compensated use of state-owned land. Among them, land leasing has advantages in its short-term nature, flexibility, and low cost.[14] As regards land owned by the collectives, leasing is among the transfer methods of the right to contracted management of land, and approval shall be obtained if used for non-agricultural purposes.[15] This means that there is the possibility of leasing lands owned by the collectives for natural gas development.

4. Temporary use of land

The Regulation for the Protection of Petroleum and Natural Gas Pipelines does not concern itself with the temporary use of land in pipeline construction, and the Real Right Law does not have a general provision on the temporary use of land, so the temporary use of land in natural gas development resorts to Art 57 of the Land Administration Law. After the approval by the competent authority, a natural gas development enterprise must sign contracts for temporary use of land with the relevant land administrative departments or rural collective organizations or villagers' committees. The approval, once obtained, means that the owner of land has agreed, and the amount of compensation depends on the contract between the pipeline enterprise and the land owner. The establishment of a right of temporary

---

[13] Liu Zhifei, Qin Fenghua, ibid, 24–6.
[14] Zhao Nan, 'Talk about the Advantages of Leasing State-owned Land' (2008) National Land and Resources, added edition 1, 60–1.
[15] Art 8 of the Rural Area Land Contracting Law: 'contracting land in rural area shall abide by laws and regulations to protect land resources for rational development and sustainable use. The land in the contract shall not be used for non-agriculture purpose without approval in accordance with law'.

use of land equals in essence the expropriation of the right to use the land, for the right to the temporary use of land constrains or replaces the former right to use the land, and will come to an end in two years when the former rights are restored. However, the process to establish the right is different from expropriation.

Article 121 of the Real Right Law prescribes that:

> Where the usufructuary right is terminated or its exercise is affected for reasons of taking or expropriation, the usufructuary right holder has the right to obtain corresponding compensations in accordance with articles 42 and 44 of the present Law.

This ensures that the usufructuary right holder affected by expropriation shall be compensated. The temporary land-use contract in the Land Administration Law only concerns pipelines enterprises and land owners, excluding holders of land-use rights and other right holders of land as parties to the contract. This exclusion not only conflicts with current provisions of the Real Right Law, but also violates the standards of equality and rationality. Considering the fact that the stakeholders affected most by temporary use of land are the holders of land-use rights rather than land owners, the related contracts and compensation should weigh the specific circumstances of the subject directly affected. Considering all this, the Land Administration Law should be amended to add parties to the contract for temporary use of land so as to be in line with the Real Right Law; at the same time, it is suggested that in making special laws for natural gas, provisions for the temporary use of land and compensation therefor be considered. Some local compensation measures concerning the temporary use of land in natural gas matters have considered these problems and can serve for reference. For example, the 'Circular of the Office of the People's Government of Huanggang Municipality on the Compensation Standard for Temporary Use of Land and Removal Placement in Natural Gas Project' requires that

> reconstruction of the house is free from matching fees for city infrastructure, plan management fees and various extra fees. The relevant local authority shall provide the removed persons with house sites so as to encourage the reconstruction of a private house, and also acreage compensation for reconstruction. Water conservancy facilities, water irrigation channels, road change shall, in principle, be repaired or compensated by the construction unit subject to former scale, level and standard.[16]

5. *The public easement as a means of resolving problems of preference of land-use rights*

(a) Public easements in different countries

Based on the intervention of public power in ownership, the easement provided by administrative law occurs in countries with a civil law system such as France

---

[16] 'Circular of the Office of the People's Government of Huanggang Municipality on the Compensation Standard for Temporary Use of Land and Removal Placement in Natural Gas Project', available at <www.dongao.com>.

and Japan. Such an easement, which represents the public interest and replaces the prior easement for the private interest, is called a public easement.[17] The public easement means that the owner of real estate or the holder of the right to use land shall tolerate some encumbrance for the public interest, such as for electricity supply, petroleum and natural gas, communications, public security, fire protection, urban infrastructure, or aviation.[18]

In contrast with general easement in civil law, public easement in the civil law system is characterized mainly by:

a. Difference in method of obtaining it. Article 639 of the Civil Law Code of France provides: 'the easement arises out of natural circumstances on the site, or legal duties, or contract between owners'. As for the methods of obtaining a public easement, most scholars think it is suitable for direct provision by laws, and should be free. The reason is that the public easement is regulated by administrative laws.[19] It is worth discussing whether it is reasonable that a public easement is brought into administrative laws to impose an encumbrance without any compensation. In contrast to France, the elements of jurisprudence for public easement in the United States of America are the police power; and where the legal provisions cause material injury to the property of the citizen, the citizen may request a court to confirm that it constitutes taking, and claim compensation.[20]

b. Difference in purpose and transferability. The purpose of the establishment of a traditional easement is the facilitation of land use and the better employment of the economic value of land, so the transfer of the easement is permitted. However, a public easement may not be transferred at will due to its public interest purpose. Its purpose is the special use for public interests, such as the protection of wild animals and plants, clean air and water, scenic beauty, the maintenance of public amusement, and the protection of history and culture. Because the establishment of a public easement is intended to meet the need of public use, the authorities or utility enterprises may not abandon or transfer it at will, and it cannot be the subject matter of compulsory enforcement by the court.[21]

c. Difference in remedy. The public easement is under the protection of police power (such as licence and punishment). After suffering infringement such as the illegal issuance of a licence by the authorities, or an omission by the authorities,

---

[17] Xiao Zesheng, 'Double Property Structure for Public Things: Public Easement and Viewpoint of its Establishment' (2008) Zhejiang Journal, issue 4, 138.

[18] Yang Changji, 'Suggestions for Legislation of Public Easement' (2006) Spot Report of Law, issue 12, 35–6.

[19] Xiao Zesheng, 'Double Property Structure for Public Things: Public Easement and Viewpoint of its Establishment' (2008) Zhejiang Journal, issue 4, 138.

[20] Fifth Amendment of the US Constitution 'nor shall private property be taken for public use, without compensation'.

[21] See Wang Mingyang, *The Administrative Law of France* (1997) 330.

any third party (entity or individual other than the party to the public easement) may bring an administrative lawsuit to the court for access to a remedy. However, because the easement in civil law cannot be protected by police power, the usual ways of access to remedy are civil methods such as negotiation, mediation or civil litigation, instead of administrative or even criminal methods.[22]

In the United States, public easement means an easement established on private land for the purpose of the public interest. The two common types of easement in relation to the development of natural gas are the right of way for pipelines and the utility easement.[23] Such rights may be established by the federal government, states, counties, cities and utility enterprises for the purpose of public interest. The utility easement usually covers fields such as electricity, petroleum and natural gas, communication, water, sewerage, and pipelines. Its advantage lies in economy, for it does not include the taking of ownership, and it allows coexistence with existing rights. The general procedure to set up such an easement is as follows. First, friendly negotiation for purchase is carried out. In case the negotiation fails, the taking procedure will be initiated by government, and the holder of the property right must be sufficiently compensated on the basis of fair market value. Generally speaking, the scope of compensation includes two parts: loss of property, and damage to remaining property. If a natural gas pipeline belongs to an interstate project, it must be licensed by the Federal Energy Regulatory Commission (FERC),[24] and the federal licence generally equals proof of public use. In negotiations for easements, there is little room for negotiation on the location and time of pipeline construction. However, there is much more room to negotiate compensation, the scope of use, and the effects on agriculture. Over time, many new easements have been established alongside existing easements, because of reduced costs and the involvement of fewer interested parties, so that gradually utility corridors have come into being. For example, a parcel of land may have been first used for electricity transmission lines, and then for natural gas pipelines, or for water pipelines, on the easement or alongside. However, this tendency increases the need to coordinate the land-use relations among the various pipelines and other utilities.[25]

In a word, the fundamental difference between public easement in the civil law system countries such as France and Japan and that in the United States is that in the former it is prescribed by laws and the emphasis is on its compulsoriness; while, in the latter, 'public' is only the description of the purpose

[22] ibid, 331.

[23] Transportation Research Board of the National Academies, *Transmission Pipelines and Land Use: A Risk-Informed Approach* (2004), 35–8, available at <www.trb.org>.

[24] See FERC, 'Gas Pipelines', available at <www.ferc.gov>.

[25] 43 CFR § 2801.5 'Designated right-of-way corridor means a parcel of land with specific boundaries identified by law, Secretarial order, the land-use planning process, or other management decision, as being a preferred location for existing and future rights-of-way and facilities. The corridor may be suitable to accommodate more than one type of right-of-way use or facility or one or more right-of-way uses or facilities which are similar, identical, or compatible.'

of easement, without prescribing its compulsoriness. Under ordinary circumstances a public easement in the United States is established by negotiation based on free will, but if negotiation fails, then governmental power may be applied to compulsorily establish the easement and to pay compensation based on fair market value.

(b) Establishment of the public easement in China

a. Establishing public easement in natural gas development. The Reply Letter, previously discussed, notes that the West-East Gas Transmission Project is a national key infrastructure construction project approved by the State Council, and that the management of the Project shall be carried out in accordance with the Regulation for the Protection of Petroleum and Natural Gas Pipelines. The construction unit is entitled to underground rights-of-way after the completion of the Project. The rights and duties of underground rights-of-way for the pipelines may be agreed in a form of contract concluded with the competent authorities for land of the people's governments in relevant counties or cities. Such an underground right-of-way specified by this Reply is in essence a public easement, but the Reply is only for the West-East Gas Transmission Project and is not of general application. For other pipelines for oil or natural gas, it is uncertain whether the Reply applies. In addition, the Reply does not make it clear whether land-use rights for non-pipeline purposes, such as for natural gas exploration and development operations, are in the nature of public easement. Future legislation for natural gas shall make specific provisions to make the public easement available for natural gas development.

For underground natural gas pipelines, the powers granted and the restrictions imposed in the easement within the most directly affected zone (as defined by specific technical norms) should be similar to general rights to use construction land. In this zone the use of land for the pipeline restricts other land right holders to the greatest extent, and the pipeline enterprise should possess the powers and functions necessary to ensure the normal operation of pipelines. The law should therefore impose compulsory provisions which cannot be excluded by contract.

Article 15 of the existing applicable Regulation for the Protection of Petroleum and Natural Gas Pipelines provides that:

within 5 meters on each side of the middle line of the pipeline, it is forbidden to take soil, dig pools, construct other buildings and structures, or plant any kind of plants with deep roots. Within 50 meters on each side of the middle line of the pipeline and around any site for pipeline facilities, it is forbidden to use explosives, to cut into a mountain for quarrying, to build large buildings or structures. On the patrol road over the underground pipeline facilities, it is forbidden to drive motor vehicles. On the pipeline facilities at or above ground, it is forbidden to walk.

Moreover, the restriction of land use except the key zone also may be brought into the public easement. However, due to a slight reduction of the requirements on security, the intervention of the public laws should be weakened to a moderate extent, and the related parties are granted more sufficient room for free negotiations.

b. Conflict of rights in underground projects should be solved by public easement. In accordance with the Regulation for the Protection of Petroleum and Natural Gas Pipelines, when crossing other ground or underground projects, a natural gas pipeline enjoys a right of priority, which is in exclusion of the provision of the Real Right Law that an easement shall be with the consent of the existing usufructuary right holder. Obviously, the existing laws and regulations of China in relation to natural gas pipelines imply some contents of a public easement, but they fail to specify and define it. However, a question may arise. The right of priority of a natural gas pipeline on land use is stipulated by the Regulation for the Protection of Petroleum and Natural Gas Pipelines. If rights of priority are also stipulated by other legislation on communications or drainage pipelines, how is one to deal with the conflict between such rights? It is evident that the key is not only to introduce the public easement in such a field by the adoption of a future petroleum and natural gas law, but also to make systematic and complete norms on the establishment of public easements for all qualified activities, including the resolution of conflicts. In consideration of the tendency of pipelines to form utility corridors, the related laws may refer to the right type of 'partitioned ownership of building' for ground building to specify exclusive rights and public rights.

c. The relationship between public easements and the real right law. The essence of the public easement is its significance in public law. Whereas taking concerns the entire ownership of the land, and expropriation is not involved in a perpetual right, the public easement is therefore supplementary to the current system on taking and expropriation.

Article 163 of the Real Right Law specifies that where any usufructuary right such as the right to the contracted management of land, the right to use house site, etc, on the land has already been established, the land owner may not establish any easement without the consent of the aforesaid usufructuary right holder. In accordance with that provision, without the consent of the land owner and the usufructuary right holder, the natural gas developer may not acquire easement. That is inconsistent with the characteristic that the public easement need not obtain the consent of the holder of a land-use right in civil law countries. It is clear that the civil law of China fails to define the public easement with such meaning.

The public easement in the civil law system grants a right of priority to utility enterprises, based on the public interest relating to the responsibility of land right holders in administrative law, and the land right holders do not obtain compensation for their losses. In the writer's opinion, the public easement to be established in the future legislation of China should be a compound right for public interest, also allowing free negotiations to some extent between both parties. The public easement should be based on the fundamental framework of laws such as environmental law, energy law and real right law, which would produce a result that would be consistent with taking and expropriation, and would avoid disruption to the existing legal system. Therefore, the public easement should in the future be established in the Real Right Law, with its specific provisions in special laws such as the Petroleum and Natural Gas Law.

In this way, the public easement should be defined as a new kind of right with the concurrent attributes of both public and private law. The establishment, acquisition, exercise, change, disposal and conflict resolution for such a right should be provided specifically by laws and regulations. The special law should state that the laws on the environment, resources, and energy directly and specifically restrict the availability of the public easement with its public interest purpose, non-transferability, compensation for land owners, and land-use right holders' remedy through civil and administrative methods. It should be strictly limited to governments, utilities, and some large state-owned enterprises with administrative powers and functions. As far as the development of natural gas is concerned, the provisions on the public easement for natural gas development in the special law should be detailed and operational, so as to avoid confusion with general easements or general powers in administrative laws, and to avoid the chaos that is likely to flow from the confusion.

If public easement in the United States is a completely private right, while public easement in the civil law system is completely brought into the administrative legal system, the public easement which should be established in China will be a compound right, merging the advantages of two legal systems, concurrently with the nature of public and private rights. Such a public easement can be established on non-construction land, so that it need not pass the procedure for transforming rural land into construction land. It simplifies the examination and approval formalities, and it may avoid the complete change of land use, because it is possible to impose some restriction on the existing land use.

The acquisition of a public easement, based on its characteristics as a public right, must follow a licensing procedure similar to that for the construction land-use right, that is, the applicant must obtain the licences of competent land authorities and planning authorities before it signs a contract with the owner or usufructuary right holder of land. Specifically speaking, obtaining all the necessary licences means that the land owner or usufructuary right holder consents to the establishment of an easement that meets the needs of the project, the laws and regulations, and the technical standards, and the parties agree on the specific compensation. If the parties fail to negotiate such a contract, fair and reasonable terms must be decided by a third party, in order to avoid injury to the interests of farmers, who lack a mechanism for equal dialogue in the course of the transformation of rural land into construction land.

The establishment of public easement requires registration, to maintain the stable operation of natural gas facilities. Moreover, similar to the public easement in civil law systems such as in Japan and France, based on the consideration of the public interest, a public easement may not be transferred and abandoned at will. In summary, because of the strategic importance of natural gas development, it is impossible that a public easement could possess the character of a merely private right. Instead, it has an extremely strong character as a public right.[26]

V. Conclusion

The root causes of conflicts between rights of land use and the development of natural gas include natural conditions, system, and practice. Such conflicts of rights exist through the phases of exploration, exploitation, and transportation of natural gas. They include conflicts with land ownership, the right to the contracted management of land, the right to use construction land, and the right to use house sites; and also include the restrictions arising from neighbouring relations and easements. Following the principle of the combination of the autonomy of private law and the intervention of governments, the methods of conflict resolution include not only methods of private law such as transfer and leasing contracts, but also methods of public law intervention such as licence, taking, expropriation, and allotment. The public easement as a new kind of compound right, with the advantages of methods of private law and public law, causes little disruption of the current legal system. It is urgent to establish the public easement in order to solve the problem of preference for rights of land use in natural gas development. The writer suggests that the Real Right Law introduces in principle the public easement, and that special laws of natural resources such as the Petroleum and Natural Gas Law make specific provisions for the public easement for the development of such natural resources. Obviously, the public easement is significant not only for the development of natural gas, but also for the resolution of conflicts between land use and the development of other public utilities.

---

[26] Xiao Jun, 'Discussion on the Object of Compensation for Loss of Urban Underground Space Use' (2008) Journal of China University of Geosciences (social science edition, issue 3) 20–3.

10

Got Title; Will Sell: Indigenous Rights to Land in Chile and Argentina

*Lila Barrera-Hernández**

[P]roperty—at least alienable property—corrupts the moral subject.[1]

I. Introduction

It is January 2008 and Patricia Troncoso teeters on the brink of death. Troncoso is the last of the imprisoned activists who refuses to end a hunger strike over the Chilean government's treatment of indigenous peoples.[2] Though her famine is self-inflicted, it is also emblematic. Throughout South America, indigenous peoples are being pushed to extinction through government action (and inaction) which deprives them of their lands and seriously compromises their access to life-sustaining resources. To a considerable extent, the government's attitude towards indigenous land rights is a result of a desire to attract investment to the energy and energy-related sectors. Though investor companies may appear to benefit from these tactics in the short term, it is doubtful that they will be better off in the long run as sustainability is compromised.

II. The problem with indigenous property rights and natural resource development

Mainstream law and economics theory advocates traditional private property rights, ie those that are *exclusive* and *tradeable*, as a pre-condition to economic

* Adjunct Assistant Professor, Faculty of Law, University of Calgary, Canada, and Abogada, Buenos Aires, Argentina; email: lila.kbh@gmail.com.
[1] C. M. Rose, 'The Moral Subject of Property' (2007) 48 Wm & Mary L Rev 1897 at 1919.
[2] 'Chile: 'Dejará el gobierno morir a Patricia Troncoso?' (24 January 2008), available at <www.servindi.org>; see also, J. Aylwin, 'Chile: Huelga de hambre y comisionado indígena' (31 January 2008), available at <www.servindi.org>.

development. Tradeable property rights incentivize 'rational' market operators to maximize the social value of property by responding to the market's signals. It follows that protecting traditional private property rights is a pre-requisite to efficient and dynamic market economies that can deliver growth and prosperity. This point is strongly advocated by world-renowned Peruvian economist, H. de Soto whose claim to fame rests on the argument that facilitating access to formal property rights over land to the dispossessed is the best tool to combat poverty. According to de Soto, obtaining legal title to the land they occupy empowers the poor by unleashing its transactional value. Through their ability to mortgage, sell or otherwise leverage the value of land, the (newly titled) poor can enter the market and prosper.[3]

Unfortunately, there is no one-size-fits-all solution to combating poverty, and indigenous peoples' relationship to land provides a case in point. Indigenous relations to land and resources stress the collective over the individual, the spiritual over the material. When incorporated into western legal systems, this special relationship generally translates into property and other rights to land and resources characterized as communal and inalienable, and barred from carrying encumbrances such as mortgages or similar tools used to raise capital. In addition, the particular relationship that ties indigenous peoples to the land results in behaviour that defies what is expected of property rights holders under Western liberal law and economics theory. Their approach to land challenges the conventional (market-based) wisdom regarding the wealth-maximizing behaviour of property holders.[4] As a result, solidifying indigenous rights over land and resources could potentially undermine the operation of the free market, and, because those rights are generally inalienable, lock up otherwise valuable resources. This prompted one South American leader, Peru's president Alan Garcia, to compare indigenous peoples of the Amazon to 'the vegetable garden keeper's dog' (*el perro del hortelano*) who, as the Spanish saying goes, does not eat, and prevents everyone else from eating too.[5]

Despite its obvious limitations in explaining the diversity and complexity of human behaviour in relation to land,[6] the law and economics approach dominates current thinking on property over land and economic development.[7] Turned on its head, it tells us that indigenous land rights, typically collective, stripped of

---

[3] H. de Soto, *El Misterio del Capital* (2001), on which see further Watson Hamilton and Bankes in this volume.

[4] In her book tracing the saga of the Wichi in Argentina, M. Carrasco, includes very detailed first-person accounts of the difficulties that indigenous persons face when attempting to define their relation to the land in western terms. See M. Carrasco, *Tierras Duras* (2008). See also, E. Dannenmaier, 'Beyond Indigenous Property Rights: Exploring the Emergence of a Distinctive Connection Doctrine' (2008) Wash U L Rev 53.

[5] A. García, 'El síndrome del perro del hortelano' in *El Comercio*, 27 October 2007, available at <www.elcomercio.com.pe>.

[6] For a critique of the law and economics approach to land ownership see: E. M. Peñalver, 'Land Virtues' (2009) Cornell L Rev 821.

[7] de Soto, above n 3.

their transactional value by the restrictions generally placed upon them, and out-side the reach of rational wealth-maximizing operators, do not deserve the same protection as traditional private property, or—at least—are not held in such high regard. Though not explicitly, this negative expression of the law and economics argument is the paradigm in place in many parts of South America, and particu-larly the Southern Cone, in connection to traditional indigenous territories and those peoples' struggles to assert their rights.

As shall be illustrated below, in relation to Chile and Argentina, governments pay lip-service to culturally correct indigenous land rights, but generally fail to follow up in practice by aligning local rules and action with the level of protec-tion that such recognition entails. Instead, they promote individual property in a veiled attempt to incorporate indigenous lands to the market and they delay rec-ognition and titling of traditional lands. In the latter case, maintaining indigen-ous rights to property in a legal limbo is a convenient way of unlocking valuable resources from under the grip of indigenous groups.

III. The international law connection

Land and resource rights are at the centre of international human rights discus-sions concerning indigenous peoples. Vindication of indigenous territorial rights in the Southern Cone and throughout Latin America is grounded in international human rights law and practice. Most claims are anchored on Convention 169 of the International Labour Organization concerning Indigenous and Tribal Peoples in Independent Countries (ILO 169),[8] the only non-assimilationist indi-genous rights instrument with binding force.[9] In addition, the Inter-American Human Rights System of the Organization of American States (OAS), may be the most active international dispute resolution forum currently dealing with indigenous rights issues. The United Nations Special Rapporteur on the situation of human rights and fundamental freedoms of indigenous people is also very active in the area. What follows is a brief overview of the objectives and functions of ILO 169, the Inter-American System, and the Special Rapporteur.

A. ILO 169

Concluded in 1989, ILO 169 was the first international instrument to deal with indigenous rights in a non-assimilationist fashion, and remains the only pro-gressive, legally-binding instrument on the subject. ILO 169 is of great relevance in Latin America which accounts for 14 out of its 20 total ratifications, includ-ing those of Argentina and Chile. Its application is backed by the prestige and

---

[8] Available at <www.ilo.org>.
[9] Its predecessor, ILO 107 was clearly assimilationist and focuses on indigenous labour protection.

experience of the International Labour Organization, the oldest specialized agency of the UN, with long standing monitoring and enforcement procedures.[10]

Infused by the principles of respect and participation, ILO 169 recognizes indigenous and tribal peoples as a clearly distinct stakeholder group with a 'right to decide their own priorities for the process of development as it affects their lives, (...) and the lands they occupy or otherwise use'.[11] Indigenous land rights are dealt with in no uncertain terms under Art 14, which states that:

1. The rights of ownership and possession of the peoples concerned over the lands which they traditionally occupy shall be recognised. In addition, measures shall be taken in appropriate cases to safeguard the right of the peoples concerned to use lands not exclusively occupied by them, but to which they have traditionally had access for their subsistence and traditional activities. Particular attention shall be paid to the situation of nomadic peoples and shifting cultivators in this respect.

2. Governments shall take steps as necessary to identify the lands which the peoples concerned traditionally occupy, and to guarantee effective protection of their rights of ownership and possession.

Governments are specifically instructed to take special account of the importance of the cultural and spiritual relationship between indigenous peoples and their territories, particularly the 'collective aspects of this relationship'.[12] Regarding mineral and sub-surface resources, governments must consult indigenous peoples 'before undertaking or permitting any programmes for the exploration or exploitation of such resources pertaining to their lands'.[13]

B. The Inter-American System

The Inter-American Human Rights System (IAHR System) provides recourse to people in the Americas who have suffered violations of their human rights and have been unable to find justice in their own country. The IAHR System follows two main documents: the American Declaration on the Rights and Duties of Man (1948),[14] and the American Convention on Human Rights (1969), which expands and updates the principles and rights contained in the Declaration.[15] Though the right to property is included in the 1948 and 1969 instruments, it is generic and does not cater to the peculiarities of indigenous land tenure. To

[10] ILO members must address requests for information resulting from complaint procedures initiated before the Organization and must present periodic reports on the status of legislation and practice in relation to the matters dealt with in its Conventions and Recommendations regardless of ratification.
[11] Art 7.
[12] Art 12.
[13] Art 15.2.
[14] OEA, AG/RES. 1591 (XXVIII-O/98). OEA/Ser.L.V./II 82 doc 6 rev 1 at 17 (1992).
[15] American Convention on Human Rights, O.A.S. Treaty Series No. 36, 1144 U.N.T.S. 123 entered into force July 18, 1978, *reprinted* in Basic Documents Pertaining to Human Rights in the Inter-American System, OEA/Ser.L.V/II.82 doc 6 rev 1 at 25 (1992).

bridge that and other gaps, the OAS is currently working on the final revision of the American Declaration on the Rights of Indigenous Peoples.[16]

The institutional pillars of the system are the Inter-American Commission on Human Rights, based in Washington, DC, and the Inter-American Court on Human Rights, located in San José, Costa Rica. Rather than having adjudicatory powers, the Commission functions as a fact-finding and conciliatory body. It is empowered to receive, investigate, and analyse individual allegations of human rights violations, conduct on-site visits, observe the general human rights situation in member states, and publish reports of its findings. It may recommend the adoption of measures to improve the protection of human rights in specific cases. Where all else fails, it can also send a case to the Inter-American Court for adjudication.

Standing requirements for petitioning the Commission are broad, allowing any citizen of a member state to petition regardless of harm. Petitions may proceed against the state and its agents or against any person where it can *prima facie* be demonstrated that the state failed to act to prevent a violation of human rights or failed to carry out proper follow-up after a violation, including the investigation and sanction of those responsible. The requirement of exhaustion of local remedies that is common to international tribunals also applies to the Commission's jurisdiction.

The highest level of recourse within the System is the Inter-American Court. The Court has both advisory and adjudicatory powers.[17] However, only states and the Commission have a right to submit a case to the Court.[18] If a breach is found, the Court can order a state to take specific measures to ensure the enjoyment of the right or freedom violated. It can also order remedies and compensation.[19] Its judgments are binding and establish precedents.

Over the last decade, the System has intervened in numerous cases involving indigenous peoples. The case law and opinions of the Inter-American System seem to be increasingly supportive of indigenous land claims.[20]

C. The UN Special Rapporteur

Among the main functions of the Rapporteur is the ability to conduct fact-finding country visits to assess the situation of indigenous peoples. As a result of those visits the Rapporteur issues reports with findings and recommendations

---

[16] For additional information see, Indian Law Resource Center website, available at <www.indianlaw.org>.

[17] Statute of the Inter-American Court on Human Rights, OAS Res. 448 (IX-0/79), Arts 1 and 2, available at <www/oas.org>.

[18] Inter-American Court on Human Rights, Rules of Procedure.

[19] American Convention on Human Rights, Arts 62 and 63.

[20] L. Barrera-Hernández (1), 'Sovereignty over Natural Resources under Examination: The Inter-American System for Human Rights and Natural Resource Allocation' (Spring 2006) XII Annual Survey of International & Comparative Law, 43.

to improve the conditions of indigenous peoples in the country. Former Special Rapporteur, R. Stavenhagen, visited Chile in 2003. No Rapporteur has visited Argentina to date.[21]

IV. Chile

A. Background

In the investment community Chile has a reputation of being a safe and dynamic market backed by sound and steady free-market policies and institutions, as well as a long-standing commitment to trade liberalization. From 2003 to 2008, foreign direct investment inflows quadrupled.[22] Mining, forestry, and energy are among the sectors most favoured by investors, with energy and mining expected to account for 70 per cent of investment in 2009–2012.[23] However, Chile's model economy comes at a very high price for its indigenous minority.

For all their efficiency and diligence in facilitating investment, when it comes to recognizing and implementing indigenous rights to land and resources, Chile's institutions move at a surprisingly glacial pace, and display such duplicity and lack of serious political will that the entire international human rights community has been called upon to intervene in one way or another.[24] This contrast sets the stage for continuous and protracted conflicts between government, industry, and indigenous groups.[25] Whether the disputes have to do with natural resource extraction or energy development, the common denominator is the struggle for access to traditional indigenous territories and resources.

Of the numerous conflicts currently underway,[26] hydroelectricity development in the Bio Bio River system provides a good illustration of Chile's treatment of indigenous claims to ancestral territories and resources. Although the case may not be one of the most resounding ones today, it was the first one to test the newly democratic state's commitment to protecting indigenous rights, particularly to land and resources. Its long history provides a unique window into what may be viewed as a systematic and deliberate pattern of exclusion and discrimination on behalf of a narrowly conceived notion of development.

---

[21] See Office of the United Nations High Commissioner for Human Rights, available at <www2.ohchr.org>.

[22] Chile claims to have more bilateral or regional trade agreements than any other country. US CIA World Factbook, available at <www.cia.gov>.

[23] The Economist, Forecast (17 February 2009), available at <www.economist.com>.

[24] IWGIA, *The Indigenous World 2008*, Copenhagen (2008), available at <www.iwgia.org>.

[25] Indigenous peoples make up around 10% of the country's population: J. Alwyn, 'Indigenous Rights in Chile' (1999) ILB 72, available at <www.austlii.edu.au>.

[26] Logging in indigenous land is also very contentious. See articles published in Indigenous People's Issues Today, available at <www.indigenousissuestoday.blogspot.com>.

B. Indigenous territories and the law

In 2001 Chile created a 'Truth Commission' (Comision Verdad Histórica y Nuevo Trato) to look at the historical evolution of relations between indigenous peoples and the state. Its report, including the Commission's advice on advancing indigenous democratic participation and the recognition and enjoyment of their rights, was issued in 2003.[27] The extensive report details a pattern of state-sponsored oppression which, through fraudulent and violent methods, managed to eradicate indigenous peoples from the vast majority of their ancestral territories. While the Chilean army played an undeniable part, often the agents of this oppression were natural resource concession-holders.

In the early days of the republic's consolidation, obeying the mandates of 'civilization', indigenous peoples were cornered into reservations. The goal was to force the disappearance of the indigenous, ie 'barbaric', identity through assimilation. This initial thrust managed to strip indigenous groups of most of their territories. However, given their stubborn resistance to full assimilation, the state's approach later changed to one of 'integration'.

To promote integration the law mandated that the remaining communal land holdings be parcelled out and titled to individual indigenous persons. Individual property rights enabled those persons' integration into mainstream society by opening the doors to the formal economy, particularly through their newly acquired ability to sell their lands to non-indigenous parties. Most importantly, from the point of view of law and economics, indigenous lands could enter the market and fulfil their economic development potential.[28]

After a short-lived attempt at reversing these practices and implementing a more equitable system of land tenure that ended with the 1973 military coup,[29] the approach described above was reinstated and intensified. Claiming concern for legitimating individual indigenous property rights, Decree 2568 of 1979 deepened the division and dissolution of indigenous communities and nearly wiped out what was left of indigenous land holdings. Notwithstanding the high hopes that accompanied the return to democracy in 1990, a 1993 Indigenous Law[30]—still in force today—solidified and reinforced the landscape of land tenure inherited from the military dictatorship.

---

[27] Chile, Informe Comisión Verdad Histórica y Nuevo Trato 2001–2003, available at <biblioteca.serindigena.org>.
[28] As reported by the Commission, the main legal vehicles used were Law 4169 of 1927 and Decree Law 4111 of 1931.
[29] The 1950s saw the rise of a pro-indigenous movement that ended in 1973 with the military coup that overthrew Allende.
[30] Ley Indígena 19.253, Establece normas sobre protección, fomento y desarrollo de los indígenas, y crea la Corporación Nacional de Desarrollo Indígena, available at <www.conadi.cl>.

The Indigenous Law recognizes indigenous ownership in those registered *occupied* lands assigned and/or titled to indigenous persons or communities[31] under the early state's indigenous reservation and settlement laws, as may be accredited by existing documentation (Art 12.1) or by judicial determination. Article 12.2 also designates as indigenous lands those that '*have been* historically occupied and *are* possessed',[32] by indigenous persons provided they are recorded in the Indigenous Lands Registry created for that purpose. The change of tense highlighted signals a deliberate willingness to restrict its application to *presently* occupied lands, ie a minimal portion of traditional lands. To make matters worse, the letter of the law is somewhat contradictory in that recording of historical possession requires proof of title. Neither the law nor the Indigenous Lands Registry's regulations provide any specific guidance regarding alternative means of accreditation of ancestral ownership outside written title.[33] On the contrary, Art 54 of the Indigenous Law confines the application of indigenous custom as a source of law to the resolution of controversies amongst indigenous persons. Also, Chile's Constitution establishes that the manner in which property is acquired can only be determined by law,[34] and the property rules contained in the Civil Code, applicable by default, do not contemplate traditional or customary indigenous uses as a source of property rights over land and resources. Hence, Art 12.2 is inoperative in practice.[35]

Perhaps the most problematic issue with the Indigenous Law is its glaring omission of *unoccupied* ancestral lands, which make up a disproportionately large piece of traditional indigenous territories. Although the Indigenous Law recognizes indigenous ownership in any (registered) lands awarded by the government to indigenous persons or communities, it does not link this type of conveyance to restitution of ancestral lands. In fact, the process set up under the special 'Land and Water Fund', an indigenous land titling programme, allows authorities to swap indigenous lands for other lands if the lands prioritized in the claim are ineligible.[36] Further, the law does not recognize property rights to natural resources and only refers to the conditions of use.

By law, communal indigenous lands cannot be sold to non-indigenous persons, and cannot bear encumbrances unless under authorization from the government agency in charge of indigenous affairs, ie the Corporación Nacional de Desarrollo Indígena—CONADI. Interestingly, although communal lands cannot be rented or put under third party administration under any circumstances,

---

[31] 'Indigenous' is defined in the law. A person or community must meet the law's requirement in order to be recognized as owner under the law. Recognition as indigenous person or community also requires registration and other procedures determined in the law. An in-depth discussion of the issues and hurdles raised by those requirements is beyond the scope of this chapter.

[32] Emphasis added.

[33] Decreto Supremo 50, Art 6; an exception applies to Easter Island peoples under Art 69.

[34] Art 19.24.

[35] Chile, *Código Civil*, available at <www.unhcr.org/refworld>. G. Aguilar Cavallo, 'El título indígena y su aplicabilidad en el Derecho chileno' (2005), available at <www.scielo.cl>.

[36] CONADI, Fondo de Tierras y Aguas, <www.conadi.cl>.

the same prohibition does not apply to individual indigenous property. Contrary to the recommendations issued by the UN Special Rapporteur on Indigenous Rights, the law also contains several provisions allowing for division and titling of communal property. The Rapporteur noted that while titling of individual parcels was slow and insufficient, reconstruction and restitution of traditional communal lands, though essential, was non-existent.[37] Another incentive to individual property is that individual plots can be swapped for non-indigenous lands which automatically convert into indigenous lands and free up the original tract. As illustrated by the Bio Bio River case study below, the operating philosophy behind the law is too obviously one of dividing and conquering.

Recently, Chile's president unveiled a new policy on indigenous peoples reaffirming her administration's commitment to continued progress.[38] However, shortly after its issuance, the government infuriated activists by attempting to curtail the protection due to indigenous peoples under ILO 169 at the time of the Convention's ratification and local implementation.[39] After repeated attempts to make explicit reservations were rejected by the ILO, the government eventually ratified ILO 169 as is but sneaked into the ratification document a reference to the correspondence that had taken place between the government and the ILO.[40] The idea behind that move is that the strategically placed reference could eventually come in handy as interpretative data and allow Chile to restrict domestic application of ILO 169. Further evidence of the fact that Chile has not fully embraced the principles of ILO 169 is the recently proposed constitutional amendment addressing indigenous issues, and the manner in which it is being handled. Contrary to the requirements of ILO 169, the Senate report originating the proposal is being debated behind closed doors and without the participation of indigenous peoples. According to a member of the UN Indigenous Forum with access to the report, the proposal insists on subordinating ILO 169 to Chilean law and generally cancels any gains deriving from its ratification, including rights to land and resources.[41] This latest development is entirely consonant with Chile's approach to the case below.

C. Harnessing the Bio Bio: applied doubletalk

In 1989 the Chilean government approved an ambitious hydro-electric development plan for the upper Bio Bio River area on traditional indigenous Mapuche lands: the Pangue-Ralco project. The Pangue-Ralco project consisted of the

---

[37] Naciones Unidas, Consejo Economico y Social, Informe del Relator Especial, E/CN.4/2004/80/Add.3, (17 November 2003), available at <www.politicaspublicas.cl>.

[38] Available at <www.conadi.cl>.

[39] See Mapuche newsletter, Mapuexpress, 'La "Declaración Interpretativa" de Chile al Convenio 169. Un Desafío al Derecho Internacional y un Error Estratégico del Gobierno de Bachelet' (9 January 2008) and related articles, available at <www.mapuexpress.net>.

[40] Note that the ILO does not allow any reservations to its Conventions. The instrument of ratification and the correspondence are available at the Planning Ministry's site, <www.mideplan.cl>.

[41] B. Clavero, 'Chile: Reforma Constitucional Cancelatoria de Derechos Indígenas' (8 March 2009), available at <www.clavero.derechosindigenas.org>.

construction and operation of a series of dams to be built along the Bio Bio River as well as the additional support infrastructure for electricity generation. The project was to be undertaken by a newly privatized company, ENDESA, with funding from the International Financial Corporation (IFC), a subsidiary of the World Bank Group. Once completed, the project would supply electricity to mostly urban areas outside the Bio Bio region and represent 18 per cent of the country's supply.

Mapuche representatives raised concerns about the environmental and social impacts of building the proposed series of dams on the Bio Bio. With the assistance of environmental organizations, and backed by CONADI, they argued for closer government scrutiny of the proposal before approval of the first dam: Pangue.[42] The legal battle that ensued ended with the Supreme Court's dismissal of the Mapuches' claims as exaggerated and premature and cleared the way for developing the first dam.[43] Pangue was completed in September of 1996 and ENDESA forged ahead with its plans to build the Ralco dam, 27 kilometres upstream from Pangue. The expected social and environmental impacts of Ralco were far greater than those of Pangue, including the displacement of 91 Mapuche families. Opposition grew and, amidst much turmoil,[44] the families refused to be relocated.

Ralco confronted Chilean authorities with a conflict between the 1982 Electrical Services Law, which included sweeping powers to expropriate lands in the public interest,[45] and the Indigenous Law. According to the Indigenous Law, relocation could only take place with the consent of the affected indigenous peoples. In addition, compensation could not take the place of an actual re-assignation (swap) of lands which would also require approval from CONADI.[46] Despite CONADI's objections to relocation and the opposition of the Mapuche families, after obtaining environmental approval,[47] ENDESA proceeded to secure the necessary land rights for the project. While on the one hand, the company entered into direct negotiations with the affected peoples, on the other, it continued to press for expropriation under the Electrical Services Law.

[42] L. Nesti, 'The Mapuche-Pehuenche and the Ralco Dam on the Bio Bio River: The Difficult Protection of Indigenous Peoples' Right to (Their) Land' (undated), available at <www.unisi.it>.

[43] L. K. Barrera-Hernández (2), 'Indigenous Peoples, Human Rights and Natural Resource Development: Chile's Mapuche Peoples and the Right to Water' (2005) XI Annual Survey of International & Comparative Law 1.

[44] The World Bank and the IFC were repeatedly denounced by members of civil society for approving the project without a full EIA as required by World Bank policy, and for alleged abuses resulting from the project's implementation. See American Anthropological Association, Committee for Human Rights, 'The Pehuenche, the World Bank Group and ENDESA S.A.' (20 April 1998) available at <www.new.aaanet.org>.

[45] Ley General de Servicios Eléctricos, D.F.L. 1 de 1982, Cap.V. Chile, Diario Oficial de 13 de septiembre de 1982.

[46] ibid, Art 13.

[47] Environmental certification for Ralco was obtained in June 1997 and was challenged by the Mapuche. See, Nicolasa Quintreman y Otras contra CONAMA, ENDESA S.A., Acción de Nulidad de Derecho Público, available at <www.xs4all.nl>.

ENDESA secured the final concession permits for Ralco in two controversial decrees issued by the Ministry of the Interior.[48] Decrees 31 and 32, issued in March 2000, were based on an interpretation of the Indigenous Law that contradicted CONADI's position regarding expropriation of indigenous lands. According to the decrees, the requirements of Art 13 of the Indigenous Law could only apply to voluntary disposition of indigenous property and not to other protected uses of land that triggered expropriation, such as is the case of hydroelectricity development under the Electrical Services Law. In other words, development has priority over indigenous rights.

Decrees 31 and 32 of 2000 and the resulting concession were denounced as illegal before the National Assembly and several judicial actions were launched. The complaints and legal action did not stop the project's progress.[49] Faced with increasing pressure, most Mapuche families eventually negotiated with the company the fate of their individual land holdings. However, in December 2002, a few Mapuche women whose lands and families were the last remaining obstacle for the completion of Ralco filed a complaint before the Inter-American Commission for Human Rights. The complaint was based, *inter alia*, on the right to property of the 1969 American Convention on Human Rights which Chile ratified with reservations that shelter the government's discretionary powers with regard to expropriation.[50]

Because by that time Ralco was 70 per cent complete, the petitioners requested the Commission to issue precautionary measures to avoid the serious and irreparable harm that would ensue from completion and the imminent flooding of the reservoir. The precautionary measures were granted,[51] but, unfortunately, the Commission was never able to consider the merits of the case which, among other things, would have forced it to consider Chile's reservation on the right to property. Instead, the parties agreed to enter into negotiations which resulted in a 'Final Amicable Agreement' (the Amicable Agreement—AA) between Chile and the petitioners that the Commission approved on 11 March 2004.[52]

In the AA the government makes broad promises directed at advancing the rights of indigenous peoples. The AA also refers to the terms of a prior set of compensation agreements made with the participation of ENDESA, ie the September

[48] See webpage of Alejandro Navarro, Member of the House of Representatives of the National Assembly, Debate 36 (4 April 2000), available at <www.navarro.cl>.

[49] Barrera-Hernández (2), above n 43. See also C. J. Bauer, 'Slippery Property Rights: Multiple Water Uses and the Neoliberal Model in Chile' (Winter 1998) 38 Nat Resources J 109.

[50] Art 21.2 reads: 'No one shall be deprived of his property except upon payment of just compensation, for reasons of public utility or social interest, and in the cases and according to the forms established by law.' Chile's reservations require that the Inter-American tribunals abstain from making 'statements concerning the reasons of public utility or social interest taken into account in depriving a person of his property.' *Pact of San Jose*, Costa Rica, available at <www.oas.org/juridico/English/treaties/b-32.html>.

[51] OEA, Comisión de Derechos Humanos, Informe No 30/04, Petición 4617/02, Solución Amistosa, M.J. Huenteao Beroiza y Otras, Chile (11 March 2004), available at <www.cidh.oas.org/>.

[52] For details of the Agreements of 16 September 2003, see <www.mapuexpress.net>.

16 Agreements, as final settlement of the subsisting individual claims in consideration of which the petitioners desisted in all existing and future legal and administrative claims with the exception of those required to execute the settlement agreement. That part of the agreement is in the nature of a regular, private and individual compensation agreement concerning land where the indigenous status of the claimants does not come into consideration. Similarly, the remainder of the AA does not contain any specific recognition of the Mapuches' right to own, control, or manage land, water, or other resources. Rather, it is limited to a set of rules to guide management of the Upper Bio Bio area incidentally including activities directed at implementing individual provisions of the Indigenous Law regarding indigenous lands. To be clear, although the government commits to procuring lands for those peoples indirectly impacted by the dam and not covered in the compensation agreement with ENDESA,[53] it does so as mitigation and compensation for the development's impacts. The AA does, however, oblige the authorities to take important steps regarding legal recognition of indigenous rights. It also requires the government to ensure the peoples' participation in future development plans in the area, as well as to impede any future mega-development in the area, particularly for hydroelectricity generation. To achieve the latter, the government vowed to declare the Upper Bio Bio a specially protected area.[54]

Although backed by the Inter-American Commission's supervisory powers, the AA has already proven to be of little effect. Chile's reluctance to embrace and enact indigenous rights can be traced in the follow-up reports submitted to the Commission. It is also manifest in its attitude towards ratification of ILO 169 and the proposed constitutional amendment. In addition, the government continues to lend its unwavering support to large-scale development in indigenous territories, the latest example of which is ENDESA's affiliate's, Colbún SA, Angostura Dam proposal, also in the Bio Bio area. The proposal and the government's—initially—positive reaction to it, have generated renewed unrest among the indigenous population.[55]

The proposed Angostura Dam will be situated in the Middle Bio Bio and requires the relocation of 43 families, including some of the families that were relocated as a consequence of the Pangue-Ralco project. Of those 43, only 17

[53] S. Larrain, 'Caso RALCO: Oscuridad jurídica y compensaciones públicas' (24 August 2003), available at <alainet.org/active>.

[54] OEA, Comisión de Derechos Humanos, Informe No 30/04, ss 2 and 3, above n 51. The Agreement was immediately denounced by Mapuche leaders and organizations who accused the government and ENDESA of negotiating in bad faith. See compilation of opinions and declarations by the Mapuche community and its leaders available at <www.mapuexpress.net>. See also, J. Aylwin, 'Ralco: Un conflicto mal resuelto y sus lecciones' available at <www.mapuexpress. net>; Kolectivo Lientur, 'Entrevista con Rodolfo Stavenhagen, Relator de la ONU. "La demanda mapuche no es violenta"' (24 July 2003), available at <www.derechosindigenas.cl>.

[55] R. Huenteau and B. Quintreman, Denuncia ante CONAMA (10 December 2008), available at 'Nuevamente presentan proyecto hidroeléctrico en el Bio Bio' (9 December 2008), available at <www.radio.uchile.cl>.

have legal title to the land. According to the EIA summary prepared by Colbún, there are no legally recognized, ie *registered*, indigenous communities or lands in the directly impacted area.[56] Though the practical reality may be different, by adhering to the strict letter of the law, the proponent need not concern itself with any requirements in connection with indigenous peoples' protection. In fact, the Indigenous Law is not even referred to in the summary section of the EIA devoted to the legal framework applicable to the proposal or anywhere else.

The environmental approval process is still under way. However, to add insult to injury, when confronted by indigenous leaders arguing, *inter alia*, an infringement of the 2004 AA, the Environment Minister, A. L. Uriarte, said that she ignored its existence and contents.[57] Colbún on the other hand, claims that the Agreement is not applicable to Angostura because of its location in the *Middle*, and not the Upper, Bio Bio.[58] Indigenous leaders have vowed to present a new claim before the Inter-American Commission.

Beyond highlighting the weaknesses of the Indigenous Law, an additional consequence of the Ralco-Pangue case, was to expose and discredit CONADI as the independent and impartial custodian of indigenous interests, including indigenous property interests in, and access to, land.[59] CONADI had been conceived under the auspices of the 'Nueva Imperial Agreement'[60] finalized during the transition to democracy as a tool to end the marginalization of Chile's indigenous peoples. CONADI's creation by the Indigenous Law was welcomed by Chile's indigenous peoples who considered that its composition, including eight elected indigenous representatives, was an important step towards the recognition of their rights. However, at the height of the Ralco conflict, CONADI's Director, Mauricio Huenchulaf, who had adopted a strong position in support of the rights of the affected Mapuche, was fired. According to Huenchulaf's declarations to the press, he had become an obstacle to the implementation of the government's economic development plans. His successor, Domingo Namuncura, was also asked to resign.[61] From then on, the government took care to designate pro-government appointees. Thus Ralco marked the start of a steady decline in

---

[56] The EIA mentions 30 individuals who identify themselves as indigenous. Colbún, EIA, Proyecto Central Hidroeléctrica Angostura, Resumen Ejecutivo (August 2008) Contra: L. Gonzalez Bertoni, Ficha de Observaciones Ciudadanas, Proyecto: Central Hidroeléctrica Angostura (10 December 2008).

[57] 'Porqué los representantes Mapuche tienen que instruir a la Ministra de Medio Ambiente?' (13 December 2008), available at <www.mapuexpress.net>; Santiago Times, 'Mapuche Oppose New Biobio Dam Project' (1 December 2008), available at <www.patagoniatimes.cl>; 'Mapuche Present to Environmental Ministry their opposition to a new dam on the Bio Bio River' (26 November 2008), available at <www.globaljusticeecology.org>.

[58] Unrepresented Nations and Peoples Organization, 'Mapuche: opposition to power plants' (22 December 2008), available at <www.unpo.org>.

[59] Law 19.253 of 1993, Art 39, available at <www.conadi.cl>.

[60] Available at <www.politicaspublicas.net>.

[61] 'Renunciado director de la Conadi fustigó duramente al gobierno' Chile, El Diario Austral (27 April 1997).

the Commission's reputation.[62] Particularly in relation to CONADI's handling of the Land and Water Trust, one commentator laments that under CONADI the Trust was transformed from a mechanism of restitution of ancestral lands to one of indigenous relocation at the market's service.[63]

Perhaps the most disturbing aspect of the ongoing conflict over indigenous lands is an ostensible retreat in the area of human rights guarantees and the criminalization of indigenous dissent. 'The government views indigenous protest as a security issue and an obstacle to investment, and it therefore follows a policy of social discipline, deploying the police force in areas of conflict.'[64] To date a considerable number of indigenous protesters have been routinely harassed, detained, charged, and incarcerated, some under counter-terrorism laws or before military tribunals.[65] Despite token gestures by the government, lately, the harassment has extended to entire communities and their supporters.[66] A few cases have been taken to the Inter-American System[67] and several UN bodies, church dignitaries, and human rights organizations have called on Chile to desist from the persecution of indigenous protesters and to establish an Ombudsman office. The government, however, continues to drag its feet, and the violence on both sides continues to escalate[68] leaving the country vulnerable to outside disruptive influences which can take advantage of the underlying chaos to advance their own agendas.[69]

---

[62] The deterioration of relations between the government of Chile and indigenous organizations is well documented in J. Aylwin O., 'Los Conflictos en el Territorio Mapuche: Antecedentes y Perspectivas' (2000) 3:2 Perspectivas 277, available at <www.2.estudiosindigenas.cl>; and Nesti, above n 42. See also, 'Letter from the National Indigenous Commission to BID' Santiago de Chile (3 February 2001).

[63] IWGIA, above n 24.

[64] ibid at 225.

[65] P. Sepulveda, 'Indígenas-Chile: Gobierno revive ley antiterrorista' (22 February 2009), available at <www.ipsnoticias.net>.

[66] E. Varela, an award-winning documentary maker is awaiting trial on charges of terrorism. At the time she was documenting the Mapuche conflict. 'Se inicia juicio oral a Elena Varela en Rancagua' *Clarin*, 17 March 2009, available at <www.elclarin.cl>.

[67] See CIDH, *Victor Manuel Ancalaf Llaupe v Chile*, Informe Admisibilidad No 33/07, Petición 581–05 (2 May 2007); and, *Juan Patricio Marileo Saravia Y Otros v Chile*, Informe Admisibilidad No 32/07, Petición 429–05 (2 May 2007), available at <www.cidh.org>. In a case before the Inter-American Court, Chile was required to take all necessary measures to guarantee access to information. See *Claudio Reyes y Otros v Chile*, Sentencia de 19 de Septiembre de 2006, Serie C 151, available at <www.corteidh.or.cr>. Chile denies discriminatory application of the Anti-Terrorist Law, IAHRC, Public Hearings of the 134 Period of Sessions, Human Rights Situation in Chile (21 March 2009), available at <www.cidh.org>.

[68] IWGIA, above n 24.

[69] Colombian authorities have recently reported that a detained Mapuche had been receiving training from the terrorist group known as FARC. Servindi, 'Chile-Colombia: Mapuche recibió entrenamiento de las FARC' (30 April 2009), available at <www.servindi.org>. The US State Department has also voiced concern about potential terrorist affiliation of Mapuche activists. 'Chile-EE.UU.: Acusan a coordinadora Arauco Malleco protagonizar "atentados terroristas"' *Servindi*, 17 June 2009, available at <www.servindi.org>.

V. Argentina

A. Background

Over the last few years, Argentina has lost much ground as an investment destination compared to the privileged position it enjoyed when neo-liberal-oriented policies and laws were in full swing. Nevertheless, it continues to be a country rich in natural resources, with vast expanses of unexploited land. Energy supply, however, has not kept pace with demand and renewed efforts to expand supply are vital to economic growth. Accordingly, the country is looking for opportunities to attract investment and revitalize the sector and the economy. As a result, much of its land is coveted today by agribusinesses hoping to grow biofuel crops.[70] In addition, efforts to increase hydrocarbon exploration and production will eventually translate into developers keen to gain access to those areas rich in subsurface deposits and to criss-cross the land with pipelines and support infrastructure. Finally, with water and land in abundance, traditional large-scale hydropower development and flooding of large tracts of land, is also an option.

B. Indigenous territories and the law

Argentina's treatment of indigenous peoples after its independence from Spain in 1816 was not very different from that of its contemporaries in other parts of America. As famously labelled in 1845 by D. F. Sarmiento, then future president of the country, in his book: *Facundo: Civilización o Barbarie*,[71] indigenous peoples were barbarous savages, whose isolation, nomadic lifestyles, and close proximity to nature, precluded them from living a civilized life and from contributing to the country's progress. His thinking, as reflected in the following quote, anticipates de Soto's theories. Sarmiento says:

> [Tribal] society exists, even if it is not affixed to a determined place on the land (...). But progress is suffocated, because there cannot be progress without permanent possession of land (...) which unleashes man's industry, and allows him to expand his acquisitions.[72]

Following the mandate of the first national Constitution of 1953, the 'civilized' governments of the second half of the century sought to 'colonize public lands',[73] which included most lands occupied by indigenous peoples, and to extend 'civilization' to the confines of the territory. The means utilized, ie military campaigns,

---

[70] Though Argentina has introduced mandatory biofuel blend targets, most of its expanded biofuel crop production is intended for export.

[71] D. F. Sarmiento, *Facundo: Civilización o Barbarie* (1845).

[72] ibid at 33.

[73] Constitución de la República Argentina 1953, Art 67.16. Art 67.15 charges authorities with the evangelization of 'indians'.

were not so civilized. As in Chile, indigenous peoples were forcibly displaced, and their lands allocated to those who had contributed to the 'civilization' efforts.[74]

Though isolated instances of laws granting property rights to specific indigenous groups as reparation existed, most legal activity was aimed at incorporating indigenous peoples to 'a civilized and productive life'. To accomplish that, several instruments provided indigenous survivors with limited rights to lands.[75] In some instances land was granted on a trial basis for a certain period of time, after which the indigenous settlers were eligible to accede to full ownership.[76] Setting up reservations on public lands and granting their members a lifetime usufruct of the land was another option.[77] A 1945 law forbade the elimination of reservations or any reductions in the size of federal lands used or occupied by indigenous peoples, regardless of the nature of their title, without the favourable opinion of the authorities. Thus, in general, indigenous people's permanence on the land was at the government's will and discretion.[78] A 'productive', ie sedentary, Western-style lifestyle seemed to be the principal determinant of their undisturbed possession.[79]

The 1994 constitutional reform in Argentina, signalled a radical turn in the country's treatment of indigenous peoples, at least on paper. Article 75.17 of the Constitution empowers the National Assembly, together with the provinces:

> To recognize the ethnic and cultural pre-existence of indigenous peoples of Argentina.
> To guarantee respect for the identity (. . .); to recognize the legal capacity of their communities, and the community possession and ownership of the lands they traditionally occupy; and to regulate the granting of other lands adequate and sufficient for human development; none of them shall be sold, transmitted or subject to liens or attachments. To guarantee their participation in issues related to their natural resources and in other interests affecting them.[80]

The new approach is consistent with the 1992 ratification of ILO Convention 169,[81] which is ranked on a par with the Constitution in Argentina's normative hierarchy.

However, not all national legislation currently in force strikes the same tone. The 1985 Indigenous Law subjects indigenous property rights to land to similar

[74] G. Sanchez, *La Patagonia Vendida* (2007).

[75] Equipo Federal de Trabajo, 'Propiedad comunitaria' (4 December 2008), available at <www.newsmatic.e-pol.com.ar>.

[76] Ley 12636.

[77] M. I. Valdata, 'Biblioteca Popular Etnica' (undated) available at <www.portal.unr.edu.ar/institucional/secretarias/sec-ext-univ/proyectos/bibliotecapopularetnica.pdf>.

[78] Decreto Ley 9658/45, Boletín Oficial (7 May 1945), available at <www.indigenas.bioetica.org>.

[79] W. Delerio, 'Mecanismos de tribalización en la patagonia: desde la gran crisis al primer gobierno peronista' (2005) *Memoria Americana*, no.13, available at <www.scielo.org.ar>.

[80] Constitución de la Nación Argentina 1994, available at <www.argentina.gov.ar>. [Translation provided by the source.] The right to property is guaranteed; expropriation for reasons of public interest requires authorization and prior compensation.

[81] Ley 24.071 (4 March 1992), available at <www.bioetica.org>.

assimilationist criteria as its predecessors, ie actual physical settlement, as well as personal or communal undertaking of productive activities such as agriculture and forestry.[82] Though productive activities may be conducted according to traditional customs, failure to settle, personally work the land, or meet legal productivity requirements results in the forfeiture of any lands acquired as a consequence of the Indigenous Law's application.[83] Abandonment is also penalized with the loss of property rights. Moreover, title to communal property can be granted solely to registered indigenous communities[84] and is extinguished with the cancellation of the registration.[85] Similar to Chile's approach, title may also be granted on an individual basis to indigenous persons. While communal registration requires accreditation of ethnic ancestry, no similar requirement is necessary for individual claimants, potentially making it easier to access land as an individual than as a community.[86] The law does not prohibit sale in absolute terms; land can be sold 20 years after acquiring title.[87]

Just like in its neighbour to the west, in Argentina, the operating policy seems to be that of divide and conquer. That it is so may not come as a surprise after verifying that the 1985 law is only a slight improvement on the indigenous colonization law of 1958 which concerned indigenous *persons* individually rather than as a people.[88] Thus, despite the recognition of indigenous rights manifest in the ratification of ILO 169 and the guarantees included in the Constitution, their implementation is conveniently stuck in the past. No evidence has been found of any attempt to strike down the 1985 Indigenous Law as unconstitutional. On the contrary, enactment of regulations under its authority in 1996 may be taken as confirmation of its validity within the existing regime.[89]

---

[82] Ley 23.302, Crea Comisión Nacional de Asuntos Indígenas, as am. (30 September 1985), available at <www.derhuman.jus.gov.ar>.

[83] Decreto 155/1989, Decreto Reglamentario de la Ley 23302 sobre Política Indígena y Apoyo a las Comunidades Aborígenes, Boletín Oficial (17 February 1989).

[84] Under Argentine law, in order to accede to registration the aspiring registrant must adopt and abide by certain organizational requirements. In her book, *Tierras duras*, documenting an indigenous community's saga to obtain legal title to its lands in the province of Salta, Argentina, M. Carrasco provides an anthropologist's view of the conceptual and practical difficulties posed by the requirement to adopt a western-style organizational structure as a pre-condition to the materialization of their constitutional rights. Carrasco, above n 4.

[85] Argentine authorities may also rely on the intricacies of the law regarding proper legal representation of a communal organization to undermine indigenous claims. Such was the position of Salta's public attorney in the case before the Inter-American Commission on Human Rights. Report No 78/06, Petition 12.094, Admissibility, Aboriginal community of Lhaka Honhat, Argentina (21 October 2006), para 59, available at <www.cidh.oas.org> (Petition 12.094).

[86] ibid and Resolución 4811/1996 (8 Oct. 1996), available at <www.indigenas.bioetica.org>. The preamble to this regulation refers to self-identification as the main recognition criterion. This position is in consonance with ILO 169 ratified in 1992.

[87] Art 11.

[88] Decreto Ley 3964/58, Boletín Oficial (24 March 1958). The 1958 law was very much in synch with the prevailing approach of the day. Its contemporary, ILO's Convention 107 of 1957, is openly integrationist.

[89] Resolución 4811/1996, above n 86.

Argentina being a federal country, provincial law adds another layer of opacity to the picture. Indeed, provincial law concerning indigenous rights is frequently at odds with constitutional guarantees. One obvious example is Salta's 1998 Constitution. Article 15 on indigenous peoples recognizes those peoples' property rights over *public* lands, clearly narrowing the scope of the federal guarantee.[90] Jujuy, on the other hand, did not even bother to amend its 1986 Constitution, which still refers to them in unambiguously assimilationist terms.[91] Neither did Rio Negro, which only recognizes indigenous peoples' rights to lands over which they have actual possession.[92]

Buenos Aires, however, is the most creative; it manages to recognize and deny indigenous rights at the same time. Article 36.9 of its Constitution reads:

The province vindicates the existence of those indigenous peoples in its territory, guaranteeing respect for their ethnic identities, the development of their cultures, and *family* and communal *possession* of those lands that they *legitimately* occupy.[93]

By adding the reference to family, it anticipates the possibility—not contemplated in the national constitution—of individual rights over land. However, again unlike the national constitution, the extent of those rights is limited to possession. It also begs the question of what is meant by 'legitimate occupation'.

All of the provinces mentioned are home to a good share of the country's indigenous population. Because of the concurrent jurisdiction over indigenous issues, the discrepancies and contradictions pose a real challenge. As illustrated by the cases below, the practical application of the law renders very discouraging results as indigenous groups confront provincial authorities determined to make room for development, mostly for energy or energy-related activities.

C. The case of the Wichi and Mapuche peoples: doubletalk in stereo

The Wichi peoples' Lhaka Honhat Association's fight for their traditional territory spans over two decades. Like the Ralco case in Chile, it transcended national borders, and is now being dealt with by the Inter-American System on Human Rights. At issue is the Association's insistence on the allocation of a single, undivided tract of public land free from non-indigenous occupants.[94] Salta's provincial authorities insist on (and have actually acted upon) individual titling or titling to sub-groups, interspersed with non-indigenous settlers, as well as on developing infrastructure projects in the public lands claimed by the indigenous occupants.

---

[90] In the same article, it refers to the need to promote negotiated solutions to issues of access to public lands by indigenous and non-indigenous settlers. Constitución de la Provincia de Salta (1998), available at <www.sinca.cultura.gov.ar>.

[91] Constitución de la Provincia de Jujuy, Art 50 (1986), available at <www.jujuy.gov.ar>.

[92] Constitución de la Provincia de Rio Negro, Art 42, available at <www.intertournet.com.ar>.

[93] Constitución de la Provincia de Buenos Aires (1994), available at <www.gob.gba.gov.ar>. [Emphasis added.]

[94] For a first person explanation of the rationale for this demand see: Carrasco, above n 4.

In its petition to the Commission, Lhaka Honhat requested precautionary measures, *inter alia*, to halt individual titling and the construction of an international bridge and other works within the territory claimed. For its part, the federal government (the party officially named in the proceedings) offered to broker a friendly solution between the province and the Association. It even advanced a proposal consistent with its obligations under international law, but has not acted to block the province's actions. On the contrary, the petitioners have argued that, despite its role as mediator, the federal government authorized works in relation to hydrocarbon development and other infrastructure projects in the areas claimed without consulting the local indigenous population.[95] This is particularly surprising in light of the federal government's recognition that:

the National Institute of Indigenous Affairs (INAI) considers that construction of the international bridge over the Pilcomayo River (…), as well as other roads and various buildings, is appreciably changing the way of life of the indigenous communities, for which reason it would have been advisable to hold consultations and to produce an environmental impact study of those projects.[96]

Moreover, and notwithstanding the declaration above, federal authorities consistently refused to demand that the province respect the country's supreme law, including its international obligations under ILO 169.[97] Instead, they relied on their ability to persuade Salta to come to a friendly settlement and went on record justifying their position on the basis of a Supreme Court decision declaring the matter as one of provincial jurisdiction.[98] In the meantime, while the Commission delayed its decision on the precautionary measures in an attempt to broker a friendly outcome, the international bridge on Wichi land was completed.

After years of negotiations, the Association ended up urging the Commission to issue its decision. The negotiation phase was closed and the petition is now pending resolution. However, given the position taken by Argentina and the Supreme Court's precedent, even in the case that the Commission recommends that indigenous land rights be honoured as petitioned, it is doubtful that federal authorities will make any strong attempt to bring Salta into compliance. Moreover, as far as the impact of development on indigenous lands and peoples is concerned, their negative impacts are already being felt.[99]

The experience with Lhaka Honhat exposes the weakness of indigenous territorial claims despite Constitutional protections and ILO 169. Both federal and provincial authorities seem to view indigenous ownership as a hindrance to development and are ignoring their claims. Federalism offers an excellent cover

[95] Petition 12.094, para 42.
[96] ibid, para 52.
[97] Hernán Mascietti, 'El articulo 15 de la Constitución salteña. Constitución y jerarquías constitucionales en materia indígena' available at <www.bioetica.org>.
[98] Petition 12.094, para 53.
[99] Carrasco, above n 4.

for perpetuating the status quo. For as long as the claims remain unresolved and authorities can resort to their respect for federalism and the constitutional division of powers to explain away their inaction, infrastructure development in indigenous territories, including energy development, may continue virtually undisturbed. Indeed, not much has changed since breaking ground in the development of the Nor-Patagonia hydroelectricity complex in Mapuche territory back in the 1960s.

Though the Nor-Patagonia Hydroelectric Project, including the Chocón, Alicura and Piedra del Aguila dams, is relatively old, its development, starting in the 1960s through to 1990, is illustrative of the precarious position indigenous peoples might find themselves in when faced with development interests.[100]

For construction of the first dam, El Chocón-Cerros Colorados, the Mapuche Painemil reservation, which had been granted the right to use the land under the reservations' law, was simply wiped out and its inhabitants forced to relocate.[101] The other two dams also required relocation of Mapuche families. However, because those families were not titled owners and, instead, were traditional occupants or were only entitled to the use of reservation lands, Hidronor S.A. did not negotiate directly with them. Instead, the state had to intervene as owner of the public lands. Compensation was limited to the value of any improvements, including permanent structures. In some cases, payments never reached their intended target.[102] Moreover, Hidronor, only recognized as impacted those persons and groups that were directly affected by flooding of the reservoirs, and ignored the community's claims based on the collective and indivisible nature of their rights.[103]

On top of the practices described above, provincial empowerment stemming from the 1994 constitutional amendment which, in addition to concurrent power over indigenous matters, gave the provinces control over natural resources within their territories, seems to have a further negative impact on indigenous peoples. As informed by the UN Refugee Agency in its latest report on Human Rights Practices in Argentina 'many provinces evicted indigenous communities from ancestral lands to sell the land to multinational companies, particularly for petroleum, mining, soy industries, and tourism development.'[104] The practice

---

[100] The mega hydroelectricity projects developed in the Argentine side of the Mapuche territory did not receive the type and amount of attention that the ones in Chile did. In part, that can be explained by the tumultuous history of Argentina during that period. Another reason may have been the general lack of awareness of indigenous issues and scarce legal development of indigenous rights internationally. By the time that Argentina ratified ILO 169, the last works of the Nor-Patagonia projects had long been completed.

[101] A. O. Balazote and J. C. Radovich, 'Grandes represas hidroeléctricas: efectos sociales sobre poblaciones Mapuches en la Región del Comahue, Argentina', in S. Coelho dos Santos and A. Nacke, *Hidreletricas e povos indígenas* (2003).

[102] ibid.

[103] ibid.

[104] UNHCR, Bureau of Democracy, Human Rights, and Labour, 2008 Country Reports on Human Rights Practices—Argentina (25 February 2009), available at <www.unhcr.org>. The same information is posted on the site of the USA Department of State, <www.state.gov>.

of evicting and developing first, and negotiating later, has become increasingly bolder as provincial authorities try to take advantage of the deep pockets of developers and foreign investors to advance their own agendas.[105] Not even the 2006 emergency law issued by the federal government to impose a four-year moratorium on all evictions of registered indigenous communities from traditional lands, pending demarcation and titling,[106] can stop provincial authorities from forging ahead with their plans.[107] That may be due to the fact that the law only applies in cases of 'actual, traditional, and public possession, that is irrefutably accredited'.[108] Indigenous customs and use of land are such that, at times, some portions of their territories may appear vacant, opening the door to land grabs by settlers and even the authorities, thereby precluding actual possession as required by the law. In this sense, the moratorium law is in tune with the framework law which subjects indigenous ownership rights to actual and productive possession.

Thus, for example, the province of Chubut, rich in mineral and energy resources, is considering passing a special eviction law that authorizes summary eviction in cases of interference with the use of real property or with any interest in private or public lands in the terms of the Criminal Code, Art 181, even before the person evicted has been formally charged.[109] The law has been denounced by several organizations including the National Institute against Discrimination, Xenophobia, and Racism (INADI). INADI considers that the law will have particular negative impact on the Mapuche living on government lands, finds that the law is against ILO 169 and other binding human rights instruments, and calls on the governor of Chubut to veto it.[110] The National Indigenous Affairs Institute (INAI), however, is remarkably silent on the issue despite the federal government's duties under ILO 169.

Even provinces not normally associated with the energy industry, like Santiago del Estero and Chaco, are actively attempting to attract energy-related investments by displacing indigenous peoples and clearing lands to make room for soy bean production for biofuel. In 2007, Santiago del Estero co-sponsored the Buenos Aires Biofuels Congress.[111] Shortly thereafter seven farmers were

[105] For a detailed account of the newly-forged friendships between local authorities and some of the most powerful investors in the world see Sanchez, above n 74.

[106] Ley 26160, Boletín Oficial (29 November 2006), available at <infoleg.mecon.ar>.

[107] Sánchez, above n 74; INADI, Delegación Jujuy, Desalojo violento a familias de la comunidad guaraní Jazy Endy Guazú, available at <www.delegacion.inadi.gov.ar>. See also, UN, ECOSOC, Written statement submitted by the Permanent Assembly for Human Rights (ADPH), E/CN.4/2005/NGO/246 (8 Mar 2005), available at <www.apdh-argentina.org.ar>.

[108] Ley 26160, Art 2, above n 106. [Translation by the author.]

[109] Bill 187/08, available at <puertae.blogspot.com/2009/02/ley-de-desalojos-letra-por-letra.html>. Under Argentine criminal law, charges can only be placed if the prosecution has met a minimum standard of proof (semi-plena prueba).

[110] See <www.inadi.gov.ar>.

[111] UNHCR Refworld, Minority Rights Group International (1), *World Directory of Minorities and Indigenous Peoples—Argentina: Overview* (May 2008) available at <www.unhcr.org/refworld>.

summarily evicted from their land.[112] In Chaco, only about 15 per cent of public lands slated to be titled to indigenous groups remain in the province's hands. The rest have been cleared and allocated to soy producers.[113] The Lhaka Honhat case and Salta's refusal to grant communal title has also been tied to the province's thirst for biocrop investments. In fact, one of the Association's grievances relates to the continued granting of logging permits in Wichi territory as a precursor to extensive farming.[114]

Rather than a lack of information and resources for demarcation and titling,[115] often used to explain inactivity, at the root of the problem is an evident lack of political will on the part of Argentina's authorities to find a satisfactory solution to indigenous claims. Strained federal-provincial relations and a broken governance system[116] allow indigenous claims to fall conveniently between the cracks. Once there, lack of political will paired with lack of accountability[117] ensures that they remain there.

More than a decade has elapsed from the constitutional amendment that recognized indigenous rights to land, yet no framework law has been issued that deals with its implementation in its entirety. Despite immemorial occupation, for as long as indigenous lands remain untitled they will be regarded as publicly owned property liable to be sold to the highest bidder[118] while rights and claims are relegated to legal limbo. As mentioned above, the federal moratorium law suspending evictions has not brought any relief to untitled indigenous peoples in Argentina. According to Minority Rights Group International,

indigenous claimed land continued to be sold on a massive scale to multinational companies in 2007, particularly for petroleum, open-cast mining and genetically modified soy industries. The result is that Argentina's indigenous peoples continue to be evicted from ancestral lands to make way for these enterprises.[119]

Rather than endlessly waiting for communal title to be granted, perhaps the best chance for an indigenous person to obtain title to the lands he or she has

---

[112] A similar case was reported in the province of Jujuy. See: 'Argentina: Indigenous Guaraní Resist Eviction by Soya Growers' (3 September 2008), available at <climateandcapitalism.com>.

[113] Minority Rights Group International (1), above n 111.

[114] Other indigenous groups and even Greenpeace have taken the government of Salta to Court on this issue. See eg, Corte Suprema de Justicia de la Nación, Recurso de hecho deducido por la Comunidad Indígena del Pueblo Wichi Hoktek T'Oi en la causa Comunidad Indígena del Pueblo Wichi Hoktek T'Oi c/ Secretaría de Medio Ambiente y Desarrollo Sustentable (11 July 2002) available at <www.bioetica.org>.

[115] As documented by Carrasco, several universities and NGOs have developed complete studies and are ready and available to help. Carrasco, above n 4.

[116] L. K. Barrera-Hernández (3), 'Sustainable Energy Development in Latin America and Donor Driven Reform: What Will the World Bank Do?' in *Regulating Energy and Natural Resources* (Barton et al, eds, 2006).

[117] Ibid.

[118] UNHCR Refworld, Minority Rights Group International (2), *State of the World's Minorities 2008—Argentina* (11 March 2008), available at <www.unhcr.org/refworld>.

[119] Ibid.

been living on is through claiming adverse possession whenever, as any other individual, he or she can prove twenty years of uninterrupted possession.[120] This may be a very market friendly solution which bodes well for developers, and even gets a nod from the authorities, but it is culturally inadequate and morally indefensible.

VI. What does this mean for developers?

For as long as current laws and practices remain in place, access to indigenous lands, titled or untitled, seems to be the least of a developers' troubles. Some companies may be happy to take advantage of the murkiness that surrounds indigenous property rights and take a fait accompli approach to socially sensitive projects by doing first and negotiating later. However, if experience in neighbouring countries is any indication, in the long term, the odds are against them. Already, increasing levels of conflict and insecurity are a powerful reminder that development cannot be sustained if indigenous land issues are routinely ignored.[121]

A case in point is Peru where, today, similar laws and practices are imposing a heavy toll on the oil and gas industry. Although hydrocarbon companies active in Peru have had indigenous lands-related troubles of their own, nothing compares to the wave of protests unleashed by the government's approach to liberalization of the land market in indigenous territories.[122] Through a series of decrees that encourage individual titling, and by persistently ignoring indigenous grievances in connection with their territories,[123] the current Peruvian administration has managed to rekindle past and existing disputes and has placed the oil and gas industry operating in indigenous territories in an extremely precarious position.[124] In addition, one need not be reminded that years of government neglect of legitimate social grievances are at the root of the popularity of such private industry-averse regimes as those of Hugo Chavez in Venezuela, and Evo Morales in Bolivia.

Distributional justice is doubly compromised when developers enter indigenous territories. Added to a precarious legal situation in relation to traditional

---

[120] The frequent use of this practice is referred to by Sanchez, above n 74.

[121] Following the reasoning of Alexander and Peñalver, failure to protect indigenous rights, means failure to protect the rights of the private developers. See G. S. Alexander and E. M. Peñalver, 'Properties of Community' (2009) 10 Theoretical Inquiries in Law 127.

[122] For a day-by-day account on the developments of the indigenous protest see articles posted in <www.servindi.org/actualidad>.

[123] For a detailed account of Peru's approach to indigenous land rights see, L. K. Barrera-Hernández (4), 'One Step Forward, Two Steps Back: Peru's Approach to Indigenous Land and Resources and the Law' in *Sustainable Futures: Comparative Perspectives on Communal Lands and Individual Ownership* (L. Godden and M. Tehan, eds, forthcoming).

[124] R. Rumrrill, 'Perú: Estado de emergencia contra los pueblos indígenas amazónicos' (12 May 2009), available at <www.servindi.org/actualidad>.

lands and resources, as is evidenced by the cases discussed and is the typical pattern in the region, indigenous peoples bear the negative impacts of development and are generally excluded from enjoying their benefits. The more enlightened private developers are finding ways of ensuring that some of the benefits reach indigenous communities. However, private companies cannot fill the void resulting from government neglect, and their actions only reach a few communities. A more permanent way of ensuring that development is compatible with respect for indigenous rights and culture needs to be found.

As mentioned at the beginning of this chapter, there is an increasing trend towards the internationalization of disputes between indigenous peoples and their governments as is clear from a review of the docket and decisions of the Inter-American Commission and the Inter-American Court on Human Rights.[125] Having their companies' actions scrutinized by an international tribunal in connection to allegations of human rights abuses is not what developers are looking for when they invest in a country. Governments should understand that ignoring indigenous claims to land and resources is not sound development policy.

VII. Conclusion

More than four centuries after bishop Bartolomé de las Casas dreamed of building a fair society in the Spanish-speaking Americas, where indigenous peoples and western colonizers could coexist,[126] a viable formula has yet to emerge. Attempts to fit indigenous land tenure systems to western-style property law moulds have been relatively sustainable when the collective nature of the indigenous relationship to land is respected and translated into collective title. However, despite legal and policy commitments to the contrary, some governments like those of Argentina and Chile, continue to push the 'productive frontier' further into indigenous territories. They do so by dragging their feet on settling claims to communal titling while making it easier for indigenous persons to obtain individual title and enter the land market than to obtain communal title.[127] However, contrary to what de Soto predicts, individual title does not leave indigenous property-holders any better off. Once individual title is conveyed, and without the mutual protection and strength that comes from communal ownership and management, indigenous persons become easy prey of the market and often end

---

[125] Barrera-Hernández (1), above n 20.

[126] B. De las Casas, *Brevísima relación de la destrucción de las Indias* (1542).

[127] Where indigenous groups lose faith in their ability to defend their communal lands, they choose private title. T. M. Hayes, 'The robustness of Indigenous Common-property systems to Frontier Expansion: Institutional Interplay in the Mosquitia Forrest Corridor' (2008) 6(2) Conservation and Society, 117 at 125.

up landless and poor.[128] The right to exclude becomes first and foremost a 'right to acquire' to be exercised by those who understand the system and can bear the transaction costs that legal ownership entails. The hand of the market is blind to issues of distributional justice. Welfare, which property is so uniquely designed to protect, as Watson Hamilton and Bankes explain in their chapter, becomes an abstraction shielding blatant inequalities. A system combining property and governance may be better able to bridge the gap between western-style development and respect for indigenous culture and lifestyles. ILO 169, with its emphasis on participatory rights alongside territorial guarantees, may hold the key.

---

[128] M. Colchester et al, 'Indigenous land tenure: challenges and possibilities' in *Land Reform 2004/1* (P. Groppo, ed, 2004), available at <www.fao.org>; and, M. Moore, 'Negative Impact of World Bank Land Policies' (11 February 2005), available at: <www.foodfirst.org/>.

11

The Scope and Limitations of the Principle of National Property of Hydrocarbons in Mexico

Jose Juan Gonzalez[*]

I. Introduction

This chapter analyses the scope and limitations of the principle of national property over natural resources of the subsoil established by Art 27 of the Mexican Constitution. The research discusses the difference between state and national property from a comparative perspective. In addition, the chapter describes the evolution of the constitutional and legal framework regarding the role private investment has played in the public monopoly of oil exploration and exploitation. From this analysis, the chapter proposes the adoption of a new approach to make effective the principle of national sovereignty over oil resources without excluding the possibility of private investment participating in oil exploration and exploitation.

II. Models of property over natural resources in the subsoil

From a comparative analysis of natural resources law it is possible to identify three different models of property over natural resources of the subsoil: i) the so-called regime of *accessio*; ii) the national property model; and iii) the model of absolute property of the state.[1]

Under the regime of *accessio* all substances placed in the soil belong to the land owner. Thus, if the land is owned by private parties, the natural resources of the subsoil are under private dominion. This system rules the property of oil

[*] Professor, Department of Law, Universidad Autónoma Metropolitana, Mexico, and Director of the Mexican Institute for Environmental Law Research; email: jjgonzalez@gonzalezasociados.com.
[1] See R. Garza Garza, 'El derecho Mexicano de la explotación petrolera y los contratos de burgos' (2005), available at <www.itesm.mx>.

resources in the United States of America[2] and partially in Canada.[3] This regime is also applicable to property in forest resources in Mexico.[4]

The national property model distinguishes between property in land and property of other natural resources whose nature is different from the soil, such as hydrocarbons. According to this model, property of resources in the subsoil is vested in the state. In consequence, the state has the exclusive right to grant concessions to exploit such resources under the terms and conditions it establishes. This system governs property in waters[5] and mineral resources in Mexico,[6] as well as property in hydrocarbons in Argentina,[7] Brazil,[8] and Peru.[9]

The model of absolute governmental or state property consists of recognizing the absolute property of the state over natural resources, excluding the possibility of any kind of private property. The model also prohibits the possibility of private parties participating in the exploitation of such resources. This is the legal

---

[2] In that country, although oil and gas laws vary by state, the laws regarding ownership prior to, at, and after extraction are nearly universal. An owner of real estate also owns the minerals underneath the surface, unless the minerals are severed under a previous deed or an agreement.

[3] In Canada some oil and gas rights are held privately in fee simple or in other types of freehold estates, but the foundation of Canada's oil and gas has been the exploitation of minerals that are owned by the provincial governments. S 109 of the Constitution Act 1897 explicitly grants the ownership of all lands, mines, minerals and royalties to the original provinces of Ontario, Québec, Nova Scotia and New Brunswick. After the entry of British Columbia, Prince Edwards Island and Newfoundland into Canada, they were granted ownership of the mineral resources from the federal government. Only the provinces of Alberta, Saskatchewan and Manitoba were not originally granted ownership of the mines and minerals upon entry into Canada. At the time, these interests remain vested in the federal government. With the exception of freehold estates, the federal government still owns and administers the mines and minerals located outside the provincial boundaries in the three Territories. The federal government has also retained mineral ownership of areas off Canada's coasts. See Blakes Lawyers, 'Overview of oil and gas in Canada' (2008), available at <www.blakes.com>.

[4] According to Art 5 of the General Act For Sustainable Development of Forests, the property in forest resources corresponds to the people or communities that own the lands where such resources are placed.

[5] See National Waters Act, Diario Oficial de la Federación 1 December, 1992, as amended on 18 April 2008.

[6] See Mining Act, Diario Oficial de la Federación 26 June 1992, as amended on 26 June 2006.

[7] In 2007 Argentina adopted a legal framework under which, even though hydrocarbons belong to the state, concessions to explore and produce hydrocarbons may be granted to private parties. In addition, according to the Transference Law passed in that year, concessionaires have full ownership of the hydrocarbons once extracted. In exchange for these rights, concessionaires are required to pay the provincial states a royalty calculated on the basis of the hydrocarbon production. See A. Hyder and T. Chevalier, 'A protected bay for energy investors' (2008) 5 Latinlawyer, available at <www.Latinlawyer.com>.

[8] On 9 November 1995 the Brazilian Constitution of 1988 was amended to break the public monopoly on all oil activities, allowing the federal government to contract with any private or government company to carry out exploration, exploitation, production refining and distribution of hydrocarbons. See R. Seroa da Mota et al, 'Hydrocarbons in Latin America—Case of Brazil' (2008), available at <http://servicios.iesa.edu.ve/Portal/CIEA/brazil_damotta_d1.pdf>.

[9] Under the 1995 Land Law passed during the Fujimori regime, subsoil resources remain the property of the State. See R. Smith, 'Can David and Goliath Have a Happy Marriage? The Machiguenga People and the Camisea Gas Project in the Peruvian Amazon' in *Communities and Conservation. Histories and Politics of Community-Based Natural Resources Management* (J. Broosius, A. Tsing and C. Zener, eds, 2005) 231–57.

regime currently in force in Russia,[10] Bolivia,[11] and Venezuela[12] in regard to oil and hydrocarbon resources.

For decades, policy makers and scholars have held that the Mexican Constitution, as passed in 1917, established the absolute state property over natural resources in the subsoil. Consequently, they assert that the state has the absolute property of hydrocarbon resources as well as the exclusive right to exploit such resources.[13] However, as will be analysed in this chapter, this argument is based more on an ideological than on a constitutional or legal basis.

In fact, although during the nineteenth century property in hydrocarbons in Mexico was governed by the model of *accessio*;[14] the Mexican Constitution of 1917 introduced a property regime based on the national property model that made possible the private exploitation of oil resources through concessions granted by the state. As will be explained, the introduction of absolute state property was the result of a series of constitutional and legal reforms passed during the years 1940 to 2008.

III. Property in hydrocarbon resources under the Mexican Constitution of 1917

The Mexican Constitution of 1917 did not adopt the classic patrimonial model expressed in the institution of private property as it was drafted by the authors of the Declaration of the Rights of Man and Citizen of 1789 or by the Code Napoleon of 1804.[15]

Article 27 of The Mexican Constitution of 1917 established a property system based on the following principles:[16]

A. The original property of the nation over all lands and waters in the national territory.

---

[10] The Russian government has the right to control and define priorities in every part of the gas and oil industries (including pipelines). See C. Fracese, 'Hydrocarbon resources in Russian foreign and domestic politics in *Energy in the 21st century: risks, challenges, perspsective* (2007), available at <http://www.cartografareilpresente.org/article126.html>.

[11] In Bolivia, on 1 May 2006 President Morales issued the Supreme Decree No 28701 nationalizing the hydrocarbons resources of the country.

[12] In 1957 the Law that reserves to the state the industry and commerce of hydrocarbons nationalized the oil resources in that country.

[13] This chapter will discuss if such a system really is in force in Mexico.

[14] During those years different legal bodies establishing that the land owner also owns the subsoil resources were passed. See, for instance, the Mining Code of 1884, the Law of Petroleum of 1901, and the Mining Act of 1909.

[15] See M. Diaz, 'El régimen jurídico ambiental del subsuelo en México' in *PEMEX, ambiente y energía. Los retos del futuro* (C. Carmona, ed, 1995) 35–42.

[16] See J. Ma. Serna de la Garza, 'El régimen constitucional de la propiedad en México' in *Derecho comparado Asia-México. Culturas y sistemas jurídicos comparados* (J. Ma. Serna de la Garza, ed, 2007) 473–94.

B. The consideration of private property as a right acquired from the nation and, in consequence, subject to the statute of limitation and expropriation.

C. The direct dominion of the nation over those natural resources that had a strategic importance for the economic development: waters, minerals, and hydrocarbons.

All the same, contrary to what the majority of specialists in energy law have held, the original text of Art 27 did not nationalize hydrocarbon resources. This Article kept the principle of public dominion of hydrocarbons that was in force during the times Mexico was a colony of Spain,[17] but allowed participation of private parties in the exploitation of oil resources.[18] In that regard, Art 27, para 6 stated that nation's domain over hydrocarbon resources was inalienable and not subject to the statute of limitations.[19] However, this Article authorized the federal government to grant concessions for exploitation of such resources to individuals or corporations constituted in accordance with Mexican laws.[20]

In addition, the Regulatory Act of Art 27 of the Constitution in the field of petroleum passed by the Federal Congress in 1925[21] recognized the rights acquired by foreign petroleum companies on the basis of the non-retroactivity of the Constitution of 1917[22] and widely governed a regime of concessions that comprised the exploration, exploitation and transport of oil and hydrocarbons resources.[23] Confirming these criteria, by 1934 the Supreme Court of Justice recognized that Art 27 had no retroactive effect. In consequence, the Law of 1925 that established the procedure for private parties to request recognition of their acquired rights was, in accordance with the Supreme Court criteria, absolutely constitutional.[24]

---

[17] See Handersson Bady Casafranca Valencia, 'Ponencia sobre la propiedad de los recursos naturales en los territorios de pueblos indígenas Perú: La pobreza de los ricos territorios indígenas y recursos naturales' (2008), available at <www.dar.org.pe/hidrocarburos>.

[18] In 1910 President Francisco Madero introduced a tax of 3 cents per barrel of oil and a tax of 20 cents per ton of petrol extracted by private companies.

[19] According to Raúl Jimenez, Art 27 of the Mexican Constitution establishes the absolute property of the nation over hydrocarbons resources as well as the direct and exclusive exploitation of hydrocarbons by the nation: R. Jimenez, 'Elementos historicos para la interpretación del régimen constitucional del petróleo de los mexicanos' in *El petroleo en la historia y la cultura de Mexico* (Jose Alfonso Suarez, ed, 2008), 99–118.

[20] See A. Gersherson, 'Hechos históricos importantes del petróleo en México' (2009), available at <http://prdleg.diputados.gob.mx/publicaciones/libros/petroleo_cultura/petroleo-cultura-57–61.pdf>.

[21] Diario Oficial de la Federación, 25 December 1925.

[22] For some scholars the promulgation of such Law was the result of the 'Bucarely Treaties' between the Mexican and United States governments. In such Treaties the United States of America recognized the governments that emerged from the Mexican revolution only on condition that the Mexican governments did not apply Art 27 of the Constitution to the titles of property of petroleum companies issued by Porfirio Díaz.

[23] See Arts 7, 8 and 9.

[24] See 'El Aguila'. *Compañía Mexicana de Petróleo v Mexican Government* (1934) AR 88/28.

IV. The process of nationalization of hydrocarbons

The first step toward the nationalization of the oil sector was not taken until 1938, when the Mexican government expropriated foreign oil companies' facilities. However, even after the expropriation it could not be said that the constitutional principle of the nation's absolute property governed property in the subsoil resources in Mexico.

To nationalize this sector, it was necessary to introduce another principle into the Constitution: the principle of direct and exclusive exploitation of hydrocarbons by the nation.[25] Addressed to reach this objective, in 1940 a constitutional reform was passed to modify the sixth paragraph of Art 27 in the following terms:[26]

In the case of petroleum, and solid, liquid or gaseous hydrocarbons no concessions or contracts will be granted and the respective regulatory law shall determine the manner in which the nation shall carry out the exploitation of such products.

Since that time the Mexican government has assumed the monopoly of oil exploration, exploitation, refining and distribution of oil and other products derived from it.

One year before, a Law in the field of petroleum had been passed to forbid concessions.[27] However, despite the constitutional reform, this Law was repealed in 1941 by the Regulatory Law on petroleum that made possible the participation of private companies in the oil industry through the so-called 'contracts of risk'.[28] According to the Law of 1941, through contracts of risk, exploration and exploitation activities could be conducted by private companies and compensation for the services such companies provided could consist of a payment in cash or of a percentage of the products obtained.[29]

Between 1949 and 1951, a number of contracts of risk were allocated to foreign oil companies.[30] Such contracts concerned hydrocarbon resources under a surface area of almost 4,000 square kilometres of the Mexican territory. The payment to companies consisted of the total reimbursement of their expenses and investments, plus 50 per cent of the value of the hydrocarbons produced by the

---

[25] In his address to the Congress of 1938, President Cárdenas stated: '… to avoid as far as possible future problems to Mexico that estranged interests could cause it will be submitted as a matter of sovereignty that no concession of subsoil will be granted concerning petroleum and that the State has the absolute control of oil exploitation.' See J. Cárdenas, 'La irreformabilidad constitucional en materia de petroleo hidrocarburos' in *Exclusividad de la Nacion en Materia de Petroleo* (J. A. Almazan, ed, 2008) 66–7.

[26] Diario Oficial de la Federación, 9 November 1940.

[27] ibid, 30 December 1939.

[28] ibid, 18 June 1941.

[29] See M. Becerra, *Análisis constitucional de los aspectos más relevantes de la reforma energética* (2008), available at <http://www.senado.gob.mx/reforma_energetica/content/foros/docs/20mayo2008_7.pdf>.

[30] In Bolivia, the Capitalization Act of 1996 introduced risk-sharing contracts for oil exploration and production.

perforated oil wells, in addition to compensation of between 15 and 18.5 per cent of the production value over a period of 25 years.[31]

Given that such contracts were in contradiction to the constitutional principles as defined in 1940, in 1958 a fourth Regulatory Act of Art 27 of the Constitution in the field of petroleum was passed by Federal Congress. The new law created a legal system establishing absolute property in the nation over oil and hydrocarbon resources coupled with a public monopoly in the oil sector that included all activities related to the construction and operation of the infrastructure.

The Act of 1958 constituted an important step towards the configuration of a regime of absolute state dominion over hydrocarbon resources. This Act forbade for the second time private participation in the oil industry. Article 2 stated: 'Only the nation may carry on the different exploitations that constitute the oil industry in the terms of the following article.' Article 3 complemented that provision by stating that the oil industry comprises the exploration, exploitation, refining, transport, storage, distribution and direct sales of petroleum products obtained from its refining; the exploration, exploitation, elaboration and direct sales of gas; as well as the transport and storage indispensable and necessary to interconnect their exploitation and elaboration.

A new step towards the nationalization of hydrocarbons was made in 1960 when Art 27 of the Mexican Constitution was modified again to introduce into its sixth paragraph the following text:[32]

In the case of petroleum, and solid, liquid or gaseous hydrocarbons neither concessions *nor contracts* will be granted, nor may those that have been granted continue, and the nation shall carry out the exploitation of these products, in accordance with the provisions indicated in the respective Regulatory Law. [emphasis added]

The reform of 1960 established also that the absolute domain of the nation over subsoil resources includes the continental shelf, seabed and subsoil of the submarine areas of the islands.[33]

Finally, to conclude the process of nationalization of the oil industry, in 1982 Arts 25 and 28 of the Mexican Constitution were amended to establish that the oil industry is a strategic economic area and in consequence is a monopoly of the Mexican state. In consequence, in regard to hydrocarbon resources, by 2008 the Mexican Constitution established a system of absolute state property with prohibition of concessions or contracts and a system of oil exploitation based on a state monopoly. However, as will be analysed, legislation passed on those constitutional bases has established quite different regimes that make possible private participation in the oil industry.[34]

---

[31] The contracts were cancelled until 1970 by the Director General of Pemex, Jesus Reyes Heroles.

[32] Diario Oficial de la Federación, 20 January 1960.

[33] This reform made it possible for PEMEX, the public monopoly currently in charge of oil exploitation, to have control of oil fields located in the Campeche Area.

[34] Such legislation is clearly unconstitutional: see Cárdenas (above n 25) 69–78.

V. Re-privatization of the hydrocarbon exploitation industry by secondary legislation

Notwithstanding the above, the Act of 1958 has been modified a number of times to allow private investment in the oil sector. In May 1995 the Federal Congress passed modifications to the Regulatory Act of Art 27 of the Constitution in the field of petroleum.[35] This reform allowed the private sector to build, operate and own systems of transport, storage and distribution of natural gas and other products derived from petroleum; in these cases such products are not designated to be used as commodities for basic industries and in the specific case of gas for the basic petro chemistry.[36] As an adjunct to these modifications, the Regulation of Natural Gas was approved by the Executive. This regulation defines three types of activities subject to governmental permission: transport, storage, and distribution. In the same year, a constitutional reform expressly excluded secondary petrochemicals from the public monopoly of the oil industry.[37] In 1996 the Regulatory Act was modified again to restrict further the areas where the transport, storage, and distribution of gas and other products derived from petroleum can only be carried out by the state and to allow a wider participation of private parties in such activities.[38]

Eventually, in 2008 the law was modified to provide a legal basis for the public petroleum company, PEMEX, to contract multiple services and to enable private companies to participate in activities of exploration and exploitation.[39] Article 5 of the law (as amended in 2008) states: 'The Federal Executive, through the Ministry of Energy, shall grant exclusively to "Petroleos Mexicanos" and its subsidiary organisms the assignment of areas for oil exploration and exploitation'. However, Art 6 clarifies the meaning of the cited provision by stating: ' "Petroleos Mexicanos" and its subsidiary organisms may contract with private parties and corporations, works and services required for the best realization of its activities. The payments established by such contracts shall be in cash and in no case shall the property of hydrocarbons may be transmitted to contractors for the works or services provided or for the works executed, nor can private parties and corporations be subscribed contracts for sharing production or contracts comprising percentages of production or the value of sales of hydrocarbons or their derivates.'

Basically the reform of 2008 reintroduced the contracts of risk that had been prohibited by the constitutional reform of 1960 with the unique difference that, according to the new legal text, payments for such contracts cannot consist of transmitting any property rights over hydrocarbon resources.

---

[35] Diario Oficial de la Federación, 11 May 1995.
[36] See Arts 3 and 4.
[37] Diario Oficial de la Federación, 2 March 1995.
[38] Diario Oficial de la Federación, 13 November 1996.
[39] ibid, 28 November 2008.

The analysis of these constitutional and legal reforms allows us to assert that while the Mexican Constitution postulates the model of absolute property of the nation over hydrocarbon resources, according to secondary legislation property in hydrocarbon resources in Mexico is governed by the model of national property as it is defined in the first section of this chapter. This issue will be discussed in the next section.

VI. The current constitutional regime of property and exploitation of hydrocarbons in Mexico

The Mexican Constitution of 1917 (as amended in 1940, 1960, and 1982) contains three principles that govern the public policies and provide the basis for legislation regarding the property and exploitation of hydrocarbons: (1) the absolute and inalienable dominion of the nation over hydrocarbons (not subject to the statute of limitations); (2) the right to exclusive and direct exploitation of hydrocarbons by the nation (which supposes the prohibition of granting concessions or contracts to private persons or companies in that field); and (3) the treatment of hydrocarbons and basic petro chemistry as strategic areas reserved to the public sector.[40] However, the real scope of such principles is defined by legislation in a quite different sense. Paragraph four of Art 27 of the Constitution states:

In the nation is vested the direct ownership of all natural resources of the continental shelf and the submarine shelf of the islands; of all minerals or substances, whether in veins, ledges, masses or pockets, constituting deposits of a nature distinct from the components of the earth itself such as ... *solid mineral fuels, petroleum and all solid, liquid and gaseous hydrocarbons*. [emphasis added]

In addition, Art 27, para 6 adds that:

in the case of petroleum, and solid, liquid or gaseous hydrocarbons no concessions or contracts will be granted nor may those that have been granted continue, and the nation shall carry out the exploitation of these products, in accordance with the provisions indicated in the respective Regulatory Law.

Finally, the Mexican Constitution does not grant to the nation the property of the oil industry infrastructure but establishes a regime of direct and exclusive right of exploitation of hydrocarbons by the nation in Art 28 in the following terms:

In the Mexican-United States monopolies, monopolistic practices, practices interfering with commerce and tax exemptions shall be forbidden under the law ... The functions performed in an exclusive manner by the state in the following strategic areas shall not constitute monopolies: postal service, telegraphs and radiotelegraphy; *petroleum and any*

---

[40] See generally J. Cárdenas, 'Constitución y normas en materia petrolera' (2008), available at <http://stj.col.gob.mx/STJ/CJI/jaimecardenas.doc>.

other hydrocarbons; basic petrochemical; radioactive minerals and generation of nuclear energy; electricity and other activities explicitly established by the laws enacted by the Congress of the Union.[41] [emphasis added]

Notwithstanding the above, the principle of absolute dominion recognized by the Mexican Constitution is far from the model of absolute property of the state referred in the first section of this chapter. In fact, the property regime established by the Mexican Constitution of 1917 regarding resources of petroleum and other hydrocarbons is modulated by legislation passed under the above-mentioned constitutional principles.

As a result of the series of the amendments referred to above, the current Regulation under Art 27 of the Constitution in the field of petroleum allows private investment in a number of activities regulated by the legislation. In consequence, the constitutional principle of exclusive right of exploitation of hydrocarbons has a very limited scope. Thus it is possible to assert that the absolute monopoly of the Mexican state over the oil industry was never fully established.

At the moment the state retains property in the natural resources, but in the oil industry private participation is only limited in the cases of oil refining, transport, storage and distribution as well as in activities related to the basic petrochemical industry. It makes a new constitutional reform unnecessary.

The real limitation for private participation in the oil sector is not the principle of public dominion over hydrocarbons but the prohibition of private investment in those activities, which is nowadays reserved for the public monopoly of PEMEX and its subsidiary entities.

VII. Towards a new interpretation of the principle of national property

The participation of private parties in the exploitation of hydrocarbons is the dominant trend even in those Latin American countries where the regime of *accessio* rules the property system of hydrocarbons (as in Brazil and Argentina) as well as in those that postulate the absolute dominion of the state over such natural resources (as in Bolivia and Venezuela).

However, the process of privatization of hydrocarbons that Latin American countries have experienced in the last decades indicates that the new debate focuses more on the methods of participation of private companies in the oil industry than on the prohibition or authorization of such participation. In that regard, it is possible to assert that risk sharing contracts have substituted concessions as a method to make possible private participation in the oil sector. Risk

---

[41] The transcribed paragraph has to be interpreted in the sense that the state has the exclusive right to exploit the strategic areas mentioned, and even if such exclusivity constitutes a monopoly it is not prohibited by the Constitution.

sharing contracts are less controversial than concessions because they avoid the issue of a possible constitutional reform.

In the specific case of Mexico, private investment in the oil industry has practically no limits. The current Regulatory Act of Art 27 of the Constitution (1958, as amended in 2008) confirms the principles of absolute public dominion and the exclusive right of the nation to exploit hydrocarbons established by the Constitution,[42] but at the same time allows private parties to build and operate systems for the transport, storage, and distribution of gas. In this way, those interested in carrying out such activities simply need a permit granted by the Regulatory Commission of Energy.[43] In addition, although under Art 4 of the Oil Regulation Act the exploration and exploitation of oil and gas are a monopoly of the public company 'Petroleos Mexicanos', Art 6 allows this company and its subsidiary organisms to contract with private persons and corporations to undertake the works and services that their activities require, including those related to exploration and exploitation. Finally, as noted before, secondary petro chemistry is no longer an activity reserved to the state by the Constitution.

In consequence, the principle of absolute public dominion of the nation over hydrocarbons does not imply the absolute public monopoly of the oil industry.[44] Mexico's constitutional and legal regime in regard to hydrocarbons seems to be closer to the national property model than to the model of governmental or state property.

Conversely, the Mexican model of national property over hydrocarbons does not mean that Mexican citizens participate in the benefits generated by oil exploitation.[45]

---

[42] According to Art 1 of the Regulatory Act of Art 27 of the Mexican Constitution (as amended in 2008), the direct, inalienable and non-prescriptive ownership of all hydrocarbons located into the national territory, including the continental shelf and the economic exclusive zone, is vested in the nation. Art 2 adds that in accordance with Art 25, para 4 and Art 27, para 6, only the nation can exploit hydrocarbons that constitute the oil industry.

[43] The Regulatory Commission of Energy was created by Law of the Federal Commission of Energy. Diario Oficial de la Federación, 31 October 1995.

[44] Art 27 of the Constitution establishes the principle of absolute public dominion of natural resources and the public monopoly of exploitation of oil and the products derived from it, but this monopoly does not include all the stages of the oil industry; such monopoly is restricted just to primary production (basic petro chemistry). In consequence, the governmental monopoly over the oil industry has had a more ideological than constitutional basis. See Jimenez (above n 19).

[45] Thus, although oil exploitation presupposes a kind of partnership between the land owner and the nation, under the expropriation rules the only economic benefit for the land owner consists of compensation calculated on the basis of commercial value of the land without taking into account the value of the oil and hydrocarbon resources. To access natural resources in the subsoil, the nation is obliged to buy, rent or expropriate the soil under private property, in accordance with the procedure established by the second paragraph of Art 27 of the federal Constitution and its Regulatory Act in the field of expropriation. In many cases such fragmentation of property rights has generated social conflicts. In other cases land owners consider it unfair that they do not have any economic advantage resulting from the exploitation of natural resources beneath their lands.

VIII. The social investment principle as a necessary complement to the national property principle

It seems likely that the Mexican process of privatization of the oil sector will continue in the future, and it could take one of two possible avenues: either the country opens the sector to all private foreign or national investors (as happens in Brazil, Argentina, and Peru), or it restricts private investment to certain Mexican investors. The first possibility is highly criticized because it is identified with a loss of national sovereignty over natural resources. The second possibility seems consistent with constitutional principles of public dominion, but is still questionable as it confronts the constitutional principle that reserves this strategic area to the monopoly of the state.

As analysed in this chapter, private participation in the oil industry is not new in the Mexican regime. In fact, the absolute prohibition only lasted from 1958 to 1995. Private investment has always seemed necessary to complement public investment in this sector. Nevertheless, given that a constitutional reform seems to be impossible in the following years, it is necessary to explore other alternatives in order to improve the energy sector.

The last three Mexican presidents have tried to modify the Constitution in order to have a more flexible model of absolute public dominion in the field of petroleum and hydrocarbons. However, such reform is unnecessary and is likely to be prevented by social pressure.

Public opposition to constitutional reform is due more to the idea that privatization principally benefits foreign companies than to the privatization itself. So, an alternative form of opening the sector is to limit private participation to Mexican people, as already occurs in Argentina and Brazil.

One possible means of implementing this idea is to invest the savings of Mexican workers, without modifying the model of absolute property but stressing the national character of such absolute property. In other words, the term 'nation' has to be interpreted in the sense of referring not to a governmental monopoly but to a social enterprise that belongs to all Mexican people.

In 2004 the Law of Social Security was amended to establish the System of Savings for Retirement.[46] According to this legislation, each worker has to have a retirement account that is managed by authorized private companies called AFORES.[47] Such companies are allowed to invest workers' savings in productive activities.

According to official data, currently the System of Savings for Retirement has 37,513,270 affiliates and manages a total of 1 billion pesos (US $7.4 billon).[48] Politicians have asserted that this sum of money is large enough to build many

---

[46] Diario Oficial de la Federación, 11 August 2004.
[47] AFORES mean Companies for Management of Retirement Funds.
[48] See <www.consar.gob.mx>.

refining plants[49] without the support of foreign investors. Workers' savings may also be invested in other opened areas of the oil industry. [50]

Further, in 2008 the Executive sent to the Congress a bill for a new Organic Law for PEMEX.[51] Article 41 of this bill regulates the so-called 'citizen bonuses'. The 'citizen bonuses' are instruments of debt issued by PEMEX that can only be subscribed to by Mexican individuals and AFORES. However, this bill has not been approved yet by the Congress.

IX. Conclusion

As shown in this chapter, the original text of the Mexican Constitution did not establish the model of absolute property of the state over hydrocarbon resources. The principles governing hydrocarbons' property and exploitation are the result of a process of constitutional reforms aimed at establishing the sovereignty of the Mexican nation over hydrocarbons and other natural resources. However, this process had not yet concluded when the secondary legislation started turning back the privatization of the energy sector.

Private investment in the oil industry has been a constant feature of the Mexican economy. All the indicators suggest that the process of privatization will continue in subsequent years even without modifying the Constitution, which appears to be unnecessary.

Thus, the only way to preserve national sovereignty over hydrocarbons is to allow AFORES to invest the savings of Mexican workers in the oil industry. An association of this nature between workers and the government could give a different meaning to the principle of national dominion over hydrocarbons established by the Constitution, harmonizing it with the right of exclusive exploitation and allowing private investment in the hydrocarbons sector.

Allowing the Mexican people to invest in PEMEX does not violate the Constitution, but rather complements the constitutional rules currently in force. Implementing the idea of citizen bonuses could mean that in Mexico, unlike in other countries, hydrocarbon resources are not the property of the nation as an abstract concept, but the property of the people.

---

[49] According to official data, building a new refinery in the State of Hidalgo would cost US $10 million.

[50] For instance, in 2008 a representative advanced for the consideration of the Federal Congress an initiative to modify Art 43 of the Law of Systems of Savings for Retirement and Art 109 of the Law of the Institute of Security and Social Services for Government Workers so as to allow AFORES to invest workers' savings in productive activities related to energy generation, gas production and petro chemistry.

[51] See 'Reforma Energética. Iniciativa para fortalecer PEMEX' (2008), available at <www.pemex.com>.

12

Legal Models of Petroleum and Natural Gas Ownership in Brazilian Law

*Yanko Marcius de Alencar Xavier**

I. Introduction

The exploration and production of oil and gas in Brazil have been government monopolies for a considerable time. Under this model, these mineral resources belong to the government, and are to be used in accordance with the national interest. In addition, the regulation of the oil and gas sector in Brazil was for many years strongly characterized by action of the state as a financing and planning agent. The state-run company,[1] *Petrobras—Petróleo Brasileiro SA*—maintained exclusive control of all oil industry activities in Brazil for four decades following its establishment in 1953.[2]

The state's monopoly over the petroleum industry was confirmed—and indeed extended—by the Brazilian Federal Constitution of 1988. However, by the mid-1990s, as a large importer of petroleum and without the financial means to expand oil activities, Brazil's oil industry needed private investment.[3] Moreover, the global wave of market liberalization of the 1990s, the increasingly competitive nature of the international oil market, and pressure from international oil companies who were keen to exploit Brazil's extensive oil and gas reserves, all provided arguments for the opening of the oil sector to wider participation.

In 1995, Amendment No 9 to the 1988 Federal Constitution changed the legal structure of the state monopoly, and established a new regulatory framework for the Brazilian oil industry. Although government monopoly has been retained, the amended Constitution and the Oil and Natural Gas Act (Federal

* Yanko Marcius de Alencar Xavier is Professor of Energy Law, Department of Public Law, Federal University Rio Grande do Norte, Natal, Brazil; email: ymxavier@ufrnet.br.
[1] Petrobras is a private corporation, with a majority of private stockholders, in which the Federal Union has a majority of voting shares.
[2] Federal Law No 2004/1953.
[3] P. Valois, 'A evolução do monopólio estatal do petróleo' (2001) Lumen Juris 116–17.

Law No 9478/1997) allow private companies to exercise ownership over oil and gas through concession contracts and the payment of fees and surtaxes to the government. The opening of the petroleum market has permitted a very large influx of money from national and international companies, which has been sufficient to increase the number of proven oil reserves and enhance energy security.

Nevertheless, the global energy crisis, the gradual rise of oil and gas prices, and the recent discoveries of new reserves in Brazilian deep waters (the so-called 'pre-salt' fields) have led to renewed political debate about the legal structure of oil industry activities, with arguments being made for it to be changed back in the direction of greater governmental participation. Over the course of the past century, the balance of public and private involvement in the Brazilian petroleum industry has in fact undergone a number of changes, as this chapter will discuss. As the Brazilian Congress prepares to debate the bills sent by the President regarding new rules in the exploration of oil and natural gas in the pre-salt and in other 'strategic' areas, the history of the changing legal framework of petroleum exploration may indicate what lies ahead for legal analysts and investors alike.

II. Private entities in the history of the Brazilian oil industry

Since the late nineteenth century, there have been a number of legal regimes governing oil and gas exploration and production. The regime adopted in the 1891 Federal Constitution (Art 72 § 17) assured the full rights of the owner of the surface land over all resources in its subsoil. Since the adoption of the Federal Constitution of 1934, however, Brazil has distinguished ownership of the soil (land surface) from ownership of the subsoil. This is confirmed by Art 176 of the current (1988) Federal Constitution, which provides that oil and gas reserves and mineral resources found in the subsoil belong to the Federal Union.[4] To the extent that private individuals or corporations are allowed to explore these resources by the Federal Union, royalties are to be paid to the Brazilian state.

A. From free enterprise to regulation

The change in approach in the 1934 Federal Constitution came about despite considerable scepticism about the existence of petroleum in Brazil.[5] However, although there was at the time no national petroleum industry, exploratory searches for oil on Brazilian territory were under way. Notwithstanding the reservation of the ownership of oil to the Federal Union, the 1934 Constitution

---

[4] Since the beginning of the Republican period, the federal government in all its branches has been constitutionally named 'Union', or 'Federal Union' for all domestic legal purposes.

[5] M. Vaitisman, *O petróleo no império e na república* (2nd edn, 2001) 170–1.

allowed for the grant of exploration licences, and gave both the Federal Union and the member state jurisdiction over the authorization and supervision of oil exploration (Art 119 § 3). Under this system, exploration licences were to be granted exclusively to Brazilian citizens or Brazilian corporations, and a 'domanial' system was established, by which the owner of the topsoil had priority in the exploration or participation in the profits.[6] In accordance with these provisions, several corporations searched for signs of oil across the Brazilian territory. However, private participation in the exploration of state-owned oil generated intense debate about the meaning of national sovereignty in this context.[7]

B. Government monopoly and Petrobras

Following the fall of the 1937–1945 civil dictatorship, a new democratic Constitution was enacted in 1946. This post-war Constitution re-established personal liberties, but allowed for a more active participation of the federal government in economic matters. Although the 1946 Federal Constitution did not include specific rules on petroleum industry activities, Art 146 established that the '[Federal] Union might, by way of a special law, intervene in the economic domain and monopolize a certain industry of activity'—including the oil industry.

Populist sentiment, symbolized by the 'O Petróleo é nosso' ('the oil is ours') movement, became increasingly influential in the 1950s and led to the enactment of Federal Law No 2004/1953, which established Petrobras during the second Vargas government (1951–1954). A new era had begun in the Brazilian oil industry: the age of government monopoly.

According to Art 1 of Federal Law No 2004/1953, the government monopoly, under Art 146 of the 1946 Federal Constitution, included: the exploration and production of oil, rare gases, and other hydrocarbonic substances; the refining of domestic and imported oil; the transportation by sea of domestic or imported oil products; and the transportation by pipeline of oil and rare gases. The state monopoly would be exercised by Petrobras, and the federal government would retain a majority of voting shares (Art 10). The national oil market became synonymous with Petrobras.[8] The governance of the state monopoly was granted to Petrobras and to the newly-created National Petroleum Council (CNP; Art 2, I and II). Petrobras was given the right to expropriate private property, as well as to pay indemnities to proprietors of the topsoil for damages related to the activities developed on their land (Arts 24 and 30).

---

[6] A. R. Barbosa, *A natureza jurídica da concessão para exploração de petróleo e gás natural* in *Temas de Direito do Petróleo e Gás Natural II* (P. Valois, ed, 2005) 5–6.

[7] G. Cohn, *Petróleo e nacionalismo* (1968) 170.

[8] Art 6 of Law No 2004/1953 established as Petrobras's mission the following activities concerning oil (derived from reserves or shale) and its products: exploration, production, refining, selling, transportation, and other similar activities.

Among the legal obligations established by law, Petrobras was responsible for maintaining a minimum of oil reserves (Art 31) and for providing any information requested by Congress regarding corporate decisions (Art 33). Additionally, the CNP was granted the competence to supervise domestic oil supply (Art 30).

Until 1967, the federal monopoly rested purely on statute, since, although monopolies were generally authorized by the 1946 Federal Constitution, it did not mention specific activities by name. However, the 1967 Federal Constitution not only reaffirmed state ownership of mineral reserves (subject to the continuing right of the owner of the topsoil to receive royalties on oil income (Art 161, § 2)),[9] but also explicitly included in its text the state monopoly over oil exploration and production (Art 162), although the monopoly over the remaining activities of the industry remained a matter of statute only. The separation of the property of the riches of the subsoil from that of the soil was included in the constitutional text (Art 161).

The public monopoly over the oil sector was intended to protect the public interest, provide for national defence, and maintain a non-profit character.[10] The Brazilian government acted both as producer and supplier,[11] although the oil and gas industry was classified as an economic activity with the status of a public monopoly, rather than a regular government-run service. The rigid structure of the domestic market, closed to competition, was based on the idea of protection of the public interest due to the strategic position of petroleum in the world.

C. The evolution of the government monopoly: Petrobras and risk contracts

Following the first oil crisis of 1973,[12] there was a need for new investment in order to increase national oil production and reduce dependence on foreign sources. In that same year, President Ernesto Geisel and the CNP announced the possibility of granting private corporations the right to act in exploration activities under 'risk contracts' and through a bidding process. In this system, the lessee takes on the risks of the enterprise and is paid according to the discoveries they make and the costs of exploration and production.

---

[9] A. R. Barbosa, 'A natureza jurídica da concessão para exploração de petróleo e gás natural' in *Temas de Direito do Petróleo e Gás Natural II* (P. Valois, ed, 2005) 3.

[10] ibid at 21.

[11] L. M. D. Nascimento, *A água produzida na extração de petróleo: o controle estatal sobre o seu uso, tratamento, reaproveitamento e descarte* (2007) 34.

[12] The oil crisis following the Yom Kippur War led to an increase in oil prices from $2.90 to $11.65, Brazil produced at the time only 20% of the oil that was consumed domestically. The second oil crisis in 1979 raised the price from $13.00 to $34.00. In the previous year, Braspetro, the international branch of Petrobras, had been created. See C. Barreto, 'Geopolítica do petróleo: tendências mundiais pós-Guerra do Iraque de 2003' in *Brasil: situação e marco regulatório* in *Estudos e pareceres: direito do petróleo e gás* (M. R. D. S. Ribeiro, ed, 2005) 9.

In the same period, the Plan of [Economic] Goals adopted by the 1964–1985 military regime determined that Brazil should reach a production of 500,000 barrels per day by the end of the 1980s—an amount which justified the adoption of risk contracts.

Foreign companies—including Shell, BP, ELF, Pecten, Exxon, Texaco, Total, Marathon, CONOCO, Hispanoil, and Penzoil—and three Brazilian companies—Paulipetro, Azevedo Travassos, and Camargo Corrêa—signed risk contracts with Petrobras. The first contracts were signed in 1975 for a 12-year period. It was the first attempt to open the domestic market after 20 years of rigid public monopoly.

The model failed due to unimpressive results and political pressure. The political opposition to the military regime argued that risk contracts were unnecessary, since Petrobras was capable of sustaining the required investment and technological development itself. On the other hand, governmental authorities argued that the failure was due to the excessive rigidity of the contracts and the high risks of the fields over which the contracts had been granted.[13]

D. Enlarged government monopoly in the original text of the 1988 Federal Constitution

The 1987–1988 Constitutional Convention, which followed the re-establishment of full democratic civil rule in 1985, established the foundations of the oil and gas regulation present in the original text of the 1988 Federal Constitution. The state monopoly on oil and gas was extended even further to include not only exploration and production, but also refining, import, export, and maritime and pipeline transportation (Art 177)—the new structure of the federal monopoly did not even allow for new 'risk contracts'. The separation of the property of the resources of the subsoil from that of the topsoil was kept, granting the land surface owner the right to receive royalties over the income from oil exploration (Art 20; Art 176).

State monopoly was founded on the 'principles of the economic order' established in the current Brazilian Constitution (Art 170), that is, oil and gas exploration had the aim of effecting social change, based on 'national sovereignty', 'free competition', and the search for 'full employment', in accordance with a 'Democratic Rule of Law'. However, private capital could not be applied in oil and gas activities belonging to the state monopoly (Art 177, § 1). This constitutional provision ensured that all costs and risks were to be borne by the Federal Union, which could not grant any right or participation to any other entity or corporation.[14]

[13] J. Dias and M. Quagliano, *A questão do petróleo no Brasil: uma história da Petrobras* (1993) 131–3; 145. Roberto G. de Souza points out some reasons for the failure of risk contracts: Petrobras's geologists were forbidden to be contracted by the corporations; the technical ineptitude of foreign corporations when evaluating national workers; and the lack of interest of foreign countries in developing projects in Brazil. See R. G. de Souza, *Petróleo: Histórias das descobertas e o potencial brasileiro* (1997) 230–1.

[14] With the exception of the division of public revenue with, or the distribution of proportionate compensation to, the member states and municipalities in which the federally-owned resources were explored: Art 20 § 1.

E. State reform and the new model of state monopoly: Constitutional amendment number 9 and the Oil and Natural Gas Act

Since the 1950s, Petrobras had expanded the national oil production infrastructure, created jobs, trained new professionals, undertaken the mapping of resources in the continental shelf and sedimentary basins, collected data and technical information, and paid dividends to the federal government.[15] Its performance was strategic to the organization of the oil economy, to the structure of the Brazilian energy demands, and to the national economy as a whole. The recovery of the world oil market, the discovery of giant offshore oilfields (Campos and Albacora), and increased onshore production (in Bahia and Rio Grande do Norte) had all made clear the technological advantages to Brazil of Petrobras's ongoing activities. Nevertheless, because it was a vertically-integrated corporation, whose activities covered all stages of the oil supply chain, the large structure of Petrobras demanded a great amount of public investment, which the federal government was not able to provide, and innovative strategies, which the corporation was unwilling or unable to develop. After several economic plans had failed in the 1980s and early 1990s, the Brazilian government had considerable internal and external debt, and inflation had spiralled out of control. Consequently, severe budget restrictions meant fewer resources for state-run corporations, including Petrobras. The perceived advantages of a large and exclusive public oil corporation vanished within a context of economic and financial crisis.

The uncertainties in the responsibilities of different governmental bodies and Petrobras regarding the organization of the sector, the gradual economic inefficiency of the monopolistic model, and the need for an expansion of oil transportation and storage systems seemed to be the major problems of the Brazilian oil industry.[16] The gigantism of governments in Latin America was at that time considered to be a central economic problem: the Welfare State conceived by the Brazilian Constitution, for example, was not sufficient to meet the needs of citizens, public utilities worsened,[17] and questions were raised about the actual benefit that the activities of state-owned companies provided to the general public.

---

[15] Petrobras is, according to 2006 data, the world's 14th largest oil company, with a production of 1,912,733 bpd of oil and profits of over $ 12 billion. It employs 48,558 workers, and has operations in Brazil and other countries, including Argentina, Bolivia, Colombia, the United States, Ecuador, Nigeria, Peru, Trinidad and Tobago, and Venezuela. In Brazil, it runs over 7,200 gas stations and 16,000 kilometres in pipelines across the country. It is the domestic leader not only in exploration and production, but also in fuel distribution (see: <http://www.petrobras.com.br>).

[16] A. R Chequer, *A flexibilização do monopólio e a Agência Nacional do Petróleo* in *Direito Empresarial Público* (2002) 317.

[17] B. Brodbekier, *Poder regulamentar da administração pública* in (2003) 233 Revista de Direito Administrativo, 150. Marcos Jurena argues that a large government generates high costs for all society and that high taxation is not fair in a context in which the state does not provide high quality public utilities (M. S. Vilella, *Desestatização—privatização, concessões, terceirizações e regulação* (4th edn, 2001) 131).

Against this background, the National Plan of Privatization (*Plano Nacional de Desestatização*, or PND), established by Federal Law No 8031/1990 and regulated by Federal Law No 9491/1997, was adopted with the following goals: an expansion of public utilities in a competitive environment; the sale of state-run companies or of government shares in corporations; and the delegation of governmental obligations to private entities by way of licences, permissions, or authorizations.

1. *Constitutional Amendment Number 9/1995*

Eight years after the promulgation of the 1988 Federal Constitution, Constitutional Amendment No 9/1995 paved the way for reform of the oil sector. The text of Art 177 was altered with the introduction of clauses which moderated the state monopoly.[18] The Federal Union, while retaining a firm legal monopoly over the industry, was allowed to license private companies to exercise the activities described in the Article (Art 177 § 1). According to some authors, this introduced what is known in Brazilian administrative law as 'flexibilization', or a 'monopoly by government choice'. In other words, constitutional rules allowed the government to choose between maintaining a single state-owned corporation in charge of all oil and gas activities, or licensing both private and public corporations.[19] However, others argue that if the government does not choose to license private corporations, Petrobras remains, by default, the only company entitled to explore the activities of the state monopoly.[20]

Because of the contrast between the social welfarist model of government embodied in the original text of the 1988 Federal Constitution, and the economically liberal ideas that underpinned Constitutional Amendment No 9/1995, questions were raised about the constitutional validity of the amendment. However, in 2005, the Brazilian Supreme Court held[21] that, according to Arts 20 and 177 of the Federal Constitution, the concept of government monopoly in the oil industry must not be confused with that of property: that is, (1) public ownership of oil, gas, and other mineral resources, and (2) the exercise of activities related to these natural resources are two different legal concepts. In the Court's view, there is no unconstitutionality in the development of petroleum activities by other companies besides Petrobras, since such economic activity does not imply ownership of the resource that is explored.

---

[18] Brodbekier, above n 17 at 151. Other names have been given to the process of change initiated by Constitutional Amendment No 9/1995. cf A. Ferreira, *A desmonopolização do mercado* in *Temas de direito do petróleo e gás II* (P. Valois, ed, 2005) 32–3.

[19] A. D. Moraes, *Regime jurídico da concessão para exploração de petróleo e gás natural* (2001), 12 April 2009, available at <http://jus2.uol.com.br/doutrina/texto.asp?id=2426>.

[20] A. R. Barbosa, *A natureza jurídica da concessão para exploração de petróleo e gás natural* in *Temas de Direito do Petróleo e Gás Natural II* (P. Valois, ed, 2005) 24–5.

[21] *Ação Direta de Inconstitucionalidade* (Writ of Unconstitutionality) No 3273, brought by the governor of the State of Paraná before the Supreme Court regarding the constitutionality of specific rules included in the Oil and Natural Gas Act, 22 April 2009, available at <http://www.stf.jus.br>.

2. *The Oil and Natural Gas Act and the creation of the National Agency of Petroleum, Natural Gas and Biofuels (ANP)*

The text of Art 177 § 1 of the current Federal Constitution, as modified by Amendment No 9/1995, introduced a new framework of oil and gas regulation in Brazil. In order to enforce the new constitutional rules, a new legal text had to be published; a law which would aim to ensure oil and fuel supply throughout the Brazilian territory, establish the conditions for new licences, and create the structure of the agency responsible for the regulation of the new model of government monopoly (Art 177 § 2 of the Constitution).[22]

The Congress approved, with modifications, the bill sent by the President, which became the Oil and Natural Gas Act (*Lei do Petróleo*, Federal Law No 9478/1997), which regulated the entire domestic oil industry and created the National Agency of Petroleum, Natural Gas and Biofuels (*Agência Nacional do Petróleo, Gás Natural e Biocombustíveis*—ANP),[23] responsible for enforcement, regulation, and implementation of public policies in the oil and gas sector. The Act included guiding principles for national energy policy and activities belonging to the state oil monopoly, established not only the ANP, but also the National Council of Energy Policy (*Conselho Nacional de Política Energética*—CNPE), and repealed Federal Law No 2004/1953. In Chapter III, the Act provides that the exercise of the government monopoly of oil industry activities may be granted through concession or authorization to companies incorporated according to Brazilian Law and with headquarters located in Brazil (Art 5).

In the upstream petroleum industry, the Act defined the activities involved in exploration and production. These activities are to be exercised through concession of, and public bidding for, exploration blocks.[24] The process is conducted by the ANP, and the Act specifies certain terms that must be expressly included in the contract (Art 43).[25]

The ANP was closely based on the American model of regulatory agencies.[26] The agencies operate within a special constitutional and statutory framework,

---

[22] A. Ferreira, *A desmonopolização do mercado* in *Temas de direito do petróleo e gás II* (P. Valois, ed, 2005) 45–9.

[23] The agency was renamed *Agência Nacional do Petróleo, Gás Natural e Biocombustíveis* (National Petroleum, Natural Gas, and Biofuels Agency) by Federal Law No 11097/2005.

[24] Exploration blocks are delimited by the ANP (cf Resolution No 08/2003 of the CNPE, available at <http://www.mme.gov.br/mme/menu/conselhos_comite/cnpe.html>). The delimitation must consider the availability of geological and geophysical data, the potential of areas, and environmental concerns. The bidding involves, among other aspects, the offer of a signature bonus and the presentation of a minimum exploration programme.

[25] eg, the definition of the block included in the concession and the term and duration of the contract.

[26] In Brazil, the agencies are fully integrated into the Executive Branch, although, unusually, their directors serve for fixed terms, determined by law: cf O. M. de Medeiros Alves, 'Agências reguladoras e proteção do consumidor de serviços de telecomunicações' (2001) 226 Revista de Direito Administrativo 219–29. The question whether the directors of federal regulatory agencies can be dismissed by the President before the end of their respective terms remains

which includes regulatory, supervisory, and planning powers.[27] Their regulatory powers are threefold: the enactment of new rules, the enforcement of the law, and the power to hand down administrative sanctions.[28] This means that the powers of the agency are considerable, but limited:[29] the ANP has broad regulatory power (Art 8), but it shares power to regulate the market with the Ministry of Mines and Energy (*Ministério de Minas e Energia*—MME) and the CNPE.[30]

3. *Private interests and the oil industry in Brazil: authorization and concession*

According to the current Brazilian regulatory structure, private corporations may make economic use of oil and natural gas resources—that is, they may legally profit in all stages of the oil industry, including exploration. There are three legal instruments by which a private entity may be granted the use or exploration of a public good in Brazil (concession, permission, and authorization), two of which are included in the Oil and Natural Gas Act (authorization and concession).

An 'authorization' is, in Brazilian administrative law, a unilateral, discretionary, and temporary licence,[31] by which the licensee is granted the right to use the public good without prior bidding.[32] It is defined and regulated in Arts 5 §§ 2, 53, 56, and 60 of the Oil and Natural Gas Act. Authorizations are typically used for licences related to oil and natural gas transportation (by pipeline or by sea), imports, and exports. Because they are unilateral, they may be revoked at any time by the government for reasons of public interest, which significantly increases the risks for investors.

A 'concession' is a different kind of administrative licence with the following characteristics, among others: it is bilateral in nature (that is, it creates typical contractual obligations for both the licensing authority and the licensee), it depends on prior bidding, and the exploration and use of the public resource are established in a contract.[33] The Oil and Natural Gas Act established that exploration and production activities must be granted through concession contracts and that their risks are to be borne exclusively by the licensee (Art 23).

---

unsettled: see O. M. de Medeiros Alves, 'Demissão de dirigente de autarquia nomeado a termo: discussão renovada' (2002) 13 Revista Jurídica In Verbis 161–71.

[27] C. A. B. de Mello, *Curso de direito administrativo* (13th edn, 2000) 611.

[28] M. Gentot, *Les Autorités Administratives Indépendantes* (2nd edn, 1994) 41.

[29] H. L. Meirelles, *Direito Administrativo Brasileiro* (2000) 326. See also C. A. Sundfeld, 'Introdução às agências reguladoras' in *Direito administrativo econômico* (C. A. Sundfeld, ed, 2002) 26–7.

[30] The ANP also takes part in multilateral government committees, such as the National Environmental Council and the Administrative Council for Economic Defence.

[31] Although some authors view it as bilateral in nature: see S. J. L. D. Farias, *Regulação jurídica dos serviços autorizados* (2005) 66–9.

[32] M. S. Z. D. Pietro, *Direito Administrativo* (19th edn, 2006) 658.

[33] ibid at 661–3.

4. *The concession of 'exploration blocks' and the ANP bidding rounds*

The ANP is the authority with the legal competence to issue licences. Following the guidelines set by the Act and other applicable rules, it defines 'exploration blocks': specific physical areas over which oil exploration and production activities may be developed. These blocks are then offered, through a process of public auction, to corporations, individually or in consortia, that are granted the right to explore the block, and to develop, at their own risk (Art 26 of the Act), the means of extraction of oil and natural gas, if the exploratory phase leads to satisfactory results.[34] The licensee's ownership over any oil and natural gas extracted in its area is, nonetheless, not absolute, as trade in both commodities is also regulated by the ANP, notwithstanding the overwhelming influence of market forces (for instance, on prices).[35] Since 1998, the ANP has organized ten[36] 'bidding rounds' of public auction of exploration blocks,[37] as well as the so-called 'Round Zero'.[38]

III. The 'pre-salt' mega-reserves and the search for a new legal structure

A. The discovery of the 'pre-salt' reserves and early public debate

On 31 January 2007, the CNPE published a new resolution aiming to organize new bidding rounds for oil and gas exploration blocks. The resolution authorized the ANP, under the supervision of the Ministry of Mines and Energy, to perform geological studies on sedimentary basins with considerable future prospects. On 8 November 2007, soon before the ANP's Ninth Bidding Round, Petrobras announced the discovery of a large oil and natural gas field (the 'Tupi' field) in ultra-deep waters, under layers of salt, 280 kilometres off the coast of Santos, with an estimated five to eight billion barrels of oil equivalent (boe). After the announcement, 41 exploration blocks close to the Tupi Field were excluded from the Ninth Bidding Round.[39] Offshore blocks were also removed from the Tenth

---

[34] L. M. C. D. Castro, *Contratos de concessão: uma análise jurídica na indústria do petróleo e gás no Brasil* (2004) 15, 26.

[35] The Brazilian Supreme Court declared that the constitutional provision of Art 176 of the 1988 Federal Constitution allowed the federal government to transfer the risks and results of oil activity through contract. For other related aspects of the Court's opinion, see above n 21.

[36] cf <http://www.brasil-rounds.gov.br/index_e.asp>.

[37] The edicts, contracts, and other documents relating to all bidding rounds are available at <http://www.anp.gov.br/petro/rodadas_de_licitacoes.asp>.

[38] In 1998, the ANP entered into specific agreements with Petrobras, as foreseen by Art 33 of the Oil and Natural Gas Act—the so-called 'Round Zero'—under which Petrobras kept its rights over 282 fields, covering an area of over 450,000 km², for three years.

[39] Despite the legal instability brought about by the unilateral move of the Brazilian government, the Ninth Bidding Round yielded a record amount of 2.1 billion Brazilian Reals ('Balanço da 9ª Rodada da ANP', Estado.com, 14 August 2009, available at <http://www.intelog.net/site/

Bidding Round amidst proposals for tax changes and a new regulatory structure for the so-called 'pre-salt' fields.[40] Although, the existing legal structure seems to be, at least in theory, perfectly compatible with the exploration of new and larger reserves, change is considered to be necessary, essentially for political reasons.

The government's initial proposals involved changes in the tax structure applicable to the new resources. At least two models were among those suggested:[41] an increase in royalty fees on the oil and gas extracted in highly productive areas; and amendment of the rules governing the collection of special government surtaxes.[42] The suggested increase in tax rates worried investors, but it had the merit of avoiding a rupture in the current structure for the regulation of the oil and gas industry, since such proposals could be enacted with relatively few legislative changes.

Subsequently, however, several government authorities suggested that an entirely new regulatory model might be necessary for the new 'pre-salt' areas.[43] The crucial argument behind this proposal was that the current concession model, adopted during the 1990s, included a high premium due to the considerable risks involved in most licensed exploration blocks—risks which do not seem to be present in the case of 'pre-salt' areas. It is thus argued that keeping the current legal structure in place, even for the exploration and production of pre-salt reserves, would damage legitimate national interests.

On 17 July 2008 a Presidential Decree established an inter-ministerial commission responsible for studying and proposing changes to the legal structure of oil and gas exploration and production in the new oil fields of the pre-salt area.[44]

The pre-salt stratum extends from the state of Espírito Santo to the state of Santa Catarina, covering nearly 160,000 km². There are doubts about the actual amount of petroleum in it (up to 100 billion boe) and about the viability of its extraction. Great technical challenges will be involved and high investment will be needed for the extraction of oil and natural gas in an area which is 300 kilometres away from the coastline and 7,000 metres below the surface of the ocean.

Sources in the Ministry of Mines and Energy estimate that investment of approximately \$270 billion will be needed for the exploration of the area,[45] while other studies suggest that investment requirements might be as much as \$1

default.asp?TroncoID=907492&SecaoID=508074&SubsecaoID=715548&Template=../artigos-noticias/user_exibir.asp&ID=534604 >).

[40] 'The next oil giant?', The Economist Intelligence Unit Viewswire, 12 August 2009, available at <http://www.economist.com/daily/news/displaystory.cfm?story_id=13348824>.

[41] 'ANP defende alteração das normas para pagamento de participações especiais', O Globo Online, 12 August 2009, available at < http://oglobo.globo.com/economia/mat/2007/12/05/327463573.asp>.

[42] Currently, licensees for areas with production of less than 450 million m³ of oil do not have to pay the special surtax; specific conditions apply to areas of the continental shelf.

[43] 'New regime sought by big hitter', Financial Times, 12 August 2009, available at <http://royaldutchshellplc.com/2008/06/30/new-regime-sought-by-big-hitter/>.

[44] Available at <http://www.planalto.gov.br/ccivil_03/_Ato2007–2010/2008/Dnn/Dnn11699.htm>.

[45] 'Brasil precisa de US\$270 bi para reservas do pré-sal, diz Lobão' G1, 14 April 2009, available at <http://g1.globo.com/Noticias/Politica/0,,MUL1049770–5601,00-BRASIL+PRECISA+DE+US+BI+PARA+RESERVAS+DO+PRESAL+DIZ+LOBAO.html>.

trillion.[46] Considering these steep and disparate estimates, the price of oil in the world market will be a key factor in any decision-making process in the pre-salt area. Petrobras has indicated that investments in pre-salt exploration are practicable at prices ranging from a minimum of $40 to $50 per barrel of oil equivalent.[47]

The initial debate over a new legal model for the exploration and production of pre-salt fields occurred at a time of record-high prices of oil in the world market: in June 2008, soon before the Presidential Decree on the matter was published, the price of a barrel of oil (Brent and West Texas Intermediate) reached a level of almost $150. The vertiginous decline of oil prices in the following seven months (an almost $100 fall) added new elements to the viability debate, which was revived by the slight recovery of oil prices in the second quarter of 2009.

On 28 March 2009, at a press conference that took place in Chile, the Brazilian President declared that a Fund designed to reduce poverty and strengthen national education could be formed out of the pre-salt income.[48] The Brazilian government had indicated from the outset of public debate regarding the new exploration areas[49] that the new regulatory model might be inspired by the Norwegian twofold model, [50] with a production-sharing system being introduced for pre-salt areas, while the current concession model would be kept for all other blocks. In addition, a new state-owned corporation would be created to manage the fund.

B. The government proposals

The proposals of the inter-ministerial commission were delivered to the President on 5 August 2009.[51] On 31 August, President Luiz Inácio Lula da Silva finally presented to the nation the set of legal measures prepared by the inter-ministerial

---

[46] 'Petróleo e etanol devem dar novo status ao Brasil até 2020', BBC Brasil, 11 August 2009, available at <http://www.bbc.co.uk/portuguese/lg/noticias/2009/03/090330_brasil_bric_energia.shtml>.
[47] 'Gabrielli: crise afetou debate para explorar pré-sal', Agencia Estado, 11 August 2009, available at <http://www.estadao.com.br/noticias/economia,gabrielli-crise-afetou-debate-para-explorar-pre-sal,344697,0.htm >.
[48] 'Lula anuncia criação de fundo social com dinheiro do petróleo', G1, 22 April 2009, available at <http://g1.globo.com/Noticias/Mundo/0,,MUL1062632–5602,00-LULA+ANUNCIA+CRIACAO+DE+FUNDO+SOCIAL+COM+DINHEIRO+DO+PETROLEO.html>.
[49] 'Governo deve anunciar marco do pré-sal em abril', G1, 22 April 2009, available at <http://g1.globo.com/Economia_Negocios/0,,MUL1062162–9356,00-GOVERNO+DEVE+ANUNCIAR+MARCO+DO+PRESAL+EM+ABRILFONTE.html>.
[50] The Norwegian twofold petroleum exploration model involves the participation of the state both by way of a semi-privatized corporation (originally Statoil, founded in 1972, now StatoilHydro) and by a public fund or portfolio which manages oil exploration licences in specific geographic areas (the state's Direct Financial Interest, Statens direkte økonomiske engasjement—SDFI, founded in 1985), managed, since 2001, by a fully state-owned corporation, Petoro AS. cf R. Solberg, 'The new structure of the Norwegian state's interests on the Norwegian continental shelf', International Financial Law Review—Supplement—Nordic Region, 11 August 2009, available at <http://www.iflr.com/Article/2027301/Oil-and-gas.html>.
[51] 'Lobão: Lula recebeu 3 projetos com regras para pré-sal', Estadão.com, 11 August 2009, available at <http://www.estadao.com.br/noticias/economia,lobao-lula-recebeu-3-projetos-com-regras-para-pre-sal,414188,0.htm>.

commission, and four bills were sent to Congress overhauling the legal structure of oil exploration.[52]

The first bill[53] establishes a specific set of rules regarding the exploration of oil and natural gas in the pre-salt and in other 'strategic' areas. It also alters the 1997 Oil and Natural Gas Act, and grants to Petrobras pre-eminence or even exclusive rights in the distribution of oil and natural gas whenever the Federal Union chooses to do so.

The second bill[54] includes the creation of a new fully federally-owned corporation, the Empresa Brasileira de Administração de Petróleo e Gás Natural SA—PETRO-SAL. Like Norway's Petoro AS, it will administer all production-sharing contracts between the Ministry of Mines and Energy and corporations allowed to explore the newly discovered areas, but will not be responsible for any direct exploration or distribution activities.

The third bill[55] creates the Fundo Social ('Social Fund'). This will receive part of the financial proceeds of the exploration of oil and natural gas in the new areas, as well as of the royalties paid to the Federal Union, and its goals will include poverty reduction and environmental sustainability.

The fourth bill[56] authorizes the Federal Union to grant to Petrobras exclusive research and exploration rights over oil and natural gas resources in new areas, with no need for any prior bidding process.

IV. Concluding remarks

There seem to be both political and financial motives for the legal changes that are being studied by government authorities. As the current Minister for Mines and Energy has recently stated, the '1997 Oil and Natural Gas Act was written at a time in which the nation imported 40 per cent of its oil consumption, and the exploratory risks of our sedimentary basins were deemed to be high', a situation which has clearly changed.[57]

---

[52] 'Lula encaminha projetos de lei sobre o pré-sal ao Congresso', Agência Brasil, 31 August 2009, available at <http://www.agenciabrasil.gov.br/noticias/2009/08/31/materia.2009–08-31.8146387483/view>.

[53] Projeto de Lei No 5938/2009, available at <http://www.planalto.gov.br/ccivil_03/Projetos/PL/2009/msg713–090831.htm>.

[54] Projeto de Lei No 5939/2009, available at <http://www.planalto.gov.br/ccivil_03/Projetos/PL/2009/msg714–090831.htm>.

[55] Projeto de Lei No 5940/2009, available at <http://www.planalto.gov.br/ccivil_03/Projetos/PL/2009/msg715–090831.htm>.

[56] Projeto de Lei No 5941/2009, available at <http://www.planalto.gov.br/ccivil_03/Projetos/PL/2009/msg716–090831.htm>.

[57] Edison Lobão, 'Uma nova fronteira', Ministério de Minas e Energia, 11 August 2009, available at <http://www.mme.gov.br/mme/noticias/destaque3/destaque_0029.html>.

In general terms, there does not seem to be any unconstitutionality in the introduction of different regulatory models for different kinds of oil fields (land, regular deep-sea, or the new pre-salt areas), since the 1988 Federal Constitution does not establish a single model for the licensing and exploration of the state's oil and natural gas resources. Nevertheless, experts have already questioned whether it is constitutionally permissible for the government to privilege Petrobras above all other corporations in the exploration of the new areas.[58]

The four bills, now under the scrutiny of Congress, will probably be considerably altered in the coming months. However, their content will have to be thoroughly analysed by investors, and the new legal texts will certainly be scrutinized by Brazilian courts for any sign of unconstitutionality in their specific details, as well as the ever-present risk of breach of current contracts.

[58] See G. A. de Toledo, 'A questão do pré-sal', O Estado de S Paulo, 4 September 2009, available at <http://www.estadao.com.br/estadaodehoje/20090904/not_imp429374,0.php>.

13

Who Owns the Economy? Property Rights, Privatization, and the Indonesian Constitution: The *Electricity Law* Case

*Simon Butt and Tim Lindsey**

I. Introduction

On 21 May 1998, Soeharto, President of Indonesia for 32 years, stepped down amidst economic and monetary crisis and social and political unrest. The economic calamity—a flow-on from the collapse of the Thai baht in July 1997 that had caused many foreign investors to re-evaluate their portfolios in Indonesia[1]—unravelled much of the economic development achieved during Soeharto's time in power. Indonesia lost 13.5 per cent of its GDP in 1997 alone, and its currency plummeted from Rp 2,000 per US dollar to almost Rp 20,000 by February 1998. Soeharto's resignation ushered in the so-called 'Era of Reformasi', and, within a year, Indonesia had begun amending its previously 'sacred' Constitution of 1945.

Prior to Soeharto stepping down, the Indonesian government had sought foreign financial assistance, primarily from the International Monetary Fund (IMF). As a condition for the injection of more than US$ 10 billion,[2] the Indonesian government was required to commit to 'far-reaching' reforms, the content of

* Senior Lecturer, Sydney Law School and a member of the Centre for Asian and Pacific Law, University of Sydney, Australia; email: s.butt@usyd.edu.au; and Professor of Asian Law, Director of the Asian Law Centre, Director of the Centre for Islamic Law and Society and ARC Federation Fellow in the Law School, University of Melbourne, Australia; email: t.lindsey@unimelb.edu.au. NB this chapter draws in part on S. Butt and T. Lindsey, 'Economic Reform When the Constitution Matters: Indonesia's Constitutional Court and Art 33' (2008) 44 (2) Bulletin of Indonesian Economic Studies 239, and S. Butt and T. Lindsey, 'The People's Prosperity? Indonesian Constitutional Interpretation, Economic Reform and Globalization' in *Pushing Back at Globalization: Asian Regulatory Perspectives* (J. Gillespie and E. Peerenboom, eds, forthcoming 2009).
¹ R. McLeod, 'Dealing with the Bank System Failure: Indonesia 1997–2003' (2004) 40(1) Bulletin of Indonesian Economic Studies 95 at 95.
² See the IMF's website: <www.imf.org>.

which was effectively dictated by the IMF, leading a group of other multilateral financial institutions.[3] These so-called 'conditionalities' required Indonesia to commit to restructuring a range of key state enterprises so as to make them more efficient, including through privatization.[4] One focus was the electricity sector, run primarily by the State Electricity Company (Perusahaan Listrik Negara, or PLN). The Indonesian government pledged to 'improve its performance'—particularly to 'restore commercial viability, improve efficiency, and attract private investment'[5]—and to enact a new Electricity Law, largely to establish a legal and regulatory framework for competition in the electricity market.[6]

Meeting these conditions has, however, not been straightforward. One impediment has been the understanding of property rights entailed by so-called 'Indonesian Socialism', which embraces the view that property and resources have a social function, and which is said to be encapsulated in Art 33 of the 1945 Constitution. Reflecting a broad mix of Leftist, nationalist and anti-colonial ideals that were influential at the time the Constitution was first drafted,[7] Art 33 grants the state control over natural resources and essential industries, with the expectation that the Indonesian people—particularly the poor—will benefit from them. Clearly, Art 33 provides for significant government intervention in the economy and has, from 1997, been a rallying point for opposition to market-oriented policies 'pushed' by multilateral lenders and donors.

During rounds of constitutional amendments between 1999 and 2002, debates raged over Art 33's desirability, but the provision was eventually retained. During the course of the constitutional amendments a Constitutional Court (Mahkamah Konstitusi, or MK) with the power of legislative review was also established, making the Constitution enforceable for the first time in decades.[8]

---

[3] T. Lindsey, 'The IMF and Insolvency Law Reform in Indonesia' (1998) 34(3) Bulletin of Indonesian Economic Studies 119 at 119. This assessment is based in part on Lindsey's personal observations of IMF interaction with Indonesian authorities in Jakarta in 1998.

[4] Letter of Intent, 7 September 2000, point 62; see also Letter of Intent, 20 January 2000, point 70, available at <www.imf.org>.

[5] Letter of Intent, 20 January 2000, point 77, available at <www.imf.org>.

[6] Supplementary Memorandum of Economic and Financial Policies, 16 March 1999, point 20, available at <www.imf.org>.

[7] See P. Venning, 'Determination of Economic, Social and Cultural Rights by the Indonesian Constitutional Court' (2008) 10 Australian Journal of Asian Law, 100; B. Susanti, *Neo-liberalism and Its Resistance in Indonesia's Constitution Reform 1999–2002* (LL.M. Thesis, University of Warwick, 2002) 4; V. R. Hadiz, 'The Failure of State Ideology in Indonesia: the rise and demise of *Pancasila*' in *Communitarian Politics in Asia* (Chua, Beng Huat, ed, 2004) 152; M. M. Al'Afghani, 'Constitutional Court's Review and the Future of Water Law in Indonesia' (2006) 2(1) Law Environment and Development Journal 5; 'Ekonomi Indonesia di Masa Datang', Pidato Wakil Presiden RI 3 Februari 1946 (copy on file with authors); and, generally, S. E. Swasono et al (eds), *Mohammad Hatta: Demokrasi Kita, Bebas Aktif, Ekonomi Masa Depan* (1992) 5–8. For a discussion of further reforms and the Indonesian legal system more generally, see T. Lindsey (ed), *Indonesia: Law and Society* (2nd edn, 2008).

[8] For details of these amendments and the text of the Constitution before and after the amendments, see T. Lindsey, 'Indonesian Constitutional Reform: Muddling Towards Democracy' (2002) 6(1) Singapore Journal of International & Comparative Law 244, on which this paragraph draws. For a discussion of constitutional review in Indonesia, see J. Asshiddiqie, 'Setahun Mahkamah

Significantly, the statutes that have since been tested in this new court include some of those introduced to provide a legal basis for the IMF conditionalities and the notions of property they imply.

This chapter focuses upon the Constitutional Court's interpretation of Art 33 and its implications, uncertain as they are, for property ownership and privatization in Indonesia. We begin by setting out Art 33 and aspects of the debates in 2001 in the MPR (Majelis Permusyawaratan Rakyat or People's Deliberative Assembly, entrusted with amending the Constitution) which resulted in the retention of that Article without amendment. After briefly discussing Indonesia's new Constitutional Court and its jurisdiction, we turn to the Court's treatment of Art 33, focusing on the Court's very first decision: the *Electricity Law* case.[9] In this decision, the MK found Law No 20 of 2002 on Electricity to be in breach of Art 33, and struck down the Law. Subsequently, the Court has heard three further cases in which the statute under review was said to breach Art 33. In the *Oil and Natural Gas (Migas) Law* case,[10] applicants sought a review of Law No 22 of 2001 on Oil and Natural Gas. In its decision, the MK made slight alterations to the Law to bring it into line with the requirements of Art 33.[11] In the *Forestry Law* case,[12] a group of many applicants[13] unsuccessfully disputed the constitutionality of Law No 19 of 2004 on the Stipulation of Interim Law No 1 of 2004 on Amendments to Law No 41 of 1999 on Forestry as a Statute.[14] In the *Water Resources (SDA) Law* case,[15] almost 3,000 individuals and several NGOs requested that the MK review Law No 7 of 2004 on Water Resources. A majority of the MK upheld the constitutionality of the Law, finding that the Law did not in fact divest the government of control over water resources. The Law merely made it possible for the state to grant to the private sector a right to exploit water. The government retained power to make policy and regulations, manage water resources and grant permits for water exploitation.[16]

Although all four Art 33 decisions raise questions that are of critical importance for economic policy in Indonesia, the *Electricity Law* case is the most significant

Konstitusi: Refleksi Gagasan Dan Penyelenggaraan, Serta Setangkup Harapan', in *Menjaga Denyut Konstitusi; Refleksi Satu Tahun Mahkamah Konstitusi*, (R. Harun, Z. A. M Husein and Bisariyadi, 2004). See also P. Stockmann, *The New Indonesian Constitutional Court; A Study into its Beginnings and First Years of Work* (2007).

[9] MK Decision No 001–021-022/PUU-I/2003.
[10] MK Decision No 002/2003.
[11] 'MK "Koreksi" Sebagian Materi Undang-Undang Migas', Hukumonline, 21 December 2004.
[12] MK Decision No 003/2005.
[13] The application was brought by 11 environmental or human rights NGOs, 81 Indonesian citizens who lived in locations where mining companies were operating in protected forests, and other environmental activists.
[14] 'Mahkamah Konstitusi Tolak Batalkan UU Kehutanan', Hukumonline, 7 July 2005.
[15] MK Decision No 058–059-060–063/2004 and 008/2005.
[16] *SDA Law* case, at 496–9; 'Mahkamah Konstitusi Ogah Membatalkan UU Sumber Daya Air', Hukumonline, 19 August 2005. Two MK judges dissented, however: 'Mukhti dan Maruarar, Dua Hakim yang Ajukan Dissenting Opinion UU SDA', Hukumonline, 17 August 2005.

of the four for the purposes of this chapter, given that the statute in question was enacted as a direct response to the IMF's loan conditionality requirements. This chapter, therefore, largely confines itself to discussion of this case. We show that through its interpretation of Art 33, the Constitutional Court has attempted to thwart government efforts at providing greater scope for the private sector to participate in the generation and supply of electricity. Many aspects of its decision reflect or adopt arguments raised by MPR members who favoured the retention of Art 33 during the 2001 constitutional amendment debates. These members advocated concepts similar to interpretations of Indonesian Socialism that so animated the drafters of the 1945 Constitution.

Nevertheless, we will show that the Indonesian executive has circumvented the effect of the Constitutional Court's decision in the *Electricity Law* case. It did so by issuing a government regulation, a form of subordinate legislation, which contains provisions that have a similar effect to those in the Law, but over which the Constitutional Court has no powers of review. The boundary between state and private sector involvement in the energy and natural resources sector in Indonesia remains, therefore, a highly contested issue—both politically and legally.

II. Article 33: the people's economy

Article 33 of the Constitution reads:

1. The economy shall be structured as a common endeavour based upon the family principle.
2. Branches of production which are important to the state, and which affect the public's necessities of life, are to be controlled by the state.
3. The earth and water and the natural resources contained within them are to be controlled by the state and used for the greatest possible prosperity of the people.

The 'family principle' (asas kekeluargaan), as commonly described, takes a paternalistic view of the nation as a family and the state (or, more commonly, the 'ruler') as head of that family.[17] According to the formal Elucidation to Art 33, as originally included in 1945:

Art 33 embraces economic democracy under which production is carried out by all, and for all, under the leadership or supervision of members of the community. The main priority is the prosperity of the community, not the prosperity of individuals.

This is because the economy is structured as a collective endeavour based on the family principle. A business entity along these lines is a cooperative.

The economy is based on economic democracy, prosperity for all people!

Therefore, branches of production which are important for the state and which affect the lives of most people must be controlled by the state. If not, control of production might

---

[17] Susanti, above n 7 at 4.

fall into the hands of individuals in power, who might exploit the people. Only businesses which are not important for the lives of many people may be left in private hands.

The land and water and natural resources in the earth are the fundamentals of community prosperity. For this reason, they must be controlled by the state and used for the greatest prosperity of the people.[18]

However, prior to the establishment of the MK in 2003, Art 33 had never been subject to binding interpretation. Questions about its precise implications abounded, not least because of the somewhat obscure and grandiloquent style in which the original text was drafted. Since the MK's appearance, though, both policy makers and the MK have been forced to confront a series of related and complex legal questions, which we discuss further below. What does 'controlled by the state' mean? How much scope is there for private sector involvement in these sectors? What is the meaning of 'common endeavour'? And does Art 33 require the MK to assess government policy?

Although, as mentioned above, Art 33 was originally inspired by socialist and nationalist ideals, it survived the shift of the Indonesian state from the Left under Soekarno to the Right under Soeharto. Because Art 33 was unenforceable and often disregarded, it had allowed Soeharto and his inner circle to amass great wealth, including by establishing state monopolies over the exploitation of these natural resources and essential industries, without distributing the benefits in the way Art 33 seems to require—that is, to the citizenry. Nevertheless, Art 33 also survived the major overhaul of the Constitution that took place after Soeharto's fall. In 2001, the MPR retained the 'People's Economy' as the constitutional basis for Indonesia's economy, and paras (1)–(3) of the Article escaped the deliberations untouched, although the Elucidation to Art 33 was deleted.[19] However, the retention of Art 33 did not proceed without significant debate, opposition and political fervour in the MPR, along lines similar to those which emerged when Art 33 was first conceived on the eve of independence.[20]

Among the MPR members, and the senior government officials, 'experts' and commentators called in for the debates, three views prevailed on the desirability of retaining Art 33.[21] The first group might be seen as neo-liberal, although its members would not describe themselves as such.[22] This group, made up

---

[18] The Elucidation is the formal explanatory memorandum that accompanies most Indonesian regulations and is often read as if it were part of the regulation itself. The Elucidation to the 1945 Constitution has, however, always been controversial, as when the Constitution officially came into force on 18 August 1945, the Elucidation was not included. It was later promulgated in the Government Gazette in 1946. See also Susanti's translation of the Elucidation to Art 33: Susanti, above n 7 at 30.

[19] There was, however, some minor tinkering. The MPR added Arts 33(4) and 33(5):
'4 The national economy is to be run on the basis of economic democracy, and the principles of togetherness, efficiency which is just, sustainability, environmentalism, and independence, maintaining a balance between advancement and national economic unity.

5 Further provisions to implement [Art 33] will be provided in legislation.'

[20] H. M. Yamin, *Naskah Persiapan Undang-Undang Dasar 1945* (1959).

[21] These debates are available at <www.mpr.go.id>.

[22] See Susanti, above n 7, ch 4

largely of experts and commentators from outside the legislature, tended to support the types of economic liberalization policies pushed by the IMF. Some argued that Indonesia's 1997 economic collapse was, in part, the result of excessive government control over economic resources under Art 33.[23] Others argued that free-market capitalism had become 'mainstream' in the world economy, leaving Indonesia no choice but to adopt it in order to participate more substantially in global trade.[24] Others pointed to Indonesia's WTO membership and the IMF conditionalities, which required Indonesia to—'like it or not' 'open itself up and liberalize', and to become competitive in global markets.[25] These ideas manifested in proposals to amend Art 33 to limit state intervention, such as by dropping Art 33(2) altogether,[26] something that would, presumably, have allowed branches of production to be sold off to, or managed by, the private sector.

A second group pushed for a 'middle ground' between liberalism and socialism—a 'social' market system.[27] According to Susanti,[28] most members proposing this model sought an essentially socialist economy but with enough 'free market' to enable participation in global markets. Most proponents of this view, however, failed to describe its features in any detail. For example, one Golkar party member who appeared to support this system stated:

... it is ok to go to the left, ok to go to the right, but not ok to go too far either way...[29]

Most MPR members, however, took a third view, favouring state protectionism and, hence, the retention of Art 33.[30] Proponents detested the free market as unjust, 'very evil', or otherwise being unable to guarantee prosperity for ordinary Indonesians.[31] As one commentator stated during the debates:

If someone says that competition is good, I say that competition is good if we win. If competition is the way that we are re-colonized, then competition is bad.[32]

An economic system with high levels of state involvement was preferable, they contended, largely because it was the system most likely to ensure the 'prosperity of the people' (*kemakmuran rakyat*). This system was referred to variously by members as the family principle, collective endeavour based on the family

[23] See Susanti, above n 7 at 11.
[24] Drs Achmad Hafidz Zawawi (F-PG), Risalah Rapat Komisi A Ke-3 L St MPR, 6 August 2002 at 39.
[25] Dr Prasetiono (ISEI), Risalah Rapat Ke-17 PAH I, 21 February 2000 at 14.
[26] See Susanti, above n 7 at 66.
[27] Dr Sri Adiningsih (Tim Ahli), Rapat Pleno Ke-13 PAH I, 24 April 2001 at 28; Drs Achmad Hafidz Zawawi (F-PG), Risalah Rapat Komisi A Ke-3 L S MPR, 6 August 2002 at 39.
[28] See Susanti, above n 7 at 69–70.
[29] Ir Ahmad Hafiz Zawawi, M.Sc. (F-PG), Risalah PAH I Rapat Ke 20, 27 March 2002 at 31–2.
[30] See Susanti, above n 7 at 9.
[31] Erfan Maryono (LPTP), Risalah PAH I Rapat Ke-8, 28 February 2002, at 29–30.
[32] Adi Sasono (CIDES), Risalah PAH I Rapat Ke-8, 28 February 2002 at *223*.

principle, or the principle of the people's economy (*ekonomi keraykatan*), commonly translated as 'Indonesian Socialism'.[33]

What form should state intervention take? MPR members highlighted two main activities. First, the state should ensure that all Indonesians have the opportunity to participate in the economy and to share in its spoils,[34] including those arising out of the exploitation of natural resources,[35] with priority for cooperatives and small-medium enterprises over individual endeavours.[36]

Secondly, the state should protect the weak from domination by the economically strong, whether domestic or foreign.[37] According to one member, this did not require the absence of competition, but did require protection from excessive competition:

In an *asas kekeluargaan* house, we have [several] children. We want all of them to advance; they must compete with each other to advance. But they cannot kill each other. The disabled and disadvantaged must be looked after. If the father allows the strong to win, the strong will eat more... The weak will die because they cannot take back their food.[38]

Many of those in the third category justified their rejection of the free market system by emphasizing that the asas kekeluargaan system had been developed by Indonesia's 'founding fathers' in 1945, including Indonesia's first Vice-President, Mohammad Hatta. Members appealed also to Indonesia's national ideology— Pancasila—devised by Indonesia's first President, Soekarno.[39] The principles of Pancasila are contained in the Constitution's Preamble and one of them is the principle of 'Social Justice'.[40] Advocates pointed also to another part of the

---

[33] See Susanti, above n 7 at 10.

[34] H. Ali Marwan Hanan, S.H. (Menkopukm), Risalah PAH I Rapat Ke-5, 25 February 2002 at 22; M. Hatta Mustafa, S.H. (F-UD), Risalah PAH I Rapat Ke 20, 27 March 2002 at 9.

[35] A. H. Hafild, 'Membumikan Mandat Pasal' (1999) 33 UUD 45, Wahana Lingkungan Hidup Indonesia, available at <http://www.pacific.net.id/~dede_s/Membumikan.htm>.

[36] Drs Ali Masykur Musa (F-KB), Risalah Rapat Komisi A Ke-3 L St MPR, 6 August 2002 at 41; Drs Hj.Chairunnisa (F-PG), Risalah Rapat Komisi B Ke-2 St MPR, 4 August 2002 at 9.

[37] Mayjen. Tni Affandi, S.IP (F-TNI/Polri), Risalah PAH I Rapat Ke 20, 27 March 2002 at 23.

[38] Ir A.M. Luthfi (F-Reformasi), Risalah PAH I Rapat Ke 20, 27 March 2002 at 35.

[39] Drs Sutjipno Mayjen. Pol. (Purn) (F-PDIP), Risalah PAH I Rapat Ke 20, 27 March 2002 at 44; Harjono, S.H., MCL. (F-PDIP), Risalah PAH I Rapat Ke 20, 27 March 2002 at 56.

[40] The full text of the Preamble is as follows (the Pancasila state ideology is italicized). 'Whereas freedom is the inalienable right of all nations, colonialism must be abolished in this world as it is not in conformity with humanity and justice; And the moment of rejoicing has arrived in the struggle of the Indonesian freedom movement to guide the people safely and well to the threshold of the independence of the state of Indonesia which shall be free, united, sovereign, just and prosperous; By the grace of God Almighty and impelled by the noble desire to live a free national life, the people of Indonesia hereby declare their independence. Subsequent thereto, to form a government of the state of Indonesia which shall protect all the people of Indonesia and their entire native land, and in order to improve the public welfare, to advance the intellectual life of the people and to contribute to the establishment of a world order based on freedom, abiding peace and social justice, the national independence of Indonesia shall be formulated into a constitution of the sovereign Republic of Indonesia which is based on the *belief in an Almighty God, just and civilised humanity, the unity of Indonesia, democracy guided by the inner wisdom of deliberations amongst representatives and the realization of social justice for all of the people of Indonesia.*'

Preamble which states that one of the purposes of independence was to create public welfare.[41] Presumably, these members thought that the free market could not appropriately guarantee this welfare.

Disappointment with the state's economic performance since Indonesia's independence was constantly raised during the debates, and prompted some members to question, rather rhetorically, whether asas kekeluargaan or ekonomi kerayakatan were to blame. Most concluded that it was the misinterpretation of the principles, rather than the principles themselves, that had caused these economic problems.[42]

III. The Constitutional Court

Constitutional amendments made in 2000 and 2001 required that Indonesia's first Constitutional Court (Mahkamah Konstitusi, or MK) be established by 17 August 2003. Art 24C[43] of the amended Constitution provides for the jurisdiction of the new court, granting it the power to make first and final—and binding—decisions in the review of statutes (Undang-undang) for conformity with the Constitution; to determine disputes concerning the authority of the state organs whose power is derived from the Constitution; to dissolve political parties; and to determine disputes on the results of a general election.[44] It also has the power to make decisions concerning the opinion of the national legislature (Dewan Perwakilan Rakyat, or DPR) regarding alleged violations of the Constitution by the President and/or Vice President—in other words, the power to have the final say in any impeachment proceedings.[45]

The MK has thus far reviewed the constitutionality of dozens of statutes. The MK cannot, however, review other types of laws below the level of statute such as government, ministerial, and Presidential regulations. Government regulations are a very common form of law in Indonesia and their legal status clearly ranks below that of a statute (Art 7(1) of Law No 10 of 2004 on Lawmaking). They are not subject to the legislative process; rather, they are usually drafted by government departments and signed into law by the President.

---

[41] H. Ali Marwan Hanan, S.H. (Menkopukm), Risalah PAH I Rapat Ke-5, 25 February 2002 at 19.

[42] Dr Sri Adiningsih (Tim Ahli), Rapat Pleno Ke-13 PAH I, 24 April 2001 at 28; Hobbes Sinaga, SH, MH (F-PDIP), Risalah PAH I Rapat Ke-20, 27 March 2002 at 10; Ir Ahmad Hafiz Zawawi, M.Sc. (F-PG), Risalah PAH I Rapat Ke 20, 27 March 2002 at 31). One expert, for example, mused that the 'family principle' (asas kekeluargaan) had been misinterpreted as the one-family principle (asas keluarga)—that is, the Soeharto family (Dr Sri Adiningsih (Tim Ahli), Rapat Pleno Ke-13 PAH I, 24 April 2001 at 28; see also Ir A.M. Luthfi (F-Reformasi), Risalah PAH I Rapat Ke 20, 27 March 2002 at 34).

[43] Unless otherwise stated, all references to 'Articles' are references to Articles of the 1945 Constitution of the Republic of Indonesia as amended.

[44] Art 24C(1); Art 10(1) of the MK Law.

[45] Art 24C(2); Art 10(2) of the MK Law.

These types of lesser laws fall firmly and exclusively within the review jurisdiction of the Mahkamah Agung (Supreme Court): Art 24A(1) of the Constitution. As will be seen below, this division of the review jurisdiction between the Constitutional and Supreme Courts is highly problematic, largely because the Supreme Court has not exercised its review jurisdiction regularly or vigorously. Hence the passing of regulations rather than statutes has thus come to be seen by government as one way to avoid MK intervention in its legislative programme.

The new MK has so far made important, if often controversial, contributions to the implementation of the amendments to the Constitution that brought it into being. It appears to be emerging as a professional and determined—even energetic—guardian of the new Constitution.[46] This has, on occasion, brought the new court into tension—and sometimes, as this chapter will show, conflict— with the executive branch.

IV. The MK's decision in the *Electricity Law* case[47]

As mentioned above, the enactment of the Electricity Law appeared as an IMF 'conditionality' in a Letter of Intent sent by the Indonesian government to the IMF. The Electricity Law and the statutes challenged in other Art 33 cases spawned significant controversy in the media and debate in the DPR, mainly because they sought to privatize elements of the sectors with which they respectively dealt.[48] They also sparked fears that prices would rise as a consequence of the relinquishment of state control.[49]

Hukumonline, Indonesia's leading and influential legal information and commentary website, described the effect of the Electricity Law as changing the sectoral policy from monopoly to competition.[50] Prior to the Law's enactment in

[46] See, for example, A. Irmanputra Sidin, 'Saat Harimau Itu Diompongkan Hakim: Pasal Eks PKI', Kompas, 26 February 2004 at <http://www.kompas.com>. See also Harman, Benny K. and Hendardi (eds), *Konstitutionalisme, Peran DPR, dan Judicial Review; Jaringan Informasi Masyarakat (JARIM) dan Yayasan Lembaga Bantuan Huku, Indonesia (YLBHI)*, 1999; and Harun, Refly, 'Bikin Lembaga Zonder KKN' in *Menjaga Denyut Konstitutsi; Refleksi Satu Tahun Mahkamah Konstitusi* (Refly Harun, Zainal A.M Husein and Bisariyadi, eds, 2004) 309.
[47] The MK publishes its decisions on its website <www.mahkamahkonstitusi.go.id> and also in hard copy. We refer to the soft-copy versions, as found on the website, in this chapter. All translations are our own, unless otherwise indicated.
[48] 'Dihujani Minderheidsnota, DPR Setujui RUU Sumber Daya Air', Hukumonline, 20 February 2004; 'Pasca Disetujuinya RUU SDA, Petani se-Bandung Somasi Komisi IV', Hukumonline, 20 February 2004; 'Undang-Undang Sumber Daya Air Terus Menuai Gugatan', Hukumonline, 4 August 2004; 'Mengapa Judicial Review UU Sumberdaya Air?', Walhi website, 28 July 2004, available at <http://www.walhi.or.id/kampanye/air/privatisasi/040728_judrevuuair_li/>; 'Akibat Privatisasi, Layanan Publik Jadi Barang Dagangan', Hukumonline, 15 February 2003.
[49] 'Ini Dia, Kelemahan RUU SDA Versi LSM', Hukumonline, 18 March 2004; 'Kampayne menolak privatisasi dan komersialisasi sumberdaya air', Walhi website, 14 April 2005.
[50] See, for example, 'Akibat Privatisasi, Layanan Publik Jadi Barang Dagangan', Hukumonline, 15 February 2003.

2002, the state electricity company was, in essence, the sole, generator, distributor, transmitter, and seller of electricity.[51] The Law, however, provided much greater scope for private sector involvement in the sector. Using the rhetorical and often vague style that is common in Indonesian legislative drafting, the Introductory Considerations of the Electricity Law state that:

[e]lectricity must be provided efficiently through competition and transparency in a climate of healthy industry, through regulations that treat all business entities equally and provide a just and even benefit to consumers (Part b).

In the framework of fulfilling national need for electricity and the creation of healthy competition, equal opportunity to participate in the electricity industry must be given to all business enterprises (Part c).

Consistent with this theme, the Law prohibited government monopolies in designated 'competition areas', 'unbundled' the 'provision of electricity' into several activities, including generation, transmission, distribution, and sale, and allowed different entities to perform these activities.[52] Only in areas 'not ready for competition', could the state retain its monopolies.

The applicants in the *Electricity Law* case used some of these criticisms of the Law as bases for constitutional argument before the MK. It is to these arguments that we now turn.

A. Parties' arguments

The applicants in the *Electricity Law* case contended that a myriad of their constitutional rights had been damaged by the Electricity Law.[53] We will limit our discussion, however, to the arguments relating to Art 33.

The first applicant argued that the privatization of electricity—an important branch of production—contradicted Art 33 of the Constitution.[54] The second applicant argued that the Law's unbundling of the provision of electricity undermined the state's control, as required under Art 33(2) of the Constitution. In this way, there would 'no longer be protection for the majority of people who could not afford…electricity'.[55] The third applicant argued that free competition would cause an electricity crisis in Indonesia, as was already occurring outside

---

[51] While private power companies existed in Indonesia prior to 2002, most had exclusive power purchase agreements with state-owned PLN. See, for example, W. J. Henisz and B. A. Zelner, *The Political Economy of Private Electricity Provision in Southeast Asia* (2001); D. Hall and E. Lobina, 'Private and Public Interests in Water and Energy' (2004) 28 Natural Resources Forum 268.

[52] See Arts 8(2), 16 and 17 of the Electricity Law.

[53] The first applicant alleged its rights under Arts 1(3), 28C(2), 28D(1), 28H(1), 33(2) and 33(3) of the Constitution had been damaged; the second applicant alleged a breach of Arts 27(2), 28D(2), 28H(1), 28H(3), 33(3) and 54(3); and the third applicant claimed its Art 28A, 28C(1) and 28H(1) rights had been breached.

[54] *Electricity Law* case at 342–3.

[55] ibid at 343.

Java, criticized unbundling, and argued that leaving the market to determine prices was inconsistent with Art 33's emphasis on 'the people's prosperity'.[56]

In response, the government put forward several arguments. First, it emphasized that the Law was 'desirable' because the government was having difficulties meeting demand for electricity by itself.[57] Private-sector capital was, therefore, necessary to meet this demand. Secondly, the government contended that competition would help to make the provision of electricity more transparent and efficient, and it would assist in ensuring the 'sufficient supply of electricity throughout Indonesia at an affordable price'.[58]

Thirdly, the government argued that it had decided to focus on regulating, rather than operating, the sector, because 'Government's function is to govern'.[59] In this context, the government claimed that it would still 'control' the sector: it would determine policy, regulate and supervise the sector under the Law.[60] It could, therefore, ensure that those operating in the sector were providing a sufficient supply of electricity to meet the needs of the population.

Fourthly, the government acknowledged that 'competition' in the electricity sector would not be successful through the whole of Indonesia. In anticipation of this, the government had allowed monopolies to remain in areas of Indonesia where competition would not ensure the adequate provision of electricity.[61] In these places, prices would be set only to recover costs.[62]

Fifthly, the government noted that it would maintain complete control over some sectors of the electricity industry. The state would remain in control of distribution and transmission and the private sector could be involved in only the sale and production of electricity.[63]

B. The MK's decision

The Court's decision focused on the state's obligation to 'control' important branches of production under Art 33(2) of the Constitution. It held that Arts 16, 17(3) and 68 of the Law, which sought to introduce competition and unbundling in the electricity sector, conflicted with Art 33(2) of the Constitution because they would, in fact, result in a relinquishing of control in the sense intended by that Article. It therefore declared them to be invalid.[64]

The Court, however, also found that competition and unbundling were at the 'heart' of the Law. Quite extraordinarily, it therefore declared the entire statute invalid on the grounds that it was not in line with 'the soul and spirit' of Art 33(2),

---

[56] ibid at 343–4.
[57] Indeed, a government expert argued that PLN was incapable of meeting demand for electricity, despite electricity 'being second only to food in importance to human life': *Electricity Law* case at 339–40.
[58] ibid at 337, 340.   [59] ibid at 338.   [60] ibid at 337, 340.   [61] ibid at 338.
[62] ibid.   [63] ibid.   [64] ibid at 349–50.

which, according to the Court, 'forms the basis of the Indonesian economy'.[65] The Court argued that it had no choice but to do this, because it believed that the invalidity of only a small part of the Law would 'cause chaos that would lead to legal uncertainty' in the Law's application.[66] The MK then reinstated the previous Electricity Law (Law No 15 of 1985) on the logical basis that Art 70 of the 2002 Law—which declared the 1985 Law to be no longer in force—was, itself, no longer valid.

The most important aspect of the MK's decision was that merely regulating the electricity sector was insufficient to constitute 'control by the state' as required by Art 33(2). It is useful, however, to dispose first of some of the Court's responses to other arguments raised by the parties before returning to a more detailed discussion of this point.

The MK rejected most of the government's arguments in favour of privatization. First, the Court held that the increased transparency and reduced corruption that competition was presumed to bring was outweighed by the importance of the state fulfilling its (binding) obligations under Art 33.[67]

Secondly, the MK expressed doubts that privatization would necessarily improve capacity, quality and price. The Court emphasized the testimony of an English expert,[68] who argued that restructuring of the electricity sector in Britain had not resulted in lower prices and greater efficiency. Instead, the Court said, many jobs had been lost and investors had enjoyed high returns. The expert also stated that Thailand, South Korea, Brazil and Mexico had delayed or 'put off' restructuring for these reasons.[69] The Court stated that the suggestion that the market would naturally provide available, evenly-distributed and affordable electricity was 'far from realistic'.[70]

In any event, the Court held that the government could improve the sector and attract private-sector capital without privatization. According to the Court, PLN could seek financial assistance from, or work in partnership with, the domestic or foreign private sector. The Court also suggested that PLN delegate its functions to another state enterprise, or regional state enterprise with PLN as a holding company, although it did not explain what this might achieve.[71]

Thirdly, the Court held that the state's obligation to ensure public prosperity would not necessarily be achieved by allowing competition, because the private sector would prioritize its own profits and would concentrate on established markets—primarily in Java, Madura and Bali. The Court believed that

---

[65] ibid.
[66] *Electricity Law* case at 349–50. The Court did not, however, go so far as to invalidate contracts or licences signed or issued under the Law, allowing them to continue until they expired.
[67] ibid at 348–9.
[68] David Hall, Director of the Public Services International Research Unit, University of Greenwich, London.
[69] *Electricity Law* case at 342.
[70] ibid at 331.
[71] ibid at 348.

cross-subsidies from these established markets would be required to support 'less competitive' parts of Indonesia and that such subsidies could not be obtained from the private sector.[72] In this context, competition would 'tend to undermine state enterprises and may not guarantee the supply of electricity to all parts of the community'.[73]

It is worth noting here that many of the MK's arguments are similar to those made by the MPR members in 2001 in favour of the retention of Art 33, mentioned above. These similarities are considered in the conclusion to this chapter.

C. Controlled by the state?

As indicated earlier, a crucial issue in all four Art 33 cases has been the Court's definition of the phrase 'controlled by the state' contained in both Art 33(2) and 33(3). Clearly, the Court saw Art 33 to be one of the Constitution's most fundamental provisions. In the *Electricity Law* case, for example, the Court even observed that state control over important areas of production 'could be said to be the entire paradigm and legal ideal of the Constitution'.[74]

In the *Electricity Law* case, the Court's discussion about the nature of obligations placed upon the government by this phrase was extensive, and was referred to in the *Migas* and *SDA Law* cases. The judges discussed whether 'controlled by the state' in Art 33(2) required only that the government regulate important branches of production, or whether it imposed more onerous obligations upon the state such as to own and operate the means of sale, supply and distribution— even if this required prohibiting the private sector from operating in those areas. Further, was the state required to take control over industries which were already being run by the private sector, if they became important enough to fall within Art 33(2)?[75]

The Court referred to testimony provided during hearings by Prof Dr Harun Alrasid, a highly-regarded Indonesian constitutional law expert, who interpreted 'controlled by the state' to mean 'owned' by the state.[76] The Court also referred to the written submission of the State Enterprises Minister, who interpreted 'controlled by the state' to mean 'regulated, facilitated and operated by the state', but 'dynamically moving towards the state only regulating and facilitating'.[77]

The Court itself took the view, however, that Art 33 required more than ownership over important branches of production in the civil law sense. Because 'state control' exists within the Constitution's framework of 'public law, political

---

[72] ibid at 347.
[73] ibid.
[74] ibid at 330.
[75] ibid at 329–30. The MK stated (at 330) that any such takeovers must be carried out in accordance with just laws.
[76] ibid at 332.
[77] ibid.

democracy and economic democracy' (which it did not define), the Court stressed that the Indonesian people have ultimate power, and thus hold collective ownership, over those branches of production.[78] The Court argued that the civil concept of 'ownership' was therefore insufficient because it did not, in itself, necessarily provide for the welfare of the people or social justice, as is required in the Constitution's Preamble. According to the Court:

> Viewing the Constitution as a system as intended, 'controlled by the state' in Art 33 has a higher or broader meaning than civil law ownership. The concept of state control is a public law concept related to the principle of peoples' sovereignty adhered to in the Constitution, in both politics (political democracy) and economics (economic democracy). Within this concept of peoples' sovereignty, it is the people who are recognized as the source, owners and also the holders of the highest authority in the state, in accordance with the doctrine 'from the people, by the people and for the people'. This concept of highest authority encompasses public collective ownership by the people.
>
> If 'controlled by the state' means only ownership in the civil sense, then the control will be insufficient to achieve the 'greatest prosperity of the people', rendering the mandates to 'advance public wellbeing' and 'to create social justice for all Indonesian people' in the Elucidation to the Constitution impossible to achieve. Nevertheless ... civil ownership must be recognized as a logical consequence of state control, which also encompasses collective public ownership by the people over the sources of those [natural] assets.[79]

Further, the Court refused to accept that 'controlled by the state' could be interpreted merely as the government's right to regulate. According to the Court, the government would have inherent power to regulate, even if the phrase 'controlled by the state' was not contained in Art 33.[80] 'Controlled by the state', therefore, must have a broader meaning. The Court argued that, in light of the people's sovereignty over all natural resources and public ownership of those natural resources, the people, through the Constitution, had 'provided a mandate to the state to make policy, organize, regulate, manage and supervise to achieve maximum welfare for the people'.[81]

The government exercises the state's administrative function by issuing and revoking permits, licences and concessions . The DPR, using legislative power, and the Government, through Government regulation, exercises the regulatory function of the state . The management function is exercised through share ownership mechanisms and/or through direct involvement in the management of State Owned Legal Entities ... which, through the state, that is, the government, uses its control over those natural assets so that they are used for the greatest prosperity of the people. Similarity, the state, that is, the government, exercises the state's monitoring function ... to ensure that the state's control over the sources of assets is truly exercised for the greatest prosperity of the people.[82]

---

[78] ibid at 333.
[79] ibid at 332–3.
[80] ibid at 333.
[81] ibid at 334.
[82] ibid at 334. *Migas Law* case at 208–9.

D. Scope for private sector involvement?

The Court interpreted Art 33(2) as requiring state control over important existing branches of production—even if this requires prohibiting the private sector from operating in those areas or leads to the state taking over from the private sector areas that have become important.[83] Significantly, however, it did not prohibit all private-sector involvement in the electricity industry. Rather, the Court held that the government could allow private sector involvement, provided that it did not extinguish its own control.[84] The Court also stated that the civil 'ownership' included in the concept of control did not require 100 per cent government ownership. Rather, the MK required only that the government own sufficient shares in the enterprise to enable the government to 'control' decision and policy-making.[85]

Further, the Court stated that the government could, from time to time, reassess the 'importance' of these branches of production. If the government thought that a particular industry—such as electricity—was no longer of sufficient importance to the people, then policy, organization, regulation, management and supervision could be left to the market.[86]

To support these conclusions, the Court engaged in 'historical interpretation', in which it reflected on the Elucidation to Constitution as it stood before it was deleted during the amendment process. To do so was, of course, an act that severely strained the limits of the MK's authority, given that the whole purpose of deleting the Elucidation was precisely to prevent it being used to interpret the Constitution. Be that as it may, the MK emphasized that there should be economic democracy for the welfare of all and that the government should remain in control of important areas of production, because if production were to fall 'into the hands of someone powerful, the community could be afflicted', a claim the Court did not explain further.[87] The MK also referred to the interpretation of Art 33 proposed by Mohammad Hatta.[88] According to Hatta, the Indonesian government should control essential areas of production, but if it cannot meet demand, then it should seek foreign loans and, as a last resort, allow foreigners to invest in production.[89]

It is critical to note here that the Court has left it to the national legislature to decide whether particular branches of production are 'important' and therefore subject to state control. For example, in the *Electricity Law* case, the Court accepted that electricity was sufficiently 'important' because the importance

[83] *Electricity Law* case at 329–30.
[84] ibid at 336.
[85] ibid at 334–6, 346. Similar comments were made in the *Migas Law* case at 210–11.
[86] *Electricity Law* case at 335.
[87] ibid at 331.
[88] ibid at 332.
[89] ibid at 331–2, citing Mohammad Hatta, *Kumpulan Pidato II*, compiled by I. Wangsa Widjaja and M. F. Swasono, PT Toko Gunung Agung, Jakarta, 2002, at 231.

of electricity was emphasized in the Law itself.[90] This is significant, because it could potentially give latitude to a government to legislatively—and thus, in all likelihood, definitively—re-categorize a branch of production as no longer 'important', thus removing all legislation on that branch of production from the jurisdiction of the MK (at least so far as Art 33 is concerned).

E. The MK and government policy

In some of the cases it has decided thus far the Court has gone to great lengths to emphasize that it lacks jurisdiction to assess government policy.[91] The Court did not discuss the boundaries of its judicial review jurisdiction in the Art 33 cases. Yet Art 33(2) appears to establish an obligation on the government to enact laws that further the peoples' welfare and hence a constitutional right that citizens and legal entities can seek to enforce. It is arguable, then, that, contrary to the MK's apparent concern to refrain from entering the domain of public policy, it is, in fact, obliged to ensure that legislative policy in cases involving state control over natural resources furthers the peoples' welfare.

Indeed, some of the Court's arguments in the *Electricity Law* case set out above were, in essence, a critique of privatization. That is, the Court's stance appears to be that privatization cannot guarantee the prosperity of the people, as required by Art 33(2). Determining whether government control is exercised to further peole's welfare appears to verge on, or might, in fact, constitute, the MK intruding into what the MK itself defines as the constitutional 'corridor' within which the DPR can legitimately exercise discretion when legislating.[92]

The extent to which the Court will continue to enter the policy debate is unclear, and should be clarified by the Court as it hears more Art 33 cases. Many questions remain, such as how the Court will assess whether public prosperity is, in fact, being achieved. For instance, how would the Court view legislation that imposes a short-term financial burden but anticipated long-term economic benefits? Would Indonesia's electricity price rises of 2005, had they been established by statute,[93] be reviewable by the Court on the basis that they could reduce 'the people's welfare'? If so, would the Court have upheld the application because of the economic hardship the price rises caused for the poor, even if they freed up budgetary resources for the provision of other services? Or would the Court have rejected it on the basis that fuel subsidies were crippling the Indonesian economy and hence reducing general welfare levels? Courts elsewhere have been reluctant

---

[90] *Electricity Law* case at 345.
[91] MK Decision No 006/2003, reviewing Law No 30 of 2002 on the Corruption Eradication Commission (the *KPK Law* case).
[92] *KPK Law* case at 95.
[93] In fact, the electricity rises were introduced via Presidential Regulation No 55 of 2005: 'Kenaikan BBM Diajukan Judicial Review', Hukumonline, 14 October 2005.

to enforce constitutional prohibitions on privatization, at least in part precisely to avoid having to answer difficult questions of policy such as these.[94]

In the authors' view, the MK might now be well-served by delineating more precisely the issues that it thinks it is competent to assess and those that should be left to the legislature. Like many other superior courts around the world that conduct judicial review, the MK faces the practical, political and perennial question of the precise extent to which unelected judges should be able to overrule the opinions of the majority of a democratically-elected legislature. Of course, the MK's constitutional mandate is to do precisely that—review (in certain circumstances) the constitutionality of statutes produced by the legislature—but that does not free the Court from considering the political implications that inevitably arise from the exercise of that mandate. This is particularly true if the Court does not, in future cases, fully explain the degree of state control Art 33 requires.

As mentioned at the outset, the effect of the MK's decision in the *Electricity Law* case has been to create potentially significant impediments to government's capacity to implement economic policies pushed by the IMF and other donors. The implications of this decision for donors were, at time of writing, unclear but they have probably been placated by the government's aggressive (and, in our view, subversive) regulatory response to the MK's decisions on privatization, which we now describe.

F. Statutory resurrection by government regulation and a pre-emptive strike?

In January 2005, around two months after the MK handed down its decision in the *Electricity Law* case, the government issued a regulation the full title of which was 'Government Regulation No 3 of 2005, Amending Government Regulation No 10 of 1989 on the Provision and Exploitation of Electricity'. Part (a) of the Preamble to the Regulation reveals its intent:

...in the framework of increasing the availability of electricity for the public interest, the roles of cooperatives, State Owned Enterprises, Regional State Owned Enterprises, the *private sector*, community groups and *individuals* must be increased [our emphasis].

The government regulation was not framed as a formal and direct replacement of the Electricity Law struck down by the MK,[95] but it certainly appears to attempt to mitigate, even nullify, much of the effect of the MK decision. It has

---

[94] T. Daintith and M. Sah, 'Privatisation and the Economic Neutrality of the Constitution' (1993) PL 465; D. Feldman and F. Campbell 'Constitutional Limitations on Privatisation' in *Comparative Law Facing the 21st Century* (J. W. Bridge, ed, 2001).

[95] Although the MK's invalidation of the Electricity Law is mentioned in passing in the Elucidation to the Regulation.

even been described as being 'not much different'[96] from the Electricity Law the MK invalidated and Hotma Timpul, a Jakarta lawyer, has said it was just a re-enactment of the Electricity Law 'in new clothes'.[97] Indeed, even a senior government official, J. Purnowo, the Electricity Management Administration Director, has admitted that the regulation was passed to provide certainty for private sector investors in the aftermath of the MK's decision.[98] More specifically, he hoped that the regulation would enable PLN to invite the private sector to compete for tenders.[99]

The main objections appear to centre around Arts 6 and 11 of the regulation. Article 6 states that, provided that it does not damage the interests of the state, a permit can be provided to a cooperative or 'another enterprise' to provide electricity in the public interest or in its own interest. Article 6(2) and (3) provides that such 'other enterprises' can include the private sector and individuals. Article 11 states that permit holders can buy and sell electricity. These provisions appear to directly contravene the MK's decision in the *Electricity Law* case, because they allow the state to evade its obligations under Art 33 by relinquishing its 'control' over the provision of electricity to the private sector. It appears, therefore, that the government has successfully circumvented the decision.

The irony is that the MK can do nothing to remedy the apparent unconstitutionality of the electricity regulation, because, as mentioned earlier, it cannot review lower-level laws. It is, therefore, likely that the regulation will remain in force and applicable, a result that threatens to make a farce of the whole judicial review process.[100]

IV. Conclusion: teething problems?

The MK Art 33/privatization cases show that the Art 33 'People's Economy' debate between state and market and between global economic orthodoxy and local political discourses is quite clearly still alive in post-Soeharto Indonesia and, indeed, has even been revived by the MK. The debate continues now to have

---

[96] Personal communication with Fultoni, Secretary of KRHN (Konsorsium Reformasi Hukum Nasional (National Legal Reform Consortium), 8 May 2005. See also 'PP Listrik Swasta Diajukan Uji Materiil', Hukumonline, 17 July 2005.

[97] 'PP Listrik Swasta Diajukan Uji Materiil', Hukumonline, 17 July 2005.

[98] 'Pemerintah Segera Keluarkan PP Kemitraan Swasta Sektor Ketenagalistrikan', Hukumonline, 14 January 2005.

[99] 'Pemerintah Segera Keluarkan PP Kemitraan Swasta Sektor Ketenagalistrikan', Hukumonline, 14 January 2005.

[100] It should also be noted that the government also attempted to circumvent the anticipated effect of the *SDA Law* case, mentioned earlier. After the MK had begun hearing the *SDA Law* case, but before its decision was handed down, Government Regulation No 16 of 2005 on the Development of a Drinking Water Availability System was issued. This regulation appears to achieve part of what the SDA Law aims to do—allow for private sector involvement in the provision of drinking water.

potentially enormous implications for both politics and the economy. This is true, in particular, for the continuing process of transfer of state assets into the hands of private business that forms so important a part of economic reform orthodoxy in post-Soeharto Indonesia, and which was a central feature of the post-1998 reform agenda sponsored by the IMF, the World Bank and other donors.

The independence of the Court and the sincerity with which it approaches its constitutional tasks have been impressive so far.[101] But if the Court is too ambitious and its decisions are too far-reaching and unpalatable to government, it runs the risk of being ignored by the government or having its decisions rendered meaningless—or even of having its powers curtailed through future legislation or constitutional amendment.

Further, the more directly the MK enters debates over legislative policy, the more likely it is to face stiff resistance—and even, as in the *Electricity Law* case, subversion—from government. Resistance or non-compliance has resulted, even though the MK has in the decisions discussed in this chapter appeared to give effect to the views of many MPR members on the continuing need for state intervention in the Indonesian economy. This resistance from DPR members and the government is somewhat incongruous, given that the majority of the MPR members who approved the retention of Art 33 and the establishment of the Constitutional Court were also members of the DPR which enacted the Electricity Law. In reality, then, the Court has been forced to mediate the inconsistencies caused by the differing political and economic imperatives of the DPR and the MPR, which, in turn, were to a large extent a result of the imposition of the IMF's conditionalities.

Resistance is all the more likely if, as we have shown, some aspects of the Court's decisions and their implications are unclear or inconsistent, making compliance difficult. The same is true if the Court runs head-on into major planks of economic policy, such as privatization and property rights.

---

[101] See S. D. Harijanti and T. Lindsey, 'INDONESIA: General Elections Test Constitutional Amendments and New Constitutional Court' (2006) 4(1) International Journal of Constitutional Law 138.

PART III

PROPERTY RIGHTS, MARKETS, AND REGULATION

14

Ownership Models for Water Services: Implications for Regulation

*Sarah Hendry**

I. Introduction

Water is essential for life and also for health and dignity, it has an economic value to agriculture and industry, it is used for recreation and has a spiritual and cultural dimension. The complexity of its multiple uses lead to tension, especially in those regions where it is under increasing pressure. Traditionally, water has been seen as a 'public good' in some way, appropriate to the culture and legal system of the society in question—whether as *res communis* in Roman law,[1] public ownership in modern civil codes,[2] concepts of public trust or public right,[3] or religious or customary duties to provide water to humans and animals in need.[4] At the same time, there may be concepts of private rights in some waters such as spring waters.[5] This makes the property regime for water more complex than that of land or other 'fixed' resources. These debates belong to the world of water resources management, and rights in water as a resource are considered elsewhere in this book by Lee Godden in particular.

This chapter is instead concerned with the provision of water services—drinking water and sanitation, the latter of which may or may not involve waterborne disposal through a sewerage system. However, partly because of

* Lecturer in Law, IHP-HELP Centre for Water Law, Policy and Science (under the auspices of UNESCO), Graduate School of Natural Resources Law, Policy and Management, University of Dundee, United Kingdom; email: s.m.hendry@dundee.ac.uk. My thanks to colleagues, and the editorial team, for their input into earlier drafts. All errors and misconceptions remain the author's own.
[1] Institutes of Justinian, Book II Title I, Trans. R. W. Lee, *The Elements of Roman Law* (1956).
[2] See eg the French Civil Code Art 538.
[3] See eg the National Water Act 1998 s 3 (South Africa).
[4] Thus the Islamic system so provides; D. Caponera and M. Nanni, *Principles of Water Law and Administration* (2nd edn, 2007) ch 5.
[5] See, eg, in a civilian jurisdiction, the French Civil Code Art 642; see also B. Clark, 'Migratory Things on Land: Property Rights and a Law of Capture' (2002) vol 6.3 Electronic Journal of Comparative Law, available at <www.ejcl.org>.

social concepts of water as a public resource, water services may be seen as something that states should provide for no charge, or at a price far below the actual cost of the service. This causes many difficulties as states seek to give citizens access to water supply and sanitation, because of the need for high levels of capital and operational expenditure. The concept of ownership as applied to water resources is a very different creature to the concept of ownership of the assets of water services providers, whatever legal form those providers may take.

Water services, and the failure to provide these essential services to many of the world's poorest citizens, have been accorded increasing importance in global policy agendas on water, environment, development, and public health, as water is a cross-cutting issue. United Nations estimates widely used as benchmarks[6] suggest that in 2000, out of a world population of six billion, 1.1 billion lacked 'improved' water supply and 2.4 billion lacked 'improved' sanitation.[7] Water and sanitation impact on health, food security and poverty alleviation and the UN Millennium Development Goals[8] include halving the number of people without 'safe' water globally, and improving sanitation for 100 million slum dwellers, by 2015.[9] At the Johannesburg Summit, the international community reaffirmed its commitment and clarified the goal of halving the number of people without access to 'safe' drinking water, and in addition a commitment to halving the numbers without basic sanitation.[10] Since Johannesburg, the Human Development Report 2003[11] has stressed the social good achieved by adequate public services, including water services, whilst the Second World Water Development Report clarified the paramount role of water in improving public health[12] and the Human Development Report 2006 was increasingly critical of the lack of global progress.[13] Although some progress has been made towards achieving at least the water supply target, the world's population continues to increase as does the proportion living in an urban environment. Globally, the scale of the problem cannot be under-estimated.

[6] These figures were first produced by WHO/UNICEF, *Global Water Supply and Sanitation Assessment* (2000) available at <www.who.int>. Since then, some progress has been made in service delivery, yet the global population continues to expand; see UNDP, *Human Development Report 2006 Beyond Scarcity: Power Poverty and the Global Water Crisis* (2006) 5 available at <www.hdr.undp.org>.
[7] For an explanation of 'improved' water services, see UN, *Water, A Shared Responsibility The United Nations World Water Development Report 2* (2006) 224–5 available at <www.unesco.org>.
[8] UN Millennium Declaration UN General Assembly A/RES/55/2 2000 available at <www.un.org>.
[9] UN Roadmap towards the Implementation of the UN Millennium Declaration UN A/56/326 2001 available at <www.un.org>.
[10] UN Report of the World Summit on Sustainable Development (2002) A/Conf.199/20 incorporating the Johannesburg Declaration and Plan of Implementation II.8 available at <www.un.org>.
[11] UNDP, *Human Development Report 2003* (2003) especially chs 4 and 5, available at <www.hdr.undp.org>.
[12] *World Water Development Report* 2 (above n 7).
[13] UNDP (above n 6).

In the last 30 years, in the post-industrial world, governments have favoured the 'privatization' of essential services as a means of shedding the burden of capital investment,[14] and to achieve greater efficiency in delivery of the service. The capital burden is especially high in water, where there is a natural monopoly, high fixed costs and a long pay-back period.[15] Meantime the efficiency argument diminishes, as evidence increases that efficiency is effectively achieved by regulation, not by the markets.[16] Yet this solution has been promoted in the developing world, where the scale of the problem, and the level of unmet need, is acute.

'Privatization' is a loose term and can be used to describe many different structures, which will be discussed further below; it will be used here to mean any involvement of the private sector in provision of water or sanitation services. It also brings highly polarized socio-political responses. Despite moves throughout the 1990s to increase the private sector's role, it is still the case that only around 5 per cent of water services globally have been fully divested,[17] and perhaps 15 per cent are provided through some other mechanism that engages with the private sector. In the United Kingdom, the divestiture in England and Wales[18] was and is unusual; the 'Scottish model', whilst moving from local government to regional board to public corporation in the same time period, still has more commonality with the rest of the world. The English water companies are amongst the most highly regulated in the world; traditionally, the private sector requires a high degree of economic regulation to control both the drive to maximize profit and the tendency to monopoly. But from a global perspective, the attention is shifting—not necessarily away from private sector involvement, but certainly towards a greater focus on how to regulate the public sector. The public sector, just as the private, has a tendency towards monopoly, and can benefit no less from more rigorous economic management, whilst perhaps being more likely to achieve social and environmental goals.

This chapter will examine the different ownership models operating in England and Scotland, along with structures for their regulation and control. It will also draw on examples from other jurisdictions, particularly South Africa and Australia. In both South Africa and Australia there is a mixture of public and

[14] For an overview of the privatization era, from a UK perspective, J. Vickers and G. Yarrow, *Privatisation: An Economic Analysis* (1988). 'Privatization' will be defined further below.
[15] See I. Kessides, *Reforming Infrastructure: Privatisation, Regulation and Competition* (2004) World Bank Policy Research Report WB/OUP available at <www.econ.worldbank.org>; Public Private Infrastructure Advisory Facility and Water and Sanitation Programme, *New Designs for Water and Sanitation Transactions: Making Water Work for the Poor* (2002) available at <www. ppiaf.org>; J. Winpenny, *Report of the World Panel on Financing Water Infrastructure* (2003) (The Camdessus Report) available at <http://www.financingwaterforall.org>. This examined how to improve funding for water services in order to achieve the Millennium Development Goals and in the longer-term, provision for all by 2025.
[16] S. Renzetti and D. Dupont, 'Ownership and Performance of Water Utilities' in *The Business of Water and Sustainable Development* (J. Chenoweth and J. Bird, eds, 2006).
[17] See ibid Chenoweth and Bird, 'Introduction'.
[18] Water Act 1989.

private sector involvement; in both there is provision by local government, with consequences for ring-fenced funding, economic audit and business planning; in both there is already disaggregation of bulk and individual supply, and moves to commercialize or corporatize public supply. In Queensland, we note that the public and private sectors are subject to parallel, but essentially similar, regulatory, business planning and reporting arrangements.[19] The chapter will assess the role of regulation and of governance, as well as structures of ownership, and will draw conclusions as to the importance of ownership of this industry, compared to the role of effective regulation and good governance. Perhaps the correct question is not 'does ownership matter,' but rather, in what way does it matter, and how can the effects of ownership be addressed in the regulatory framework?

II. Competition and vertical integration

Water services tend to be natural monopolies. There will only be one set of networked pipes, for either water or sewerage, and unless the whole system is divested, these networks at least will usually remain in public ownership. In order to bring the benefits of competition to water services, there are a few options. One is to use 'competition by comparison', the English model, where an economic regulator compares the performance of regional suppliers, using the best performers as benchmarks for setting targets for the rest. Another is to establish competition 'for the market', by inviting private sector participants to tender for aspects of the service provision. A third is to disaggregate the components of the industry. These options are not mutually exclusive; unless the entire system is to be sold, or its management transferred under a long-term contract, it will be necessary to disaggregate the supply chain before opening sections of it to competition.

If the water services industry is vertically integrated, then bulk abstraction of raw water from source, its treatment, and the distribution of drinking water through the networks, will all be provided by one entity. So too will off-take of waste water through the sewerage networks, treatment, and discharge of the treated waste. Alternatively, separate bodies may be involved in bulk supply, treatment, and distribution to consumers. This is the case, for example, in South Africa, where regional water boards are responsible for bulk supply,[20] and also in Queensland, Australia, where there are two major suppliers of bulk water, each with a different legal structure but both in the public sector.[21] In both of

---

[19] In terms of economic regulation, see the Queensland Competition Authority Act (Qld) 1997; Part 3 applies to public agencies, and Part 5A to 'non-government agency suppliers'.

[20] Water Services Act 1997 s 29 (South Africa).

[21] SunWater is a government-owned corporation under the Government Owned Corporations Act (Qld) 1993 and the Government Owned Corporations Regulation 2004 SL No 166. SEQWater is constituted as a company under the Corporations Act (Qld) 1990, but the shares are held by the Queensland government and various local governments.

these jurisdictions most urban water services are provided by local authorities, although in rural areas the supply of domestic water services may be integrated with the provision of irrigation water,[22] and other service providers may also be authorized. It is notable that in South Africa there is a statutory duty to utilize the public sector if this is possible.[23] Such a duty may be a useful law reform option internationally to limit negative perceptions of privatization.

The question of vertical disaggregation can be separated out from the public–private debate for any one aspect of the service. It is arguable that of itself, the separation of components of the industry is beneficial in terms of competition policy and the management of the natural monopoly tendencies of water, as is accepted in other services that tend towards monopoly. However, it is also likely that a disaggregated industry will engage the private sector in some components of the service. Small steps towards disaggregation, with concomitant market liberalization, have taken place in Scotland, with the opening up to competition of retail services to business customers (discussed further below); in England, where there is a highly integrated system through regional private companies, the government and the regulator are now looking at much more substantial disaggregation.[24] Whilst disaggregation in itself may have positive consequences in reducing the concentration of monopoly power, it does not necessarily affect the perception of private provision of these services as negative. Furthermore, the networks at least will remain a monopoly, and other elements of the service may well be provided by only a few key players.

III. Models for water services provision

A. Public sector options

As already noted, the majority of water services globally are provided through the public sector, and often by local government. This was the case in Scotland, prior to the mid-1990s, when water services were provided by the 'top tier' regional councils.[25] It is also the case in South Africa and Queensland.[26] Alternatively, there may be a national or regional board, agency or public corporation. This is the case in Scotland now, since the establishment of Scottish Water as a national

---

[22] In Queensland, through water authorities, or private owners of infrastructure; Water Act (Qld) 2000 s 370(c). In South Africa, through water services providers that are not municipalities; Water Services Act (above n 20) s 22. These may include Water Users Associations.

[23] Water Services Act 1997 (South Africa) s 19(2).

[24] M. Cave, *Independent Review of Competition and Innovation in Water Markets* (2009) available at <http://www.defra.gov.uk>.

[25] Local Government (Scotland) Act 1973.

[26] In South Africa, municipalities are water services authorities and may also be water services providers, Water Services Act 1997 s 20; in Queensland, water services providers may be local governments, Water Act (Qld) 2000 s 370(a), and this includes the majority of the registered providers.

public corporation in 2002.[27] As will be explored below, this public sector monopoly hides behind it a substantial tranche of private involvement in aspects of sewerage services.

The advantages of a separate institution for water services include a clear focus on the service and transparency regarding costs and tariffs. If instead services are provided by local government, there are many other competing demands on resources, and the financial management of any particular service may be obscured. On the other hand, there is, or should be, a high level of political accountability, and it is also possible to make any necessary trade-offs, between price and levels of service, at a local level.[28]

B. Models for the private sector

If the political decision is made to seek some private sector involvement in service provision, almost certainly to secure capital investment, then there are several different forms in which to do so, each necessitating different contractual or regulatory models and seeking different allocations of risk and opportunity. Generally, the shorter the term of the contract, the less risk there is, and therefore the less opportunity for profit. Longer-term arrangements tend to allocate more responsibility and more risk, whereby the investing company will seek greater opportunities to profit from the arrangement. The World Bank has analysed these models intensively in terms of improving service delivery in the developing world.[29]

As noted, the terminology is not exact; this chapter uses the term 'privatization' to refer to any model that engages the private sector, but 'divestiture' to mean a complete sale of the assets. Apart from the use and misuse of the particular word, the various options discussed below may be called different names in different jurisdictions. As with roses, the smell, not the name, is the defining factor; in any particular jurisdiction it is necessary to look behind the terminology to establish the reality of the contractual and regulatory arrangements.

In the short term, with service or management contracts lasting perhaps three to five years, private companies may provide specific services such as IT support, transport services, or metering, to an existing public service provider. These contracts may involve flat-rate payments to the provider, or perhaps a system of incentive payments to improve performance. There is no transfer of assets, no responsibility for investments, and little risk. These types of contracts are widely used, and relatively

---

[27] Water Industry (Scotland) Act 2002.
[28] Thus in Queensland, small rural service providers may be able to agree a reduced set of service standards with their communities; Department of Natural Resources and Water, *Guidelines for Implementing TMP: Service Standards Implementation Guide* (2001) section 6 available at <http://www.nrm.qld.gov.au>.
[29] See especially World Bank/Public-Private Infrastructure Advisory Facility, *Approaches to Private Sector Participation in Water Services* (2006) available at <www.worldbank.org>; and for a broader analysis also J. Delmon, *Water Projects: A Commercial and Contractual Guide* (2001).

unproblematic, though they still need careful drafting and effective enforcement; but they have no impact on ownership and will not be considered further here.

C. Long-term arrangements

Longer-term arrangements include leases, concessions, and variants on Build-Own-Operate (BOO) schemes. Leases and concessions, which may be for periods of 25 or 30 years, do not involve transfer of the asset base. Concessions will include investment in maintaining and perhaps extending the infrastructure base, so bring a high degree of risk to the concessionaire. These have been common in countries that have adopted a 'French model' for water services provision, and the two largest private sector providers of water services in the world are both French, Veolia and Suez. However, given recent and very public failures in some of these concession contracts,[30] the major private players are less inclined to bid for concessions, and are now much more likely to look for more tailored and less extensive projects such as the provision of treatment plant.

BOO schemes and their variants are particularly useful for a single treatment plant, whether drinking water or waste water.[31] Variants include Build-Operate-Transfer, or Build-Own-Operate-Transfer. Although there are clearly differences, this chapter will refer to them all as BOO schemes. These schemes usually involve a private sector operator building new plant and operating it for a defined period of time. The operator will contract with the water services provider, and receive a price probably based on volume (of water supplied or waste water treated). This does involve risk, if demand changes during the contract or if there is a specific price review mechanism within the contract.

The plant may remain in the ownership of the public provider, or it may be owned by the private entrant to the market. The private entrant will be responsible for funding the investment in the plant, but the land on which it is built may be owned by the public provider, in which case at the end of the contract the residual asset will revert. Perhaps crucially for the political decision-makers, the consumer of the service will still be billed by, and otherwise deal with, the public sector provider. This may help to minimize the political risk, if consumers are simply unaware that elements of the service are being provided commercially. Yet it may be at the expense of transparency, which is one of the goals of the current policy agenda to bring better governance to water services. Governance will be considered further below.

---

[30] They have led to political and social dissent and to legal actions, primarily arbitrations at the International Centre for the Settlement of Investment Disputes; see eg in Argentina, *Compañía de Aguas del Aconquija SA & Vivendi Universal v Argentine Republic,* ICSID Case No ARB/97/3 (Award of Tribunal of 21 November 2000) and *Azurix Corp v Argentine Republic,* ICSID Case No ARB/01/12 (Award of Tribunal of 14 July 2006); in Bolivia, *Aguas del Tunari SA v Republic of Bolivia,* ICSID Case No ARB/02/3; and in Tanzania, *Biwater Gauff (Tanzania) Limited v United Republic of Tanzania* (ICSID Case No ARB/05/22) (Award of Tribunal of 24 July 2008).

[31] For a detailed analysis of these schemes see J. Delmon, *BOT/BOO Projects: A Commercial and Contractual Guide* (2000).

BOO schemes were introduced in Scotland in the 1990s to build new waste water treatment plants, in order to comply with European Community rules on waste water treatment.[32] The European Union has been a significant driver for investment in water services in the UK jurisdictions and across the Community, with several key European Commission water directives[33] requiring new plant. In developed countries, where public sector borrowing may be available at advantageous rates, BOO schemes are likely to work out more expensive across the lifetime of a project than public sector investment, but they remove the burden of capital investment from the public purse. They have been widely used in the UK for projects ranging from schools and hospitals to the London Underground, where they are commonly referred to as the Private Finance Initiative or simply Public Private Partnerships, but they have attracted a negative press. The Scottish government has been looking at alternative ways of funding these types of projects generally[34] but they are unlikely to be used again in water services. However they did provide nine schemes, with an equivalent capital value at the time of over £650 million (around the same as the following five years' worth of public sector capital investment in waste water treatment).[35] The nine schemes include 21 treatment plants and currently treat 50 per cent of Scotland's waste water. The BOO schemes are managed within the same regulatory framework as Scottish Water's public provision, but they provide a model for private sector engagement, financing, political accountability, and legal accountability.

D. Divestiture

The idea that the entire asset base be divested into private hands is perhaps the purest of the privatization options, yet it is rarely found in water services. Concessions, which may last for 30 years and transfer all investment decisions and risks, nonetheless keep ownership of the plant, network and other infrastructure in public hands. Divestiture alone sells assets to the private operator, as well as transferring investment decisions and operational risk. As the World Bank notes, the differences may not be as great as they appear.[36] In England, the incumbent suppliers are also licensed, for 25-year periods, and without a licence their ownership of the assets is useless to them. As discussed further below, the licences are

---

[32] Council Directive 1991/271/EEC on Urban Waste Water Treatment [1991] OJ L 135/40.

[33] Including ibid; also Council Directive 1980/778/EEC on the Quality of Water Intended for Human Consumption [1980] OJ L 229/11, and Council Directive 1976/160/EEC concerning the Quality of Bathing Water [1976] OJ L 31/1. Later revisions of these Directives have continued to require additional investment.

[34] Scottish Government, *Taking Forward the Scottish Futures Trust* (2008) available at <http://www.scotland.gov.uk>.

[35] Scottish Executive, *Water Quality and Standards 2000–2002* (1999) available at <http://www.scotland.gov.uk> para. 4.9.

[36] See above n 29, World Bank/PPIAF, 11.

effectively another layer of regulation. Nonetheless the political implications of divesting the assets are often significant. England and Wales sold off water services after 1989, as part of the programme of privatization of both services and industries under Mrs Thatcher's administration. To do so, it was necessary to establish an economic regulator to practise 'competition by comparison' across regional monopolies. Broadly the same model has been operating since.

It is important to note that the English model has been able, at least to an extent, to meet the needs of both the companies and consumers. The former require to make a return on their investment, and the latter to have an acceptable service at an affordable price, where environmental protection and other wider social goals are also met. This has been achieved by the complex regulatory framework. Renzetti has argued that in developed countries, it is regulation—of prices, service standards and the environment—rather than competition itself which improves efficiency,[37] and his analysis would support one conclusion of this chapter, that effective regulation is key to better performance whether services are provided by the public or private sector; there is similar evidence in studies within developing countries.[38] This conclusion can be extended to argue that ownership is not the critical focus. A comparison between Scotland and England shows that a very similar regulatory model, applying to both public and private providers, apparently mitigates both the predatory instincts of the corporate world and the inefficient practices of the state-owned entity.

E. Corporatization and commercialization

In recent years, the private sector provision of water services has been the subject of increasing criticism.[39] In addition, following high-profile failures of privatization initiatives in several countries, including Bolivia, Argentina and Tanzania,[40] the companies themselves have become more reluctant to invest in developing countries, where the need is greatest. This reluctance is only likely to be heightened by the prevailing financial crisis. Thus attention turns back to the vast majority of services provided by the public sector, and ways to make those services more effective and more efficient, using better regulatory models. Part of this may involve the 'commercialization' or 'corporatization' of the service, whereby commercial principles are applied to the public provider.

---

[37] Above n 16.
[38] L. Anwandter and T. Ozuna, 'Can Public Sector Reforms Improve the Efficiency of Public Sector Utilities' (2002) Environment and Development Economics 7: 687–700.
[39] See eg M. Finger and J. Allouche, *Water Privatisation* (2002), especially ch 3; World Development Movement, *Going Public—Southern Solutions for the Global Water Crisis* (2007) available at <www.euractiv.com>, or the work of the Public Sector International Research Unit at the University of Greenwich, available at <www.psiru.org>.
[40] Above n 30.

In Queensland, Australia, water authorities, which operate in rural areas and often provide both irrigation and domestic water, are bodies corporate and statutory bodies, established by regulation and operating in a defined area.[41] The larger 'category 1' authorities have more statutory obligations particularly regarding commercialization and performance planning.[42] In addition, there is relevant provision in local government law[43] for the 125 councils and 32 Aboriginal and Torres Strait Islands community councils that are designated as water services providers. Water and sewerage services are business activities which may be subject to National Competition Policy.[44] If a council has a 'significant business activity', determined by a financial threshold, there are certain competition requirements.[45] Councils must undertake a public benefit assessment to determine if the activity should be corporatized, commercialized, or subject to full cost pricing. Commercialization requires the provision of the service through a business unit which is still part of the council. Corporatization requires the service to be provided through a separate entity with full corporate reporting procedures. In both cases there will be full cost pricing but there may also be community service obligations, under the direction of the council,[46] effectively allowing for subsidy. Thus commercialization does not necessarily equate to full cost recovery, but it certainly does aid transparency as to the true costs.

Similar approaches are seen in South Africa, perhaps less developed. There is some general provision affecting local and municipal government, that is, water services providers, under the Municipal Systems Act 2000.[47] Councils should adopt a tariff policy for municipal services including service agreements.[48] The policy should reflect equity, the user pays principle, provision for basic services, and a lifeline tariff; it should reflect all costs and facilitate financial sustainability. There should be surcharges where appropriate and maybe special tariffs for commercial and industrial users to encourage local economic development. The policy should foster the economic, efficient and effective use of resources, recycling and other environmental objectives. Any subsidization should be fully disclosed and tariffs may differentiate, for example between users or areas as long as there is no unfair discrimination. There is a duty to adopt bylaws to effect the policy, and model bylaws have been published by DWAF with considerable detail on, *inter alia*, obtaining a connection, subsidies, metering, disconnections,

---

[41] Water Regulation (Qld) 2002 SL No 166.

[42] Water Act (Qld) 2000 Part 5.

[43] Local Government Act (Qld) 1993.

[44] Council of Australian Governments, 'National Competition Policy and Related Reforms Agreement' (1995) Communique and Attachment available at <http://www.coag.gov.au>.

[45] Local Government Act (Qld) 1993 Ch 8.

[46] Where water services are provided by local government, they are provided for by the Local Government Act (Qld) 1993 ss 677–678. For other providers, see the Water Act (Qld) 2000 s 998.

[47] Municipal Systems Act 2000 (South Africa).

[48] ibid ss 74–75.

and debt recovery.[49] This commercialized approach has been heavily criticized in southern Africa.[50] The critics may find some justification in the current litigation in Johannesburg over entitlement to a free basic water supply.[51] However the desirability of transparency, regarding costs and charges, and subsidies, is surely not in doubt; it is an essential prerequisite of a better service, whether public or private. Facilitating this information is the purpose of commercialization in the public sector. A strong policy framework and effective regulatory structure should then be able to protect those most in need whilst still enabling sound investment decisions with appropriate levels of service.

IV. 'Good governance' in water services

The question of governance is very popular at present with policy makers and academics; 'good governance' of water is important both for the management of water resources[52] and the provision of services.[53] The three objectives of improving governance are closely linked; transparency, public participation, and accountability.

A. Transparency

Transparency requires that information be provided, particularly on tariffs and levels of service. To do so it is necessary to separate out the particular service from other activities of the same provider. Such separation is a particular problem where the provider is a local government, but a problem where commercialization may assist. Information may be made available through general freedom of information legislation, or specific provisions in a sectoral law. Thus the EC Environmental Information Directive[54] applies to public authorities, but this is broadly defined to include any natural or legal person providing relevant services (affecting the environment) under national law. During the passage of this Directive there was considerable debate about the need to ensure that private

---

[49] DWAF, *Model Bylaws Pack Model Credit Control and Debt Collection Bylaws; Model Water Services Bylaws* (2005) available at <http://www.dwaf.gov.za>.

[50] D. McDonald and G. Ruiters (eds), *The Age of Commodity: Water Privatisation in Southern Africa* (2005). This book takes the view that even minimal private participation or partnership, including the commercialization or corporatization of public service providers, amounts to the 'commodification' of water services and should be resisted.

[51] *City of Johannesburg v L Mazibuko* (489/08) [2009] ZASCA 20 (25 March 2009).

[52] P. Rogers and A. Hall, 'Effective Water Governance' (2003) Global Water Partnership TEC Paper 7; M. Solanes and A. Jouravlev, 'Water Governance for Development and Sustainability' (2006) UN/CEPAL.

[53] M. Rouse, *Institutional Governance and the Regulation of Water Services: the Essential Elements* (2007).

[54] Directive 2003/4/EC on Public Access to Environmental Information [2003] OJ L 41/26.

water services providers were covered.[55] In addition, in the UK, detailed sectoral rules in water services require significant provision of information to the regulators. This requirement is a core part of the business model. Much of the information is then made available to the public.

In England, the principal reporting requirements are set out in legislation,[56] but they are minimal. The economic regulator, OFWAT[57] must prepare and publish a forward work programme annually,[58] and report to the Secretary of State.[59] There is a public register,[60] provision for publication of advice by the Secretary of State and OFWAT[61] and a general duty on undertakers to supply information.[62] There are specific duties requiring undertakers to provide information regarding compensation paid for breach of performance standards for water and sewerage services.[63] These basic reporting requirements do not reflect the substantial volume of reported information emanating from OFWAT. Far more detailed information is required from the service providers under the terms of their licences, confirming the view that the conditions of appointment effectively make another layer of regulation applying to undertakers in England and Wales. OFWAT requires an annual return on activities in the previous financial year (the 'June return') and this is the primary source of information.[64] Extensive guidance is available from OFWAT as to what is required in the June return, both from the undertaker and from the auditors and reporters who confirm certain of the contents.[65] OFWAT then produces four reports based on the information in the June returns.[66] In January, undertakers provide a principal statement along with their charging scheme for the coming year. This enables the regulator to check that price increases are within the permitted limits, and charges for the year from April are then approved. In the spring OFWAT reports on tariff

---

[55] COM 2000/0402/Final section 6.

[56] Water Industry Act 1991.

[57] Initially, the economic regulator was the Director General of the Office for Water Services (OFWAT). Since the Water Act 2003, and in line with UK best practice on regulation, the Director General has been replaced by a board, the Water Services Regulatory Authority, on whom the statutory functions are now conferred. The general practice, which I follow in this chapter, is to refer to the Authority as OFWAT.

[58] Water Industry Act 1991 s 192.

[59] ibid s 192B.

[60] ibid s 195 provides for a register, containing details of appointments, terminations and transfers; variations of areas; directions, consents and determinations; enforcement orders, undertakings and special administration orders.

[61] ibid s 201.

[62] ibid s 202.

[63] ibid s 38A and s 95A respectively.

[64] OFWAT, 'Information Note: Information for regulation and the June return' (undated) available at <http://www.ofwat.gov.uk>.

[65] OFWAT, *June Return 2009 Reporting Requirements* (2009) available at <www.ofwat.gov.uk>.

[66] *On Security of Supply, Leakage and the Efficient Use of Water; Levels of Service; Water and Sewerage Service Unit Costs and Relative Efficiency;* and *Financial Performance and Expenditure.* OFWAT's Reports are available from <www.ofwat.gov.uk>.

structures and charges. This annual process then fits into the five-yearly review of prices, the Periodic Review.

It might be thought that such extensive provision for regulatory returns is aimed at the control of the private profit motive. However, it could just as easily be interpreted as simply a highly centralized system for ingathering all of the data that might be required to effectively control both prices and service standards; this chapter posits that such data collection should be required for both public and private sector provision. Such a system is clearly an aid to transparency; yet serious questions remain as to the capacity of the consumers of the service to make sense of the material gathered. Due to the complexity, volume and technical nature of much of the information flow, there are significant problems of asymmetry of information, and in developing countries especially these potentially affect regulators as well as consumers. If there is a weak, underfunded or inexperienced regulator, seeking to manage a well-resourced transnational corporation, then the balance of power will favour the company. The same will go for a small local authority seeking to contract with such a company. Even in developed countries access to information and the expertise to use it can be a problem, especially where economic regulation is being introduced. It is a problem for regulators as well as consumers, and can be a problem when dealing with public sector entities as much as private. There is evidence of this problem in Scotland where in the early days of the Water Industry Commissioner he found it very difficult to obtain accurate data from Scottish Water and its predecessors, for both operational efficiency and capital investment.[67]

B. Participation

Likewise, we look to both general and sectoral rules to facilitate public participation in water. Again there is an EC Directive,[68] which (like that on access to information) stems from the Aarhus Convention[69] and wider global policy.[70] Public participation is now a core governance principle, but is also part of the sustainable development agenda; indeed, participation is just one of a number of parallels between sustainable development and governance.

When we turn to the sectoral rules to determine in more detail how participation should work in water services, we are aware of the tendency (in the UK and

---

[67] Scottish Parliament Finance Committee, 2nd Report 2004 (Session 2), *Report on Scottish Water* (2004) SP Paper 125; Water Industry Commission, *Costs and Performance 2002–03* (2003) ch 5 on efficiency, Water Industry Commission, *Investment and Asset Management 2002–03* (2003) ch 5 on the capital programme.

[68] Parliament and Council Directive 2003/35/EC Providing for Public Participation in Respect of the Drawing Up of Certain Plans and Programmes in Respect of the Environment [2003] OJ L 156/17.

[69] Convention on Access to Information, Public Participation in Decision-making and Access to Justice in Environmental Matters (UN/ECE) (Aarhus) 38 ILM (1999) 517.

[70] Declaration of the UN Conference on Environment and Development (Rio) A/CONF.151/26 Principle 10.

many other countries) to undertake extensive paper-based consultation, but not necessarily facilitate actual involvement.[71] Thus the assumption is that interested consumers will access the returns and reports identified above, make sense of them, and respond accordingly. This is 'a big ask', and may not be very realistic. To facilitate the engagement of the public, in England there are certain high-level duties placed on the regulator in order to further the interests of consumers. They will be examined in detail below.

In both Scotland and England there are specific consumer bodies established to represent views and provide a channel between regulator, providers, and the public. The current body in England is the Consumer Council for Water[72] which, unlike its predecessor, is independent from OFWAT.[73] Its powers and functions were also extended, including representing customers to regulators, suppliers and other bodies, providing information to consumers, requiring information from the service providers, conducting investigations, and resolving certain complaints. In Scotland, similarly, the Water Customer Consultation Panels have been given an extended role including independent investigation and making recommendations not just to the economic regulator, but also to ministers and other agencies.[74]

A separate agency is one model, but it is expensive to provide and may not always be feasible. An alternative, used in both Scotland and England before the last round of reform, is to have the economic regulator represent customers, but this still leaves the question as to how the views of customers can be effectively ascertained, especially if there is a high level of unserved poor. Community groups or NGOs may not truly reflect the views and wishes of the whole community. The mechanisms or bodies selected may be 'hijacked' by sub-interest groups, or those with the time and personal resources to attend meetings, read documents, and so forth. Nonetheless we can see participation as a critical goal, helping both the provider and the regulator to make trade-offs, and, especially, to determine the appropriate level of service as against the price.

C. Accountability

In some ways, accountability is the most difficult of the governance principles to address. Whether public or private, water services are a political issue; politicians

---

[71] For a discussion of the ascending forms of public engagement, the classic article, still widely used and much-adapted, is S. Arnstein, 'A Ladder of Citizen Participation' (1969) 35 J Am Inst Plan 217.

[72] Water Act 2003 Pt 2.

[73] In England, regional Customer Service Committees, later known by their public face as 'WaterVoice', were established under the Water Act 1989. They were part of OFWAT, and appointed by the Director General. As theory and practice of regulation has developed in the UK, and potential conflicts emerged, WaterVoice began to function separately from OFWAT. This separation was completed and enacted by Part 2 of the Water Act 2003.

[74] Water Services (Scotland) Act 2005 s 3.

may want to maintain control over tariffs. Politicians may make short-term political decisions to keep tariffs low, without a good strategy to ensure that services
can be maintained and expanded. The alternative is to hand tariffs to a regulatory
body, which itself must be adequately resourced, especially if the provider is a
transnational corporation. Again, whether public or private, both regulators and
service providers will have legal responsibilities towards the customers; this time
the rules will inevitably be in the sectoral legislation. But the existence of duties
does not necessarily mean that there are effective remedies. So in England, there
are duties on the water companies, but often they are enforced by the regulator
rather than the customer. And the regulator may have other duties, including
enabling the company to make a return on its investment, that will prevent it pri-
oritizing its duties towards the consumer.[75] This has led to recent changes in the
law in England, to shift the regulatory focus, but not necessarily to give the consumer any more power;[76] in the UK jurisdictions, the law relating to the enforcement of statutory duties by individuals is notoriously problematic.[77] Additional
problems of liability and legal accountability emerge where there are public–
private partnerships; so in Scotland, the most recent reforms to water pollution
control were expressed in a way that could make both Scottish Water and the
operators of the BOO schemes liable in a criminal prosecution.[78]

One way to improve accountability and make duties enforceable by the consumer as well as the regulator is to enshrine water services obligations into constitutional law, through bill of rights provisions.[79] It is not within the scope of this
chapter to enter the hugely complex debate around a 'human right to water',[80]
but we can look at the recent South African litigation as an example in the specif-
ics of water services provision. Litigants can use the constitutional provision as a
mechanism, but it is only an additional tool to enforce the universal service obligation,[81] and the commitment to a certain level of 'free basic water' for the poorest,[82] which are in the sectoral law and surrounding policy framework. Duties of

---

[75] *Marcic v Thames Water Utilities Ltd* [2004] 2 AC 42 (HL).

[76] Water Act 2003 s 39, inserting new ss 2A–2E into the Water Industry Act 1991, replacing
s 2(2). These provisions will be analysed further below.

[77] S. Hendry, 'Statutory Duties: Worth the Paper They Are Written On?' (2005) Journal of
Planning and Environment Law 1145; I. Roberts and C. Reid, 'Nature Conservation Duties: More
Appearance than Substance' (2005) 17 Journal of Environmental Law and Management 162.

[78] Water Environment (Controlled Activities) (Scotland) Regulations 2005 SSI 2005/348 rr 5,
40(1)(a), 40(1)(o).

[79] See eg Constitution of South Africa Act, 1996, c 2 ss 7–39. The environment is addressed in
s 24, and water in s 27.

[80] See eg UN General Comment 15, *The Right to Water* (2002) E/C.12/2002/11; C. de
Albuquerque, *Report of the independent expert on the issue of human rights obligations related to access
to safe drinking water and sanitation* (2009) A/HRC/10/6; S. McCaffrey, 'The Human Right to
Water Revisited', in *Freshwater and International Economic Law* (E. Brown-Weiss, ed, 2004) 93;
P. Jones and R. Ordu, 'A Bibliography of Primary and Secondary Sources of Law on the Human
Right to Water' (2007) UUSC Environment Program available at <www.uusc.org>.

[81] Water Services Act 1997 (South Africa) ss 3(1), 11(1).

[82] DWAF, *Strategic Framework for Water Services* (2003) available at <www.dwaf.gov.za>.

supply, including specific service standards and high-level obligations, will also be in that sectoral law. Mechanisms for holding the providers accountable may also be found in water services legislation, but can be supplemented by the general legal regime, for example judicial review. Indeed it is arguable that the key to better service provision lies in the reform of the public sector, not just the water service itself, as that may be partly private, but of access to justice and broader principles of governance outwith the 'water box'.[83]

Governance is an overarching concept, applicable in many situations and to many activities, and in that regard it has some similarities to the sustainable development agenda. The governance debate may also facilitate a more nuanced approach to the polarized debate around 'privatization'. Governance, like effective regulation, is not dependent on the ownership model; it is possible to identify bad practice in the provision of water services in both public and private sectors. Both good regulation and good governance are required in each.

V. The English model

When Scots lawyers go out into the world—and not just the world of water—they are used to being presented with an English legal framework that is confidently described as 'UK law' or a 'UK structure'. In water services, this is particularly inapposite; the divergence between Scotland and England is complete—at least in terms of an analysis of ownership. Yet in other regards there may be significant similarities, so a comparison of these two approaches, with so many other variables accounted for, may shed some light on a topic shrouded in ideological positioning.

The history of the privatization of the English and Welsh water industry is well known and will be examined only briefly here.[84] In the 1980s, towards the end of the Thatcher-era divestitures, attention turned to water and sewerage, which at that time were provided by regional water authorities. The Water Act 1989 was the privatizing legislation in England and Wales, and also established the National Rivers Authority as the environmental regulator for water.[85] In 1991 there was consolidating legislation in the shape of the Water Industry Act 1991, which as amended remains the principal legislation framing water services in England today.[86]

Full divestiture of water services is unusual globally, because most states prefer to retain long-term ownership of the asset base, but England has served as an

---

[83] The idea that water management decisions—and decision-makers—must emerge from outside the 'water box' is the key theme of the 3rd World Water Development Report, World Water Assessment Programme, *The United Nations World Water Development Report 3: Water in a Changing World* (2009).

[84] See eg K. Bakker, *An Uncooperative Commodity: Privatising Water in England and Wales* (2003).

[85] Now the Environment Agency under the Environment Act 1995 Part 1.

[86] Water Industry Act 1991. Major amendments have been made by the Water Industry Act 1999, the Water Act 2003 and now the draft Floods and Water Bill, available at <www.defra.gov.uk>.

exception and a different global model for water services reform. Where owner-ship as well as management is divested, then economic and social (including envir-onmental) regulation becomes the principal role of government, and the model for privatizing water followed that used in other service privatizations under Mrs Thatcher's government, particularly gas and telecommunications. In water how-ever, there is much less expectation that the need for regulation will fade away as the market develops. This is partly because of the natural monopoly tendency, and partly because of the social and environmental implications. In theory, disaggregation creating competition can facilitate some economic deregulation; in practice the proposition is debatable, but even if it were true, the need for social and environmental regulation is certainly not likely to wither away.

Although the asset base was transferred to the new companies in its entirety, the companies are licensed by the Secretary of State through OFWAT to provide ser-vices, with licences lasting at least 25 years and in theory terminable by the state on at least 10 years' notice. The conditions of appointment which OFWAT imposes upon undertakers are effectively a parallel control regime operating in addition to the Water Industry Act and its secondary regulations.[87] The conditions signifi-cantly lessen the degree to which we can equate ownership with control in this highly regulated field. Disputes over conditions of appointments are determined by the Competition Commission,[88] and there is a system of enforcement orders to ensure either performance of a statutory duty or compliance with a condition of appointment.[89] There are financial penalties for contravention of conditions of appointment, contributing to another company contravening the same, or failure to achieve performance standards.[90] There is also a procedure for the making of special administration orders in the event that a water supply provider becomes insolvent, providing a default provision to ensure constancy of supply.[91]

VI. Economic regulation under OFWAT

In England the economic regulation of water is comprehensive. There is provi-sion for charging schemes, approved by OFWAT. The control of prices is found

---

[87] The Instruments of Appointment currently in force are available from OFWAT <www.ofwat.gov.uk>. The power to impose conditions is in the Water Industry Act 1991 s 11.

[88] Water Industry Act 1991 ss 12–17.

[89] ibid s 18. These orders are available to both OFWAT and the Secretary of State.

[90] ibid ss 22A–22F.

[91] ibid ss 23–26. These orders are made by the court on the application of the Secretary of State or OFWAT and will ensure that the statutory functions of the WSP are still carried out by another company, if necessary splitting those by function or area. Petitions for winding up of the companies will not be granted nor may there be a voluntary winding up or petition for administration under the Insolvency Acts. The special administration order will take account of the interests of creditors and members but will give priority to ensuring constancy of supply to customers; licensed suppliers are also subject to these orders.

in the Conditions of Appointment;[92] Condition B sets out controls on charges. For 'competition by comparison' to function, there must be enough companies operating to provide robust comparators, so mergers require a degree of control over and above that required generally by competition law and policy. OFWAT has responsibility for competition but the Competition Commission has concurrent jurisdiction.[93] The Office of Fair Trading has a duty to refer certain mergers to the Competition Commission, where the turnover value of the company being taken over is £10 million or more.[94] The Commission must consider whether the merger will prejudice the ability of OFWAT to make comparisons amongst undertakers, and decisions require a two-thirds majority.[95] In considering such prejudice or adverse effects, it must weigh up any countervailing customer benefits. However, uniquely to the water market, customer benefits will only prevail where they are substantially more important than the prejudice to OFWAT, or where taking account of these benefits would not prevent a solution to the prejudice. The rules therefore respond to the particular nature of water services, especially the lack of direct competition.

Competition by comparison has inherent difficulties. A report looking at the financial structure of the industry in England and, specifically, at the moves by some companies towards structures with lower equity and higher debt, concluded that diversity of financial models was probably desirable, as was regulatory stability.[96] Some merger activity was to be expected and would not necessarily diminish the future of comparative competition. Bakker has suggested that there is a contradiction between regulating for stability and efficiency on the one hand and regulating for reasonable returns on equity on the other, and that the result has been an increasingly constrained regulatory environment with too little room to manoeuvre compared to other areas of business, that has simply made operating in this environment unattractive to public companies.[97]

VII. Scotland's water: 'safe clean affordable public'?

The history of the non-privatization of Scotland's water supply industry by the Conservative administrations (those of John Major and Margaret Thatcher) is less well known. It was a difficult time in Scotland, politically and economically; and the public campaign to keep 'Scotland's water...safe clean affordable and

---

[92] Above n 87.
[93] Competition Act 1998. The Competition Commission was set up to replace the Monopolies and Mergers Commission, and has various functions relating to the water industry.
[94] Water Industry Act 1991 ss 32–35.
[95] ibid s 34.
[96] DEFRA and OFWAT, *Structure of the Water Industry in England: Does it Remain Fit for Purpose?* (2003) available at <www.ofwat.gov.uk>.
[97] K. Bakker, 'From Public to Private to ... Mutual? Restructuring Water Supply Governance in England and Wales' (2003) 34(3) Geoforum 359.

public' reflected not only an attachment to public water supply, but also several other deeply-felt political grievances.[98] Nonetheless, there was a strongly held view in Scotland that water services should remain public. In a local referendum in Strathclyde in 1994, on an unusually high turnout of 71.5 per cent of the eligible voters, 97.2 per cent voted 'no' to privatization.[99]

The Strathclyde referendum followed a series of government consultations on options for the delivery of water and sewerage services in Scotland, to accompany the disbanding of the regional councils and their replacement by a single tier of unitary authorities.[100] One option was full divestiture; in the event, due at least in part to the political and public pressure, the decision was taken to maintain public sector provision by the creation of three regional water authorities,[101] in the form of non-departmental public bodies. Such public bodies were not considered, at least in the 1990s, to require as high a level of regulation as the private sector. Nonetheless a degree of formalized economic control was needed along with a system of customer representation, and the Water Industry Act 1999 made provision for an economic regulator, the Water Industry Commissioner.[102] The Commissioner did not have the same powers as the Director-General of OFWAT; in particular, he did not set charges but rather advised the ministers.[103] Very soon after the Commissioner began work, it became clear that further institutional reform would be helpful, and one proposal that emerged was to amalgamate the three regional bodies, whilst keeping them in the public sector.

Considerable further support was given to this proposal by the Commissioner's second strategic review of charges,[104] which indicated that if the three authorities were retained, prices would rise in real terms by between 23 and 31 per cent. If there was a single authority, prices would rise by only 8.4 per cent. A wide-ranging Parliamentary inquiry also strongly recommended a unitary authority.[105] The arguments were irresistible and the Executive proceeded to bring forward proposals for the creation of Scottish Water. The Bill was passed in February 2002[106] and the new corporation began operating on 1 April of the same year. Scottish Water is a state monopoly, vertically integrated and serving almost the whole

[98] S. Hendry, 'Scotland's Water—Safe Clean Affordable Public' (2003) 43 Natural Resources Journal 491.

[99] J. Arlidge, 'Scottish Tories Urge Rethink of Water Plan', *The Independent*, 2 April 1994 available at <www.independent.co.uk>.

[100] Scottish Office, *The Case for Change* (1991); Scottish Office, *Shaping the New Councils* (1992); Scottish Office, *Water and Sewerage in Scotland: Investing in the Future* (1992); Scottish Office, *Shaping the Future: the New Councils*, Cm 2267 (1993).

[101] Local Government etc (Scotland) Act 1994. In the title, water and sewerage were the 'etc'.

[102] Water Industry Act 1999 Part II; this Act was primarily English legislation, and the last piece of Westminster legislation to address Scottish water services.

[103] ibid s 13.

[104] Water Industry Commission, *Strategic Review of Charges 2002–2006* (2001) available at <www.watercommissioner.co.uk>.

[105] Scottish Parliament, *Report on the Inquiry into Water and the Water Industry* (2001) (Transport and Environment Committee Report No 9 of 2001).

[106] Water Industry (Scotland) Act 2002.

population (over 95 per cent of the population for water, and over 90 per cent for sewerage).[107] The remainder are served by private water supplies and, usually, septic tanks. As noted, limited market liberalization has been introduced[108] for the largest industries, but this only extends to retail (billing and customer services) rather than supply.

There were significant difficulties in adapting to the new regime for economic and financial planning,[109] including the lack of data noted above, and a perceived lack of consideration for the impact of steeply rising water rates for small business customers, identified by the Finance Committee of the Scottish Parliament.[110] The Finance Committee recommended the replacement of a single commissioner with a committee, as discussed above; the Water Industry Commission now determines charges, and does not advise ministers.[111] Disputes are appealed to the UK Competition Commission, which has the expertise to examine the Water Industry Commission's economic analysis, charging scheme, and licensing activities.[112] The price determinations are made within policy objectives set by the ministers.[113] Under the new regime, Scottish Water is required to produce, *inter alia,* an annual return, which is the largest annual information request. The format and content is closely based on the OFWAT June return. This has a number of advantages in allowing the Water Industry Commission to carry out some comparative analysis of Scottish Water against English undertakers. Meantime the Water Industry Commission has required technical information from Scottish Water to be certified by a Reporter, as also happens in England, Queensland and other jurisdictions.

As we move through the third full strategic review of charges in Scotland, it begins to look possible to regulate the public sector in a similar manner to the private sector and thereby to institute comparable efficiencies, whilst still maintaining a public sector ethos.[114] This has been attempted by setting up a sector-specific regulator on the OFWAT model, and requiring similar regulatory returns. If water services are provided by government, then separation of water services and their budgets will first require the adoption of principles of commercialization—just as they were applied to Scottish Water, and much more effectively than to its predecessors. This is a consequence of the regulatory framework.

---

[107] Scottish Executive, *The Water Services Bill: The Executive's Proposals* (2001) para 2.2.

[108] Water Services (Scotland) Act 2005.

[109] S. Hendry, 'Water for Sale? Market Liberalisation and Public Sector Regulation in Scottish Water Services' (2008) 16 Utilities Law Review 153.

[110] See Scottish Parliament Finance Committee (above n 67).

[111] Water Industry (Scotland) Act 2002 s 29B.

[112] Water Services etc (Scotland) Act 2005 (Consequential Provisions and Modifications) Order 2005 SSI 2005/3172.

[113] Water Industry (Scotland) Act 2002 s 29D.

[114] The Draft Determination has been issued for comment: Water Industry Commission, *The Strategic Review of Charges 2010–2014: The Draft Determination* (2009) available at <www.water-commission.co.uk>.

It is true that in both Scotland and England there is use of comparators for determining optimum efficiency and targets across the spectrum including service standards, customer relations and indeed leakage. Some of these optimal targets could be set without regional comparators, but others probably could not. One solution, begun in Scotland and being more extensively considered in England, is the disaggregation of the industry, which will bring changes to the ownership structure for the component parts.[115] It is also true that Scotland and England have much in common, including some aspects of the general legal systems and many socio-cultural, political and economic contexts. Nonetheless, within the relatively narrow range that these comparators present, the one factor that does not appear to alter the effectiveness of the regulatory structure is the ownership of the industry itself.

VIII. High-level duties and social regulation

Although Scotland has a mixed legal system and England does not, one can agree that today the Scottish system bears more similarities to the common law world than to the civilian jurisdictions.[116] Certainly in terms of regulatory law and regulatory structures, the Scots approach to such regulation is little different from that in England. The similarity is borne out by the classical analysis of Ogus,[117] comparing economic and social regulation in common law and civilian industrialized nations, and in particular the role of the courts, the use of contract law to manage the private sector, the shape and form of the regulator, and the mechanisms of enforcement.

The use of statutory duties can be seen as part of an Anglo-American approach to providing regulated services. Water services legislation in Scotland and in England makes extensive use of statutory duties. Statutory duties in England are particularly instructive as they control a private sector world. Because of this, the high-level general duties fall not upon the service providers, but upon the Secretary of State and the regulator.[118] These duties have been substantially amended by the Water Act 2003, specifically to improve the protection of consumers. Originally, the first of these was 'to secure the carrying out of the functions of water undertakers', and the second was to ensure that the companies were able to make a reasonable return on their capital.[119] Secondary to these were the duties to protect

---

[115] Water Services (Scotland) Act 2005; and for England, see above n 24.

[116] Though of course a common law world may be no less homogenous than the civilian; see eg P. De Cruz, *Comparative Law in a Changing World* (3rd edn, 2007) 232–3.

[117] A. Ogus, *Comparing Regulatory Systems: Institutions, Processes and Legal Forms In Industrialised Countries* (2002) Centre on Regulation and Competition Working Paper No 35.

[118] Water Industry Act 1991 s 2.

[119] ibid s 2(2).

customers, to promote economy and efficiency and to facilitate competition.[120] There were then subsidiary environmental and recreational duties.[121] However the revised law gives the furthering of the 'consumer objective' as the first duty.[122] The 'consumer objective' is further defined as protecting interests of consumers 'wherever appropriate by promoting effective competition'.[123] There is a further requirement to give special (but not exclusive) regard to certain groups of consumers, including the sick and disabled, pensioners, those with low incomes, and those in rural areas. This may go some way to satisfying the concerns of those who feel that the privatized industry has resulted in high charges that discriminate against some groups, particularly where water metering is in place. There are other new duties in s 2, *inter alia* requiring the Secretary of State and the Authority to 'promote economy and efficiency', to 'contribute to the achievement of sustainable development' and 'to have regard to principles of best regulatory practice'. There are also new general duties regarding water conservation applying to the Secretary of State, the undertakers and all public authorities[124] and new duties to promote water efficiency; undertakers already had a duty to provide 'an efficient and economical water supply'.[125] For the most part, these changes reflect concerns over the social agenda; in the context of economic regulation, that would include environmental regulation.

In Scotland, the general duty of the ministers and Scottish Water is simply 'to promote the conservation and effective use of ... water resources ... and the provision of adequate water supplies throughout Scotland'.[126] The general function of the Water Industry Commission was to promote the interests of customers,[127] although under the Water Services (Scotland) Act 2005 this function was amended to the promotion of the interests of persons whose premises are or are likely to be connected to the public system;[128] the Water Industry Commission has no such duty to those served by a private entrant to the market, but continues to regulate the wholesale provision of services by Scottish Water to those new entrants.

These high-level duties are important as they set the context within which regulatory decisions are made, and they also affect the enforcement of other duties, especially in qualifying more specific duties of supply falling on the service providers themselves.[129] Further, they are significantly different as between Scotland and England precisely because of the different ownership models. Where there is private sector involvement, the duty to serve the interests of the poorest and most vulnerable must be placed on the regulator, as it will conflict

---

[120] ibid s 2(3).   [121] ibid s 3.   [122] ibid s 2A(a).

[123] ibid s 2B, reflecting provision made for other services in the Utilities Act 2000 ss 9, 13.

[124] Water Act 2003 ss 81–83.

[125] Water Industry Act 1991 s 37.

[126] Water (Scotland) Act 1980 s 1.

[127] Water Industry (Scotland) Act 2002 s 1(2).

[128] Water Services (Scotland) Act 2005 s 1.

[129] *Marcic* (above n 75).

with the private interests of the companies themselves and those that fund their activities. The analysis of the structure and operation of the economic regulation in England and in Scotland evidences considerable similarities, but the provision for social regulation is more extensive in England, as a direct result of the ownership model.

IX. Conclusions

The provision and regulation of water services is highly contentious and deeply polarized. It involves very complex issues, technical, social, economic and legal. There is a great deal of scope for a nuanced debate, yet this is rarely found, even in academia. It is not the case that ownership does not matter, but the correct questions are why and how it matters. It does not matter, as is often argued, because of economic efficiency. That can be achieved by regulation, with competition where appropriate and feasible. It matters because of the social, political and environmental concerns. It matters because of deeply held views that water should be 'free', or at least that it should not be subjected to private profit. Proposals to introduce the private sector, especially in a vertically integrated structure, usually result in intense opposition. The traditional debate is an economic debate, and suggests that the private sector requires economic regulation to control prices and to enable a return on capital. Yet the public sector may also tend towards inefficiency, and again may demonstrate monopoly characteristics. The Scottish experiment indicates that rigorous economic regulation is necessary, desirable, and effective in the public sector, just as it is to control the behaviour of firms; we see this also in Queensland, where both sectors are subject to similar regulatory, business planning and reporting arrangements. Ownership, then, is not the distinguishing factor for economic regulation.

However ownership may be a highly significant variable when considering social regulation, for both consumers and the environment, and when trying to manage the socio-political agendas and improve governance. Where the service, or key components, remain in the public sector, there may be less resistance to price increases, as long as they can be justified by improvements in the service, and as long as there are adequate mechanisms for transparency in providing information and public participation in the decision-making process. Accountability is certainly not problem-free in the public sector, but there is the long-stop of the ballot box. Although the drive to engage the private sector arose from a need for investment, which has not diminished, the private sector is increasingly reluctant to so engage. Other ways forward must be found, and will continue to involve public authorities. It is heartening to see that ways can be found to regulate public authorities for economic efficiency. It is rewarding to consider that a focus on the public sector may negate, or at least lessen, some of the social concerns prevalent in water services. As the world's population increases, water resources deteriorate, and demand soars, it is essential to move away from entrenched positions. This will be much more likely if those defining the terms of the debate recognize the nuanced complexity of the options and consequences of ownership models, but it will also be more likely with recognition that in most places, a well-structured and managed public sector is the way to provide these services in the future.

15

Eminent Domain and Regulatory Changes

*Luis Erize**

I. The ownership of natural resources: two competitors for one single source and the lease concept

Ownership of natural resources has been a sensitive issue throughout the years, not only as a source of international conflicts over boundaries[1] but also within national territories. This raises a number of related issues.

The first consideration is related to the nature of these resources: they are not created by man, nor are they the result of a combination of man and nature, but become, independently from any transformation, a value in themselves. But they do not participate in the complexities of the so-called 'tragedy of the commons' or at least not fully, since such goods require considerable technical and economic means to be discovered, developed, become marketable and able to be consumed.

The open access to common property by everybody at no cost makes for the premature depletion of the resource (the land of the commons), a source for the economic theory of externalities. This theory operates in any activity, though with various degrees (global warming is but one of the consequences, and, more generally, there is an unavoidable environmental impact present in any human intervention).[2]

The sophistication of the technology and the concentration of the capital needed for the exploration, development and exploitation of natural resources makes for a complex relationship between the given (nature) factor and the added value

* Managing Partner of Abeledo Gottheil Abogados, Buenos Aires, and former Adjunct Professor of Constitutional Law, National University of Buenos Aires, Argentina; e-mail: erize@abeledogottheil.com.ar.

[1] A tragic example is the Chaco wars between Bolivia and Paraguay. This originated in the mistaken perception that the much cherished reserves were in the disputed area; in fact they were further to the west.

[2] J. Roberts, D. Elliott and T. Houghton, *Privatizing Electricity—The Politics of Power* (1991) 15–16 describe such effects with regard to energy production.

(extraction and processing) factor, and for sophisticated and capitalized business entities apt to face the mining risk.

The 'tragedy of the commons' considers the over-exploitation of a scarce resource by those that are not holders of such resources, when the resource becomes commercial. There is a need to internalize the externalities, that is to say, those costs that relate to the consumption of the resource, to the extent they are not borne by the consumer.[3] Externalities and their economic calculation in market terms may be dealt with through various mechanisms for the allotment of such costs. Even if conclusions are generally drawn for mechanisms of internalization of costs provoked by environmental damage, the problem is the same for energy, to the extent the externalization of certain costs is also present. Generalized subsidies for energy consumption have the same effect.

As a matter of policy, it is very difficult to determine if the common citizen prefers to live a life of higher taxes and lesser income, rather than eventually being charged with a cost directly related to the benefit of his or her consumption of the service or good. The 'tragedy of the commons' thus reappears as a recurrent economics discussion.

There is always one possible competitor to accumulate both eminent domain over natural resources and their exploitation: the state. However, when some combination of private effort and state activity exists, disputes arise. The limits to what can be labelled as eminent domain have been discussed in the courts in Argentina. In *Prov de Buenos Aires v SA Empresas Eléctricas de Bahía Blanca*, the Federal Supreme Court held that:

> The circumstance that companies' assets are subject to public interest, pursuant to a concession of the same nature, authorizes state protective measures reasonably necessary for an appropriate service supply, but does not justify their assimilation with eminent domain or their comparison with the police power in an extent involving substantial ignorance of the property right.

With the supposedly unlimited fiscal resources based on taxation imposed on generations to come, and discounted cash flows not being a particular concern, the Sovereign can direct its focus to long-term planning in order to ring-fence the unexploited natural resources and reserve them for exclusive development by the Sovereign, either directly, or indirectly by private operators acting in the name of and for the sake of the Sovereign. This can occur through a variety of contracts.

However, such an aim requires substantial conclusions and policy definitions with respect to the entire spectrum of economic activities. A clear shift to command economy policies results, as a balance is seldom reached between large

---

[3] See L. Erize, 'Dependent Variables in the Selection of Stimuli or Charges for an Environmental Policy' in *Symposium on Tax and Financing Aspects (Including Stimulae) for Environmental Protection* (1978).

tracts of the state's reserved areas of economic activity, on the one hand, and private initiative, on the other.

Reaching extremes, generations may be sacrificed on the altar of some pharaonic state objective. The furious combat between state or state command economies and market economies has declined in intensity, hand in hand with the decline of the influence of ideologies. However, the debate between the attributes of Sovereignty (in the form of nation-states) and globalization trends (which rely on the economic theory of the advantages of competitivity and open markets) is never-ending.

The countries strongly influenced by immigration (the United States and, to a lesser extent, other developed countries, including Argentina) have from the outset adopted a model open to foreign populations (both as to their initiative and to their accumulated savings (capital)) to the extent that these countries have reflected such openness as a main target and credo in their Constitutions.

These principles were set forth not without effort or conflict, as the United States and Argentina have proved by the similarity of the common tragedy of civil war, after their respective independence wars.

This leads to the discussion of the so-called eminent domain theories, whether of the federal or state governments, versus open access and efficient exploitation of natural resources. There is also a shift from this discussion into one of regulatory change, as we will address below.

In an old publication, Morineau[4] discussed the differences between numerous authors on the constitutionality of the notion that the subsurface resources belong in a direct way to the state (instead of interpreting such eminent domain as indirect, to allow the rights granted to a private party to be equated to a full property right, though subject to a number of conditions for its exploitation). According to the author, the rights to exploit are not to be assimilated to rights *in rem*, which would otherwise preclude the state from altering them in the future.

The resolution of such tensions in international arbitration awards has been a continuous trend, and the early summary of the most relevant ones can be seen in an article by Lauterpacht.[5] This article revisits *BP/Lybia, Topco, Liamco, Aminoil, Aramco, Sapphire* and other cases and introduces the protection of rights under a different perspective than one of legal substance of the rights, by defining instead their extent and efficacy under international law.

The concept of eminent domain has appropriately been defined by an Argentine Scholar, Professor M. Marienhoff,[6] more as an emanation of public powers (potestas) than an outright property right, referring thus to the authority of the Sovereign to legislate and to set forth rules applicable to the private parties

---

[4] O. Morineau, 'Régimen Constitucional del Subsuelo de México' in *Los Derechos Reales y el subsuelo de México* (1948) 197–296.

[5] E. Lauterpacht, 'Law and Policy in International Resource Development' (1993) 11 JERL 145.

[6] *Tratado del Dominio Público* (1960) 37.

(subject however to the limitations set forth by the constitutional guaranties vested in the latter).

The two main issues that appear constantly in this sector are:

- the Sovereign rights and authority over underground natural resources (eminent domain) versus the acquired rights (and thus, property rights) by holders of title to exploit such resources (with respect to reserves, as well as to the hydrocarbons produced); and
- the limits to regulatory powers, especially facing what is now being invoked as a *state of necessity*, whether as an exception to international law standards' enforcement or as a modification of the latter (supposedly with temporary effects, and with no limitation on the duty to compensate the affected investor with an award of damages).

In Argentina, the Hydrocarbons Law (HL), s 1, assigned to the national government the eminent domain, as an 'inalienable and imprescriptible' property over the subsurface oil and gas (the reservoirs). After the amendment enacted by Law 24,145, such eminent domain belonged to the provinces where they are located, upon the expiry of the present concessions. Later, section 124 of the National Constitution, amended after the 1994 reform, granted to the provinces the eminent domain on 'all natural resources' located in their respective territories. Such rights may not restrict the rights to explore and exploit hydrocarbons within the areas granted in existing permits or concessions by the national government. The exploitation concession holders are granted the exclusive right to exploit the oil fields subject to the concession granted for which purpose a title is vested upon them. The right to the crude oil and natural gas, once produced, belongs to the concession holder, as set forth in such documents, as authorized by the HL and by Law No 24,145.

The nature of the eminent domain is affirmed not only in the HL[7] but also in the Argentine Constitution, which refers to it as *dominio originario* in the new section 124. Differences arise in practice from the same concept, as shown in the HL of Argentina and, for example, in the Constitution of Mexico, Art 27.[8]

Sovereigns expand the concept of security of supply to justify control and intervention in sectors that are earmarked as 'strategic', and, when needed, as being the subject of geopolitics, to exclude mere market economics. But those decisions are necessarily linked with fiscal and monetary policies, closely related to policies regarding strategic considerations for the energy field. Trade balance may be affected by the need of non-self-sufficient countries to make substantial energy imports payments, and pressures arise by the level of impoverishment of

---

[7] L. Erize, 'Argentina's Exploration Plan: The Return of Exploration Permits and Exploitation Concessions' (1992) 10 JERL 241.

[8] E. Murphy, 'The Dilemma of Hydrocarbon Investment in Mexico's Accession to the North American Free Trade Agreement' (1981) 9 JERL 262 n 13 explores the concept applied in this country.

the population brought by massive devaluations, the most notorious instrument of the *Seigneuriage* on its domestic currency, to make ends meet through a change of the trade balance under a controlled foreign exchange.

The matter of the foreign exchange risk concerns the monetary policy, which is an aspect of the sovereignty of the country by which the government has the authority of fixing exchange rates.

'Monetary power' is:

the expression that the monetary sign chosen by the state as currency converts the same in the unit of official value related to which all other values must be measured; in addition, that unit benefits—to the exclusion of all the others—of exorbitant privileges: the obligatory use (forced acceptance), the payment of all debts and credits (legal tender) and permanent fixation of value in principle (nominalism).[9]

As a consequence of national sovereignty, the national government has the power to issue and print money and determines its value, which exercise may not be opposed by the judiciary in the absence of any arbitrary conduct. But a limitation is required to the abusive exercise of such sovereign monetary and foreign exchange policies, because otherwise it would mean that the executive would have the possibility of arbitraging between the net worth of the members of the community in order to produce a transfer of income from one sector to the other, in the way it best suits its interests. This is clearly unconstitutional.

The monetary sovereignty of the state and its capacity of 'seigneuriage'[10] results in its ability to establish the currency with legal tender effects and also its value, which however must not be abused. The value of money is destroyed by expansive monetary policies, in which case the community reacts by destituting such currency of any transactional value, provoking an important growth of money velocity,[11] and reducing its value in each new transaction, in a spiral that in extreme cases leads to hyperinflation.[12]

E. Colombatto and J. Macey[13] maintain that:

[T]he choice of the exchange rate regime is neither random nor arbitrary. In particular, we maintain that the influence of orthodox exchange economies in many transition economies is modest; rather, rent-seeking phenomena are more likely to prevail, while technicalities may be taken advantage of in order to provide shelter vis-à-vis potential criticism, or to disguise partially the welfare-redistribution effects implied.

---

[9] D. Carreau, 'The Monetary Sovereignty at the End of the 20th Century: Myth or Reality?' in *Souveraineté Étatique et Marchés Internationaux à la Fin de 20ème Siécle* (2000) 491.

[10] A. Nussbaum, *National and International Monetary Law* (1954) 44 ff.

[11] This means the rate at which the stock of money is turning over each year (P. Samuelson and W. Nordhaus, *Economics* (12th edn, 1998)).

[12] An important recollection of the manipulation of monetary policies and fiscal policies can be seen in B. Fi Hiemenz and P. Trapp, *Argentina: The Economic Crisis in the 1980s* (1985).

[13] E. Colombatto and J. Macey, 'New Stories on Exchange Rate Policies in Transition' in *Economic Dimensions in International Law—Comparative and Empirical Perspectives* (1997) 371.

But the allocation of resulting losses through the exercise of regulatory powers goes beyond foreign exchange policies. A foreign exchange policy consists in fixing the exchange rate and the conditions of access to such market by the parties subject to such control. This is complemented by the monetary policy, thus making the size of the local currency supply depend entirely on the free will of the government itself, but its abuse does have severe consequences.

The attempt to arbitrage between the different sectors, pretending to transfer the consequences of devaluation from one sector to the other, constitutes an abuse of such powers. Such allocation of losses goes beyond foreign exchange policies. A foreign exchange policy consists in fixing the exchange rate and the conditions of access to such market by the parties subject to such control. This is complemented by the monetary policy, thus making for the other term of the foreign exchange equation.

Thus, government decisions not only determine the amount of money supply, but also the creation and expansion of the other monetary aggregates (the most important of which is constituted by current accounts and term deposits within the banking system, that operate as fiduciary money) which are also regulated by the government. But if the value of the local currency is to be fixed, the control of its expansion and of the access to the foreign exchange market is quite different from the power to establish differentiated methods of cancellation of monetary obligations, which exceeds the exercise of sovereign power in monetary and exchange policies.

The Public Emergency Law issued by Argentina during the 2002 crisis went beyond this, by reducing USD tariffs to the level of their nominal local currency values, pre-devaluation, without adjustments. Within four months, the Law declared, this should have led to a restoration of the economic equation of the concessionaires and licensees, by means of the adaptation of the respective contracts.

Instead of doing so, and without attempting to comply with such instruction by the legislature, the Executive declared that the emergency was still present and interfered in the determination of prices in the entire energy prices chain, by means of an array of regulations. Under this cover the government continuously fixed and readjusted the mechanisms of the transfer of economic and legal consequences of monetary and exchange policies, in an unpredictable way.

The argument of the *Fait du Prince* is of an entirely different nature: the state invokes special prerogatives inherent to Sovereign power, but the use of such prerogative is entirely the result of a specific policy rather than an unforeseen event of an instantaneous nature. Devaluation, whether as a result of the easing of prior exchange restrictions (free or dirty flotation) or of the fixing of an official exchange rate, is unrelated to the various price control policies that apply to contracts or transactions agreed to, or complied with, after the date of the devaluation, or as from the change of exchange policies. As explained below, the recurring argument to convert energy term contracts and tariffs quoted in dollars into domestic currency at a discriminatory rate, applied singly to them, is not the result of *Seigneuriage*, but of strict price control policies that should be obliged to respect property and acquired rights, or otherwise compensate for the losses.

As with monetary policies, fiscal policy can mask other, less evident purposes of steering the economic factors so as to reach a *de facto* or creeping expropriation of the activities targeted, and either change the nationality of the investors, their relationship with the state, the passage to the state of the activity itself, or the larger part of its income.

The perception of this shift is felt by many. G. K. Foster[14] states:

States have learned that overt nationalization programs...have a chilling effect on investment, raise diplomatic tensions and expose states to the prospect of large damages awards in favour of investors. As a result, in recent years states have tended to a more subtle approach when effecting takings. Now they generally seize control of foreign-owned assets only indirectly, through domestic entities subject to their influence or through the imposition of regulatory burdens or tax penalties which undermine the value of an investment.

In the following two sections, the past, present and future of Argentine regulations are analysed in the light of the dialectic interplay between state intervention policies and private business initiative. In section IV, a description is given of the new scenarios resulting from these changes.

II. The history of hydrocarbons exploitation in Argentina

Argentina is no exception to the dialectic noted above. Oil and gas were reserved mainly for the state, with sporadic[15] and controversial fishing expeditions to lure investors and oil companies to engage in such activities at various stages and levels. The failure of both experiments (measured in objective terms evidenced by the deficit of the commercial trade of an oil producing country)[16] led to the enactment by a military government at the end of the 1960s (but kept basically in force until present times as it proved to be an adequate legal instrument) of a hydrocarbons law regulating the upstream in full recognition of fork-in-the-road

---

[14] G. K. Foster, 'Managing Expropriation Risks in the Energy Sector: Steps for Foreign Investors to Minimize their Exposure and Maximize their Prospects for Recovery when Takings Occur' (2005) 23 JERL 37.

[15] The 'California' episode, never brought into practice, is an example, as well as the short lived 'batalla del petróleo'1958–1962 ending with the annulment of the oil service contracts of Argentina's President Frondizi era.

[16] We refer to the annulment of the crude oil production contracts decided in 1963 (Decree 744/63). The fall in the production reserves of crude oil in the 1980s can be appreciated in *The Argentina of the 90's—Economical Performance in a Context of Reforms* (D. Heimann and B. Kosakoff, eds, 2000) 1–82. The periods between the years 1972 and 1975, and most of the 1980s also show such stagnation and the fall in hydrocarbons production, coincident with the dissociation of local prices with respect to the international ones.

policies, since basically it considered both avenues, leaving it for the governments to make the difficult choice of which road to take.

The present legal framework implements the HL, No 17,319, enacted in 1967 and Law No 24,145 enacted on 13 October 1992, with new additions to further grant eminent domain to the Provinces[17] (the so-called *Ley Corta*, Law No 26,197). The HL allows the enforcement of different oil policies:

- either production sharing or service contracts entered into with Yacimientos Petrolíferos Fiscales (YPF), the then state-owned oil company, on the one hand; or
- exploration permits and exploitation concessions granted to the private sector, on the other hand.

The constitutional reform that introduced s 124, last paragraph ('the original eminent domain of the natural resources existing in their respective territories belongs to the provinces') was issued in 1994, thus ending a long history of conflicts between the provinces and the nation over the eminent domain of such natural resources, including oil and gas. The 'original' or eminent domain is not a right *in rem*, as a grant of a property right. This right over subsurface oil and gas is the basis permitting an extended regulation of their extraction and exploitation, and the right to collect fees or royalties on the production; but the oil and gas, once in the surface, belongs to the entity that was authorized to produce it, although subject to the above-mentioned regulations.

The rights of the exploitation concession holders to take possession of all hydrocarbons extracted from the oilfield and to freely dispose of them as a consequence of the nature of the concession granted results from mining law and administrative law. The exploitation rights may be assimilated to those referred to in Art 128 of the Mining Law Code (though application by analogy may be disputed as per the limits set forth for this in Art 388 of the Mining Law Code). The property only reverts to the state at the end of the concession (as even the Venezuelan government has recently admitted indirectly, by stating that it has the intention to retain title over mines *after* their respective concession periods expire).

After an initial call for bids in 1967, the HL, issued by a military government, was not used in the following decades for the grant of concessions such as the ones now considered. But the Law was instead extensively applied by the 1983–1989 government, with the Houston Plan launched in 1985, superseded from then on by a set of exploration permits, exploitation concessions and joint operating agreements by the private sector oil companies with YPF, the state-owned corporation that was later subject to privatization as well.

---

[17] Court of Appeals, Rosario, Panel IV, 5 April 1982, Jurisprudencia Argentina. 982–III–753; T. de Pablos, in *Comentarios a la Ley de Hidrocarburos* (La ley, 134–1403); E. Catalano, *Mining Law Course* (1995) 413.

Following the HL's second alternative, that allowed the Executive to trust the private sector with the exploration and exploitation of oil and gas, twenty exploration permits were awarded at the end of the 1960s. No new exploration permits according to the HL were granted thereafter, and it was only after Law No 21,778 (the risk contracts law of 1978) that exploration was resumed by the private sector.

The Houston Plan (1985) established services contracts for the exploration and exploitation of oil and gas, with specific exploration and exploitation periods, different from the ones established in the Risk Contracts Law or the HL. Work commitments were set forth (seismic options or exploratory well), allowing YPF to take up to a 50 per cent participating interest in a joint venture upon reimbursement of its share in some of the costs incurred, and delivering to YPF all the crude oil produced, at international oil prices for equivalent oil with a 20 to 30 per cent discount for royalties and fees to be paid to YPF. The last call, at the end of 1989, under the Houston plan proved to be unsuccessful, as few companies showed interest.

Exploration permits were resumed through a substantially different framework, as they were the consequence of awards of bids called under the Argentina Exploration Plan enacted by decree 2178/91 of 31 October 1991,[18] and of the reconversion of some of the so-called 'Houston contracts', described below.

The energy sector is a particularly sensitive area, as it was entirely monopolized by the government in the past and was a fertile ground for hidden deficit financing. Prior to 1993, YPF, by then state-owned, had been trusted with (1) all oil field operations, where it tried to compensate for its own inefficiency by making service agreements with private sector oil companies, (2) transport pipelines, and (3) regulations of the downstream industry (which it did by fixing all prices—on crude oil and gasoline, transport tariffs, and refineries' margins). More than 60 per cent of the total refinery capacity in Argentina was owned by YPF itself.

Since energy policies are not decided in a political vacuum, the military regimes of the late 1960s and 1970s continued with a state monopoly of these resources, and various and ever-changing private assistance patterns.

Many different forms of exploitation services contracts had been experimented with in the past, overlapping partially in different periods. Several model contract layers piled up, from public works contracts to service contracts, contracts of reimbursement accounts or capital accounts, risk service contracts (the result of the military view of a 'peripheral privatization'), incremental production curve contracts, and finally the so-called 'Houston contracts'.

This continued until the return in the 1990s to classic exploration permits and exploitation concessions, which are now stigmatized. No plans are now implemented to do otherwise, imposing however an 'end of the pipeline' progressive

---

[18] See L. Erize, 'Argentina's Exploration Plan: The Return of Exploration Permits and Exploitation Concessions' (1992) 10 JERL 233.

statization, by once again (a) controlling the entire downstream through regulated or interfered energy prices, and (b) creating state (federal as well as provincial) oil companies, which benefit from a privileged status.

A sweeping privatization trend in the 1990s to solve the 1980s energy crisis led to the oil and gas industry, as well as the power industry as a whole being trusted to the private sector. This was completed with a massive restructuring of the midstream and downstream rules of the game, and the full use of the options the HL allowed for the granting of new oil and gas exploration permits and exploitation concessions.

Decree 1589/89 gave the option in s 1 to contractors of the Houston plan to amend their contracts according to the new deregulation, in order to have free disposal of the crude oil produced when a commercial discovery was made. Decree 2411/91 gave YPF the power to renegotiate the contracts, as well as the risk service contracts of Law No 21,778, and to convert them into exploration permits and exploitation concessions under rules similar to the ones established in the Argentina plan. The property in oil and gas produced thus reverted to the new exploitation concession holder according to s 6, HL (s 5, decree 2411/91, reproducing s 6, HL).

Decrees 1055, 1212 and 1589 of 1989 produced an important deregulation of the local hydrocarbons industry.[19] Decree 1055 established international bids to be called to assign in concession to the private sector underexploited (marginal) areas, previously held by YPF and for association (joint operating agreements) with YPF to obtain an increased hydrocarbon production in certain main fields reserved for YPF. The principle of free disposition of the oil obtained by contractors through these and other contracts was also established in this decree.

A call for bids was made in 1990 for entering into joint operating agreements with private sector operators for four so-called central areas, which accounted at the time for 14 per cent of Argentina's oil production. This was followed thereafter by additional bids, to share with YPF an equal (later on increased, and nowadays ranging up to 90 per cent interest in some cases) interest in joint ventures, holding the rights on the areas for the next 25 years.

Until the enactment of Decrees 1055 and 1212, all contractors had to deliver the oil and natural gas to the refining companies (mainly YPF, Shell and Esso) within Argentina. The distribution of the crude oil to be processed was done formerly by the Secretary of Energy through the 'crudes' table', fixing quotas for each refinery, as well as the price. This was no longer required from then onwards, and the export and import of hydrocarbons and by-products were then exempted from all import/export taxes, tariffs, duties, and present or future withholdings.

---

[19] The framework under the Law No 23,696 and the decrees themselves was confirmed by Laws 25,148, 25,645 and 25,918, and their validity enforced in court cases as eg in *Pérez Companc v DGA*, 14.09.00 (El Derecho, 196) 27.

Massive investment led to a dramatic increase in energy output and reduction of prices, in a remarkable achievement that avoided the pitfalls of similar reforms throughout the world.[20]

Significant capitals and financing flow led to the continuous expansion of the production of natural gas, crude oil and electricity generation, and the expansion of networks and the capacity of compression of natural gas transmission systems.

The associated capital flow cannot be achieved without a reasonably stable horizon of profitability, now put under a question mark.

The magazine 'Petrotecnia Argentina', of the Argentine Institute of Oil and Gas, as well as the reports by ENRE and ENARGAS, the regulatory agencies for electricity and the natural gas frameworks, give a clear idea of the indexes of the growth of all variables, with the exception of prices, during the 1990s. In the reports of ENARGAS and ENRE the process of incorporation of new economic agents[21] in the electricity and natural gas markets may also be seen, as well as the origin of capitals, and the high level of dispersion of such agents. There has been a large increase of the number of power producers in the electricity market during the decade, a significant incorporation of high-level technology and the investment of US $ 12 billion in acquisitions and new plans.[22]

The economic crisis developing since the end of the 1990s finally exploded at the end of 2001, and with it the continuity of such rules of the game, amidst a massive default of both monetary and legal commitments by the state, which scrambled to reach a balance amongst the different sectors of the economy.

III. Energy as a balancing factor for re-distributing wealth

The end result is that, after overcoming the economic crisis, the cross-subsidies imposed as a burden on the energy sector led to a standstill of investments. This resulted in an ever-increasing energy crisis, the increase in gas and fuel oil imports and the decrease in oil and natural gas reserves, with an over-blown demand caused by ridiculously low energy consumer prices controlled by the government. In the path of the asymmetric allotment of transfers of risk that has been attempted as a consequence of the crisis, the transfer of the regulatory risk to the

---

[20] A. Ramos and R. Martínez, 'The Investment Process in Argentina. Impact of Political Reforms and Decision Making Process in Scenario of Certain Changes', in Heimann and Kosakoff (above n 16) at 177–233, refer to the important investment process made in infrastructure sectors by an annex to the important foreign direct investment flow in Argentina. Their conclusions were that in the process of investments in the 1990s: '1) investments . . . [were] up again; 2) the same was financed largely with a higher level of external savings . . . 5) the contribution of the private sector increased; 6) there was a higher participation of the foreign capital'.

[21] 'Agents' includes all the different entities that are present in the different regulated markets: power producers, oil and gas producers, pipeline licensees, distributors, etc.

[22] F. Mezzadri, President of the Argentine Chamber of Investors in the Electric Energy Sector, El Cronista, 10 July 2003.

investor is used as a way of selective price controls, and in such a way as a concrete anti-inflationary instrument in order to solve the emergency.

Thus, the attributes of property rights (the right to exploit resources, and sell them at competitive prices, in a market that sooner or later interchanges with international prices) are separated from its ownership through regulations that may, in extreme situations, lead to the inability to enjoy any economic benefit from the business.

Specific commitments had been made by the state to respect a number of guaranties set forth by regulatory decrees and incorporated by reference in the concession decrees regarding the exploration and exploitation of hydrocarbons. In the case of bilateral investment promotion and protection treaties which have what is called an 'umbrella clause', such investment agreements are relevant specifically under the operation of such clause if international arbitration is commenced. But other bilateral treaties contain a specific clause allowing the investor to invoke the more favourable treatment.[23]

This protection is necessary especially in the case of mature projects, with sunken costs, highly leveraged or with extremely long return periods, where investments have already been made (as in power generation, transportation and distribution, natural gas downstream, and in oil and gas mature fields).

The resulting lack of investments raises from governments the concern to replace such an absence by means of segregation of markets, different pricing for new consumers (or 'incremental' consumption) or producers, and/or incentives or tax holidays, but the permanence of such dual track is doubtful.

The accumulation of succeeding regulations based on the emergency has been gradually replacing the system that was in place by a new re-regulated system. A major change in the provisions of term contracts has been effected by means of leaving aside of the systems of determination of prices that were established in the past. In the case of natural gas, the government in the past only intervened to determine a reference price resulting from a technical evaluation (to compute the median price of the aggregate of supply contracts made). Such mechanism was abandoned, on the argument that the conditions of the market had been profoundly altered. The government took the reading of a previous evaluation, the price of natural gas at nominal value in 2001 pesos (for example, Resolution 2614/02). Thereafter, in the following resolutions this freeze was imposed not only on the price of natural gas but also, indirectly, on the price of the electric

---

[23] W. Ben Hamida, 'La Clause Relative au respect des Engagements dans les Traités d'Investissement' in *Le Contentieux Transnational relatif à l'Investissement* (2006) 97, makes reference to the clause generally incorporated in Bilateral Investment Protection Treaties (BIT) signed by France, which include *la clause relative à la préservation de la norme la plus favorable* instead of the umbrella clause, which allows the investor to call the rights resulting from specific engagements signed with the host state, to the extent that they are more favourable than the principles set forth in the specific BIT, thus granting international protection to such rights, which have to be respected by the host state (quoting P. Juillard, *Le réseau français de conventions bilatérales d'investissement: à la recherche d'un droit perdu?* (1987) at 50–2).

energy, with a pass-through[24] of these reduced natural gas prices, in nominal pesos of pre-devaluation times, for each relevant period, although the government always insisted that this situation was provisional.

When the transfer of wealth from the suppliers of energy to large customers is provoked by changes imposed by the Executive and confirmed as well as by the regulatory agencies, the argument in the social context ceases to have meaning.[25]

Resolution 208/2004 of the Ministry of Federal Planning and Public Works confirmed an agreement with the oil and gas producers on natural gas prices according to Decree 181/2004 and set forth a pathway for gradually increasing the formerly capped prices (since 2002) until the end of 2007.

After the end of such transition, the goal to which the government was committed, namely, returning to unregulated prices, subject only to free market rules (meaning in practice that the natural gas price would have to find a natural ceiling constituted by the substitute fuel at import parity prices), was replaced by an ambiguously-worded policy, linking such commitment to a set of conditions in the future, as defined by the authority, provided that a plurality of natural gas producers and a transparent market and security of supply would by then have been created. This was against the letter and scope of the HL, as well as of the three decrees made at the end of 1989,[26] which had assured that local prices would be related to international prices.

Resolution 503/04 represents a breach of the HL, since the latter had instituted a system of guaranties in case of restrictions on the marketing of natural gas. In effect, at the time of the HL, where the commercialization of natural gas was entrusted to the government, the Resolution stated that whenever such natural gas production was called for by the government, the prices should assure 'a fair profitability of the corresponding investment, taking into consideration the special characteristics and conditions of the field'. It is only with such a condition that the law established that the government could further regulate such commercialization. In each of the reconverted contracts or bids that led to oil and gas exploitation concessions, more specific guaranties are included.

Resolution 503/04 introduced a system of priority of consumption of natural gas and of transportation that interfered with the otherwise free rights to reach firm contracts with special customers. By invoking security of supply, ENARGAS was authorized to re-nominate volumes of gas to be transported (preserving in such a way the load factor in the pipeline) in the dispatch order set forth pursuant to Annex I of the Resolution. This meant that natural gas transporters are

---

[24] A total of 50% of electric energy in Argentina is generated with natural gas; the price of natural gas is transferred to the power consumer, included in the tariff rate payable by the latter (*pass-through*). When the government imposed a natural gas price cap reduction for reducing the power tariff, the natural gas producers were forced to adjust their prices accordingly.

[25] See statements of Repsol in the Argentine newspapers of 4 August 2003, *El Cronista* (at 3); *Ambito Financiero* (at 7); and *La Nación* (at 2).

[26] Decrees 1055/89, 1212/89 and 1589/89, that were the grounds for the oil and upstream gas deregulation.

to re-route natural gas injected in the pipelines by natural gas producers that have contracted interruptible transportation capacity, to give priority of supply to distributors, at prices fixed as per Resolution SE 208/04, in case of possible short-ages. The lack of supply by natural gas producers, it was alleged, would other-wise affect customers that are ranked with priority rights[27] for distribution. But non-interruptible contracts, including those of the power producers that had in the past contracted on a firm basis, were left aside. Natural gas producers, the shippers through the gas pipelines, were affected by such regulations, and had to face conflicts with their foreign counterparts for the non-delivered gas because of such eventual re-nomination or re-routing.

The objective of the Price Path Recovery Agreement was never met. Regarding the implementation of the last step of the price path and the free market for the industrial consumers and power generators, Resolution SE 752/05 implemented a new protection mechanism called 'Additional Permanent Injections', which set gas prices at the former levels stated by Resolution SE 659/04 and later by Resolution SE 752/05. Hence, the committed free market for large consumers was discarded, and replaced by a new price intervention against the letter and intent of the Price Path Recovery Agreement.

Natural gas exports at free, international prices were subject instead to a with-holding tax of 20 per cent of the export price, pursuant to Decree 645/04. In 2006, the Ministry of Economy and Production issued Resolution No 534/06, that further increased to 45 per cent the export withholding tax. Resolution 503/04 of the Secretary of Energy established different rules for the priority of dispatch of natural gas for the domestic market, breaching the status agreed upon on 21 April 2004. These changes established as the basis for the assessment of nat-ural gas exports withholding tax the price fixed for the sale of natural gas under the Framework Agreement between Argentina and Bolivia dated June 2006, in order to reduce domestic prices. Later on, by Note 57/08 the Customs Authority advised that the contractual price taken as a guideline for the export tax assess-ment had increased to over US $17 per million British Thermal Units (BTU) (inter natural gas produced by the regas plant temporarily imported for such purpose). On 13 March 2008, the Ministry of Economy and Production issued Resolution 127/2008 and established a fixed 100 per cent export withholding tax rate for natural gas,[28] computed on the basis of 'the highest price established for this good in any such natural gas import agreements'. This in effect acted as a prohibition to export, raising the price of Argentine-sourced export gas above the Bolivian export gas price to Argentina.

---

[27] The ENARGAS note 305/04 set forth a specific ranking, through priority supply rights: first, residents and customers with levels of consumption up to 9000 m3 per day, then holders of firm transportation and distribution contracts, and thereafter natural compressed gas stations with firm contracts and metering devices.
[28] The Resolution modifies the 45% fixed rate set by Resolution MEP No 534/06, which was expressly computed on the basis of the price established in the Agreement ENARSA/YPFB.

On 10 October 2006, the Ministry of Economy and Production issued Resolution No 776/2006, which applies to export duties. In December 2006, the National Congress enacted Law No 26,217, that extends for five years (until 2013) export duties established by s 6 of Law No 25,561, the rules issued pursuant to emergency legislation being in force for such a term until otherwise decided.

On 14 June 2007, the Secretariat of Energy of the Nation issued Resolution SE No 599/2007, which ratifies the proposal for the 'Agreement with Natural Gas Producers 2007–2011'. The 'agreement' (to be signed by the gas producers within five days or else be subject to a discriminatory, even more damaging treatment) with natural gas producers is designed to assure supply of the then current level of aggregate domestic natural gas consumption, at the expense of prior export commitments to Chile, under the threat of a severe price reduction for the reallocation of natural gas from non-subscribers to the agreement, to be first chosen, in case of unsupplied demand, to satisfy the latter at lower prices.

The resolution, thus applicable to those that signed the Agreement as well as to those who did not sign (the latter, however, to rank worse than the signatories, for being dispatched first at the lowest prices imposed by such regulation, as per Resolution SE 882/05, and according to Resolution SE 1886/07), instituted a price segmentation that was not in accordance with the former commitment stemming from the prior 'Agreement' 2004–2007, both in the terms of volume reserved and on the destination of gas and its remuneration. The former agreement was not honoured and was superseded by the new one, which was imposed on the producers under warnings of confiscation of the entire gas production at lower prices than those that should have been applied according to the former price path agreement, thus breaching the legitimate expectations of investors in such fields.

The matter of the breach of legitimate expectations is considered in a number of ICSID awards.[29] Legitimate expectations should be relied on, on the basis of a stable legal and business framework. The full analysis on the subject is made by Dolzer:[30]

Meeting the investor's central legitimate concern of legal consistency, stability and predictability remains a major, but not the only, ingredient of an investment-friendly climate in which the host state in turn can reasonably expect to attract foreign investment. Thus, no inconsistency between the interests of the host state and those of the investor in regard to the creation of a stable legal framework of the host state will be diagnosed. Built upon this joint perspective of host state and investor, underlying the agreement on an investment treaty, the standard of fair and equitable treatment will nevertheless not be understood to amount to a stabilization clause but will leave a measure of governmental space for regulation. ... Changes of government may lead to special problems in this context

---

[29] *Enron*: § 252: *Tecmed* 115; *CME* 611; *Occidental v Ecuador; Pope & Talbot, Oxy v Ecuador*, 1 July 2004, § 183, *Enron*, § 267, *CMS* final, § 274.

[30] R. Dolzer, 'Fair and Equitable Treatment: A Key Standard in Investment Treaties', The International Lawyer, Spring 2005 at 87.

as well as in the second area of concern, being the stability of long-term arrangements and commitments, which may be re-evaluated by governments following the one which accepted the obligation toward the investor.

In the case of crude oil exports, the export withholding, first set a 20 per cent level as per Decrees 310/02 and 809/02 (further increased to 25 per cent by Resolution Minister of Economy 337/04) was later on increased through Resolution of the Minister of Economy 532/04 of 4 August 2004. This imposed an additional, windfall rate, as a consequence of which on top of the 25 per cent withholding a variable 3 per cent to 20 per cent, in the case of rising export prices, would be added. This amounts in total to an overall 45 per cent withholding when export prices strike US $ 45 per barrel of West Texas intermediate oil (WTI) equivalent, making in the aggregate an approximate 37 per cent withholding.

Furthermore, alleging security of domestic supply principles, Resolution SE 876/05 re-established the export contracts registry submitting it to these restrictions as per Resolution SE 1679/04 and Decree 645/02. Resolution 1338/06 adds to the system provided by Decree 645/2 products such as gas, fuel oil and its mixes (diesel oil, aerokerosene or jet fuel, lubricants, asphalts, coke and derivatives for petrochemical use).

Resolution SE 394/07 (and Resolution SE 127/08) provided that the withholding tax would increase as the international price increases. Based on a special formula, a cut-off value was set, which in effect is the after-tax export income to be collected by the exporter, where the international price is above US $ 45 per barrel. The exporter's income remains fixed and dissociated from international price increases. In this way, a price cap was established both in the export market as well as the domestic one. Paradoxically, in Venezuela, where the oil fields are much more productive than in Argentina, a similar export tax (known as a contribution for the windfall prices in international markets, or windfall profits tax) was assessed whenever the Brent price exceeds US $ 70 per barrel (a higher threshold than in Argentina), but taking 'only' 50 per cent of the difference (in Argentina, 100 per cent), increasing to 60 per cent if the international price goes above US $ 100 per barrel.

The withholding tax on oil and gas exports also touched previously exempted areas, including the Special Customs Area of the Province of Tierra del Fuego, thus making customs law rulings apply retrospectively.

The government stated it was going to use such Decree 645/04 resources to build up a new oil and gas competitor, a company to be formed by the federal state. The resources drained from the natural gas upstream industry were thus meant to be used by the government to provide for the same infrastructure and investments that the national gas producers could not make on account of such deprivation.

The indirect impact of the increase of exports withholding on the domestic price of a tradeable product such as crude oil is evident, though it requires modelling to assess the elasticity of domestic demand to different price levels, to conclude how the export withholdings impacts on the same.

The rules under which the economic actors make their decisions are of substantial importance, as the consequences may differ if there is a command economy or a deregulated or free market economy. Reducing the income of one sector by imposition and forecasting the consequences in the other sectors requires at least a weighted analysis of the incidence of that sector in the general economy, in the balance between savings, investments and consumption, which should be of paramount importance to further estimate money velocity, fiduciary money expansion (M3), deficit and taxation. The exercise of an unlimited power banning exports, establishing export duties at several times the export price itself, the forced re-directing of supplies and discriminatory pricing used as a weapon against non-consenting natural gas producers, was established on account of a continuing emergency, but has been preserved ever since despite a phenomenal gross national product growth during 2002 and 2008.

In accordance with the natural gas agreement by the industry with the government, the only commitment set forth was of an aggregate of historic production to be supplied. The further increase of volumes through regulations went beyond such agreement.

The further Agreement 2007/2011, referred to above, signed by the oil companies to avoid being penalized with the lowest ranking gas prices, was not only the end of the former agreement's promise that the market would return to its deregulation and free market practices, but was also soon subject to a complementary Resolution (No 1070/08), which established that the price variations were to be finally absorbed for the purpose of funding government-planned subsidies for LPG to consumers.

The Gas Supplementary Agreement (Resolution SE 1070/08) provides that the increases derived from the agreement shall be distributed as follows:

- 65 per cent, for a trust fund to subsidize the sale prices of LPG (LPG Fund), with a specified annual budget.
- The remaining 35 per cent to be received by the producers, provided that they join the agreements with the Argentine government (2007–2011 Gas Agreement and Supplementary Agreement).

In the event that the percentage applied to the LPG Fund (65 per cent) is not enough to fill the estimated amount of revenue to the annual budget, the Secretariat of Energy is authorized, with the intervention of ENARGAS, to increase such percentage to cover the shortfall. However, it was provided that this increase 'shall not exceed 100 per cent of the funds effectively received by producers resulting from this restructuring'. On 9 February 2009, the Secretariat of Energy decided by means of a letter to the signing producers to transfer to the LPG Fund 100 per cent of the amounts received as a result of the increase of natural gas to the residential demand and to the Compressed Natural Gas (CNG) stations granted by Resolution 1070/08. Likewise, it was provided that the method set forth in the letter shall be maintained as long as the Trust Fund financial needs so require.

The background to this is the grave energy supply crisis caused by the so-called emergency regulations that, affecting severely the economic equation of the overall energy market, caused selective power and/or natural gas supply cuts for limited periods of time, and restrictions imposed for power and natural gas exports. Thus the government exported the crisis to neighbouring countries, disregarding firm authorizations to export that had been granted to gas producers. The government thus interfered with financial agreements, which had enabled the construction of international natural gas pipelines, and left the international market for natural gas produced in Argentina in a high level of uncertainty, both in terms of quantity approval and price. An additional burden on the return of the investment in such pipelines and natural gas production committed to exports was soon added (Decree 645/04).

The demand for energy consumption expanded, caused by the growth rate of industrial activity since it hit a rock bottom low in 2002, therefore making for a swollen natural gas demand over and above traditional growth rates (further increased by the conversion of car engines to compressed natural gas instead of gasoline, to take advantage of the natural gas frozen prices). The natural gas industry shortage of supply developed as a consequence of the impact of the reduction and freezing of natural gas prices, and with it, of power prices, which explains the lack of sufficient exploratory wells and of the development of existing ones as from 2002.[31] Gas transmission is also at its limit if daily peaks of demand in winter times are considered, and pipeline capacity expansion is left to be financed by trust funds by the government. That funding is supposed to be refunded through special levies or 'charges' imposed on specific groups of natural gas consumers, payable on top of the tariffs, thus capturing part of the existing rent of the supply remuneration. Open seasons are being called for receiving Irrevocable Purchase Offers, as described below.

Supply and demand simply did not match, and because of it, a shortage occurred. The 'first come, first served' attitude that underlies the open access transportation system terminates, and conflicts arise between the different sectors. Rationing, its first manifestation being the limitation of volumes of natural gas according to the past pattern of each consumer's demand, comes as the first answer. It is a new form of making ration coupons. To avoid them, rising prices should be the consequence, both to choke off excessive consumption as well as to expand the necessary production and investments.[32] The forecast for energy shortages proved to be correct, as a consequence of the rationing of natural gas

---

[31] Infobae, 23 February 2004, at 14, commenting on the Instituto Argentino del Petróleo y del Gas figures evidencing the fall in the drilling of exploratory wells, while the natural gas demand continued to expand, even during recession years (2001–2003). The last quarter of 2003, compared with the same period of 2002, showed an expansion of 85% in the demand by Independent Power Producers, 23% for Natural Compressed Gas, and 16% for the industry.

[32] The concept is taken from Samuelson and Nordhaus (above n 11) at 392–3.

supply[33] and power supply for industrial purposes even during the summer period, with the anticipation of a worsening situation for the winter period, unless hydrology helps (Argentina has an energy matrix that includes 50 per cent of the power generation by hydro, except in dry years). Exports to Chile (natural gas)[34] and Uruguay (power) were hastily curtailed, to the dismay of such countries, and imports were hastily set—electricity from Brazil,[35] fuel oil from Venezuela,[36] and natural gas from Bolivia (but a lead time is necessary there).

Such flows were redirected (up to the amounts that the inland transportation system allows) to serve distribution networks. Exports were first reduced, the energy shortage gap being partially filled by importing gas from Bolivia, which in 2004 was three times the domestic, frozen price, and its substitute for thermal energy units, fuel oil, was six times the energy equivalent price level of domestic natural gas.

To further assimilate such measures with the concept of rationing, Disposition 27/04 of the Sub-Secretary of Fuels, as complemented by Resolution SE 265/04 and SE 503/04 referred to a 'Programme of Rationalization of Natural Gas Exports', establishing that exports are to be made only after domestic customers are supplied, export ceilings are to return to their 2003 levels, and that the value of such re-routed gas is assessed at international price levels in certain cases.

Later on these were further limited by Resolution SE 659/04 of 17 June 2004 as to the remuneration to be paid to the natural gas suppliers with export supply contracts, since the re-routed gas to the domestic market would be paid with no distinctions (previously set forth in Resolution SE 27/04, which in some instances provided for the respect of international prices for the re-routed gas), making such gas supply to the domestic market payable at the level of domestic prices designed in July 2005 for large customers. Though such price was considerably higher than the present domestic price, it was lower than the then current export prices.

Finally, the state attempted to reduce the growing gap between investment (as a result of the disincentives introduced by the governmental measures in contrast with the concession terms) and demand trends, by introducing in Resolution SE 24/2008 a new gas programme (Gas Plus Programme) that deregulates (again) the gas price, but only for the gas that comes from the 'new gas projects' (Gas Plus Projects). This category only applies if the Secretariat of Energy approves

---

[33] *Ambito Financiero*, 17 February 2004, at 7, announcing such shortages for the northwest of the country; *El Cronista*, 29 January 2004, to the same effect.

[34] *Ambito Financiero*, 1 April 2004, at 4; *El Cronista*, 1 April 2004, at 4; Infobae, 31 March 2004, at 9.

[35] *Ambito Financiero*, 1 April 2004, at 3. Infobae, 20 May 2004, at 9, stated that a complex triangular export scheme involving Brazil, Uruguay and Argentina had been signed to solve the deficit of energy supply from Argentina to Uruguay. However, by Resolution SE 161/06 (2 February 2006) a transitory Regime for Electric Energy Trade was enacted as per the relevant agreement between Brazil and Argentina, for the years 2006–2008, to allow firm capacity and interruptible supply term contracts to be made.

[36] *El Cronista*, 31 March 2004, at 4.

the particular project as a Gas Plus Project. The programme further reinforces the negative effects in the current production and reserves from existing projects, stalled due to the interference in the gas pricing.

In 2008, the government implemented the Gas Plus Program to create an incentive for producers participating in the above-mentioned supply agreements to increase production in unexploited areas, areas under exploitation with particular geological characteristics (eg 'tight gas'), areas that have not been in production since 2004, or new fields in areas otherwise under production (Secretary of Energy Resolution 24/2008). Gas produced in these new areas can be freely marketed without being subject to the conditions imposed by the natural gas producers' agreement, but the Secretary of Energy (with the approval of Ministry of Federal Planning, Public Investment and Utilities) has to authorize the associated costs and approve a reasonable rate of return for each project (in fact, it is a cost plus regulation).

Decree 2014 provided for a similar programme, focused on crude oil. The Oil Plus Program sets forth incentives for the increase in oil production, considering as a base the first semester of 2008. Each barrel of oil produced that exceeds this base will receive tax credit certificates provided it complies with the increase of the reserve replacement index (RRI) requirement. 'Strategic' investments such as oil and gas exploration and development are the subject of tax incentives under Law No 26,360.

There is no difference between the 'old' gas (gas produced by the existing fields and facilities) and the 'new' gas (produced from new fields), except for the time when such investments were made (the former investments were made relying on the legitimate expectations of the legal framework and concession granted in the early 1990s, whilst new investments are supposed to be made under a new de-regulated scheme), reserving controls on prices for the existing production projects. The same gas will be remunerated differently, denying to the older investments the remuneration set forth in the legal framework granted formerly to them, while granting a more beneficial treatment to the new investments by denying rights as per the earlier commitment, while instituting new, additional rights to the new production in the terms of the recent regulation. Different treatment in like circumstances is thus incurred, for the same activity and kind of product, and based only on whether the investments were made before or after the current government's time.

The differential pricing for old and new investments (whether in power[37] or in gas production[38]) represents an evident proof of discrimination, reinforced by the requirement of the joint acceptance of such double regime, as the *new gas* pricing is not to be applied unless continuity of supply under the existing production

---

[37] Resolution SE 1281/2006 (Programme Energía Plus). Pursuant to Note SE No 234/2008, the generation commercially qualified after 5 September 2006 ('new generation') is exempted from the invoice level restrictions imposed on generators by Resolution SE 406/2003.

[38] Resolution SE 24/2008 (Programme Gas Plus).

flow is assured at the lower price by the same producer. This is a condition precedent to reducing the otherwise applicable price restrictions for the denominated *new natural gas* or *new oil*. The marketing price of the Gas Plus is not the product of a free market because such price must be approved by the Secretariat of Energy according to the associated costs with an allowance for a reasonable rate of return on each project.

Discrimination is also evident when agreed energy prices (according to well-established market rules incorporated in the title and rights of the investor) are set aside by the action of the government for the benefit of certain categories of consumers (in essence, subsidies to the latter, but funded by the energy producers), with no fiscal sacrifice by the government. In this respect, there is a swing from one of the parties to the other, in order to switch the acquired benefits of the supplier, passing such benefit to the consumer, with a direct impact on the profit and loss statements of both (losses for the supplier and gains for the consumer).

It is one more confirmation of the transfer of wealth to consumers, by:

- The combination of increasing export withholding taxes ranging to punitive export custom duties (*retenciones*), as per Resolution 127/08, to bar natural gas exports without a formal revocation of prior permits or of new ones, forcing the producers to dump such volumes in the domestic market (reinforcing what the *additional injections* mechanism—the redirecting of export meant natural gas to the domestic demand at the request of any large consumer—was intended for); and
- Subsidies to reduce the natural gas domestic demand by means of substitute, subsidized fuels to be supplied by ENARSA, or gas from Bolivia at higher than the locally controlled prices, with funds extracted from consumers of a certain level through specific 'charges'.

Decree No 2067/2008 sets forth the so-called 'tariff charges', to be paid, even retrospectively, by the large customers of transport and distribution of natural gas, as well as by the consumers that have supply agreements from the producers, regardless of whether the natural gas they receive is or is not the higher priced natural gas from Bolivia, purchased by ENARSA.

The closed circle makes the natural gas production sector pay for the substitute fuels necessary to meet the demand, in its turn reducing the natural gas price by the thus reduced natural gas demand.

Such natural gas aggregate demand was already being benefited by the domestic market ring-fencing, thus completing the segregation between international prices and local prices. It reaffirms the shift of the energy matrix to the supply by the government-administered, substitute fuel import business, once it has insulated the consumers from any possible resulting energy price increase. ENARSA's brokerage business is also strengthened by completing its many tasks as one more *gendarme*, with vested interests in the energy business, as a supplementary control agency, and as an imposed partner in new offshore projects, for example.

The sterilization of the impact of such substitute fuel, to be consumed by power producers instead of natural gas, on the determination of the spot price of electricity, was already effected by the power regulations amendments in breach of the electricity law principles. The over-cost of the substitute fuel in the place of the natural gas price (or the gas from a re-gasification plant vessel docked in an Argentine port for solving winter gas shortages) is subsidized by the government with the income of the natural gas export withholding taxes (Res 121/08 of the Ministry of Production, and Disposition 30/08 of the Secretary of Control and Coordination).

The slump of the international market of oil prices in the first half of 2009 has reduced the gap between the same and the domestic prices, and dried up the flow of export withholding revenues. But this can only forecast a future lack of reaction of the oil industry in case of a rise of crude oil international prices, as the regulations that capture for the government any additional income from international prices remain in place (except for the friendly *new oil* and *new gas* plus programmes, mainly in the hands of new entrants). The second half of 2009 is likely to see the materialization of severe labour union conflicts caused by the lack of exploration and development activity in the oil and gas industry upstream, with resulting layoffs, up to now not implemented on account of governmental pressure.

IV. The political choices and their aftermath

When exercising their choice between (a) eminent domain, royalties-driven legislation, or (b) effective state ownership and monopoly of production, with services contracts or risk services contracts with private operators, states should always bear in mind the limited global amount of investment-directed resources, in order to make for an optimal allocation of resources for the purpose of preserving competition and promoting growth.

The provinces, like the national government has done with ENARSA, have created provincial state-owned corporations,[39] which will naturally be the vehicles for exploiting (a) the fields that are not subject to existing permits or concessions already granted to private parties, or (b) once the term of the current concessions has lapsed, the fields thus relinquished to the state. But the reach of these corporations will expand gradually so that they will become a privileged actor in the energy production field.

The role of ENARSA is being expanded to combine the role of a true oil company, theoretically bound by regulations as anybody else, with one as a policy maker, by being the arm of the regulator for intervening heavily in the market through massive purchases of natural gas from the Regas plant for covering winter shortages.

---

[39] Petrominera SE was created by Law No 3422 (modified by Law No 3919 and Law No 5231) and Provincial Decree 1814/1990. Formicruz SE (Law No 2057, modified by Law No 2690).

V. The future and how to attract new investments

In the case of administrative law concessions for public services, the Public Emergency Law No 25,561 had allowed these to be renegotiated. Law No 25,790 gave the Executive powers to enter into partial and/or transition agreements, establish periodic reviews as per pre-established guidelines and quality standards redefinitions (s 3), to allow full flexibility to redesign the terms of the same, without the limits set forth in the specific legislative frameworks (as in the Natural Gas Law and the Electricity Law) as thereafter delegated to UNIREN (the government's public services contracts' re-negotiation unit). This matter is still under discussion as no specific guidelines have been set forth for such authority to be exercised.

The path for the oil and gas exploitation concessions, which do not involve public services, was different, as no re-negotiation is considered. But the oil and gas market has been fragmented to the point of non-recognition, by establishing different brackets of new and old hydrocarbons, priced differently, and consumer price bands making for cross-subsidies, taking from the oil industry and giving to the consumers.

The future is not only addressed by the state through these new 'oil and gas plus' experiments, but also through the extension of the existing oil and gas exploitation concessions. The HL enables a ten-year extension at the end of the concession term, to avoid investment from drying up when such concessions approach the end of their terms.

As the provinces regained eminent domain over hydrocarbon reserves, though under federal rules, provincial decrees not only granted the ten-year extension that the HC Law allows under Art 35 as from the end of the existing concession (an issue at odds with Art 35, since such extension is allowed in case the producer has complied with its duties under the concession, which has still years to go),[40] but also other rights to become contractors to the provincial state oil company at the end of such extension.

In summary, the promise to a return to an unregulated, open market and to the historic assurances is reinstated only for a hypothetical future, in exchange for accepting the current, restricted status.

VI. Policy making, statesmanship, and elections

Throughout Latin America a mounting voice is being heard: at best, the governments' take is considered unsatisfactory; worse, a new wave of state intervention will follow, with a deep involvement going beyond classic interest percentage thresholds. Worse still, there have been recent announcements of the nationalization of the exploitation of natural resources, and especially of hydrocarbons.

---

[40] But as the HC Law does only refer to not less than six months' prior notice, and not a time window, it can generally be said that this is feasible.

The title of the oil industry's rights on the oil fields is said to have been insti-tuted by an earlier generation of politicians. The government assault starts by reviewing terms; this is a quest to control prices, raise indirectly the government's take through levies or withholdings, or through a set of taxes and imposed costs. Sympathy with increasingly aggressive labour strikes, tolerance of violent actions, disruption of activities, and pickets complete the picture.

Control agencies and a judiciary subject to pressure allow for a round of ever-continuing fines. Targets established by regulation increase their thresholds and allow hostile mobilization of theoretical environmental concerns, amidst consid-erable media coverage, in a never-ending process. The most telling examples are the conflicts arising in the Andean region: the most recent indigenous peoples' clashes in Peru, and the Ecuador cases.[41] Exports are curtailed to re-direct flows to internal consumption, becoming an active part of international politics, where the goals exceed the energy supply and demand concerns.

Many Latin American governments have introduced retroactive changes to the oil and gas exploitation concessions or oil service contracts, through: (a) the review of contractual terms, reclassifying them so as to impose huge increases in retroactive taxes; (b) 'migration', re-negotiation or re-adaptation of the contract terms on the basis of ill-defined criteria; or (c) the plain incorporation of the state as a full partner (to be financially or economically carried by the original title holders). The creation of new state-owned energy companies anticipate that these will be capitalized with an increase in the government's take.

In Venezuela, a dismantling of the former *Apertura Petrolera* was established, with the government requesting a transition to association agreements, the increase of tax thresholds, the termination of existing Operating Agreements, and the imposition of minority stakes for the investor as the only acceptable practice, in a collision between the alleged national public interest, public policy and Sovereign prerogatives, on the one hand, and international commitments made in prior bilateral investment protection treaties,[42] on the other hand.

Taking advantage of market concentration, distortions by state regula-tions introduce asymmetries in the formation of prices, while the state requests investors either to 'capitalize' (in the production capacity expansion of state-led projects) part of their income thus withheld, or postpone indefinitely the expect-ation of recovering such income. Finally, price controls are introduced indirectly by choking demand through streams of new regulations, and establishing price differentials for each market segment.

There is one classic response by the energy industry: investments dry up (exploration and development projects are suspended or archived, transportation

---

[41] A. Esan, 'Preventing Violent Conflicts Caused by Infringements of Indigenous Peoples' Rights: The Case of the Ecuadorian Amazon' (2005) 23 JERL 529, also quoting the long struggle of the *Aguinda v Texaco* case.

[42] E. Eljury and V. J. Tejera Pérez, '21st Century Transformation of the Venezuelan Oil Industry' (2008) 26 JERL 475.

bottlenecks remain unresolved, etc). Reluctantly, the industry goes to court or arbitration, while being subject to severe criticism by public powers and the further menace of retaliation. The compound effect of these measures amounts to creeping expropriation: the deprivation, at the end of the road, of property rights.

Litigation, public hearings, anti-trust clearance, plain permits, concessions transfers approval procedures, and environmental clearance procedures linger for years, and are subjected to variable rules or to a changing interpretation. This adds to frictional costs, the reinsertion or increase of the state-run companies' share to make them a part of the problem solving. New investments are linked to new rules, letting the past deal with itself. Conflict arises, and the outcome is in some cases investment arbitration, as seen below.

VII. The change of expectations and the resulting conflicts: investment protection and the national interest

The general principles of how such a dispute arises, who has standing to sue, the nature of the dispute, the extent of such international commitments and the scope of the relevant treaties, may be discussed at length, as well as the legal arguments in disputes between the host state and investors. To determine if an international breach has occurred, it is necessary to take into consideration the whole series of different acts which, together, make for a breach of the international commitment by the state.[43]

The unity of purpose can be seen by the succession of government acts that led, first, to the imposition of an agreement that would supposedly allow for a certain transition to later on recuperate existing losses, but which was shortly followed instead by a continuation of price reductions received by the producer, with an increase in the price paid by certain consumers by means of charges payable to the government on top of such reduced prices. The private sector was not able to develop due to the prior price freezing and reductions.

A set of measures may be tantamount to expropriation. Fortier states:[44]

[T]his language encompasses a potentially wide variety of state regulatory activity that may interfere with an investor's property rights in his investment...For example, taxation measures, by its very nature, could be said to be expropriatory. More particularly, they constitute a form of indirect expropriation; they have an effect that is tantamount to expropriation; and when implementing over a period of time they could also be called 'creeping expropriation'.

---

[43] As expressed in the *Chorzow Factory* case (1927, A/9 at 31), the Permanent Court described the principle that a party cannot take advantage of its own wrong as a principle 'generally accepted in the jurisprudence of international arbitration, as well as by municipal courts' (D. J. Harris, *Cases and Materials on International Law* (1998) at 48). In respect of a breach of international obligations, the state 'cannot plead the condition of its domestic law by way of absolution' (ibid at 70).

[44] L. Y. Fortier (2003) 20(1) ICSID News.

The term 'creeping expropriation' is defined in the American Law Institute Restatement of the Law III (the Foreign Relations of the United States), as state action which seeks 'to achieve the same result [as an outright taking] by taxation and regulatory measure designed to make continued operation of a project uneconomical, so that it is abandoned'.[45] In the same sense: 'A creeping expropriation therefore denotes, in the paradigmatic case, an expropriation accomplished by a cumulative series of regulatory acts or omissions over a prolonged period of time, no one of which can necessarily be identified as the decisive event that deprived the foreign national of the value of its investment'.[46]

The confiscatory practices are not restricted to the outright dispossession of fixed assets. Thomas Franck states:

If Acme [the company organized by the Investors in the hypothetical example] can demonstrate that it could not fairly be expected to resume profitable operations or find a purchaser as long as the new regime of costs and controls persists, and that the tax regime has specifically skewed against it to drive it out of business, the government's action will not escape categorization as 'uncompensated taking' merely by proclaiming itself a revenue measure. For example, if an increase in fares sufficient to cover the new levies were prohibited by law, or by the economics of competition by alternative carriers, it stands to reason that Acme's operations have been made impossible, and, in effect that it has been expropriated by the Government without compensation.[47]

The many issues regarding when governmental measures of the sort described above may constitute a creeping expropriation were considered in the *BG Group Plc v Argentina—UNCITRAL Rules*—award of 24 December 2007, at §§ 258–266. Citing the authority of *Starret Housing Corporation, Impregilo, Lauder, Pope & Talbot*, the award concluded that creeping expropriation occurs when governmental measures, even if gradually, but cumulatively, have effectively neutralized the benefit of the property of the investor; and if the investor's activity continues, then the issue is to determine if compensation by way of damages is due, on account of a breach of the fair and equitable treatment incorporated in the relevant treaty.[48] As expressed by Kunoy:[49]

---

[45] Restatement, vol I, section 712, reporter's note 7 (1987).

[46] W. M. Reisman and R. Sloane, 'Indirect Expropriation and its Valuation in the BIT Generation' (2003) 74 British Yearbook of International Law 128. Boston University School of Law, Working Paper Series, Public Law and Legal Theory, Working Paper No 06–43, <http://www.bu.edu/law/faculty/scholarship/workingpapers/2006.html>.

[47] T. Franck, *Fairness in International Law and Institutions* (1997) at 464; quoting Sir Robert Jennings and Sir Arthur Watts in *Oppenheim's International Law*, Vol 1 (9th edn, 1992) at 915.

[48] The BG Tribunal relied on the award in *Waste Management II*: (*Waste Management Inc v United Mexican States*, ICSID Case No ARB(AF)/00/3, award of 30 April 2004, § 98), and it referred itself to the *SD Myers, Mondev, ADF* and *Loewen* decisions (BG, § 292) to conclude that a breach had been incurred, quoting (§ 296) as also *Revere Copper and Brass Inc v Overseas Private-Investment Corp.* award of 24 August 1978, 56 International Law Reports 258 at 1331.

[49] B. Kunoy, 'The Notion of Time in ICSID's Case Law on Indirect Expropriation' (2006) 23 J International Arbitration 341.

Terms such as 'disguised expropriation',[50] 'taking',[51] measures that are 'tantamount to expropriation or nationalization'[52] or 'any direct or indirect measure... having the same effect against investments'[53] should therefore be regarded as indirect expropriation.[54] The common thread running through this nomenclature is that, in each case, the investor is not deprived of its property interest by means of any formal measure. Therefore the temporal determination of the indirect expropriation, for purposes of valuation, is indeed very difficult. Determining 'when governmental action that interferes with broadly-defined property rights ... crosses the line from valid regulation to a compensable taking'[55] is not without complexity.

Thomas Waelde[56] states:

There is now a formal recognition in virtually all modern BITs and MITs that expropriation can not only consist in a formal transfer of the property right, but also by a 'regulatory taking', ie regulatory and other governmental action which in effect destroys the normal, legitimately expected functioning and economic value of the operation.

Necessity is neither an excuse for exempting a compensation obligation, nor may it be invoked, if such difficulties are to a certain extent self-generated by the state. Article 25 of the ILC Articles on State Responsibility states that in order to acknowledge that a state of necessity exists which excuses state responsibility, such measure must (a) constitute the sole means of protecting an essential interest against a serious and imminent danger, and (b) not seriously affect an essential interest of the state or states towards which the obligation exists, or of the international community as a whole. In addition, necessity cannot be invoked as an excuse (i) if such international obligation excludes the calling of such state of necessity, (ii) if the government has contributed to its development, or (iii) if it excludes compensation. By s 27(b), full compensation for any effective loss caused by such measures is due as soon as the period of the emergency lapses (as per s 27(a)). As stated in *Gabcikovo-Nagymaros* by the ICJ, the state concerned is not the only judge as to whether such requirements are met.[57]

---

[50] Elettronica Sicula SPA (ELSI), Judgment, (1989) 15 ICJ Reports §§ 116–119.

[51] In the Second Restatement 'taking' was defined as a 'conduct attributable to a state that is intended to and does, effectively deprive an alien of substantially all the benefit of his interest in property even though the state does not deprive him of his entire legal interest in the property', American Law Institute, *Second Restatement on Foreign Relations Law of the United States* (1962), s 192.

[52] See *United Kingdom-Ukraine BIT*, 10 February 1993, TS (24) 1993 Cm 2192, Art 6(1).

[53] See *Argentina-Sweden BIT*, 22 November 1991, entered into force 28 September 1992, Law No 24,117, Art 4(1) (Argentina).

[54] For commentary on the scope and implications of the different types of indirect expropriation, see B. Kunoy, 'Developments in Indirect Expropriation Case Law in ICSID Transnational Arbitration' (2005) 6 J World Investment and Trade 474.

[55] *Marvin Feldman v Mexico*, ICSID case No ARB (AF)/99/1, 16 December 2002, § 100.

[56] T. Waelde, 'Multilateral Investment Agreements (MITs) in the Year 2000' in *Souveraineté étatique et marchés internationaux à la fin du 20 ème siècle* (2000) at 408.

[57] *Gabcikovo-Nagymaros (Hongrie-Slovaquie)*, CIJ Recueil 1997, 40; quoted by J. Crawford, *The Articles of the ILC on the Responsibility of the State* (2003) at 219.

The act of state doctrine constitutes no excuse for international commitments, or else such principles would be void, and not even the state of necessity could be argued as a possible excuse for international commitments. A balance has to be reached between contract stability (*pacta sunt servanda*) as opposed to public power prerogatives and, on account of the doctrine of *rebus sic stantibus,* to the need to confront fundamental changes that turn upside-down the existing framework applicable at the time the contracts were entered into (*la problematique de l'équilibre entre la stabilité contractuelle et la nécéssité de faire face aux changements fondamentaux qui bouleversent les données existantes auparavant au moment de la conclusion des contrats*).[58]

The reports by the International Law Commission state that no state of necessity may be invoked by the state as a cause of exclusion of the illegal nature of an act not in conformity with one of its international obligations, if such act does not constitute for the state the only means to protect an essential interest against an imminent and serious danger (Art 26), or if the state itself has contributed to such state of necessity.[59] This rule also applies when *force majeure* is invoked as a cause for the exclusion of responsibility (Art 24) if such *force majeure* occurs in conjunction with the behaviour of the state that invokes it. Section 27 states that even the declaration of the existence of a state of necessity is without prejudice to the respect of such international obligation if and when the circumstance excluding such illegality no longer exists, and to the issue of indemnification of damages and material losses effectively caused.[60]

There has been a substantial controversy as to the situation resulting from stabilization clauses, either established by statute or by domestic law.[61] A complete history of the vagaries of politics, sovereign theories, and pendulum changes on this subject is described by Professor P. Stevens,[62] who clearly sets forth the nature of the problem:

Once oil was discovered and the investment sunk in development, relative bargaining power switches in favour of the host government which then tries to increase its fiscal take by changing the terms of the original contract...... A period of resource nationalism inevitably leads to less investments and a shortage of crude oil.

---

[58] Prologue by A. El-Kosheri, to S. Salama, *L'Acte du Gouvernement—Contribution à l'étude de la force majeure dans le contrat international* (2001) V–VI.

[59] *Obligations Multilatérales, Droit Impératif et Responsabilité Internationale des États* (2003) at 271

[60] ibid.

[61] See A. Maniruzzaman, 'The Pursuit of Stability in International Energy Investment Contracts: A Critical Appraisal of the Emerging Trends' (2008) 1 J World Energy Law and Business 121 for an exhaustive research of applicable bibliography and examples, either by freezing the applicable domestic law at the time of the contract and/or the investment, or by requiring that any amendments be compensated. See also A. Faruque, 'Validity and Efficacy of Stabilization Clauses, Legal Protection vs Functional Value' (2006) 23 J International Arbitration 317.

[62] P. P. Stevens, 'National Oil Companies and International Oil Companies in the Middle East: Under the Shadow of Government and the Resource Nationalism Cycle' (2008) J World Energy Law and Business 5.

Fouchard, Gaillard and Goldman[63] refer to stability clauses, commenting that arbitral court precedents generally validate stabilization clauses (quoting numerous international court precedents beginning with the *Texaco* case (with a commentary by Pierre Lalive),[64] *Aminoil*,[65] *Agip v Congo*[66] and others).

VIII. Sovereignty over natural resources, without prejudice to international law and international commitments

There should be no conflict between state sovereignty and private investments in the energy sector. It is the right of the Sovereign to make the choices it deems preferable in terms of national resources and their exploitation. In general, the design of domestic policies falls within the sovereign power, and it is only limited by international law, whether customary or treaty law, to the extent that an international law breach is deemed to have been incurred.

Regardless of the discussion whether general principles of international law would be applicable to limit such intent to make domestic law prevail, treaties set precise standards. The legitimate expectations generated for the investor limit the Sovereign's right over natural resources and its rule-making power, to preserve the maintenance of a contractual balance.[67]

There is a reaction to the recognition of general principles of international law as a third source of international law, besides custom and treaties.[68] As stated above, international arbitration has reaffirmed the authority of such general principles, whether as a category of its own or supported by either customary international law or treaty law. So many awards have allowed compensation in case of expropriation (*Sapphire v NIOC*,[69] *Texaco v Libya*,[70] ICSID awards such as *Alcoa Mineral*,[71] *Kaiser Bauxite*,[72] *Reynolds Jamaica*,[73] *Klöckner*,[74] *Letco*,[75] and *AAA's*

---

[63] P. Fouchard, E. Gaillard and B. Goldman, *Treaty of International Commercial Arbitration* (1996) 806.

[64] J. Lalive, Un grand arbitrage pétrolier entre un gouvernement et deux sociétés privées étrangères (arbitrage *Texaco Calasiatic v Gouvernement Lybien)*, JDI (1982) 844.

[65] *Aminoil*, JDI (1982) 869.

[66] *Agip v Congo*, Rev, Crit. DPI (1982) 92.

[67] Such as in *Aminoil*, §§ 96 and 159.

[68] C. Leben, 'Quelques Réflexions théoriques à propos des contrats d'État' in *Souveraineté étatique et marchés internationaux à la fin du 20 ème siècle* (2000) at 159 ff.

[69] *Sapphire International v NIOC*, Award (15 March 1963) (1967) 35 International Law Reports 136.

[70] *Texaco Overseas Petroleum Company and California Asiatic Oil Co v Libya* (1978) 17 ILM 1.

[71] *Alcoa Minerals of Jamaica Inc v Jamaica* (ICSID Case No ARB/74/2).

[72] *Kaiser Bauxite Company v Jamaica*, ICSID Case No ARB/74/3, Decision on Jurisdiction, 6 July 1975 (1993) 1 ICSID Reports 296, 303.

[73] *Reynolds Jamaica Mines Limited and Reynolds Metals Company v Jamaica*, ICSID Case No ARB/74/4.

[74] *Klockner v Cameroon*, Award, 21 October (1983) 2 ICSID Reports 4.

[75] *Liberian Eastern Timber Corporation (LETCO) v Republic of Liberia*, ICSID Case No ARB/83/2, Award (31 March 1986).

Revere Copper and Brass[76]) that they have long since established a clear path for compensation in case of a regulatory taking or an outright expropriation, even where they are related to the exploitation of natural resources.

In the case of creeping or indirect expropriation,[77] regulatory taking[78] can adopt a very varied group of measures, each of them seemingly a consequence of the exercise of regulatory power, but in essence applied with a view to severely impairing the economic balance under which the investment was made.

[76] *Revere Copper and Brass Inc v Overseas Private Investment Corporation*, Award (24 August 1978) (1978) 17 ILM 131.

[77] Art 15 of the ILC Articles on State Responsibility refers to the identification of a series of actions or omissions that, together with others, make for an international breach, in which case the breach is deemed to have occurred as with the first of the series.

[78] R. Higgins, 'The Taking of Property by the State: Recent Developments in International Law' (1982) 176 Recueil des Cours 331.

16

Restrictions on Foreign Investment in the Energy Sector for National Security Reasons: The Case of Japan

*Kazuhiro Nakatani**

I. Introduction

Article 3 of the OECD Code of Liberalization of Capital Movements provides that a state can restrict foreign investment when it considers it necessary for the maintenance of public order or for the protection of its essential security interests.[1] However, the concepts of public order and essential security interests are vague and the interpretation of these concepts is open to each state.

States often impose restrictions on foreign investment in the energy sector and Japan is no exception.[2] In May 2008, the government of Japan, in an unprecedented move, ordered The Children's Investment Master Fund (TCI), a British hedge fund, to drop a bid to raise its stake in J-Power, the biggest wholesale electric company in Japan.

The J-Power/TCI case[3] posed the problem as to whether foreign ownership holdings in strategic energy companies like J-Power would threaten Japan's national security and/or public order. J-Power has the controlling ownership of a large amount of energy infrastructure in Japan, including hydroelectric dams, electricity transmission facilities and nuclear facilities. Even if the foreign

---

* Professor of International Law, University of Tokyo; email: nakatani@j.u-tokyo.ac.jp.

[1] For the growth of concern about energy security in the international community, see B. Barton, C. Redgwell, A. Rønne and D. N. Zillman, 'Introduction', in *Energy Security: Managing Risk in a Dynamic Legal and Regulatory Environment* (B. Barton, C. Redgwell, A. Rønne and D. N. Zillman, eds, 2004) 3; D. Yergin, 'Ensuring Energy Security' (2006) 85 Foreign Affairs 69.

[2] See eg control mechanisms for the United States, introduced by the Foreign Investment and National Security Act 2007, see also changes to the Investment Canada Act; or the Russian law, On the Procedure for Foreign Investment in Companies Strategically Important for the Defence and National Security of the Russian Federation, enacted in 2008.

[3] Though we may call it a 'case' for convenience's sake, the J-Power/TCI affair did not go before a court or tribunal but was conducted through an administrative and governmental process with a final Ministerial Order.

ownership of a component of the company's shares is far less than 50 per cent of the total shares, foreign shareholders can influence the basic policy of the company by pursuing an activist role in the shareholders' meetings. Consequently, in the long run this capacity for influence would affect Japan's energy security. By contrast, the expropriation of any company, even a strategic company, by the government is difficult in modern Japan because it is considered to infringe upon private ownership and it requires a large sum in compensation.[4] Therefore, such expropriation is almost impossible in modern Japan, except for the purpose of relieving bankrupt banks as a prudential measure for financial stability. Given such restrictions therefore, the prohibitive order in the J-Power instance was the only available measure, and the strongest form that governmental intervention could take. The Japanese government for the first time exercised this power in accordance with its Foreign Exchange and Foreign Trade Act (FEFTA).[5] This fact reveals just how important the government considered J-Power to be for Japan's energy security.[6]

Although this decision was implemented in accordance with the FEFTA, some commentators cast doubt on this decision, arguing that it would shrink foreign investment and it would be contrary to the Japanese government's campaign to promote foreign investment.[7]

In this chapter, after surveying international rules and Japanese laws on this subject, the nature and content of the order by the government of Japan in the J-Power/TCI case are considered.[8]

II. International rules concerning restrictions on foreign investment

The OECD Code of Liberalization of Capital Movements, which is binding on member states,[9] aims to eliminate restrictions on capital movements between the member states. However, Art 3 of the Code provides clearly that restrictions

---

[4] Constitution of Japan 1946 Art 29.

[5] Act No 228 of 1 December 1949.

[6] On Japan's energy security, see K. Nakatani, 'Energy Security and Japan: The Role of International Law, Domestic Law, and Diplomacy' in *Energy Security: Managing Risk in a Dynamic Legal and Regulatory Environment* (B. Barton, C. Redgwell, A. Rønne and D. N. Zillman, eds, 2004) 413.

[7] Prime Minister Fukuda announced at the World Economic Forum in Davos in January 2008 that he aimed to double the amount of foreign direct investment stock in Japan by raising it to the level of 5% of GDP by 2010.

[8] In the future, some foreign funds and SWFs (Sovereign Wealth Funds) in particular, might be interested in having more stocks in Japanese energy companies, like J-Power and TEPCO (Tokyo Electric Power Company).

[9] On the binding nature of the Code, see G. Guillaume, 'L'Organisation de coopération et de développement économiques et l'évolution recent de ses moyens d'action' (1979) Annuaire français de droit international 79.

on capital movements based on public order or national security are permitted. The same Article provides as follows:

> The provisions of this Code shall not prevent a Member from taking action which it considers necessary for:
> (1) the maintenance of public order or the protection of public health, morals and safety;
> (2) the protection of its essential security interests;
> (3) the fulfillment of its obligations relating to international peace and security.

This Article allows each OECD member state to take measures which 'it considers necessary', which means that this provision is explicitly *subjective*.[10] According to the *User's Guide*,[11] this Article is intended to address exceptional situations. In principle, the provisions allow members to introduce, reintroduce or maintain restrictions not covered by reservations to the Code stipulated in Art 2,[12] and, at the same time, exempt these restrictions from the principle of progressive liberalization. However, in recent years, members have been encouraged to lodge reservations when they introduce restrictions for national security concerns, rather than keeping these restrictions outside the disciplines of the Code. This has not only the advantage of enhancing transparency and information for users of the Code, it also constitutes a first step towards eventual liberalization, especially when national security is not the predominant motive for restrictions, ie when it is accompanied by economic considerations.[13]

Japan considers that there are several categories of restrictions on foreign investment. The first is based on 'the maintenance of public order or the protection of public health, morals and safety' (Art 3(i) of the Code) and it includes the restriction on foreign investment in the drug manufacturing and biological products manufacturing sectors. Secondly, the restriction on foreign investment that is based on 'the protection of its essential security interests' (Art 3(ii) of the Code) includes the restriction on foreign investment in the aeroplane manufacturing, weapons, nuclear energy and space development sectors.[14] Restrictions on foreign investment in a wholesale electricity utility, like J-Power, is considered to come into the latter category.

[10] See K. Yannaca-Small, 'Essential Security Interests under International Investment Law', in *International Investment Perspectives* (OECD, 2007) 93 at 95. *Subjective* means that the member state can decide whether the situation in the state necessitates taking the measures.

[11] OECD, *Code of Liberalization of Capital Movements and Current Invisible Operations: User's Guide* (2008) 34.

[12] According to Art 2(b) of the OECD Code of Liberalization of Capital Movements:

A Member may lodge reservations relating to the obligations resulting from paragraph (a) when:
(i) an item is added to List A of Annex A to this Code;
(ii) obligations relating to an item in that List are extended;
(iii) obligations relating to any such item begin to apply to that Member; or
(iv) at any time, in respect of an item in List B.
Reservations shall be set out in Annex B to the Code.

[13] ibid.

[14] See Gaikoku Kawase Boeki Kenkyuu Group (ed) [Study Group on Foreign Exchange and Trade (ed)], *Kaisei Gaitame Hou* [Revised FEFTA] (1998) 481–2.

In accordance with Art 2 of the Code, Japan has lodged reservations relating to investment by non-residents in (1) primary industry related to agriculture, forestry and fishing, (2) mining, (3) oil, (4) leather and leather products manufacturing, (5) air transport, and (6) maritime transport.[15] Japan has also lodged reservations in terms of direct and/or indirect foreign capital participation in the Nippon Telegraph and Telephone Corporation (NTT) where foreign holdings must be less than one-third of the total share ownership.[16]

In making such reservations Japan follows a similar approach to many other developed countries. Indeed recent declarations of the G8 Summits, which Japan supports as a member, refer to national restrictions on foreign investment on national security grounds. For example, para 11 of the *Heiligendamm Summit Declaration on Growth and Responsibility in the World Economy* on 7 June 2007 provides as follows:

...we remain committed to minimizing any national restrictions on foreign investment. Such restrictions should apply to very limited cases which primarily concern national security. The general principles to be followed in such cases are non-discrimination, transparency and predictability...[17]

Similarly, para 6 of the *Hokkaido Toyako Summit Leaders Declaration on World Economy* on 8 July 2008 provides as follows:

Any foreign investment restrictions should be very limited, focusing primarily on national security concerns, and should adhere to the principles of transparency, predictability, proportionality, and accountability.[18]

Although these declarations are soft law instruments and have no binding force under international law, they have high political persuasive value. These declarations set the international standards on this point and they serve as the *de facto* limitation to the reservation made by a member state based on national security grounds.

To sum up, states can restrict foreign investment if they adhere to the principles of transparency, predictability, proportionality, and accountability.[19]

---

[15] OECD, *Code of Liberalization of Capital Movements* (2009) 84.
[16] ibid.
[17] <http://www.g-8.de>.
[18] <http://www.mofa.go.jp/policy/economy/summit/2008/>.
[19] Restricting foreign investments in the service sector has to satisfy the rules under the General Agreement on Trade in Service (GATS) as well. Under the GATS, investments in the service sector come under the third mode of trade in service (Art 1 para 2(c)). Restrictions on foreign investment in the service sector can be a breach of Art 2 (most-favoured-nation treatment), Art 16 (market access) and Art 17 (national treatment), although the latter two provisions are applicable only in sectors where specific commitments are undertaken. However, the restriction can be justified when it is necessary to protect public morals and to maintain public order (Art 14(a)) and when it is necessary for the protection of its essential security interests (Art14*bis* para 1(b)). According to *The Commentary: WTO General Agreement in Trade in Service* (in Japanese) (Economic Bureau, Ministry of Foreign Affairs, 1996) 144, the word 'essential' in Art 14*bis* para 1(b) was inserted with an intent to prevent the abuse of this Article.

III. Japanese laws concerning restrictions on foreign investment

Under Japanese Law, there are two types of restrictions on foreign investment. One is the restriction based on the FEFTA.[20] A large number of industries including the energy-related sector come under this category. The other group is restrictions based on the laws which regulate particular industries, such as air transport and broadcasting.

As to the former category, Article 27 of the FEFTA provides as follows:

(1) When a foreign investor intends to hold the inward direct investment, which means holding 10 per cent or more of shares of a Japanese company, and the investment is considered to have the possibility to disturb national security, the maintenance of public order or the protection of public safety, the investor shall notify in advance to the Minister of Finance and the Minister having jurisdiction over the business.

As far as the energy sector is concerned, the minister having jurisdiction means the Minster of Economy, Trade and Industry. The notice must include the business purpose, amount, time of making the investment and other matters specified by Cabinet Order (paras 1 and 3).

(2) Whether the investment is considered to have the possibility to disturb national security, the maintenance of public order or the protection of public safety is determined by governmental order according to the industrial sector to which the company belongs.

The electricity industry as discussed below is one of the sectors which falls under this category (para 3).

(3) The Minister of Finance and the Minister having jurisdiction over the business, after the review of the investment, may recommend, after hearing opinions of the Council on Customs, Tariff, Foreign Exchange and other Transactions, the investor to change or discontinue the investment if they find that the investment is considered to disturb national security, the maintenance of public order or the protection of public safety (para 5).

(4) If the investor refuses to accept the recommendation, the Ministers may order the investor to change or discontinue the investment (para 10).

The Cabinet Order specifies the sectors for which prior notification before making an investment is required (as mentioned in Art 27 para 1). As far as the energy sector is concerned, the following sectors are included: (a) manufacturing of nuclear reactor, turbines for nuclear power, generators for nuclear power and nuclear materials, (b) mining of oil and natural gas, (c) electricity business (power plant, transformer substation, electricity business office), (d) gas business (gas manufacturing factory, gas supply facility, gas business office), (e) heat supply business,

---

[20] Act No 228 of 1 December 1949. An unofficial translation of this Act is available at <http://www.cas.go.jp/jp/seisaku/hourei/data/FTA.pdf>.

(f) oil wholesale business, and (g) fuel resale businesses, including filling stations. J-Power, as a major energy utility, comes under the category of an electricity business and therefore Art 27 is applicable when a foreign company intends to hold ten per cent or more of the shares of J-Power. The following discussion considers the nature of the Order issued by the Cabinet in the J-Power situation.

IV. Order by the Japanese government to discontinue further investment in J-Power

The Children's Investment Master Fund (TCI) is a London-based hedge fund. Electric Power Development Co Ltd (J-Power) is a major electricity supplier and a leading wholesale electricity utility in Japan. It was established in 1952 as a government-affiliated corporation. In 1997, the Japanese government decided to privatize the J-Power utility. J-Power was listed on the Tokyo Stock Exchange in 2003, when all the state-owned shares were sold off. In 2004, the privatization process was completed. J-Power is a central institution in Japan's electric power supply system and it has a wide range of functions in the energy sector in Japan. First, it is set to be the key player in the nuclear fuel cycle in Japan as the corporation is constructing the Ohma nuclear power plant. Secondly, the corporation is responsible for the maintenance of the national electric power network through the operation of transmission and substation facilities. Finally, the organization also comprises a wholesale electric power company that provides the backbone of electric power supplies within the country.[21]

On 15 January 2008, the Minister of Finance (MOF) and the Minister of Economy, Trade and Industry (METI) received a notification from TCI in accordance with Art 27 para 1 of the FEFTA. TCI already held a 9.9 per cent stake in issued stock of J-Power. At this time, TCI notified the ministers of its intention to increase its acquisitions in J-Power to up to 20 per cent of the shares in the company. Subsequently, a series of interviews with TCI over six meetings were conducted by the MOF and the METI. In addition, two meetings of the Special Subcommittee on Foreign Companies of the Committee of Custom, Foreign Exchange and other Transactions of the Council on Customs, Tariff, Foreign Exchange and other Transactions, were held. These meetings occurred on 11 and 15 April, respectively. TCI was given full opportunity to express its opinion at the Special Subcommittee meetings. At the second meeting on 15 April, the Special Subcommittee reached a consensus on the following conclusion:

(1) We recognize the possibility that 'maintenance of public order' may be disturbed through the investment. Thus, we request the Japanese Government to take an appropriate measure to address the threat.

---

[21] Ministry of Finance, Ministry of Economy, Trade and Industry, Recommendation to TCI (16 April 2008), <http://www.enecho.meti.go.jp/english/080513.htm>.

(2) *J-Power* has power transmission lines totalling 2,400 kilometers all over the country, including the inter-regional transmission lines which connect Japan's four islands respectively. *J-Power* also owns a frequency power converter station which enables it to interchange electric power between eastern and western Japan. Its long-term capital spending contributes to a national stable supply of electricity, and the company is planning to construct a nuclear power plant in Ohma which is vital for implementing the government's nuclear policy/nuclear fuel-cycle policy.

(3) If *TCI* increases its stake in *J-Power*, even if accompanied by the proposals made by *TCI*, the possibility that the planning, operation, and maintenance of key electric power facilities, and the implementation of nuclear policy/nuclear fuel-cycle policy could be adversely affected cannot be denied as this would be dependent on the behavior of *TCI* as a major share holder.

(4) It is obviously important to attract more Foreign Direct Investment (FDI) inflows for the further growth of the Japanese economy. Since FDI, in general, promotes productivity improvement and the economic efficiency of our industry through the introduction of excellent technology, human resources and management skills. Furthermore, FDI has a positive effect on strengthening sound corporate governance in Japanese companies. Since FEFTA has adopted the general principle of freedom of transaction in 1980, all FDI prior notifications, including approximately 760 in the last three years, have been approved. We believe that we must maintain this openness to foreign investment in Japan.

(5) On the other hand, we should take an appropriate action if the maintenance of the public order were to be disturbed as a result of an unrestrained investment activity. From this point of view, many governments, including the government of Japan, regulate FDI in the electric power industry as a critical infrastructure pursuant to the OECD Code of Liberalization of Capital Movements, and/or own state electricity companies, so that stable electricity supply, as an essential public service for its people, is secured for long-term.

Paragraphs (2) and (3) stress the crucial importance of J-Power for energy security in Japan. Paragraphs (4) and (5) explain that the restriction is compatible with the OECD Code of Liberalization of Capital Movement, as well as with Japan's general policy to attract more FDI. Therefore, it was reasonable for the Subcommittee to have reached this conclusion, especially in view of the importance of J-Power to the Japanese economy. The Subcommittee did not consider the TCI to be a trustworthy shareholder.

Taking this opinion into consideration, on 16 April 2008, the Minister of Finance and the Minister of Economy, Trade and Industry made a recommendation[22] to TCI, based on Art 27 para 5 of the FEFTA. In accordance with the legislation, it was recommended that TCI discontinue the proposed inward direct investment that was stipulated in the notification. The grounds given for discontinuing the investment were that the investment was likely to impede the stable supply of electric power and Japan's nuclear and nuclear fuel cycle policy, and to disturb the maintenance of public order. On the same day, the ministers made a statement that Japan's policy to promote foreign direct investment was

---

[22] Available at <www.enecho.meti.go.jp/english/080416.htm>.

unchanged. The intention of the ministers was to indicate that restricting foreign investment based on national security grounds was very exceptional, and that it was compatible with the general principle to promote FDI.

On 25 April 2008, TCI informed the ministers by notice of its refusal to accept the recommendation. On 8 May 2008, TCI submitted an explanation to the ministers pursuant to the Administrative Procedures Act.[23] On 13 May 2008, the ministers ordered TCI to discontinue the inward direct investment as stipulated in the notification based on Art 27 para 10 of the FEFTA.[24] This was the first time that an order based on this provision had been issued. In regard to the possibility of disturbing the maintenance of public order, the Order stated:

(1) TCI has made various proposals as a shareholder to J-Power officially and unofficially. For example, it requested J-Power to commit to a minimum target ROE [return on equity] of 10% and target ROA [return on assets] of 4%, and requested the management to be accountable for meeting these targets. However, the fund did not clarify specific methods to realize its requests.

(2) In response to our request to TCI to explain in detail its specific ideas to improve the management of J-Power, TCI disclosed its policy to introduce outside directors and resolve cross shareholdings in order to promote sound corporate governance. However, TCI did not present its management policies on issues related to adverse effects on the construction and operation of Ohma nuclear power plant, a decrease of capital investment and repair expenses for core facilities, and damage to J-Power's financial strength.

(3) For this reason, we recognized that there is a possibility that, through TCI's further acquisition of J-Power's shares and its use of shareholders' rights, the management of J-Power and its planning/operation/maintenance of backbone facilities such as electric power transmission lines and the nuclear power plant may be affected, and thus a stable supply of electric power and Japan's nuclear policy and nuclear fuel cycle-related policy may be affected.

(4) Meanwhile, TCI stated in its explanation that TCI has never intended to disturb the stable supply of electricity in Japan or Japan's nuclear/ nuclear fuel cycle policy and further that TCI would not make such a proposal. However, TCI requested J-Power to adopt management targets and requested J-Power's management to be accountable for meeting the targets, but did not clarify the method to accomplish the targets. Therefore, in the screening process of the notification, the government acknowledged the possibility that the stable supply of electricity or Japan's nuclear/nuclear fuel cycle policy may be affected through, for example, a freeze or significant delay in the construction of Ohma nuclear plant or a decrease in capital investment and repair expenses for core facilities, as a direct or indirect influence of J-Power meeting TCI's requests.[25]

Paragraphs (1) and (3) of the Order revealed that, although TCI behaved only as an active shareholder, it had little interest in Japan's long-term energy security, or in becoming a stable shareholder. Paragraph (2) explained that TCI's greater influence over J-Power would badly affect Japan's long-term energy security.

[23] Act No 88 of 1993.
[24] Available at <www.enecho.meti.go.jp/english/report/080513–3.pdf>.
[25] ibid 3–4.

Furthermore, the Order refutes arguments raised by TCI. TCI stated in its explanation that such a decision was inconsistent with the Supreme Court decision in the *Izumi-Sano City Civil Centre* case,[26] under which 'clear and imminent breach of interests protected by law' and 'specific predictability' are necessary to constitute a 'possibility' of the type contemplated in the Order. In response to this argument, the Order stated:

> ...the Supreme Court case referred by *TCI* is a case where the decision was made on the relation between a refusal by the Izumisano-City to allow a specific group to use the civic center based on the 'possibility to disturb public order' as stipulated in the relevant ordinance, and the 'freedom of expression' as protected by Article 21 of the Constitution.[27] However, the case has little to do with the interpretation of FEFTA, which is related to the property rights protected by Article 29 of the Constitution.[28]

TCI also raised an argument that there was no possibility that investment and repair expenses for backbone facilities would be inappropriately reduced because the Minister of Economy, Trade and Industry may order J-Power to keep corporate financial reserves as required by the Electricity Enterprises Law.[29] In response to this point, the Order stated,

> ...the Electricity Enterprises Law regulates the activity of the electricity companies on the premises they construct nuclear power plants and other facilities on a *voluntary* basis.[30] Therefore, the Law imposed no legal obligation on the future investment activities of the private electricity companies; for example, the Law does not require private electricity companies to make capital investment or pay repair expenses or to operate nuclear power plants and the nuclear fuel cycle. Thus, the Law does not cast aside the possibility of the maintenance of public order being disturbed.[31]

V. Analysis of the J-Power situation for foreign investment in the energy sector

To clarify the legal problems concerning the restriction of foreign investment in the energy sector in Japan, there is a range of matters to which attention is drawn.

---

[26] Supreme Court (Third Chamber) Judgment, 7 March 1995, available at <www.courts.go.jp> (in Japanese).

[27] Art 21 of the Japanese Constitution provides: 'Freedom of assembly and association as well as speech, press and all other forms of expression are guaranteed. No censorship shall be maintained, nor shall the secrecy of any means of communication be violated.'

[28] Art 29 of the Japanese Constitution provides: 'The right to own or to hold property is inviolable. Property rights shall be defined by law, in conformity with the public welfare. Private property may be taken for public use upon just compensation therefor.'

[29] Available at <www.enecho.meti.go.jp/english/report/080513–3.pdf>, 6.

[30] Emphasis added by the author.

[31] Above n 24.

First, as mentioned above, it is clear that states have the discretion to restrict foreign investment if they do not contravene the principles of transparency, predictability, or proportionality when imposing such restrictions. As the Order that was directed to TCI is completely based on the FEFTA, it seems *prima facie* to satisfy these principles.

Secondly, according to the METI, among the OECD countries, ten countries[32] restrict foreign investment in the national electric power industry in accordance with the OECD Code of Liberalization of Capital Movements. Given such measures, it is not unusual that there is regulation of foreign investment in the energy sector, including electricity, in Japan. Further, it should be emphasized that the J-Power/TCI case is the *only* situation where the government of Japan prohibited foreign direct investment. The very exceptional character of this situation should not be generalized to give the impression that Japan is not open to foreign investment.

Thirdly, it is undeniable that J-Power's role as a major supplier of electricity is of crucial importance to the 127 million people living in Japan. Long-term management planning is required for the stable supply of electricity. Therefore it is not wise to pay excessive dividends to shareholders of electricity utilities in the short term, without fully considering the long-term investment needs in relation to the construction of power plants and other long-term costs for the provision of infrastructure and plant.

Fourthly, there is a need to consider the function of so-called 'golden shares'. As a means to prevent mergers and acquisitions, private companies have sometimes instituted a system of golden shares. These golden shares allow the holder (usually government) the *veto* power on matters of vital importance for the company. Under Japanese company law, it is possible for a company which is listed on a stock exchange to introduce the golden shares system.[33] The internal rules of the Tokyo Stock Exchange do not completely preclude an already listed company from introducing a golden share system. However the Tokyo Stock Exchange is very cautious about permitting a listed company to issue golden shares because it considers that the golden shares might be incompatible with the principle of equality of shareholders and that they might harm existing shareholders' rights. There is no international rule which hinders Japanese companies from introducing a golden shares system. This lack of regulation is very different from the

---

[32] Japan, United States, Slovakia, Switzerland, Iceland, France, Finland, Austria, Canada and Korea. METI, Annex 2 to the Order of 13 May 2008, <http://www.meti.go.jp/press/20080513001/04_02.pdf> 3 (in Japanese).

[33] Companies can issue golden shares in accordance with Art 108 of the Companies Act (Act No 109 of 2006). That Article provides:

'A Stock Company may issue two or more classes of shares with different features which have different provisions on the following matters...

(viii) Such of the matters to be resolved at a shareholders meeting that require, in addition to such resolution, a resolution of a Class Meeting constituted by the Class Shareholders of such class shares.'

situation of companies in the European Union. In the EU, the European Court of Justice has usually concluded that golden shares are incompatible with Arts 43 (freedom of establishment) and 56 (free movement of capital) of the Treaty establishing the European Community.[34] However, the only Japanese company which has introduced the golden shares system is INPEX Corporation, a major oil and gas exploration and development company. INPEX did introduce the system when it was listed on the Tokyo Stock Exchange in 2006. J-Power did not introduce the golden shares system when it was listed on the Tokyo Stock Exchange in 2003. Although as noted, it is not prohibited for a company which is already listed on a stock exchange to introduce the golden shares system, J-Power did not choose to introduce such a system when TCI sought to increase its share-holding. If such a system had been introduced, then it is possible that the Order to discontinue the investment could have been avoided.

More widely, it needs to be considered that, without doubt, the general trend of the government of Japan is toward promoting foreign direct investment. Therefore the Order to TCI is a very exceptional one based on national security. On the very day when the Order was issued, the ministers were at pains to emphasize that Japan's policy to promote foreign direct investment was unchanged, and that it would not change. Subsequently, on 26 January 2008 at the Annual Meeting of the World Economic forum in Davos, Prime Minister Fukuda stated that he would continue to advance efforts towards market liberalization, including reforms in the areas of foreign direct investment in Japan.[35]

When considering the actual governing legislation in the J-Power context, there are some specific problems. One of the key difficulties with the FEFTA is that the factors to be considered in making a decision as to whether 'national security is impaired, the maintenance of public order is disturbed, or the protection of public safety is hindered' are not provided for in the legislation. In order to improve the transparency, predictability and proportionality of any Order to discontinue foreign investment, it would be desirable for the FEFTA to expressly provide the factors to be considered in making such decisions. In this regard reference should be made to relevant United States Law. In the United States, s 721, para (F) of the Defense Production Act of 1950,[36] as amended by the Foreign Investment and National Security Act of 2007,[37] provides that the President may, taking into account the requirements of national security, consider a range of factors. The eleven factors to be taken into account include:

---

[34] See, eg, *Commission v United Kingdom*, C-98/01, [2003] ECR I-4641; but in *Commission v Belgium*, C-503/99, [2002] ECR 4809, the Court concluded that the Belgian legislation which vested golden shares in SNTC and Distrigaz was justified by the objective of guaranteeing energy supplies in event of a crisis.

[35] The Prime Minister's comments are available at <www.mofa.go.jp/policy/economy/wef/2008/address-s.html>.

[36] 50 USC App 2170.

[37] Public Law 110–49.

(1) domestic production needed for projected national defense requirements;

(2) the capability and capacity of domestic industries to meet national defense requirements;

(3) the control of domestic industries and commercial activity by foreign citizens as it affects the capability and capacity of the United States to meet the requirements of national security;

(4) the potential effects of the proposed or pending transaction on sales of military goods, equipment, or technology to any country

    (a) identified as a country which supports terrorism, as a country of concern regarding the proliferation of missile or chemical and biological weapons;

    (b) identified as posing a potential regional military threat to the interests of the United States; or

    (c) listed on the Nuclear Non-Proliferation-Special Country List;

(5) the potential effects of the proposed or pending transaction on United States international technological leadership in areas affecting United States national security;

(6) the potential national security-related effects on United States critical infrastructure, including major energy assets;

(7) the potential national security-related effects on United States critical technologies;

(8) whether the covered transaction is a foreign government-controlled transaction;

(9) a review of the current assessment of

    (a) the adherence of the country to nonproliferation control regimes,

    (b) the relationship of the country with the United States, specifically on its record on cooperating in counter-terrorism efforts, and

    (c) the potential for trans-shipment or diversion of technologies with military applications, including an analysis of national export control laws and regulations;

(10) the long-term projection of United States requirements for sources of energy and other critical resources and material; and

(11) such other factors as the President or the Committee on Foreign Investment in the United States (CFIUS) may determine to be appropriate, generally or in connection with a specific review or investigation.[38]

If Japan had possessed legislation outlining the same factors, the J-Power/TCI case would likely have come under the factor that covers the potential national security-related effects on Japan's critical infrastructure, including its major

---

[38] Among the eleven factors, (3), (6) and (10) are directly relevant to energy companies such as J-Power.

energy assets. It is highly desirable that Art 27 of the FEFTA should clearly provide such factors in order to justify the restrictions on foreign investment. The reference to explicit criteria would better serve to satisfy the principles of transparency, predictability, proportionality, and accountability.

Finally, the J-Power/TCI situation revealed a serious *lacuna* in the Electricity Enterprises Law.[39] Article 29 para 3 of the Law provides:

The Minister of Economy, Trade and Industry may, when he/she finds that the Supply Plan is not appropriate for realizing the comprehensive and reasonable development of Electricity Businesses through wide-area operations, recommend that the electricity Utilities should revise the Supply Plan.

In association, Art 29 para 4 provides:

Where the Ministry of Economy, Trade and Industry has made recommendations pursuant to the preceding paragraph, he/she may, when deeming it particularly necessary and appropriate, order the Electricity Utility to take the following measures; provided, however, that the Ministers shall not order a Wholesale Electricity Utility to take the measure set forth in paragraph 3 to

(1) supply electricity to a General Electricity;
(2) provide a cross-area wheeling service;
(3) receive electricity supply.

The problem with Art 29 para 3 is that the minister cannot *order* a wholesale electricity utility like J-Power to revise the supply plan even if the urgent revision of the plan is absolutely required for energy security in Japan. The minister can only *recommend* the revision. This *lacuna* in the law should immediately be amended.

VI. Concluding remarks

After the Order of 13 May 2008 to TCI there were a series of other developments. TCI lost a proxy battle[40] against J-Power at the shareholders' meeting on 26 June 2008. TCI's five proposals which included a doubling of dividends and a rejection of certain board members were rejected by the shareholders. The struggle

---

[39] The name of this Law can also be found translated as Electricity Business Act (Act No 170 of 11 July 1964). An unofficial translation is available at <www.cas.go.jp/jp/seisaku/hourei/data/FTA.pdf>.

[40] TCI requested that J-Power's shareholders be given the opportunity to vote on the following five proposals: (1) Proposal on stock market and cross-shareholdings (limit stock market and cross-shareholdings); (2) Proposal for outside directors (stipulate a minimum of three Outside Directors); (3) Dividend proposal (fiscal year-end dividend of ¥90 per share, for a total annual dividend payment of ¥120 per share); (4) Alternative dividend proposal (fiscal year-end dividend of ¥50 per share, totalling ¥80 per share for full year); and (5) Share buy-back proposal (company authorized to spend up to ¥70 billion to acquire its own shares), <http://www.efinancialnews.com/share/media/downloads/2008/04/2350399815.pdf>

between TCI and J-Power finally ended in November 2008, when TCI sold its entire shareholding stake back to J-Power and disappeared from the Japanese stock market. This fact seems to demonstrate that TCI had no interest in acting as a stable shareholder of J-Power.

According to a newspaper report, the government of Japan is now considering the revision of the industries which come under the restrictions for foreign investment. If the restriction is to be maintained, clear reasons have to be provided.[41] Although it is not clear from the reports whether the emerging government policy would include the revision of the FEFTA and inclusion of the factors to be considered when a decision is made to restrict foreign investment, that would certainly be a favourable step in order to promote greater accountability and transparency in the process.

VII. Appendix

Article 27 of the Foreign Exchange and Foreign Trade Act (FEFTA) (extracts only)

1. When a foreign investor intends to make an inward direct investment, etc. (excluding those specified by Cabinet Order by taking into consideration inheritance, testamentary gift, merger of juridical persons or other circumstances; hereinafter the same shall apply in this article) specified by Cabinet Order as being likely to fall under inward direct investment, etc, which requires examination pursuant to paragraph 3, he/she shall notify in advance, pursuant to the provisions of Cabinet Order, the Minister of Finance and the minister having jurisdiction over the business of the business purpose, amount, time of making the investment, etc and other matters specified by Cabinet Order in regard to the inward direct investment, etc.

3. Where the Minister of Finance and the minister having jurisdiction over the business have received a notification pursuant to the provision of paragraph 1, when he/she finds it necessary to examine whether or not inward direct investment, etc pertaining to the notification falls under any of the following inward direct investment, etc. (referred to as 'Inward Direct Investment, etc pertaining to National Security, etc' in paragraphs 4, 5, and 11), he/she may extend the period in which inward direct investment, etc. pertaining to the notification is prohibited up to four months from the acceptance of the notification.

(i) Inward direct investment, etc. which is likely to cause any of the situations listed in (a) or (b) (limited to inward direct investment, etc, which is made by a foreign investor of a member state of a multilateral treaty or other international agreement on inward direct investment, etc., which is specified by Cabinet Order and to which Japan has acceded (hereinafter referred to as 'Treaty, etc' in this item), and which is free from the obligations pursuant to the Treaty, etc. in regard to removal of restrictions on inward direct investment, etc, and inward direct investment, etc made by a foreign investor of a state other

---

[41] *Nihon Keizai Shimbun* [Japan Economic Newspaper], 28 December 2008.

than the member states of the Treaty, etc., which would be free from the said obligations if the state was a member state of the Treaty, etc)

(a) National security is impaired, the maintenance of public order is disturbed, or the protection of public safety is hindered.

(b) Significant adverse effect is brought to the smooth management of the Japanese economy. (omitted)

5. Where the Minister of Finance and the minister having jurisdiction over the business have extended the period in which inward direct investment, etc is prohibited pursuant to the provision of paragraph 3, when he/she finds through examination pursuant to the said provision that inward direct investment, etc pertaining to a notification pursuant to the provision of paragraph 1 falls under Inward Direct Investment, etc. Pertaining to National Security, etc, he/she may recommend a person who has given notification of the inward direct investment, etc to change the content pertaining to the inward direct investment, etc or discontinue the inward direct investment, etc pursuant to the provisions of Cabinet Order after hearing opinions of the Council on Customs, Tariff, Foreign Exchange and other Transactions; provided, however, the period for making the recommendation of the change or discontinuance shall be up to the expiration date of the period extended pursuant to the provision of paragraph 3 or 6, counting from the day of acceptance of the notification.

7. Any person who has received a recommendation pursuant to the provision of paragraph 5 shall notify the Minister of Finance and the minister having jurisdiction over the business of whether to accept the recommendation within 10 days from the day of receipt of the recommendation.

10. Where a person who has received a recommendation pursuant to the provision of paragraph 5 has not given a notice pursuant to the provision of paragraph 7 or has given a notice of refusal of the recommendation, the Minister of Finance and the minister having jurisdiction over the business may order the person to change the content pertaining to the inward direct investment, etc., or to discontinue the inward direct investment, etc.; provided, however, that the period for giving an order of the change or discontinuance shall be up to the expiration date of the period extended pursuant to the provision of paragraph 3 or 6, counting from the day of acceptance of the notification.

17

Ownership Unbundling and Property Rights in the EU Energy Sector

Iñigo del Guayo, Gunther Kühne, and Martha Roggenkamp[*]

I. Introduction

Since the end of the 1980s the European energy sector has been subject to many fundamental changes. Following the European Commission's (EC) 1985 and 1988 Communications on the Internal Energy Market (IEM),[1] it became clear that the general provisions of the EC Treaty (ECT) should also be applied to the energy sector. By contrast to the previous position, member states could no longer rely automatically on the concept that energy companies provide services of a general interest and, therefore, were exempted from the provisions of free movement of goods, services, capital and the general provisions of competition law.[2] As a result of the new approach, the EC issued several sets of legislation facilitating the application of general concepts of European Union (EU) law to the energy sector. As for the 'traditional' energy utilities—the electricity and gas supply sector—the Electricity Directive of 1996[3] (ED 1996) and the Gas Directive of 1998[4] (GD 1998) initiated a process of widespread change, followed by the Electricity and Gas Directives of 2003,[5] that resulted in a process of unbundling, ie, the

* Professor of Administrative Law, University of Almería, Spain; email: iguayo@ual.es; Emeritus Professor of Mining and Energy Law, Technical University of Clausthal, and Honorary Professor of Law, University of Göttingen, Germany; email: gunther.kuehne@tu-clausthal.de; and Professor of Energy Law, Groningen Centre of Energy Law, University of Groningen, and Of Counsel, Brinkhof Advocaten, Amsterdam, The Netherlands; email: m.m.roggenkamp@rug.nl.

[1] Completing the Internal Market: White Paper from the Commission to the European Council (Milan, 28–29 June 1985), COM(85) 310, June 1985, and The Internal Energy Market. Commission Working Document, COM(88) 238 final, 2 May 1988.

[2] Art 86, para 2 ECT.

[3] Directive 96/92/EC of the European Parliament and of the Council of 19 December 1996 concerning common rules for the internal market in electricity (OJ L 176, 15.7.2003).

[4] Directive 98/30/EC of the European Parliament and of the Council of 22 June 1998 concerning common rules for the internal market in natural gas (OJ L 204, 21.7.1998).

[5] Directive 2003/54/EC of the European Parliament and of the Council of 26 June 2003 concerning common rules for the internal market in electricity and repealing Directive 96/92/EC (OJ

separation of regulated network activities and commercial supply and trading activities. The trends in EU Directives regarding the energy sector have instigated successive stages of unbundling, with most recent changes impacting ownership arrangements for network and commercial activities. Ownership unbundling has the potential to radically realign ownership interests in the EU energy sector and thus affect existing property forms.

On 19 September 2007, the EC proposed a number of amendments to the existing EU energy legislation,[6] including a further step in the gradual introduction of unbundling of energy activities, the so-called *ownership* unbundling: electricity and gas companies involved in both network (transport and/or distribution) and commercial (supply and/or production) activities, legally would no longer be allowed to be engaged in those two types of energy activities, and consequently such organizations would be asked to divest ownership in one or both activities. On 22 April 2009, the European Parliament adopted a resolution on the common position of the Council, whereby a new unbundling option was given to member states, together with the two options originally envisaged by the EC's proposal. Two months later, on 25 June 2009, the European Council adopted the new rules on the IEM. The new Electricity and Gas Directives were published in the Official Journal of the EU on 14 August 2009 and entered into force twenty days after their publication. Member states are required to implement these Directives in national law within 18 months after entry into force with the exception of the rules on unbundling. These rules are to be transposed into national law after 30 months.[7]

This chapter assesses how the provision of ownership unbundling[8] when (and if) adopted by any of the member states, will affect the property rights of gas and electricity network owners. To understand clearly how such ownership may be affected, Section II briefly explains the historical background of the EU energy sector and its progressive liberalization in order to situate the moves toward unbundling. Subsequently, the various meanings of unbundling are analysed in Section III. This analysis focuses especially on ownership unbundling and whether such unbundling could be considered as an expropriation measure directed against the property rights of networks owners.

L 176, 15.7.2003), and Directive 2003/55/EC of the European Parliament and of the Council of 26 June 2003 concerning common rules for the internal market in natural gas and repealing Directive 98/30/EC (OJ L 176, 15.7.2003).

[6] Proposal for a Directive of the European Parliament and of the Council amending Directive 2003/54/EC concerning common rules for the internal market in electricity COM(2007)0528, and Proposal for a Directive of the European Parliament and of the Council amending Directive 2003/55/EC concerning common rules for the internal market in natural gas COM(2007)0529.

[7] OJ L 211, 14.08.2009 and Press release of the EC of 25 June 2009, IP/09/1038. This chapter was finalized before the Directives were published in the OJ; the authors have tried, however, to make references to the published Directives, whenever that was needed for a better understanding of the legal discussion.

[8] As the concept is understood in the recently adopted EU Directives.

Consequently, the chapter examines whether the imposition of ownership unbundling may result in the necessity for compensation. Against this backdrop, Section IV analyses the compensation issue in the broader perspective of general EU law and by reference to the European Human Rights Convention. Thereafter we discuss ownership unbundling from the perspective of two member states with contrasting views and policies; those being Germany (Section V), and the Netherlands (Section VI). Whereas Germany can be considered one of the main opponents of ownership unbundling in the EU, the Netherlands has adopted strong unbundling policies. Not only has the Netherlands introduced ownership unbundling at a transmission level but also in terms of the energy distribution companies. These two examples illustrate the difficulties in the establishment of one IEM and the varying effects on organizational and ownership structures of the recent Directives; a situation that is the subject of reflection in the final section.

II. The process of energy liberalization in the EU

A. Evolution of the energy sector

At the beginning of the twentieth century, most energy companies produced and supplied energy at the local level. Municipal or regional companies were charged with the production and supply of electricity and (manufactured) gas. Due to technical developments it became possible in the 1930s to construct long distance transportation pipelines and electricity cables. This resulted in important changes in the organization of the energy sector after World War II. Whereas some member states opted for a horizontal integration of the electricity and gas supply sector (like the Netherlands and Germany), other member states decided to vertically integrate the energy sector, ie an integration of production, transmission and supply of electricity or gas (like the United Kingdom and France).[9] In addition, the national energy markets were gradually interconnected for reasons of security of supply, linking remote producing units with customers, by means of a complex infrastructure of transport and distribution networks.

B. Liberalizing the energy market

By the time efforts were under way towards the creation of an EU IEM, there were, in most countries, a handful of energy companies, frequently belonging to the state and/or lower governments, dominating the whole of the energy chain, from production to supply. In most cases these energy companies enjoyed a legal

---

[9] For a definition of vertical and horizontal integration, for the purposes of the ED 2003 and the GD 2003, see recitals No 20 and 21, respectively.

or *de facto* monopoly. Twenty five years ago, it was generally assumed that there was no other way of arranging for the secure, effective and universal supply of energy to customers.

This status quo created a severe obstacle for the implementation of fundamental economic freedoms of the EU, such as the free movement of goods and services, regarding energy. In fact, the 1988 Communication from the EC, on the IEM (which, in turn, was a development of the 1985 White Book on the internal market)[10] considered horizontal and/or vertical integration of the industry (in particular, the integration of network businesses, with production and supply businesses) to be one of the main obstacles to the creation of a true internal EU energy market. Since the integrated monopoly owned the network, and since electricity and gas supplies are network-bound services, there were few, if any, options for a competitor to enter the business. The lack of transparency in energy tariffs and/or prices was rooted in integration, insofar as costs were not clearly attributed to a particular link in the energy chain, leading to cross-subsidies among customers and activities, and, hence, to a distortion of competition. Whether the monopoly was a legal or a *de facto* one, the outcome was that customers were exposed to the risks of any monopoly, ie either inefficient charges for the good supplied or for the services provided, or a lack of sufficient supply of the good, or of provision of the services.

The integration of the various activities leading to final energy supply to customers is the result of a natural tendency of network-bound industries, based on economies of scale as well as the character of natural monopolies of distribution and transport of electricity and gas. As opposed to most economic activities, efficiency is matched, in transport and distribution, by the existence of only one provider, within a given geographical area. Simultaneously, due to the high capital investment intensity on cables and pipelines, the main incentive for a company to invest in new network infrastructure is that it will be entitled not only to supply the gas or electricity which it transports through its network, but also that it will enjoy a monopoly to do so. Though distribution and transport networks are natural monopolies, production and supply are not.

C. Regulating the energy market

The EU liberalization process is based on the approach that the liberalization of the market must be accompanied by adequate regulation of the networks. It was assumed that specific network regulation in a liberalized energy market would lead to the emergence of electricity-to-electricity, and gas-to-gas, competition. As a result, the ED 1996, GD 1998 and the 2003 Directives provide for the possibility that consumers and suppliers should (gradually) have the freedom to choose where to buy and/or sell electricity and/or gas. Such freedom should not

[10] Above n 1.

be limited to natural boundaries but exist across the entire EU. As a consequence of this approach and the fact that the energy networks are national monopolies, the use of these networks needs regulation. The Directives thus provide two crucial regulatory instruments: the obligation of network companies to give third parties access to the grid and the obligation to separate energy supply and network activities within one integrated company. The manner in which member states have organized this unbundling differs and also depends on the national situation before liberalization. It can be noted, however, that from the beginning several member states have gone beyond the minimum requirements of the Directives.

III. Unbundling and EU energy law

A. Introduction

In order to achieve energy market liberalization, the EU has introduced specific legislation on unbundling, applying to vertically integrated energy companies, ie undertakings or a group of undertakings performing at least one of the functions of transmission or distribution and at least one of the functions of generation or supply of electricity.[11] A decisive element is the extent to which the generation/supply company controls the network company or vice versa.[12] The definition also shows that the term vertically integrated energy companies has a slightly different meaning now than before and can include energy supply companies which were considered to be horizontally integrated, ie supplying gas and electricity.

In general, the process of energy liberalization applied in the EU since 1985 has been dominated by two basic approaches to energy regulation: the structure regulation model as against the conduct regulation model. Whereas the structure regulation model focuses on the need to create the right structure for the energy market and thus allowing for competition, the conduct regulation model stresses the need to regulate the behaviour of companies in order to avoid anti-competitive conduct, rather than imposing a market structure. In general terms, European Directives and regulations are based upon the conduct regulation model. When comparing the wording of the original proposal in 2007 for the new Directives (when only two options were given to member states), and the text finally adopted by the European Parliament in the Second Reading in April 2009 (when three options were given to member states), it becomes clear that the conduct regulation model involves more regulation. As a result of the new Directives, further rules have been added to the original ones, aimed at guaranteeing that the

---

[11] See Art 2 ED and GD. The definition makes a reference to Art 3(3) of Council Regulation (EEC) No 4064/89 of 21 December 1989 on the control of concentrations between undertakings.
[12] See Note 14 January 2004 of DG Energy and Transport on Directives 2003/54/EC and 2003/55/EC on the *Internal Energy Market in Electricity and Natural Gas—The Unbundling Regime.*

networks will operate truly independently from the commercial production and/ or supply businesses. In other words, the conduct model needs more prescriptive and comprehensive rules, since, had the ownership of networks been entirely separated from the ownership of the supply company, there would not have been a need for rules to guarantee the independent operation of each entity.

B. The Electricity and Gas Directives and the concept of unbundling

1. Types of unbundling

The regulation necessary to liberalize the network-bound energy market increasingly focuses on the issue of unbundling as one of the main instruments to make energy network operators independent from commercial companies. In addition, the legislative developments indicate that the extent of unbundling increases in line with the liberalization process. In other words, whereas the first Electricity and Gas Directives of 1996 and 1998 respectively provided for a limited degree of unbundling, the recently approved amendments to the 2003 Electricity and Gas Directives aim towards the highest degree of unbundling. ie unbundling at the ownership level. Below we will present an overview of all existing and new unbundling options.

The first and weakest type of unbundling is *accounting* or *administrative unbundling*, by which integrated energy undertakings are asked to keep separate accounts for each of their production, transmission, distribution, and supply activities (and, in the case of gas, Liquid Natural Gas [LNG] and underground gas storage). Accounts are to be organized as if they were carried out by separate undertakings and with a view to avoiding discrimination, cross-subsidization and distortion of competition. This type of limited unbundling was required in the ED 1996 and GD 1998 to provide sufficient transparency. Integrated national gas and electricity undertakings were obliged to keep separate accounts for their production, transmission, distribution, and storage activities and, where appropriate, consolidated accounts for non-gas, or non-electricity activities; a balance sheet and a profit and loss account were required to be drawn up for each activity. The accounts for transmission and for distribution activities could be combined where access to the system was on the basis of a single charge for both activities. Each transmission undertaking was required to preserve the confidentiality of any commercially sensitive information it obtained from other systems or system users. In practice, this resulted in the creation of the so-called 'Chinese walls' between the regulated network and commercial supply activities. Transmission and distribution companies were supposed to operate on the basis of commercial principles.

The 2003 Directives provide for a second type of unbundling, *legal unbundling*, whereby integrated energy companies must maintain separate legal entities for each of the activities performed by the undertaking, and, in particular, for production, transmission, distribution, and supply. It was introduced to create greater transparency and a more level playing field between transmission system operators (TSO) and distribution system operators (DSO). All vertically integrated undertakings who at the same time supply gas and/or electricity and transport gas and/or electricity through a high-pressure or high-voltage grid, are required to legally separate these functions so that one of these functions is carried out by a separate company which, however, may be controlled by the other company, and can belong to the same group or holding of companies. The same requirement applies to distribution networks if they are part of a vertically integrated supply company. Experience shows that the effectiveness of the legal unbundling does depend on the way in which the operations of both companies are further regulated. The success of legal unbundling seems to depend on the extent to which the legally unbundled network company is able to operate independently from the supply company, which includes the power to make investment decisions. Legal unbundling is not considered to be sufficient to create the required level of independence and it should be accompanied by functional unbundling.

The third and more challenging step, introduced in 2003, is *functional (or managerial) unbundling*.[13] It provides for a greater degree of separation as it requires integrated energy undertakings to implement a set of detailed rules to ensure the effective independent operation and decision-making of those subsidiaries dealing with network activities within the integrated group of companies. It calls for strict independence of the operations of various companies. Such independence is to be assured through the non-involvement of personnel responsible for the management of production and supply in the network activities. This means that the day-to-day operations of transmission and distribution should rest with the network operator. Head office's control should be limited to general supervision such as the approval of the annual financial plan. The setting up of so-called 'Chinese walls' preventing exchange of commercially sensitive information between network operators and other parts of the energy company is also considered as part of functional unbundling.[14] However, both aspects (the treatment of commercially sensitive information, and functional unbundling), must be clearly distinguished, since the protection of confidential information is not subject to unbundling requirements and is an autonomous legal standard in itself.[15]

---

[13] Arts 15 ED and 13 GD.
[14] A distinction must be made between functional unbundling, whereby there are rules to guarantee the independence of the running of companies belonging to the same group of companies, and informational unbundling, whereby there are rules to guarantee that information flows properly (ie, that network companies do not reveal sensitive commercial information to suppliers, and that network companies do not treat preferentially, in information terms, the supply company belonging to the same group).
[15] Z. Zafirova, 'Unbundling the Network: the Case of Ownership Unbundling?' (2007) 2 IELTR 29–36.

2. *The implementation of the Electricity and Gas Directives in relation to unbundling*

Following the ED 1996 and GD 1998, most member states included in their legislation a requirement for administrative unbundling. However, a number of countries went beyond this minimum requirement, introducing legal and/or even ownership unbundling, in either the gas and electricity transmission sector or in both. Although not required by the ED 1996, the UK, Italy, Luxembourg, Portugal, the Netherlands, Sweden, Denmark and Spain all opted for a legal unbundling of their electricity transmission sector. The most advanced system was to be found in the UK where network and supply activities had already been unbundled in ownership terms before the EU liberalization process started. Due to national (production) interests, the number of member states going beyond the requirements of the GD 1998 was far more limited. Legal unbundling in the gas transmission sector was only achieved in Spain, Italy and the UK.

The 2003 Directives required member states to apply legal and/or functional unbundling. While implementing the 2003 Directives some member states went beyond the minimum requirement of the Directives and introduced ownership unbundling. In the UK, as in other member states, experience showed that the mere establishment of 'Chinese walls' between transmission and supply activities, did not fully protect energy companies against challenge from the competition authorities, and therefore, ownership unbundling was needed.[16] Currently, in the EU some 15 electricity TSOs and eight gas TSOs are considered as 'independent' due to ownership unbundling.[17] Another tendency, possibly the result of ownership unbundling concerns, is the further integration of grid companies.

On 13 July 2009 the EU adopted new legislation bringing the EU liberalization process one step further. As in previous Directives, unbundling is a key issue. Although the initial aim was to require member states to introduce an even stricter unbundling regime, implying divestiture of some of the assets of the company (ie ownership unbundling), the final negotiated agreement permits member states the choice between three options.

C. The new unbundling rules of the 'Third Energy Package'

1. *Third Energy Package*

Several member states for various reasons decided that legal and functional unbundling do not achieve an adequate level of independence, and have therefore opted voluntarily for ownership unbundling. These measures are in line with

---

[16] I. del Guayo, C. Redgwell, M. Roggenkamp, A. Rønne, 'Energy Law in Europe: Comparisons and Conclusions' in *Energy Law in Europe: National, EU and International Regulation* (M. Roggenkamp, C. Redgwell, I. del Guayo, A. Rønne, eds, 2nd edn, 2007) 1265. See also Platts, EU Energy, Issue 72–73, 19 December 2003, 30.

[17] Platts, EU Energy, 209, 5 June 2009.

the EC's view that the provisions of the 2003 Directives did not ensure a well-functioning market as: i) the TSO may treat its affiliate companies better than competing parties; ii) under the 2003 Directives unbundling rules, non-discriminatory access to information cannot be guaranteed as limited means of preventing TSOs releasing market sensitive information to the integrated production or supply companies; and iii) investment incentives within an integrated company can be distorted.

In order to avoid these problems, the EC proposed a third legislative package for an internal EU gas and electricity market ('Third Energy Package'). Perhaps, the most essential element of this package, adopted by the EU Parliament on 22 April 2009, is the introduction of a stricter unbundling regime for vertically integrated energy undertakings (VIU).[18] Subsequently, the European Council finally adopted the package of new energy legislation and after its entry into force, member states will have 30 months to implement in national law one option from the new unbundling provisions.

2. Unbundling in the Third Energy Package

As a result of the comprehensive debate and political deliberations on the EC's proposals, the options available to member states comprise: strict ownership unbundling, the Independent System Operator and the Independent Transmission Operator.

Strict *ownership unbundling* means that member states must ensure that the same person or persons cannot exercise control over a supply undertaking and, at the same time, hold any interest in or exercise any right over a TSO; this provision also applies vice versa, that is, control over a TSO precludes the possibility of holding any interest in or exercising any right (at least a majority share) over a supply undertaking. The EC is aware of the impact of this option on property rights. Ownership unbundling may be implemented either by direct divestiture or by splitting the shares of the integrated undertaking into the shares of the network undertaking and shares of the remaining generation and supply undertaking. An amendment sought to address the situation where some member states had introduced ownership unbundling, on a different legal basis/definition. To facilitate implementation in these member states, a caveat has been included.[19]

The EC considers that ownership unbundling is the preferred option, but has provided an alternative for member states not opting for ownership unbundling. The alternative option must, however, provide the same guarantees regarding independence of network activities and the same level of incentives to network operators to invest in new infrastructure, which may benefit all competitors. This option

---

[18] Legislative Resolution of 22 April 2009 (14539/2/2008—C6 0024/2009—2007/0195 (COD)). The 2003 Directives are repealed.

[19] Art 9 of the 2009 Directive.

is known as the Independent System Operator (ISO).[20] It enables vertically integrated companies to retain the ownership of their network assets,[21] but requires at the same time that the transmission network itself is managed by an ISO, ie an undertaking or entity entirely separated from the vertically integrated company and performing all the functions of a network operator. In order to ensure that the operator remains and acts truly independently of the vertically integrated company, special regulatory control mechanisms must be put in place.

While the EC stated in September 2007 there were no alternatives to the two previous options, as the result of amendments suggested by eight member states—France, Germany, Austria, Bulgaria, Greece, Latvia, Luxembourg and Slovakia—a third alternative was presented. The common position adopted by the Council on 9 January 2008[22] forced the EC to accept a third alternative: the introduction of an Independent Transmission Operator (ITO).[23] An ITO allows TSOs to remain part of integrated undertakings but provides for detailed rules ensuring their independence, including rules on investments, day-to-day operations, compliance, supervisory board plus a specific revision clause which can lead to legislative proposals. The EC considers that these detailed rules permit an acceptable degree of effective unbundling, and that the ITO option is therefore acceptable as part of a general compromise, provided that such option is not weaker than in the common position and contains the strongest possible features that a political compromise will allow. As far as we understand, the new ITO system tries to avoid not only divestiture (ie, ownership unbundling), but also the disadvantages (from an ownership point of view) of the ISO system, whereby the operation of the network is entrusted to a separate legal entity which does not own the network. In the case of the ITO, the running of the network system is entrusted to an entity which does own the network, but which is subject to detailed rules, related to its managerial independence.

Whatever alternative is chosen, all three options provide that for sensitive managerial functions and the investment decisions, the network operator TSO is required to submit annually for approval to the national regulator, a ten-year network development plan.[24] Indeed provisions of Chapter IV of the 2009 Gas Directive, and of Chapter V of the 2009 Electricity Directive can be understood as a set of minimum rules to be applied to every TSO. The regulator must monitor and evaluate implementation of the plan, and, in the event that the network operator does not execute an investment, the national regulator may take further measures to ensure that the

---

[20] ibid Art 14.
[21] NB the legal regime for ownership of (subsoil) energy grids in the EU may differ. It seems that under the traditional rule, the land owner owns everything permanently situated in or on his land. Differences appear to exist as to what 'permanently' means. Under traditional German doctrine, eg, grids are considered to be installed only temporarily even though their life span may last for decades. Consequently, the grids are owned by their operating company.
[22] ie after the Second Reading of the European Parliament.
[23] Arts 17–22 of the 2009 Directive.
[24] Art 22 of the 2009 Directive.

investment is made. It could, for example, oblige the network operator to build/operate the new assets or to accept the financing/constructing of them by any third party.[25]

3. An assessment

The original provisions of the draft Directives of 2007 contained innovative aspects by comparison with previous Directives. Yet, the ITO alternative is no more than a reinforced functional unbundling, with tougher rules to monitor the relationship between network and supply businesses. Obviously, the ownership unbundling, as already adopted in a number of EU member states, is still a possibility, but not as a compulsory alternative. Theoretically, ownership unbundling was not to be compulsory but it became so in practical terms, since the ISO alternative was not popular among existing member states.[26]

D. Unbundling and (national) property rights

Unbundling with its many facets and ownership unbundling raise a number of critical points as to property protection. In considering these, regard should be had to the common tradition of property protection within the essential European constitutional framework. Its basic ingredients are that, in principle, private property is generally protected against taking by the state; it is equally well established that private property can be expropriated by the state on grounds of public interest, provided that adequate compensation is afforded. The legislature also has the power to determine limitations concerning the use of property.

Beyond these generally undisputed tenets of property protection there are 'grey zones' of key relevance to issues of unbundling and property protection. First, what is to be regarded as 'property' other than corporeal objects; for example, are intangible rights (voting rights) attached to corporate shares also to be considered as 'property'? Secondly, where does the demarcation exist between 'expropriation' (subject to compensation) and 'determination of limits to the use of property' (generally not subject to compensation)? Thirdly, there are the elements and requirements of 'proportionality', and fourthly, the function of compensation. Compensation issues centre on the basic question whether property protection primarily aims at protecting the holder against loss of the substance of property or protecting against pecuniary losses.

These issues resonate in the discussion about ownership unbundling. Countries opposing ownership unbundling argued, amongst other things, that ownership unbundling is unconstitutional, since it violates the fundamental

---

[25] Art 22 para 7 of the 2009 Directive.
[26] See, further, on the issues involved by unbundling in EU law and various national laws <www.unecom.de>, the website of a research programme, led by the Jacobs University Bremen, Vienna University of Economics and Businesses, the University of Tilburg, Delft University of Technology, and Ruhr University Bochum.

right to property, imposing an expropriation with no compensation. In contrast to this position, other countries have argued that such a violation would only occur if network owners (or the owners of network companies) were forced by the Directive to sell their assets at less than the full market value. It is argued that this situation will not arise since sales of network and/or generation assets must be at full value. Consequently ownership unbundling cannot be considered an expropriation. Rather, it should be understood as a compulsory sale at market value, executed in the interests of the public good of market liberalization.

Two different approaches to the intersection of property protection and ownership unbundling that reflect such arguments are outlined below. First, ownership unbundling has been most thoroughly scrutinized in Germany and thus it may serve as an exemplary application of the property protection principles. By contrast, ownership unbundling may be primarily viewed from the perspective of the state's strategic interest in energy infrastructure, and in this respect the Netherlands can serve as a case study.

IV. EU property rights and ownership unbundling

A. Introduction

All unbundling options of the new EU Directive have a more or less severe impact on the VIU, its assets and on the exercise of its proprietary functions. This section takes a closer look at primary EU law in considering whether the measures constitute an inadmissible infringement of property rights. Thereafter we discuss the impact of EU anti-trust law on unbundling. At this point it appears appropriate to note that ownership unbundling is already a reality under present EU procedural antitrust law—apart from being implemented on a voluntary basis in some member states. Finally, we discuss the impact of the European Human Rights Convention.

B. The role of Art 295 ECT

As a general rule the ECT does not regulate national property rights. Art 295 ECT clearly states that 'this Treaty shall in no way prejudice the rules in Member States governing the system of property ownership'. Hence, EC law may govern the liberalization of the energy sector but does not regulate the way ownership of the sector is organized, ie EC law must not require the privatization of national energy companies.

Some commentators also regard Art 295 ECT as an impediment to ownership unbundling.[27] The validity of this argument is questionable. Art 295 ECT certainly

---

[27] J. F. Baur, K.U. Pritzsche, S. Pooschke and F. Fischer, *Eigentumsentflechtung der Energiewirtschaft durch Europarecht—Mittel, Schranken und Rechtsfolgen* (2008) 22.

was designed to respect member states' economic philosophies in respect of their ownership implications (private–public), but the European Court of Justice (ECJ) has narrowed the impact of Art 295 ECT by stating that the national ownership concepts are subject to the principles of the Treaty, eg the basic freedoms and the prohibition to discriminate.[28] In particular, the exercise of property functions may be restricted by Community action in order to advance the goals of the Treaty.[29] This means that neither the ISO- nor the ITO-model can be deemed to violate Art 295 ECT. Strict ownership unbundling appears to be a situation closer to the borderline. From a constructive viewpoint the rationale underlying Art 295 ECT obviously was and still is to prevent the EU from interfering with member states' property regimes by ordering the transfer (transaction between transferor and transferee) of property (in particular from public to private ownership or vice versa).[30] Unbundling, however, only focuses on the losing part (transferor). Divestiture or loss is the objective in itself, not accrual of property to any other specified individual or entity. Hence, removal of ownership is not motivated by a move to redistribute property as a matter of general economic policy but, instead, by a specific public interest (enhancement of competition in the network-bound energy industry). Art 295 ECT therefore cannot be considered to be an obstacle to ownership unbundling in the EU.

C. Unbundling under EU antitrust law

Despite objections raised by some member states to ownership unbundling, it is already being applied under current procedural law. Under Art 7 para 1 of Regulation 1/2003[31] the Commission may, in case an infringement of Art 81 or 82 ECT, require the undertaking or association of undertakings to terminate the infringement. The Commission's powers include the authority to impose behavioural or structural remedies. All remedies are subject to the principle of proportionality.

Structural remedies may be imposed only where either there is no behavioural remedy available or where any behavioural remedy would be more burdensome for the undertaking concerned than would a structural remedy.[32] Without a doubt, structural remedies will regularly result in restrictions, if not taking, of property. Not surprisingly, the explicit mentioning of the principle of proportionality in the antitrust unbundling provision of Art 7 of Regulation 1/2003 already highlights the key issue at stake in the discussion on ownership unbundling, ie the question of proportionality.

---

[28] See Case C-302/97, *Klaus Konle v Republic of Austria* (1999) ECR I-3099, 3134, marg N 38.

[29] See Case C-309/96, *Daniele Annibaldi v Sindaco de Comune di Guidonia and Presidente Regione Lazio* (1977) ECR I-7493, 7512 marg N 23 (common agricultural market).

[30] The historic purpose of Art 295 ECT was to commit the EU to respect the basic economic traditions (private-public economy).

[31] Council Regulation (EC) No 1/2003 of 16 December 2002 on the implementation of the rules on competition laid down in Arts 81 and 82 EC Treaty.

[32] Art 7 para 1 sent 3 Reg 1/2003.

The degree of voluntariness exercised in making a self-commitment by the aggrieved party is a different aspect of proportionality which has been explored by the Commission in a recent decision involving an unbundling commitment by Germany's biggest energy undertaking, E.ON AG, Düsseldorf. The decision turned upon the Commission's reading of Art 9 para 1 of Regulation 1/2003.[33] Art 9 provides the Commission with the power to adopt a decision to make commitments offered by an undertaking binding when it intends to issue a decision ordering the termination of restrictive practices and where the undertaking involved offers commitments to meet the concerns expressed by the Commission in its preliminary assessment. Among the commitments offered by E.ON, *inter alia*, was divestiture of its high-voltage transmission grid. The Commission underlined the voluntary character of the commitment as a factor contributing to the proportionality of the divestiture in conjunction with other aspects such as the difficulty of monitoring behavioural obligations.

The decision has been criticized in particular for not applying the proportionality principle with regard to structural measures as strictly within Art 9 as it is applied within Art 7 of Regulation 1/2003[34]. In addition, there is the lingering suspicion that the Commission, by embarking on the Art 9 procedure on the executive level, tries to attain its political objective of a clear-cut ownership unbundling which it has failed to attain at the legislative level. The suspicion is certainly not mitigated by the fact that in March 2009 the Commission and RWE, Germany's second-largest energy company, concluded a similar arrangement under Art 9 of Regulation 1/2003 involving RWE's commitment to divest itself of its high-pressure gas transmission network.[35]

The enforcement regime of Arts 7 and 9 of Regulation 1/2003 obviously has not encountered opposition with regard to the aspect of property protection. This can be explained on the ground that divestiture within Art 7 constitutes a sanction for a proven infringement of Art 81 or Art 82 ECT and within Art 9 is the object of a voluntary offer in view of a presumed infringement. The elements of individual accountability (Art 7) and attributability (Art 9: '*volenti non fit iniuria*') are absent in the unbundling scheme presented by the Third Energy Package. It appears that ownership unbundling, as an instrument of competition policy within the electricity and gas sector generally, raises more serious doubts as to property protection than divestiture orders that are designed to sanction individual conduct on the part of the owner.[36]

---

[33] EC-Commission, Decision of 26 Nov 2008—COMP/39.388 and COMP/39.389 (*Deutscher Stromgroßhandels- und Regelenergiemarkt*).

[34] See A. Klees, 'Das Instrument der Zusagenentscheidung der Kommission und der Fall E.ON "– Ein (weiterer) Sündenfall"' in *Wirtschaft und Wettbewerb* (WuW) (2009) 374.

[35] EC-Commission, Decision of 18 March 2009—COMP/B-1/39402-RWE.

[36] Baur, Pritzsche, Pooschke and Fischer (above n 27) at 68 explicitly reject any analogy between Art 7 Reg 1/2003 and the general discussion on unbundling of energy undertakings.

D. Property protection under EU Law with reference to the European Human Rights Convention: key elements

1. Introduction

In the absence of a codified catalogue of human rights as part of EU law, over the years the ECJ has developed a set of principles in relation to the protection of human rights, including property, on a case-by-case basis as part of primary community law. These principles have been formed in accordance with the legal traditions of EU member states and with reference to the European Convention on Human Rights and its First Protocol.[37] The right of property is well established in primary EU law.[38] This protection is further reflected in the provisions of the European Charter of Fundamental Rights, which is considered an authoritative source of European human rights law even though it will become directly binding EU law only after the Lisbon Treaty has entered into force. The realm of property protection, ie the notion of property, has been understood by the ECJ in a broad sense. 'Property' in this concept encompasses all proprietary interests exclusively attributed to a given person.[39] 'Person' is understood as being either a natural person or a legal entity, for instance a corporation. Since all three unbundling options (strict ownership unbundling, ISO, ITO) will impact upon the exercise of proprietary functions as to the transmission grids by the VIU, the realm of 'property' held by the VIU itself is affected. Indirectly, the same is true of the shareholder's interest in the parent company (VIU).

2. Distinction between taking (expropriation) and (mere) restriction of property

Under ECJ case law, the impact at law for determining the legal effect of interferences with a person's property will turn upon whether the relevant legislative or executive action has to be categorized as taking of property (expropriation) or as a mere restriction on the use of property.[40] Any action by a Community organ that results in the loss of legal ownership is permissible only upon payment of adequate compensation.[41]

This, however, does not only apply to expropriation in a formal sense, ie the authoritative transfer of property from a person to a public entity or to a third person. In keeping with practices established by the ECJ on human rights under Art 1 of the First Protocol of the European Convention on Human Rights, the

---

[37] Art 6 para 2 EU Treaty commits the EU to respect the basic rights as guaranteed by the European Convention on Human Rights.

[38] See Case 44/79, *Liselotte Hauer v Land Rheinland-Pfalz* (1979) ECR-3227, 3746, marg N 19 (1979).

[39] See Baur, Pritzsche, Pooschke and Fischer (above n 27) at 22.

[40] See Case 44/79, *Liselotte Hauer v Land Rheinland-Pfalz* (1979) ECR-3227, 3746, marg N 19 (1979); Case C-347/03, *Regione autonoma Friuli-Venezia Giulia—Agenzia reginale per lo sviluppo rurale (ERSA) v Ministero delle Politiche Agricole e Forestali* (2005) ECR I-3785, 3867 s, marg N 119 ss (2005).

[41] See ibid at 3868.

ECJ has extended the notion of expropriation to so-called *de facto* expropriations, ie restrictions on the use of property, which—while leaving the formal ownership position untouched—deprive the owner of all reasonable alternatives of using the property or of marketing it.[42]

State interferences with property that do not amount to a *de jure* or *de facto* expropriation are categorized by the ECJ as mere restrictions of property, eg, a regulatory prohibition to use certain names for products (wine).[43] Mere restrictions do not entail an obligation to compensate for the economic loss such restrictions may cause.

3. *The public interest, in particular the Community interest*

Restrictions upon the use of property may be imposed, provided they correlate with Community objectives serving the public interest. The most obvious forms of Community objectives are those enunciated in the Union Treaty (Art 2) and the ECT (Art 2), eg, the realization of an internal market or a high level of environmental protection.

4. *The principle of proportionality*

The necessary link between the action interfering with a person's property and the pursuit of Community objectives is the principle of proportionality as laid down in Art 5 para 3 ECT. Its elements are threefold: a) the action has to be appropriate for achieving the objective, b) it has to be necessary for achieving the objective pursued, and c) there has to be an adequate relationship between the adverse effect of the action on the one hand and the objective itself (proportionality in the narrow sense: end-means relationship).

The ECJ has elaborated upon the principle of proportionality and its prerequisites over many years in a series of decisions, and has recently outlined more clearly how such principles operate in cases where fundamental rights are at stake.[44] At the same time the Court has consistently underlined the considerable margin of assessment the EU law making bodies enjoy in handling the principle of proportionality.[45]

As a general conclusion the ECJ's practice concerning alleged cases of infringement of fundamental rights by Community action (legislation) is characterized by a considerable degree of restraint. This approach has been criticized by German writers[46] who—in line with the German Federal Constitutional Court—advocate

---

[42] See ibid at 3868, marg n 122.

[43] See *Regione autonoma* (above n 40) at 3785.

[44] See, eg, Cases C-20/00 and C-64/00 *Booker Aquaculture Ltd (Marine Harvest Mc Connell)* and *Hydro Seafood Ltd v The Scottish Ministers* (2003), ECJ I-7411, 7474 ss, marg N 67 ss.

[45] See, eg, Case C-280/93, *Bundesrepublik Deutschland v Rat der Europäischen Union* (1994), ECR I-4973, 5068, marg N 90 ss.

[46] See, eg, Th. von Danwitz, *Der Grundsatz der Verhältnismäßigkeit im Gemeinschaftsrecht*, in: *Europäisches Wirtschafts- und Steuerrecht (EWS)* (2003) 393, with further references.

a more active use of the principle in favour of striking down statutory provisions as incompatible with European fundamental rights. One reason for this restraint may be the more dynamic character of Community interests as compared with national public interests. Within the balancing process inherent in the proportionality test these Community interests generally tend to have the upper hand over property and pecuniary interests. Experience suggests that this will also be relevant for the Community interest of creating a functioning internal energy market. Not surprisingly complaints against Community action based upon an alleged infringement of freedom of profession or property right have not been successful so far.

E. Property protection and the Third Energy Liberalization Package

There is no question that the restrictions imposed under each of the three unbundling options on the property held by the VIU itself or by the individual shareholders constitute a serious interference with the property sphere of property holders concerned: either the ownership is formally lifted (strict ownership unbundling) or the owner, while retaining the property formally is deprived of essential functions connected to corporate property, eg in particular decision-making on investments (ISO and ITO options). In the latter option, the remaining formal ownership is to a large extent hollow. Assuming that the unbundling alternatives can be regarded as a *de jure* or at least a *de facto* expropriation their introduction is not coupled with a compensation scheme and, for that reason, constitutes a violation of the fundamental right of property. It is true that the VIU and the shareholders still derive economic benefits from their ownership position when unbundling is implemented (purchase price in case of strict unbundling, yield under the ISO and ITO options). From this perspective there would be need for residual compensation since the purchase price may be lower than the market value and the yield achieved by the investment decisions of the ISO and the ITO may not amount to what would have been achievable through investments directly implemented by the VIU.

The Community interests identified in the new Directives such as the well-functioning of an internal electricity and gas market (recitals 4b and 5) and the promotion of investments in network infrastructure (recital 8) certainly are *valid public interests* to support Community action as such.

The most difficult aspect of property-related evaluation of the unbundling options lies, however, in the *proportionality principle*. Unlike the assessment in the context of Art 7 and Art 9 of Regulation 1/2003 where a concrete, individual case situation is to be dealt with, the new Directives bring about an across-the-board systematic regime change applicable to all member states. These member states represent widely differing property concepts with regard to their energy undertakings—a situation which is bound to result in differing impacts of the new EU unbundling regime. Any evaluation, consequently, is confined to generalities with a considerable speculative element. This certainly relates to the first prerequisite: the *appropriateness* of the regime change. It can, of course, be presumed that a clearer separation between the production and supply levels (competition) on the one hand and the network level (monopoly) on the other will contribute to eliminate anti-competitive practices. Unbundling may, however, have different effects according to whether integrated ownership is public or private. Despite the required instalment of two separate public bodies for generation/supply and transmission, the ultimate responsibilities converge in the public sector and, thus, are not strictly separated. This in itself may give rise to legal problems arising out of the discriminatory effects such a regime change will have on the different existing—private or public—national ownership patterns. Whether, as recital 8 asserts, the implementation of the unbundling regime will promote investments in (trans-border) networks, may be speculative. However, it is possible that the experiences in those member states who have voluntarily introduced ownership unbundling can be applied as an example or yardstick.

Even more difficult is the assessment of *necessity*. The imposition of the unbundling regime—in staged intensity for the three options: strict ownership unbundling, ISO, ITO—would not be necessary and therefore disproportionate if—as an alternative—a milder instrument were available that would yield at least the same results as the implementation of the unbundling options. One alternative would possibly be to extend the trial period of the existing regime in order to have a better basis for evaluating the potential defects of the current situation. If need be, one could envisage partial amendments and a more rigid enforcement strategy. It has to be noted in this context that the Commission, after presentation of its proposals in 2007, has been sharply criticized for the defects in its empirical findings and database.[47] The tightening of the regulatory enforcement system, in particular the creation of ACER (Agency for the Cooperation of Energy Regulators), which is now part of the new Directive in addition to the unbundling regime, might have been in itself an alternative, at least for the time being. The proportionality principle also encompasses a time element: if improvements through the use of existing tools, including some narrow amendments appear possible, the legislature may postpone an incisive regime change the effects of which are highly speculative. The analysis of the regime change therefore is fraught with uncertainties. Such uncertainties will be multiplied when it comes to an assessment of the third prerequisite: the adequacy of the *end-means relationship*. It is submitted, however, that it will be exactly this plethora of uncertainties that would prevent the ECJ from striking down the Directive as violating the principle of property protection.

---

[47] See Baur, Pritzsche, Pooschke and Fischer (above n 27) at 52.

V. Unbundling in Germany and in German constitutional property protection

A. The German situation at the transmission level

The situation in Germany differs to some extent from other EU member states. First, and in contrast with other member states, there are several transmission system companies. The high-voltage electricity transmission system is owned and operated by four undertakings (E.ON AG, RWE AG, EnBW AG, Vattenfall Europe AG) through their transmission subsidiaries—as result of legal unbundling requirements. In the gas sector, the high-pressure long-distance pipelines are owned and operated by roughly eight undertakings, mostly affiliated with the electricity sector. The main gas pipeline operators are E.ON Ruhrgas, RWE and Verbundnetz Gas (VNG). Secondly, the ownership of these transmission companies is usually privately held. On the transmission level there is therefore no discussion about privatization. Thirdly, we have seen above that ownership unbundling is taking place not as a result of implementing Directives or as a government initiative, but as a result of antitrust actions on EU level. The government is in fact one of the fierce opponents to further unbundling and one of the initiators of the third unbundling alternative ITO. One of the main arguments against further unbundling was based on an infringement of property rights—an understandable argument in light of the specific German situation.

B. Unbundling in the light of property protection

1. Interaction between EC property protection principles and German constitutional property protection principles

Before discussing German principles of constitutional property protection it has to be clarified whether German constitutional law is applicable at all in addition to European principles of property protection.

It is by now an established rule both in the case law of the ECJ[48] and of the German Federal Constitutional Court (Bundesverfassungsgericht, BVerfG)[49] that European secondary legislation (Directives, regulations) can be judicially reviewed only on the basis of European principles of fundamental rights protection. It is true, however, that the BVerfG has left open a back door for reviewing European secondary legislation under German constitutional standards in

---

[48] See Case C-540/03, *European Parliament v Council of the European Union* (2006), ECR I-5769, marg n 105.

[49] Decision of the BVerfG of 22 October 1986 (*Solange II*), Amtliche Sammlung der Entscheidungen des BVerfG (Official Collection of the Decisions of the BVerfG), BVerfGE 73, 339, 387; Decision of 7 June 2000 (*Bananenmarktordnung*), BVerfGE 102, 147, 162.

case the level of European protection should significantly fall below the level of German protection—a proviso with some impact upon the course of events leading up to the Third Energy Package as discussed further below.

The situation is different, however, with regard to constitutional review of German implementing legislation. Here it depends on whether the underlying EU Directives are compulsory or whether they leave scope for the national legislatures. If not, ie to the extent Directives are compulsory, German implementation legislation is not subject to judicial review under German principles, but only under European standards. Things are different to the extent that European legislation gives the German legislature a margin of independent decision-making. Within this margin the German legislature can choose. In doing so, the legislature is bound by national (German) standards of fundamental rights protection. Where European Directives leave room, eg, by granting options to member states, it may be that on the implementation level the range of options is narrowed because one of the options is incompatible with German national standards.[50]

This basic German position on the relationship between EU law and German (constitutional) law, however, has to be supplemented by one aspect which obviously played a role in the Community's (Commission's) political strategy concerning ownership unbundling.

The German BVerfG, while recognizing the supremacy of EU law even over German constitutional law and, thereby, supremacy of ECJ fundamental rights review over that of the BVerfG, added a reservation. In its landmark *Maastricht* decision of 12 October 1993[51] the Court claimed a reserve competence for fundamental rights control if the general level of fundamental rights protection within the EU should fall behind the standard of protection required by the Constitution and in the protection of the essentiality of fundamental rights.[52] In later decisions the BVerfG declined to exercise fundamental rights control following the reasoning of its *Maastricht* dictum.[53] Nonetheless, the Community organs dealing with ownership unbundling were obviously well aware of the position of the BVerfG on the existence of a reserve competence and the unclear prerequisites of its implementation. Hence, there was a lingering apprehension on the European level that perhaps the compulsory introduction of strict ownership unbundling relatively soon after the second generation of Directives (2003) had become operative would be regarded as disproportionate and trigger fundamental rights control by the BVerfG under the reserve competence.[54]

---

[50] See decision of the BVerfG of 18 July 2005 (*EU Haftbefehl*), BVerfGE 113, 273, 300; Baur, Pritzsche, Pooschke and Fischer (above n 27) at 25.

[51] BVerfGE 89, 155 ss.

[52] BVerfGE 89, 174 ss.

[53] BVerfG, Neue Juristische Wochenschrift (NJW) (2000), 2015; BVerfGE 102, 147.

[54] On 30 June 2009, the BVerfG confirmed its position in *Maastricht* in another landmark decision involving the constitutionality of the Lisbon Treaty and the accompanying ratification legislation.

In the present case of unbundling the EU has made it compulsory for member states that network operation has to be independent of the competitive branches of energy supply (generation, distribution). To achieve that objective the EU legislature, however, granted three options (strict ownership unbundling, ISO, ITO). Whether the German legislature may fully use this margin, depends on German constitutional principles in general and on the property protection principles in particular.

2. *Principles of German property protection*

(a) **Article 14 Basic Law**

The normative basis for constitutional property protection is to be found in Art 14 Basic Law (BL). The provision reads:

> (1) Property and the right of inheritance shall be guaranteed. Their content and limits shall be defined by the laws.
> (2) Property entails obligations. Its use shall also serve the public good.
> (3) Expropriation shall only be permissible for the public good. It may only be ordered by or pursuant to a law that determines the nature and extent of compensation. Such compensation shall be determined by establishing an equitable balance between the public interest and the interests of those affected. In case of dispute respecting the amount of compensation, recourse may be had to the ordinary courts.

The Constitution thus distinguishes between two kinds of restriction of property:

- the determination of content and limits (*Inhalts- und Schrankenbestimmung*, Art 14 para 1, sentence 2 BL), and
- expropriation (*Enteignung*, Art 14 para 3 BL).

A textual interpretation already appears to warrant the conclusion that the difference lies in the compensation aspect: Art 14 para 1 sentence 2 BL does not say anything about compensation, whereas Art 14 para 3 BL deals with compensation quite explicitly. Modern case law as it has emanated from the BVerfG has extensively tried to demarcate the realms of both paragraphs of Art 14 BL.

(b) **The relationship between determination of content and limits of property and expropriation**

Modern case law under the leadership of the BVerfG has developed a rather formal and narrow notion of expropriation as addressed by Art 14 para 3 BL:

Expropriation means a deprivation of property in an individual case directed at a transfer of property from one person to another in order to achieve an objective of public interest.[55]

This means that all general restrictions of property imposed by law only constitute a determination of content and limits in the sense of Art 14 para 1 sentence

---

[55] See the landmark decision of 15 July 1981 (*Nassauskiesung*), BVerGE 58, 300.

2 BL.[56] There is no such thing as a regulatory expropriation or taking by statute. The German system of property protection therefore differs from European law.

(c) The proportionality principle

The proportionality principle also plays a crucial role in German constitutional law. It is relevant on two levels:

- A restriction on property effected by a state organ is lawful only if it meets the standard of proportionality. Its elements (appropriateness, necessity, adequate end-means relationship) are the same as in European law.
- In case a restriction is proportionate under these prerequisites, it may entail compensation even if it is not an expropriation (Art 14 para 3 BL) but (only) a determination of content and limits (Art 14 para 1 sentence 2 BL). Here the proportionality test intervenes on the second level. If a statutory restriction is so severe that it exceeds the limits of reasonableness for the owner, proportionality requires that the 'victim' has to be compensated (so-called 'ausgleichspflichtige Inhalts- und Schrankenbestimmung').[57] Methodologically, the aspect of compensation in such situations is part of the proportionality principle in order to make an otherwise disproportionate restriction proportionate.

This makes the difference between the ECJ and the German concept apparent. The link between expropriation, dynamic Community interests, a reduced concept of proportionality—Art 5 para 3 ECT only mentions the element of necessity—and the limited role of compensation as a mere consequence of expropriation tends to narrow the ambit of property protection. On the other hand, the separation of protection from expropriation, the extension of the three-tier principle of proportionality to all restrictions of property and the enhanced function of compensation not only as a consequence of expropriation but also as a balancing factor within the principle of proportionality outside expropriation tends to widen property protection. This wider concept has led German courts to strike down quite a number of statutory provisions on the grounds of unlawful infringement of property, particularly in the conflict area of property versus environmental protection.

C. The different models of unbundling in light of German constitutional principles of property protection

Both the ISO- and the ITO-models mean that the VIU would lose essential corporate influence on the network operator while it retains the ownership *per se*. Strict ownership unbundling would mean that, in addition, the VIU would be deprived of its formal ownership. From the principles under German law as described above it would appear that as long as there are instruments available that have a milder

---

[56] See the decision of 9 January 1991 (*Vorkaufsrecht*), BVerfGE 83, 201, 211.
[57] See, eg, BVerfG decision of 2 March 1999 (*Rheinland-pfälzisches Denkmalschutzgesetz*), BVerfGE 100, 226, 244.

impact upon the corporate structures (vertical integration) the variant 'strict ownership unbundling' (loss even of formal property) would have to be considered as not necessary and therefore disproportionate. This is exactly the reason why the Commission, from the beginning, cushioned its pro-strict ownership unbundling stance with the ISO variant and later the even milder ITO option was added. Even though the final result is a political compromise, it also reflects some legal logic within the property protection concept. The unknown factor, however, is the uncertainty about the relative ability of the options to enhance competition.

When it comes to the choice between the ISO- and the ITO-models the proportionality test is far less clear-cut. Moreover, the final judgement will depend on the details of the implementation statute.

The ISO- and the ITO-models alike seriously impact upon corporate rights of the VIU pertaining to the operation of the network. At the same time the shareholders of the VIU are also seriously affected in their participatory function, eg decision-making through exercise of their voting rights, as to network operations. In view of the seriousness of these impacts of both models the German legislature when implementing these models could be held obligated to make provisions for residual compensation under the principles of property protection as discussed in Section V.2.b and c, above.

It is also established law that the 'reliance principle' which is an element of the 'rule of law' principle enshrined in Art 20 para 3 BL requires the legislature in situations where a systematic change of law is enacted to provide for transitional norms in order to secure a 'smooth transition' for existing rights.[58]

D. Concluding remarks

The preceding discussion of EU and German property protection principles has shown the significance and complexity of the problem of ownership unbundling from the perspective of a member state like Germany which is endowed with a highly sophisticated system of fundamental rights protection in general and of property protection in particular. This legal situation has developed its political implications and contributed to a more differentiated set of options rather than to a radical and strict ownership unbundling.

VI. Ownership unbundling in the Netherlands

A. Introduction

This section presents the developments in the Netherlands, which to an important extent differ from the situation in Germany both as regards the organization

---

[58] See decision of 9 January 1991 (above n 56).

of the energy market and the discussion about property rights in relation to the unbundling of energy companies. The issue of property rights has been discussed more in relation to the ownership of electricity and gas distribution grids and less in relation to property protection.

By contrast to Germany, the number of TSOs is limited to two: one share-holding company responsible for electricity transmission and one responsible for high-pressure gas transport. Before the liberalization process started only the latter entity was partly privately owned (see further below). The distribution sector was horizontally integrated and gradually transferred into shareholding companies as of the 1970s. The shares in these companies were held by lower governments (municipalities or provinces). From the beginning of the liberalization process the Dutch government has gone beyond the minimum requirements of the Directives. As a result, it introduced legal unbundling while implementing the ED 1996 and GD 1998 or soon thereafter. Moreover, ownership unbundling was introduced on a voluntary basis for the entire network-bound energy sector, starting with the electricity transmission sector in 2000 and followed by the gas transmission sector in 2005. The unbundling at a shareholders' level on transmission level went without any major debate and led to a situation that the TSOs actively operate as infrastructure companies. However, it might be debated whether a particular activity (such as the assignment of supplier of last resort or developing subsoil gas storages) is an infrastructure or a commercial supply activity.

More recently, the Dutch government has also decided to implement ownership unbundling at the distribution level. The reasons for doing so are twofold. First, it aims to create more financial and market transparency as a result of which the grid companies will focus on their core-business (ie operation of the grid) only. Secondly, it aims to facilitate some degree of privatization of the distribution companies and that involves the possibility to privatize only the commercial supply companies, as the ownership of the network companies should stay in the hands of the government.

By contrast to the ownership unbundling on transmission level, the proposal to create ownership unbundling on distribution level led to an intense debate including the issue of property rights and the question whether this type of unbundling in fact should be considered as expropriation. Following the main principles of property protection, Art 14 of the Dutch Constitution[59] provides that:

Expropriation may take place only in the public interest and on prior assurance of full compensation, in accordance with regulations laid down by or pursuant to Act of Parliament. [...] In the cases laid down by or pursuant to Act of Parliament there shall be a right to full or partial compensation if in the public interest the competent authority destroys property or renders it unusable or restricts the exercise of the owner's rights to it.

---

[59] The Constitution dates from 1814, but was largely rewritten in 1983.

It follows from the latter part of this provision that a limitation of a person's property right is possible if such limitation is based on an Act of Parliament, is in the public interest and is fully and partially compensated. Although the wording of this provision does not explicitly refer to property rights, it is generally assumed that it applies to property rights. The principles of the European Convention on Human Rights and its First Protocol (see above) usually play an important role in disputes about property rights between government and citizens. This is illustrated by the dispute between the four main vertically integrated energy distribution companies (Nuon, Essent, Delta and Eneco) and the government following the decision to introduce ownership unbundling at the distribution level. The Court of The Hague issued a ruling on this matter in April 2009. Given such developments, we discuss ownership unbundling, as applied in the Netherlands, its correspondence with the definition used in the Third Energy Package, how it affects the privatization process and the above-mentioned ruling of the Court of The Hague regarding the intended ownership unbundling on distribution level.

B. Ownership unbundling at the transmission level

Ownership unbundling in the Netherlands is directly linked to a discussion about privatization. According to the government the privatization of energy companies (the transfer of government ownership to private investors) could only be restricted during the process of energy market liberalization and not thereafter. Therefore any change of ownership in the energy production and supply sector during this transitional period required the permission of the Minister of Economic Affairs (MEA).[60] The first requests for privatization concerned the electricity production sector. Since neither the MEA (nor Parliament) saw any objections, permission was awarded to sell the shares in a majority of the electricity production companies.[61]

As the production companies together held all shares in the legally unbundled TSO for electricity transmission—TenneT BV—any change in ownership would have a direct effect on the ownership situation. In other words, the privatization of the majority of the shares in TenneT would result in a situation where foreign energy companies also would hold a majority share in TenneT. As this was considered unfavourably, it was decided by Act of 21 December 2000[62] that the state would purchase all shares of the network company TenneT.[63] In 2001 the state (Ministry of Finance) bought all shares in TenneT for the amount of €1.157.00

---

[60] Art 93 E-Act and Art 85 G-Act.

[61] Three out of four companies—UNA, EZH and EPON—were sold around the year 2000 to E.ON (Germany), Electrabel (Belgium/France) and Reliant (USA). Some years later Reliant sold its shares again to the Dutch energy distribution company Nuon.

[62] Stb 2000, 607. This Act also provides a solution for the non-commercial stranded costs made by these companies.

[63] Art 10 of the Act of 21 December 2000, Stb 607. Since then the E-Act states in general that the state holds all shares in TenneT (Art 93a E-Act). In 2005 the legal structure of TenneT changed

(NLG 2,550,000). Currently, the company TenneT Holding BV holds all shares in TenneT TSO BV which is not only responsible for the management of the original high-voltage grid but, in addition, has been charged by a law of 2006[64] with the management of all grids of 110 kV and more. As a result, energy distribution companies have been required to transfer parts of their grid management to TenneT TSO.

The gas transmission sector is organized in a different way. The discovery of the Groningen gas field in 1959 and the need to reorganize the gas sector, has resulted in an early example of a public–private partnership as the shares in the gas transmission and supply company NV Nederlandse Gasunie (Gasunie) were partly privately owned (25 per cent Shell and 25 per cent Exxon) and partly publicly owned (directly and indirectly by the state). By contrast to the electricity transmission sector, no shares were held by lower governments and legal unbundling was not intended at the beginning of the liberalization process. To start with there was administrative and accounting unbundling and Chinese walls between transmission and supply. In order to provide market parties with more transparency, Gasunie started on its own initiative to increase the level of unbundling.[65] Following a change of government in 2002, the new MEA aimed at more liberalization and thus a complete restructuring of Gasunie involving ownership unbundling.[66] On the basis of this idea, the government started to negotiate the intended unbundling with the shareholders Shell and Exxon. Due to uncertainty about transportation tariffs and conditions in and outside the Netherlands, and the precise content of the proposed new gas directive, the negotiations could not be concluded before the entry into force of Directive 2003/55/EC. The announcement on 1 November 2004 that shareholders had reached an agreement about the reorganization of the company[67] was nevertheless a surprise as Gasunie had just been legally unbundled.

Ownership unbundling of Gasunie was achieved on 1 July 2005, with retroactive effect as of 1 January 2005. As a result the (former) Gasunie was split up into two autonomous companies: a gas transport company that continues to operate under the name of NV Nederlandse Gasunie (and again called Gasunie), and a purchasing and sales company for natural gas, Gasunie Trade & Supply BV which was transformed into GasTerra on 1 September 2006.[68] The (new) Gasunie

---

again as the state holds all shares in TenneT Holding BV and the holding holds all shares in the network company TenneT TSO BV.

[64] Act of 23 November 2006, Stb 614. This Act also provided for ownership unbundling of the energy distribution companies.

[65] To begin with Gasunie established a separate office for transportation and ancillary services on 1 April 2000.

[66] TK 2002–2003, 28109, no 4 and TK 2003–2004, no 5 as well as TK 29372, no 10, 35 and 46. The intended ownership unbundling would result in a 100 per cent state-owned network company and a supply and trading company owned by Shell and Exxon. The latter company could ultimately be split in two in order to enhance competition in the market.

[67] TK 2004–2005, 28109, no 6.

[68] The ownership unbundling was based on Art 7:662 Dutch Civil Code governing transition of an enterprise. Personnel working for Gasunie were transferred partly to Gasunie and partly to GasTerra.

consists of all of the transport assets of Gasunie, the national transmission system operator GTS and the relevant contracts belonging to it, including those for carrying out transport services and quality conversion.[69] As part of the agreement, the state (Ministry of Finance) has become the sole shareholder of the new Gasunie as of 1 January 2005. The state paid €2.78 billion for the take-over of the shares of Shell and Exxon, after deduction of all taxes.[70] The new company is operating entirely for the account and at the risk of the state.

C. Ownership unbundling at the distribution level

1. *The background to ownership unbundling*

Soon after the privatization of the electricity production sector, the political landscape completely changed and a more critical approach regarding the need for privatization emerged. After a long debate and several changes in the legal regime, a policy was introduced that energy networks and network companies, for reasons of supply security, needed to stay in the hands of the government. In other words, energy supply companies may be privatized as long as they are unbundled at the shareholder level from the network company. In 2004 the MEA went one step further by proposing that ownership unbundling should be achieved in the entire distribution sector.

A central reason for ownership unbundling is the need structurally to safeguard the public interest in a safe, reliable and reasonable energy supply. According to the MEA it is not possible to combine free grid access and a high quality grid with the commercial interests of an integrated energy distribution company. Moreover, an integrated energy distribution company could be tempted to achieve illegitimate advantages, such as the use of the grids as a security in financial transactions. Therefore, the unbundling of integrated energy distribution companies would enhance the functioning of the Dutch energy market, as it would lead to a transparent company culture and better supervision.[71] The MEA's policy intention was backed up by a report of the energy regulator stating that as existing legislation did not guarantee complete independence of grid companies, and therefore ownership unbundling would be an option as it could guarantee such independence and simplify the regulator's task as supervisor of the energy sector.[72]

---

[69] This includes the entire high-pressure and regional pipeline networks, the associated facilities and the LNG installation on the Maasvlakte, the 60% interest of Gasunie in the interconnector or the Balgzand-Bacton pipeline (BBL), Gasunie Engineering and Gasunie Research and several assets such as the main building of Gasunie in Groningen and the trade name, 'Gasunie'.

[70] Some political parties claimed that the agreed price was too high and could constitute an (illegal) state aid. They called for an investigation. Although the Netherlands Court of Audit (Algemene Rekenkamer) was charged with this investigation, no information has been given since then on this issue.

[71] Letter of 31 March 2004 of the Minister to the President of the Lower House of Parliament; Tweede Kamer, 2003–2004, 29892, no 18 and Tweede Kamer, 2003–2004, 29892, no 29.

[72] Tweede Kamer, 2003–2004, 28982, no 24.

Gradually it had become clear that the appointment of a separate grid company (ie legal unbundling) is not sufficient to create an independent network operator. The main reason for lack of independence is the fact that the (then) MEA[73] assented to the establishment of so-called 'slim' network companies rather than the envisaged 'fat' network companies. Within the concept of a 'fat' network company, all financial and operational activities had to be conducted independently from the holding so that the network company would have sufficient financial resources available to be able to decide independently about maintenance and/or investments in the grid. A network company would, for example, have complied with these requirements if the beneficial ownership of the grid was vested in the network company so as to enable the latter to conduct an independent network management.[74] The establishment of a 'slim' network company allowed these basic tenets to be set aside, however, so that the ownership of the grids could stay on the balance sheet of the holding. Time and practice have shown that the 'slim' network companies are much less independent than the legislator had anticipated. In order to safeguard the independence of the network companies, the Gas Act and Electricity Act were amended and now explicitly provide that the network companies shall hold the beneficial ownership of all networks managed by the company.[75] For reasons mentioned above, the MEA did not consider this provision to be sufficient to create an independent network company and required ownership unbundling of all energy distribution companies, ie the need to split up the company at the shareholder level.

2. Ownership Unbundling Act

The Unbundling Act of 2006[76] prohibits that the operation of energy networks and the production, trade or supply of energy (by Dutch as well as foreign parties) is carried out within the same group of companies.[77] The intended unbundling takes place at holding level (ie central control) and will result in a situation that existing shareholders—municipalities and provinces—will hold shares in both the company (or group of companies) operating the grid and the commercial

---

[73] It should be noted that several ministers with different political backgrounds have been involved in the process of privatization and unbundling.

[74] See policy rules on the Appointment of Grid Operators of 1999, at 6 and policy rules on the Appointment of Grid Operators of 2000, at 9.

[75] Art 3b G-Act and Art 10a E-Act entered into force on 1 July 2008 for existing network operators and apply to new operators as of 1 January 2007, Stb 13. These provisions were included in the law when implementing the 2003 Directives, but did not enter into force because the legislator wanted to avoid too many reorganizations of the distribution companies.

[76] Act of 23 November 2006, 614. The entry into force of unbundling provisions was made dependent on an assessment whether a company had made investment decisions conflicting with the network interests (EK 2006–2007, 30212, H). On 3 April 2007 the minister announced that such a situation had appeared and that the necessary steps would be taken for initiating ownership unbundling of the distribution companies. See TK 2006–2007, 30212, 55.

[77] Art 10b E-Act 1998 and Art 2c G-Act, provide that a grid company is not allowed to form part of a group of companies within the meaning of Art 2:24b Dutch Civil Code.

energy supply and/or production company. In case the network company is part of a group (not being a group with commercial production and/or supply companies), this group is not allowed to perform acts or activities that may be contrary to the management interest of the grid in question. This includes all acts and activities that do not relate or are not connected to infrastructural provisions or activities, as well as the provision of security by the network operator manager for the financing of activities to be carried out by legal entities or companies that are part of the group.[78] In addition, the beneficial ownership of the grids needs to be transferred to the network operators. The purpose is to create 'pure' network companies.

The distribution companies are free to decide how such ownership unbundling will be implemented, ie whether the network or the supply company is split off from the holding company or other suitable legal arrangements are instituted.[79] It means that there will no longer be a direct legal link between the commercial production/supply company and the network company. As a result of this, the latter company can no longer be involved in the decision-making process concerning the network company. There are no objections, however, to a situation that the original shareholders (ie the national and/or lower governments) hold shares in both the independent network and independent commercial production/supply company. Ownership unbundling will thus lead to the situation before liberalization as the original shareholders (lower governments) again have a direct say in the network operations. In addition, the shareholders in the commercial supply company may decide, without any government involvement, whether they wish to sell their shares, ie to privatize the supply company.

All distribution companies are currently in the process of preparing for ownership unbundling which needs to be achieved before 1 January 2011. This includes the requirement to submit before 1 July 2009 an Unbundling Plan stating a) how the assets should be divided between the commercial supply/production company and the network company, and b) the way in which the unbundling should take place and how the unbundling costs are paid for without having an impact on the tariffs. The proposed Unbundling Plan will be presented to the Competition Authority which is entitled to amend it. The Competition Authority sends the Unbundling Plan together with its reasoned opinion to the MEA for a final decision.[80]

As the goal is to create a real independent network company, the Unbundling Act has also resulted in several further regulations describing how the network operators should act independently. Binding provisions are included in the Unbundling Regulation of July 2008.[81] In addition, the Competition Authority issued guidelines explaining which activities network operators should undertake

---

[78] Art 17 paras 2 and 3 E-Act and Art 10b G-Act.
[79] See for these unbundling variants: M. M. Roggenkamp, 'Ownership Unbundling of Energy Distribution Companies: the Netherlands' (2006) 10 IELTR 240.
[80] Art IXb jo IXa Unbundling Act.
[81] Regulation Unbundling Plans, Stc 2008, nr 140, 9

themselves in order to fulfil the legal requirements concerning 'fat' network operators.[82] Within the context of the need to establish an independent network operator, demands are made on the network operator's financial management as well. For this purpose rules are laid down in a governmental decree regarding the proper financial management by the network operator.[83] The aim is to guarantee that the network companies have sufficient financial means to be able to invest in the maintenance and upgrade of the grid. It also means then in the process of unbundling it should be avoided that any losses (other then directly connected to the network company) are put on the balance sheet of the network company. The decree includes provisions requiring network operators to fulfil certain demands with regard to their creditworthiness, including their debt/equity ratios. In December 2008 the MEA agreed to amend the original requirements as a result of which the network companies at the time of unbundling must have a debt/equity ratio of 60 per cent/40 per cent.[84]

3. *The position of the energy distribution companies*

The proposed Unbundling Act raised an intense debate in the Netherlands. Whereas the MEA was of the opinion that ownership unbundling would have a large number of positive effects such as market and financial transparency (no cross-subsidization), a clear focus on grid activities (investing in and operating the grid) and the possibility for public shareholders to withdraw from the more volatile production and supply market, the distribution companies presented a set of different arguments. They argued that ownership unbundling would trigger 'change of ownership' clauses in cross-border leases they had entered into previously with US investors and which could lead to serious penalties. In addition, they argued that ownership unbundling in fact would constitute some sort of illegal expropriation and would impede the free movement of capital and thus one of the main principles of EU law.

The energy distribution companies Delta, Essent and Eneco started proceedings against the Dutch state in August 2007 claiming unlawfulness of the provisions regarding ownership unbundling based on announcements made by the MEA that the entry into force of these provisions would depend on the adoption of the ownership unbundling provisions in the Third Energy Package. In addition, they claimed that the provisions which limit the transfer of shares to public entities in fact impedes the free movement of capital. Apart from these aspects ownership unbundling is to be considered as taking of property (expropriation) according to Art 1 of the First Protocol of the European Convention on Human Rights.[85]

---

[82] Guidelines regarding supervision of Art 16Aa E-Act and 7a G-Act, Stc 2008, nr 70, 21.

[83] Decree financial management network operator, Stb 2008, 330.

[84] Tweede Kamer, vergaderjaar 2008–2009, 31 510, nr 30.

[85] Another argument raised concerns that the impact it will have on the CBL-contracts and the fact that ownership unbundling could be considered as an 'event of loss'. This element will not be

The Court of The Hague issued a ruling on 11 March 2009.[86] It argued that an announcement made by a former minister cannot bind its successor as it only indicates a political intention. Such an announcement is a political statement and does not have the same binding force as a rule of law. The Court then stated that the ownership unbundling provisions are not contrary to Art 295 ECT as the latter provision leaves it to the member states whether or not they wish to introduce rules on privatization or not, as long as the general rules of the freedom of capital, etc, apply. As the ownership unbundling only indirectly affects the provisions in the Electricity and Gas Act on privatization (the ban on privatizing network companies) the Court did not consider it necessary to discuss the impact of Art 295 ECT. As to the question whether the ownership unbundling provisions are contrary to the fundamental freedoms of the ECT, the Court ruled that energy networks are essential for security of supply and thus of a general public interest. Therefore the Court is of the opinion that there is a valid reason to restrict the free movement of capital and require ownership unbundling so that the network companies will not be faced with commercial risks taken by the integrated commercial production and/or supply company. Finally, the Court addressed the issue of whether there was a property 'taking'. The Court argued that ownership unbundling entails the situation where the holding company no longer holds the share in the network company. However, the original shareholders will not be deprived of any ownership rights. After ownership unbundling the original shareholders—the lower governments—will still hold all shares in two independent companies instead of in one integrated company. Taking into account the reason for and proportionality of ownership unbundling and the general public interest of supply security, the Court is of the opinion that the relevant provisions in the Unbundling Act strike a fair balance between the general interests and the private interests of the energy companies.

D. Ownership unbundling in the Netherlands from an EU perspective

The new Electricity and Gas Directives of 2009 define ownership unbundling as 'the need for each Member State to ensure that the same (legal) person or persons cannot exercise control over a supply undertaking and, at the same time, hold any interest in or exercise any right over a transmission system operator or transmission system'.[87] This provision also applies vice versa, that is, control over a transmission system operator precludes the possibility of holding any interest in or exercising any right over a supply undertaking. The Directive allows for a

---

discussed further in this chapter as it seems to be a specific Dutch development and of less importance in the general discussion on ownership unbundling in the EU.

[86] *Rechtbank's Gravenhage*, case Nos 293142/HA ZA 07–2538, 296094/HA ZA 07–3089 and 306147/HA ZA 08–756.

[87] Art 9 Directive 2009/72/EC and Directive 2009/73/EC. See also above section III.A.2.

situation in which the same person holds non-controlling minority interests in both a transmission system operator and a supply undertaking. However, such a minority shareholder cannot have blocking rights in both undertakings, nor can it appoint members of their boards, nor can any person be a member of the boards of both undertakings.[88]

As the Directives with regard to ownership unbundling require that the same persons cannot exercise control over the network company as well as the commercial production/supply company it seems at first sight that the Netherlands, despite its achieved level of unbundling, would not satisfy the criteria for ownership unbundling. This is consistent with the case before the last common position. The reason is that the state holds all shares in Gasunie and a 50 per cent interest in GasTerra, and therefore would not meet the requirement that the same person is not entitled to have a direct or indirect control over the supply as well as the network company. The fact that different entities within the state hold these shares (Ministry of Finance, Ministry of Economic Affairs and the state participant EBN) is basically not relevant.[89] In order to avoid the situation that the achieved ownership unbundling of Gasunie could not be considered as ownership unbundling under EU law, the proposal for the Directive was amended in the last common position limiting the direct or indirect control to a holding of a majority share.

VII. Conclusion

During the pre-liberalization period up to the 1990s electricity and gas supply systems generally were vertically integrated and monopolistic. The natural grid monopoly determined the market structure on all value adding levels: production/import, transportation, wholesale and retail distribution. In some EU member states vertical integration was centralized (national monopolies as, eg, in France and Italy), in others decentralized (vertically integrated inter-regional, regional and local monopolies as, eg, in Germany and the Netherlands).

The key idea of liberalization was, and still is, to open the market to all levels of business, other than the unavoidable monopolistic grid, to competitive structures. The only way to ensure competition is Third Party Access (TPA) to the monopolistic grid as construction of large-scale competing grids is economically disadvantageous and ecologically unwelcome. If any value is to be seen in a competitive system, it has to be fair, non-discriminatory and undistorted. In light of vertical integration being a long-standing reality in the energy market structure, there is an inherent danger of anti-competitive practices across the different

---

[88] Art 9 of the new Directive.

[89] The outcome would be similar for the distribution sector if for any reason the same principle of ownership unbundling would apply to this sector in the future and the shares in the former integrated commercial production/supply company would not have been sold to other (private) parties. This situation is known in Brussels.

branches within the integrated company. Here the idea of unbundling comes into play: separation of the levels as to accounting (accounting unbundling), to availability of business-related information and operations (functional unbundling) and the establishment of separate legal entities (legal unbundling). These forms of separation may affect the identity of the integrated company and, thereby, infringe upon the property of the integrated entity itself and of its shareholders through, eg, loss of synergy effects. That is why the EU, in its first liberalization package (ED 1996 and GD 1998), was very careful in limiting the unbundling requirement basically to accounting.

Since the EC suspected integrated companies of distorting competition across the different levels, in particular German ones (see above section V), separation was extended to functional and legal unbundling in the second liberalization package for electricity and gas (2003).

The crucial test came with the proposal put forward in 2007 by the still unsatisfied EC to mobilize the final link of the unbundling chain: the separation of grid ownership from the integrated company (ownership unbundling). There are two main reasons why ownership unbundling raises sensitive problems: (i) it constitutes a severe interference with proprietary integrity for the company and for the shareholders alike, and (ii) it releases parts of the strategic infrastructure into the unpredictability of market economy (freedom of capital transfer). Both aspects have played a dominant role in the discussions in Germany and in the Netherlands respectively.

Property protection was by far the most contested aspect within the German discussion, both from the EU and German constitutional law perspectives. Even though both systems of fundamental rights property protection basically are very similar, and the supremacy of EU law over German constitutional law is now widely accepted, critical voices in Germany appear to have had their impact: the initial addition of the ISO option to the EC's proposals and the final acceptance of the ITO alternative are, to some extent, attributable to the intense discussion in Germany about the question whether the position preferred by the EC and by the EU Parliament—clear-cut divestiture—satisfies the requirement of property protection principles.

By contrast with the German situation, unbundling in general and ownership unbundling in particular to a large extent is seen, in the Netherlands, from the perspective of the dichotomy between public and private ownership (privatization) with the strategic national interest in energy infrastructure looming in the background. Consequently, ownership unbundling, at least by the state, appears to be viewed not primarily from the property protection angle, but as an instrument to reassert the public interest in strategic infrastructure. This has led to a considerably less antagonistic attitude by the Netherlands towards the Brussels ownership unbundling initiatives, than that taken in Germany. A further reason is that the Netherlands had already introduced ownership unbundling at the transmission level and was debating a further step as the government wished to introduce ownership unbundling at the distribution level as well. The recent discussion in the Netherlands about the possible expropriation at the distribution level as a result of unbundling appears to be relatively moderate as compared with that in Germany.

As a general conclusion it may be justified to rationalize the different approaches on the basis that, as shown by the unbundling discussion, property rights, to which a strategic public interest—security of energy supply—is attached, are relatively vulnerable when restricted by state interference in furtherance of such strategic public interest. The public interest, in whatever conceptual appearance (nationalization, proportionality), will find its way to be taken into account.

Finally, will the new 2009 Directives be the final stage of the process or will another (fourth) energy liberalization package come into effect within a couple of years? Its central point then could well be compulsory strict ownership unbundling. The course followed in the past, ie a slow step-by-step approach in matters of unbundling with options to member states, was obviously a necessary compromise between the final objective and the realities as they had developed in 27 member states. One of the central stumbling blocks was the different conceptual ideas about property protection. It will have to be seen whether compulsory ownership unbundling will be imposed. It may well be that on the basis of the realities as they will evolve under the 2009 Directives this final step will be small enough to make it digestible even from a high-level property protection and proportionality perspective.

18

The Social Obligations of Ownership and the Regulation of Energy Utilities in the United Kingdom and the European Union

Aileen McHarg*

I. Introduction: property rights and regulation

The relationship between property rights and regulation can be conceptualized in various ways. Perhaps the most common conceptualization sees property rights as a limit on regulatory action. On this, natural law,[1] approach, property rights are regarded as pre-political, and as conferring upon the owner a protected sphere of autonomy. They may therefore be invoked to resist regulatory incursions, except where these are strictly necessary to protect the public interest, and usually on payment of compensation. Stereotypically (although not entirely accurately)[2] this approach is associated with the so-called 'takings' clauses in the United States Constitution,[3] under which the courts police the boundaries between lawful and unlawful interferences with property rights, including in the notion of 'takings' not only overt deprivations, but also excessive restrictions on the use or enjoyment of property.

An alternative, positivist,[4] conceptualization, sees property rights not as prior to state regulation, but in fact constituted by it. On this view, to which most modern property theorists subscribe, property is a social institution, created in order to perform social functions. A particularly clear example is the

* Senior Lecturer in Public Law, University of Glasgow, United Kingdom; email: a.mcharg@law.gla.ac.uk.
    [1] U. Mattei, *Basic Principles of Property Law: A Comparative Legal and Economic Introduction* (2000) 4.
    [2] See, eg, J. W. Singer, *Entitlements: The Paradoxes of Property* (2000); G. S. Alexander, 'The Social Obligation Norm in American Property Law' (2009) 94 Cornell LR 745; see also F. I. Michelman, 'A Skeptical View of "Property Rights" Legislation' (1995) 6 Fordham Envtl L J 409 at 416; and see further Section II A below.
    [3] 5th and 14th Amendments.
    [4] Mattei (above n 1) at 4.

creation of property rights in atmospheric emissions permits as a technique of environmental protection.[5] From this perspective, since property rights are created by regulation, regulatory reconfigurations are presumptively legitimate, and to the extent that they receive any protection at all, this is essentially parasitic upon other constitutional values, such as protection of human dignity, non-arbitrariness or non-discrimination.[6] Nevertheless, there is still a tendency to see property rights *per se* as individualistic and self-regarding,[7] with the interests of property holders therefore sometimes coming into conflict with social goals.

Clearly, the difference between these two positions is not simply between constitutional protection of property rights or not. Not all constitutions protect property rights;[8] and of those that do, not all follow the absolutist, natural law model. For example, after guaranteeing the right to (private) property in Art 14(1), Art 14(2) of the German Basic Law states that 'Property entails obligations. Its use shall also serve the public good'.[9] Conversely, what Nedelsky describes as the 'myth of property'[10] as a pre-political right can gain strong legal protection even where there is only weak constitutional support (for example, in the United States, where property is not in fact expressly declared to be a fundamental right), or indeed none at all. Blackstone's *Commentaries*, for instance, famously described the common law concept of property as an inviolable natural right,[11] and property rights have historically secured quite strong protection against government interference in the United Kingdom's unwritten constitution via presumptions of statutory interpretation and common law controls over executive action.[12]

It is not, however, my intention in this chapter to discuss constitutional protection of property rights, nor to debate their legal origins. Rather, it explores a third conceptualization of the relationship between property rights and regulation, which departs fundamentally from the individualistic assumptions of the previous two. On this third view, property rights (at least in relation to certain types or uses of property) are regarded as necessarily carrying with them obligations of a social nature. In other words, property is regarded as a social institution not merely (or even necessarily)

[5] See L. Godden, in this volume.

[6] See J. Nedelsky, 'Should Property be Constitutionalized? A Relational and Comparative Approach' in *Property Law on the Threshold of the 21st Century* (G. E. van Maanen and A. J. van der Walt, eds, 1996) 432; A. J. van der Walt, 'The Constitutional Property Clause: Striking a Balance Between Guarantee and Limitation', in *Property and the Constitution* (J. McLean, ed, 1999) esp 127–34.

[7] cf J. B. Baron, 'The Expressive Transparency of Property' (2002) 102 Columbia LR 208 at 226.

[8] See van der Walt (above n 6) at 109–33.

[9] Discussed further in Section III A below.

[10] See J. Nedelsky, *Private Property and the Future of Constitutionalism: the Madisonian Framework and its Legacy* (1990).

[11] *Commentaries on the Laws of England* (1765–79) Vol. 2, 2.

[12] See M. Taggart, 'Expropriation, Public Purposes and the Constitution' in *The Golden Metwand and the Crooked Cord* (C. Forsyth and I. Hare, eds, 1998) 104–5.

because it is socially constituted; rather, the concept of property itself is seen as inherently relational and limited by others' interests. On this view, therefore, property rights may be regarded, in effect, as a *source* of regulatory obligations.

Concern with the social obligations of ownership in fact has a long pedigree, in both property theory and legal doctrine. Seventeenth- and eighteenth-century natural lawyers saw property rights as inherently subject to moral limits.[13] Locke, for instance, viewed original acquisitions as legitimate only if enough and as good was left for others; moreover, owners were bound by a duty of charity once their own needs were met.[14] This approach also forms an important strand in contemporary property law thinking,[15] although since it is a theory about the *content* rather than the source of property rights, it does not necessarily entail a commitment to natural law.

As far as legal doctrine is concerned, two broad methods of giving legal recognition to the social obligations of ownership can be identified. One is via constitutional permission for *legislative* imposition of duties on particular classes or uses of property; the other is by attaching general obligations to (particular classes or uses of) ownership by operation of law, their precise scope and content being determined through *adjudication*. Again broadly speaking, these correspond to the two models which, according to Samuel, underpin property concepts in Western legal thought.[16] The first derives from Roman law and influences modern civilian systems. Roman law distinguished two forms of power: *dominium* and *imperium*. Whilst *dominium* involved a unitary and exclusive notion of ownership as a matter of *private* law, property holders were not actually free to do as they pleased with their property because the power of *imperium* permitted officials to regulate it as a matter of *public* law. The second model is feudal in origin and influences modern common law systems. Feudal law differed from the Roman model in two key respects. First, in relation to land, *dominium* entailed its own form of *imperium*. Accordingly, there was no clear distinction, as there was in Roman law, between public and private law. Secondly, far from ownership being an exclusive category, the feudal model was based on the idea that people could simultaneously have different interests in the same piece of land. This produced the idea that property consists of a 'bundle of rights',[17] rather than a unitary relationship between owner and thing.

The aim of this chapter is to consider the influence of ideas about the social obligations of ownership in relation to the regulation of energy utilities in two

---

[13] See S. Coyle and K. Morrow, *The Philosophical Foundations of Environmental Law: Property, Rights and Nature* (2004) ch 2.

[14] *Two Treatises of Government* (1690) II.5.27, I.42.170.

[15] See, eg, references in n 2 above, and in nn 20–22 below.

[16] G. Samuel, 'The Many Dimensions of Property' in McLean (ed) (above n 6). See also Mattei (above n 1) ch 1; G. Amato, 'Citizenship and Public Services—Some General Reflections' in *Public Services and Citizenship in European Law* (M. Freedland and S. Sciarra, eds, 1998) 146.

[17] On which see A. M. Honoré, 'Ownership' in *Oxford Essays in Jurisprudence* (A. G. Guest, ed, 1961) 112–28.

overlapping jurisdictions: the United Kingdom (UK) and the European Union (EU). This example allows examination of both common law[18] and civilian approaches[19] to the social obligations of ownership, as well as the interaction between them. It also resonates with some of the concerns that have re-awakened interest in this issue amongst contemporary property law theorists.[20] One is environmentalism, which has led some scholars to advocate models of property rights which promote sustainability.[21] Another is the desire to counter-act the potentially adverse social consequences of privatization and liberalization policies, by using the law to promote public service values.[22] Because they provide essential services and may cause enormous environmental damage (as well as for more technical reasons), energy utilities are of course subject to extensive statutory regulation at both UK and EU levels, which has focused more closely on social and environmental objectives in recent years. I do not intend to describe or evaluate these regimes in detail. Instead, my aim is to explore how more general notions of the social obligations of ownership may support, shape and/or supplement these explicit regulatory responses.

II. The social obligations of ownership and UK energy regulation

A. Social obligations in the common law tradition

Not surprisingly, more than one conception of ownership can be found within the common law tradition. There is undeniably a strong line of thought which sees social obligations, on the Blackstonian model, as being primarily *external* to the concept of ownership; they *regulate* what can be done with property rights, but do not *define* their nature or scope.[23] Nevertheless, the common law has long

[18] NB care is required when talking about the law of the UK, which in fact has three distinct legal systems: England and Wales; Northern Ireland; and Scotland. Scots law is usually classified as a hybrid between common law and civilian systems, and Scots property law is very different to that of England and Wales and Northern Ireland. Nevertheless, Scots property law remains very strongly influenced by feudalism, and in respect of the issues covered by this chapter, it largely follows the same approach as in England and Wales.

[19] The EU is technically neutral on the question of property ownership (Treaty Establishing the European Community, Art 295). However, Section III B below will argue that the approach that has evolved bears greater resemblance to the civilian model.

[20] Another important strand is concerned with questions of distributive justice, particularly in the context of land redistribution—see, eg, A. J. van der Walt, 'Dancing with Codes: Protecting, Developing and Deconstructing Property Rights in a Constitutional State' (2001) 118 S A L J 258; G. S. Alexander and E. M. Peñalver, 'Properties of Community' (2008)10(1) Theoretical Inquiries in Law.

[21] See, eg, Coyle and Morrow (above n 13); K. Gray and S. F. Gray, 'The Idea of Property in Land' in *Land Law: Themes and Perspectives* (S. Bright and J. Dewar, eds, 1998).

[22] These debates have been focused particularly on utility industries (see references below), but are not limited to them: see, eg, K. Gray and S. F. Gray, 'Private Property and Public Propriety' in McLean (ed) (above n 6).

[23] cf Coyle and Morrow (above n 13) at 82, 160.

recognized ways in which property rights are intrinsically limited by obligations owed to others.[24] Land ownership is, for instance, subject to a general requirement of reasonable use, giving rise to liability in nuisance to those adversely affected by unreasonable uses. In addition, a number of related common law doctrines—common callings, the concept of 'business affected with a public interest', and the 'prime necessity' doctrine—have at various times and in various jurisdictions been used to impose on certain business uses of property duties to allow non-discriminatory access to services or facilities, and to charge reasonable prices.[25] These doctrines applied mainly, although not exclusively, to those with *de jure* or *de facto* monopolies in the provision of services of particular public importance.

Reflecting the absence of a clear public/private distinction in the common law, some private organizations were historically also subject to what are now classed as administrative law doctrines. For instance, the rules of natural justice were at one time widely applied to private associations to protect members against arbitrary expulsion. Similarly, the *ultra vires* rule was first developed to control (privately-owned) joint stock railway companies created by private Acts of Parliament before being extended to governmental institutions.[26]

Common law non-discrimination and fair pricing doctrines were highly influential in nineteenth-century America, where earlier British authorities were used as the basis for the development of a distinct body of public utilities law. This occurred both directly via the imposition of duties at common law, in particular by extending the notion of a common carrier to the newly developing utility industries, and indirectly by using the concept of business affected with a public interest to justify statutory price regulation under the takings clauses.[27] Despite the development of extensive statutory controls, the common law continues to be a source of legal obligations for American utilities.[28] In addition, public law remedies such as *mandamus* are available against common callings in the United States,[29] whilst utility providers may be bound by the Bill of Rights under the state action doctrine.[30]

In the UK itself (and to a lesser extent elsewhere in the common law world), however, the pattern of development was different; common law non-discrimination

[24] Other examples might include the requirement on riparian owners to respect other users' interests. Honoré also lists liability to execution for debt, to taxation and to expropriation by the state as incidents of the social aspect of ownership (above n 17) at 145.

[25] For a full account of these doctrines, see M. Taggart, 'Public Utilities and Public Law' in *Essays on the Constitution* (P. Joseph, ed, 1995). See also P. P. Craig, 'Constitutions, Property and Regulation' [1991] PL 538.

[26] Sedley LJ, 'Public Power and Private Power' in *Judicial Review and the Constitution* (C. F. Forsyth, ed, 2000) 296–8.

[27] See Taggart (above n 25). This was later superseded by a general power to regulate all businesses in the public interest: *Nebbia v New York* (1934) 291 US 502.

[28] See, eg, *Gay Law Students Association v Pacific Telegraph and Telephone Co* 595 P 2d 592 (Cal 1979).

[29] D. Oliver, *Common Values and the Public/Private Divide* (1999) 203.

[30] J. McLean, 'Public Function Tests: Bringing Back the State?' in *A Simple Common Lawyer: Essays in Honour of Michael Taggart* (D. Dyzenhaus et al, eds, 2009) 189.

and fair pricing doctrines became largely obsolete, and no equivalent body of public utilities, or public services, law developed. This was attributable partly to the
imposition of very similar duties under specific regulatory statutes,[31] and cases
brought on the basis of statutory provisions sometimes assumed that equivalent
actions would be available at common law.[32] However, the British courts, unlike
their American counterparts, actually refused to expand the category of common callings to include the new utility providers,[33] and Taggart argues that this
reflected a general trend towards an absolutist model of property rights in the UK
towards the end of the nineteenth century.[34] Dealing with the adverse social consequences of private ownership was increasingly seen as a matter for Parliament:

> But the significant statutory modifications Parliament made simply overlaid the com-
> mon law and did not change it. This reinforced the cleavage between private law and
> public law, and justified the continuation of the absolutist rhetoric.[35]

Coyle and Morrow tell a similar story in relation to the development of environmental regulation. This too came to be seen as a matter of public law, based
on essentially arbitrary policy choices, and removed from the body of doctrinal
principles governing private rights.[36] In this case, though, the law of nuisance,
albeit sidelined by statutory regulation, was never entirely eclipsed by it,[37] perhaps
because it aimed to protect the interests of other property owners. The growth of
the public/private distinction did, however, eventually curtail administrative law
regulation of private property owners. Judicial review in the UK went into a general decline in the first half of the twentieth century, and when it was revitalized
from the 1960s onwards, it was (at least in England and Wales) explicitly regarded
as a species of public law, applicable only to those performing public functions.[38]

Paradoxically, the trend towards an absolutist model of ownership and the
absence of any developed body of public utilities law in the UK was reinforced
by the preference, particularly after 1945, for nationalization instead of regulated
private ownership. Nationalization has been described as 'a great economizer of
legal friction'.[39] Since the UK's legal systems do not recognize any distinct public law of property, nationalization essentially involved taking utility industries
into the 'private' ownership of the state.[40] Whilst the nationalization statutes did

---

[31] Craig (above n 25) at 540–1; Taggart (above n 25) at 249.

[32] ibid at 237; Oliver (above n 29) at 202.

[33] M. Taggart, *Corporatization, Privatization and Public Law* (1990) 30.

[34] See M. Taggart, *Private Property and Abuse of Rights in Victorian England* (2002).

[35] ibid, 140.

[36] Above n 13 at 160. Both Coyle and Morrow (ibid, 161) and Taggart (above n 34) at 175 ascribe this trend to the influence of positivism. More accurately, however, it reflects the rise of formalism.

[37] See generally Coyle and Morrow (above n 13) ch 4.

[38] *O'Reilly v Mackman* [1983] 2 AC 237; *R v Panel on Takeovers and Mergers ex p Datafin plc* [1987] QB 815.

[39] B. Schwartz and H. W. R. Wade, *Legal Control of Government: Administrative Law in Britain and the United States* (1972) 39.

[40] Honoré (above n 17) at 146.

impose some legal obligations, these were rarely the subject of litigation, and in many cases were too vague to be enforceable. Nationalization thus relied overwhelmingly on political rather than legal controls to enforce the public service missions of the industries in question.[41] Instead of challenging the absolutist conception of property rights gaining ground in the common law, nationalization effectively reinforced it, since its answer to the inadequacy of allowing essential services to be governed by the purely selfish interests of their owners was to change the identity, and therefore the motivations, of the owners, rather than altering the inherent obligations of ownership.

Thus, by the twentieth century, the imposition of social responsibilities on property holders had come to be seen in the UK as largely a matter of political choice rather than a necessary requirement of ownership as a private law concept. Moreover, the fundamental constitutional principle of parliamentary sovereignty meant that there was no need for any legal support for legislative regulation of property rights in the form of a *constitutional* doctrine of the social obligations of ownership. Although, as noted above, the British courts did protect property rights against legislative 'interference', they did so largely covertly, in the knowledge that Parliament could always have the last word.[42] This effectively foreclosed the development of any sophisticated legal understanding of the limits of private property rights in the service of social ends.

B. The social obligations of ownership and contemporary energy regulation

Interest in the social obligations of ownership was, however, reignited towards the end of the twentieth century by the trend towards privatization and liberalization of utility services. A number of writers began to speculate about revival of the old common law non-discrimination and fair pricing doctrines, and/or argued for the extension of judicial review as means of controlling private providers of essential services and upholding public service values.[43] This was particularly strongly advocated in New Zealand, where state-owned enterprises were first corporatized and then privatized initially with no regulatory oversight except general competition law.[44]

In the UK, by contrast, privatized utilities were subject to control by independent, specialist regulatory agencies—in the energy sector, the Office of Gas Supply,

---

[41] T. Prosser, *The Limits of Competition Law: Markets and Public Services* (2005) 40.

[42] See, eg, the immediate overruling, by the War Damage Act 1965, of the House of Lords' decision in *Burmah Oil Co Ltd v Lord Advocate* [1965] AC 75 that the owners of property deliberately destroyed to prevent it falling into enemy hands during wartime were entitled to compensation.

[43] See, eg, Taggart (above n 33) at 23–31 and (above n 25); Craig (above n 25); Oliver (above n 29) at 205; G. Borrie, 'The Regulation of Public and Private Power' [1989] PL 552 at 558–61.

[44] For subsequent developments in New Zealand energy regulation, see B. Barton, 'Self-Regulation, State Regulation and Co-regulation in Energy in New Zealand' in *Regulating Energy and Natural Resources* (B. Barton et al, eds, 2006).

established in 1986, and the Office of Electricity Regulation, in 1990, merged in 1999 to form the Office of Gas and Electricity Markets (Ofgem)[45]—the existence of which might be thought to render additional judicial controls unnecessary.[46] As originally conceived, the regulatory regimes were intended only as a limited incursion into the autonomy of privatized companies; a temporary application of minimal pricing, access and service quality rules until competition was properly established. Regulation was to be a technocratic, efficiency-oriented process, insulated from political influence. In fact, though, the regimes were always broader in scope and far more discretionary than the official philosophy of light-handed regulation implied. Moreover, the privatized utilities' political unpopularity and the ongoing public importance of the industries have meant that regulatory controls have became progressively stronger and more extensive.[47]

Somewhat ironically, the initial reason for giving the regulators wide discretion was to insulate them from judicial intervention, because, going by American experience, this was regarded as likely to taint the pursuit of efficiency with considerations of fairness.[48] However, the discretionary nature of the regulatory regimes can also be read as a powerful expression of the social obligations of utility industries, since it means that regulatory rules are never fixed nor final, and hence that utility companies are subject to a strong form of ongoing public accountability (albeit balanced with both procedural and substantive protections against what they regard as unreasonable demands). Unexpectedly, therefore, this has enabled the regulatory regimes to become the focus for debate about the appropriate forms of control over essential services, and, according to Prosser, has spawned for the first time in the UK an identifiable body of public service law.[49]

Nevertheless, there is arguably still a role for a more general legal conception of the social obligations of ownership to play alongside sector-specific regulation. For one thing, as noted above, the existence and current scope of statutory regulation reflects a *political* choice, rather than a legal imperative, which could change in future. Moreover, as Hendry points out in her chapter, again reflecting the public/private distinction, it is the regulator rather than the companies themselves which are subject to *general* legal obligations under the statutory regimes; the latter are merely bound by whatever *specific* duties are placed upon them from time to time by their licences or secondary legislation. Of course, these duties can be altered if they prove to be inadequate. However, aggrieved parties must

---

[45] For discussion of British energy regulation post-privatization, see A. McHarg, 'The Political Economy of Regulation: Developments in British Energy Regulation Under Labour' in Barton et al (eds), ibid.

[46] Indeed, Taggart noted that the common law regulation that he was advocating for New Zealand was so minimal that it was hardly likely to be needed elsewhere—(above n 25) at 264.

[47] See, in relation to energy regulation, McHarg (above n 45).

[48] C. D. Foster, *Privatization, Public Ownership and the Regulation of Natural Monopoly* (1992) 194; T. Prosser, *Law and the Regulators* (1997) 32.

[49] See T. Prosser, 'Public Service Law: Privatization's Unexpected Offspring' (2001) 63 Law and Contemporary Problems 63.

persuade the regulator to change the rules;[50] a process in which the balance of power is weighted in the companies' favour. Finally, notwithstanding the greater prominence of non-economic values in energy regulation in recent years, it continues to be alleged that Ofgem displays a pro-market bias that makes it reluctant to intervene, especially in pursuit of social and environmental goals.[51]

While there may therefore be a case in principle for supplementing sectoral regulation with judicial controls, it remains to be considered how much scope there is in practice for direct legal action against energy companies—and how willing judges are actually to intervene—given the existence of specialist regulation.

1. *Private law obligations*

(a) Non-discrimination and fair pricing

Although there have been recent attempts to invoke common law supply and fair pricing obligations in New Zealand,[52] there are no contemporary British examples. As before nationalization, common law controls have largely been rendered unnecessary by similar statutory provisions. Thus, the core gas and electricity network operators have licence obligations to permit non-discriminatory access to and use of their systems, and are also subject to price controls. However, neither wholesale electricity generators and gas shippers nor retail energy suppliers are currently bound by such duties (although the latter must contract with domestic consumers on request, and are subject to a range of consumer protection obligations). Of course, unlike the networks, the wholesale and retail markets are fully open to competition, and Ofgem has generally taken the view that it is preferable to rely on competition rather than regulation to protect consumers wherever possible.[53] Thus, for example, price controls were finally removed from the supply market in 2002, when the regulator considered that competition was sufficiently well established to render them unnecessary.

Nevertheless, both wholesale and retail energy markets have been dogged by repeated criticisms that competition is ineffective, forcing the regulator, usually only after considerable pressure, to undertake numerous investigations, and resulting in frequent rule changes. Most recently, for instance, the Energy Supply Probe identified a number of respects in which the retail market was not working as well as it should.[54] Although Ofgem dismissed allegations of a cartel between the six major energy suppliers, it did find evidence of barriers to entry, lack of

---

[50] Borrie (above n 43) at 559–60.

[51] See, eg, Consumer Focus, *Rating Regulators: Ofgem* (2009) ch 6. However, the regulator's general duties have recently been amended to raise the profile of sustainable development objectives—Energy Act 2008 s 83.

[52] See particularly *Mercury Energy Ltd v Electricity Corp of New Zealand Ltd* [1994] 2 NZLR 385; *Vector Ltd v Transpower New Zealand Ltd* [1999] 3 NZLR 646.

[53] Indeed, its primary duty is to 'protect the interests of existing and future consumers ... wherever appropriate by promoting effective competition'—Gas Act 1986 s 4AA(1); Electricity Act 1989 s 3A(1).

[54] Ofgem, *Energy Supply Probe—Initial Findings Report* (October 2008).

transparency, and, most importantly for present purposes, unjustifiable pricing differentials, particularly affecting vulnerable consumer groups.

In response to these findings, Ofgem has in fact imposed a temporary licence provision on suppliers prohibiting undue discrimination, as well as a requirement to use cost-reflective payment methods.[55] Nevertheless, the length of time it has taken to launch formal action against unjustifiable price discrimination suggests that there might potentially be a role for the common law to play in supplementing regulatory controls in this area. The ability to bring actions directly against their supplier would not only have provided affected consumers with immediate remedies, but would also have put pressure on the regulator to act. Importantly, although the common law doctrines appear to have been predicated on the existence of market power, they did not require *de jure* monopoly. For instance, in the leading American case of *Munn v Illinois*,[56] the Supreme Court upheld the constitutionality of a statute fixing maximum prices for Chicago grain warehouses where there was no actual monopoly but rather long-standing collusion between warehouse owners such that they did not compete on price.

Admittedly, even in the absence of specific regulatory obligations, the kind of behaviour caught by the common law rules might also constitute a breach of competition law. For example, in *Dwr Cymru Cylyngedig v Water Services Regulatory Authority*,[57] a water company was found to have abused its dominant position, contrary to Chapter II of the Competition Act 1998, by charging an excessive price for carriage of bulk water supplies, even though at the time there were no express common carriage obligations in the water sector. Similarly, Ofgem justified removal of retail price controls in the energy sector partly because of the existence of competition law as a safety net.[58] However, competition law is not directly enforceable by aggrieved individuals, so its application again depends upon the regulator's willingness to intervene.[59]

Assuming there is a gap which common law non-discrimination and fair pricing doctrines might potentially fill, the question remains whether the courts are likely to be willing to revive them. The New Zealand experience is not encouraging, especially given the greater paucity and antiquity of relevant British authorities.[60] Following *Mercury Energy Ltd v Electricity Corp of New Zealand Ltd*,[61] in which the Privy Council expressed caution about whether the defendant had a

---

[55] Ofgem, *Notice of Modification of the Standard Conditions of Electricity Licences Requiring Cost Reflectivity Between Payment Methods and Prohibiting Undue Discrimination in Domestic Supply* (August 2009).

[56] (1876) 94 US 77.

[57] [2009] 2 All ER 279.

[58] Ofgem (above n 54) at para 2.5.

[59] Albeit in this case third parties as well as regulated companies have appeal rights.

[60] There are only two, very old cases involving businesses affected with a public interest: *Bolt v Stennett* (1800) Term Rep 606; *Allnutt v Inglis* (1810) 12 East 527. As noted above, utilities were not regarded as common callings in the UK; and the prime necessity doctrine appears never to have been part of British law.

[61] Above n 52.

common law obligation to supply a prime necessity at a fair and reasonable price, even though this was accepted as common ground between the parties, the issue was squarely addressed by the New Zealand Court of Appeal in *Vector Ltd v Transpower New Zealand Ltd*.[62] Here it was held that the prime necessity doctrine had been displaced by the Commerce Act 1986, since it would be inconsistent with the light-handed regulatory scheme established by that Act for the court to engage in control of Transpower's prices.

The Court's rejection of the prime necessity doctrine was partly based on concerns about institutional competence: it feared becoming permanently involved in price-setting; a task which was not suited to the adversarial process, and for which the common law provided inadequate guidance. However, in a separate concurring judgment, Thomas J considered that there could still be a role for the common law if it focused on the duty to supply, which he regarded as the key principle underpinning the prime necessity doctrine, with the notion of fair prices essentially performing a supporting role. Thus, for example, a court might be less apprehensive about intervening where there is clear evidence of unjustified price discrimination, rather than where it was merely asked to rule on the reasonableness of prices generally. Nevertheless, the other judges in *Vector* were also concerned about institutional legitimacy:

The selection of a particular form of regulation involves consideration by the government and Parliament of fundamental issues of social and economic policy and obviously includes assessment of the trade-offs between the costs associated with particular regulatory regimes and the benefits they are expected to deliver. If upheld in this case, the doctrine of prime necessity would necessarily involve heavy handed regulatory intervention ... of a type which Parliament decided it did not wish to impose ...[63]

Experience in other areas suggests that British courts would be likely to share this concern.

(b) Nuisance

Another ground of private law liability which has been invoked against private energy companies is the law of nuisance. In *Nicholls v Powergen Renewables Ltd*,[64] a statutory nuisance action[65] was brought in respect of noise from wind turbines. The claim failed because the company had taken steps to abate the noise and, although the grant of planning permission was not conclusive, it complied with the noise limits set in the planning conditions. However, in *Clifton v Powergen*,[66] two farmers successfully claimed compensation for crops damaged by acid rain caused by burning Orimulsion at a nearby power station.

[62] Above n 52.
[63] ibid, para 61.
[64] South Lakeland Magistrates Court, unreported, 20 January 2004. For details, see S. Tromans, 'Statutory Nuisance, Noise and Windfarms', available at <www.39essex.co.uk>.
[65] Environmental Protection Act 1990 s 82.
[66] Queen's Bench Division (Technology and Construction Court), unreported, 1 August 1997.

The law of nuisance is limited in scope, and can pose significant evidential challenges,[67] reducing its potential to address the most serious environmental problems caused by energy utilities. In any case, there are again often statutory environmental duties which can be employed instead. Nevertheless, where the relevant public agencies decline to act, as in the above cases, nuisance may provide a useful additional enforcement mechanism for neighbouring property owners directly affected by environmental harms.

However, the application of the law of nuisance to regulated private companies must now be considered in the light of the House of Lords' decision in *Marcic v Thames Water Utilities Ltd*.[68] Marcic's property had been repeatedly flooded because of inadequate sewer capacity and, instead of complaining to the water regulator, he brought an action against his sewerage provider based on nuisance and on breach of the Human Rights Act 1998 (discussed further below). Regarding the former claim, the court held that the common law of nuisance could not impose on the defendant obligations which were inconsistent with the statutory scheme under which it provided sewerage services, the Water Industry Act 1991. Section 18(8) of that Act reserved power to enforce the company's statutory obligations to the water regulator and, despite an express saving for causes of action not based on the statute, the court considered that the nuisance action in this case would 'set at nought the statutory scheme', effectively supplanting the role that the regulator was intended to discharge when questions of sewer flooding arose.[69]

It is difficult to know how far this ruling applies in other contexts. The case in fact affirmed a long line of authority granting sewerage providers immunity from nuisance actions.[70] But this approach was never applied to energy companies even when acting under statutory authority,[71] and Howarth suggests that the House of Lords overlooked the significance of the fact that the previous sewerage cases all involved local authorities rather than private companies.[72] *Marcic* does, nevertheless, seem to be based primarily on a general unwillingness to interfere with the balance between conflicting priorities (in this case between infrastructure investment and affordable prices) determined by the regulator. The same reasoning would therefore appear to apply in the energy context, where there are similar provisions reserving enforcement to Ofgem.[73] This would in practice limit nuisance actions to harms caused by activities falling outwith the regulator's remit.

---

[67] See generally, Coyle and Morrow (above n 13) ch 4.

[68] [2003] All ER 89.

[69] Per Lord Nicholls of Birkenhead at para 35.

[70] See Coyle and Morrow (above n 13) at 175–6.

[71] See, eg, *Shelfer v City of London Electric Lighting Company* [1895] 1 Ch 287; *Farnworth v Lord Mayor, Aldermen and Citizens of Manchester* [1930] AC 171.

[72] D. Howarth, 'Nuisance and the House of Lords: Squaring the Triangle' (2004) 16 JEL 233 at 259.

[73] Gas Act 1986 s 28(3)(b); Electricity Act 1989 s 25(3)(b).

2. Public law obligations

The courts' unwillingness to disturb regulatory choices also acts as a barrier to the use of public law remedies against privatized utilities. There are two possible grounds for public law challenge. The first is judicial review at common law, which applies general standards of reasonableness and procedural fairness. The second is under s 6 of the Human Rights Act 1998 (HRA), which requires 'public authorities' to comply with rights contained in the European Convention on Human Rights (ECHR).[74] 'Public authority' is defined as including 'any person certain of whose functions are functions of a public nature',[75] which was clearly intended to include at least some privatized functions.[76] The breadth and flexibility of these public law duties make them potentially very useful in supplementing more specific regulatory obligations, and there have been several cases against private energy providers, as well as other utilities, on both grounds. So far, however, none has succeeded.

Two questions must be asked when invoking public law controls: first, is the body in question amenable to review; secondly, if so, has there been a breach of public law obligations?

The only case in which the amenability of a privatized utility to judicial review at common law has been expressly considered is *In the Matter of Applications by Sherlock and Morris for Judicial Review*,[77] although there have been other cases in which this was assumed without argument.[78] In *Sherlock and Morris* it was alleged that Northern Ireland Electricity had acted unlawfully in exercising its power to disconnect customers suspected of meter tampering. However, the company argued that it was not subject to review: its duty to supply electricity was purely a matter of private law, and in any case the applicants had an appropriate alternative remedy in the form of a complaint to the Northern Irish electricity regulator, which they had chosen not to exercise. Kerr J rejected these arguments, holding that it was inconceivable that discharge by a public electricity supplier of its statutory duties should be outside the common law control of public functions. Moreover, the existence of an alternative remedy did not affect the availability of review in principle, although it could be a ground on which a remedy might be refused as a matter of discretion—a ground that was ultimately successful.

Although Kerr J regarded the public nature of the function being performed by Northern Ireland Electricity as the key factor in determining its amenability to judicial review, it is notable that all the cases in which review has been

---

[74] Subject to a defence where primary legislation makes it impossible to comply with Convention rights—s 6(2).

[75] S 6(3)(b). Unless the nature of the particular act in question is private—s 6(5).

[76] See *Rights Brought Home: The Human Rights Bill* Cm 3782, 1997, para 2.2.

[77] Northern Ireland High Court, unreported, 29 November 1996 (but see discussion by A. McHarg at (1997) 8 Util Law Rev 123).

[78] *R v Minister for Energy ex p Guildford*, *The Times*, 6 March 1998; *R v Northumbrian Water ex p Able UK Ltd* [1996] 2 PLR 28; *R v Northumbrian Water ex p Newcastle and Tyneside Health Authority* [1999] Env LR 715.

sought at common law involved companies acting under statutory authority. This is important because, since the energy supply markets were fully opened to competition, energy is no longer supplied under statute. It is now a matter of contract, albeit still subject to the terms of suppliers' licences and to the statutory Gas and Electricity Codes,[79] and there is clear authority that decisions based purely in contract are not subject to judicial review.[80]

It is, of course, debatable whether energy supply is a matter of 'pure' contract. However, *James v London Electricity plc*,[81] a case brought under the HRA, confirms that the introduction of competition has changed the legal nature of the function being performed. In this case, the claimant argued that the supply of electricity is such a fundamental social utility that the party supplying it must be a public authority. Moreover, despite attempts to encourage competition, Parliament had not managed to relinquish the controls necessary to ensure that electricity supply is properly regulated. For the company, it was argued that Parliament had in the Utilities Act 2000 deliberately separated the provision of electricity supply infrastructure (which it accepted was a public function), from supply to the end user, which was a private matter of contract regulated in such a way as not to constitute the ultimate supplier a public authority. Wilkie J found the arguments finely balanced, but agreed with the respondent that under the competitive regime electricity supply was a private matter, notwithstanding continued public regulation of the terms of supply. Indeed, he noted that the fact that acts are supervised by a public regulatory body does not necessarily indicate that they are public in nature.

James is consistent with a highly formalistic approach to the scope of review more generally, whereby the courts seem to assume that freedom of contract provides sufficient protection against corporate power without inquiring into the quality of choice actually available. Whilst Parliament may decide that specific regulatory protections are necessary, judges are not prepared to add to corporate burdens by supplementing express obligations with general standards of review. Indeed, in *YL v Birmingham City Council*,[82] Lord Mance went so far as to argue that the fact of regulation suggests that the nature of the act in question is actually private.[83]

In practice, therefore, it appears that judicial review, both at common law and under the HRA, will be available in the energy sector (at best)[84] only against the monopoly network providers. Even in these areas, though, the presence of regulation may restrict the scope of public law remedies. In addition to the procedural

---

[79] Gas Act 1986 sch 2B; Electricity Act 1989 sch 6.

[80] *R v Panel on Takeovers and Mergers ex p Datafin plc* [1987] QB 815. In Scotland, judicial review applies to those exercising jurisdictions rather than public functions, but this also excludes purely contractual relationships—*West v Secretary of State for Scotland* 1992 SC 385.

[81] [2004] EWHC 3226 (QB).

[82] [2008] 1 AC 95 at para. 116.

[83] See also *Cameron v Network Rail Infrastructure Ltd* [2007] 3 All ER 24: Railtrack plc was not a public authority in respect of its rail safety functions, *inter alia*, because ensuring rail safety was the responsibility of the Health and Safety Executive.

[84] cf *Cameron*, ibid.

requirement to exhaust alternative remedies, highlighted by *Sherlock and Morris*, *Marcic* demonstrates that the regulatory regime may have a substantive effect on the question of whether public law duties have been breached.

In this case, as noted above, Marcic also claimed that his rights to respect for his home (Art 8 ECHR) and to peaceful enjoyment of his possessions (Art 1, 1st Protocol ECHR) had been breached. Although it was not disputed that Thames Water was performing public functions, and the House of Lords accepted that Marcic's rights had *prima facie* been interfered with, this claim also failed essentially for the same reasons as the nuisance action. The rights in question were not unqualified, but could be restricted where necessary in the public interest. The House of Lords took the view that the statutory scheme conferred upon the regulator the power to decide where the balance should be struck between the householder's right not to be flooded and the competing public interest considerations (including the high cost of flood prevention which would be borne by water consumers as a whole), and that this was a reasonable approach for Parliament to take. Although something had 'clearly gone awry' in this particular case, this did not cast doubt on the fairness of the scheme as a whole. The appropriate remedy was to complain to the regulator, with the backstop option of seeking judicial review *of the regulator*, not to circumvent the statutory scheme by bringing an action directly against the sewerage company.

A final practical restriction on the use of judicial review to impose social obligations on privatized companies is the point accepted in *R v Northumbrian Water ex p Newcastle and Tyneside Health Authority*:[85]

> It is perfectly clear that as a commercial organization the respondent company cannot be said to possess powers solely in order that it may use them for public good. It has its commercial obligations to its shareholders. It must exercise its powers in accordance with those obligations.

Accordingly, the company was entitled to refuse the local health authority's request that it fluoridate its water supply because it feared being exposed to potential liability.

C. Social responsibilities and political intervention

As well as through Ofgem and the courts, a final way in which the social obligations of private energy providers might be articulated is through the political process. The government and legislature have much greater freedom to intervene than either of the former institutions, and politicians have often proved more willing to respond to demands that energy companies be made to act in a socially responsible manner, whether by altering the sectoral regulatory regime, or by *ad hoc* interventions outwith the regulatory framework.

---

[85] Above n 78.

Such *ad hoc* interventions may take a variety of forms. One option is for the government to intervene directly in the ownership of a particular service provider (short of outright nationalization) in order to alter its incentive structure, or to gain leverage which can be used to pursue wider interests. For instance, in 2002, the government was instrumental in the transfer of the UK's rail infrastructure from a shareholder-owned company (Railtrack) to a not-for-profit company (Network Rail) when the former became insolvent. The government had refused Railtrack's request for more public subsidy, angered by the fact that the company was continuing to pay dividends to its shareholders. There have been no such radical ownership interventions in the energy sector.[86] However, all privatized energy companies were initially subject to so-called 'golden shares', which effectively gave the government powers to veto proposed changes in their ownership, and could also be used to extract concessions. For example, in 1995, when the regional electricity companies wished to sell the National Grid Company, the government used its golden share to ensure that the significant increase in the company's value since privatization was shared between shareholders and customers.[87] Subsequently, though, all golden shares have either expired or been redeemed.[88]

Another device which has been used to impose special obligations on energy utilities is the so-called 'windfall tax'. In 1997, the newly elected Labour Government imposed a £5.2 billion windfall tax on privatized utility profits,[89] which it justified on the basis that these industries had been sold on excessively generous terms. The tax was therefore a clawing back of some of the value of the companies on behalf of taxpayers. Nevertheless, the government was clearly taking advantage of a widespread public perception that profit-maximizing behaviour by (near-) monopoly essential service providers was of questionable legitimacy.

During 2008, a campaign for another windfall tax, this time specifically targeted at energy companies,[90] gained considerable support, due to concerns that they were profiteering from energy price increases, attributable to global oil price rises and the introduction of the European Emissions Trading Scheme. Again, the perception that companies were profiting from provision of essential services when price increases were causing hardship to consumers posed a real threat to the legitimacy of private ownership.[91] Ultimately, the government declined to

---

[86] When the nuclear generator, British Energy, experienced financial difficulties in 2002, the government took a majority shareholding in the company to prevent it going bankrupt. However, this was intended as a temporary measure to protect security of supply, and the company was sold in 2008 to Electricité de France.

[87] See A. McHarg, 'Government Intervention in Privatized Industries: The Potential and Limitations of the Golden Share' (1998) 9 Util Law Rev 198.

[88] The last was relinquished with the sale of British Energy in 2008.

[89] Finance Act (No 2) 1997 s 1.

[90] Including but not limited to energy utilities.

[91] eg, there were calls at the Labour Party conference for renationalization of the gas and electricity industries—*The Guardian*, 23 September 2008.

impose a second windfall tax, not least because energy companies threatened to stop investing in badly needed infrastructure if they did so.[92] Instead, however, it exploited the political pressure to persuade energy companies, initially, to increase their spending on voluntary social tariffs,[93] and, subsequently, to accept a substantial increase in their obligations to invest in household energy efficiency measures.[94]

These sorts of *ad hoc* interventions are, not surprisingly, often very controversial, not least because privatization was supposed to insulate the industries from short-term political influence. Unpredictable interventions, it is argued, raise the cost of capital and deter investment, whilst imposing special obligations on particular companies distorts the market and creates further inefficiencies. Moreover, intervention outwith the sectoral regulatory framework may be perceived as being unfair, since it bypasses the legal protections afforded to the companies.

As noted above, the merits or otherwise of such measures would in the past have remained a purely political matter. However, constitutional developments in the latter part of the twentieth century mean that the UK Parliament is no longer legally unconstrained, creating new opportunities for legal challenge to regulatory choices. Indeed, following the incorporation of the ECHR, the right to peaceful enjoyment of property is now explicitly recognized in the UK's legal systems.[95] Whilst Convention rights can still be overridden by legislation, s 3 of the HRA creates a strong interpretive obligation on the courts to read statutes compatibly with the ECHR wherever possible. In practice, though, the right to property is one of the weakest Convention rights. Although it does not explicitly acknowledge the social obligations of ownership, Art 1 of Protocol 1 does permit both deprivation and regulation of the use of property in the public interest. Moreover, the European Court of Human Rights has repeatedly confirmed that states have a very broad margin of appreciation to decide where to strike the balance between property rights and other interests,[96] and the domestic courts have similarly indicated that they will defer to democratic decisions in this area.[97]

A much more important constraint on the government's regulatory freedom stems from European Community (EC) law. The supremacy of EC law has replaced parliamentary sovereignty in the hierarchy of legal norms in the UK, and EC law has a direct and growing impact on the regulation of energy utilities.[98] As

---

[92] *The Guardian*, 4 September 2008.

[93] HM Treasury, *Budget 2008: Stability and Opportunity: Building a Strong and Sustainable Future*, HC 388 (March 2008) para 4.34.

[94] Department of the Environment, Food and Rural Affairs, News Release 300/08, 11 September 2008.

[95] Art 1, Prot 1, ECHR.

[96] See, eg, *Sporrong and Lönnroth v Sweden* (1983) 5 EHRR 35; *Hatton v United Kingdom* [2003] 37 EHRR 28.

[97] See, eg, *Marcic* (above n 68); *R (Countryside Alliance) v Attorney General* [2008] 1 AC 719.

[98] Indeed, the establishment of an EU-wide energy regulator has recently been agreed, although this will mainly deal with technical issues relating to cross-border network integration: Regulation 2009/719/EC, OJ 2009 L 211/1.

will be discussed below,[99] the impact of EC law on social regulation in the UK has been to some extent positive. Nevertheless, it has in some cases obliged the UK authorities to alter their regulatory approach. One example is the decline in use of golden shares, which stems in part from severe restrictions placed on the lawful use of such devices by the European Court of Justice (ECJ) at the instigation of the European Commission.[100] The remainder of this chapter therefore considers the role of ideas about the social obligations of ownership in EC law.

III. The social obligations of ownership and EU energy regulation

A. Social obligations in the civil law tradition

As already noted, civilian legal systems tend to employ different conceptions of property in public and private law. According to Art 544 of the French Civil Code, for instance, '[o]wnership is the right to enjoy and dispose of things in the most absolute manner,' *provided,* however, 'they are not used in a way prohibited by statutes or regulations'. Ideas of the social obligations of ownership are therefore most relevant as supports for public law regulation of the definition and use of property rights, and this tends to produce specific restrictions on property holders' freedom, rather than open-ended obligations towards third parties.[101]

The best known general statement of the social function of property is contained in Art 14(2) of the German Basic Law, quoted above,[102] although similar provisions appear in the Italian[103] and Spanish[104] constitutions. The 'social model' developed by the German Constitutional Court (which contrasts, and sometimes conflicts, with the individualistic approach in the Civil Code)[105] to some extent has protective implications for property owners. Since the function of property rights is to promote individual self-governance, Art 14(2) sometimes provides an absolute guarantee against state interference, not merely a right to compensation. At the same time, though, it requires property owners to act in a socially responsible manner, as determined by regulations authorized by the legislature. Moreover, the legislature itself is required to exercise its duty under

---

[99] Section III C(2).

[100] See further below.

[101] Mattei (above n 1) at 150.

[102] See text accompanying n 9. The following account draws upon G. S. Alexander, 'Constitutionalizing Property: Two Experiences, Two Dilemmas' in McLean (ed) (above n 6); R. Lubens, 'The Social Obligation of Property Ownership: A Comparison of German and US Law' (2007) 24 Arizona J of Int and Comp L 389; H. Mostert, 'Engaged Citizenship and the Enabling State as Factors Determining the Interference Parameter of Property: A Comparison of German and South African Law' (2009), unpublished manuscript on file with the author.

[103] Art 42(2).

[104] Art 33(2).

[105] See, eg, Art 903: 'The owner of a thing may, to the extent that a statute or third party rights do not conflict with this, deal with the thing at his discretion and exclude others from every influence.'

Art 14(1) to define the content and limits of property rights in such a way as to develop a 'socially just property order'. This requires it to balance the interests of owners against the public good in accordance with a proportionality test, which in practice creates a 'sliding scale' of social obligation. In other words, the degree of permissible intervention varies depending, *inter alia*, on the social importance of the type of property in question, and this can change over time.

French law takes a different, and somewhat narrower, approach to the social obligations of ownership, but one which has been particularly influential in the development of EC law. Unlike in Germany, there is no general concept of the social nature of property. Indeed, the Declaration of the Rights of Man describes property as 'a sacred and inviolable right',[106] although this is subject to a general abuse of rights doctrine which prevents rights being exercised solely to harm others. However, the Preamble to the 1946 French Constitution (incorporated by reference into the constitution of the Fifth Republic) states that: 'all property and all enterprises of which the operation has, or acquires, the character of a national public service or of a monopoly are to become public property'. The 'public service' doctrine, to which this refers, has been described as a 'foundation myth' of French public law,[107] and again similar concepts can be found in Italian and Spanish law, albeit less culturally and legally entrenched.

Despite the wording of the constitution, the French concept of public service does not require public ownership, or indeed monopoly. However, all public services, even if privately provided, are subject (at least in part) to special legal regimes, and they are still regarded as ultimately the responsibility of the state. It is, moreover, up to Parliament or the government to determine what counts as a public service, and how it should be organized. The precise implications of the public service doctrine in terms of the content of the special legal regimes are somewhat vague. It is generally said to require compliance with principles of continuity, equality and adaptability of service, which give rise to special obligations to service users (as well as special rights for service providers) enforceable before the administrative courts. However, additional principles have, in recent years, been applied to particular public services through legislation.

As with the German social clause, therefore, the French concept of public service can be seen providing general constitutional support for political determination of the social obligations of ownership, both allowing flexible responses to changing social needs.

---

[106] Art 17.

[107] J. Bell, 'The Concept of Public Service Under Threat From Europe? An Illustration from Energy Law' (1999) 5 EPL 189 at 189. The following account draws upon this article, as well as E. Malaret Garcia, 'Public Service, Public Services, Public Functions, and Guarantees of the Rights of Citizens: Unchanging Needs in a Changed Context' in Freedland and Sciarra (eds) (above n 16); and Prosser (above n 41) ch 5.

B. Property rights and EC law

According to Art 295 EC: '[t]his Treaty shall in no way prejudice the rules in Member States governing the system of property ownership'. In practice, however, it does not maintain a strictly neutral approach. The primacy of 'the principle of an open market economy with free competition'[108] in the European legal order means that EC law *de facto* employs a liberal model of property rights.[109] All economic[110] undertakings (whether in public or private ownership)[111] are, *prima facie*, subject to the free movement, competition and state aid rules, and member states can only depart from market principles where permitted by the Treaty rules, and subject to a proportionality test. Thus, for example, in the golden shares cases, the ECJ rejected the argument that this was a matter of property ownership protected by Art 295. Instead, the Court held that, even where they do not explicitly prohibit foreign ownership, such provisions constitute a restriction on free movement of capital and the right of free establishment. They can therefore be justified only by overriding considerations of national interest, and only if the government's powers are non-discriminatory, non-discretionary, and no wider than necessary to achieve the specified objectives.[112]

This model is sometimes described as Anglo-Saxon. For instance, Amato argues that the assumption that all economic activity is private, even when conducted or controlled by the state, reflects a common law rather than civilian approach.[113] Nevertheless, it may be argued that the rigid public/private distinction and constraints on state intervention contained in EC law have deeper civilian than common law roots. What appears to be missing, however, is any counterbalancing notion of the social obligations of ownership to support and shape state intervention. On the contrary, there appears to be a general presumption *against* the legality of regulatory action.[114]

The practical significance of this model was relatively limited until the late 1980s. However, once the Commission began to apply it to utility and network industries (which had hitherto been largely ignored by EC law), as part of its drive to

---

[108] Art 4 EC.

[109] See also Art 17, Charter of Fundamental Rights of the EU.

[110] EC law draws a sharp distinction between economic and non-economic activities: see J.-L. Buendia Sierra, *Exclusive Rights and State Monopolies Under EC Law* (1999) ch1.

[111] Arts 31 and 86(1) EC. Consequently, EC law indirectly favours privatization over public ownership: see, eg, W. Devroe, 'Privatizations and Community Law: Neutrality Versus Policy' (1997) 34 CMLR 267.

[112] *Commission v Italy*, C-58/99, [2000] ECR I-3811; *Commission v Portugal*, C-367/98, [2002] ECR I-4731; *Commission v France*, C-483/99, [2002] ECR I-4781; *Commission v Belgium*, C-503/99, [2002] ECR 4809; *Commission v Spain*, C-463/00, [2003] ECR I-4581; *Commission v UK*, C-98/01, [2003] ECR I-4641; *Commission v Netherlands*, C-282 & 283/04, [2006] ECR I-9141; *Commission v Germany*, C-112/05, [2007] ECR I-8995. See E. Szyszczak, *The Regulation of the State in Competitive Markets in the EU* (2007) 33–6.

[113] Above n 16 at 146, 152.

[114] Szyszczak (above n 112) at 14.

complete the internal market, it became highly controversial. Some member states (notably France) and other groups were extremely concerned about the impact of liberalization policies on public service values. The consequence has been to focus attention on the previously little-known concept of 'services of general economic interest' (SGEI), which are accorded special status within EC law.[115] This concept has become increasingly important as a vehicle for mediating the tension between competitive and public service values and, it may be argued, has developed into a proxy for the social obligations of ownership at European level.

C. Services of general economic interest and the social obligations of ownership

1. *Services of general economic interest and disapplication of the Treaty rules*

The concept of SGEI originated in Art 86(2) EC, which provides that:

> Undertakings entrusted with the operation of services of general economic interest … shall be subject to the rules contained in this Treaty, in particular to the rules on competition, in so far as the application of such rules does not obstruct the performance, in law or in fact, of the particular tasks assigned to them. The development of trade must not be affected to such an extent as would be contrary to the interests of the Treaty.

As it is used in this provision, the SGEI concept is properly described as merely a *proxy* for the social obligations of ownership. To begin with, it constitutes only a *permission*, not a requirement, for member states to impose public service obligations on undertakings. Moreover, it has nothing to say about the nature of the obligations that might be imposed. The term SGEI is not defined in EC law,[116] let alone the normative implications of such a designation. Rather, the focus of Art 86(2) is *structural* only: it permits departure from relevant Treaty rules[117] where an undertaking requires special or exclusive rights in order to support the delivery of public service obligations. Its role is to provide space for the promotion of public service goals within a market order; hence its key practical effect is on the *shape* that public service interventions must take in order to comply with EC law.

This shaping is achieved via the application of a proportionality test. Because Art 86(2) was originally interpreted as a derogation from the Treaty, this test was initially strictly applied.[118] However, it was relaxed in the 1990s, as the competition, state aid and free movement rules were increasingly applied to essential

---

[115] For general discussion of this concept see: Buendia Sierra (above n 110); Prosser (above n 41) chs 6–8; Szyszczak (above n 112).

[116] It is, however, clear that it includes energy utilities: *Commission v Netherlands, Italy and France*, C-157, 158 and 159/94, [1997] ECR I-5699, 5789 and 5815 (*Gas and Electricity Monopolies*).

[117] A similar exemption for SGEI is provided in the Services Directive, Directive 2006/123/EC, OJ 2006 L 376/36.

[118] See, eg, *BRT v SABAM*, C-127/73, [1974] ECR 313.

services.[119] According to Baquero Cruz, it has become a 'binary or switch rule' which establishes the conditions for application or non-application of the Treaty to undertakings entrusted with SGEI.[120] Nevertheless, successful invocation of Art 86(2) is still subject to conditions. For example, in the *Gas and Electricity Monopoly* cases,[121] in which the Commission tried to force a number of member states to remove exclusive rights to import and export gas and electricity in advance of legislative agreement to liberalize those sectors, the court held that it was not necessary for the member states to show that the economic survival of the undertakings in question would be threatened if their exclusive rights were removed, nor that there were no other means of fulfilling the public interest objectives entrusted to them. However, France could not justify the grant of exclusive rights to Electricité de France and Gaz de France by reference to their contribution to general environmental and regional policies because the undertakings had no specific obligations in respect of these goals. Similarly, in *Altmark*,[122] the ECJ confirmed that state measures providing compensation for the delivery of public service obligations do not constitute state aid, and hence need not be notified to the Commission, nor justified in terms of Art 87 EC. However, the public service obligations in question must be clearly defined; the basis on which compensation is calculated must be established in advance in an objective and transparent manner; the compensation must not exceed the cost of meeting the obligations, allowing for a reasonable profit; and if responsibility for discharging the public service obligations is not allocated through a public procurement procedure, the level of compensation needed must be determined by reference to the costs that a typical well-run undertaking would incur.

Thus, in general, the Art 86(2) jurisprudence seeks to reconcile protection of SGEI with competition objectives by promoting a model of public service obligations that is rule-based, residual, and detachable from the economic mission of essential service providers.

2. Services of general economic interest and the goals of the European legal order

Although the concept of SGEI continues to play the essentially negative role envisaged by Art 86(2), it has more recently also acquired a positive role as one of the general principles of EC law. Whereas Art 86(2) acts to preserve member state autonomy in relation to the pursuit of public service objectives, there is now a positive duty on both member states and the Community institutions to protect and promote SGEI. This gives SGEI a constitutional status within the

---

[119] See: *Corbeau*, C-320/91, [1993] ECR I-2533; *Almelo*, C-393/92, [1994] ECR I-1477; *Gas and Electricity Monopolies* (above n 116).

[120] J. Baquero Cruz, 'Beyond Competition: Services of General Interest and European Community Law' in *EU Law and the Welfare State: In Search of Solidarity* (G. de Búrca, ed, 2005) 176.

[121] Above n 116.

[122] C-280/00 [2003] ECR I-7747.

Community legal order, more closely resembling the approach to the social obligations of ownership in civilian legal systems.

The starting point for this transformation was the insertion of a new (French-inspired) Art 16 into the EC Treaty by the 1997 Treaty of Amsterdam. Article 16 provides that:

… given the place occupied by services of general economic interest in the shared values of the Union as well as their role in promoting social and territorial cohesion, the Community and the Member States, each within their respective powers and within the scope of application of this Treaty, shall take care that such services operate on the basis of principles and conditions which enable them to fulfil their missions.

Article 36 of the Charter of Fundamental Rights, adopted in 2000, also proclaims that:

The Union recognizes and respects access to services of general economic interest as provided for in national laws and practices, in accordance with the Treaties, in order to promote the social and territorial cohesion of the Union.

Further, when it comes into force, the 2007 Lisbon Treaty will amend Art 16 (which will be renumbered Art 14) to give the Community institutions a new legal basis upon which to adopt legislation to establish principles and set conditions which enable SGEI to fulfil their missions. It also contains an interpretative Protocol on SGEI, which sets out some of '[t]he shared values of the Union in respect of services of general economic interest within the meaning of Article 14.' These include in particular:

— the essential role and the wide discretion of national, regional and local authorities in providing, commissioning and organizing services of general economic interest as closely as possible to the needs of the users;
— the diversity between various services of general economic interest and the differences in the needs and preferences of users that may result from different geographical, social or cultural situations;
— a high level of quality, safety and affordability, equal treatment and the promotion of universal access and of user rights.

Alongside these formal texts, the Commission has also issued a series of communications on SGEI.[123] In contrast to its initial attitude, which appeared to regard public service obligations as an inconvenient barrier to completion of the internal market, it now acknowledges the role of SGEI as 'an essential element of the European model of society' and 'a pillar of European citizenship',[124] albeit

---

[123] *Services of General Interest in Europe*, OJ 1996, C 281/3; *Services of General Interest in Europe*, OJ 2001 C 17/4; *Report to the Laeken European Council: Services of General Interest*, COM (2001) 598 final; *Green Paper on Services of General Interest*, COM (2003) 270 final; *White Paper on Services of General Interest*, COM (2004) 374 final; *Services of General Interest, Including Social Services of General Interest: A New European Commitment*, COM (2007) 725 final.
[124] eg, Green Paper, ibid, para 2.

continuing to stress that 'the objectives of developing high-quality, accessible and affordable services of general economic interest and of an open and competitive internal market are compatible and should be mutually supportive.'[125]

The significance of these developments is a matter of some dispute.[126] For some, they are merely intended to reassure—and thereby neutralize—opponents of liberalization, whilst leaving the substance of EC law intact. Proponents of this view point to the vagueness of Art 16, the key terms in which—including the notion of SGEI itself—remain undefined, and to the Declaration accompanying the Amsterdam Treaty which stated that Art 16 was to be implemented with full respect for the ECJ's jurisprudence. Moreover, even when the Charter of Fundamental Rights becomes legally binding upon ratification of the Lisbon Treaty,[127] it is accepted that Art 36 does not create any enforceable rights.[128] As for the Lisbon Protocol, according to Sauter, this:

appears to add little of substance as regards SGEI ... If anything, it illustrates an inability on the part of the Member States to conceptualise within the EU legal framework what it is they want from SGEI.[129]

Others, however, most notably Ross,[130] have argued that the inclusion of Art 16 amongst the general principles of the EC Treaty creates a new teleology for EC law, which places SGEI on an equal footing with competition. According to Szyszczak,

Article 16 fits the pattern of the move within the EU from a purely *economic* community of Member States to ... a community of Member States *and* Citizens 'in a highly competitive social market economy' where national interests are recast as interests to be addressed at the trans-national level.[131]

In practical terms, the impact of the new provisions so far has been mixed. On the one hand, the Commission has resisted repeated requests from the European Parliament and Council of Ministers to prepare a draft framework directive on SGEI, which would set out minimum public service standards and general principles for the organization and regulation of such services. The Commission's 2004 White Paper concluded that there was insufficient consensus on the need for or content of such a directive,[132] and it seems to have taken the view that

---

[125] 2007 Communication (above n 123) at para 2.2.

[126] See Szyszczak (above n 112) at 219–21.

[127] NB the UK (along with Poland) has opted out of the justiciable effect of the Charter via a Protocol to the Lisbon Treaty.

[128] Szyszczak (above n 112) at 221.

[129] W. Sauter, 'Services of General Economic Interest and Universal Service in EU Law' (2008) 33 E L Rev 167 at 173.

[130] M. Ross, 'Article 16 EC and Services of General Interest: From Derogation to Obligation' (2000) 25 E L Rev 22.

[131] Above n 112 at 221 (emphasis in original).

[132] Above n 123. The only general measure enacted so far is a Commission Decision on state aid and public service compensation, adopted in the wake of the *Altmark* case (above n 122): OJ 2005 L 312/67.

the Lisbon Protocol—which emphasizes the diversity of public service missions and the need for wide discretion for member states—renders further clarification unnecessary.[133] Hence, even with the addition of a new legal basis, since the Commission has a monopoly over legislative initiative in the EU, there is unlikely in the foreseeable future to be any further fleshing out of a set of *general* rights and obligations attaching to SGEI.

On the other hand, public service obligations have increasingly been included in sector-specific legislation. This has been an important condition of the acceptability of liberalization directives, and the trend is growing both in terms of recognizing a wider range of legitimate public service objectives and in the increasingly prescriptive nature of these requirements. For example, the first electricity[134] and gas[135] liberalization directives *permitted* member states to impose public service obligations in five categories—security; regularity, quality and price of supplies; and environmental protection—and *allowed* derogation from some provisions of the directives where necessary to secure fulfilment of these objectives. In the 2003 directives,[136] these permissive provisions were retained, but in relation to electricity member states were also *obliged* to ensure that all household (and optionally small business) consumers enjoy universal service, defined as the right to be supplied with electricity of a specified quality within the territory at reasonable, easily and clearly comparable, and transparent prices. Further, for both gas and electricity, member states were required to take 'appropriate measures' to protect final customers and ensure high levels of consumer protection, particularly for vulnerable groups, and to achieve the objectives of social and economic cohesion, environmental protection, and security of supply. The recently-agreed 'third package' of liberalization measures[137] continues this process by further elaborating the existing public service requirements and adding new mandatory obligations, for instance a duty to take appropriate measures to address energy poverty.

At least part of the explanation for the increasing prescriptiveness of public service requirements is the desire for harmonization between member states, since differing levels of social intervention may act as a barrier to competition within the internal market. This has the effect of raising standards of protection within some member states. For example, writing in 2004, Brothwood argued that public service obligations in the UK energy sector fell short of that required by the 2003 directives.[138] The UK government did not agree,[139] but at the very

---

[133] See 2007 Communication (above n 123).

[134] Directive 96/92/EC, OJ 1997 L 27/20.

[135] Directive 98/30/EC, OJ 1998 L 204/2.

[136] Directive 2003/54/EC, OJ 2003 L 176/37 and Directive 2003/55/EC, OJ 2003 L 176/57.

[137] Directive 2009/72/EC, OJ 2009 L 211/55 and Directive 2009/73/EC, OJ 2009 L211/94.

[138] M. Brothwood, 'Public Service Obligations in the Electricity and Gas Sectors' (2004) 3 IELTR 48.

[139] Department of Trade and Industry, *Implementation of EU Directive 2003/54 Concerning Common Rules for the Internal Market in Electricity* (2004).

least the directives have had the effect of shoring up existing levels of social protection.

However, in terms of the *form* that public service obligations may take, the same model applies under the liberalization directives as under Art 86(2). Thus, it is expressly provided that public service obligations must be clearly defined, transparent, and non-discriminatory, as well as verifiable, published, and notified to the Commission. In addition, the right to disapply pro-competitive requirements is subject to a proportionality test. As already noted, the Art 86(2) jurisprudence continues to apply, and in fact, according to Sauter, a stricter proportionality test is used in sectors in which Community legislation has been enacted.[140]

In other words, EC law is at best a source of highly specific social obligations for private energy companies. It seems clear that Art 16 is not capable of acting as a broad and flexible source of obligations which might supplement specific regulatory requirements because it is too vague to be capable of direct effect. It has been suggested that it could be used to ground judicial review (or even liability) proceedings if member states and/or the Community institutions fail adequately to protect SGEI.[141] But even here it is probably too vague to act as more than an aid to interpretation of more concrete provisions in the Treaty or secondary legislation. By contrast, Art 86(2) *is* capable of direct effect,[142] and could therefore be used to *challenge* public service obligations which are regarded as excessively burdensome.

IV. The social obligations of ownership in the UK and the EU: An evaluation

Tracing the development of ideas about the social obligations of ownership in the UK over the past two centuries, a clear, albeit incomplete, trend towards the growth of a public/private distinction can be identified. Instead of the traditional common law approach which regarded ownership as inherently entailing social obligations, the contemporary British approach more closely resembles the civilian model. In other words, it is now seen as being primarily the state's responsibility to specify through legislation the social obligations attaching to particular classes of property holders, such as private energy providers, who are otherwise entitled as a matter of private law to pursue their own selfish interests.

This change has come about partly because of the domestic courts' unwillingness to supplement specialist statutory regulation with broadly-based legal obligations, especially where private companies operate in a competitive environment. However, the public/private distinction has been reinforced by EC law, which employs as its default model a liberal, market conception of ownership.

---

[140] Above n 129 at 186.
[141] Szyszczak (above n 112) at 220.
[142] *Corbeau* (above n 119).

This has been balanced in recent years by the increasing importance attached to the concept of SGEI, which it has been argued, can be seen as a proxy for the social obligations of ownership, justifying the imposition of a range of public service obligations on essential service providers. Whereas in domestic law the question of whether and how to impose social obligations remains largely a matter of political choice, EC law now compels member states to promote certain public service values in the energy and other utility sectors. However, it also has a disciplining effect on the form that state intervention may take. In order to minimize interference with competition, it promotes a hierarchical and legalistic model of public service protection, requiring specific, rule-based obligations in place of more general and flexible regulatory responses.

Two main justifications for this approach can be identified. First, the domestic courts appear to be motivated primarily by separation of powers-based concerns regarding the legitimacy of second-guessing decisions which have been entrusted to specialist regulators about the appropriate regulatory burdens which should be imposed on privatized utilities. In addition, and much more explicitly in relation to EC law, there is a concern that open-ended and *ad hoc* regulatory commitments will produce legal uncertainty, discriminate between undertakings, and thereby undermine efficient market outcomes.

Both justifications are, however, questionable. To begin with, such a formalistic approach to the location of regulatory power is out of step with contemporary analyses of regulation, which emphasize its pluralistic and 'decentred' nature.[143] Rather than sectoral regulators being unitary and exclusive fora for the articulation of industry standards, these accounts highlight the dispersal of regulatory authority amongst a range of both formal and informal sources, as well as the plurality of regulatory values which compete for ascendancy. The background legal rules governing property ownership are an inevitable part of this regulatory mix. Hence by refusing to impose additional social obligations on private utility providers, the courts are not being neutral, but rather are contributing towards the maintenance of a particular distribution of power within the relevant sector.

As regards the efficiency argument, the main issue here concerns the consequences of the emerging regulatory model in terms of the effectiveness of public service protection. Tightly-defined, hierarchical regulation may fail adequately to capture the values being promoted and may be unresponsive to the dynamic nature of public service demands, whilst also provoking lip-service compliance and legalistic behaviour on the part of regulated companies.[144] In addition, it is

---

[143] See, eg, C. Scott, 'Analysing Regulatory Space: Fragmented Resources and Institutional Design' [2001] PL 329; J. Black, 'Decentring Regulation: Understanding the Role of Regulation and Self-Regulation in a "Post-Regulatory" World' (2001) 54 Current Legal Problems 102.

[144] See H. De Bruijn and W. Dicke, 'Strategies for Safeguarding Public Values in Liberalized Utility Sectors' (2006) 84 Pub Admin 717; C. Scott, 'Services of General Interest in EC Law: Matching Values to Regulatory Technique in the Public and Privatized Sectors' (2000) 6 European LJ 310.

perhaps doubtful in highly imperfect markets such as gas and electricity whether the efficiency costs of broader and more flexible social obligations are really as great as implied.

It would, of course, be foolish to suggest that specific regulatory duties be abandoned altogether. The development of explicit regulatory protections for public service values is one of the major benefits of privatization and liberalization of the energy and other utility industries. Nevertheless, as I have sought to demonstrate, broader legal notions of the social obligations of ownership can and do have a role to play in supporting, supplementing and shaping regulatory responses in these sectors.

PART IV
EMERGING PROPERTY REGIMES

19

The Role of the Common Law in Promoting Sustainable Energy Development in the Property Sector

*Adrian Bradbrook**

I. Introduction

The law of real property in the majority of common law jurisdictions dates back to the feudal system of land tenure. In medieval times it became one of the three major pillars of the common law, along with contracts and torts. While some of the major principles of common law of real property were established by legislation, a surprisingly large number were developed by the courts over the centuries. These include the doctrines of adverse possession, prescription, accretion, avulsion, profits à prendre, easements, leases and restrictive covenants, to name but a few. Even in areas originally established by legislation, many important developments and modifications were established by case law. These important common law developments include the development of restrictive covenants, originally expounded in *Tulk v Moxhay*,[1] the concept of native title, established in Australia in *Mabo v Queensland (No 2)*,[2] and the notion of leases as contracts as well as estates in land.[3]

Despite this venerable history, the common law of real property can be criticized for its slowness in responding to changing societal values. Many of the principles which made sense when first adopted have proven to be anachronistic and

---

* Bonython Professor of Law, Law School, University of Adelaide, Australia; email: adrian.bradbrook@adelaide.edu.au.

[1] (1848) 2 Ph 774; 41 ER 1143.

[2] (1992) 175 CLR 1. Native title was further considered and developed in Australia by the High Court in *Wik Peoples v Queensland* (1996) 187 CLR 1; *Fejo v Commonwealth* (1999) 195 CLR 96; and *Western Australia v Ward* (2002) 76 ALJR 1098.

[3] See eg *Javins v First National Realty Corporation* (1970) 428 F 2d 1071; *Lund v MacArthur* (1969) 462 P 2d 482; *Shevill v Builders Licensing Board* (1982) 149 CLR 620; *Progressive Mailing House Pty Ltd v Tabali Pty Ltd* (1985) 157 CLR 17; *Laurinda Pty Ltd v Capalaba Park Shopping Centre Pty Ltd* (1989) 166 CLR 623.

inappropriate in later times as a result of changing values. This includes the law of leases,[4] the rule against perpetuities, which in some jurisdictions still contains absurd anachronisms in its interpretation,[5] and the law of dower and curtesy. The problem here is not that the law was inappropriate or unjust at its commencement, but rather that neither the courts nor the legislature have adopted necessary reforms over the years. While contracts and torts have changed fundamentally in many respects as a result of court decisions, the progress of reform of real property is very slow. The reason for this is unclear. One argument is the lack of parliamentary time to consider reforms, coupled with the obscurity of many issues of real property and their lack of electoral interest. Another argument is the inherent conservatism of the courts and their reluctance to make changes affecting land, the most valuable commodity of all.

While the major role for promoting sustainable energy development undoubtedly rests with the legislature, it is submitted that the courts have the capacity to play a significant supporting role in this regard. The purpose of this chapter is to consider the options available to the courts in common law jurisdictions to influence and modify real property law so as to take full account of the societal need to advance the goal of sustainable energy development. The chapter will examine the elements of sustainable energy development, will explore the extent to which the law of real property is relevant to sustainable energy and will then consider the range of legal solutions available to the courts to achieve this goal.

II. The elements of sustainable development

It is important at the outset to understand exactly what is meant by 'sustainable energy development'. The term presupposes that energy is part of sustainable development. This term has been defined in numerous contexts. The best known definition is that of the World Commission on Environment and Development (the Brundtland report),[6] which stated that sustainable development is 'development that meets the needs of the present without compromising the ability of future generations to meet their own needs'.[7]

The only comprehensive attempt to achieve an exhaustive content for 'sustainable energy' is that of the International Energy Agency (IEA). In its report, *Energy Efficiency Indicators for Public Electricity Production from Fossil Fuels,*

---

[4] A. Bradbrook, 'The Role of the Judiciary in Reforming Landlord and Tenant Law' (1976) 10 Melbourne U L Rev 459.

[5] See A. Bradbrook, S. MacCallum and A. Moore, *Australian Real Property Law* (4th edn, 2007) 402–4. See especially *Shelley's case* (1581) 1 Co Rep 93b; 76 ER 206.

[6] World Commission on Environment and Development, *Our Common Future* (1990).

[7] ibid at 87. A comprehensive list of definitions is given in D. Pearce et al, *Blueprint for a Green Economy* (1989).

the IEA has drawn up a list of energy indicators for sustainable development. There are 30 indicators, sub-divided into social, economic and environmental dimensions.[8] While these are stated to be 'indicators', in the absence of other statements of the content of sustainable energy it is submitted that the list can be used as a proxy for this purpose. Rewording and combining some of the energy indicators so as to turn them into elements of sustainable energy would give us the following comprehensive requirements of sustainable energy development:

- Energy must be universally accessible;
- Energy must be affordable;
- Energy development must satisfy health and safety requirements;
- Efficiency of energy conversion and distribution must be assured;
- Energy efficiency must be promoted in all sectors of the economy—agriculture, commercial, households and transport;[9]
- Diversification of energy supplies is essential, with renewable energy and non-carbon energy resources forming a significant proportion of electricity generating capacity;
- Energy security must be maximized;
- Strategic fuel stocks must be maintained;
- The effect of energy use and production on climate change and air quality must be considered;
- Water quality must not be compromised by energy use and production;
- Soil quality must be preserved, with particular concern given to acidification caused by energy production;
- Energy use and production must not lead to excessive deforestation; and
- Consideration must be given to the cumulative amount of radioactive waste, analysed by reference to the amount of energy produced.

III. Real property issues in sustainable energy development

Having identified the elements of sustainable energy development, we must consider the potential scope for promoting such development in the context of real property law. The areas where real property law could make a contribution are in respect of energy efficiency, renewable energy resources and carbon capture and storage (CCS).

---

[8] International Energy Agency, *Energy Efficiency Indicators for Public Electricity Production from Fossil Fuels* (2008) 11 ff. See also European Energy Agency, *Energy Subsidies in the European Union: A Brief Overview*, Technical Report 1/2004 (2004); European Energy Agency, *Energy and the Environment in the European Union*, Environment issue report no 31 (2002).

[9] 'Energy efficiency' is defined in the Energy Efficiency and Conservation Act 2000 (NZ) s 3 as: 'a change to energy use that results in an increase in net benefits per unit of energy'.

A. Energy efficiency

While energy efficiency laws have actual and potential application to all sectors of the economy, it is in the field of buildings that it has direct application to real property law.[10] Commercial and residential buildings account for approximately 30 per cent of all energy consumption,[11] so the need for energy efficiency in this sector is very great. Much has been achieved in a wide range of jurisdictions by the introduction of legislation controlling minimum standards for new buildings. These typically prescribe minimum levels of insulation required for roofs and walls, create an energy rating or labelling system, or establish a system of energy and conservation option points which requires all new buildings to score a minimum number of points from an option list that the legislation prescribes.[12] Improving energy efficiency in existing buildings is more complex, although the addition of roof insulation and/or the creation of a green building and green points programme is still possible.[13]

The role for the courts in this sector appears to be very limited as building laws are primarily statute-based. Where a building is owner-occupied little can effectively be achieved in this area until the owner sells or otherwise disposes of the property. We can identify two possible alternative approaches in this situation. The first approach would extend the notion of a common law warranty of habitability, developed by courts in the United States, from the law of leases to land contracts.[14] The vendor would warrant to the purchaser that minimum standards of efficiency materials existed in the building to satisfy the accepted standards of energy efficiency in the community. Damages would be payable to the purchaser by the courts for a breach of the warranty.

The alternative approach would be for the courts to add to the statutory list of duties imposed on vendors in many jurisdictions by creating a new implied duty to notify purchasers of all gas and electricity bills incurred by the owner in respect of the premises in the preceding one or two years. While this would not provide a purchaser with a guaranteed energy cost for the building as the circumstances of the purchaser's proposed use of the premises may differ significantly from the past use by the vendor, it would provide a rough approximation of the

---

[10] See J. Waters, *Energy Conservation in Buildings* (2003); House of Commons Select Committee on Energy, *Energy Conservation in Buildings,* 5th Report (HC Paper (1981–82) no 401-I); A. Bradbrook, *Energy Conservation Legislation for Building Design and Construction* (1992).

[11] United Nations Development Programme, *Public Policies Promoting Energy Efficiency in Buildings, Draft* (February 2008) at 13. The figure of 30% is an average of all countries. Developing countries are in the range of 20–25%, while the figure increases to 35–42% for developed countries.

[12] See generally V. Schwarz, *Public Policies Promoting Energy Efficiency in Buildings: Examples and Results* (2008).

[13] An illustration of this is the Boulder (Colorado) Revised Code, ch 10–7.5. The scheme was originally called the Energy and Conservation Options Points System. This type of legislation is explained in Bradbrook (above n 10) at 29 ff.

[14] See *Pines v Perssion* (1961) 111 NW 2d 409; *Reste Realty Corp v Cooper* (1968) 53 NJ 444, 251 A 2d 268.

likely energy costs to be incurred. Equally importantly, such an implied duty would build on the statutory system of energy labelling and would bring the issue of energy efficiency to the mind of potential purchasers as a valid consideration to take into account in determining which property to purchase. Such an implied duty is consistent with the notion of treating purchasers of buildings as consumers and providing as much information as possible to consumers.

In contrast to buildings that are owner-occupied, different laws to promote energy efficiency are required in respect of buildings that are rented.[15] Neither landlords nor tenants have any incentive to install energy efficiency measures in private commercial or residential accommodation. From the tenant's perspective, the fundamental problem is that as tenants do not own the premises they are extremely reluctant to make capital investments on the landlord's property by installing energy efficiency measures.[16] Any such measures installed by a tenant in the rented premises will become fixtures under traditional common law rules and legal title will vest in the landlord.[17] The landlord is under no legal obligation to compensate the tenant for the value of the improvements. Although tenants are given certain rights at common law to remove fixtures prior to the termination of a lease, such right of removal is limited to trade, ornamental and domestic fixtures.[18] This would appear to exclude energy efficiency measures. From the landlord's perspective, as landlords do not pay the gas and electricity supply and consumption charges in respect of their rental premises, there is little incentive for them to invest in energy efficiency measures.[19] Further lack of incentive arises from the fact that any investment in energy efficiency measures is unlikely to increase the rental or resale value of the premises.[20]

One method of increasing energy efficiency in rented buildings would be for the legislature to enact a law establishing a code of minimum energy efficiency standards for rented buildings. It could be made a requirement that no land owner may transfer a rental unit unless, within the previous five years, an inspector has inspected the unit and issued a certificate stating that the unit satisfies the

[15] See R. Counihan and D. Nemtzow, 'Energy Conservation and the Rental Housing Market' (1981) 2 Solar Law Reporter 1103; A. Bradbrook, 'The Development of Energy Conservation Legislation for Private Rental Housing' (1991) 8 EPLJ 91.

[16] Counihan and Nemtzow (above n 15) at 1105.

[17] For a discussion of the common law rules relating to fixtures, see Bradbrook, MacCallum and Moore (above n 5) 637 ff; A. Bradbrook, C. Croft and R. Hay, *Commercial Tenancy Law* (3rd edn 2009) [10.5].

[18] See eg *Smith v City Petroleum Co Ltd* [1940] 1 All ER 260; *Spyer v Phillipson* [1931] 2 Ch 183; *Concepts Property Ltd v McKay* [1984] 1 NZLR 560; *New Zealand Government Corporation v HM&S Ltd* [1982] QB 1161; *D'Arcy v Burelli Investments Pty Ltd* (1987) 8 NSWLR 317.

[19] In North America, a significant percentage of commercial and residential multi-unit buildings are master-metered, with the landlord responsible directly to the utilities for the payment of the accounts. While master-metering increases the incentive for landlords to install energy efficiency measures, it reduces the incentive for tenants to economize on the use of energy and ultimately drives up rent levels as landlords seek to recoup their outlays.

[20] California Energy Commission, *Energy Conservation in Rental Housing: Conference Proceedings*, Report P400–85-013 (1985) 3.

prescribed standard. An alternative approach would be to enact 'truth in heating' legislation, as in the State of New York, whereby all prospective purchasers and renters of residential accommodation are entitled to receive information on the past heating and cooling costs of a residence they are considering buying or renting.[21]

In the absence of legislation on this issue, the courts could imply a term of the lease that the premises comply with reasonable energy efficiency standards. The term implied could be either classified as a covenant or as a condition, the effective difference being that a condition would be classed as an essential term of the contract and would, on breach, entitle the other party to terminate the contract.[22] While most existing implied terms are classified as covenants, an implied condition exists on the part of the landlord that furnished premises are fit for habitation at the commencement of a lease.[23] While such a decision by the courts would involve extending the general principle that terms will only be implied in leases where it is necessary to give 'business efficacy' to the contract,[24] a variety of different implied lease terms have been accepted into common law jurisprudence in modern times. The implication of a further term in respect of energy efficiency requirements would simply amount to updating the relevance of the law to modern societal conditions and standards.

B. Renewable energy resources

Real property law has direct relevance to the development of solar energy, onshore wind energy and geothermal energy.

1. Solar energy

The major problem for solar energy users is that in non-tropical regions of the world the sun is never directly overhead: sunlight reaching a solar device on the solar user's land must pass through the skyspace of one or more neighbouring properties. During this passage through the neighbour's skyspace, the sunlight may be blocked by vegetation or a building, shading the solar collector panels. There is little incentive for a private land owner or an industry to install a solar appliance if the efficiency of the appliance can be ruined at any time by the erection of a building or the planting of vegetation on neighbouring land.

---

[21] NY Stat s 17–103 (1983). The regulations are contained in 9 NYCRR, s 7835.

[22] *Associated Newspapers v Bancks* (1951) 83 CLR 322; *Progressive Mailing House Pty Ltd v Tabali Pty Ltd* (1985) 57 ALR 609.

[23] *Smith v Marrable* (1843) 11 &W 5; 152 ER 693; *Penn v Gatenex Co Ltd* [1958] 2 QB 210; *Sarson v Roberts* [1895] 2 QB 395.

[24] *Liverpool City Council v Irwin* [1977] AC 239; *Karaggianis v Malltown Pty Ltd* (1979) 21 SASR 381; *Chorley Borough Council v Ribble Motor Services Ltd* (1996) 72 P&CR D32; *Edward Kazas & Associates Pty Ltd v Multiplex Pty Ltd* [2002] NSWSC 840.

Some form of legal protection for the solar user must be found. In some jurisdictions, particularly in the United States, the legislature has intervened and has created the necessary protection, in the form of a new property right for the solar user or new planning laws taking solar energy into account in new developments.[25] Local government has also intervened in some jurisdictions by making solar access a relevant consideration for the planning approval of new property developments.[26] In many common law jurisdictions, however, no remedy has been enacted.

Solar access to solar collector panels could be protected under the common law doctrines of easements or restrictive covenants, both of which could be drafted so as to prevent neighbours from allowing vegetation or buildings on their land to block the access of sunlight to the collectors at specified times during the day. The use of such doctrines has been well documented.[27] From the standpoint of the legal protection of the right of solar access, easements and restrictive covenants are of limited significance, however, as both are consensual transactions and cannot be imposed on an unwilling party. Under present authorities, there appears to be no scope for the application of implied rights in this context.

In the absence of legislation, the courts may consider that the blocking of solar access from solar collector panels of a neighbour constitutes a private nuisance.[28] While nuisance lies in tort, it relates to the unlawful interference with land or a right in relation to land.[29] In the United States, two conflicting decisions have been reported. In *Prah v Maretti*,[30] the plaintiff, the owner of a solar-heated residence, sued for an injunction to restrain his neighbour, the defendant, from constructing a residence on the defendant's property in a position that would interfere with the plaintiff's access to unobstructed direct sunlight to his solar panels. The plaintiff's residence was the first constructed in the subdivision and had been erected close to the defendant's boundary line. This maximized the likelihood of shading problems arising from any building erected on the neighbouring property. The defendant had received the necessary planning and building approval from the Planning Commission.

---

[25] See eg New Mexico Solar Rights Act s 47-3-4; Environmental Planning and Assessment Act 1979 (New South Wales, Australia) ss 26, 54, 79C.

[26] For illustrations, see A. Bradbrook, 'Solar Access Law: Thirty Years On', forthcoming (2009) EPLJ.

[27] See eg A. Bradbrook, 'The Development of an Easement of Solar Access' (1982) 5 U New South Wales LJ 229; J. Goudkamp, 'Securing Access to Sunlight: The Role of Planning Law in New South Wales' (2004) 9 Australasian J Nat Res L & Policy 59; T. Alvarez, 'Don't Take My Sunshine Away: Right to Light and Solar Energy in the Twenty-First Century' (2008) 28 Pace L Rev 535.

[28] The possibility of an action for public nuisance has been discussed and discarded in A. Bradbrook, 'Resource-Use Conflicts: The Role of the Common Law' in *Growing Demands on a Shrinking Heritage: Managing Resource-Use Conflicts* (M. Ross and O. Saunders, eds, 1992) 344; A. Bradbrook, *Solar Energy and the Law* (1984) [602] ff.

[29] *Gartner v Kidman* (1961) 108 CLR 12 at 22; *Read v J Lyons & Co Ltd* [1945] KB 216 at 136; *Newcastle-under-Lyme Corporation v Wolstanton Ltd* [1947] Ch 92 at 107.

[30] (1982) 108 Wis 2d 223, 321 NW 2d 182. Analysed recently in R. Zerbe, Jr, 'Justice and the Evolution of the Common Law' (2006) 3 J L Econ & Policy 81.

The plaintiff argued that the defendant's residence constituted a private nuisance by virtue of the shading problems. The Supreme Court of Wisconsin accepted the plaintiff's claim by a 2–1 majority. Judge Abrahamson, for the majority, noted that the defendant's argument—that he has a right to develop his property in compliance with existing legislation and private covenants, regardless of the effect that this has on the plaintiff's solar access—amounts to an argument that the private nuisance doctrine is not applicable in the present case. The court rejected this argument and also the further proposition that there is no property interest in sunlight. In relation to the right of land owners to develop their property as they wish, Judge Abrahamson noted that society has increasingly regulated, for the general welfare, the use of land by the land owner. As to the value of sunlight, the court stated that access to sunlight as an energy source is significant both to the land owner who invests in solar energy and to a society that has an interest in developing alternative energy sources. The court also noted that the policy of favouring unhindered private development in an expanding economy is no longer in harmony with the realities of modern society.[31]

The court concluded that common law private nuisance rules must adapt to changing social values and conditions, and that what is legally regarded as a nuisance in modern times would undoubtedly have been tolerated without question in former times. The court added that the fact that the defendant complied with the relevant zoning and building laws does not automatically bar a nuisance claim, although this fact is entitled to some weight.

This decision was not followed by the California Sixth District Court of Appeals in *Sher v Leiderman*.[32] In this case, the plaintiff constructed a passive solar home,[33] designed to take advantage of the winter sun for heat and light. Trees planted by a neighbour on adjoining land grew sufficiently tall to block the sun to the plaintiff's house for most of the day during winter. The plaintiff argued that the shading constituted a private nuisance. The court held in favour of the defendant, despite accepting that sunlight is important as an energy source and that the promotion of solar energy is of paramount public interest.[34] The court reasoned that it is more appropriate to protect solar access by zoning and other local ordinances than by the law of nuisance, and that it is solely within the province of the legislature to assess the relative importance of social priorities and to decide whether to change the law. The court also noted that the expansion of the nuisance law in this area would have the undesired effect of fostering ill-will and a proliferation of litigation between neighbours.

---

[31] Above n 30 at 190, citing *State v Deetz* (1974) 66 Wis 2d 1, 224 NW 2d 407.

[32] (1986) 181 Cal App 3d 645, 226 Cal Rptr 698.

[33] A passive solar device does not employ any solar collector panels or mechanical devices, but seeks to control temperature by the architectural features of the building itself. Such features include the size and placement of windows, the type of materials of which the walls are constructed, and the orientation of the building towards the sun.

[34] 226 Cal Rptr 698 at 702.

There are no direct case law authorities on this issue outside the United States. It is doubtful on analogous authorities whether the right of solar access would be protected by the law of nuisance elsewhere. Some advantages are not protected even though interference with them may cause economic loss to the land owner. Such illustrations of unprotected advantages are the enjoyment of a view, freedom from spying or observation, and the enjoyment of water percolating through undefined channels. Using analogies, the right to solar access might be likened to the traditional right to light, to a claim for an uninterrupted view or to a legal right to privacy. While the right to light has been recognized in some common law jurisdictions, the other analogous rights have been rejected by the courts. A further problem with the existing law of nuisance is that the right of solar access may be regarded as a sensitive or unusual use of the land and thus excluded from the operation of the law.[35] The law of nuisance may also be excluded in this context by virtue of the fact that there is no 'material injury to property', as required by the case law,[36] as the obstruction of sunlight does not cause any actual harmful deposits on the plaintiff's land.

While this summary of the current state of the law of nuisance suggests that the likelihood of a solar user successfully employing this principle to protect their right of solar access is dubious, it is clear from *Prah v Maretti* that judicial creativity could be employed here to create such a right. What is needed is a willingness to recognize the importance of the issue and a recognition that the courts may have a role to play regardless of the action (or lack of action) on the part of the local legislature.

2. On-shore wind energy

Serious legal problems are likely to beset a person or electricity authority who wishes to erect and operate a wind generator or wind farm. The major property-related problem is to obtain the requisite planning permission for the erection of the generator. In built-up areas of cities and towns this is likely to be difficult to obtain, as generators are likely to infringe on planning or zoning regulations and in some instances it will be difficult to comply with relevant building regulations. Objections are often made by neighbouring land owners on aesthetic grounds as wind generators are a prominent feature on the landscape. A second problem is to obtain guaranteed access to the wind. Even if wind generators are ideally situated at windy locations they may be rendered ineffective or inefficient if building developments on neighbouring land block or restrict the natural flow of wind to the rotor blades.[37]

---

[35] See eg *Robinson v Kilvert* (1889) 41 Ch D 88; *Hoare & Co v McAlpine* [1923] 1 Ch 167; *Rattray v Daniels* (1959) 17 DLR (2d) 134.

[36] *St Helen's Smelting Co v Tipping* (1865) 11 HL Cas 642, 650; 11 ER 1483, 1486; *Halsey v Esso Petroleum Co Ltd* [1961] 2 All ER 145; *Kraemers v Attorney-General (Tasmania)* [1966] Tas SR 113.

[37] A. Bradbrook, 'The Access of Wind to Wind Generators' [1984] AMPLA Yearbook 433 at 434.

The planning issue raises complex issues as the planning legislation and the local planning schemes in most jurisdictions seldom contain specific and precise controls relating to the siting of individual wind generators or wind farms. Wind generators or farms are usually classified as a permitted use, but a permit is required in each case. The issue of a permit is usually subject to determination or challenge before a state planning tribunal, which possesses a wide discretion as to whether and on what terms to grant planning approval. Many proposals for wind farms are challenged by local land owners as, due to wind velocity considerations, wind farms are usually proposed for location on exposed and highly visible sites or hilltops or close to the ocean. Additional problems are noise in the surrounding area caused by the turning rotor blades, interference with local television and radio reception, and bird deaths as a result of birds attempting to fly through rotating blades, particularly where wind generators are located in the path of migratory birds.[38] Wind energy development thus divides the environmental movement: while environmentalists support clean energy, the other reported problems often outweigh this goal.[39]

It is submitted that the role of planning tribunals in the exercise of their discretion whether to approve new wind generators or farms should be to give more weight to issues of climate change and the associated need to minimize the use of fossil fuels for generating electricity. The opposing issues of aesthetic injury and other traditional environmental concerns are of course entitled to consideration, but should be recognized as carrying lesser weight than climate change, a relatively recent issue but one that has been described as the greatest environmental challenge of the twenty-first century. The challenge is for the tribunals and courts to readjust their traditional weightings of various planning considerations to reflect this fact. At present, the evidence is mixed. Some tribunals have responded while others have not. Using Australia as an example, we can contrast recent planning decisions favourable to wind energy development in *Thackeray v Shire of South Gippsland*,[40] *Perry v Hepburn Shire Council*[41] and *Kittel & Vandepeer v District Council of Yankalilla*[42] with less favourable decisions, such as in *Hislop v Glenelg Shire Council*.[43] These decisions appear to mirror the emerging jurisprudence on climate change litigation, where the outcome of planning disputes sometimes appears to turn on the individual judge's or tribunal member's level

---

[38] For a discussion of the adverse environmental issues associated with wind energy, see A. Bradbrook, 'Liability in Nuisance for the Operation of Wind Generators' (1984) 1 EPLJ 128.

[39] For a discussion of planning issues associated with wind energy development, see A. Wawryk, 'Planning for Wind Energy: Controversy Over Wind Farms in Coastal Victoria' (2004) 8 Australasian J Nat Res L & Policy 103; A. Wawryk, 'The Development Process for Wind Farms in South Australia' (2002) 19 EPLJ 333.

[40] [2001] VCAT 739.

[41] [2007] VCAT 1309.

[42] [2002] SAERDC 131.

[43] Unreported, Tribunal Application No 1997/88762, available at <www.austlii.edu.au/au/cases/vic/aat/1997/088762>.

of concern or awareness of the significance of climate change.[44] Frequently the environmental concerns associated with individual wind farm planning applications can be satisfactorily reconciled with climate change and energy considerations by the tribunals imposing conditions or restrictions on the development without outright rejection of the proposal. Judicial education may be the long-term solution here.

In relation to the need for guaranteed access to the wind, it appears that the only effective avenues open to a wind user are either to purchase title to or a long-term lease over a sufficient tract of land upwind to ensure that no obstructions will impede the wind access, to purchase a restrictive covenant or easement restricting the use to which the upwind neighbour may put his or her land, or as a last resort to sue in nuisance.

Clearly the most effective of these options is the acquisition of a fee simple estate in the neighbouring land, but for economic reasons it is likely to be unrealistic in most situations. Unless the wind user can put the land to a profitable use that will not interfere with the access of wind to the wind generator, the cost of obtaining the land is likely to be prohibitive. The only possible exception may be in the case of a large wind farm built by a public electricity authority or private company established to supply electricity to the grid. A more financially realistic possibility is for the wind user to purchase an interest rather than an estate in land. The interest may take the form of either a restrictive covenant or an easement. In each case, of course, the neighbour may simply refuse to negotiate for the grant of an appropriate interest to protect the wind generator as such interests cannot be imposed at common law on an unwilling neighbour on the ground of public interest or for any other reason.

This leaves for the wind user the possibility of an action in nuisance against a neighbour who blocks wind access to a wind generator.[45] To date, there is no reported decision on the issue in any common law jurisdiction. There is a strong parallel here between solar and wind access in relation to the application of the law of nuisance. A major requirement of nuisance is that the right of wind access must be regarded as a 'protected interest'.[46] This may depend on whether the right of wind access can be regarded as an extension to the right to air, or whether it is

---

[44] cf *Minister for the Environment and Heritage v Queensland Conservation Council* (2004) 134 LGERA 272; *Gray v Minister for Planning* (2006) 152 LGERA 258; *Border Power Plant Working Group v Department of Energy* (2003) 260 F Supp 2d 997; *Mid States Coalition for Progress v Surface Transportation Board* (2003) 345 F 3d 520; *Pembina Institute for Appropriate Development v Attorney-General of Canada* [2008] FC 302; *Connecticut v American Electric Power* (2005) 406 F Supp 2d 265; *Massachusetts v EPA* (2007) 549 US 1; *Australian Conservation Foundation v Latrobe City Council* (2004) 140 LGERA 100. See generally J. Smith and D. Shearman, *Climate Change Litigation* (2006).

[45] For an earlier discussion of this issue, see A. Bradbrook, 'The Access of Wind to Wind Generators' [1984] AMPLA Yearbook 433.

[46] See and cf *Victoria Park Racing and Recreation Grounds Co Ltd v Taylor* (1937) 58 CLR 479; *Freeman v Shoalhaven Shire Council* [1980] 2 NSWLR 826; *Wentworth v Woollahra Municipal Council* (1982) 56 ALJR 745.

a separate novel right. The right to air, which could be enforced by an easement, was originally conceived for ventilation purposes, which is fundamentally different from the purposes of wind generation.[47] For this reason, wind access must be regarded as a claim for a separate novel right. We need to consider analogies to determine whether the right of wind access will be regarded as a protected interest. One close analogy is the right to light, which is only protected when it constitutes an easement. At common law this used to arise most frequently under the doctrine of ancient lights, which recognized an easement of light based on prescription after 20 years' continuous and uninterrupted use.[48] Implicit in these authorities is the fact that in the absence of an easement of light, the right to light is not protected by the law of nuisance. This analogy thus suggests that the right of wind access is an unprotected interest.

Other possible analogies are also unfavourable to the wind user. For example, if the right to wind access is likened to a claim of privacy, based on *Victoria Park Racing and Recreation Grounds Co Ltd v Taylor*,[49] then the right will be regarded as unprotected. The right to wind access may be likened to a claim for an uninterrupted view[50] or the right to receive television and radio reception without interference.[51] Both these rights have been held by common law courts to be unprotected interests.

Even if the conclusion that the right of wind access is an unprotected interest is later held to be wrong, there are other reasons why the law of private nuisance will be unavailable to a wind user. One reason is that wind users who sue neighbours in nuisance for blocking wind access may be met by the defence that they are making an especially sensitive or unusual use of the land. Wind generators are definitely sensitive in that they require the uninterrupted access to the free flow of the wind for their efficient operation. They are also unusual in that they are only used by a very small percentage of the population.[52] Another reason is that the neighbour responsible for blocking the wind access could in many instances argue that he or she was making an ordinary or reasonable use of the land. Although as a general rule, this defence would be unsuccessful,[53] it will succeed in the case of non-feasance.[54] Non-feasance may be argued, for example, in

---

[47] See eg *Cable v Bryant* [1908] 1 Ch 259; *Wong v Beaumont Property Trust Ltd* [1965] 1 QB 173.

[48] *Aldred's* case (1610) 9 Co Rep 57b; 77 ER 816; *Delohery v Permanent Trustee Co of New South Wales* (1904) 1 CLR 283. All Australian states and territories have since abolished prescriptive easements of light by legislation.

[49] (1937) 58 CLR 479.

[50] *Aldred's* case (1610) 9 Co Rep 57b, 77 ER 816; *Palmer v Board of Land and Works* (1875) 1 VLR (E) 80; *Harris v De Pinna* (1885) 33 Ch D 238; *Chastey v Ackland* (1895) 11 TLR 460.

[51] *Bridlington Relay Ltd v Yorkshire Electricity Board* [1965] 1 Ch 436. Cf *Nor-Video Services Ltd v Ontario Hydro* (1978) 84 DLR (3d) 221.

[52] R. Lornell and D. Schaller, *Small Power Production and Wind Energy: Regulatory Actions Under PURPA*, Report SERI/SP-635–794 (1982).

[53] *Lester-Travers v City of Frankston* [1970] VR 2; *St Helen's Smelting Co v Tipping* (1865) 11 HLC 642 at 650; 11 ER 1483 at 1486.

[54] *Bamford v Turnley* (1862) 3 B&S 66 at 83–4, 122 ER 27 at 33; *Kraemers v A-G (Tasmania)* [1966] Tas SR 113.

respect of a naturally seeded tree that blocks the access of wind to the plaintiff's wind generator. The case of 'natural use', sometimes referred to as the 'give and take' rule, would appear to be sufficient to include the case of blocking of wind access caused by buildings or trees as the erection of buildings and the planting of trees is a common use of both rural and urban land.

A final possibility is for the courts to create of their own initiative a new property right to be called a 'wind access right' and to protect it by creating a new, additional *de facto* exception to indefeasibility of title to add to the usually extensive list of statutory exceptions to indefeasibility of title created by legislation in many jurisdictions.[55] Such an approach would undoubtedly be regarded by many commentators as a bold and possibly too extreme illustration of judicial creativity, but there are precedents in this area that support such an approach. While it is true that the courts have been slow to create new property rights and that some more cautious courts have even declared that no new property interests can be created,[56] this has been contradicted in more recent times by decisions such as *Prah v Maretti*, discussed above.[57] The High Court of Australia adopted a more imaginative approach to the creation of new property rights as long ago as 1918 in *Commonwealth v Registrar of Titles (Victoria)*,[58] where Griffiths CJ stated:[59]

In the course of argument I referred to several possible easements novel in kind. For instance, an easement or servitude for the passage of aeroplanes through the super adjacent air of the servient tenement to a landing place, for the passage of electric current through suspended wires passing through that air, for the free passage of the flash from a heliograph station. Why not also the sun's rays?

In addition, some jurisdictions in the United States have created a new 'solar right' as a property interest,[60] so this proposal is not as extreme as it might appear at first glance. There are also precedents for the courts to create of their own initiative new exceptions to indefeasibility to add to existing statutory lists. Illustrations of this in Australia are overriding legislation[61] and rights *in personam*.[62]

---

[55] Real Property Act 1886 (South Australia) s 69; Land Title Act 1994 (Queensland) s 184; Real Property Act 1900 (New South Wales) s 42; Transfer of Land Act 1958 (Victoria) s 42; Transfer of Land Act 1893 (Western Australia) s 68; Land Titles Act 1980 (Tasmania), s 40; Land Titles Act 1925 (Australian Capital Territory); Land Title Act (Northern Territory).

[56] See eg *Phipps v Pears* [1965] 1 QB 76 at 82–3.

[57] Above n 30. See also *Attorney-General of Southern Nigeria v John Holt & Co Ltd* [1915] AC 599; *City Developments Pty Ltd v Registrar General (NT)* [2001] NTCA 7; *Clos Farming Estates v Easton* [2002] NSWCA 389.

[58] (1918) 24 CLR 348.

[59] ibid at 354.

[60] NM Stat Ann ss 47–3-4; Wyo Stat ss 34–22-101–106.

[61] See eg *South-Eastern Drainage Board (SA) v Savings Bank of South Australia* (1939) 62 CLR 603; *Attorney-General (NT) v Minister for Aboriginal Affairs* (1990) 90 ALR 59; *Miller v Minister for Mines* [1963] AC 484.

[62] See eg *Bahr v Nicolay (No 2)* (1988) 164 CLR 604; *Mercantile Mutual Life Insurance Co Ltd v Gosper* (1991) 25 NSWLR 32; *Say-Dee Pty Ltd v Farah Constructions Pty Ltd* [2005] NSWCA 309. This area of law is discussed in Bradbrook, MacCallum and Moore (above n 5) at [4.350] ff;

3. Geothermal energy

'Geothermal energy' may be described as the earth's heat energy.[63] It encompasses not only vapour-dominated and magmatic reserves, which are usually associated with volcanic activity, but also hot groundwater and hot dry rocks.[64] These latter two resources are widespread throughout the world.

The major property-related issue to be resolved in each jurisdiction is the ownership of the resource. Where this is not explicitly covered by legislation, the issue will be resolved by common law. This issue does not arise where geothermal resources are developed on Crown/state land, as on any legal analysis the ownership rights will vest in the Crown/state. However, the issue is of concern in respect of private lands, where claims to ownership may be lodged by both the surface land owners, by virtue of their fee simple estate, and by the Crown/state, by virtue of its rights to minerals and to groundwater.

Geothermal resources are of a hybrid nature and are capable of classification as either minerals, gas, groundwater or any combination thereof. Ownership rights at common law will depend on which classification is regarded as appropriate. The legislation that exists on this point is contradictory. In the United States, for example, some states declare the resource to be a 'mineral', and therefore subject to the relevant minerals allocative regime, some States declare it to be 'water', and therefore subject to the relevant groundwater allocative regime, while others declare it to be *sui generis*. There is also case law stating that the geothermal resource is a 'gas'.[65]

The different approaches are caused by the fact that there is much in common between geothermal resources and various other natural resources and mineral deposits in that the established regimes for the exploration, development and production of minerals could also be used for geothermal resources. Like minerals, geothermal resources also constitute a heat energy source and are probably finite in duration. This latter point is subject to dispute as often, little is known about whether individual reservoirs are recharging or about the rate of recharging. Current evidence suggests that in most cases a certain degree of recharging occurs, but that the rate of recharging will not sustain continuous production for an indefinite period. A similarity also exists between deep aquifer groundwater resources and low-temperature geothermal resources and also between the oil and gas industry and high-temperature geothermal resources in respect of the techniques used for exploration, well-drilling and production.

J. Tooher, 'Muddying the Torrens Waters with the Chancellor's Foot' (1993) 1 Australian Property L J 1; A. Moore, 'Equity, Restitution and In Personam Claims under the Torrens System: Part Two' (1999) 73 ALJ 712.

[63] S. Sato and T. Crocker, 'Property Rights to Geothermal Resources' (1977) 6 Ecology L Q 247 at 250.

[64] Hot dry rock development (HDR) involves the injection into the earth through drilled holes of cold water which becomes superheated on contact with underground heated rock and is discharged at the surface in the form of steam.

[65] *Reich v Commisssioner of Internal Revenue* (1972) 454 F 2d 1157.

Despite these similarities, however, on closer analysis the analogies between geothermal resources and minerals, gas and groundwater break down. Geothermal resources are fundamentally different from groundwater as it is the heat energy, rather than the liquid content, that constitutes the resource. Fundamental differences also exist between geothermal resources, on the one hand, and minerals, oil and gas, on the other hand, as the latter must be burned or processed in order to produce heat energy, while the former *is* heat energy and requires no such processing. An additional factor is that minerals, oil and gas can be utilized directly, while the geothermal resource can only be exploited indirectly by means of steam or water that conveys the heat energy to the land surface.

If geothermal resources are found to be neither minerals, nor gas, nor groundwater, they will be classified as *sui generis*. What would be the effect of such a determination on ownership rights in the resource? The ancient maxim, *cujus est solum ejus est usque ad coelum et ad infernos,* would suggest that geothermal resources should belong to overlying land owners merely by virtue of their location beneath their land.

There is considerable doubt whether the wide application of the maxim represents the current position at common law. Unfortunately, very few cases relevant to the maxim are concerned with the ownership of subsoil and substances beneath the earth's surface. Such authority that does exist suggests that the maxim is of only limited application. The Privy Council stated in *Commissioner of Railways v Valuer-General*[66] that in no previous case is there an authoritative pronouncement that 'land' means the whole of the space from the centre of the earth upwards: so sweeping, unscientific and unpractical a doctrine was unlikely to appeal to the common law mind. The court did not, however, substitute its own rule for determining ownership of the subsoil. The present position appears to be that the land owner has limited rights over the subsoil close to the earth's surface.[67] This proposition is supported by cases declaring entry into the subsoil to exploit a coal-seam and an underground cave to be a trespass against the owner of the overlying land.[68]

As the authorities on the operation of the maxim in respect of subsoil are sparse, in the present context a court might examine the application of the maxim to the ownership of airspace and apply the relevant authorities to the issue under discussion by analogy. These cases suggest that the maxim will be given only a limited scope. In *Lord Bernstein of Leigh v Skyviews and General Ltd,*[69] the defendants had flown over the plaintiff's land and had taken an aerial photograph of it with the intention of selling it to him. The plaintiff unsuccessfully sued the defendants in trespass on the basis of his alleged unrestricted ownership of the airspace above his land. Griffith J rejected the claim that a land owner's rights extend to an unlimited height, and stated that the rights of a land owner in the airspace above his land

---

[66] [1974] AC 328 at 351–2.

[67] See *Corbett v Hill* (1870) LR 9 Eq 671.

[68] *Bulli Coal Mining Co v Osborne* [1899] AC 351; *Edwards v Sims* (1929) 24 SW 2d 619. See also *Elwes v Brigg Gas Co* (1886) 33 Ch D 562.

[69] [1978] QB 479.

should be restricted to such height as is necessary for the ordinary use and enjoyment of his land and the structures upon it.[70] In *Graham v K. D. Morris & Sons Pty Ltd*,[71] the jib of a crane infringed the airspace of the neighbouring property at certain times when the wind blew from the north. On these occasions the jib was suspended 20 metres over the neighbour's house. On these facts W. B. Campbell J held that there was a trespass to land. His Honour stated that the plaintiff succeeded because the defendant interfered with that part of the airspace above her land which is requisite for the proper use and enjoyment of that land'.[70] The judge indicated that the proper use and enjoyment was affected inasmuch as the overhanging of the jib could adversely affect the market value of the property. By inference the judgment suggests that there would be no trespass if the infringement of the airspace did not adversely affect the use and enjoyment of the land.

These latter authorities support the proposition that private ownership of the airspace does not extend to a height beyond that which can reasonably be held to be within the control of the occupier, which appears to represent the current law. This is consistent with the earlier decision in *Electric Telegraph Co v Salford Overseers*[72] where the court determined the case on whether the plaintiff had exclusive occupation of the airspace affected.

This conclusion, linked with the earlier discussion concerning the application of the maxim to the ownership of subsoil, suggests that the maxim only operates to a limited distance above and below the land and that the test is one of the land owner's exclusive occupation. It is impossible to specify a precise height or depth on the limitation of the land owner's rights. In the context of mineral and energy rights, the exact depth of the land owner's rights may increase as the technological capacity to exploit the deep subsoil increases, although there is no direct authority for this proposition.

In the context of geothermal resources, it is arguable that if the technology exists to exploit the geothermal resources, then the maxim would operate to give ownership of the resources, all of which lie deep within the earth's crust, to the surface owner. On the other hand, there is no authority where a land owner has been declared to be the owner of such a deep layer of the subsoil. The preference of the present writer is for the latter proposition, which appears to better reflect the current state of the authorities.

If this conclusion is correct, it follows that the geothermal resources are *res nullius* and will become owned by the first person to reduce them into possession.[73] In the absence of any statutory management regime for geothermal resources, the rule of capture would operate to allow the surface owner to exploit the resource to the maximum extent possible on his land regardless of whether his operations cause the resource to be drained from underneath neighbouring land.[74]

---

[70] ibid at 488.   [71] [1974] 1 Qd R 1.   [72] (1855) 11 Exch 181.   [73] ibid at 4.
[74] M. Crommelin, 'The Legal Character of Resource Titles' (1998) 17 Australian Mining and Petroleum L J 57.

In summary, there are two possible alternative conclusions as to ownership of the resource if the resource is regarded as *sui generis*: first, the *cujus est solum* maxim will vest the resource in the overlying landowner; secondly, the resource will be *res nullius* and will only be subject to ownership when it is reduced into possession. As a practical matter however, it appears that the effective result in both cases will usually be the same even if the resource is *res nullius*: access to the resource can only be obtained by the overlying land owner or by developers allowed entry onto the overlying land with the landowner's consent. Thus, exclusive control over access to the resource is effectively, if not legally, the equivalent of ownership.

C. Clean fuel technologies

A variety of industrial processes have been explored in recent years to consider whether the use of fossil fuels can be made less polluting. This concern has been driven mainly by the climate change debate and the need to reduce atmospheric carbon emissions, the majority of which emanate from the burning of fossil fuels. Coal is the greatest concern as it produces the most emissions. In this regard the major issue affecting property rights is the emerging technology of carbon capture and storage (CCS).[75] This has been defined as 'the process consisting of the separation of CO_2 from industrial and energy-related sources, transport to a storage location and long-term isolation from the atmosphere'.[76] The process involves reinjecting the carbon formed by the burning of fossil fuels into underground storage areas in geologically stable areas. This technology has been strongly supported by governments in Europe, Australia and the United States, and a number of pilot projects have been conducted in these areas.[77] The motivating factor behind this interest is the economic need to keep utilizing coal for electricity generation for the indefinite future, as coal is the most plentiful form of fossil fuels.

In Europe and Australia, the major focus in relation to CCS is off-shore storage. In order to facilitate CCS, public international law has been modified by

---

[75] For a discussion of the legal issues associated with CCS, see R. Ashcroft, 'Carbon Capture and Storage: A Need for Re-Conceiving Property Interests and Resource Management in the Australian Legal System' [2008] LawAsia J 48; N. Bankes and M. Roggenkamp, 'Legal Aspects of Carbon Capture and Storage' in *Beyond the Carbon Economy: Energy Law in Transition* (D. Zillman, C. Redgwell, Y. Omorogbe and L. Barrera-Hernandez, eds, 2008) at 344 ff; J. Moore, 'The Potential Law of On-Shore Geological Storage of CO2 Captured from Coal-fired Power Plants' (2007) 28 Energy L J 443; A. Warburton et al, 'Geosequestration Law in Australia' in *Climate Law in Australia* (T. Bonyhady and P. Christoff, eds, 2007) 142; J. Fahey and R. Lyster 'Geosequestration in Australia: Existing and Proposed Regulatory Mechanisms' (2007) 4 J European Env & Planning Law 378.

[76] International Panel on Climate Change (IPCC), *Special Report on Carbon Capture and Storage* (2005) 3.

[77] See the presentations at the United Nations Department of Economic and Social Affairs Expert Group Meeting on Carbon Capture and Storage and Sustainable Development, September 2007, available at <www.un.org/esa/dsd/dsd_aofw_ene/ene_egm0907_presentations.shtml>.

way of recent amendments to the Protocol on the Prevention of Marine Pollution by Dumping of Wastes and Other Matter 1996.[78] The purpose of the amendments is to exclude CCS schemes from the legal definition of 'dumping' and so avoid the operation of the Protocol.[79] Australia has enacted new legislation, the Offshore Petroleum and Greenhouse Gas Storage Act 2006 (Cth), creating a legal management scheme for the exploitation of CCS. This legislation adopts a similar model of management as for the exploitation and development of off-shore petroleum reserves. It reasserts government ownership and control of the seabed in Commonwealth waters and creates new property interests in the form of greenhouse gas assessment permits, greenhouse gas holding leases, greenhouse gas injection licences and greenhouse gas search authorities. These rights are purely statute-based and have no common law component.

Different property issues arise in the case of on-shore CCS activities. Again, legislation specific to CCS may resolve this issue. This has occurred in three Australian states, which have declared that ownership rights of underground depleted reservoirs and stored CO_2 vest in the Crown.[80] In the absence of such legislation, at common law we must consider the respective rights of private companies and/or the government to the underground storage areas.

To determine this question, we need to know in each case whether the disposal of CCS will be into an aquifer or into an underground gas or coal formation.[81] Where disposal is into an aquifer, the matter will be resolved by reference to the prevailing water law regime, which in most countries is statute-based. Where disposal is into a coal or oil or gas formation, the relevant legislation governing these resources may in some cases specify the ownership rights in the use of the depleted reservoir. As in most cases petroleum resources are vested by legislation in the Crown/state, it would follow that the ownership of the depleted reservoir automatically follows. In other cases, however, the legislation may fail to clarify ownership rights in the depleted reservoir. It is here that the common law may have a role to play.

As in the case of geothermal energy, the starting point for the discussion is the common law maxim, *cujus est solum, ejus est usque ad coelum et ad infernos*.[82] The analysis above in the context of geothermal resources shows that in the case of underground caves and subsoil the land owner's claim extends only to a limited distance above and below the land and that the test is one of the land owner's exclusive

---

[78] (1997) 36 ILM 1.

[79] See A. Weeks, 'Subseabed Carbon Sequestration as a Climate Mitigation for the Eastern United States: A Preliminary Assessment of Technology and Law' (2007) 12 Ocean and Coastal L J 245; R. Purdy and I. Havercroft, 'Carbon Capture and Storage: Developments Under European Union and International Law' (2007) 4 J European Env & Planning Law 3.

[80] Petroleum Act 2000 (South Australia) ss 5, 10; Greenhouse Gas Geological Sequestration Act 2008 (Victoria) ss 14, 16; Greenhouse Gas Storage Act 2009 (Queensland) s 27.

[81] See Bankes and Roggenkamp, above n 75, 352 ff.

[82] See above nn 66–71 and accompanying text.

occupation.[83] It is impossible to specify a precise height or depth on the limitation of the land owner's rights. In the context of mineral and energy rights, the exact depth of the land owner's rights may increase as the technological capacity to exploit the deep subsoil increases, although there is no direct authority for this proposition.

As in the context of geothermal resources, it is arguable that if the technology exists to exploit the depleted reservoirs, then the maxim would operate to give ownership of the resources, all of which lie deep within the earth's subsoil, to the surface owner. On the other hand, there is no authority where a land owner has been declared to be the owner of such a deep layer of the subsoil. The preference of the present writer is for limiting the ownership rights of the surface owner, as this appears to better reflect the current state of the authorities. It would follow that ownership of the storage sites would vest at common law in the Crown/state. The only obligation on the Crown/state would be to compensate the overlying surface landowner for any actual land disturbances or losses caused by the industrial processes associated with the storage.

It should be noted, however, that the cases on the application of the *cujus est solum* maxim were largely decided on the basis on the depth of land for which the surface owner could reasonably exploit. Such cases predate all modern considerations of CCS technology. It is thus possible (although not certain) that later court decisions might extend the depth of the subsoil belonging to the surface owner so as to take account of the new technological possibilities.

A further unresolved issue is whether for legal purposes we must distinguish between the hole in the ground and the inserted gases to determine property rights. As discussed by Ashcroft,[84] the uncertainty is caused by doubt expressed by the Privy Council in *Borys v Canadian Pacific Railway Co*[85] as to whether the *cujus est solum* maxim applies to fungacious resources. While in most common law jurisdictions gases are in Crown/state ownership, this legislation is arguably limited to gases in their natural state and does not extend to gases like carbon under CCS that have been 'converted'.

These two areas of uncertainty in the law are disturbing in that they militate against active investment in land-based CCS. Clarification is required, either by further case law or by legislation.

IV. The role of the courts

This chapter has focused on the possible avenues open to the courts to develop the law relating to sustainable energy development. Perhaps the greatest advantage of court intervention in this field is that the courts are more likely than the legislature

---

[83] Above nn 72–74 and accompanying text.
[84] Ashcroft (above n 75) at 54 ff.
[85] [1953] AC 217.

to appreciate the impact and significance of applying principles of property law in new contexts and to be able to ensure that property law principles are correctly applied. Many parliamentarians are not legally trained, and although they have legal advisers, property law is a complex area of legal reasoning and principle more conducive to interpretation and application by the judiciary.

A second major advantage of court intervention is where Parliament fails to act on an important societal issue for fear of electoral unpopularity or backlash. An illustration of this was the native title issue in Australia, where the High Court established a new legal regime in this area in its decision in *Mabo v State of Queensland (No 2)*[86] after many years of political indecision and inaction.

A final advantage is that the common law is able to offer a more nuanced approach to resolving disputes than legislation. Legislation requires a determination in advance by parliamentary counsel and parliamentarians of the whole range of possible disputes and the appropriate manner of their determination. In other words, what is required is 'crystal-ball gazing'. In contrast, common law can be interpreted at the time of each dispute by the courts with the benefit of the actual facts before them. While courts are bound by the doctrine of precedent, there remains considerable flexibility for courts to distinguish or to refuse to apply past cases on a variety of grounds. A considerable range of flexibility exists even under a legalistic approach to judicial determination.[87] This on-the-spot determination with knowledge of the particular facts advances the likelihood of a fair resolution to the dispute at hand.

However, while the courts in common law jurisdictions have the power to create new principles of property law in the absence of conflicting legislation, we must recognize that there are significant limits on what the courts can realistically achieve in promoting sustainable energy development. The following represent the major of these limitations:

- The courts' power to create new law is subject to the ability of the legislature at any time to introduce legislation overturning their decisions. The courts therefore cannot act in a manner that would not have the support of Parliament.
- The courts cannot initiate litigation themselves, and can only act on any issue when a relevant case appears before them. Thus, the courts have to wait for litigants to appear, which is a random and haphazard process. In an area where the law is not established, it is a very risky financial enterprise for people to litigate in the hope that a judge will create new precedent by deciding in their favour. Litigants are at considerable financial risk in taking legal action as if they are unsuccessful they will normally be required to pay the costs of the opposing party. In this area, where large sums of money are not normally in dispute in

---

[86] (1992) 175 CLR 1.
[87] See generally J. Gava, 'A Study in Judging: Sir Owen Dixon and McDonald v Dennys Lascelles' (2009) 32 Australian Bar Review 77.

issues involving renewable energy resources or energy efficiency, potential litigants would be discouraged by the high costs of litigation.

- Potential litigants would be further discouraged by the fact that in all common law jurisdictions court decisions are subject to at least one and often two or more rights of appeal.
- Despite the doctrine of precedent, judicial decisions can easily be distinguished by later courts on various legal grounds. This compounds the parties' costs and acts as a disincentive to litigate in an area involving novel legal issues.
- There is no method for harmonizing the views and actions of judges on new issues. Some judges would undoubtedly regard sustainable energy development more seriously than others. It is thus a matter of chance for litigants as to which judge is assigned to hear their case, as this may well determine the outcome of their dispute.
- One of the major issues retarding the development of renewable energy technologies is legislative barriers, the majority of which predate the modern concern for sustainable energy and which were enacted in other contexts to achieve other goals. Their application to renewable energy technologies is often accidental and unintended by the legislature.[88] The courts are powerless to intervene in this context. Their powers are thus severely limited.

V. Conclusion

While the major role in advancing sustainable energy initiatives and policies rests with the legislature, this chapter has shown that the courts have an important subsidiary role to play in this regard. The application of the property law measures discussed above will not only encourage the production and use of technologies and products supporting sustainable energy but will also provide legal clarification and certainty on the rights of those using such technologies and products. As has always been the case in the energy sector, legal clarification is an essential prerequisite to large-scale investment. Investment is one of the major keys to sustainable energy development.

This chapter also illustrates the potential breadth of the role of property law in the area of energy and natural resources. Far from being a moribund area of ancient concepts and principles, property law can be applied to the resolution of a range of modern societal issues. We must remember that property law is the basis for important still-developing areas of law such as intellectual property, taxation and family property.

---

[88] For examples and discussions of such legal barriers, see A. Bradbrook and A. Wawryk, 'Energy, Sustainable Development and Motor Fuels: Legal Barriers to the Use of Ethanol' (1999) 16 EPLJ 196; D. Taubenfeld and H. Taubenfeld, 'Wind Energy: Legal Issues and Legal Barriers' (1977) 31 Southwestern L J 1053; L. Coit, *Wind Energy: Legal Issues and Institutional Barriers* (1979).

A word of caution should be sounded. While the chapter has focused on the positive role that the courts are capable of exercising in promoting sustainable energy development, it is possible that common law may be used to create legal barriers to its promotion. Much of this potential problem lies in the realm of torts,[89] where a wind user or solar user may be liable for damage caused to neighbours or passers-by as a result of negligence or under strict liability pursuant to the rule in *Rylands v Fletcher*.[90] A more serious concern is liability under the law of nuisance for such possible damage as blade-throwing, fire, structural collapse, injury to television reception, glare or aesthetic injury.[91] The common law is thus a 'two-edged sword' in this regard.

In conclusion, it is submitted that even if the major reforms in the field of sustainable energy development are undertaken by the legislature rather than the courts, this would not remove the need for a fundamental reappraisal by the judiciary of the need to promote sustainable energy development. As the courts have the power to influence the practical effect of any legislation by their interpretation, it can be argued that a change in the attitudes of the judiciary is one of the major keys to the realization of sustainable energy development. As explained by one legal commentator:

Adequate response of the law to the needs of society depends on the willingness of judges to re-evaluate old answers to new problems and to be receptive to social realities. Only through judicial willingness to re-examine established rhetoric in light of harsh realities, and judicial amenability to necessary improvements, can really significant changes occur.[92]

---

[89] A. Bradbrook, 'The Tortious Liability of the User of a Solar Energy System' (1983) 14 Melbourne U L Rev 151; A. Bradbrook, 'The Liability of the User of a Wind Generator in Tort for Personal Injuries' (1986) 15 Melbourne U L Rev 249.

[90] (1868) LR 3 HL 330.

[91] L. Coit, *Wind Energy: Legal Issues and Institutional Barriers* (1979); A. Bradbrook, 'Nuisance and the Right of Solar Access' (1983) 15 U Western Australia L Rev 148; A. Bradbrook, 'Liability in Nuisance for the Operation of Wind Generators' (1984) 1 EPLJ 128.

[92] D. Loeb, 'The Low Income Tenant in California: A Study in Frustration' (1970) 21 Hastings L J 287 at 315–16.

20

Governing Common Resources:
Environmental Markets and
Property in Water

*Lee Godden**

> The most rigid defenders of the momentary legal definition of 'property'
> apparently think 'property' refers to something as substantive as atom and
> mass. But every good lawyer and every good economist knows that 'prop-
> erty' is not a thing but merely a verbal announcement that certain tradi-
> tional powers and privileges of some members of society will be rigorously
> defended against attack by others.[1]

I. Property rights as governance of common resources

Environmental markets, in concert with the rise of property-based instruments
to regulate natural resources, have gained ascendancy in many areas, once the
preserve of more traditional forms of legal regulation. Prominent among the
trends has been the development of cap and trade regimes that utilize property
rights as specific instruments to achieve 'efficiencies' in the regulation of common pool resources such as water, and increasingly in emerging 'resources' such
as greenhouse gas emissions. Adoption of property rights is regarded as instituting a system that prevents the 'tragedy of the commons'. This chapter critically
explores this view by considering the emergence of new forms of property rights
in common pool resources. It then examines a case study of the emergence of
water property rights and market-based mechanisms in water law. The primary

* Professor of Law, University of Melbourne, Australia: email: l.godden@unimelb.edu.au. The
author would like to acknowledge the research support provided by Australian Research Council
Grant Discovery Project 86558, 'Responding to Climate Change: Australia's Environmental Law
and Regulatory Framework'. Research Assistance was provided by the Melbourne Law School
Legal Resource Centre, and editorial assistance by M. Power.
[1] G. Hardin, 'Foreword' in *Should Trees Have Standing: Towards Legal Rights for Natural Objects*
(C. Stone, ed, 1974) i at xii.

focus is upon Australia, although some comparisons are made with other jurisdictions. Finally, the chapter analyses experience with the use of property rights
and trade in water to suggest some potential opportunities and challenges that
property rights and cap and trade regimes may pose for the governance of common pool resources more widely.

II. Property rights: changing models of environmental and natural resource management

The advent of neo-liberal or market-based forms of environmental and natural
resource management over the last few decades obscures the fact that property
rights have long formed the basis for law and regulation of the natural world over
much of the globe. These property rights may pertain to formalized systems of private property or less technologically formalized customary systems of entitlement
and utilization of natural resources. Indeed, many gradations and different forms
of property rights are conceivable: from private property, to state-vested property,
to common property and any number of 'quasi proprietary' rights.[2] Most legal
systems have a core body of rules and normative frameworks that define the relationship between individuals and/or groups, and the lands, waters and resources
that are occupied and used. Such assumptions about the nature of the environment and human relationship to the environment are typically conceptualized in
legal rules in terms of various gradations of access and control which are seen as the
hallmarks of 'property'. In most modern western democracies, historically these
rules revolve around the protection of private property rights. There is only consequential protection for environmental and natural resources as a concomitant of
the legal protection afforded to an individual's economic interest in the land.

Underlying traditional approaches to property law is a pervasive notion that, if
something is designated as property, then property owners have a legal right to
use and control that object—whether land or natural resources—largely without
restriction. There is a famous property law dictum that states that a man (sic) has
sole, despotic dominion over his property. Historically this was inaccurate, and in
contemporary terms there are strong qualifications to legal control over land and
resources that property ownership confers.[3] Nonetheless, a powerful association is
retained between property and use at will. Anthropological insights offer a different
perspective on property rights and natural resource utilization and exchange processes. They illuminate the interrelationships between laws, normative grounds and
institutional practices that mediate between property and systems of allocation,

---

[2] R. Connor and S. Dovers, 'Property Rights Instruments: Transformative Policy Options' in
Property Rights and Responsibilities: Current Australian Thinking (Land and Water Australia, 2002)
119 at 122.
[3] For a discussion see A. Gardner, R. Bartlett and J. Gray, *Water Resources Law* (2009) 542–3.

distribution and use, whereby individuals and groups negotiate for strategic advantage or to gain status. In this manner, property concepts are 'thick' language and cultural constructs with resonances deep into a given society and locale.[4]

Re-appraisals of property rights have sought to refocus attention upon the relational basis and normative function of property law.[5] Where the contextual basis of land-oriented property regimes is now more strongly emphasized, it has enhanced the capacity to have regard to the situated, environmental aspects of property rights. Regulatory models centred on private property, in association with default rules such as civil actions in negligence/nuisance to protect property rights, came to be regarded as less effective in achieving long-term sustainability than more 'purpose-built' environmental legislation. Since the second half of the twentieth century, recognition of the importance of environmental protection and natural resource integrity has become more accepted.[6]

The rise of ecological thought was an important driver for the introduction of broad schemes of environmental law and integrated natural resource management that emerged from the 1970s onward.[7] Developments in environmental protection at an international level had parallels in most western democracies. Since then a comprehensive legislative and institutional framework has been implemented in most jurisdictions. Typically there is government involvement, principally through departments of environment but with significant institutional responsibilities for land and water management within many other government departments, including market regulatory authorities. Sustainable development has achieved prominence as a primary guiding principle informing regulatory objectives.[8] Adaptive governance strategies within the overarching ideal of sustainable development have significant appeal in natural resource management where ongoing management arrangements can be adjusted and improved. Property rights, as traditionally interpreted, as imposing systems that define and secure entitlements at a given point in time, in many ways are counter-intuitive to an adaptive management approach. This tension between secure and certain rights, and the need for ongoing monitoring and adjustment in the management of natural resources remains critical to determining whether market environmentalism as the 'new wave' of property rights regulation is able to achieve sustainable outcomes.[9]

---

[4] *Changing Properties of Property* (F. von Benda-Beckman, K. von Benda-Beckman, and M. G. Wiber, eds, 2006).

[5] J. W. Singer, *Entitlement: The Paradoxes of Property* (2000); J. W. Singer, 'The Social Origins of Property' (1993) 6(2) Can J L Juris 217.

[6] T. O'Riordan, *Environmentalism* (2nd edn, 1981) ix.

[7] D. Fisher, 'The Impact of International Law upon the Australian Environmental Legal System' (1999) 16 EPLJ 372.

[8] J. Peel, 'Ecologically Sustainable Development: More than Mere Lip Service?' (2008) 12 Australasian Journal of Natural Resources Law and Policy 1.

[9] A. Pye, 'Water Trading Along the Murray: A South Australian Perspective' (2006) 23 EPLJ 131 at 144; cf K. Casey, 'Water Entitlements: Across the Property Spectrum' (2008) 27 Australasian Res and Env L J 294 at 301.

More recently, the parameters for the regulation of the environment and natural resources have shifted under prevailing economic discourses. The present
phase is characterized by the growing ascendancy, even dominance, of market
mechanisms and deregulatory approaches.[10] Such perspectives offer an at times
competing and at other times a congruent approach to the previously dominant
discourse of 'ecology', that gave precedence to western scientific knowledge as
the basis for environmental and natural resource governance, management structures and institutions.

A. Market environmentalism

Market environmentalism—denoting a complex of regulatory, structural economic social, cultural and institutional changes—has assumed an increasing
role in natural resource management and environmental protection over the last
two decades.[11] These influences, fashioned by both global and local factors, have
reshaped many aspects of the interface between common pool resources, and
the governing models of environmental and natural resource management across
many countries.

The property-rights model is now advocated as an increasingly viable basis
for environmental and natural resource laws, albeit that the resurgent forms
are quite different in many respects from the previous property rights model.
Accordingly, there now exists a wide spectrum of legal and regulatory instruments and approaches that are potentially available to govern environmental
and natural resources. At one end of this spectrum, free-market environmentalists contend that—provided property rights in relation to the environment and
natural resources are well-defined and protected through liability rules—transactions amongst those causing and suffering from environmental degradation
can achieve an outcome where negative environmental externalities are internal-
ized, with limited need for government regulation.[12] Similarly, the introduction
of tradeable rights in resources is regarded as allowing resources to be used by
the most efficient and highest-value user.

In this manner, regulatory power can be devolved from the state to the market. Generally, the impetus for market-based models accords with the perspective
that environmental problems and natural resources degradation is the result of
either poorly defined property rights in resources or an inadequate accounting for
environmental costs and externalities.

---

[10] P. Kinrade, 'Towards Ecologically Sustainable Development: The Role and Shortcomings of
Markets' in *Markets, the State, and the Environment: Towards Integration* (R. Eckersley, ed, 1995)
86 at 86.
[11] R. Eckersley, 'Markets, the State and the Environment: An Overview' in Eckersley, ed, ibid,
1 at 7.
[12] See, eg, T. L. Anderson and D. Leal, *Free Market Environmentalism* (2000).

1. Perceived advantages of market mechanisms

Advocates for transition to a market-based model have achieved most success in recent years, although there has been ongoing debate over the advantages of market tools since the late 1980s.[13] Market-based approaches have become pervasive in specific environmental sectors, such as greenhouse gas emission mitigation.[14] More widely, the claims made in favour of a market-based model typically suggest it has lower cost and greater efficiencies. Market tools, as regulatory mechanisms, it is argued, can enhance positive social behaviour towards environmental compliance through market pricing of resources or the property system rather than direct government intervention via legislative standards and penalties.[15] Such tools are regarded as less prescriptive; with flexibility as to how compliance is achieved.[16] Proponents also contend that such approaches have the potential to promote better environmental outcomes as it gives an economic incentive for efficient resource utilization.[17]

In contrast, other commentators indicate that historically, property rights are oriented to relatively narrow interactions where the contribution of individuals to environmental and natural resource degradation can be readily identified and quantified. Faced with increasingly diffuse, complex environmental problems and natural resource degradation, the transaction costs associated with private bargaining on the basis of property rights may become prohibitively high, as it is difficult to determine who is responsible for resource degradation and to what extent. Typically this phenomenon is identified as the failure of property-based and market regimes to deal with 'third party effects', including intergenerational equity concerns.[18] In such instances of 'market failure' government regulatory intervention may be more appropriate, and indeed may be warranted by the need to engage the wider public interest.

Despite a wide spectrum of regulatory tools being available to governments, property based approaches have exhibited a strong resurgence as a governance model in the environmental and natural resource fields. In large measure, this resurgence relies on the theory—embedded in market environmentalism—that private property owners are best placed to manage environmental outcomes

---

[13] See, eg, B. A. Ackerman and R. B. Stewart, 'Reforming Environmental Law' (1985) 37 Stan L Rev 1333.

[14] See M. Passero, 'The Nature of the Right or Interest Created by a Market for Forest Carbon' (2008) 2 Carbon and Climate L Rev 248 at 249.

[15] N. Gunningham, 'Bringing the "R" Word Back In: Regulation, Environment Protection and NRM', An Academy of the Social Sciences Policy Roundtable Canberra, 4 August 2009 (copy on file with author).

[16] For discussion see Ackerman and Stewart (above n 13).

[17] See K. Casey, 'Water Entitlements: Across the Property Spectrum' (2008) 27 Australasian Res and Env L J 294 at 301.

[18] For a discussion of ecologically sustainable development and intergenerational equity see *Walker v Minister for Planning* (2007) 157 Local Government Environment Reports Australia 124, 147–55.

under their control because it is in their long-term interests to do so.[19] A similar 'wise-use' assumption underlies many legal regimes for natural resources, such as administrative schemes for fishing rights where various individuals hold transferable quotas entitling them to a given portion of the total allowable catch for a species.[20] In each instance the 'allocation' is a result of interplay between government processes and individual 'rights'. Even under market environmentalism, there are few systems where the property rights are entirely 'free-standing', as typically there are gradations in the degree of governmental control and oversight.[21]

2. Re-designing property rights

By contrast to the physically-referenced concept of property at common law, one of the significant trends of market environmentalism has been the need to articulate new dimensions of property rights. These emerging property rights do not pertain so directly to physical orientations, even though these 'rights' may be claimed as furthering the sustainability of the environment and natural resources. For example, trading in water entitlements requires a redesign of property-based instruments away from land-oriented definitions of property. Historically in common law systems, water use entitlements were typically expressed as riparian rights,[22] and were regulated by law as concomitant of land holding. The emerging property rights in common pool resources that form the foundation of new models of market regulation typically contemplate a distinct entity that exists, and can be regulated, largely independently of land holding. However, while the governance mode is one that contemplates a separation of the tradeable resource rights and land holding, such independence often remains counterfactual at a practical level.

Generally speaking, the emerging property 'rights' are created by statute, even though such statutes may employ a terminology derived from traditional property law schema.[23] Thus the new property in common pool resources such as water rights, biodiversity credits, carbon credits and ecosystem 'services' are created by legislation (albeit often in association with private law forms, such as contract) in order for the market-based strategy to be implemented within an existing legal system.[24]

Thus, what is different about current utilization of property frameworks under market environmentalism is that the 'property rights' are more tenuous in their linkages to 'land' or place. Indeed, the essence of newly emerging property forms

[19] D. Fitzpatrick, 'Evolution and Chaos in Property Rights Systems; The Third World Tragedy of Contested Access' (2006) 115 Yale L J 996 at 1006.
[20] R. O'Connor and B. McNamara, 'Individual Transferable Quotas and Property Rights' in *The Politics of Fishing* (T. Gray, ed, 1998) 81.
[21] *Yanner v Eaton* (1999) 201 CLR 351 (HCA).
[22] D. Fisher, 'Markets, Water Rights and Sustainable Development' (2006) 23 EPLJ 100.
[23] See B. Barton, in this volume.
[24] For an early example of this, see the creation of forestry rights in NSW, protected in the Conveyancing Act 1916 (NSW) Pt 6 Div 4.

is their very lack of explicit 'land' connection and the enhanced capacity to be freely alienable and traded. Where once property rights connoted an attachment to place, the virtue of emerging models of property rights in common pool resources, such as water, biodiversity and sequestered carbon, is that they can function as commensurate values. These values are related to exchange and trade rather than a specific land and place, as the older institutions of property and law are reshaped to meet new social, economic and political imperatives that drive the new forms for managing the environment and natural resources. These new managerial forms are directly correlated with a re-emergence of exchange and contractual forms of regulation. Edgeworth argues that '... individual consumer choice driven by specifically individual and differentiated goods and services, rather than universal state provision of standard, uniform goods and services [has become] the axial principle of public policy and social organisation'.[25] In this context market environmentalism exemplifies a regulatory mechanism of 'new property', that can explain the shift in water law from state provision to market exchange as a public policy position.

B. Common pool resources—is property necessary?

While these new normative agendas surround emerging resource property systems and institutions,[26] in most instances there is limited acknowledgement of the view that property and natural resource systems are social governance constructs.[27] Classical economic models do acknowledge, indeed they assume, 'relationships'; but they typically focus on simplified, exchange and transactional relations between individuals and forms of economic organization. According to economic perspectives, '[p]roperty rights of individuals over assets consist of the rights, or the powers, to consume, obtain income from, and alienate these assets. Obtaining income from and alienating assets requires exchange; exchange is a mutual ceding of rights'.[28]

In the current era of globalization and overarching economic regulation, this character of fungibility has been critical as it allows resources to be made transferable, and ultimately, the subject of transactions.[29] In other words, property rights function in the market. This fact often is glossed over by lawyers in conceptualizing property and obscured by theoretical analyses,[30] although acutely highlighted by the identification of private property with efficiency parameters in many classical economic models. Models, such as the social cost theory of private property,

[25] B. Edgeworth, *Law, Modernity, PostModernity: Legal Change in the Contracting State* (2003) 136.
[26] ibid.
[27] cf Fitzpatrick (above n 19) at 1009.
[28] Y. Barzel, *Economic Analysis of Property* Rights (1989) 2.
[29] Edgeworth (above n 25) at 135–6.
[30] C. Rose, 'The Moral Subject of Property' (2007) 48 WMLR 1899 at 1895.

developed by Coase,[31] implicitly require a market or at least some form of organizational capacity that allows exchange. Accordingly, the property rights in market environmental frameworks for governing common pool resources typically comprise a mixture of default legal and quasi-legal rules that comprise a form of 'ownership' predicated upon market exchange.[32]

1. Evolution towards private property?

Indeed, under the impetus of strongly articulated constructs of 'ownership' and market exchange constructs, influential property theories typically regard the evolution toward private property and formal resource management systems as virtually inevitable.[33] Within law, Demsetz is credited with advancing the argument that rising resource values will precipitate the establishment of property rights where the benefits of private ownership are greater than the associated costs.[34] Under evolutionary models of property law that adopt this cost/benefit formula, property rights will emerge from the 'primordial soup'[35] when benefits to be gained from capturing resource rents (ie profits from land and resource use) outweigh the costs of internalization of externalities and of enforcement. Demsetz's theory held that when a resource was plentiful an open access regime would prevail with little need for 'ownership'. Ownership, it is argued, is the paramount form of property right,[36] although in most common law systems, for example, ownership as such is not a designated right *per se*, but conceived as a bundle of rights.[37] With increasing scarcity (and thus value) the competition for resources leads to the instigation of ownership by 'self interested' (ie utility maximizing) individuals through physical or technological means, or by bargaining with other claimants. Yet, as Fisher suggests, there is a need to delineate what is meant by the designation of 'property' in common pool resource contexts,[38] as no simple, broad type of property regime will fit the physical characteristics and technological requirements of diverse resources. Pertinently, Fisher contemplates a distinction between various rights of access, use and control, all of which may pertain as 'property' in environmental and resource governance contexts.[39]

Moreover, the highly contingent character of these evolutionary property theories is now being acknowledged, and '[c]ontrary to Demsetzian formulations, property rights do not necessarily emerge where their gains outweigh their

---

[31] R. Coase, 'The Problem of Social Cost' (1960) 3 J L & Econ 1.
[32] P. Mennell and J. Dwyer, 'Reunifying Property' (2002) 46 St L U L J 599 at 602.
[33] M. Trebilcock and P. Veel, 'Property Rights and Development: the Contingent Case for Formalization' (2007) University of Toronto, Faculty of Law Research Paper No 10, 55, 69–71.
[34] See discussion by Fitzpatrick (above n 19) at 998.
[35] See Rose (above n 30).
[36] H. Demsetz, 'Toward a Theory of Property Rights' (1967) 57 Am Econ Rev 347, H. Demsetz, 'Toward a Theory of Property Rights II: The Competition Between Private and Collective Ownership' (2002) 31 JLS 653.
[37] See J. Watson-Hamilton and N. Bankes, in this volume.
[38] D. Fisher, 'Rights of Property in Water: Confusion or Clarity' (2004) 21 EPLJ 200 at 203.
[39] ibid.

costs, or as a natural consequence of constrained cost-minimization decisions by resource participants'.[40] Yet until recently, most property theory developed in environmental and resource contexts have routinely adopted the cost-benefit formulation to explain the emergence of property rights. Coase, in his widely-adopted model, uses the evolutionary framework as a resolution to the social cost problem of externalities; which have particular pertinence for problems of environmental and natural resource degradation. Externalities basically comprehend the disadvantages or negative utilities of the use of land and exploitation of resources. Pollution is a classic externality in industrial and urban societies. Coase argued that in a world without transaction costs, those affected by externalities would bargain with the land or resource user either to receive compensation or to induce a change in the land or resource use. Under such impetus, the land or resource might be transferred and it would then be in the hands of the party who valued it most.[41] The assumptions being that this 'owner' would efficiently monitor land and resource use, exclude those without access and/or usufructary rights, and bear the consequences of the negative utilities for surrounding users.

Such an assumption hinges on the implied view that a lack of private property rights will remove incentives to take on such 'efficiencies' and ultimately lead to dissipation of the resource.[42] The limitations and imprecision of the 'tragedy of the commons' consequences that this scenario suggests have been vigorously debated.[43]

2. Critiques of the efficiency concept

Within common law countries, many jurisprudential analyses have levelled criticisms against attempts to construct the notion of 'efficiency' within the paradigm of law-and-economics as an ethical norm. The major criticism is that efficiency, as a component of overarching wealth maximization strategies, does not deal adequately with the distributive disparities.[44] Moreover, many common pool resource models related to social cost theories have subsequently proven difficult to implement across a range of empirical situations, especially where there is weak governmental regulation.[45] Nonetheless, the purported causal association between private property and efficient resource allocation and use remains strongly persuasive in international and national policy contexts, resurfacing in diverse countries and situations.[46]

---

[40] Fitzpatrick (above n 19) at 1000.

[41] Coase (above n 31), as discussed in Fitzpatrick (above n 19) at 1006.

[42] D. Lueck, 'Contracting into the Commons' in *The Political Economy of Customs and Culture; Informal Solutions to the Commons Problem* (T. Anderson and R. Simmons, eds, 1993) 43 at 43.

[43] Hardin in his original thesis called for overt centralized regulation. It was the influence of theorists such as Richard Posner that associated formal property rights with prevention of the commons tragedy. See, eg, R. Posner, *Economic Analysis of Law* (1983).

[44] See, eg, R. Dworkin, 'Why Efficiency?' (1980) 8 Hof L Rev 563; D. Kennedy and F. Michelman, 'Are Property and Contract Efficient?' (1980) 8 Hof L Rev 711.

[45] Trebilcock and Veel (above n 33) at 10.

[46] For a representative example see B. H. Thompson Jr, 'Tragically difficult: the obstacles to governing the commons' (2000) 30 EL 241.

3. Property rights and efficiency

The adoption of Coase's social cost model as the underpinning theory for many aspects of market environmentalism, in conjunction with evolutionary models of property law, has further reinforced a perceived disjunction between the wastefulness of the commons and the careful husbandry of private property as the appropriate means to enhance net social utility.[47] A further extrapolation has occurred that links efficiency of resource exploitation with sustainable outcomes. For example, in Australia under the impetus of national competition policy reforms, sustainability concepts have been pared down to equate with 'wise-use' measures that historically derive from resource economic frameworks.[48] By contrast, some more acutely localized empirical studies[49] suggest that common property governance remains strongly viable.

In this vein, Ostrom's research has provided a more nuanced conception of the varied rights, including proprietary rights that may pertain over common pool resources. Her analysis, by strong reference to empirical data, challenges the view that the formal institution of private property alone can provide effective governance for common pool resources.[50] Specific analyses of common pool resources, such as fisheries, demonstrates that a complex interplay of operational rules govern everyday activities—such as the access to the fishery resource and the capacity to take resources from the common pool. A distinction is drawn between operational rules and rights. Rules are defined as 'generally agreed upon and enforced prescriptions that require, forbid or permit specific actions for an individual'[51] and these 'rights' can be articulated along a spectrum from authorized users to 'owners' of the resource.

Ostrom's highly influential work in common pool resource governance emphasizes the distinction between rights at an operational level (ie to withdraw fish) and 'higher order' rights at a collective choice level. Collective choice rights are regarded as most significant as 'the authority to devise future operational level rights is what makes collective choice rights so powerful'.[52] Ostrom's approach offers some valuable counterpoints to formal legal schema for determining property. In particular, her empirical research identifies a plurality of sources for collective choice rules. The insight that effective governance of communal resources incorporates both formal legal rule making and informal norm setting in social and cultural arenas is of particular relevance to the use of property-based

---

[47] R. Barnes, *Property Rights and Natural Resources* (2009) 63.

[48] For a specific discussion of the influence of economic theories in the evolution of property in resources see A. Scott, 'Property Rights and Property Wrongs' (1983) 16 Can J Econ 555 and A. Scott, *The Evolution of Resource Property Rights* (2008).

[49] Hardin (above n 1).

[50] E. Ostrom, *Governing the Commons: The Evolution of Institutions for Collective Action* (1990).

[51] E. Schlager and E. Ostrom, 'Property-Rights Regimes and Coastal Fisheries: An Empirical Analysis' in *The Political Economy of Customs and Culture: Informal Solutions to the Commons Problem* (T. L. Anderson and R. T. Simmons, eds, 1993) 13 at 15.

[52] ibid.

instruments to regulate environmental resources.[53] Typically, prevailing instruments are very crude in their incorporation of diverse social and cultural values. Moreover, where the physical movement of resources is precipitated by property and trade regimes, the structural change and community impacts that are associated with market exchange are generally inadequately captured.[54]

Further, there remains the knotty problem of transaction costs for formal property systems. Transaction costs are associated with capturing resource rents, the protection and enforcement of rights, and any ultimate transfer of property. Transaction costs, in enforcing property rights in legal systems, even by such prosaic means as suburban fences, is a costly and time-consuming activity—a factor often disregarded in many assessments of the efficiency of property and trading regimes.[55] Moreover, as many empirically grounded studies acknowledge, the enforcement of property rights and its corollary, exclusivity, in the absence of direct physical coercion, will depend on either normative communal 'coercion' or state institutional systems for delineating property rights and ensuring their competent administration.[56]

In the context of state institutional and administrative systems, the rigid demarcation between informal and formal rules, practices and sanctions has been blurred by the increasing array of regulatory tools adopted by governments, including behavioural change modes of governance in the environmental and natural resource areas. Thus while the 'new' market environmentalism property rights frameworks are strongly advocated for common pool resource governance, such instruments are typically implemented as part of a wider regulatory strategy.[57] Arguably it is getting the regulatory tool mix 'right' that is seen as the most pressing problem for effective governance in determining the long-term sustainable outcomes for common pool resources, rather than the viability of any one regulatory instrument or tool.[58] Yet a shift towards a spectrum of modes of governance also poses challenges for the state. The use of a multiplicity of strategies and instruments risks making policy objectives too diffuse to be effective.

Therefore, despite regulatory ambiguities and practices, many adherents of economic-oriented analyses continue to frame the problem of environmental and common pool resource degradation as amenable to singular approaches based around market instruments. The advocacy of this 'solution' to the problem is predicated on the view that environmental assets lack a value in the market, and

---

[53] C. Ferreyra, 'Imagined Communities, Contested Watersheds and Water Governance' (2008) 24 Journal of Rural Studies 304.

[54] L. Godden, 'Water Law Reform in Australia and South Africa: Sustainability, Efficiency and Social Justice' (2005) 17 JEL 182.

[55] M. Omura, 'Property Rights and Natural Resource Management Incentives: Do Transferability and Formality Matter?' (2008) 90 Am J Ag Econ 1143 at 1151.

[56] Fitzpatrick (above n 19) at 1000.

[57] B. Morgan and K. Yeung, *An Introduction to Law and Regulation: Text and Materials* (2007) 3.

[58] C. Biesaga, 'Water Markets: No Substitute for Effective Governance', paper delivered to 'Systemic and adaptive water governance': Reconfiguring Institutions for social learning and more effective water managing? 5 December 2008, The University of Melbourne (copy on file with author).

that value can be best expressed through property rights. To provide empirical context for the foregoing assessment of such arguments, the following section considers the instigation of water markets and water trading regimes as one proffered solution to the problem of governing common resources.

III. Market tools: trading in water as a common pool resource

The instigation of water 'property' that can be transferred or traded has been occurring for many years in particular countries, although these schemes have become more formalized with the advent of market environmentalism. Water transfers denote both acquisition of new water units or a reallocation of existing entitlements,[59] but the use of the term 'transfer' highlights the premise that such transfer requires the relocation of water.[60] The capacity of the new property forms to mobilize resources was identified above as a distinguishing characteristic. Transferability is an important aspect of new property in water, as it is part of the wider shift away from continually developing new sources of water to meet emerging economic and social demands. While typically most water transfers involve short distances, the very movement of water out of locations may disrupt established social and economic patterns,[61] engender conflicts over water use, and pose a threat to the long-term viability of ecosystems. In specific instances such transfers may be part of explicit or implicit policy agendas to institute structural change through water markets.[62]

Primarily, it is common law countries where water scarcity pertains due to climatic features that have introduced water property and trading. Accordingly, jurisdictions such as Australia,[63] the western states of the USA,[64] and to a lesser extent South Africa[65] and some countries in Central and South America have established water trading regimes under water legislation.[66] However, given the

---

[59] A. D. Tralock, 'Water Transfers: A Means to Achieve Sustainable Water Use' in *Fresh Water and International Economic Law* (E. Brown Weiss, L. Boisson De Chazournes and N. Benasconi-Osterwalder, eds, 2005) 35 at 37.

[60] Fisher (above n 38).

[61] Godden (above n 54) at 192.

[62] Productivity Commission, *Water Rights Arrangements in Australia and Overseas* (2003).

[63] See Water Act 2007 (Cth) ss 97–99; Water Management Act 2000 (NSW) s 71Q; Water Act 1989 (Vic) ss 62, 33S–33Z, 46–46A; Water Act 2000 (Qld) Part 6; Water Act 1992 (NT) s 22B(5)(c); Natural Resources Management Act 2004 (SA) Ch 7, Pt 3; Water Management Act 1999 (Tas) s 60, Pt 6 Div 4; Rights in Water and Irrigation Act 1914 (WA) s 5C(3), Sch 1 cl1, ss 29(1)(a), 31(1), 34; Water Resources Act 2007 (ACT) s 26.

[64] Arizona Revised Statutes §§ 45–172, 45–1001–1063; Arkansas Code Annotated §15–22–304; California Water Code §§ 109, 2100, 1610; Idaho Code Statute Annotated § 42–222; Indiana Code § 13–2–9–8; Kansas Statutes Annotated (Water Appropriation Act 1945) § 82a-701(g); Kentucky Revised Statutes § 151.150(1); Montana Code Annotated (Water Use Act 1973) § 85–2-102; Nevada Revised Statutes § 533–345; Annotated Statutes of New Mexico § 72–5-22 & 23.

[65] National Water Act 1998 s 25.

[66] See, eg, the Chilean Water Code 1981, the Peruvian Water Resources Law 2009 and the Mexican National Water Law 2002.

wide variability in how water rights, property and trading are defined in respective jurisdictions, care should be taken with any suggestion that all such schemes entail fully transferable water property and established trading systems.

Indeed, as Hodgson's analysis indicates, although there is a concern to encourage adoption of formal 'property' rights in water to avoid 'damaging economic consequences',[67] the formalization of water rights may not always be accompanied by fully fungible and transferable water entitlements.[68] Nonetheless, Hodgson's analysis reinforces the pervasiveness of the view that formal property rights are a necessary step to avoiding the 'tragedy of the commons' (or in market environmental terms, 'damaging economic consequences').

The instigation of fully fungible water rights typically occurs where the market is seen as the most efficient (and economical) arrangement to permit reallocations of water. Clearly it is possible to reallocate water rights through administrative and institutional processes. In theory, water rights can be reduced or re-distributed by governments. In the context of market environmentalism though, the explicit redistribution of water allocations by governments is generally seen as politically unpalatable and economically inefficient, particularly where governments have constitutional imperatives to compensate when water rights are acquired for re-distribution.

Tarlock identifies a number of drivers for the introduction of water markets in the USA under the general economic efficiency argument of moving water from low value to high value uses.[69] Diffuse, non-state power groups developed to disrupt existing institutional capacity to mediate water demands, in favour of sectoral interests such as urban water supply needs. He points to the adoption of water market philosophies by mainline environmental groups in the mid-1980s who opposed new storages as important to this shift. Concurrent changes in federal water policy to a more devolved pattern of administration and funding also precipitated enhanced receptivity to water markets. Old and new stakeholders demanded a seat in the 'multiparty bargaining processes that characterize many allocation conflicts ...'.[70] While a confluence of interests developed to push water markets, there remained two key objections. The first is that water markets are sound in theory, but legal and institutional barriers will result in prohibitive transaction costs. Secondly, water transfer is 'immoral' as it commodifies water and removes communal values. 'Many communities object to being de-watered and to the consequent loss of political and economic power and viability that follows.'[71]

These factors advanced for and against water markets typify debates around market environmentalism more generally. With this background of competing assessments of water property in mind, this chapter turns to consider Australia as it is a

---

[67] Productivity Commission (above n 62) at 24.
[68] ibid at 5–6.
[69] ibid at 38–9.
[70] ibid at 40.
[71] ibid at 41.

paradigm example of the adoption of market-based property approaches to water governance designed around explicit efficiency goals. The example of water trading in Australia provides one of the most acute case studies available to explore the feasibility of cap and trade property-based schemes for common pool resources.

IV. Market mechanisms and water trading in Australia

Market-based measures for environmental and natural resources management are distinguished by underpinning economic theories that support their implementation.[72] Until the last decade or so, the theories of market tools were more discussed than used in Australian law. While recent years have seen the increasing use of property instruments in association with cap and trade schemes, the use of market mechanisms is less pervasive than might be expected given the overarching policy commitment by Australian federal and state governments to such approaches. At the federal level, a major reorientation of Australia's climate change policy since 2007 has seen the federal government release draft exposure legislation for a carbon pollution reduction scheme, with a projected implementation date of 2011.[73]

In addition, state governments in Australia have legislated to separate rights to carbon in timber from the land on which trees are grown,[74] paving the way for carbon offset trading.[75] These initiatives build on a number of legislative developments supporting market-based instruments at the state level and include several pilot trading schemes, such as the Hunter River salinity trading scheme. Many proposals are now emerging for trade in ecosystem services, which embrace various aspects of biodiversity conservation, drought and flood mitigation projects or the stabilization of the climate.[76] As these services have not been traded in the past on a market basis, regulating their provision typically is regarded as requiring the creation of property rights in ecosystems or specific components of ecosystems.

---

[72] S. Bell and J. Quiggin, 'The Limits of Markets: The Politics of Water Management in Rural Australia' (2008) 17 Environmental Politics 712.

[73] Carbon Pollution Reduction Scheme Bill 2009 (Cth); Australian Climate Change Regulatory Authority Bill 2009 (Cth); Carbon Pollution Reduction Scheme (Consequential Amendments) Bill 2009 (Cth); Carbon Pollution Reduction Scheme (Charges – General) Bill 2009 (Cth); Carbon Pollution Reduction Scheme (Charges – Excise) Bill 2009 (Cth); Carbon Pollution Reduction Scheme (Charges – Customs) Bill 2009 (Cth).

[74] See Carbon Rights Legislation Amendment Act 1998 (NSW), amending Pt 6 Div 4 of the Conveyancing Act 1919 (NSW); Forestry Rights (Amendment) Act 2000 (Vic), amending the Forestry Rights Act 1996 (Vic); Forest Property Act 2000 (SA) s 3A; Forestry and Land Title Act 2001 (Qld), inserting Pt 6B into the Forestry Act 1959 (Qld); Forestry Rights Registration Act 1990 (Tas); Carbon Rights Act 2003 (WA).

[75] A. Thompson and R. Campbell-Watt, 'Carbon Rights—Development of the Legal Framework for a Trading Market' (2004) 2 NELR 31.

[76] For one such proposal see J. Agius, 'Biodiversity Credits: Creating Missing Markets for Biodiversity' (2001) 18 EPLJ 481.

However, by far the most fully implemented property rights/cap and trade scheme in operation in Australia is the water trading scheme operating in the Murray-Darling Basin.[77] Even so, '[w]ater markets in Australia have revealed themselves to be uneven in development and a little unpredictable in nature'.[78]

V. Water markets in the Murray-Darling Basin

The National Water Initiative agreed by the Council of Australian Governments in 2004[79] brought policy trends in favour of water trading to the surface, drawing on a national water law reform agenda,[80] and national competition policies designed to address what was perceived as a looming tragedy of the commons in the Murray-Darling Basin (MDB).[81] Market environmentalism formed the underlying rationale as Pye comments: '...water reforms were originally driven and underpinned by economic rationalism. However, they have been delayed in implementation because even those continuing to push market theory have had to acknowledge that the market and improved efficiencies were not going to provide the desired environmental outcomes...'.[82]

The most controversial element of the water law reforms in Australia over the last three decades has been the separation of an entitlement to water from land holding.[83] Effectively these legal changes instituted a system of property entitlements that could then be made the subject of trade.[84] As Fisher notes, '...in the context of tradable water entitlements,...before the possibility of widespread trading in water can occur, there is a need for property right arrangements formally to be put in place'.[85] These arrangements for instituting property in water marked a significant change in the governance of water as a common pool resource within Australia. Concurrently there was the recognition that the environment itself required a water 'entitlement', generally referred to as an environmental flow or an environmental water reserve.[86] Water law reforms were orchestrated by intergovernmental agreements and incentive payments to state jurisdictions

---

[77] A. Pye, 'Water Trading Along the Murray: A South Australian Perspective' (2006) 23 EPLJ 131.

[78] Gardner, Bartlett and Gray (above n 3) at 566.

[79] Council of Australian Governments, *Intergovernmental Agreement on a National Water Initiative* (2004) (National Water Initiative).

[80] See Attachment A to the Communique, Council of Australian Governments' Meeting, Hobart, 25 February 1994, available at <http://www.coag.gov.au>.

[81] Productivity Commission, *Water Resources and Waste Disposal* (1992).

[82] Pye (above n 77) at 146.

[83] J. McKay and H. Bjornlund, 'Recent Australian Market Mechanisms as a Component of an Environmental Policy' in Land and Water Australia (above n 2) 137 at 138.

[84] D. Fisher, *Implementing the National Water Initiative: A Generic Set of Arrangements for Managing Interests in Water* (2006) 1, available at <http://eprints.qut.edu.au/6355/>.

[85] Fisher (above n 38) at 200.

[86] See, eg, Water Act 1989 (Vic) s 4A.

to implement water law reforms, largely based upon market parameters[87]—an approach reinforced by the National Water Initiative. A key goal of the National Water Initiative is 'a nationally-compatible, market, regulatory and planning based system of managing surface and groundwater resources for rural and urban use that optimizes economic, social and environmental outcomes'.[88]

The recent introduction of new federal water legislation, the Water Act 2007 (Cth), has provided an overarching jurisdiction for water planning and trading across the basin. However, much of the detailed implementation of water plans and trade will remain with state governments, which historically have had the main responsibility for water governance. More generally, water plans are to provide for both 'secure ecological outcomes' and 'resource security outcomes' through the designation of shares in the consumptive pool of water and rules regarding water allocation and trade.[89]

There is not a single national water market in the MDB. 'Instead markets largely operate within states, catchments, water systems and zones, although this appears to be changing slowly. There is a developing interstate water market.'[90] Central to the introduction of water trading in the MDB has been the emergence of water property rights,[91] largely as a consequence of government institution of scarcity through regulation creating a cap on extractions of water in the basin to address historic levels of over-allocation.

Administrative institutions and practices for water management in the MDB had resulted in highly over-allocated water resources across most water catchments. Over the twentieth century, a complex institutional structure of multi-level water instrumentalities developed, largely to satisfy consumptive demand for water. Continual pressure for more water supply resulted in levels of consumptive entitlements beyond environmental capacity in many catchments.[92] As a result, natural systems in most parts of the MDB are highly degraded with threatened ecological collapse in many sections—a tragedy in progress. In addition, there is intense conflict and competition between water users over scarce water resources, with irrigated agriculture (which uses by far the largest share of water) and major regional cities facing uncertain futures.

This situation has been accentuated under climate change scenarios of sustained water scarcity and highly variable levels of precipitation,[93] accompanied

---

[87]   Fisher (above n 38).
[88]   National Water Initiative (above n 79) at [23].
[89]   ibid at [37].
[90]   Gardner, Bartlett and Gray (above n 3) at 556.
[91]   M. Bond and D Farrier, 'Transferable Water Allocations—Property Rights or Shining Mirage' (1996) 13 EPLJ 215.
[92]   A. Gardner, and K Bowmer, 'Environmental Water Allocations and their Governance', in *Managing Water for Australia: the Social and Institutional Challenges* (K. Hussey and S. Dovers, eds, 2007) 48 at 50.
[93]   R. Jones et al, *Future impacts of climate variability, climate change and land use change on water resources in the Murray Darling Basin: Overview and Draft Program of Research* (2002).

by dramatic changes in inflow to major storages across the MDB, but reaching critically low levels in the southern part of the Basin.[94] The capacity of legal and regulatory structures to provide a sustainable balance between consumptive and environmental water requirements will be critical to the long-term viability of the MDB. Therefore, the implementation of water trading in these circumstances provides a litmus test for whether property rights and water trading regimes can achieve both efficiency and environmental sustainability.

Progress in implementing water trading varies widely across the jurisdictions within the MDB, even though there was an agreement '...to establish by 2007 compatible institutional and regulatory arrangements that facilitate intra and interstate trade, and manage differences in entitlement reliability, supply losses, supply source constraints, trading between systems, and cap requirements'.[95] These measures were aimed at reducing the transaction costs that Tarlock identified as barriers to effective implementation of market approaches. However, water trades are not free of regulatory restraint; they exemplify blended modes of market and state regulation. For instance, the 'Principles for Trading Rules' specified by the National Water Initiative include permission for trades to be refused on the basis of inconsistency with a relevant water plan and the principle that '[t]rades must not generally result in sustainable yields being exceeded'.[96]

A. Unbundling reforms to facilitate water trade

The state of Victoria is the most advanced in adopting a water governance system that most fully replicates the goals of the National Water Initiative. It is an instructive example of the working of environmental markets and the substantial implementation of a cap and trade regime. A significant overhaul of water management arrangements in Victoria during the 1980s led to the Water Act 1989.[97] Yet the key process was to clarify and protect consumptive-based rights to water by conversion to a formal Bulk Entitlement allocated to water authorities.[98] This secured to authorities the legal right to divert water and to sell it to individual customers such as urban consumers and irrigators, thereby establishing the foundations for a legal, regulated water market. Such entitlements are the basic entity from which the government creates the individual water rights that are open to trade. Tweaking at the margins of the existing entitlement scheme has also provided for some relatively limited environmental water allocations.[99]

---

[94] ibid.

[95] National Water Initiative (above n 79) at [60].

[96] ibid at Sch G, [4]–[5].

[97] P. Tan, 'Irrigators Come First: Conversion of Existing Allocations to Bulk Entitlements in the Goulburn and Murray Catchments, Victoria' (2001) 18 EPLJ 154 at 154–5.

[98] J. Pigram and B. Hopper, (eds), *Transferability of Water Entitlements: Proceedings of an International Seminar and Workshop* (1990).

[99] A. Foerster, 'Victoria's New "Environmental Water Reserve:" What's in a Name?' (2007) 11 Australasian Journal of Natural Resources Law and Policy 145.

The most recent round of reforms in Victoria[100] introduced measures targeted at individual water 'rights' to support environmental protection, as well as water trading and pricing initiatives. The Water (Resource Management) Act 2005 introduced measures for the facilitation of trade, including water registration and recording facilities for water trade, adoption of a legal status for environmental water (that can include water purchased/traded for environmental sustainability purposes), and assessments of the long term sustainability of the water resource— all in the context of severe climatic change.

More specific unbundling reforms were contained in 2006 amendments and included s 6A of the Water Act, which stages the conversion of existing individual water rights (largely those supplying irrigation water) into water shares, water-use licences and delivery services. A water share is a new form of entitlement that constitutes a percentage share of the available water resource in a catchment or storage. Existing water entitlements will be progressively brought under the unbundled scheme. Thus water allocations at law constitute a share, based upon available water in the relevant system—up to a maximum amount. Water shares equate in various ways with a 'property right', but their statutory character renders it problematic as to whether they are directly equivalent to common law 'landed' property interests.[101] The exact legal status of these water shares will be tested in coming months when the Australian High Court determines whether the conversion of existing groundwater entitlements to a water 'shares' scheme constitutes an acquisition of property that is compensable.[102]

Water shares can be freely traded, although there is a limit set. Currently, only 10 per cent of water shares can be held independently of land holding. Pursuant to s 33F of the Water Act, the minister may issue a water share upon application or under a contract of sale,[103] subject to certain restrictions.[104] The key trading provisions are in Division 5 of the Act. Section 33S facilitates water trade, as it allows for the 'owner' of a water share to transfer the share to another person (an 'owner' can be a tenant in common). There is provision for a transfer of future rights, and transfer of water on a temporary basis (for example, for one irrigation season).

Water trade is subject to various regulatory approvals, many of which have an environmental role, such as salinity management constraints. Water trade into certain areas of rising water table remains highly regulated. Delivery fees are attached to water shares to recover water infrastructure costs.[105] Fees owed to an authority are a charge on the share. Moreover, an unbundled water share

---

[100] Government of Victoria, *Securing our Water Future Together: Victorian Government White Paper* (2004).

[101] Doug Fisher initially argued that such entitlements should be treated as administrative dispositions: see above n 38.

[102] Transcript of Proceedings, *ICM Agriculture Pty Ltd v Commonwealth* (High Court of Australia, French CJ, Gummow, Hayne, Heydon, Crennan, Kiefel and Bell JJ, 24–27 August 2009).

[103] See Water Act 1989 (Vic) s 33G.

[104] See Water Act 1989 (Vic) s 33JK.

[105] See generally Water Act 1989 (Vic) Part 3 Div 9.

does not stand alone, as it is a requirement that a holder of a water share must have a water-use licence.[106] Licences contain standard water-use conditions. In many respects, the model of water share and water licence appears analogous to landed property interests, such as a fee simple with associated development/use consents.

The unbundling has required many new layers of administration, including a comprehensive water register that supports '... the monitoring of, and reporting in relation to, records and information about water-related entitlements and allocation and use of water resources'.[107] Water shares now form an accepted component of general property, whether it is part of an individual's estate or company assets. While water entitlements have reached this legal categorization in a practical sense, the more critical issue is the extent to which such property rights are carrying out the perceived function of transfer, and enhanced efficiency and sustainability.

B. Inter-jurisdictional and inter-catchment water trade

In the MDB, it is possible to trade water interstate as well as inter-catchment, but interstate trade is subject to specific agreements being entered into between various state governments which relate to the imposition of the MDB 'cap' and interstate extraction agreements.[108] The interstate arrangements for water trade have been politically contentious and were hammered out over a long and fraught process that commenced in 1914. The current iteration of the Murray-Darling Agreement appears as Schedule 1 to the federal Water Act. The Murray-Darling Agreement regulates the amounts of water that each state can 'withdraw' from the river system as well as maintaining checks on salinity levels and the volume of passing flows moving downstream to South Australia. At a Commonwealth level, the Water Act requires substantive involvement of trading regulators, as the minister is to prepare water trading rules on the advice of the Australian Competition and Consumer Commission.[109]

Wide-reaching changes have been introduced into Australian water law and regulation in line with central tenets of environmental marketization. Water property is in place, it is being actively traded; but what are the outcomes for achieving sustainability of water? The critical point still to be discussed is how the water trade operates alongside the 'cap' component of the cap and trade system. This issue has been even more fraught than the unbundling process that produced water shares as a form of water property.

As noted, water governance arrangements to date have been largely state government-based, in terms of the primary legislation and organizational frameworks.

---

[106] Pursuant to Water Act 1989 (Vic) s 64J it is an offence to use a water share without a licence.
[107] Water Act 1989 (Vic) s 84.
[108] This is now subject also to the new federal water legislation: Water Act 2007 (Cth).
[109] Water Act 2007 (Cth) Pt 4.

In the past there was limited federal coordination and variable attempts to negotiate competing state interests through the Murray-Darling Ministerial Council,
together with associated political agreements. Reforms, including adoption of
market-based instruments and water trading, were characterized by only incremental change.[110] The implementation of the MDB 'Cap' in the mid-1990s
was an attempt to set limits on water extraction across the Basin, binding on
state governments. It is illustrative of the difficulties encountered in negotiating
competing regional interests in water allocation and management.[111] The MDB
diversion limit was implemented in 1994 with water allocations 'capped' at the
level of existing development of water resources, which were already recognized
as badly over-allocated. Despite such inadequacies, water trade and the associated water governance system remains predicated around the institution of a cap
designed to encourage sustainable use through water trade.

Yet despite the extensive institutional and legal structures creating water property and water trade, as Connell states, 'governments [of the MDB]...have not
yet succeeded in establishing effective institutional processes that can protect
[water resources] from continuing degradation and reduction'.[112] Indeed, the
failure of participating jurisdictions across the MDB to agree on more sustainable levels of water extraction was a major driver for the development of a federal
water plan and consequent legislation in 2007. The federal legislation also seeks
to mediate the existence of classic upstream/downstream user conflicts and represents yet another attempt to introduce a sustainable diversion limit. It is unclear,
however, exactly how this more stringent cap will be implemented beyond the
rubric of general water resource planning. The Water Act specifically excludes the
compulsory acquisition of water 'rights',[113] and instead the Commonwealth government is to rely on a willing seller formula to acquire water entitlements that
form environmental water holdings.

In summary, water markets have been reasonably successful in allowing individuals some flexibility to meet water supply and demand problems, particularly
under the extreme climate change-induced scarcity of recent years, and in pre-
cipitating a shift from low-value to high-value water uses.[114] Water trading has
been much less successful at addressing the core problems of over-allocation of
water. This highlights the point that in any cap and trade system, trade in property rights alone (ie reallocation) cannot achieve meaningful outcomes in the face
of weak and poorly implemented 'caps'. Thus property in water, by itself, cannot
achieve long-term sustainability. This seeming truism is manifest most clearly in

[110] For discussion see S. Clark, 'The Murray-Darling Basin: Divided Power, Co-Operative
Solutions?' (2003) 22 ARELJ 67, and D. Connell, *Water Politics in the Murray-Darling Basin* (2007).
    [111] D. Connell, 'Contrasting Approaches to Water Management in the Murray-Darling Basin'
(2007) 14 Australasian J of Env Man 6 at 9–12.
    [112] ibid at 25.
    [113] Water Act 2007 (Cth) s 255.
    [114] Biesaga (above n 58).

the current widespread 'market failure' of water markets across the MDB, where the federal government has committed billions of dollars to 'buy-back' water for environmental purposes in the face of the imminent collapse of many ecosystems. Indeed, some commentators are suggesting that a triage system will have to be put in place as only some sections of the Murray-Darling system will be able to be saved. Early in 2009, the relevant federal minister conceded that Ramsar wetlands near the mouth of the Murray River were likely to be irretrievably 'lost' due to dramatically reduced flows reaching the river mouth.

The politically sensitive nature of water markets and water trading can be gauged by the fact that in early 2009, the South Australian government committed to mounting a legal challenge in the High Court to the limits placed on water trade out of catchments by the Victorian government.[115] Victoria maintains a four per cent cap on trading water out of any irrigation district in a year and a ten per cent cap on trading overall in line with sustainability objectives. The four per cent cap is due to rise to six per cent by 2010 and will be abolished by 2014. Nonetheless, South Australia has pressured the federal government to use funding imperatives to induce Victoria to lift the trading limits. This example neatly highlights the problems of using water trade to 'solve' environmental problems and underlines the seemingly intractable conflicts over water use. Victoria maintains the controls to prevent increasing salinity in the river waters, while South Australia maintains it requires increased flows from Victoria to arrest the ecosystem decline at the mouth of the Murray.

C. Assessing water trading to date

Over twenty years of water law reform in Australia has been ambitious in its scope. It has introduced innovative measures to drive major structural change hinged upon the adoption of market-based instruments and water property. In terms of newly emerging forms of property, the water law reform has been far reaching. Its aspiration was to promote trade in water access entitlements 'with different characteristics, including variations in security of supply, across a much wider area than has previously been the case'.[116] However critics point out that the underlying assumption that the market once established will essentially be self-sustaining has not proven feasible. In addition, there are already significant difficulties emerging as more comprehensive water trading and institutional implementation proceeds.[117] These difficulties include reconciling tensions between efficiency of allocation through transfer and the requirement that the water law reforms 'complete the return of all currently over-allocated or overused

---

[115] M. Pelly and G. Lower 'States join High Court fight on water buyback', *The Australian*, 17 August 2009.

[116] D. Connell, S. Dovers and R. Quenton Grafton, 'A Critical Analysis of the National Water Initiative' (2005) 10(1) Australasian J of Nat Res 81 at 94–5.

[117] ibid.

systems to environmentally-sustainable levels of extraction'.[118] Inherent problems in reconciling private efficiency goals with public sustainability outcomes
for water management are exacerbated when dealing with the complexities posed
by the Australian federal system.

Finally, the new property forms are clearly the product of statute, and as such
exist in a co-regulatory space with extensive government oversight, and 'intervention' in the market; albeit often at a substantial remove. Older administrative
forms of water regulation characterized by more direct lines of control and discrete
policy mediation between competing interests posed a particular set of regulatory
conundrums. A new set of conundrums arise with market environmentalism in
determining the extent and nature of government intervention into the market that
will be necessary to secure environmental and social outcomes, and to effectively
regulate water trades. Given these challenges, the economic, political, and social
transaction costs of Australian water management will continue,[119] one suspects
largely almost irrespective of the specific regulatory instruments adopted. Thus
while market mechanisms and new forms of property rights will continue to play a
role in the governance of 'common pool' water resources within Australia, they are
unlikely to offer a single panacea for long-entrenched management problems that
are produced by scarce water resources. Indeed, many factors influencing the overall
effectiveness of regulation, such as inter-jurisdictional tensions, inadequate funding
and co-option of policy agendas by powerful stakeholders, are generic challenges
that will impact as much upon market mechanisms as more traditional regulatory
approaches.[120] In addition, the success of market tools, particularly tradeable property schemes, is likely to depend upon effective and sufficiently stringent levels of
federal regulation to mediate long-standing conflicts. In this context, the enthusiasm for market tools may need to be tempered as Lyster remarks:

> ... policy-makers in Australia need to ensure that before rushing to the market, they are
> confident that the services that are traded are properly evaluated and accounted for. They
> need to consider whether natural resource markets need to be regulated so as to achieve
> ecologically sustainable outcomes. This is in spite of the fact that such regulation is coun-
> ter-intuitive to a free market economist's vision for such a market.[121]

VI. Lessons for cap and trade schemes

From the case study of water property and trade in the MDB in Australia, it
is clear that the property rights regimes over common pool resources that have
emerged under market environmentalism are substantially different from the

---

[118] National Water Initiative (above n 79) at [23] (iv).
[119] Connell et al (above n 116) at 86.
[120] Eckersley (above n 11).
[121] R. Lyster, '(De)regulating the Rural Environment' (2002) 19 EPLJ 34 at 57.

traditional view of property, typically associated with land-related schema. As an example of a comprehensive (although still incompletely instituted) cap and trade scheme, the experience with water trading can inform the understanding of other emergent property forms in common pool resources. While the experience with water trading may not be directly transferable to all situations where tradeable permits pertain, including emissions trading schemes, nonetheless sufficient similarities exist between respective cap and trade approaches for some analogies about communal governance to be drawn.

At the very least there needs to be a clear recognition that such property rights in cap and trade schemes are nested within implicit structural change paradigms. Governments are not absent from these social and economic changes; simply operating at a distance. These new property concepts remain as firmly embedded in social and relational contexts as traditional modes and are just as open to 'stakeholder' power structures which influence questions of the allocation *and* distribution of rights.[122] Moreover as Tarlock identifies, governments typically choose market-based environmental reforms to re-allocate water rights as direct acquisitions are seen as inefficient (ie it is governments in this instance that are 'least cost'-oriented). Yet experience with water trading has rendered the least cost alternative of water trade highly problematic with the onset of severe resource degradation where public spending becomes imperative. Governments create property and markets ostensibly to avoid the tragedy of the commons, but then may price themselves out of effective agency when market failures require government interventions. Emissions trading schemes are also predicated upon the idea of least cost structural change by stimulating innovative technologies, but experience with Australian water trade suggests that while individual structural adjustments are feasible, aggregate change is more difficult to achieve.[123] Retention of a diversity of regulatory tools to achieve widespread re-structuring seems necessary.

Perhaps though, the most telling lesson from the water property case study in the MDB is that property alone cannot solve entrenched problems of resource use and common pool management. Such conclusions fly in the face of the extensive literature on common pool resources and their governance that posit property rights as the panacea. This literature accepts that property is necessary to prevent the tragedy of the commons, but does not ask whether it is sufficient. Property, trade and transfer of resource entitlements must subsist in tandem with realistic 'caps' if the tragedy is to be prevented. After all, Hardin's prescription was for strong governance, not necessarily private property. Hardin was well aware of the limitations of property as a device of effective governance when he noted, '[b]ut every good lawyer and every good economist knows that "property" is not a thing but merely a verbal announcement that certain traditional powers and privileges

---

[122] This is exemplified by the influence of trade exposed industries obtaining favourable permit allocations under the proposed Australian Carbon Pollution Reduction Scheme.

[123] N. Durrant, 'Legal Issues in Biosequestration: Carbon Sinks, Carbon Rights and Carbon Trading' (2008) 31 UNSWLJ 906.

of some members of society will be rigorously defended against attack by others'.[124] In this light it is worthwhile reflecting that as this chapter is being compiled there are a series of claims based around traditional powers and privileges in the use of water in the MDB that are being rigorously defended in the Australian High Court. Irrigators seek to defend their claim to property in water against the government; proclaiming the age-old inviolability of property as a civil 'right' that cannot be taken and perhaps not even 'adjusted' by governments, no matter how compelling the public interest benefits of water sharing.[125] By contrast, a downstream state asserts its rights to a new property in water, to the fungibility of water freed by water trade that would shift water downstream as yet another form of water sharing.[126] Perhaps, then, we might rework Hardin's homily to suggest that what lawyers might have told economists is that the institution of property in resources may introduce as many conflicts as it resolves. Market environmentalism offers innovative approaches for common pool resource governance and 'sharing', but property brings with it a long and contested history.

---

[124] Hardin (above n 1).

[125] Transcript of Proceedings, *ICM Agriculture Pty Ltd v Commonwealth* (High Court of Australia, French CJ, Gummow, Hayne, Heydon, Crennan, Kiefel and Bell JJ, 24–27 August 2009).

[126] South Australian Premier Mike Rann has publicly committed to a challenge in the High Court, arguing that Victoria's caps on water trading are unconstitutional: Mike Rann, 'High Court Challenge to Victoria's 10 per cent Cap' (Press Release, 29 April 2009). However, despite expectations that the challenge would be on foot by the end of July, no legal action has yet been taken, apparently due to diplomatic progress towards an agreement between the two states: Michael Pelly and Gavin Lower, 'States Join High Court Fight on Water Buyback' The Australian Online (National), 17 August 2009.

21

The Significance of Property Rights in Biotic Sequestration of Carbon

*Alastair Lucas**

I. Introduction

The international climate change regime under the Kyoto Protocol to the United Nations Framework Convention on Climate Change[1] provides considerable scope for biotic sequestration on agricultural and forested land to offset carbon emission as part of the national strategies to meet greenhouse gas (GHG) emission reduction commitments. However, the capacity of terrestrial sinks for carbon sequestration is finite, and in any event the result is not removal from the carbon cycle, but merely redistribution of carbon between the biosphere and the atmosphere. The result is that carbon sequestration through land use changes is an interim and not an ultimate strategy to reduce carbon emissions from energy consumption. Nevertheless, some countries have developed, or are in the process of developing, offset systems that rely on market trading of emission reductions and offsets. The focus of this chapter is Canada where there is legislation in the province of Alberta and a federal scheme under development. Under such schemes, biotic offsets on private lands are likely to be structured through private rental contracts for use of sequestration capacity. For these transactions to be viable and effective the nature and ownership of sequestration rights must be reasonably certain. If these rights are property rights of definable character, the legal principles and legislation that secure and protect property rights will be available to parties to sequestration rights transactions. If there is significant uncertainty, legislative clarification will be required.

This chapter explores the role of property rights in the design of appropriate legal structures for biotic carbon sequestration. The objective is a regime that permits creation of biotic sequestration rights that can be integrated into offset trading systems. Two main issues will be explored, building on earlier, broader-scale,

---

* Dean and Professor, Faculty of Law, University of Calgary, Canada; email: a.lucas@ucalgary.ca.
[1] United Nations Framework Convention on Climate Change (9 May 1992, 1771 UNTS 165) 7 (accession by Canada 4 December 1992, entered into force 21 March 1994).

preliminary research:[2] (1) defining foundational legal rights to carbon sequestration potential and sequestered carbon, and (2) shaping a property rights regime for sequestered carbon. This will be done in a particular context—in effect a case study—namely, private and public or 'Crown' lands in the province of Alberta, Canada.

First, these issues are placed in the broader international, national and provincial context. Relevant Kyoto Protocol provisions, the proposed federal offset credit scheme, and existing provincial legislation under which biotic carbon offsets can be created and traded are reviewed. Then, ownership of carbon sequestration potential and sequestered carbon is assessed in the absence of legislation to determine the legal character of these property rights and thus who owns them where title to land is split. Taking into account what the common law is likely to say about ownership of sequestration rights, the remainder of the chapter looks at characterization of a property rights regime that will best support sequestration transactions to produce valuable offset credits.

II. Biotic carbon sequestration—carbon offset systems

Parties to the Kyoto Protocol have, through a series of negotiations, recognized and defined the ways in which 'Land Use, Land-Use Change and Forestry' activities fit under the Protocol. Cropland and grazing land management and revegetation are the subject of Art 4(4) which provides that:

[*The Parties shall decide which*] additional human-induced activities related to changes in greenhouse gas emissions by sources and removals by sinks in the agricultural soils and the land-use change and forestry categories shall be added to, or subtracted from, the assigned amounts for Parties included in Annex I.... such a decision shall apply in the second and subsequent commitment periods. *A Party may choose to apply such a decision on these additional human-induced activities for its first commitment period*, provided that these activities have taken place since 1990 (emphasis added).

Ultimately, in the Marrakech Accords,[3] the parties agreed to include these activities, as well as forest management, to be counted only during the first commitment period of 2008–2012. Canada was a strong supporter. But subsequent research revealed doubts about whether Canada's managed forests might, because of forest fire and mountain pine beetle forest damage, actually be a net source of carbon

---

[2] S. Kennett and A. Lucas, 'Transaction Costs and Other Issues for Carbon Sequestration on Agricultural Land; Defining the Legal and Policy Agenda' (2004) 14 J Environmental Law & Practice 47 at 48; S. Kennett, A. Kwasniak and A. Lucas, 'Property Rights and the Legal Framework for Carbon Sequestration on Agricultural Land' (2005–2006) 37 Ottawa L Rev 178.

[3] Affirmed at first meeting of the Parties, Montreal, 2005: <www.unfccc.int/resource/docs/cop7/13a02.pdf>.

dioxide. In the end, Canada decided not to include these biotic sinks in its Kyoto Protocol commitments.[4] But even if biotic sequestration activities are not eligible to meet Kyoto targets, they remain relevant to achievement of Canadian national targets—a 20 per cent reduction from 2006 emission levels by 2020 and 60 per cent by 2050.[5]

Canadian federal response has not yet moved beyond a series of policy papers. The most recent policy paper, *Regulatory Framework for Air Emissions*, describes offsets as, '... emission reductions that take place outside the domain of regulated activities'.[6]

The 'regulated activities' in climate change regimes are industrial GHG emissions, for which 'caps' would be established under statutory authority. The federal system contemplates complying with caps in a number of ways, including reducing emissions, contributing to a technology fund, reducing emissions below their caps, and purchasing (in an emissions trading market) emission credits created by other parties and by non-regulated actors.

The non-regulated offsets category is where biotic carbon sequestration would fit. Biotic carbon offsets would be purchased and used by regulated emitters toward their emission cap obligations. This must be additional to emissions reduction that would have occurred in the absence of the regulatory system or other government programmes. Offset credits would be issued only where emission reduction can be quantified and verified.

Meanwhile, the province of Alberta, acting under constitutional powers based on provincial property, civil rights and public natural resource management,[7] has already developed a system for biotic carbon sequestration. This was built on an initial inventory and assessment of agricultural sequestration potential by a government–industry working group.[8] The group concluded that while sequestration of as much as 5 Megatonnes per year is possible, the ability of soil to absorb carbon declines after six or seven years.

This work was reflected in the Climate Change and Emissions Management Act 2003. However, biotic sequestration was given limited attention. 'Carbon sinks' were recognized, with 'sink' defined as:

a component of the environment that removes or captures gases from the atmosphere through natural processes and includes, without limitation, plants and soil.[9]

---

[4] See Canadian Forest Service, *Is Canada's Forest a Sink or a Carbon Source?*, Science-Policy Notes (October 2007): <www.cfs.nrcan.gc.ca/news/544>.
[5] Environment Canada, *Turning the Corner: An action plan to reduce greenhouse gases and air pollution* (April 2007): <www.ecoaction.gc.ca/news-nouvelles/20070426–2-eng.cfm>.
[6] Environment Canada, *Regulatory Framework for Air Emissions* (2007), Catalogue No: En84–53/2007: <www.ec.gc.ca/doc/media/m_124/report_eng.pdf>.
[7] N. Bankes and A. Lucas, 'Kyoto, Constitutional Law and Alberta's Proposals' (2004) 42 Alberta L Rev 355.
[8] Climate Change Central, *A Basis for Greenhouse Gas Trading in Agriculture*, Discussion Paper C3–01(a) (2002).
[9] Climate Change and Emissions Management Act, SA 2003 c-16.7, s 1(e)(i).

It is stated that 'a sink right is a property right'.[10] The provincial cabinet is authorized to make regulations concerning 'emission offsets, credits and sink rights', including the manner and conditions by which these rights may be 'created, obtained, distributed, exchanged, traded, sold, used, varied and cancelled'.[11]

The overall scheme of the Act and its major regulations, establishes emission intensity limits for large scale emitters (more than 100,000 tonnes per year) with an offset trading system as a key element of the compliance system. This includes agricultural offsets, which were the subject of complex quantification protocols to ensure that offsets are real and demonstrable, quantifiable and measurable, and additional in the sense of not being required by law at the time the action was initiated.

The aim of both existing provincial and proposed federal offset systems is to motivate private actors, including the corporate sector, to create offset projects including biotic sequestration projects. Under both schemes, it is also for private actors to create the market necessary for trading of emission credits generally.

III. Property rights

Essentially, both schemes rely on private actors being motivated to use their property, or acquire property on which to undertake sequestration actions. It is critical therefore to determine who owns what. In the case of private land, this question will be determined by the general law of property as it may have been modified by statute. For public (state-owned property), an analysis is required of the relevant legislation and the granting instruments by which public lands and the resources on them are allocated to private parties for development. In both cases, the most relevant question concerns ownership of the rights and powers required to create readily marketable offset credits.

A. Ownership of sequestration potential and sequestered carbon

The question for policy makers concerns ownership for the purpose of clarifying claims and reducing transaction costs for creation of government certified offsets. In Canada, this has been framed by the assumption that agricultural offsets will be created by aggregators entering into contracts with land owners for sale of sequestration and sequestration potential.[12] This government perspective is purely instrumental—how can the most effective and efficient offset system be created?

Property rights questions have emerged when the ownership question is posed by land owners. They want to know what they have to sell. Their concern is whether and how they will benefit from any proposed offset system. So they

---

[10] ibid s 5.9.
[11] ibid s 5.
[12] Kennett and Lucas (above n 2) at 48.

begin with their property, asking whether, as between them and other owners or potential owners of interests in their land, they own sequestered carbon and sequestration potential as part of their property rights. These other owners and potential owners include private parties and public entities.

This latter question—the land owners' ownership question—is considered next. The question is broken down into two parts: first, what, apart from legislation, is the legal character of sequestration potential of land and sequestered carbon; and, secondly, who owns these rights?[13]

B. Divided ownership rights

The common law concept of property as a bundle of rights accommodates divided ownership rights for a particular parcel of land. How does biosequestration fit this concept? An important perspective is that there may be two property rights components of biosequestration: (1) the 'sequestration potential' of land—the ability of soil and vegetation to absorb and retain atmospheric carbon, and (2) 'sequestered carbon', that is, carbon actually retained by the soil and vegetation. The former is a potential product or value of the land; the latter is an existing attribute or product of the land. While realization of the ultimate value of other products of the land requires removal, the essential value of carbon sequestration is in retention.

For agricultural land, particularly cropland or rangeland, the soil is the primary carbon reservoir. On wooded land valued for forestry purposes, the carbon storage medium is the vegetation including root systems. The legal issue is: who has the legal title to the stored carbon and to the carbon sequestration potential that permits this carbon storage to be realized?

Clarity of ownership is important for any biotic carbon sequestration initiative. It confirms the initial ownership of rights—the beginning state of play for a system of certification and marketing of biotic carbon sequestration rights[14]—and gives purchasers reasonable assurance about title and marketability of their acquisitions. Clear ownership is also critical for the integrity and objectives of a sinks policy and offset trading system. Without it, double counting of sinks-based offsets may compromise the operation of the system.[15] Of course, like purchasers of surface land, these purchasers would have to exercise due diligence and perhaps rely on land registration systems[16] to ensure their ownership. The risk of ownership defects must be manageable if there are to be potential purchasers of biotic carbon offsets.

---

[13] Kennett, Kwasniak and Lucas (above n 2).

[14] I. Liepa, *Greenhouse Gas Offsets: An Introduction to Core Elements of an Offset Rule* (2002) s 3.0, App A, <www.climatechangecentral.com/resources/discussion_papers/GHG_offsets.pdf>.

[15] ibid.

[16] As under the Alberta Land Titles Act, R.S.A. 2000, c. L-4[ALTA].

There is potential for different categories of owners of marketable biotic carbon sequestration rights,[17] just as agricultural or forest land is allocated for cropping or for grazing, logging, etc. The difference is that these latter rights and sale transactions are well understood, while biotic carbon and carbon sequestration potential are novel.

Rosenbaum, Schoene and Mekouar have outlined various possibilities for carbon sequestration potential. Their first possibility is that the land owner (the fee simple owner) owns the sequestration potential and stored carbon so that the rights may:

(A) not be separate property rights, but nonetheless be the subject of related property rights such as easements or restrictive covenants;

(B) be separate real property rights that may be characterized as coming within a recognized category of property rights such as profit à prendre;[18] or

(C) be forms of personal property or of another category of property other than real property.[19]

A second possibility is that carbon sequestration potential and stored carbon are 'public goods', either (a) incapable of ownership like air, or (b) owned by the state or state sub-unit.

The first possibility—that the land owner owns carbon sequestration potential and sequestered carbon, and the possible legal character of this right is discussed next. Is it part of the fee simple absolute?[20] More specifically, is it a surface right or a mineral right? Or is it personal property? Discussion then turns to the second possibility—is it a public good?

1. Part of the 'fee simple absolute'?

In property law terms a land owner's legal interest, a fee simple absolute estate, unless otherwise limited, has been expressed by the maxim, *cujus est solum, ejus est usque ad coelum et ad infernos*—'the owner...has everything "up to the sky and down to the centre of the earth"'.[21] Thus, a fee simple absolute estate includes

---

[17] Emission Reduction Trading Protocol Team, *A Basis for Greenhouse Gas Trading in Agriculture* (2002) 10, <www.climatechangecentral.com/resourdes/discussion_papers/basis_for_grnhse_trading.pdf>.

[18] The right to enter another person's land to remove something from the land; E.Burn and J. Cartwright, eds, *Cheshire and Burn's Modern Law of Real Property* (17th edn, 2006) 640 [Cheshire and Burn].

[19] K. Rosenbaum, D. Schoene, and A. Mekouar, *Climate Change and the Forest Sector: Possible National and Subnational Legislation* (2004) 32–3: <ftp://ftp.fao.org/docrep/fao/007/y5647e/y5647e00.pdf>.

[20] That has been characterized as 'perpetual': R. Megarry and W. Wade, *The Law of Real Property* (6th edn, C. Harpum, M. Grant and S. Bridge, 2000) 64 [Megarry and Wade].

[21] ibid 56–7 [footnotes omitted]; Cheshire and Burn, above n 18, 173. Note, however, that this maxim has not been applied without limit to air space and has been described as 'a useful point of departure' for courts, but a colourful and 'fanciful phrase' of limited validity: B. Ziff, *Principles of Property Law* (4th edn, 2006) 82.

the soil and anything growing in it, as well as the underlying minerals. The fee simple absolute right contemplates realization of the potential of the land in various ways, including growing crops, grazing animals, erecting buildings and structures and removal of minerals and organic matter. These uses are, of course, subject to statutory planning and other regulatory restrictions. Uses, including planting, tilling and otherwise managing land use, line up convincingly with soil and vegetation management, particularly tree planting and no-till agriculture, necessary to effect carbon sequestration.[22]

2. *Surface and mineral rights*

Another potential legal characterization of rights to carbon sequestration and sequestered carbon is as mineral rights.[23] These are well-recognized property rights that flow from the fee simple absolute owner's presumptive ownership to the centre of the earth.

The mineral estate can be severed from the surface estate, and this kind of severance is common, either in initial grants from the state or as a result of reservations in sales by fee simple owners. The possibility that biotic sequestration rights are included in these severed mines and minerals is enhanced by judicial statements that mines and minerals are not definite terms, and are presumed to be used in the widest sense.[24] Ultimately however, everything depends on the intentions of the parties to the granting document. Experience with analogous ownership disputes, such as split oil and natural gas estates in the Canadian western provinces, suggests that courts are likely to approach issues case by case and focus on the intentions of the parties in the legal instrument they chose to use.[25] Legal issues will thus be characterized as matters of interpretation rather than more general ownership principle. As the Supreme Court of Canada stated in *Anderson v Amoco Canada Oil and Gas*,[26] issues of 'broad ownership theory [are] not required to be determined in this appeal'.[27]

3. *Personal property*

Could carbon sequestration rights be personal property, or some separate category other than land? If so, there could be great difficulty with lack of access for

---

[22] In *Earl of Falmouth v Thomas* (1832) [1824–34] All ER Rep 357, 1 Cr & M 89 (Ex Ct), the court held that the right to crops and the benefit of work, labour, and material that are incorporated into the land are inseparable from it and are interests in land. Numerous courts have found that profits of the soil, such as trees, forage, mines, minerals, peat, or the soil itself, are part of the realty and are interests in land. The owner of the fee may separately convey the right to remove these interests—a 'profit à prendre': Cheshire and Burn (above n 18) at 640–2.

[23] ibid at 174.

[24] *Attorney General v Earl of Lonsdale* (1827) [1824–34] All ER Rep 666, 57 ER 518 (Ch); B. Jones and N. Bankes (eds), *Canadian Oil and Gas* (2nd edn, 1993) para 3.112.

[25] See *Borys v CPR Co* [1953] AC 217, [1953] 2 DLR 65 (PC).

[26] [2004] 3 SCR 3, 241 DLR (4th) 193.

[27] ibid, para 36.

biotic carbon offset owners to land registration systems, and perhaps uncertainty as a result of other kinds of carbon offsets based on geological carbon sequestration being characterized as real property rights.

Attempting to answer this question by applying common law real and personal property distinctions is problematic. On its face, if personal property is, unlike land, not fixed and finite, the answer seems obvious. But common law real and personal property distinctions are complex—originally based largely on procedural rules, and subject to evolution. Leases, initially developed as contractual rights and considered personalty, became recognized as estates in land—'chattels real'.[28]

Carbon sequestration rights too may be created by contract, and the idea of sequestration potential gives them an air of incorporeality. But incorporeal interests such as profits à prendre (which include oil and gas leases) and easements have long been recognized as property rights. The essence of biotic sequestration rights is not removal of produce of the land. Rather, it is maintenance and enhancement of the land's carbon sequestration qualities. But the essence, as with removal, is control so that the sequestration qualities and potential of land can be managed to benefit the right holder. Thus, rights to sequestered carbon and sequestration potential at least present an analogy to profits à prendre.

In any event, biotic sequestration rights concern physical characteristics of land. Sequestered carbon is finite, fixed in relation to particular land, and permanent (though variable)—all characteristics that distinguish realty from personalty.[29] Consequently, biotic sequestration rights are not likely to be characterized as personal property.

4. A public good?

The question here is not whether sequestration potential and sequestered carbon is a 'public good' in the economic sense of being indivisible and non-excludable. Rather, the inquiry involves two possibilities: (1) is it public property for which the title is vested in a government,[30] and (2) is it common property or 'non property'[31] that may be used, and in a sense owned, by the public or a significant portion of the public? The latter would be analogous to environmental resources or media such as clean air.[32] Similarly, at common law, flowing water can be appropriated and used (and these rights are recognized as property rights), but not owned.

But biotic sequestration rights seem not to fit comfortably in either category. If they are public property owned by government, the government claim must be

---

[28] Megarry and Wade (above n 20) at para 3–009.
[29] Ziff (above n 21) at 69.
[30] A claim to government ownership of sequestration potential and sequestered carbon on private land raises legal and policy issues beyond the scope of this chapter.
[31] Ziff (above n 21) at 7.
[32] See, eg, International Institute for Sustainable Development, *On the Great Plains: Use of Common Property*: <www.iisd.org/agri/gpcommonprop.htm>.

based on reservations in original grants, or perhaps on statutory takings. Evidence that these rights have been addressed by governments in these ways is unlikely to be found. As to common property, the idea immediately raises the likelihood of disputes with private land owners claiming biotic sequestration rights. The latter can raise their rights of exclusion as surface owners[33] and point to the 'centre of the earth' ownership presumption,[34] which has received judicial recognition, at least concerning air space.[35] Ultimately, given the novelty and uncertain nature of these rights and their function in GHG emission reduction regimes, as well as the high value that the law places on clarity and security of fee simple land owners' rights and individual autonomy,[36] the 'public good' theory is unlikely to prevail.

5. Conclusions on ownership

This brief property law analysis suggests that, in the absence of legislation, it is unlikely that courts will characterize sequestration potential and sequestered carbon as new property rights or rights separate from the core fee simple interest in land. They are likely to be considered real and not personal property. The legal character of mineral rights and the principles of interpretation of property-granting instruments provide little support for characterization of these rights as mineral rights. Several factors, including the physical association of carbon with soil and vegetation and the law's treatment of air as opposed to subsurface rights, suggest that specific legislation or agreement aside, biotic sequestration rights will normally be the property of the surface owner and not public or common property.

C. Property rights to support an offset system

The common law property rights analysis suggests that a statutory offset system that provides for transferable sequestration rights cannot simply be based on common law rights. Statutory definition of biotic sequestration right is necessary to clearly separate sequestration rights from land owners' broader fee simple rights. At the same time, common law property categories must be taken into account in the design of legislation because they are critical data for interpretation of legislation that defines new property rights. This property rights analysis informs, but as Nigel Bankes has pointed out,[37] does not directly address the functional elements of the property rights on which a claim to sequestration potential and

---

[33] For a discussion in relation to water rights, see Australian Commonwealth Department of Agriculture, Fisheries and Forestry, *An Effective System of Defining Water Titles* (Research Report) (ACIL Tasman in association with Freehills) 17–19, <www.lwa.gov.au/products_list.asp>.

[34] Megarry and Wade (above n 20) at 56–7.

[35] Though there are virtually no cases concerning the extent of subsurface private rights: Ziff (above n 21) at 84.

[36] ibid at 90.

[37] Professor N.D. Bankes, Faculty of Law, University of Calgary, personal communication.

sequestered carbon can be based that will support a marketable sequestration right. Thus, Kennett et al proceeded to identify the key elements of any sequestration transaction. They argue that six characteristics of a property rights[38] regime are necessary to support a sequestration transaction. These are:

1. *Separation of transferable sequestration rights from ownership of land*

Parties to sequestration transactions should be able to freely transfer legal interests in carbon rights, particularly sequestration potential, sinks, sequestered carbon and sinks-related effects, in relation to particular land. The objective is to clear away uncertainties caused by common law property interest categories discussed above and distinctions between property and non-transferable personal interests such as licences and permits. This is necessary because carbon sequestration is likely to be a secondary use for which less than fee simple ownership will be required.

2. *Direct definition of sequestration rights*

Parties to sequestration transactions should be able to define their interests directly in relation to the carbon assets that are the subject of their transaction. This differs from indirect definition of sequestration rights by reference to land owner obligations such as no-till or low till farming, or abstention from clearing vegetation. In the latter case, the legal rights of purchasers of sequestered carbon or sequestration services would be limited to monitoring or control of land use practices. This could result in uncertainty about transferability and ownership of biological offsets produced by sequestration activities.

3. *Parties' flexibility to define implications of sequestration rights*

Here, there are two perspectives. One is the need, given the broad range of possible sequestration transactions, of parties to define with as much precision as possible, the terms of their contractual relationship. A key factor is the temporary nature of biological sequestration, and the corresponding need for parties to specify and limit the term of their relationship and thus the risk inherent in it. The other perspective is that of governments and the international community, focusing on the need to reduce transaction costs by, as far as possible, promoting standard 'rental' agreements, and ensuring consistency with carbon credit certification under international instruments.

4. *Sequestration rights 'running with the land'*

The need to sequester carbon over long periods is not necessarily consistent with land owner interests, which may include land use changes and land dispositions. If contractual instruments are used, an obvious problem is privity of contract—third parties are not bound by contractual land use restrictions and obligations.

A solution is structuring sequestration interests so they run with the land and bind subsequent purchasers. Direct connection between sequestration rights and particular land is thus maintained. In these circumstances, further protection

---

[38] Kennett, Kwasniak and Lucas (above n 2) at 187–94.

would result if sequestration interests could be registered on title under statutory land registration systems. This provides notice and facilitates verification.

5. *Conflicting interests*

A property regime for sequestration transactions should avoid, to the extent possible, conflict between sequestration rights and other legal interests. Conflicts may arise between farmers or ranchers (primary owners) who wish to market sequestration rights, and holders of grazing interests or perhaps of conservation easements in the same land. Can the primary owner act independently? If sequestration is enhanced as a result of the activities of grazing or conservation interest holders, do they own the incremental sequestration rights?

One response is that models for addressing this kind of problem exist in the case of surface-mineral ownership disputes and disputes concerning mineral rights split ownership. Basic property and contract law and the judicial process can resolve these disputes. But this may be costly and time consuming, thus increasing risk and consequently transaction costs.

Legislative definition can, for example, give priority to sequestration rights and provide for compensation to interest holders who incur loss. A statutory regime could include public registries to provide notice, and holding provisions when sequestration agreements are being negotiated.

6. *Legal uncertainty and transaction costs*

Kennett et al identified the potentially high costs of dispute resolution as transaction cost factors. Others are inherent in the discussion of key regime characteristics above. These factors underline the need for clearly defined legal categories of sequestration rights and relatively simple mechanisms for creating and transferring legal interests in carbon assets. It is clear that a property rights regime for carbon sequestration cannot be addressed in isolation, but must be viewed against the broader elements of carbon offsets regimes.

The importance of fair and efficient dispute resolution must be underlined. It has been noted that a mechanism—ideally a designed mechanism—for resolving disputes about ownership of property, the subject of sequestration activities, on which offset credits are based—is an important characteristic of a legal regime for biotic carbon sequestration.[39] A dispute resolution mechanism would be beneficial for resolution of several other types of disputes.[40] Some disputes centre on the registration and certification systems proposed for federal and provincial offset systems. Another set of issues concerns disputes about liability for non-performance of carbon removals on which offset credits are based.

In the absence of specific legislation, common law procedural fairness principles may be available to applicants and other persons affected by decisions under offset

[39] Climate Change Central, *Proceedings of Carbon Offsets Workshop* (3 July 2008): <www.carbonoffsetsolutions.ca/policyand registration>.

[40] See A. Lucas and O. Daudu, *Disputes and Dispute Resolution in the Offsets System* (March 2006), BIOCAP Canada Research Integration Synthesis Paper: <www.biocap.ca>.

legislation to register and to certify carbon removals through biological sequestration.[41] If, for example, sequestration rights are conveyed under rental-type agreements to carbon aggregators, the latter would be applicants for registration and certification of sequestration projects and issuance of offset credits. Under fairness principles, applicants, as well as holders of other legal interests in the land, would be entitled to reasonable notice of decisions to be made, 'fair hearing', in the sense of an opportunity to respond to issues raised concerning an application, an impartial and independent decision maker, and in certain cases, to reasons for decision.

Judicially established functional criteria, including the relative formality of the decision, the nature of the statutory scheme (including whether there is an appeal), the importance of the decision to affected persons, and procedural choices of the decision maker, suggest that persons affected directly by registration decisions would at least have the opportunity to make written representations and receive brief written reasons for decisions.[42] Decisions on certification and compliance, which have potentially greater economic and personal impact on those affected, would require greater procedural rights including opportunity (depending on the particular circumstances) for an oral hearing.

Issues include project ownership, whether proposed projects are within the scope of offset systems, whether carbon renewals are quantifiable and will be achieved during registration periods, whether there is real environmental benefit, whether carbon removals are surplus (in excess of regulatory requirements), whether reductions can be verified, and whether there is double counting of reductions. Another set of issues concerns compliance decisions that may, for example, require replacement of unsupported credits (as a result of post-credit issuance information or events) by proponents.

Alleged denial of procedural fairness, as well as issues concerning the scope of authority under offsets legislation, may potentially be taken to court in judicial review proceedings by affected parties. Notwithstanding considerable judicial deference to decision makers' expertise, courts are likely to address and decide what they consider to be legal issues of statutory interpretation or fundamental scope of legal authority.

This significant potential transaction cost risk could potentially be mitigated by establishment of specialized internal appeal processes that do not reach general courts. In addition, consensual dispute resolution procedures, such as mediated negotiation processes, could be established to avoid even the time and cost of internal appeal processes.

The result of this assessment of characteristics of a property rights regime necessary to support biotic sequestration transactions is summed up by Kennett et al in the following criteria:

---

[41] Based on judicial functional criteria, including the nature of the decision power, the relationship between the decision maker and affected persons, and effects on other persons subject to the decision, it is likely that the threshold for procedural fairness is crossed: Lucas and Daudu, ibid.

[42] *Baker v Canada (Minister of Citizenship and Immigration)* [1999] 2 SCR 817.

- Sequestration rights should be distinct legal interests that are separate from ownership of land on which sequestration activities will take place and that are freely transferable.
- Sequestration rights should be defined directly as legal interests in carbon assets (ie sequestration potential, carbon sinks, sequestered carbon and sinks-based emissions offsets) that have implications for the control over land use, as opposed to relying on indirect mechanisms that merely create rights and obligations relating to land use.
- Parties to sequestration transactions should have considerable flexibility to determine the nature and extent of their respective rights and obligations relating to land use.
- Sequestration rights and the associated obligations regarding land use should 'run with the land', binding subsequent purchasers and allowing parties to sequestration transactions to transfer their respective interests in carbon assets.
- The substantive definition of sequestration rights and the associated procedural mechanisms should be designed to reduce the risk of overlap and conflict with other property interests and associated land uses.
- The substantive and procedural components of the property rights regime and the broader legal framework for carbon sequestration on agricultural land should be designed to reduce legal uncertainty and other sources of transaction costs.[43]

IV. Ownership uncertainty—the example of dispositions

A. Under the Alberta Public Lands Act

1. The legislation

The Public Lands Act 2000 provides that the minister may grant grazing leases 'for the purpose of grazing livestock'.[44] This does not contemplate cropping or land management. Leases can be assigned, but ministerial consent is required. If assignment is refused (and criteria are not set out in the Act or regulations), leases are to be cancelled, or withdrawn.[45] The regime also contemplates shorter term dispositions—grazing permits of up to one year and grazing licences of up to ten years.[46]

There is also provision for 'miscellaneous dispositions' for purposes not specifically provided for under the Act or regulations.[47] This includes exploration approvals by which agricultural potential of public land can be investigated as a

---

[43] Kennett, Kwasniak and Lucas (above n 2) at 194.
[44] Public Lands Act RSA 2000 c P-40, s 102(1).
[45] ibid, s 110.
[46] ibid, Div 4.
[47] ibid, s 123.

step toward a potential agricultural lease. A specific assessment process for grazing leases is included.[48] There is no mention of carbon sequestration.

In December 2008, Alberta issued a Land-Use Framework[49] that is intended to develop and implement:

> ...a land-use system that will effectively balance competing economic, environmental and social demands.[50]

It addresses carbon sequestration only incidentally, under 'private land stewardship tools'.[51] There is no mention of carbon sequestration or sequestration potential on public lands, even though this potential is recognized in other policy documents.

A 'Guidance Document' concerning carbon offset creation under the Climate Change and Emissions Management Act 2003 and the Specified Gas Emitters Regulation 2007 contemplates sequestration projects on Crown land.[52] However, it does so most clearly in a section headed 'Ownership',[53] which lists examples of circumstances in which ownership questions can arise. The prescription is that:

> Legal ownership of the GHG reductions and removals must be established by contract or other legal agreement to qualify under the Alberta system.[54]

Attention was given to carbon sequestration in the Alberta agricultural and forest sectors beginning in 2001. Climate Change Central, a public–private partnership, carried out the inventory, measurement, and verification of potential for land management practices to increase soil carbon absorption and retention.[55] The project team developed models and pilot projects, including a scheme for carbon sequestration on Métis settlement lands in the province. This led to establishment by the province of complex quantification protocols for low or no-tillage agricultural projects, to ensure that projected carbon reductions are credible.[56]

However, the Climate Change Central research concluded that sequestration is feasible, but that sequestration potential is a declining land quality. Further, among key constraints on realizing this potential, uncertainty concerning sink

---

[48] ibid, s 34(1).

[49] Government of Alberta, Department of Sustainable Resources, *Alberta Land-Use Framework*, December 2008, online: <www.landuse.alberta.ca/documents/Final_Land_Use_Framework.pdf.>.

[50] ibid, 6.

[51] ibid, 34.

[52] Alberta Environment, *Offset Credit Project Guidance Document under the Specified Gas Emitters Regulation* (February 2008), <www.assembly.ab.ca/lao/library/egovdocs/2008/alen/165331.pdf>.

[53] ibid, 4.

[54] ibid.

[55] Climate Change Central (above n 8).

[56] Quantification Protocol for Tillage Management System (2008) <www.environment.alberta.ca/documents/Tillage_Protocol_v1.3_Feb_08.pdf>, and Additional Guidance for the Interpretation of the Tillage Protocol Management System (2008).

ownership was identified.[57] So was the need for an effective dispute resolution system.[58] Agricultural sequestration potential continued to be emphasized when the Climate Change and Emissions Management Act was amended, but the ownership issue was not resolved.

2. Assessment

It can be seen that this system for agricultural carbon sequestration does not go far toward addressing the six criteria outlined above. First, free transfer of sequestration rights is achieved in principle when an agricultural offset is certified. But ownership uncertainty may still undermine an offset credit's credibility, and thus its value. Direct definition of sequestration rights remains an open question. It depends first on interpretation of the Public Lands Act and leases or other disposition documents issued under the Act to determine whether or not biotic carbon sequestration rights are included in dispositions. The second issue is the terms of rental contracts that may be used for sale of rights to sequestered carbon and sequestration potential for creation of offset credits. These are not specified or even described in the legislation or in guidance documents for carbon offset certification.

Parties to sequestration transactions do retain flexibility to define the terms of their contractual relationship. But, the other side of this issue, namely standardization to reduce transaction costs, is not yet addressed clearly by government. Nor is it clear that Alberta sequestration rights, once created, will run with the subject land. Similarly, clear mechanisms for dealing with conflicting rights are not, or not yet, part of the regime. The need for fair and efficient dispute resolution has been recognized, but does not seem to have moved beyond discussion of alternatives by participants at Climate Change Central workshops. The result is that legal uncertainty and potential for higher than necessary transaction costs remain.

B. New legislation

The ownership problems identified could be addressed by new legislation or legislative amendment. 'Carbon sequestration rights' could be defined under the Public Lands Act and addressed in leases or other documents for allocation of public lands. Legislation to establish the carbon offset system should be enacted or amended to provide for standard rental contracts for rights to carbon sequestration potential and sequestered carbon that are flexible enough to permit parties to clearly allocate risks among them. These sequestration rights should be specified to run with the land to which they are related. This new legislation should provide for a dispute resolution system (probably a form of mediated negotiation) to resolve ownership, among other issues that may arise in the quantification and certification of biotic carbon offset credits.

---

[57] Climate Change Central (above n 8).
[58] ibid, 8–10.

V. Conclusions

Carbon sequestration potential and sequestered carbon is emerging as a novel property interest. It is the foundational property right for creation of offset credits that may be used to meet international and national GHG emission reduction targets.

While there is some value—particularly improving understanding of the legal nature of these carbon sequestration rights in the context of analogous interests under national property law systems—in analysing the legal character of rights to carbon sequestration potential and sequestered carbon, the core question should not be legal characterization of the right but rather how the property right should be structured in functional terms to most effectively support a marketable carbon offset right. Factors that should be addressed include separation of transferable sequestration rights from land ownership, direct definition of sequestration rights, parties' flexibility to define implications of sequestration rights, carbon sequestration rights running with the land and effective dispute resolution.

22

Community Based Property Rights and Resource Conservation in India's Forests

Lavanya Rajamani*

Natural resource-dependent communities, by virtue of their dependence on resources to which the state or others may have legal title, are vulnerable to losing their lands, access to resources and means of subsistence. Community based property rights typically encompass several rights, including rights to ownership, use and transfer. They derive their authority from the local community in which they originate and operate. Formal legal recognition of community based property rights to natural resources is considered optimal by these communities, but it remains contentious in most countries. Few countries, for a variety of historical reasons, provide formal legal recognition to community based property rights. A recent exception to this, however, is the controversial and hard-won Scheduled Tribes and Other Traditional Forest Dwellers (Recognition of Forest Rights) Act 2006 in India.[1] This Act recognizes that Scheduled Tribes and other traditional forest dwellers are integral to the survival and sustainability of the forest ecosystem, and that their rights to ancestral lands and their habitat were not adequately recognized in the consolidation of state forests during the colonial period as well as in independent India.[2] It therefore seeks to right this historical wrong by vesting forest rights and occupation in forest land in forest dwellers that have lived in forests for generations.[3]

This chapter explores the provenance, possibilities and limits of formal legal recognition of community based property rights through a case study of the Scheduled Tribes and Other Traditional Forest Dwellers (Recognition of Forest Rights) Act 2006. This chapter will trace the antecedents of this Act, and consider the implications of formal legal recognition of community based property rights

* Professor, Centre for Policy Research, New Delhi, India; email: lavanya.rajamani@cprindia. org. I am grateful to Shankar Gopalakrishnan, Campaign for Survival and Dignity, for enlightening conversations, useful references and innumerable leads.
[1] Scheduled Tribes and Other Traditional Forest Dwellers (Recognition of Forest Rights) Act 2006, available at <http://www.forestrights.nic.in/doc/Act.pdf> (hereinafter Forest Rights Act, 2006).
[2] Preamble, Forest Rights Act 2006.
[3] ibid.

for natural resource protection. Through the case study, this chapter will also explore the notion of community based property rights, its conceptual moorings, and its recognition in international human rights doctrine.

I. The laws of the jungle

The dramatic images evoked by Kipling's *Jungle Book* set in India—of dense lush forests across which charismatic mega fauna, slithering serpents and chattering monkeys roam—has long since given way to a reality governed by 'scientific forestry,' commercial plantations, single-species conservation projects, large-scale mining and forced evictions of forest dwellers. Systematic and reckless commercial exploitation—accelerated by the colonial encounter, characterized as a 'watershed' in the ecological history of India[4]—has reduced India's forest cover from an estimated 85 per cent two thousand years ago[5] to 20.6 per cent today.[6] Even this meagre 20.6 per cent represents tree cover rather than natural forests, so it includes plantations, orchards, sugarcane fields and the like.[7]

Be that as it may, the depleted forests of India are and have been home to millions of scheduled tribes and other forest dwellers.[8] Scheduled tribes, 84 million of them, account for 8.2 per cent of India's population.[9] Many of them identify themselves as *Adivasis*, the Hindi term for indigenous or original inhabitants.[10] *Adivasis* are the internationally recognized indigenous people of India,[11] and 60.1 per cent of India's recorded forest lands lie in the 187 *Adivasi* districts.[12] *Adivasis* are among the poorest and most disadvantaged of Indians.[13] Only 23.8 per cent

---

[4] M.Gadgil and R. Guha, *This Fissured Land: An Ecological History of India* (1992) 116.

[5] M. Poffenberger and C. Singh, 'Communities and the State: Re-establishing the Balance in Indian Forest Policy' in *Village Voices, Forest Choices* (M. Poffenberger and B. McGean, eds, 1996) 56 at 57.

[6] Of this 1.6% is very dense forest, 10.1% is moderately dense, and 8.8% is open: Executive Summary, Forest Survey of India, *State of Forests Report*, 2005, available at <http://www.fsi.nic.in/sfr2005/executive_of_summary.pdf>.

[7] By some accounts, therefore at least 12.4% of the country's recorded forest area has no forest cover: see the website of the Campaign for Survival and Dignity, available at <http://www.forestrightsact.org>.

[8] The term scheduled tribes refers to those tribes that have been notified in accordance with Art 342, Constitution of India, 1950, available at <http://indiacode.nic.in/coiweb/welcome.html>.

[9] Statistics drawn from the Census of India, Government of India, 2001, available at <http://www.censusindia.gov.in/Census_Data_2001/India_at_glance/scst.aspx>.

[10] B. Bhukya, 'The Mapping of the Adivasi Social: Colonial Anthropology and Adivasis' (2008) 43 Economic and Political Weekly 103.

[11] Minority Rights Group International, *World Directory of Minorities and Indigenous Peoples—India: Adivasis* (2008) available at <http://www.unhcr.org/refworld/docid/49749d14c.html>.

[12] Forest Survey of India, *State of Forests Report*, 2005.

[13] See R. Guha, 'Adivasis, Naxalites and Indian Democracy' (2007) 42 Economic and Political Weekly 3305 (arguing that on the whole the *Adivasis* have gained the least and lost the most in six decades of Indian democracy); see also M. Shah, 'First You Push Them In Then You Throw Them Out' (2005) 40 Economic and Political Weekly 4895.

of *Adivasis* are literate, 49.5 per cent of them live below the poverty line, 28.9 per cent have no access to medical care, 43.2 per cent have no access to safe drinking water,[14] and 62.9 per cent are landless.[15] The plight of the *Adivasis* is the result of centuries of state-led dispossession, a dispossession the Forest Rights Act, 2006, seeks to address and remedy.

A. The legacy of the colonial encounter: dominion and imperium

Notwithstanding liberal attempts to relegate colonialism and the imperial project to apologetic footnotes in world history, colonialism left a profound legacy in the once-colonized world, in particular on laws governing the access and use of natural resources. There are two primary reasons for this enduring legacy. First, the central mission of colonialism—the conquest of non-European people—was designed to establish and maintain political and economic superiority. To do this, the colonizers employed a centralized authoritarian system of law and governance, systems which many post-colonial societies inherited. Secondly, colonial law was designed to garner control over and facilitate the exploitation of natural resources rather than to limit it, another purposive design-feature post-colonial societies inherited. Law was central to and complicit in the colonial enterprise, and the colonizers in leaving their laws behind left the nascent states with the tools to perpetuate the conquest and marginalization of people. These laws nurtured '*dominion* over things' which as Maurice Cohen, the property rights theorist has noted 'is also *imperium* over our fellow human beings'.[16]

Forest laws in India provide a fitting example. The colonial laws established *dominion* by enclosing forests and *imperium* by alienating forest dwellers. In doing so they also converted forests from biological resource systems into commodities.[17] As Guha notes, the customary use of the forest rested on 'a moral economy of provision' while colonial scientific forestry rested on 'a political economy of profit'.[18]

The commercial imperatives of British colonial forestry—the demand for timber to serve the needs of ship-building and railway construction—fostered both an increasing intensity of natural resource use as well as dramatic changes in forms of management and control.[19] Inspired by B. H. Baden-Powell, who argued that the 'Oriental sovereign' had the right to dispose of forests and wasteland as they wished, a right transferable to their British successor, the early forest

---

[14] A. Maharatna, *Demographic Perspectives on India's Tribes* (2005) ch 2.

[15] Ministry of Rural Development, Government of India, *Report of the Expert Group on Prevention of Alienation of Tribal Land and its Restoration* (2004), available at <http://www.rural.nic.in/>.

[16] M. Cohen, 'Property and Sovereignty' (1927)13 Corn L R 8 at 13.

[17] See the discussion on commodification in Watson Hamilton and Bankes' chapter in this volume.

[18] R. Guha and M. Gadgil, 'State Forestry and Conflict in British India' (1989) 123 Past, Present and Future 141 at 172.

[19] ibid.

laws sought to establish total state control over forests.[20] The Indian Forest Act 1878, converted forests on which peasants and rural populations had previously unfettered rights of use into centrally managed state forests on which they had defined 'privileges'.[21] It permitted the state to expand commercial exploitation of forests, while simultaneously restricting local subsistence use.[22]

The colonial government was well aware that the land over which they were thus extending dominion was subject to long standing customary rights. When the 1878 Forest Act was drafted the Madras Board of Revenue argued against it, on the grounds that '[t]here is scarcely a forest in the whole of the Presidency of Madras which is not within the limits of some village and there is not one in which so far as the Board can ascertain, the state asserted any rights of property unless royalties in teak, sandalwood, cardamom and the like can be considered as such, until very recently. All of them, without exception are subject to tribal and communal rights which have existed from time immemorial and which are as difficult to define as they are necessary for the rural population.... [in Madras] the forests are, and always have been common property. ...'[23]

The colonial encounter brought the western liberal tradition of individual rights and private property to countries such as India, where a diverse and inclusive set of technologies of resource use—hunter-gatherers, shifting cultivators, nomadic pastoralists, subsistence and cash crop agriculturists and planters—and property relations—private, communal, corporate or state managed—were in operation.[24] Loosely defined, culturally fixated community property rights systems of resource access, use and management had been in operation for centuries in India's forests. In the absence of any lens through which to view these systems, the existence of an imperialist mission to 'civilize' the natives, as well as the 'need' to obtain and control access to natural resources for ship-building, railways and such like, the colonial powers incorporated their conceptions of exclusive property into local regimes. Only two types of property rights were recognized, respected and sanctioned—private and governmental, all other forms were seen as inefficient, engendering over-exploitation, and therefore subject to strict controls.

The Indian Forest Act 1927 that replaced the 1878 Act further consolidated state *dominion* over forests, and *imperium* over forest dwellers. It allowed the state to

---

[20] B. H. Baden-Powell and J. S. Gamble (eds), *Report of the Proceedings of the Forest Conference 1873–75* (1875) cited in R. Guha, 'Dietrich Brandis and Indian Forestry' in *Village Voices, Forest Choices* (M. Poffenberger and B. McGean, eds, 1996) 86, 93.

[21] See K. Sivaramakrishnan, 'Colonialism and Forestry in India: Imagining the Past in Present Politics' (1995) 37 Comparative Studies in Society and History 3, 14 highlighting the contribution of B.H. Baden-Powell who argued that villagers did not acquire rights by prescription because they used the forest without any distinct grant or licence, all customary usages were therefore merely privileges.

[22] R. Guha, 'The Prehistory of Community Forestry in India' (2001) 6 Environmental History 213 at 216.

[23] Remarks by the Board of Revenue, Madras, 5 August 1871, in Proceedings No 43–142, March 1878, Legislative Department, National Archives of India, New Delhi.

[24] Above n 18 at 141.

notify forest or waste land as reserved forests,[25] and by so doing extinguish existing individual or community rights over the forest.[26] It provided access to forest and forest produce, but as a 'privilege' extended at the discretion of forest officials acting under relevant rules.[27] It also created the categories of protected and village forests. Protected forests may be carved out of any land on which the government has a proprietary interest, provided private rights have been inquired into and recorded in a settlement.[28] Village forests refer to forest lands which the state assigns to a village community,[29] but to which the provisions on reserved forests would apply.[30]

The state *dominion* and *imperium* approach had profound implications both physical—in terms of the use and abuse of the resource base, and social—in terms of the alienation, protest and conflict it engendered amongst forest dwellers. The devaluation of cultural, social rights to hold land in community with others led to the conversion of a well-organized culturally defined common property regime into an open access system. Scholars studying common property regimes in Africa and Asia have questioned the 'tragedy of the commons'[31] thesis by exploring the distinction between open access and common property regimes.[32] While common property regimes have a strong internally enforced code of regulation and responsibility, open access systems do not and the costs of over-exploitation are externalized. In devaluing common property systems, the state externalized the costs of over-exploitation thereby reducing the local people's incentives to conserve the natural resource. Common property systems, it is argued, acquire the character of open access systems thereby leading to resource destruction.[33]

The state *dominion* and *imperium* approach also led to systematic and ongoing dispossession of *Adivasis* and other forest dwellers from their lands, denial of access to their means of subsistence, and criminalization of their economic, social and cultural practices, many of which revolved around the forests, on which their very presence was rendered illegal. Although procedures for 'settlement' of certain rights existed, the largely unlettered peasants found the task of proving their customary rights difficult, especially in the face of a hostile and often inept forest bureaucracy. Needless to say this fomented resistance and conflict of differing kinds from major rebellions to passive non-compliance, and the history of forestry in India has been the history of intense social conflict.[34]

---

[25] Indian Forest Act 1927, s 3.

[26] ibid, s 9.

[27] ibid, s 10 in particular s 10(5), which reads, 'the practice of shifting cultivation shall in all cases be deemed a privilege subject to control, restriction and abolition by the State Government'.

[28] ibid s 29.

[29] ibid, s 28(1).

[30] ibid, s 28(3).

[31] G. Hardin, 'The Tragedy of the Commons' (1968) 162 Science 1243.

[32] See generally B.McCay and J. Acheson, *The Question of the Commons: The Culture and Ecology of Communal Resources* (1987).

[33] Interestingly this is a point that the Assistant General of Forests acknowledged in an affidavit filed before the Supreme Court of India in the *Forest* Case. See P. Prabhu, 'The Right to Live with Dignity' (2006) 552 Seminar 14.

[34] Above n 22 at 216.

B. Forest law and governance in modern India: centralizing decision-making

The drafters of the Indian Constitution placed forests in the state list,[35] and the forest departments of individual states continued to administer the Indian Forest Act 1927. The effort to consolidate forests and integrate princely states continued in various states and with it the alienation of forest dwellers and their rights. In many cases declarations of state ownership were not followed up either by surveys and settlements of existing rights or by demarcation on the ground, leaving property rights over these lands in considerable uncertainty.[36]

In response to increasing concerns about the pace of deforestation in 1976, the 42nd Amendment Act moved forests from the State to the Concurrent list, thereby authorizing the Parliament to legislate over forests.[37] This led to the Forest Conservation Act 1980, which requires states to obtain prior central approval for de-reserving reserved forests and for converting forest land to non-forest purposes.[38] This effectively froze legal land use in a fifth of India's land,[39] thereby also freezing the attendant inequities on the ground.

The Forest Conservation Act 1980, centralized decision-making on fundamental questions relating to the use of India's forests. The reach of this decision-making power is particularly problematic. Neither the Indian Forest Act 1927 nor the Forest Conservation Act 1980, defines a 'forest'. The Supreme Court of India[40] offered a definition, the 'dictionary' one, and extended the reach of the Forest Conservation Act 1980, 'to all forests irrespective of the nature of ownership or

---

[35] The Constitution of India 1950, Art 246 (creating three lists, Union, State and Concurrent, contained in the seventh schedule to the Constitution, prescribing the areas in which the Parliament, the Legislatures of States, and both respectively, have competence to legislate).

[36] M. Sarin, 'Who is encroaching on whose land?' (2002) 519 Seminar 69.

[37] The Constitution (Forty-Second Amendment) Act, 1976, available at <http://indiacode.nic.in/coiweb/amend/amend42.htm>.

[38] Forest Conservation Act 1980 s 2, available at <http://www.envfor.nic.in/legis/forest/forest2.html>.

[39] Campaign for Survival and Dignity, *Endangered Symbiosis: Evictions and India's Forest Communities* (2004) ch 1.

[40] A word of explanation, public interest jurisdiction in India, after early case law that liberalized *locus standi*, has assumed a life of its own, quite apart from anything seen in any other jurisdiction. Public interest litigation is characterized by a collaborative approach, procedural flexibility, judicially-supervised interim orders and forward-looking relief. It typically involves numerous parties and stakeholders, *amicus curiae*, and fact-finding/expert/monitoring/policy-evolution committees. Once an issue catches the attention of the Court, it will often take immediate steps to address the problem, and simultaneously set in motion an investigative and policy evolution process. This process may take several years or even decades, but in this period it will continuously monitor administrative action, and ensure compliance with court orders. In some public interest environmental cases, the Court has passed over 200 orders in two decades. Needless to say there are numerous concerns with such an assumption of jurisdiction on the part of the Courts, some of which have been identified in L. Rajamani, 'Public Interest Environmental Litigation in India: Exploring Issues of Access, Participation, Equity, Effectiveness and Sustainability' (2007) 16 JEL 1.

classification thereof'.[41] In so doing, the Court brought within the purview of the state a wide array of lands, used to serve different ecological and livelihood functions, many of which were community, private or disputed lands.[42]

The role of the Supreme Court in the field of forest governance is worth dwelling on. In *TN Godavarman Thirumulkpad v Union of India and Ors*,[43] faced with a case of mismanagement on a tract of forest land, the Court assumed to itself the task of protecting all the forests and wildlife of India. Since 1996 it has passed numerous far-reaching orders including *inter alia*: that no forests, national park or wildlife sanctuary can be de-reserved without its explicit permission; and no non-forestry activity will be permitted in a national park or wildlife sanctuary even if prior approval under the Forest Conservation Act 1980 has been obtained. It has also imposed complete bans on the movement of cut trees and timber from the seven North-Eastern states, and on felling of trees in 'any forest, public or private' in Jammu and Kashmir, Himachal Pradesh, and the hill regions of Uttar Pradesh, and West Bengal.[44] To monitor compliance with its numerous orders, and to provide it with recommendations, the Court ordered the appointment of a Central Empowered Committee, a quasi-judicial authority, with powers to peruse and assess the reports and affidavits placed before the Court, summon officials, receive evidence, and process complaints arising out of the enforcement of the Court's orders. [45]

Such judicial policy making and governance is problematic at several levels, but in the context of the rights of forest dwellers, a particular feature of this judicial overreach has manifested itself. Public interest litigation as it has evolved in India offers tremendous scope for a judge's value preferences to play out. The Supreme Court of India is perceived to consist of urban middle-class intellectuals. It is therefore seen as more likely to be receptive to others of their ilk, certain social and value preferences (for instance, the right to a clean environment rather than the right to livelihood), and certain modes of argumentation over others (technical rather than social). Well-intentioned though it may have been, the approach of the Court to the issue of forest rights bears this out. In a bid to conserve forests—for 'environmental' reasons and through scientific means that excluded people from parks—the Court rode roughshod over the private and community property rights of forest dwellers. It also, in an Interlocutory Application filed by the *Amicus Curiae* in the case, directed various states to report to the Court on the steps needed to clear encroachments, and to indicate the steps they had already taken to clear earlier encroachments.[46] Although this order did not direct evictions, pursuant to this order, the Ministry

---

[41] *TN Godavarman Thirumulkpad v Union of India and Ors* (1997) 2 SCC 267.

[42] Above n 36; see also above n 39.

[43] Writ Petition Number 202 of 1995, and numerous orders therein.

[44] *TN Godavarman Thirumulkpad v Union of India and Ors* (1997) 2 SCC 267.

[45] Central Empowered Committee, constituted by the Supreme Court of India by order dated 9 April 2002 in Writ Petitions 202/95 & 171/96, Notification, Gazette of India Extraordinary, Ministry of Environment and Forests, 18 September 2002. The Central Empowered Committee is currently composed of three foresters and two wildlife conservationists.

[46] Ministry of Environment and Forests Notification, 3 May 2002.

of Environment and Forests issued a directive to all states to summarily evict 'all illegal encroachment of forestlands' before 30 September 2002. This blanket order led to a spate of reportedly brutal evictions of *Adivasis* from forest lands.[47] It is this spate of evictions, and the reaction to it, that provided the immediate impetus for the campaign that led to the Forest Rights Act 2006.[48]

II. The Forest Rights Act 2006: recognizing rights and democratizing governance

Notwithstanding sporadic attempts to recognize and resolve *Adivasi* property rights over forest lands, the Forest Rights Act 2006, is the first comprehensive legislative effort to right the historical wrong suffered by forest dwellers in relation to their lands.[49] This Act generated in preparation, and continues to generate in implementation, fierce opposition.[50]

There are those who argue that regularizing settlements in and around forest land will subject forest ecosystems, and vanishing wildlife, already under pressure from development projects, mining, and farming, to intense pressure. The need of the hour therefore is to conserve and expand the resource base, not to open it to further human intervention.[51] Some warned that this Act 'if given effect to, would be the biggest man-made ecological disaster in post-independence India, a case of laws being framed to ensure that the future generations shall see no forests and wildlife'.[52]

---

[47] J. Dreze, *Tribal Evictions from Forest Land* (2005), available at <http://pmindia.gov.in/nac/concept%20papers/evictions.pdf>; see also S. Joshi, 'Deep in the Woods' in *Down to Earth* (15 January 2003) available at <www.downtoearth.org.in>.

[48] This campaign was spearheaded by the Campaign for Survival and Dignity, a coalition of grassroots organizations and peoples' movements across 10 states. See their website available at <http://forestrightsact.org>.

[49] The National Forest Policy, 1988, available at <http://www.envfor.nic.in/nfap/detailed-policy.html>, recognized a range of tribal rights on forest lands. In 1990 the Commissioner for Scheduled Castes and Scheduled Tribes submitted a Report detailing a framework for resolution of property rights disputes between the state and forest dwellers. See *Twenty-ninth Report of the Commissioner for Scheduled Castes and Scheduled Tribes, 1987–89*, submitted to the President of India on 28 May 1990. The Ministry of Environment and Forests thereafter issued a set of six circulars which covered guidelines to deal with encroachments and disputed claims on forest land, disputes regarding pattas/leases/grants involving forest land and conversion of forest villages into revenue villages. Ministry of Environment and Forests Circulars, 18 September 1990. There have also been parallel efforts to protect Scheduled Tribes, notably through the Panchayats (Extension to the Scheduled Areas) Act (PESA) 1996, which gives *Adivasi* communities the power to manage their natural resources.

[50] See generally M. Rangarajan, 'Fire in the Forest' (2005) 40 Economic and Political Weekly 4888.

[51] Editorial, 'The Problem', Forests and Tribals Symposium (2005) 552 Seminar 12; See also U. K. Karanth and P. Bhargav, 'Defragmenting Nature', Forests and Tribals Symposium, (2005) 552 Seminar 59.

[52] P. V. Jayakrishnan, 'Is there a Need for this Bill?' Forests and Tribals Symposium (2005) 552 Seminar 23.

In a similar vein, wildlife conservationists mocked the Act as a 'novel tool for patronage and immense vote gathering ability' and predicted 'the end of conservation'.[53]

Others argue that providing forest-dwelling communities with a permanent stake would strengthen not weaken the conservation regime.[54] They also argue that the opposition to the Act stems from an 'elitist ideology, which lends itself to justifying the legal construct of colonialism and internal colonialism, including the dictum of *res nullius*, arbitrary takeover of resources without the rule of law, state monopoly over resources and an inherent mistrust by the colonial state of its subjects'.[55] That this Act is contested terrain is evident from the fact that nine cases are currently pending before the Supreme Court of India[56] and various High Courts[57] challenging the Act and/or orders under it as unconstitutional.

A. Recognizing community based property rights

The Forest Rights Act secures property rights for forest dwellers in relation to forest land. These rights secure individual or community tenure or both, and include:

- *Land rights* such as the right to hold and live in the forest land, community tenures of habitat and habitation for primitive tribal and pre-agricultural groups, rights in and over disputed lands, and rights to *in situ* rehabilitation including alternative land in case of illegal evictions;
- *Access, withdrawal and use rights* such as community rights like *nistar,* the right of ownership, and access to collect, use, and dispose minor forest produce, community rights of uses or entitlements such as fish, grazing and traditional seasonal resource access of nomadic or pastoralist communities;
- *Customary rights* recognized under traditional or customary law, or traditional rights customarily enjoyed, subject to safeguards for wildlife protection;
- *Protection rights* such as the right to protect natural resources in the customary manner; and

[53] H. Dang, 'The End of Conservation', Forests and Tribals Symposium (2005) 552 Seminar 50; see also V. Thapar, 'The Tribal Bill, Moving beyond Tigers', *The Indian Express*, 21 October 2005.
[54] P. Prabhu, 'The Right to Live with Dignity', Forests and Tribals Symposium, (2005) 552 Seminar 14.
[55] ibid.
[56] *Bombay Natural History Society and Ors v Union of India and Ors*, Writ Petition 50/2008; and *Wildlife First and Ors v Union of India and Ors*, Writ Petition 109/2008.
[57] *JV Sharma and Ors v Union of India and Ors*, Writ Petition 21479/2007 (Andhra Pradesh High Court), *Sevanivrutta Vana Karmachari Sangh v Union of India and Ors*, PIL 21/2008 (Bombay High Court), *V Sambasivam v Union of India and Ors* Writ Petition 4533/2008, *TNS Murugadoss Theerthapathi v Union of India and Ors*, Writ Petition 533/2008 (Madras High Court, Madurai Bench), *Retired Forest Officers Association v Union of India and Ors*, Writ Petition 1392/2008 (Karnataka High Court), *Retired Forest Officers Association v Union of India and Ors,* Writ Petition 4933/2008 (Orissa High Court), and *Ramesh Jauhri v Union of India and Ors*, Writ Petition 10301/2008 (Madhya Pradesh High Court, Jabalpur Bench). For updates on these cases see <www. forestrightsact.org>.

- *Intellectual property rights* such as community rights over intellectual property relating to biodiversity.[58]

Much of the controversy relating to the Act stems from concern about the nature, context and extent of these property rights over land that many consider as the patrimony of the nation. Those engaged in the public debate bring their own conception of property rights to bear, conceptions driven primarily by Western understandings of property, from which, arguably, the Forest Rights Act seeks to depart.

A property right, at its simplest, is the authority to undertake particular actions related to a specific domain.[59] The predominant conceptualist view is that property comprises a bundle of rights, which includes the rights to access, withdrawal, management, exclusion and alienation.[60] In this view, many consider the right to exclude as critical to the labelling of a thing as property.[61] Such rights are typically protected and defended by law. The conceptualist analysis relates primarily to private state controlled individual rights.

The Forest Rights Act, in contrast, recognizes a bundle of rights, but ones that derive from communities, and have thus far, been enforced by communities. Rights of access, use and withdrawal as they relate to minor forest produce, and fish from water bodies, are examples. These rights derive their authority from the community within which they operate, not from the state in which they are located.[62] Law is not constitutive here. These rights are not brought into existence, and constituted by law; instead they predate law but are recognized, respected and protected by subsequent law.

For such community based property rights however, membership in a defined community is central. In the case of the Forest Rights Act, membership is determined based on whether the person or community 'primarily reside in' and 'depend on forests or forest lands for bona fide livelihood needs'.[63] If they are members of a Scheduled Tribe these two conditions will suffice, if not, then they will have to prove that they have resided in the area for three generations prior to 13 December 2005 (a generation being defined as 25 years).[64] In establishing entitlement to forest rights, in addition to the usual documentary evidence, 'statements of elders' can also be submitted.[65] There is considerable uncertainty at the margins in determining membership in this community. First, it is unclear whether both conditions need to be fulfilled or whether one will suffice. Secondly, the requirement for primary residence, some argue, will exclude most rightful claimants who

[58] Forest Rights Act 2006 s 3.
[59] J. Commons, *Legal Foundations of Capitalism* (1968).
[60] See generally Watson Hamilton and Bankes, in this volume, and references contained therein.
[61] T. Merrill, 'Property and the Right to Exclude' (1998) 77 Neb L Rev 730.
[62] See generally D. Barstow Magraw and L. Baker, 'Globalization, Communities and Human Rights: Community-Based Property Rights and Prior Informed Consent' (2007) 35 Den JILP 413.
[63] Forest Rights Act 2006 s 2(c), (o).
[64] ibid, s 2(o), and Explanation.
[65] Scheduled Tribes and Other Traditional Forest Dwellers (Recognition of Forest Rights) Rules 2007, available at <http://tribal.nic.in/writereaddata/mainlinkFile/File1036.pdf>, Rule 13(i).

depend on the forest for their livelihood but who live on the margins of what is technically classified as forest land.[66] Thirdly, the term 'bona fide livelihood needs' is left undefined, leaving open the question of whether and if so, how much, and to what end, minor forest produce, for instance, can be sold.[67]

The Forest Rights Act recognizes a bundle of rights that can be held independently or in conjunction with each other. Some of the rights, as for instance, rights to previously occupied land, encompass the right to exclude—one that Western property rights theorists view as critical—but others, as for instance rights to minor forest produce, do not encompass a right to exclude, that right being reserved for the state. Further, the Act makes it clear that the rights recognized and vested by the Act can be inherited but not alienated or transferred.[68] This prohibition is in keeping with the community-based nature of the property rights. Since it is membership in a defined community that gives rise to these property rights, it follows that these rights cannot legitimately transcend the community context. This prohibition is also in keeping with the notion that these rights are recognized and protected because traditional forest dwellers are integral to the 'survival and sustainability of the forest ecosystem'.[69] Presumably others would not be.

The rights provided under the Forest Rights Act are not absolute. In critical wildlife habitats of national parks and sanctuaries where the presence and activities of forest dwellers are likely to cause irreversible damage to wildlife, and where co-existence is not an option, the Act permits the creation of inviolate spaces for wildlife. There are however safeguards to ensure that resettlement packages are provided to forest dwellers and that the 'free informed consent' of the *gram sabha* (village assembly) is obtained.[70]

B. Democratizing forest governance

Another interesting stick in the bundle of rights recognized by the Forest Rights Act is the right to protect, regenerate or conserve or manage any community forest resource which they have been traditionally protecting in the customary manner.[71] Forest conservation in India has been premised on the notion that the state (whether represented by the forest department, the Supreme Court in its policy-making avatar, or the Central Empowered Committee) is the sole arbiter of the public good, and that scientific forestry is the answer to the conservation dilemma. In recognizing the rights of traditional forest dwellers to conserve and

---

[66] See O. Springate-Baginski et al, *Indian Forests Rights Act 2006: Commoning Enclosures, Institutions for Pro-Poor Growth Working Paper* (2008).

[67] The Rules define 'bona fide livelihood needs' but in so doing curiously restricts its application to produce resulting from self-cultivation. See above n 65, Rule 2(b).

[68] Forest Rights Act 2006 s 4(4).

[69] Forest Rights Act 2006, Preamble.

[70] ibid, s 4(2).

[71] ibid, 3(1)(i).

manage forests this Act empowers traditional forest-dwelling communities to participate in the governance of forest resources. Scholars argue that this is central to the effort at 're-commoning enclosures'.[72]

In the same vein, the Act also empowers holders of the forest rights as well as the *gram sabha* to protect wildlife, forest and biodiversity, and to preserve the habitat from 'any form of destructive practices affecting their cultural and natural heritage'.[73] Although there is no explicit requirement for prior informed consent from the *gram sabha*, it could be argued that this right empowers forest communities to question and rescind decisions of the government to divert forest land for non-forest purposes. This is a significant power in the hands of the forest communities.[74] It is worth noting that the states with the highest proportion of forest cover in India—Orissa, Jharkhand, and Chhattisgarh—also have the largest coal reserves, and 50,000 hectares of forest land are expected to be diverted to coal mining in the next seven to eight years for *Coal India* alone.[75] Forest communities could potentially bring such coal mining to a halt. It is evident that, even absent explicit requirement for their consent, forest communities are being seen as vested with such powers. The Ministry of Environment and Forests, in a bid to implement this Act, recently sent a letter to state governments highlighting the need for clearance from the *gram sabha* for all non-forest projects on forest lands.[76]

C. In step with international law

Both the move towards recognizing community based property rights and democratizing natural resource governance, in particular relating to indigenous lands, are in step with emerging trends in international law. Numerous international legal instruments recognize that in keeping with the right to enjoy their culture,[77] indigenous people have rights of ownership, collective or individual, over lands that they have traditionally owned, occupied, or used.[78]

---

[72] Above n 66.

[73] Forest Rights Act 2006 s 5; see generally M. Gadgil, 'Empowering Gram Sabhas to Manage Biodiversity: The Science Agenda' (2007) 42 Economic and Political Weekly 2067.

[74] See generally M. Gadgil, 'Let Our Rightful Forests Flourish, National Centre for Advocacy Studies', Working Paper Series No 27, November 2008 (arguing that vesting forest communities with powers to protect has tremendous potential to strengthen conservation).

[75] P. Ghosh, 'Local Administration to Clear Forest Projects' *Mint*, 4 August 2009; see also N. Sethi, 'Gram sabha nod must for mining proposals' *Times of India*, 4 August 2009.

[76] Ministry of Environment and Forests Advisory to the States on the Forest Rights Act, 30 July 2009, F. No. 11–9/1998-FC, available at, http://www.envfor.nic.in/mef/Forest_Advisory.pdf

[77] See, eg, International Covenant on Civil and Political Rights, Art 27.

[78] See, eg, Convention Concerning Indigenous and Tribal Peoples in Independent Countries, Art 14; and UN Declaration on the Rights of Indigenous People 2007, Preamble, Art 26 available at <http://www.un.org/esa/socdev/unpfii/en/drip.html>, see generally Convention on the Elimination of All Forms of Racial Discrimination (CERD), Art 5; Proposed American Declaration on the Rights of Indigenous Peoples, available at <http://www.oas.org/>; and, CERD General Recommendation 23, Art 5, A/52/18, annex V (1997) (calling upon states to recognize and protect 'the rights of indigenous peoples to own, develop, control and use their communal lands, territories and resources').

Several international human rights bodies have sought to protect these rights. The Human Rights Committee in *Chief Bernard Ominayak and Lubicon Lake Band v Canada*[79] and *Sara et al v Finland*[80] held that indigenous peoples' protected right to enjoy their culture had been threatened by logging and industrial development activities on their lands. The Inter-American Court of Human Rights in the *Awas Tingni* judgment[81] emphasized the importance of land to indigenous people. The Court noted that, '[i]ndigenous groups, by the fact of their very existence, have the right to live freely in their own territory; the close ties of indigenous people with the land must be recognized and understood as the fundamental basis of their culture, their spiritual life, integrity, and their economic survival'.[82] The Court recognized that the right to land is 'not merely a matter of possession and production, but one intertwined with the preservation of their cultural and spiritual legacy'.[83] In subsequent cases, the Inter-American Court has recognized the right to restitution for the loss of property, and to alternative land.[84] The African Commission on Human Rights has also sought to protect the right to property, among other rights, of indigenous people.[85]

[79] Communication No 167/1984, CCPR/C/38/D/167/1984. This complaint was brought by the leader of the Lubicon Lake Band, an indigenous tribe living in Alberta, Canada that had initiated several legal actions to halt industrial development on land on which it claimed to have traditional rights. A settlement offer from the government was rejected. The complaint alleged violations of the Band's right to self-determination and pursuit of economic and social development contrary to Arts 1–3 of the ICCPR. It was argued that the development threatened the existence of the indigenous people. The Human Rights Committee found violations of Art 27 but also Canada's proposal on how to correct the situation admissible.

[80] Communication No 431/1990, UN Doc CCPR/C/50/D/431/1990 (1994). This case was brought by Finnish citizens of Sami origin, reindeer herders of Lapland, who were opposed to the passing of the Wilderness Act which extended state ownership to wilderness areas of Lapland. The Sami complained that logging and development of the area would make reindeer herding impossible, and that their rights under Art 27 of the ICCPR to enjoy their culture had been violated. The Human Rights Committee held that the Samis should have taken recourse to domestic tribunals first but directed that Finland must stop development activities till such recourse is concluded.

[81] *Case of the Mayagna (Sumo) Indigenous Community of Awas Tingni*, Judgment (2001) Inter-Am Ct HR (Ser C) No 79. The Court ruled that in light of the Nicaraguan Constitution's recognition in general terms the rights of indigenous peoples to their land, it was a violation of these rights to grant the community's traditional lands to logging companies. The court also ordered Nicaragua to formally recognize the lands of the Awas Tingni and refrain from any action that could undermine the Community's interest in those lands. See also *Community of San Mateo de Huanchor and its members v Peru* (2004) Case 504/03, Report No 69/04, Inter-Am CHR, OEA/Ser.L/V/II.122 Doc 5 rev 1 at 487. This case addressed the environmental and health impacts from mining contamination in San Mateo de Huanchor, Peru, and engaged the right to personal security, right to property, rights of the child, right to fair trial and judicial protection and the progressive development of economic, social, and cultural rights.

[82] *Awas Tingni*, above n 81, at para 150.

[83] ibid.

[84] *Yakye Axa Indigenous Community v Paraguay* (2005) Inter-Am Ct HR (Ser C) No 125; see also *Sawhoyamaxa Indigenous Community v Paraguay* (2006) Inter-Am Ct HR (Ser C) No 146 and *Case of Moiwana Village v Suriname* (2005) Inter-Am Ct HR (ser C) No 124 at 54–5.

[85] *Decision of the African Commission on Human and People's Rights, Communication 155/96*, The Social and Economic Rights Action Center and the Center for Economic and Social Rights/Nigeria, (2002) ACHPR/COMM/A004/1. The Commission found Nigeria's participation in, and failure to

The Forest Rights Act recognizes the right to land, and to restitution and alternative land in the case of illegal eviction.[86] The Act also provides, as discussed above, for participation in forest governance. It does not however specify the extent of control that forest communities wield over forest resources. If the state decides to grant mining concessions on forest lands to *Coal India*, what recourse might forest communities have? They have a right to protect these resources, and the Ministry of Environment and Forests has interpreted the Act so as to require consent from the *gram sabha* before forest lands are diverted for non-forest purposes.[87] In this respect, at least in the Ministry's interpretation, the state is under a duty to obtain consent from the forest communities. It is more than a duty to merely consult. This too is in step with international legal developments.

In addition to international instruments that prescribe a duty to consult indigenous people about development plans on their lands,[88] the recent case of the *Saramaka People*[89] before the Inter-American Court of Human Rights is instructive. The Court held that the state has a duty to consult the indigenous people about development plans affecting their lands, and in cases of 'large scale development or investment projects', the state is required not only to consult, but to obtain the 'free, prior and informed consent' of the affected group.[90] The Court explained that in determining whether the state is under a duty to consult or to obtain consent relating to resource use, the test is whether the resources are 'inextricably related to the survival of the group'.[91]

D. Forest rights, democratic governance and climate change regulation

An emerging area of international regulation with considerable implications for forest rights and governance is climate change. For indigenous communities, climate impacts are likely to fundamentally alter their way of life, affecting a set of internationally protected rights, in particular the right to the benefits of their culture,[92] and the right to freely dispose of natural resources.[93] The ill-fated *Inuit* Petition before the Inter-American Commission of Human Rights

---

put an end to, the environmental devastation of Ogoniland in the form of oil spills and water contamination violated the Ogoni peoples' rights to life, health and property, in addition to other rights.

[86] Forest Rights Act 2006 s 3.

[87] See above n 76.

[88] See, eg, Convention Concerning Indigenous and Tribal Peoples in Independent Countries 1989, Art 15; and UN Declaration on the Rights of Indigenous People 2007, Art 32.

[89] *Saramaka People v Suriname* (2007) Inter-Am Ct HR (Ser C) No 172.

[90] ibid at para 134.

[91] ibid at para 122.

[92] Universal Declaration of Human Rights, Art 27; International Covenant on Economic, Social and Cultural Rights, 1966, Art 15; and American Convention on Human Rights, Art XIII.

[93] International Covenant on Civil and Political Rights, Art 1; International Covenant on Economic, Social and Cultural Rights, Art 1.

highlighted these.[94] In addition, policies and measures to reduce emissions from deforestation in developing countries (REDD), which is on the agenda of the climate negotiations,[95] may also, unless sensitively designed, trespass on indigenous rights.[96] The decentralized rights-based approach favoured in the Forest Rights Act, albeit in step with trends in international law, is yet to influence India's negotiating position on REDD issues at the climate negotiations.

India has placed a considerable emphasis in the recent past on its potential for engaging in REDD activities.[97] India argues that while reducing deforestation and degradation saves carbon, conservation and sustainable management of forests adds carbon. And, similar financial incentives should be offered for saving and for adding carbon.[98] Reasonable though this position appears on the surface, it is worth noting that while increasing plantations at the expense of natural forests, which arguably is what is occurring in India,[99] may well result in net carbon added, it is not the same thing as saving natural forests. India is arguing for a definition of forests: 'in terms of crown density, which should include natural as well as industrial/short rotation plantations, or in the alternative, if technologically possible, a forest definition based on a minimum default biomass/carbon stocks per unit area'.[100] To view forests in such a uni-dimensional fashion—while faithful to the 'scientific forestry' method and the historical legacy of the forest department in India—misconceives the enterprise of forest conservation. Forest conservation cannot be equated to tree planting. In addition to nurturing

[94] In their 2005 petition before the Inter-American Commission on Human Rights the Inuit people claimed that the impacts of climate change, caused by acts and omissions of the United States, violated their fundamental human rights—in particular the rights to the benefits of culture, to *property*, to the preservation of health, life, physical integrity, security, and a means of subsistence, and to residence, movement, and inviolability of the home.

[95] Para 1(b) (iii) Decision 1/CP.13, *Bali Action Plan*, in FCCC/CP/2007/6/Add.1 (14 March 2008).

[96] At COP-14 in Poznan in December 2008, US, Canada, New Zealand, and Australia reportedly deleted lines relating to indigenous peoples' rights in the text on REDD. See D. Adam, 'Indigenous Rights Row threatens Rainforest Protection Plan' *The Guardian*, 9 December 2008.

[97] 'India's Forest and Tree Cover: Contribution as a Carbon Sink', Ministry of Environment and Forests, Government of India, 10 August 2009 (noting that India's forests are sufficient to neutralize 11.4% of India's emissions).

[98] J. Kishwan, Director General, Indian Council of Forestry Research and Education, REDD Presentation: India, Accra, 22 August 2008.

[99] Under the Forest Conservation Act 1980 and Rules, if forest land is diverted, with the permission of the central government, to non-forest uses, the user agency has to pay to bring other land under 'compensatory afforestation'. In 2002 in the *Godavarman* case the Supreme Court directed that these payments as well as payments for the 'Net Present Value' of the forests being destroyed, were to be deposited in a specialized central fund, to be administered by a body called the Compensatory Afforestation Management and Planning Authority (CAMPA). CAMPA currently has US $2.5 billion in it. This situation is revealing both in that the sums deposited in the CAMPA fund indicate that significant diversions of forest land have been permitted, and that compensatory afforestation is seen as sufficient to address such diversion.

[100] Views from India to UNFCCC on REDD, Views on issues related to further steps under the Convention related to reducing emissions from deforestation in developing countries: approaches to stimulate action, Submissions from Parties, FCCC/SBSTA/2007/MISC.14/Add.2 (14 November 2007).

biodiversity, forests provide subsistence ecosystem services—minor forest produce, grazing lands, water bodies—for forest dwellers, all of which vanish with plantations.

In its submissions to the inter-governmental negotiating process tasked with crafting a post-2012 climate agreement, India makes only a fleeting reference, couched in preambular language, recognizing the 'efforts of communities' and that the 'needs of local and indigenous communities should be addressed' whilst action is taken to reduce emissions from deforestation.[101] Notwithstanding the Forest Rights Act, India does not appear to envisage a participatory role for forest communities in the efforts to reduce emissions from deforestation. It does not refer to the need for 'prior informed consent' for REDD projects, or for benefit sharing of REDD profits with forest communities.[102]

III. Conclusion

This chapter sought to explore the provenance, possibilities and limits of formal legal recognition of community based property rights through a case study of the Forest Rights Act 2006 in India. The Forest Rights Act marks a significant departure from the colonial legacy of forestry laws in India both because it recognizes and vests community based property rights in forest dwellers, and because it seeks to democratize forest governance. Given its contested birth, however, the extent to which this Act will be implemented and the extent to which the fundamental ideological shifts that underlie and inspire this Act will influence the governance of and negotiations on forests remains to be seen.

---

[101] Submission by the Government of India on reducing emissions from deforestation in developing countries: approaches to stimulate action, Ideas and proposals on the elements contained in para 1 of the Bali Action Plan, Submissions from Parties, FCCC/AWGLCA/2009/MISC.4 (Part I), at 112 (May 2009).

[102] Mexico, Bolivia, and Tuvalu, among others, have supported active participation of indigenous groups in REDD decision-making, as well as in sharing of benefits that may accrue. See Issues relating to indigenous people and local communities for the development and application of methodologies, Submissions from Parties, FCCC/SBSTA/2009/MISC.1/Add.1 (17 April 2009).

Index